WORKS ISSUED BY
THE HAKLUYT SOCIETY

Series Editors
Gloria Clifton
Joyce Lorimer

PEDRO PÁEZ'S *HISTORY OF ETHIOPIA*, 1622
VOLUME I

THIRD SERIES
NO. 23

# DONATIONS

The Christensen Fund, San Francisco, California
The Calouste Gulbenkian Foundation, Lisbon
The Embassy of Spain in Addis Ababa
   with contributions from:
      Nestlé
      Explosivos Rio Tinto
      Maxam International
      España Acción Cultural Exterior

# PEDRO PÁEZ'S
# *HISTORY OF ETHIOPIA,*
# 1622

## VOLUME I

Edited by
ISABEL BOAVIDA, HERVÉ PENNEC and
MANUEL JOÃO RAMOS

Translated by
CHRISTOPHER J. TRIBE

*Published by*
*Ashgate*
*for*
THE HAKLUYT SOCIETY
LONDON
2011

Published for The Hakluyt Society by

Ashgate Publishing Limited
Wey Court East
Union Road
Farnham
Surrey GU9 7PT
England

Ashgate Publishing Company
Suite 420
101 Cherry Street
Burlington
VT 05401–4405
USA

Ashgate website: http://www.ashgate.com

**British Library Cataloguing in Publication Data**
Páez, Pedro, 1564–1622.
Pedro Páez's History of Ethiopia, 1622.
Volume 1. – (Hakluyt Society. Third series)
1. Ethiopia – History. 2. Ethiopia – Politics and government – Early works to 1800. 3. Ethiopia – Religion – Early
works to 1800. 4. Ethiopia – Foreign relations – To 1889. 5. Ethiopia – Social conditions. 6. Prester John
(Legendary character) – Early works to 1800.
I. Title II. Series III. History of Ethiopia, 1622 IV. Boavida, Isabel. V. Pennec, Hervé. VI. Ramos, Manuel João.
963–dc22

**Library of Congress Cataloging-in-Publication Data**
LCCN: 2011903959

ISBN 978-1-908145-00-0
ISSN 0072 9396

Typeset by Waveney Typesetters, Wymondham, Norfolk

MIX
Paper from
responsible sources
FSC® C018575
www.fsc.org

Printed and bound in Great Britain by the
MPG Books Group, UK

# CONTENTS

## VOLUME I

## *HISTORY OF ETHIOPIA*

BOOK II

Book II of the History of Ethiopia, which deals with the faith that the Prester John and his vassals profess, the ecclesiastical rites and ceremonies that they perform and other matters relating thereto

# VOLUME II

BOOK III
Which reports some histories of emperors of Ethiopia, with the missions that fathers of the Society undertook to this empire at the time of each of them

BOOK IV

Which deals with the last three emperors that there have been in it until today and with the missions that the fathers of the Society have undertaken to this empire during their time

# FIGURES AND MAPS

## Volume I

## Volume II

# PREFACE

This book contains an annotated English translation of the *História da Etiópia* by the Spanish Jesuit missionary priest Pedro Páez (or Pêro Pais in Portuguese), 1564–1622, who worked in the Portuguese missions in India and then in Ethiopia. His history of Ethiopia was written in Portuguese in the last years of his life and survives in only two manuscripts. The translation, by Christopher J. Tribe, is based on the new Portuguese critical edition of the text by Isabel Boavida, Hervé Pennec and Manuel João Ramos, which was published in 2008.[1] They are also the editors of this English version.

Páez's learned but often polemical work is a major contribution to the political, social, cultural and religious history of Ethiopia in the sixteenth and early seventeenth centuries, and to the history of early Portuguese and Spanish missions in Africa and India, and Western European attempts to come to terms with non-European cultures.

As will be explained in detail in the Introduction, Páez's language (Portuguese with Hispanicisms), the organization of his material, his extensive use of long quotations from other works (here indicated by the use of italic), and the history of the manuscripts and their eventual publication, are all complicated. To avoid excessive footnoting the editors have condensed a great deal of the historical, religious and linguistic annotation, and personal and place names, into a Glossary placed at the end of volume II. Readers are advised to consult the Introduction and Glossary before starting on the text in order to understand the method of presentation.

---

[1] Pedro Páez, *História da Etiópia*, ed. Isabel Boavida, Hervé Pennec and Manuel João Ramos, Lisbon, 2008.

# ACKNOWLEDGEMENTS

The cost of translating and publishing this work has been considerable, and beyond the normal means of the Hakluyt Society. The editors and the Hakluyt Society wish to express again their enormous gratitude to the donors whose financial support has made this publication possible, and who are listed more prominently on the Donations page. These are The Christensen Fund, based in California, with particular thanks to Dr Wolde Gossa Tadesse, programme officer for the African Rift Valley (Ethiopia), for his assistance; The Calouste Gulbenkian Foundation, Lisbon, with particular thanks for their help to Mr Rui Vilar, president of the Foundation (and present Chair of the European Foundation Centre), and Mr João Pedro Garcia, Director of the Foundation's International Department; The Spanish Embassy in Addis Ababa, with particular thanks to D. Rafael Dezcallar de Mazarredo, Spanish Ambassador in Berlin and former Spanish Ambassador in Ethiopia, who first decided to give support to this edition, and his successors at the Embassy who have continued to take an interest in the project. The Spanish Embassy donation was supported by generous contributions from the European Union Delegation in Addis Ababa, Nestlé, Explosivos Rio Tinto, Maxam International, and España Acción Cultural Exterior.

Others have helped in this work with advice and editorial assistance. We wish to thank Dr Christopher J. Tribe, who undertook the long and difficult task of translation and contributed substantially to the annotation; Professor Clive Willis, who read the whole work for us before it was approved for publication; Professor Joyce Lorimer, the Hakluyt Society series editor who prepared the book for publication; and others who in one way or another have assisted in the publication: Dr Joan-Pau Rubiés, Michael Walsh, and the staff of Ashgate Publishing who have seen these volumes though the press.

Manuel João Ramos
Lisbon

# ABBREVIATIONS

| | |
|---|---|
| *Ab* | *Abbay* |
| *ACIHMPEC* | *Actas do Congresso Internacional de História: Missionação Portuguesa e Encontro de Culturas* |
| *ACISE* | *Atti del Convegno Internazionale di Studi Etiopici* |
| *AE* | *Annales d'Éthiopie* |
| *Aeth* | *Aethiopica* |
| *AHSI* | *Archivum Historicum Societatis Iesu* |
| *AIUON* | *Annali dell'Istituto Universitario Orientale di Napoli* |
| *Ar* | *Archaeologia* |
| *ArE* | *Archiva Ecclesiæ* |
| ARSI | Archivum Romanum Societatis Iesu, Rome |
| BA | Biblioteca Ambrosiana, Milan |
| BGUV | Biblioteca General, Universidad de Valencia |
| BNM | Biblioteca Nazionale Marciana, Venice |
| BPB | Biblioteca Pública, Braga |
| *BrsO* | *Bessarione, Rivista di Studi Orientali* |
| *BSGI* | *Bolettino della Società Geografica Italiana* |
| *BSGL* | *Boletim da Sociedade de Geografia de Lisboa* |
| *BSOAS* | *Bulletin of the School of Oriental and African Studies* |
| *CC* | *Civiltà Cattolica* |
| *CIDGERA* | *Congresso Internacional Damião de Góis na Europa do Renascimento. Actas* |
| *CMP* | *Congresso do Mundo Português* |
| *CSCO* | *Corpus Scriptorum Christianorum Orientalium* |
| *DA* | *Dossiers de l'Archéologie* |
| *DHDP* | *Dicionário de História dos Descobrimentos Portugueses* |
| *DHMPPO* | *Documentação para a História das Missões do Padroado Português do Oriente* |
| *DI* | *Documenta Indica* |
| *DSRAPA* | *Dipartimento di Studi e Ricerche su Africa e Paesi Arabi* |
| *EAe* | *Encyclopaedia Aethiopica* |
| *EBCA* | *Extrait du Bulletin de Correspondance Africaine* |
| *EC* | *Enciclopedia Cattolica* |
| *ED* | *Euntes Docete* |
| *EGJ* | *Ethiopian Geographical Journal* |
| *ETF-HM* | *Espacio, Tiempo y Forma – Historia Moderna* |
| *JA* | *Journal Asiatique* |
| *JAH* | *Journal of African History* |

| *JES* | *Journal of Ethiopian Studies* |
|---|---|
| *JSS* | *Journal of Semitic Studies* |
| *LCC* | *Les Cahiers Coptes* |
| *LHPI* | *Literatura e História para uma Prática Interdisciplinar* |
| *MEFREM* | *Mélanges de l'École Française de Rome – Moyen Âge* |
| *MEFRIM* | *Mélanges de l'École Française de Rome – Italie et Méditerranée* |
| *MHSI* | *Monumenta Historica Societatis Iesu* |
| *MRAL* | *Memorie della Reale Accademia dei Lincei* |
| *NAS* | *Northeast African Studies* |
| *O* | *Orientalia* |
| *OC* | *Oriens Christianus* |
| *OCP* | *Orientalia Christiana Periodica* |
| *P* | *Paideuma* |
| *PC* | *Povos e Culturas* |
| *PG* | *Patrologiæ Græcæ* |
| *PICES* | *Proceedings of the International Conference of Ethiopian Studies* |
| *PL* | *Patrologiæ Latinæ* |
| *PO* | *Patrologia Orientalis* |
| *QSE* | *Quaderni di Studi Etiopici* |
| *RÆSOI* | *Rerum Æthiopicarum Scriptores Occidentales Inediti a sæculo XVI ad XIX* |
| *RANL* | *Rendiconti della Accademia Nazionale dei Lincei* |
| *RC* | *Rivista delle Colonie* |
| *RHM* | *Revue d'Histoire des Missions* |
| *ROC* | *Revue d'Orient Chrétien* |
| *RRANL* | *Rendiconti della Reale Accademia Nazionale dei Lincei* |
| *RS* | *Revue Sémitique* |
| *RSE* | *Rassegna di studi etiopici* |
| *S* | *Studia* |
| *SÆ* | *Scriptores Æthiopici* |
| SOAS | School of Oriental and African Studies, University of London |
| *TEI* | *The Encyclopaedia of Islam* |
| *Xav* | *Xaveriana* |

# WEIGHTS AND MEASURES

*almude*:  unit of capacity (c. 16.8 litres).

*calões*:  a large jug (from the Tamil *kalam*); unit of capacity equivalent to one *almude* (c. 16.8 litres).

*cruzado*:  a gold coin used in the Portuguese empire (initially issued by Afonso V (1438–81) when trying to organize a crusade against the fall of Constantinople by the Turks in 1453).

*cubit*:  a forearm's length.

*fanega*:  a Portuguese unit of dry measure, equivalent to 55.5 litres.

*oquêa*:  'Gold is given by weight in little pieces, and the usual weight is called an *oquêa*, which is exactly eight Venetian coins in weight, and a half *oquêa*, after which they gradually go down to a very small weight' (Páez, bk I, ch. 21).

*pataca*:  a silver coin of the Portuguese empire.

*qoros*:  a unit of weight in the duodecimal system, equal to twelve loads. See Pankhurst, 'A Preliminary History of Ethiopian Measures, Weights and Values – Part 3', p. 47.

*quartagos/ quartãos*:  a unit of dry measure, equivalent to 55.5 litres.

*real*:  a Spanish and Portuguese gold coin.

*ṣāḥl*:  a Ge'ez word meaning goblet, here used as a unit of capacity.

*sequin*:  a former gold coin of the Republic of Venice introduced in 1284, a former gold coin of Malta, introduced c. 1535, and a former gold coin of Turkey, introduced in 1478. Worth 16 reales.

*span*:  the breadth of a spread hand from the tip of the thumb to the tip of the little finger.

# CHRONOLOGY OF ETHIOPIAN MONARCHS
## (1270–1632)

| Reign | Name | Throne name |
|---|---|---|
| 1270–1285 | *Icûnu Amlac* / Yekunno Amlāk | Tasfa Iyasus / Yoḥannes |
| 1285–1294 | *Agba Ceôn* / Yagbe'a Ṣeyon | Sālomon |
| 1294–1299 | Five sons of Yagbe'a Ṣeyon who ruled in succession | |
| 1299–1314 | *Udm Eraâd* / Wedem Ra'ad | |
| 1314–1344 | *Amd Ceôn* / 'Āmda Ṣeyon | Gabra Masqal |
| 1344–1371 | *Zeîf Arâd / Zeifa Arâd* Sayfa Ar'ad | Newāya Krestos |
| 1371–1379 | Newāya Māryām | Wedem Asfare, Germā Asfare |
| 1379/80–1413 | *David* / Dāwit | Qwastāntinos |
| 1413–1414 | *Tedrôs* / Téwodros | Walda Anbassā |
| 1414–1430 | *Isaac* / Yesḥāq | Gabra Masqal |
| 1430 | *Andreas* / Endréyās | |
| 1430–1433 | *Hezbnânh* / Hezba Nāñ | Takla Māryām |
| 1433–1434 | Śārwa Iyasus | Meḥreka Nāñ |
| 1434 | 'Āmda Iyasus | Badel Nāñ |
| 1434–1468 | *Zara Iacob* / Zar'a Yā'eqob | Qwastāntinos |
| 1468–1478 | *Bedâ Mariâm* / Ba'eda Māryām | Dāwit |
| 1478–1494 | *Escandêr* / Eskender | Qwastāntinos |
| 1494 | *Amd Ceôn* / 'Āmda Ṣeyon II | |
| 1494–1508 | *Naôd* / Nā'od | Anbassā Badār |
| 1508–1540 | *Lebenâ Denguîl* / Lebna Dengel | *Onâg Çaguêd* / Wanāg Sagad, Etana Dengel, Dāwit |
| 1540–1559 | *Glaudeôs* / Galāwdéwos | *Athanâf Çaguêd* / 'Aṡnāf Sagad |
| 1559–1563 | *Minâs* / Minās | *Adamâs Çagued* / Admās Sagad, Wanāg Sagad |
| 1563–1597 | *Zerza Denguîl* / Śarṣa Dengel | *Malâc Çaguêd* / Mal'ak Sagad |
| 1597–1603 | *Iacob* / Yā'eqob | *Malâc Çaguêd* / Mal'ak Sagad |
| 1603–1604 | *Za Denguîl* / Za Dengel | *Athanâf Çaguêd* / 'Aṡnāf Sagad |
| 1605–1607 | *Iacob* / Yā'eqob (restored) | *Malâc Çaguêd* / Mal'ak Sagad |
| 1607–1632 | *Suseneôs* / Susneyos | *Seltân Çaguêd* / Śelṭān Sagad |

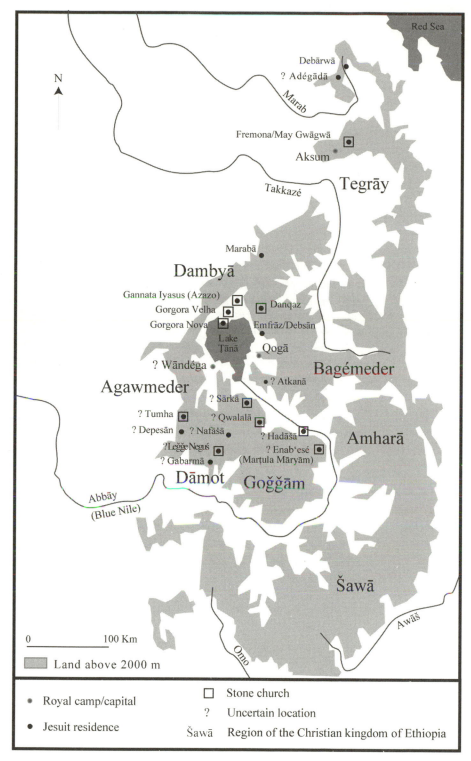

Figure 1. Map of the Catholic churches and Jesuit residences in Ethiopia in the early seventeenth century.
Drawn by H. Pennec and M. J. Ramos. Base map: R. Oliver, Geography section, City of London Polytechnic (Pankhurst, 1982).

El señor que por su infinita misericordia me llamo a la Compañia, estando yo muy lejos
dello, me a dado deseos muy eficaces de padecer trabajos por su amor, y en servicio de
la Compañia, y aunque es verdad que estos deseos los he tenido desde que estube en el novi-
ciado, con todo eso no eran de suerte que me forçasen a sacar esto; solo deseaua, y pedia
a nro señor me embiase V. P. al Iapon, o a la China, sin que yo lo pidiese: Pero
ahora no me parece cumplilia con lo que Dios nro señor me da a sentir sino pidiese a
V. P. alguna mision destas, y digo destas, por lo mucho que yo me inclino a ellas
pero no por esto no me sera de grandisimo consuelo qualquiera otra, a que V. P. me
mandare yr, aunque estoi cierto me faltan todas las buenas partes que para semejantes
misiones se requieren, porque delante de nro señor me atrebo a dezir que no me parece
soy para executar el mas minimo ministerio en que pienso se occupa la Compañia, sola
la confiança que tengo en el que puso en mi coraçon tan vehemente deseo, me hara
atrever a esto, y que no me parezcan dificultosos qualesquier trabajos, ni peligros aunq.
sean de muerte. Antes en solo pensar de morir por su amor Reciuo tanto contento q.
aunque no se me diese otro premio por ello, con este daria muy bien pagado. y ansi pa.
amor deste señor pido a V. P. me mande embiar a parte donde pueda dar la vida
por aquel, que la libro de tantos peligros, y tempestades como tenia en el mundo; este nro
guarde a V. P. por muchos años como puede y todos sus hijos deseamos. de Belmonte y
de Mayo 8. de 587.

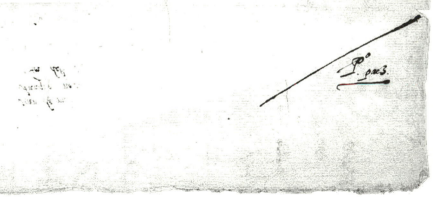

Po. paez.

Figure 2. Petition letter (*littera indipeta*) by Pedro Páez, 8 May 1587.
ARSI, MS Fondo Gesuitico 758, ff. 84–84v.

Belmonte.

P. Pedro Pablo. Mayo. 8.

_____

155.

Al P.e Claudio Aquaviua General de
la Comp.a de Jesus N.tro

Roma.

# INTRODUCTION

## 1. The Need for a Critical Edition of Páez

The writing process makes a written text linear. This linearity, however, is merely its physical appearance. Beneath the surface extend interwoven layers that place it in a corpus of context and authority, situate it, point to possible meanings for it, and provide it with organic substance. Some texts show these webs, making visible the subtle – or not so subtle – ideological threads of which they are composed. They are written in part by rewriting other texts, and they themselves will be reinterpreted and rewritten in future. They have the weight of citations that confirm or refute. They show the marks of the process through which they are constructed, like semantic palimpsests, and they bear witness to the steps in the creation of new texts.

All this is true of the *História da Etiópia* (*History of Ethiopia*) that the Jesuit priest Pedro Páez (or Pêro Pais) spent almost a decade drafting in Ethiopia until his death. This work, now published in full in English for the first time, was written both as historiographic material and as an ethnographic document. It should be seen as one element in an organized body of texts that made up the literature on Ethiopian society produced by the Society of Jesus throughout much of the seventeenth century. This specific context would confer added interest on any one of the several works about Ethiopia written in that period, which raises the question of why the organizers of this edition have chosen to focus on Pedro Páez's book.

The *History of Ethiopia* is generally acknowledged to be an essential source for several different areas of study – from the history of the Catholic missions in that country and the relations between the European religious orders, to the history of art and religions; from the history of geographical exploration to the ideological contextualization of the Ethiopian kingdom; from material culture to Abyssinian political and territorial administration; and from an analysis of local circumstances to changes in human ecology in the Horn of Africa and the Indian Ocean. This is indeed a multifarious literary monument, a repository of empirical knowledge on the political geography, religion, customs, flora and fauna of Ethiopia and, albeit to a lesser extent, southern Arabia. In addition to some unexpected rhetorical ingenuity, it blends features of a travel narrative and a historical-ethnographic monograph with those of a chronicle, in that it relates the activities of the Jesuit missionaries on the ground in their Ethiopian mission and reworks a wide variety of documents, including the first translations into a European language of a large number of Ethiopian literary texts, from royal chronicles to hagiographies.

No less important is the fact that Páez's book served as the basis for two other histories of Ethiopia, which transformed the text that he had constructed according to the rules of *confutatio* by purging it of its polemical passages. The first of these works deriving from

1

the rewriting and rearrangement of Páez's manuscript was penned by Father Manuel de Almeida (1581–1646) but only published in 1907–8 by Camillo Beccari.[1] The second, authored by Father Baltasar Teles (1595–1675), which for reasons discussed below was published in 1660 long before its primary source, was in turn an abridged and recast version of Almeida's manuscript.[2]

Pedro Páez's *História da Etiópia* remained unpublished until the twentieth century, when two versions in the original Portuguese appeared, based on the only two manuscripts known to exist. MS Goa 42 in the Archivum Romanum Societatis Iesu (ARSI) was published by Camillo Beccari in *Rerum Æthiopicarum Scriptores Occidentales Inediti* (*RÆSOI*), vols II and III, in 1905–6. MS 778 in the Biblioteca Pública de Braga, Portugal (BPB), a seventeenth-century copy, was published in three volumes by Civilização Editora, Porto, in 1945–6, with a palaeographic reading by Lopes Teixeira, a bio-bibliographic note by Alberto Feio and an introduction by Elaine Sanceau.

The Porto edition was based purely on a reading of the latter copy of Páez's text, which was most probably made from the original manuscript after certain passages in it had been revised and censored.[3] The critical apparatus in this edition, which is limited to Sanceau's brief, impressionistic and unstructured introduction and Feio's bio-bibliographic note, is virtually non-existent. There are also several omissions in the palaeographic reading that were not picked up at the proofreading stage, which sometimes affect the overall meaning of a passage. The edition did serve its purpose of disseminating the text and making it more widely available to researchers and scholars, but it has been out of print now for many years. Beccari's edition, in contrast, was based entirely on his reading of the ARSI manuscript, written by Páez himself. The editor updated the Portuguese spelling according to the rules of the time but he did not systematically mark out the author's own revisions or amendments to the text. However, not only is this edition difficult to find,[4] but the introduction and notes were written in Latin, a hurdle for most readers in the twenty-first century.

In view of the importance of Pedro Páez's text to Jesuit missionary literature on Ethiopia and more generally to sixteenth- and seventeenth-century European literature on Africa, we decided to carry out a comparative analysis of the two manuscripts in order to produce a critical, annotated edition in Portuguese, which could then serve as a basis for translations into other languages. The bulk of the work was done between 2000 and 2002, and involved establishing the editing criteria; systematically investigating direct and

[1] Almeida, 'Historia de Ethiopia a alta ou Abassia, imperio do Abexim, cujo Rey vulgarmente he chamado Preste Joam'. Parts of Almeida's work (bk I, chs 1–22; bk II, ch. 22; and bk III, part of ch. 2) were later translated into English and edited by Beckingham and Huntingford in *Some Records of Ethiopia 1593–1646 Being Extracts from The History of High Ethiopia or Abassia by Manoel de Almeida Together with Bahrey's History of the Galla*.

[2] Teles, *Historia Geral de Ethiopia a Alta ou Preste Ioam e do que nella obraram os Padres da Companhia de Jesus, composta na mesma Ethiopia pelo Padre Manoel d'Almeyda, natural de Vizeu, Provincial e Visitador, que foy na India. Abreviada com nova releyçam e methodo pelo Padre Balthasar Telles, natural de Lisboa, Provincial da Provincia Lusitana, ambos da mesma Companhia*. The work was republished in an abridged version as *História Geral de Etiópia-a-Alta* by A. de Magalhães Bastos in 1936, and as *História da Etiópia*, 2 vols, in 1989. An abridged English translation appeared in 1710: Balthazar Tellez, *Travels of the Jesuits in Ethiopia*.

[3] The copy therefore could not have been produced 'under the author's supervision', as Feio suggested on p. xxvii.

[4] The original edition of Beccari's work has long been out of print, as has the small facsimile edition published in Brussels in 1969.

indirect sources of information on Páez;[1] comparing, checking and establishing where appropriate the text by means of a comparative reading of the manuscripts; modernizing the spelling and revising the punctuation; creating the notes and glossary entries and writing the introduction. The new Portuguese edition was published in Lisbon by Assírio & Alvim in 2008.

Páez's *History of Ethiopia* is an interesting historiographic object for research into the literary, political and ideological universe of the religious missions to Ethiopia.[2] It also deserves to be seen as a notable example of the efforts made by many missionaries in the sixteenth and seventeenth centuries to record ethnographic details about non-European lands. Unfortunately, the work as presented in its earlier Portuguese editions tended to be taken by scholars of Ethiopian history and anthropology as a primary source and used as if it were an original manuscript entirely divorced from the rich context of both European and Ethiopian written materials, of which it is part. Since the Porto and Rome editions were not accompanied by any systematic critical apparatus, they did not encourage the kind of intertextual approach through which the denser meanings of the work could be explored.

It is quite clear that the discursive strategy followed by Páez in his book derives from his explicit objective of refuting Dominican criticism that the Society of Jesus had been granted the privilege of exclusive rights to the Ethiopian mission. The author therefore makes highly selective use of oral and written sources to support this specific argument. Nevertheless, the vast majority of scholars who have habitually referred to his work have made much of its plain, unrhetorical, spontaneous character and the aptness of its linguistic and ethnographic commentary on Ethiopia. As a result, they have treated it as a reliable research tool, as if it were an objective, unchallengeable repository of information and events. Such an assumption, of course, has made it much easier for them to select and manipulate individual details without having to carefully situate them within either the internal context of the work or the external context of what came before and after it.

The *History* has often been used in this way not only because the poorly developed critical apparatus of the Rome and Porto editions allowed it to happen, but also because the views expressed by the editors in their respective introductions even encouraged such use. In the introduction to the first volume of the collected works that includes Páez's book, Beccari begins by emphasizing the importance of publishing the *History*, because until then the only works available were by Jesuit fathers who were not familiar with the mission territory.[3] He then goes on to say that the publication of Páez's book gives readers access to a more authentic view of the history of Ethiopia and the Jesuit mission and of

[1] This research was carried out in the Archivo del Real Convento de Predicadores de Valencia, the Biblioteca de la Universidade de Valencia, the Archivum Romanum Societatis Iesu, the Arquivo Distrital de Braga, the Biblioteca Nacional de Lisboa, the Biblioteca Ambrosiana di Milano, the Biblioteca Nazionale Marciana di Venezia, and the library of the School of Oriental and African Studies, University of London.

[2] See, for example, Beiene, *La politica cattolica di Seltan Sägäd*; Aregay, 'Legacy of Jesuit Missionary Activities'; and Pennec, *Des jésuites au royaume du prêtre Jean*.

[3] Beccari was referring particularly to Teles's *Historia Geral de Ethiopia a Alta ou Preste Ioam* (1660), and the *Historiæ Societatis Jesu* by Nicolò Orlandini *et al.* (1615–1750). At least two other works could be added: the 'Adição à Relação das coisas de Etiópia' by Fernão Guerreiro (1611), and the *Historia Æthiopica* by Hiob Ludolf (1681). Although Beccari published 14 volumes of documents relating to the Jesuit mission in Ethiopia, he did not have access to the collections of the Braga Public Library (BPB), nor did he republish the collection of annual letters that had first been published in the 17th century – the *Lettere Annue d'Etiopia, Malabar, Brasil e Goa, dall'Anno 1620 fin'al 1624*, Rome, 1627.

the role that the Portuguese played in it.[1] In the introduction to the Porto edition, Elaine Sanceau sees Páez's book – insofar as it is a *refutatio* of the immoderate 'fictions' and 'false-hoods' that Luis de Urreta, a Dominican friar from Valencia, had written about Ethiopia in 1610–11[2] – as the sincere expression, 'without ornaments of rhetoric', of the Jesuit missionary's desire to make 'known the truth about Ethiopia'.[3]

In editing the present edition, we are very aware that Pedro Páez's book is much less than, but at the same time much more than, a 'true' and 'sincere' presentation of Ethiopian history and ethnography. We therefore hope that the publication of a critical, annotated version may enable future readers to see how carefully constructed and how polemical the book really is.

## 2. Biography of Pedro Páez

Pedro Páez Xaramillo was born in 1564 in the Castilian village of Olmeda de las Cebollas (now Olmeda de las Fuentes), a mere fifty kilometres or so east of Madrid. In 1582, at the age of eighteen, he joined the Society of Jesus and served as a novice for two years. He then attended the Jesuit college in Belmonte (Cuenca province), where his theology teacher was Tomás de Iturén. He developed a lasting friendship with Iturén, with whom he corresponded quite regularly during the years when Páez was a missionary in India and Ethiopia, at least until 1617, which is the date of his last known letter, in reply to one from Iturén dated 1614.[4]

On 8 May 1587, Páez sent an *indipeta*[5] (Fig. 2) to the Jesuit General of the time, Claudio Acquaviva (1581–1615). His application was processed and accepted relatively quickly and in March 1588 he was authorized to travel to Goa, the capital of the Portuguese State of India. On arriving in September that year, he enrolled in the theology course at St Paul's College. He did not finish his studies because, in January 1589, the Provincial of the Society in Goa, Pedro Martins, selected him as assistant to Father Antonio de Montserrat to accompany him on a mission to Ethiopia.[6] Because of this, Páez was hurriedly ordained a priest that same month.

This was not the first mission that the Society of Jesus had organized to that country. A contingent of missionaries had arrived there in 1557, only to be thoroughly frustrated

---

[1] Beccari, 'Notizia e saggi di opere e documenti inediti', p. iv. For Beccari, who was himself a Jesuit, it was clearly important to recover and promote the importance of the Jesuits' mission in Ethiopia by publishing the documents that reported their history.

[2] See section 3.1 '*The History of Ethiopia*: the Origins of a Polemical Work', below.

[3] Sanceau, 'Introdução', pp. xviii, xx.

[4] Beccari, *RÆSOI*, 11, p. 382.

[5] See Fig. 2. *Indipetae* were letters of application that future Jesuit missionaries sent to their superiors in Rome stating their desire to undertake a mission to the 'Indies'. The *indipeta* sent by Pedro Páez (ARSI, Fondo Gesuitico 758, f. 84–84v) is one of the 14,067 petitions of this kind held in the Roman Archives of the Society of Jesus, dating back to 1580 (Lamalle, 'La Documentation d'histoire missionnaire'). Páez's *indipeta*, together with an Italian translation, was published in 1905 by Father Tacchi Venturi in 'Pietro Paez apostolo'.

[6] Páez says in the *History of Ethiopia*, some thirty years later, that they left Goa 'on the afternoon of 2nd February 1588' (bk III, ch. 15, vol. II, p. 106). However, the letter he sent from Baçaim to Tomás de Iturén, dated 16 February 1589 (see Beccari, *RÆSOI*, 11, pp. 3–6), shows that the decision to send the two fathers to Ethiopia was made no earlier than the beginning of 1589.

in their hopes of converting the Orthodox Ethiopians to Roman Catholicism, a desire which had originally been voiced by the Society's founder, Ignatius of Loyola, as well as by the pope and the Portuguese crown, which sponsored the undertaking.[1] The decision to send more missionaries to the then almost inaccessible land of Ethiopia was made by the king of Spain and Portugal, Philip II (Philip I). As had been the case with the first diplomatic contacts between Portugal and Ethiopia in the first half of the sixteenth century, Philip's objectives in relation to that part of eastern Africa were both strategic and diplomatic. By renewing ties with the Christian kingdom of Ethiopia, the king hoped to increase pressure on the southern flank of the Ottoman empire, reduce its influence in the Red Sea and thus consolidate the Iberian hegemony in the Indian Ocean, as well as resurrect a highly symbolic alliance between Ethiopian Christendom and Counter-Reformation Europe. There were also practical ecclesiastical reasons: since the missionaries sent in 1557 were now dead or very old, the descendants of the Portuguese community in Ethiopia were presumably deprived of any spiritual support from the Catholic Church.

Philip decided to entrust his confidant, the governor of India Manuel de Sousa Coutinho, with his plan for a new mission to Ethiopia. Coutinho then wrote to the Jesuit Provincial in Goa asking him personally to organize the logistics of the initiative. Páez describes the person selected by the Provincial to carry out the mission as follows: 'The father with whom I am leaving is called Antonio de Montserrat, of Catalan nationality, highly competent in these affairs and particularly skilled in dealing with these kings: he was one of those who were in the kingdom and at the court of the Mogor [the Grand Mughal], and moreover he knows the necessary languages well enough. This mission is being carried out because it has been insistently called for by Our Lord [the king of Spain]. On receiving the king's letters, the viceroy [of India] came straight to our house to ask Father Martínez, the provincial of this province, for some fathers for this mission.'[2]

For the provincial, Father Antonio de Montserrat may have been just the man for the job, with his competence and skill 'in dealing with these kings'. Montserrat together with some other Jesuits had been sent to the court of Jalāl ud-Dīn Muhammad Akbar, or Akbar the Great, whom the Portuguese called the Grand Mughal (reigned 1556–1605),[3] in the hope of persuading him to convert to Catholicism, a project that proved to be 'chimerical'.[4] The fact that the authorities in Goa equated the Grand Mughal, a Muslim monarch, with the ruler of Ethiopia, a Christian king, is surprising to say the least, and suggests that they had not entirely grasped the problems that the missionaries sent to Ethiopia in 1557 had had to face. To a great extent their difficulties had concerned religious issues on which Ethiopian Christianity differed from Roman Catholicism.

Further information on Father Antonio de Montserrat is supplied by the Catalogue of the Province of India for 1599 (these details from ten years later in fact cover practically

---

[1] See Pennec, *Des jésuites au royaume du prêtre Jean*, pp. 47–71, 87–92, 116–25.

[2] Letter from Pedro Páez to Tomás de Iturén, from Bassein (a port on the west coast of India) on 16 February 1589 (Beccari, *RÆSOI*, 11, pp. 3–6).

[3] See Glossary: Gelaldîn Acabar / Jalāl ud-Dīn Muhammad Akbar / Akbar the Great. A new political order emerged in the Indian subcontinent in the 1570s, when the Mughals expanded from the Ganges valley to form an empire with access to the Indian Ocean in the west and to the Bay of Bengal in the east (Subrahmanyam, *Portuguese Empire in Asia*, p. 146).

[4] Subrahmanyam, *Portuguese Empire in Asia*, p. 147.

the whole of his life, since he died the following year).[1] He was sixty-three years old at the time and had joined the Society of Jesus forty-three years before. He had studied Latin, logic and cases of conscience, and took his vows as spiritual coadjutor on 1 January 1579.[2] Although he was a learned theologian he did not formally study theology to obtain the status of professed Jesuit. The highest rank within the Society of Jesus was that of professed – even the general was just one professed among others.[3] This rank was usually awarded after years of theological studies (four years, without counting the years spent studying the humanities and arts),[4] which Antonio de Montserrat had not done. That did not prevent him from having had adequate training and, as the Instructions of the Society state, those accepted to take the three vows to be spiritual coadjutors 'will usually be men who, while not having the knowledge and talent as preachers that our Institute requires of the professed, are so deserving and so deeply pious that the decision will be made, in our Lord, that they should be admitted'.[5]

The provincial of Goa therefore decided to send Antonio de Montserrat, a fifty-two-year-old priest with plenty of experience on the ground but little formal theological training, and Pedro Páez, at that time an apparently highly motivated twenty-five-year-old who had no practical experience at all and had not yet finished his training. This choice suggests that, although the provincial was formally obeying the royal decision emanating from Madrid, he preferred not to send more than one qualified priest to a land where missionary activity had previously failed, via a risky sea and land route that was most unlikely to be successful. Since neither Montserrat nor Páez was a professed Jesuit, they were therefore not really qualified to confront Ethiopian Orthodox theologians in conciliar debate.[6]

By this time the ambitious plans to convert the kingdom of the 'Prester John' to Catholicism, put forward by Ignatius of Loyola, had in practice been abandoned by the Society. Although political considerations (notably the rivalry among religious orders for mission lands)[7] played a part in the resurgence of interest in Ethiopia, the explicit reason for reviving the mission for the Provincial of the Society in Goa was the chance to offer spiritual support and administer the holy sacraments to a small Catholic community (of no more than 800–1,200 members) living in an Orthodox kingdom which was regarded in Europe as heretical, Judaistic and permeated with Islamic influences.

The two fathers left Goa for Ethiopia on 2 February 1589, but their boat sank within sight of Dhofar, on the southern coast of the Arabian peninsula. The travellers were saved by a vessel flying the Turkish flag and were immediately imprisoned and taken ashore as hostages. They were afterwards taken overland to San'a' in Yemen, where they remained for two years, and later they served as oarsmen on a Turkish galley that plied the Red Sea. After seven years they were at last ransomed by the Portuguese authorities in Goa for a tidy sum, and they arrived back in Portuguese India in December 1596. There, Pedro Páez

[1] ARSI, MS Goa 24 II, f. 321v.
[2] Ibid., f. 283: 'P. António de Monserrate natural de Vig. de Ausona, Bispado e Prov.a de Catalunha, de 63 años; 43 da Comp.a, estudou latim, logica, e casos, ... fez os votos de coadiutor spiial ao pr.o de janr.o de 79'.
[3] Loyola, *Écrits*, p. 517, n. e.
[4] Ibid., p. 518.
[5] Ibid. p. 519.
[6] Ibid., pp. 100–109.
[7] See Introduction, section 3.1, below.

attempted to resume his theological studies, but in February 1597 he fell seriously ill and was bedridden for eight months. Once restored to health, he was sent to Salsette island (now occupied by the city of Mumbai) in charge of the spiritual administration of four Catholic villages. In early 1601 he departed for the Portuguese fortress of Diu on the Gujarat coast, hoping to be able to set off again for Ethiopia and resume the mission with which he had been entrusted twelve years previously.

Meanwhile, an Indian secular priest named Melchior (or Belchior) da Silva had been sent from Goa to the Ethiopian kingdom in 1598 after news had arrived in Goa of the death of Father Francisco Lopes, the last survivor of the 1557 mission. An Indian priest had been chosen because of the obvious difficulties of sending European members of the Society via routes dominated by the Ottomans. After he arrived at Fremona (originally Māy Gogā or Māy Gwāgwā), in Tegrāy,[1] where most of the descendants of the Portuguese soldiers who had arrived there half a century before still lived, Father Melchior da Silva sent a grim report back to Goa. He mentioned the 'deplorable' state, both materially and spiritually, to which the Luso-Ethiopian community had been reduced and stressed that its members were about to lose their Catholic identity and embrace Ethiopian Orthodoxy.[2]

This information must have spurred the Jesuit hierarchy in Goa into supporting a new attempt to send missionaries to Ethiopia. In 1603, Páez finally reached his goal after disguising himself as an Armenian merchant and sailing on Turkish vessels to the port of Meššewā' or Massawa (which he spells Maçuâ), now in Eritrea. In May that year he was welcomed by the members of the Luso-Ethiopian community at the residence in Fremona.

Pedro Páez's arrival in Ethiopia marks the beginning of what may be considered the second phase of the Jesuit mission in that country. Over the next two years, four more missionaries (Fathers António Fernandes, Francisco António de Angelis, Luís de Azevedo and Lorenzo Romano) were sent, a clear sign that the Provincial in Goa had changed his mind about this mission, perhaps moved by the optimism of Páez's early letters about the Ethiopian court's readiness to embrace a possible diplomatic and religious entente.

Between 1603 and 1621–2 the scope of the Jesuit fathers' activities in Ethiopia expanded considerably. Initially, the royal court only allowed them to attend to the Catholic community's religious needs and to take charge of the education of Luso-Ethiopian children. Soon, however, they began to extend their influence to non-Christian peoples living in areas recently conquered by the Ethiopian royal armies and, later, even to traditionally Orthodox areas. Having been made landholders by royal privilege, they became more and more involved in tense political struggles at court as a monastic order competing with the Orthodox Church. This situation allowed the king to free himself from the traditional, constraining influence of the Order of Dabra Libānos and the Orthodox regular clergy. In addition, the members of the new mission had embarked on a programme of translating Catholic religious texts, as well as producing regular letters and documents to send to Rome and Goa. Páez tells us that soon after arriving in Ethiopia he had started translating the *Cartilha*, a catechism for children, into Amharic, the spoken

---

[1] The northern region of Ethiopia, bordering Eritrea.
[2] Beccari, *RÆSOI*, 1, p. 416 (summarized in Guerreiro, *Relação anual*, I, p. 361); see Pennec, *Des jésuites au royaume du prêtre Jean*, pp. 111–15.

language of the Christian kingdom. He was helped in this by one of the Portuguese descendants, João Gabriel, known as the 'captain of the Portuguese'. From 1612 onwards, the five Jesuit missionaries systematically laboured to translate catechetic and liturgical texts and a number of Biblical commentaries into Ge'ez, the liturgical language of the Ethiopian Orthodox Church. Their primary aim was to provide further tools of Catholic doctrine for use in disputations with Orthodox theologians, in which the missionaries engaged under the patronage of the king and certain influential courtiers.

As the superior of the Ethiopian mission, Pedro Páez also assumed the task of establishing and developing diplomatic contacts with the Ethiopian court. He took the initiative of offering King Za Dengel (reigned 1603–4) and his two successors an alliance with the Iberian crown,[1] on condition that they joined the Catholic faith and proclaimed their obedience to Rome. The Jesuit fathers' missionary efforts only really began to bear fruit in 1607, when the pretender Susneyos took the throne. This king showed a fresh willingness to reorganize the system of political influence in the kingdom, within a social and demographic context that was rapidly changing, mainly because of the arrival in the Christian highlands of several nomadic Oromo groups from the south (supposedly from the Great Lakes region).[2] As a result, the missionaries allowed themselves to be dragged by the king and his brother, *Ras* Se'elā Krestos, into a complex power struggle between the royal court, the landholding nobility and the Orthodox clergy, as rivals to the influential monks of the Order of Dabra Libānos.[3] Prior to the succession of Susneyos, the Catholic missionaries had been confined to Fremona and a few other fairly peripheral communities. Subsequently, however, as the king allowed them to found new residences and colleges[4] and granted them greater freedom of movement, Pedro Páez started to live in the royal camp for long periods of time. He gradually gained the trust of Susneyos and his immediate family circle, accompanied him on several tours and expeditions, and acted as his adviser not only on religious matters but also on substantially political, diplomatic and even military affairs.

It was above all because of Páez's influence – at least, this is the interpretation given by Jesuit writers[5] – that King Susneyos agreed to join the Catholic faith in 1621. He subsequently publicly announced his obedience to the Roman pontiff and proclaimed an edict condemning as heretical a number of Ethiopian Christian practices (observance of the Sabbath, circumcision and yearly baptism) and some fundamental doctrinal principles of monophysite Orthodoxy (the oneness of the divine and human nature of Christ, the specificity of the Trinity concept and the prominence of Old Testament theology).

---

[1] There is no suggestion in the documentation consulted that Pedro Páez had received specific instructions from the viceroy in Goa or from Philip II to propose such an alliance.

[2] Note that Susneyos had spent part of his youth living among the Macha Oromo. On the first (documented) presence of the Oromo in Ethiopia and on the immediately preceding war of resistance by the Christian kingdom against the Somali and 'Adāli invaders led by Aḥmad ibn Ibrāhīm al-Ghāzi (known as Grāññ or Granh, which means 'left-handed'), see: Abir, *Ethiopia and the Red Sea,* pp. 75–7, 133–76; Ramos, 'Machiavellian Empowerment and Disempowerment'; and Ficquet, 'La Fabrique des origines oromo'.

[3] See Pennec, *Des jésuites au royaume du prêtre Jean*, ch. 4; Pennec and Derat, 'Les Églises et monastères royaux'; and Ramos, 'Machiavellian Empowerment and Disempowerment', pp. 196–8.

[4] See the map of Catholic churches and Jesuit residences in Ethiopia in the early 17th century (Fig. 1).

[5] This simplistic, self-congratulatory interpretation needs to be thoroughly reviewed: see, for instance, Aregay, 'Legacy of Jesuit Missionary Activities', pp. 45 *et seq.*

# HISTORIA ECLESIASTICA POLITICA, NATVRAL, Y MORAL,

## DE LOS GRANDES Y REMOTOS Reynos de la Etiopia, Monarchia del Emperador, llamado Preste Iuan de las Indias.

*MVY VTIL Y TROVECHOSA TAR todos estados, principalmente para Predicadores.*

## A LA SACRATISSIMA Y SIEMpre Virgen MARIA del Rosario.

Compuesta por el Presentado Fray Luys de Vrreta, de la sagrada Orden de Predicadores.

Con tres Tablas muy copiosas.

Año 1610.

CON PRIVILEGIO.
En Valencia, en casa de Pedro Patricio Mey.
A costa de Roque Sonzonio mercader de libros.

Figure 3. Frontispiece of *Historia ... de la Etiopía* by Friar Luis de Urreta, 1610.

# HISTORIA
## DE LA SAGRADA ORDEN
### DE PREDICADORES,

En los remotos Reynos de la Etiopia.

TRata de los prodigiosos Sátos, Martyres, y Cófessores, Inquisi-
dores Apostolicos, de los Cóuentos de Plurimanos, dóde viuen
nueue mil frayles: del Alleluya con siete mil: y de Bedenagli, de
cinco mil monjas: con otras grandezas de la Religion
del Padre santo Domingo.

DIRIGIDA AL REVERENDISSIMO MAESTRO
el P.F. Luys Ystella, quõdam Vicario general de la sagrada
Orden de Predicadores; y al Presente, Maestro del
Palacio Sacro Apostolico.

POR EL PRESENTADO FR. LVYS
de Vrreta, hijo del Conuento de Predicadores
de Valencia.

CON PRIVILEGIO

Impressa en Valencia, en casa de Iuan Chrysostomo Garriz,
junto al molino de Rouella. Año 1611.

Figure 4. Frontispiece of *Historia de la Sagrada Orden de Predicadores* by Friar Luis de Urreta, 1611.

Páez started writing his *History of Ethiopia* in 1613 or 1614, fulfilling a request made by the Jesuit hierarchy in Rome. He then embarked on a vast ethnographic, historical and literary survey of Christian Ethiopia. He collected oral statements from church, monastic and court authorities; he researched manuscripts on the political and religious history of the country; and he travelled through several regions subject to the Christian monarchy, visiting important religious sites. The extensive documentation that he compiled served as the basis for the immense fresco of the *History of Ethiopia*. The work was apparently almost finished when its author died of a violent fever at the Jesuit residence in Gorgorā, on the northern shores of Lake Ṭānā, on 20 May 1622, just a few days after King Susneyos had publicly declared his obedience to Rome.[1]

## 3. The Reasons for Writing the *History of Ethiopia*: Commissioning a Refutation

The *History of Ethiopia* started out, at least, as an attempt to refute the fanciful view of the Christian kingdom of Ethiopia propounded by a Dominican scholar from Valencia, Spain, which had been published in two volumes in 1610–11. To understand why Páez's work was commissioned and written, we must first look at the reasons and objectives that lay behind the composition and publication of this other work, within the context of the relations between the Order of Saint Dominic and the Society of Jesus in the Iberian Peninsula. Indeed, rather than being a strictly Ethiopian matter, the *History of Ethiopia* owes its existence primarily to a European – Iberian – issue: the disputes between these two religious orders over mission lands, interspersed with political intrigue involving the royal courts of Portugal and Spain.

*3.1. The* History of Ethiopia: *the Origins of a Polemical Work*
In the early seventeenth century, the lands of eastern Africa were the subject of a politico-religious campaign waged by Dominican priests, which took the form of two very different literary tomes that shared the same purpose. The first was published in Évora, Portugal, in 1609 under the title *Etiópia Oriental, e vária história de cousas notáveis do Oriente*,[2] written by Friar João dos Santos, a Dominican missionary in the lands of Mozambique held under the Portuguese Oriental enterprise. The second work, printed in two volumes in Valencia in 1610–11, was by Master Friar Luis de Urreta (c. 1570–1636); its first volume bore the title *Historia eclesiástica, política, natural, y moral, de los grandes y remotos Reynos de la Etiopia, Monarchia del Emperador, llamado Preste Juan de las Indias*,[3] while the title of the second was *Historia de la sagrada Orden de Predicadores, en los remotos Reynos de la Etiopia*.[4] These publications suffered very different fates: whereas João dos Santos's work – particularly its first part – became widely disseminated through

---

[1] See Pennec and Ramos, 'Páez, Pedro (1564–1622)'.

[2] 'Eastern Ethiopia, and varied history of notable things of the East'. A highly abridged English translation was published by Samuel Purchas in *Hakluytus Posthumus or Purchas His Pilgrimes*, II, bk xi, ch. 12.

[3] '*Ecclesiastical, political, natural and moral history of the great and remote Kingdoms of Ethiopia, monarchy of the Emperor called the Prester John of the Indies*'. It is divided into three books, with 33, 15 and 6 chapters, comprising a total of 731 pages. See Fig. 3.

[4] '*History of the Sacred Order of Preachers in the Remote Kingdoms of Ethiopia*'. It comprises 20 chapters and 410 pages. See Fig. 4.

being paraphrased by other authors (notably the Jesuit priest, Father Alonso de Sandoval),[1] Urreta's books elicited an indignant reaction from the Society of Jesus. Both, however, can be read as apologies for the Dominican Order, particularly as regards missionary activity. They claim precedence for the Dominicans in this field and stress the idea of missionary exclusivity, upholding the order's right to establish missions without competition in certain lands regarded as peripheral, at a time when the Society of Jesus was expanding the geographical range of its activities. In *Etiópia Oriental*, for instance, Santos removed any reference to the early Jesuit missions in eastern Africa,[2] while in the *Historia ... de la Etiopía* Urreta claims a primordial role for the Dominicans in the conversion of the Ethiopian kingdom to Catholicism, which he attributes to a group of eight friars preachers in the early fourteenth century.[3] His purpose was 'to show that the Prester John's *Abexins* have never been and are not schismatic and separate from the Roman Church, but Catholic and obedient to her',[4] and to give substance to his claim that there had been a prior Dominican presence in that country, pre-dating the Jesuits' arrival by at least two and a half centuries. By means of this device – almost a *reductio ad absurdum* – the Dominican Urreta hoped to invalidate *a priori* the papal privilege granted to the rival Jesuits to establish a mission in Ethiopia.

The dispute over missionary lands took the battle between the two orders for influence in the Spanish court out beyond the confines of the Iberian peninsula. It had become more acute in the period around the turn of the century with the controversy over the Jesuit Luis de Molina's (1536–1600) thesis on free will, *Concordia liberi arbitrii*, on the question of grace and predestination.[5] The movement criticizing Molina's ideas had begun within the Society of Jesus itself (the work had in fact been praised by its censor, the Dominican friar Bartolomeu Ferreira). However, the two religious orders soon radicalized their positions, and the accusations which had initially been levelled against the author of the thesis came to be more broadly directed against the Society as a whole. Even the king and the pope were drawn into the dispute, to the point that, in 1607, Pope Paul V (1605–21) banned the opponents from accusing each other of heresy, in an attempt to put an end to demands that he should excommunicate the Jesuits involved in the controversy.[6] This context, which has only summarily been sketched out here, adds new meaning to the following passage from the Prologue to the first part of João dos Santos's *Etiópia oriental*: 'And there is even more reason for us to recognize this mercy from God, for we have been raised in the bosom of Christianity and fed on the milk of

---

[1] See Lobato, ed., 'Introdução' to Santos, *Etiópia oriental*, 1999, pp. 32–6. The work in question by Sandoval is *Naturaleza, policia sagrada i profana, costumbres i ritos, disciplina i catecismo evangélico de todos Etiopes* (Seville, 1627).

[2] Santos, *Etiópia oriental*, 1999, pp. 488–90, where he deals with 'the foundation of the house of St Dominic in Mozambique'. (The English version makes only a brief mention of the 'Convent of Dominicans' in Mozambique, on p. 249.) See Lobato, 'Introdução', 1999, p. 12.

[3] According to several Dominican writers, particularly Serafino Razzi, Friars Luis de Urreta and João dos Santos identified these friars with the Nine Saints venerated by the Ethiopian Orthodox Church (Santos, *Etiópia oriental*, 1999, pp. 427–9, but not mentioned in Purchas's English version; Urreta, *Historia de la Sagrada Orden*, 1611, pp. 13–30).

[4] Guerreiro, 'Adição à Relação das coisas de Etiópia', p. 287.

[5] Molina, *Concordia liberi arbitrii cum gratiae donis diuina praescentia, prouidentia, praedestinatione et reprobatione ad nonnullos primae partis D. Thomae articulos*, Lisbon, 1588.

[6] Reinhard, *Paul V*, pp. 433–8; Hilaire, ed., *Histoire de la papauté*, pp. 345–6.

the Catholic doctrine and Law of Grace'. The writer continues with an exhortation to emulate the Dominican and Augustinian religious who spread and taught it.[1] This comment may be taken together with Urreta's allegations about Judaistic heretics who went to Ethiopia from Portugal in about 1555 and were expelled by a king loyal to the Catholic teachings of the Dominican missionaries, after which they spread the calumny that Ethiopian Christianity was schismatic.[2] Although Urreta identified those involved as 'perfidious Jews' numbering more than three hundred and reserved great consideration for Bishop Andrés de Oviedo, the superior of the first Jesuit mission, the date given coincides exactly with the year when the first group of Jesuits left for India en route for Ethiopia. His comment therefore appears to be a veiled insinuation about the perfidy of the Jesuits who, at the time when he was writing, upheld theses considered heretical and had indeed labelled the Ethiopian Church schismatic.

When, in the 'Prologue to the readers' in his *Historia ... de la Etiopía*, Urreta set himself up as the defender of the truth, comparing himself to 'another Curtius in the chasm in Rome, thinking it to be the lesser evil to be censured and reprehended than not to say many new things that are written here',[3] could he have foreseen how strongly the Jesuits would react? In any case, he had been the first to fan the flames of the controversy by claiming that the Ethiopians were Catholic and that any information to the contrary had been maliciously invented by Portuguese Jews. Soon, however, the situation would be reversed, as if some higher force of justice was using the Dominican friar to rearrange the chessboard of the religious dispute. The commissions that had questioned the two ambassadors sent by the Ethiopian monarchy to Portugal on different occasions had concluded in 1514,[4] and confirmed in 1528–9,[5] that Ethiopian Christianity included practices regarded as non-Catholic, such as the keeping of the Sabbath and the Old Testament prohibitions on eating certain foods. Believing that such practices were deviations resulting from the long isolation of the Ethiopian Church and that they needed to be expurgated, the pope and the king of Portugal wrote to the Ethiopian king and metropolitan urging them to relinquish these suspiciously Judaistic aspects of their religion and to lead the faithful back to the Catholic truth. By claiming that Ethiopia was a Catholic kingdom as a result of the evangelizing activities of Dominican friars, and insinuating that the Society of Jesus and the Portuguese had had a negative, corrupting influence on the Ethiopian Orthodox faith, Urreta set in motion a rhetorical machine that would cast his own work into literary limbo. The Jesuits' reaction was organized with the clear aim of neutralizing the principal ideas put forward by Urreta.[6]

Luis de Urreta had been born in Valencia. He entered the convent of Preachers (Dominicans) there, and professed in 1588. He then gained a master's degree in theology. As far as can be ascertained, he never set foot outside the Dominican province that covered Aragon, Catalonia and Valencia, throughout which he travelled as a preacher

---

[1] Santos, *Etiópia oriental*, p. 58.

[2] Urreta, *Historia de la Etiopía*, pp. 614–15.

[3] Ibid., 'Prólogo a los lectores'.

[4] After questioning Mateus, a merchant originally from the Armenian community in Egypt, who was sent to Portugal by the Ethiopian queen regent Elléni at the end of the first decade of the 16th century.

[5] After questioning Ṣaggā Za Āb, an Ethiopian monk sent as an ambassador by King Lebna Dengel. See Aubin, 'Le Prêtre Jean devant la censure portuguaise', p. 186 and pp. 201–4.

[6] Boavida, 'História e fábula', p. 189.

every year during Lent. When he died – on Maundy Thursday, 1636 – he left so many notes and miscellaneous writings in his cell that a fellow friar remarked at that time that 'it was almost a library'.[1] Many of these papers were subsequently lost at the time of a celebration held in the monastery, when they were used to cover some decorations.[2] Apart from his books on Ethiopia, he left a few manuscripts: one a historical miscellany in two volumes, and also the *Combite de la naturaleza*.[3] The notes on Urreta in the catalogues of Dominican writers emphasize his simple, candid nature, which led him to accept everything that his informant told him about Ethiopia as the truth.[4]

The idea that Urreta was ingenuous began with his refuters. It is interesting to see how the blame for the 'lies' that he narrates gradually shifts away from the writer himself and comes to be attributed first and foremost to his informant. Nonetheless, a number of questions arise with regard to this informant, whose role was to lend authority to many of the topics discussed in the *Historia ... de la Etiopía*. To explain who he was and how they met, Urreta says that there arrived 'at this holy convent of Preachers, of the noble city of Valencia, an Ethiopian gentleman from the kingdom and city of Fatigar in Ethiopia called Iuan de Baltasar, a military knight of the Order of Saint Anthony the Abbot and of the guard of the king of Ethiopia called Prester John of the Indies, with some originals and papers, part in the Ethiopic language and part in Italian, poorly put together, but qualified and true'.[5] There is evidence that some individuals from Abyssinia did travel to Italy, and one of them may well have gone on to Spain. The possibility that they are one and the same person cannot be ruled out, but neither can the hypothesis that João Baltazar was a product of Urreta's pen.[6] The 'Relazione dell'Africa, suoi dominii, proprietà e costumi, dettata da Giovanni Abissino e scritta da Piero Duodo nel 1578'[7] suggests that a certain John the Abyssinian was passing through Italy on his way to Germany to venerate the relics of the three Magi, thus associating his journey with the complex web of fable surrounding the imaginary kingdom of 'Prester John'.[8] He was forty-two years of age at

---

[1] Falcón, '*Historia de algunas cosas más notables*', BHUV, MS 204, p. 644.

[2] Agramunt, '*El Palacio Real de la Sabedoría*', BHUV, MS 148–9, II, pp. 512–13. The writings in notebooks were handed to Friar Josef Agramunt, who had them bound.

[3] The 'Invitation of Nature'. These manuscripts were apparently still in the monastery library in the mid-18th century (see Rodríguez, *Biblioteca Valentina*, p. 310).

[4] See Gimeno, *Escritores del Reyno de Valencia*, p. 333; C. Fuentes, *Escritores dominicos del Reino de Valencia*, p. 334.

[5] Urreta, *Historia de la Etiopía*, 1610, unpaginated.

[6] The records of the Royal Convent of Preachers of Valencia that are held in the convent archive and in the General Library at the University of Valencia were searched, and no mention was found of the arrival, stay or even death of any Abyssinian or Indian. These records have been dispersed at various times in their history – to the Dominican convent in Palma de Mallorca, the Archive of the Kingdom of Valencia, the Archivo Histórico Nacional, and into private hands. See Robles, 'Manuscritos del Archivo del Real Convento de Predicadores de Valencia', pp. 350–51.

[7] 'Account of Africa, its dominions, properties and customs, dictated by John the Abyssinian and written by Piero Duodo in 1578', BA, cod.,R. 101, ff. 139r–176r. See Revelli, 'Una relazione'.

[8] The relics of the three Magi were supposed to have been brought from the Orient to Milan and later taken to Germany. Johannes von Hildesheim reports this transfer and explains the link between the Magi and Prester John by claiming that the Magi had instituted the patriarchate of Saint Thomas in India, had enthroned Prester John as his successor, and had built the city where he reigned (Hildesheim, *Historia trium regum*, ff. 33–4). On the association of the mythological Prester John complex with Ethiopia, see Ramos, *Essays in Christian Mythology*, pp. 104–25.

the time of this report, which sets out what was known about Ethiopia in Europe at that time, together with other miscellaneous pieces of information. Another account, the 'Relatione del Gran Regno degli Abissini ouero d'Ethiopia fatta da don Baldassari Abissino Cavallero dell'Ordine di Sant Antonio', records the presence of a certain Balthazar the Abyssinian in Rome in about the last decade of the sixteenth century.[1] If these two were the same person, it would mean that he had been on pilgrimage in Europe for nearly twenty years, and if he was also the person who, some fifteen years after meeting Monsignor Migliore, was a guest of the Dominicans in Valencia, he must have spent half his life outside his native land. Another possibility suggested by Urreta in the *Historia ... de la Etiopía* is that in the meantime he had returned to Ethiopia and once again set out for Europe, a sterling venture for a seventy-year-old man.[2] Urreta added that the purpose of this journey was to 'print this history', the existence of which was due to him.

This man, first called John, then Balthazar, then John Balthazar (or João Baltazar in Portuguese), had apparently found his vocation as a teller of stories that offered the same view of a wondrous Ethiopia as was found in the Prester John legends of medieval Europe. He may have been a refined, cultured impostor who knew what his listeners wanted to hear, or a simple informant whose words were manipulated to coincide with that European view of Ethiopia, or he may have been a skilful invention designed to legitimize the contemporary version of the old ideas about Ethiopia through his authority as an eye witness. This last hypothesis is supported by the details of his itinerary (mentioned above) and his identity. In the 'Relatione del Gran Regno degli Abissini' he is said to be from the kingdom of 'Fatigar' (i.e. Faṭagār), which belonged to the 'house' of the descendants of Balthazar, one of the three Magi. The figure was thus endowed with personal prestige, not only because he had been born in the region associated with that house, but also because he bore the patronym of the holy lineage (except in Duodo's 'Relazione'); this placed him close to the throne because, as he asserted, the emperor was chosen from among the first-born of the three Ethiopian houses of the line of the three Magi.[3] Faṭagār was an outlying region lying roughly between the River Awāš and the slopes of Mount Enṭṭoṭo,[4] an odd location for a land granted as a privilege to a lineage touched with holiness. The other name of this wandering knight, John, was associated with the 'presters', to whom he was also linked through the name Balthazar. This highly ingenious construction presents him as an authentic historical figure, to the extent that historians have accepted him as such without reservation.[5]

These 'Relationi' may well have been disseminated in manuscript form, not least because Urreta's work repeats and expands on the information they contain while also appealing to other authorities on historiography, hagiography and geography. It is interesting to note that the 'Relatione del Gran Regno degli Abissini' refers to the conversion of the peoples subject to the Manicongo and the king of Monomotapa by the 'Jesuit

[1] 'Account of the Great Kingdom of the Abyssinians or of Ethiopia done by Don Balthazar the Abyssinian Knight of the Order of Saint Anthony', BNM, MSS Italiani, cl. 6, n° 332. The account was written at the request of Monsenhor Migliore, the bishop of San Marco, Cosenza, Commander General of the Order of the Holy Spirit and chaplain to Pope Sixtus V (1585–90).

[2] 'He was approaching seventy when he arrived in Europe' (Urreta, *Historia de la Etiopía*, 1610, p. 7).

[3] 'Relatione del Gran Regno degli Abissini', BNM, MSS Italiani, cl. 6, n° 332, ff. 2r and 13r.

[4] Wolde Aregay, *Southern Ethiopia and the Christian Kingdom*, p. 46.

[5] For example Caraman, *Lost Empire*, p. 130.

Fathers true Apostles of the Lord Jesus Christ',[1] which brings us back to the original context for the *Historia ... de la Etiopía* and the *Historia de la Sagrada Orden de Predicadores.*

The fantastic vision of Ethiopia laid out by Urreta, in which the perfect city of men is ideally presented as a mirror of divine harmony, needs to be understood in terms of its rhetorical content rather than being reduced to a mere collection of 'lies', as it was by its Jesuit refuters.[2]

### 3.2. *The Refutation*

As Fernão Guerreiro and other Jesuit writers had done previously in the 'Adição à relação das coisas de Etiópia', albeit more generically (and infinitely more succinctly), Pedro Páez responded to his superiors' request to counter the Dominican arguments. In his extended refutation, running to 538 folios, he set out the 'truth' about that country. This was based on his long years of familiarity with, observation of and participation in Ethiopian life, as well as abundant oral statements and local writings that he had collected, and supplemented with references to Jesuit letters and reports, such as the one by Father Francisco Álvares. The *History of Ethiopia* is thus the result of twenty years' personal experience, and it offers its readers not only a detailed presentation of the country's history but also a rich, original, ethnographic description of Ethiopian society at a time when the kingdom was undergoing profound change due to the social and cultural readjustments caused by the last tremors of the war with the Muslim populations and the tensions arising from the incorporation of the Oromo into the Ethiopian power context. The work also reveals how Páez intricately wove in the story of the Jesuit mission as a supremely important episode in the overall narrative, in which he felt he played a leading role.

The panorama painted by the *History of Ethiopia* goes far beyond a disparaging view of a barbaric society dominated by an heretical faith and in urgent need of reform and of being led back to the 'true faith'. It is a complex work that represents a decisive step in the development of European knowledge about that part of Africa. Since the mid-sixteenth century, the Jesuits had been engaged in an attempt to spiritually reconquer the Prester John's kingdom, but had suffered a setback during the mission under Bishop Andrés de Oviedo, who had only been allowed to provide spiritual support to the Portuguese community established there since the 1540s. They therefore felt deeply hurt by the assertions made by Urreta, a member of a competing order, and sought to refute them by various means.

Although insufficient details are available to decide precisely who gave the orders and who carried them out, there are clues suggesting some plausible hypotheses. The Portuguese Jesuit Fernão Guerreiro (1550–1617) had been in charge of publishing the annual reports sent from the mission lands since the beginning of the century. In 1611, a few months after the first volume of Urreta's *Historia ... de la Etiopía* had been printed, he issued the annual letters for 1607 and 1608 with the authorization of the general of the order, Father Claudio Acquaviva, together with an 'Addition to the Report on the affairs of Ethiopia, with more extensive information on them, very correct and very different

---

[1] 'Padri Giesuiti veri Apostoli dal Signore Giesu Christo'in 'Relatione del Gran Regno degli Abissini', BNM, MSS Italiani, cl. 6, n° 332, f. 25v.

[2] The editors of this volume are currently undertaking a critical re-reading of Urreta with a view to producing a new edition of his works.

from that which Father Friar Luis de Urreta followed in the book that he printed on the History of that empire of the Prester John'.[1] In this 'Addition', Guerreiro wrote a long appraisal of Urreta's book based on the documentation available in the files on Ethiopia, that is to say the letters from the missionaries in Ethiopia, from the kings of Spain and Portugal and from the Catholic popes.

Guerreiro apparently did not undertake this task on his own initiative, as part of his duties as compiler of the annual letters sent back from all the mission lands; rather, it was part of a plan drawn up within the higher echelons of the Society. The main reasons for publishing the reports on the overseas missions were to stimulate missionary zeal among the students at the Jesuit colleges and to disseminate a dynamic image of the Society by providing models of courage, fervour and self-denial in the various regions where mission-aries were at work.[2] The practice was encouraged and formed part of the propaganda strategy managed by the hierarchy and put into operation through the discipline of obedi-ence. It is thus likely that Guerreiro's appraisal of Urreta's work was the result of a decision made centrally in Rome, particularly since the authorization emanated from General Acquaviva himself. This was the beginning of the polemic against Luis de Urreta, which was to continue until the middle of the seventeenth century.

Meanwhile, in the latter half of 1611, the second volume of Urreta's work was published under the title *Historia de la Sagrada Orden de Predicadores, en los remotos Reynos de la Etiopia*.[3] Here Urreta described in detail his claims for the Dominicans' pioneering missionary activity. Soon afterwards, between 1613–14 and 1616, the Jesuit provinces of Portugal and Goa, apparently acting jointly and concurrently, commissioned three works from three separate authors to refute and delegitimize the Dominican friar's books by widely publicizing the Jesuit case against the allegation that Ethiopian Christianity was Roman Catholic and challenging the insinuation that the Society of Jesus had installed itself there under false pretences. A Latin version, aimed at a wide audience, was entrusted to Father Nicolau Godinho (1561–1616), whose work *De Abassinorum rebus deque Æthiopiae Patriarchis Ioanne Nonio Barreto, & Andrea Oviedo* came off the press in 1615. The chronicler Diogo do Couto (1542–1616) wrote a lay version in Portuguese, now lost, entitled *Historia do Reyno da Ethiopia, chamado vulgarmente Preste João, contra as falsi-dades, que nesta materia escreveo Fr. Luiz Urreta Dominicano*.[4] After the author's death the manuscript was sent to the archbishop of Braga, Dom Aleixo de Meneses,[5] which shows how much the Church hierarchy and even the political authorities were interested in the

---

[1] Guerreiro, 'Adição à Relação das coisas de Etiópia', pp. 287–380. Regarding the various editions, see Sommervogel, *Bibliothèque des écrivains de la Compagnie de Jésus*, III, pp. 1913–15. In 1614, the Jesuit Pierre du Jarric published a French version inspired by Guerreiro's reports as *Histoires des choses plus mémorables*, bk III (Carayon, *Bibliographie historique de la Compagnie de Jésus*, p. 109).

[2] The letters sent back by missionaries and these annual compilations were read out at meal times in the colleges to inspire students to want to go off on missions themselves (Masson, 'La Perspective missionnaire dans la spiritualité des Jésuites', p. 1032; Laborie, *La Mission jésuite au Brésil*, pp. 10–11; Manso, *A Companhia de Jesus na Índia*, p. 85).

[3] 'History of the Holy Order of Preachers, in the remote Kingdoms of Ethiopia.' The opinion of the qualifier of the Holy Office, who happened to be a friar in the same monastery as Urreta, is dated 14 May 1611. This marks the point at which the book began to be typeset by the printer, Juan Crisóstomo Garriz.

[4] 'History of the Kingdom of Ethiopia, vulgarly called Prester John, against the falsehoods which Friar Luiz de Urreta the Dominican wrote on this matter.'

[5] Machado, *Bibliotheca Lusitana*, I, p. 649.

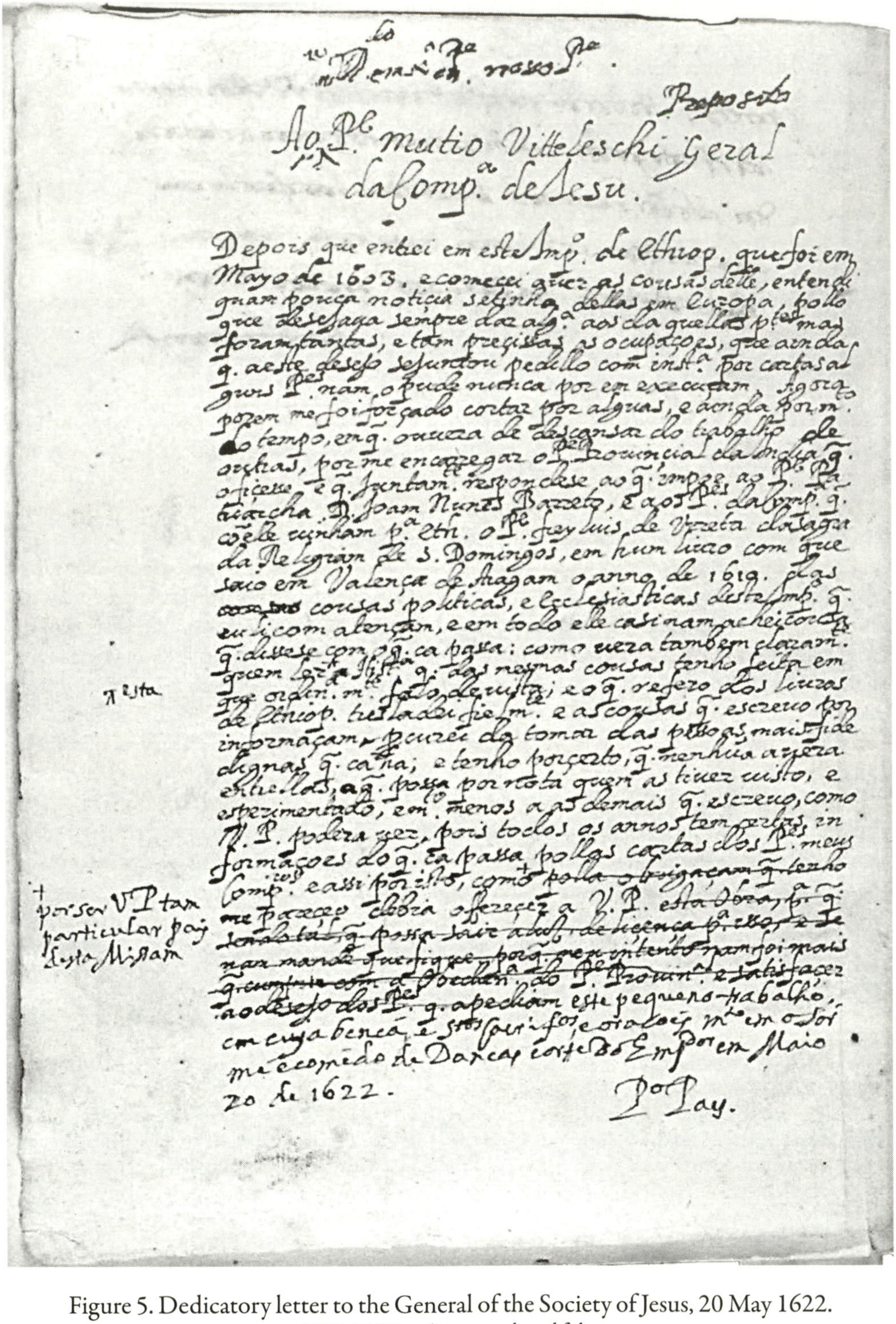

Ao P.e Mutio Vitteleschi Geral da Comp.a de Jesu.

P.o Pay.

Figure 5. Dedicatory letter to the General of the Society of Jesus, 20 May 1622.
ARSI, MS Goa 42, unnumbered folio.

issue, since Dom Aleixo had a seat on the Council of State in Madrid. The request for a third version was sent to the highlands of Ethiopia, where the direct testimony of the missionaries themselves was called on to provide a basis for the argument, establishing the principles of truth and discursive authority. Pedro Páez, the mission superior, took this task upon himself and laboured on it until the end of his life.

There is nothing in the correspondence of the Society's general, Claudio Acquaviva, to suggest that he himself had given the order for one of the missionaries in Ethiopia to devote himself to drawing up a refutation of Urreta's works *in situ*. The only information that we have is given by Páez in the dedicatory letter to the *History of Ethiopia*, where he says that he wrote it at the request of his superior, the provincial of Goa.[1] When might that request have arrived in Ethiopia? In 1903, Camillo Beccari proposed that Páez had begun the *History of Ethiopia* in 1620 and finished it in 1622.[2] In 1905, Beccari revised his views and made the rather vague statement in his critical introduction that 'Father Páez wrote his work during the last years of his life',[3] suggesting that no more precise details could be found at the time. Alberto Feio, who published the Braga manuscript in 1945–6, noted in his 'biobibliographical notice' to the Porto edition that Páez had begun to write the book in 1607.[4] He based his argument on a comment made by Father Luís de Azevedo in a letter to the provincial of Goa, dated 22 July 1607, concerning Father Páez's state of fatigue caused by intense writing.[5] This reference alone, however, is not enough for us to assert that he was writing the *History of Ethiopia*. Furthermore, it would pre-date the publication of Urreta's works in Valencia, and it is quite certain that without them Páez's *History* would not display the structure that it does, at least in its first three books, in which he makes constant reference to Urreta's volumes. In the fourth and last book he refers to the reign of Susneyos, translates a version of this king's chronicle that was not written before May 1619,[6] transcribes correspondence between Susneyos, Philip III of Portugal (II of Spain) and the pope written subsequent to 1607, and describes the frustrated attempt by Father António Fernandes to reach the East African coast via southern Ethiopia in 1613.

The chapters in book I[7] correspond almost directly to the thematic arrangement of book I of Urreta's *Historia ... de la Etiopia*,[8] and set out a sequential arrangement of points for refutation. In books II and III, Páez's aim is to discuss matters relating to the Ethiopians' faith and religious practices (book II)[9] and to place the events of the first Jesuit mission in context (book III).[10] The rhetorical strategy Páez adopts here is the same

---

[1] See Fig. 5 and p. 58, below.

[2] Beccari, *RÆSOI*, 1, p. 3.

[3] Beccari, *RÆSOI*, 2, p. xxx.

[4] Feio, 'Notícia bio-bibliográfica', in Pêro Pais [Pedro Páez], *História da Etiópia*, I, p. xxx.

[5] Beccari, *RÆSOI*, 11, p. 134.

[6] See Pennec, *Des jésuites au royaume du prêtre Jean*, p. 291.

[7] The manuscripts of the *History* do not actually mention a book I, although the existence of books II, III and IV make it implicit. After the dedication and the prologue to the reader, Páez goes straight into chapter 1; this first part, comprising 37 chapters, is termed book I for the sake of convenience.

[8] The title of Urreta's book I is 'Libro primero del govierno temporal, costumbres, y cosas más notables del Imperio de la Etipía, Monarchia del Preste Juan'.

[9] 'Book II of the History of Ethiopia, which deals with the faith that the Prester John and his vassals profess, the ecclesiastical rites and ceremonies that they perform and other matters relating to them.'

[10] 'Which reports some histories of emperors of Ethiopia, with the missions that fathers of the Society undertook to this empire at the time of each of them'.

as in book I: he first presents the 'true' facts, ratified by first-hand knowledge or the use of the European and Ethiopian documentary sources that he had to hand. Then he quotes passages of varying lengths from Urreta's books that he considers inaccurate or false, which he refutes from his own experience or that of informants whom he considers reliable, or from the Ethiopian documentation available. Finally he concludes by confirming what he has written and stressing the 'truth' of his assertions in contrast to the 'fables' and 'lies' contained in the Dominican's work. In book IV,[1] Páez attempts to incorporate the history of the second Jesuit mission into the history of Ethiopia, but he makes no reference to Urreta's *Historia ... de la Etiopía*, most probably because the time period discussed is later than Urreta's work.

## 4. The Manuscript: from its Drafting to its Travels

### 4.1. The Early Stages in Drafting the Manuscript

We know that Pedro Páez had copies of both of Urreta's works in his possession, not only because he says so in the prologue to the *History*, but also because he refers to them and quotes directly from them on many occasions. How and when he obtained these copies are questions that cannot be answered directly from the available information. Neither the Society's official records nor his own correspondence provide any hint about their arrival in Ethiopia, and so we can only draw some logical inferences based on circumstantial evidence. As Urreta's second volume was printed in 1611, they could have been sent via India, leaving Lisbon in March–April 1612[2] to arrive in Goa in September, and departing from there for Ethiopia early in 1613. In a less optimistic scenario, they could have arrived a little later, but Páez certainly had them in his hands in 1614, as we shall see. Thus, in 1613 or 1614, he set about reading them[3] assiduously so as to be able to refute point by point everything he considered mistaken or false. He felt he 'had a duty to contradict his [Urreta's] lies by declaring the truth.'[4] Another volume that probably arrived at that time was the *Annual Report* with Father Guerreiro's 'Addition', a welcome acquisition for Páez, who used it as source material for the first mission and the beginning of the second and quoted from it extensively.[5]

The most significant clues to when Páez set to work on the refutation, which also corroborate the hypothesis outlined above, are to be found in two letters penned in his own hand. The first, dated 4 July 1615, was written in Gorgorā and addressed to the Provincial of Goa, Father Francisco Vieira, who had commissioned the refutation. At a certain point in the letter, Páez asks whether Father Francisco had received the document that he had sent him the previous year summarizing the evidence he had garnered from letters in order to refute what had been written by 'the friar from Valencia' – a

---

[1] 'Book IV of the History of Ethiopia, which deals with the last three emperors that there have been in it until today and with the missions that the fathers of the Society have undertaken to this empire during their time'.

[2] Ships would normally sail in March or April so that they could round the Cape of Good Hope by the end of July, before the monsoon. If there were no delays, it was possible to sail from Lisbon to Goa in six months. See Chaudhuri, 'O estabelecimento no Oriente', p. 189.

[3] The letter of dedication, however, mentions only the first volume (see p. 59 below).

[4] P. 62.

[5] For example, on pp. 153, 353 below, and vol. II, pp. 20–23, 29–30.

clear reference to Luis de Urreta.[1] It must therefore have been in 1614, probably July,[2] that Páez sent the Provincial the first outline of the work that was to occupy him for the rest of his life. It follows that he must by then have received both the commission and Urreta's books and, even if he had not read them from cover to cover – a task that he found particularly vexing, as he later admitted[3] – he must at least have sketched out an initial outline of the *History of Ethiopia*.

The second letter was dated 20 June 1615 and addressed to Father Tomás de Iturén. In it, Páez wrote:

> When I was about to conclude this letter, I received one from Your Reverence of 1614, with which I was greatly consoled through hearing such recent news from Your Reverence; but I cannot reply to it since the bearer of this one is hurrying me too much. Your Reverence may later have a full report of the matters of this empire; because obedience now requires me to respond to two books that have come out in Valencia on the matters of Ethiopia, in which they condemn the information given from here to the Supreme Pontiffs by the Patriarch Andrés de Oviedo and the other fathers of the Society who died here and, consequently, that which I have given.[4]

Here Páez points out that he is fully occupied with writing a response to the account of Ethiopia published in Valencia, having recently received an order that he could not refuse under his oath of obedience. His use of the word 'now' suggests that he had only recently been charged with the commission.

In 1613 or 1614, then, Páez must have received copies of Urreta's works via Goa, together with a request for a critical review. His report was sent to Goa in 1614, where it was approved by the provincial, and in 1615 Páez was formally commissioned to write the refutation.

A letter from Father Diogo de Matos to the General of the Society, dated 2 June 1621, supplies a further important detail for the story of how the *History of Ethiopia* was written:

> Residence of Gorgorrâ. ... There reside in it at present Father Antonjo Fernandez, superior of this mission,[5] and Father Pero Paes, who both, in addition to working hard on the administration of that church and the cultivation of the Portuguese and Abyssinian Catholics from the whole kingdom of Dambiâ, who are many and widely scattered, and being extremely busy, one with the history of Ethiopia, the other with the refutation of all its errors ... .[6]

Although Páez had informed Father Iturén in 1615 that he was working on the refutation of Urreta's books, clearly he had not yet finished by 1621 or even 1622, since the *History* makes several references to that year.[7]

---

[1] 'o religioso de Valencia', BPB, MS 779, doc. XIb, f. 154.

[2] The Jesuit fathers made use of the period between June and September (the *keramt*, or rainy season, when travel in the Ethiopian highlands was impracticable) to catch up on their correspondence.

[3] See p. 30 below.

[4] Beccari, *RÆSOI*, 11, pp. 359–60. The letter was written in Spanish.

[5] Father António Fernandes was one of Páez's companions who had arrived in Ethiopia in 1604 (see vol. II, p. 187). In 1619 he was the acting superior of the mission, replacing Father Páez.

[6] This does not refer to the refutation of Urreta's books, with which Páez had been commissioned, but to the theological refutation of Ethiopian dogmatic material considered erroneous by the Jesuits (Beccari, *RÆSOI*, 11, p. 484).

[7] See below pp. 143, 424, 428, and vol. II, p. 272, for instance.

Figure 6. Autograph copy of a letter by Father António Fernandes, 14 October 1641.
ARSI, MS Goa 40, *Historia Aethiopiae 1630–1659*, f. 178.

## 4.2. Was the Manuscript Completed in 1622?

After almost twenty years in Ethiopia, Pedro Páez died there of a high fever in May 1622. The actual date of his death raises a number of questions, in that the details vary from one writer to another, but for the present purposes this issue is relevant to the completion of his manuscript.

In the annual report from Ethiopia for 1621–2, dated 28 June 1622, Father Diogo de Matos stated that Páez had passed away on 20 May.[1] Father Manuel de Almeida, however, placed his death in the first few days of the month,[2] and Baltasar Teles cut through the vagueness by specifying 3 May.[3] Diogo de Matos's date of 20 May would appear to be the more reliable, not only because the document is contemporary with Páez's death,[4] but also because the autograph manuscript of the *History of Ethiopia* held in the Roman Jesuit Archives (ARSI) bears that date, 20 May 1622, at the foot of the dedication to the general of the order, Father Muzio Vitelleschi. Hence Páez could not have died at the beginning of May 1622.[5]

While this dedication helps to solve one problem, it raises a number of others. Páez succumbed to a high fever, and it is therefore somewhat implausible to imagine the man writing and signing the dedication in the *History of Ethiopia* while feverish and on his deathbed. In the autograph manuscript a few lines have been crossed through towards the end of the dedication. Beccari mentioned this in a note, but he did not remark on the fact that the final five lines, which immediately follow the part struck through, had been written in a different hand, as may be seen in Figure 5. The difference is not particularly striking at first glance, but a closer look reveals differences in the shapes of several letters, particularly the capitals D, E and M. Before we attempt to identify the correcting – or censoring – hand, the last dozen lines or so of the dedication as written in ARSI, MS Goa 42 are given below in translation, showing the phrases crossed out and those added (in square brackets).

> ... as Your Paternity will be able to see, for every year you receive good information on what happens here in the letters from my companion fathers. And because of this, and ~~because of the obligation that I have~~ [because Your Paternity is so particularly the father of this mission], it seemed to me that I should offer Your Paternity ~~this work, so that, if it is such that it may be published, you may give permission for that, or if it is not then order it to be left; because my intention has been merely to comply with my obedience to the Father Provincial and to satisfy the desire of the fathers who have asked for it~~ [this little work, in whose blessing and holy sacrifices and prayers I very much commend myself to the Lord. From Dancas, the emperor's court, 20 May 1622.
>
> Po Paes]

[1] BPB, MS 779, doc. XVI, ff. 215–25, 'Carta annua desta missão de Ethiopia do anno 621 e 622' by Father Diogo de Matos, 28 June 1622 (copy in very poor condition). This letter was quoted in part by A. Feio in the introduction to the 1945 edition of Pais, I, pp. xxxiv–v. It was also published in an abridged Italian version as *Relatione d'Ethiopia degli anni 1621–22*, 1627, pp. 45 *et seq.* (see Beccari, *RÆSOI*, 2, p. xxviii).

[2] Beccari, *RÆSOI*, 6, p. 360. Modern writers who use the information given by Almeida include Kammerer, *La Mer Rouge, l'Abyssinie*, p. 356; and Beiene, *La politica cattolica di Seltan Sägäd I*, p. 149.

[3] Teles, *História geral de Etiópia-a-Alta do Preste Ioam*, p. 357 (only the year is specified in the English translation); this date (3 May 1622) is repeated by Caraman, *Lost Empire*, p. 132.

[4] Almeida was to arrive in Ethiopia two years after Páez's death and, moreover, he only began working on Páez's manuscript after 1626.

[5] The day is omitted in the Beccari edition, no doubt through an oversight, even though the date is quite clear in the manuscript (ARSI, MS Goa 42, published in *RÆSOI*, 2, p. 4).

The corrections made did not favour Páez. The change from 'this work' to 'this little work' was clearly due to modesty, a virtue to be cultivated by all missionaries, but it might also be interpreted as an attempt to diminish the value of Páez's work. The main part that was crossed through was the request that the work be published, a clear sign that the author wanted to see it in print. What seems strange, however, is that this request for permission was addressed straight to the general of the Society, Father Muzio Vitelleschi, bypassing the rest of the hierarchy, since the refutation had been commissioned by the province of Goa, to which the Ethiopian mission was attached.

At the time of Páez's death, who could have added those final phrases? The choice is limited, since the mission was then reduced to just four people: the superior, António Fernandes, was temporarily in the province of Dambyā with Luís de Azevedo, ready to go wherever he was needed; António Bruno was in Goǧǧām, and Diogo de Matos was in the province of Tegrāy.[1] The last two were a long way from where Páez died, which was at Gorgorā in Dambyā, and they had both arrived in Ethiopia only a short time previously, in 1620,[2] so they may be ruled out of this investigation. The one who appears to be most directly implicated is the father superior. According to the information given by Manuel de Almeida, Pedro Páez had been visiting the royal court and had returned to Gorgorā with a fever. Father António Fernandes had then looked after him and done everything he could to cure him.[3] In terms of opportunity, the mission's superior was well placed to make the changes to the dedication, either on his own initiative or at Páez's bidding. Indeed, a comparison of the last lines of the dedication (Fig. 5) with letters written by Fernandes (Fig. 6) supports this hypothesis, since there are obvious similarities in handwriting style, particularly in capital letters such as P and D.

Returning to the date added at the end of the dedication, which we have suggested is the best pointer to the date when the work was completed and when its author died, it would seem plausible that, as Father Fernandes signed on behalf of his companion who lay dying of fever, he would have been careful to record it correctly.

A difference in handwriting constitutes another problem raised by examination of the ARSI manuscript. Book II of the *History of Ethiopia* is written in a different hand from the other three books, which were drafted by Páez himself.[4] An undeniable pointer to Páez's authorship of the second book, however, is its structural consistency with the rest of the work, no matter who actually penned it, since it maintains the internal organization, the rhetoric of refutation, and the references to personal experience, written as it is in the first person singular. Páez may have dictated the content of Book II before his death, or another missionary may have been charged with writing it out posthumously from notes left by Páez.

There is one argument in favour of the second hypothesis, since the manuscript had still not been sent to Goa when Father Manuel de Almeida arrived in Ethiopia in January 1624.[5] In a letter dated 8 May of that year, written from the residence in Gorgorā to General Muzio Vitelleschi, Almeida stated:

---

[1] Beccari, *RÆSOI*, 11, p. 520.

[2] Ibid., p. 473.

[3] Beccari, *RÆSOI*, 6, p. 360.

[4] This was pointed out by Beccari in his edition, *RÆSOI*, 2, p. xl. See Figs 7 and 8.

[5] Beccari, *RÆSOI*, 5, p. 338.

We are sending hence this year the book of the affairs of Ethiopia that Father Pero Paes, who is in glory, wrote: I ask the fathers superior of India to have it copied out there and, leaving one copy in Goa, to send the others to Your Paternity: and I ask Your Paternity to have it printed just as it was written by the father in Portuguese, because I believe it will have much authority as it was written by a native Castilian father and also impugns Friar Luis de Urreta [...]. Once printed just as the father wrote it, it could, if Your Paternity sees fit, be copied and printed in Latin so that it may circulate in all parts of Europe.[1]

If the manuscript of the *History of Ethiopia* had been finished by 20 May 1622, as the dedicatory letter suggests, why was it still in Ethiopia two years later? Either the manuscript was in fact finished and the mission superior held it back, making no move to send it to India with the annual letters for that or the following year, or it was still incomplete and was only finished in the period before Almeida arrived as the visiting father to the mission, or perhaps even after his arrival, between January and May 1624. Since it is difficult to be sure one way or the other, the only conclusion that can be drawn is that it is impossible to give an exact date by which the drafting of the *History* was complete.

The superior António Fernandes played a significant part in the process. If the manuscript was in fact finished on Páez's death, then he appears to have stopped it from being sent to India. If book II was unfinished and had to wait for Manuel de Almeida to arrive to be copied or composed from the notes left by Páez, then again it shows Fernandes's intention to withhold the work, or at least his total lack of interest in it. In fact, it seems to have been Almeida who took it upon himself to publicize the manuscript; he was very enthusiastic about it when he heard of the large set of notebooks among Páez's belongings. He saw the work as an excellent form of propaganda to defend Jesuit interests against the claims of the Dominicans. As he pointed out in his letter to General Vitelleschi, the fact that the author of the *History* was a Spaniard was enough to counter any argument based on nationalism. In his view, Páez's manuscript ought to be printed without delay, and his suggestion of a Latin translation confirms that he believed the work deserved to be widely distributed so as to achieve its purpose as propaganda.[2]

### 4.3. A Manuscript Unfit for Publication, or Was It?

Years later, Páez's manuscript returned to Ethiopia in the baggage of Patriarch Afonso Mendes, but no steps had been taken to implement Manuel de Almeida's enthusiastic recommendations.

According to the letter Almeida wrote as the mission visitor on 8 May 1624, Páez's manuscript was to be included in the bundle of documents shipped to India that year.[3] Everything points to the fact that it was in fact sent and that it reached its destination, because one of the last folios (f. 537) bears a note written by Patriarch Afonso Mendes on 4 December 1624 in Baçaim (Bassein, now Vasai),[4] a trading post north of Goa where the Jesuits had a residence. This note in the patriarch's hand bears no connection with the

---

[1] Beccari, *RÆSOI*, 12, p. 51.

[2] This topic is discussed in greater detail by Pennec, *Des jésuites au royaume du prêtre Jean*, pp. 249 *et seq.*

[3] Beccari, *RÆSOI*, 12, p. 51.

[4] ARSI, MS Goa 42, f. 537. Beccari recognized the importance of this folio and transcribed it in *RÆSOI*, 3, p. 508. See Fig. 9.

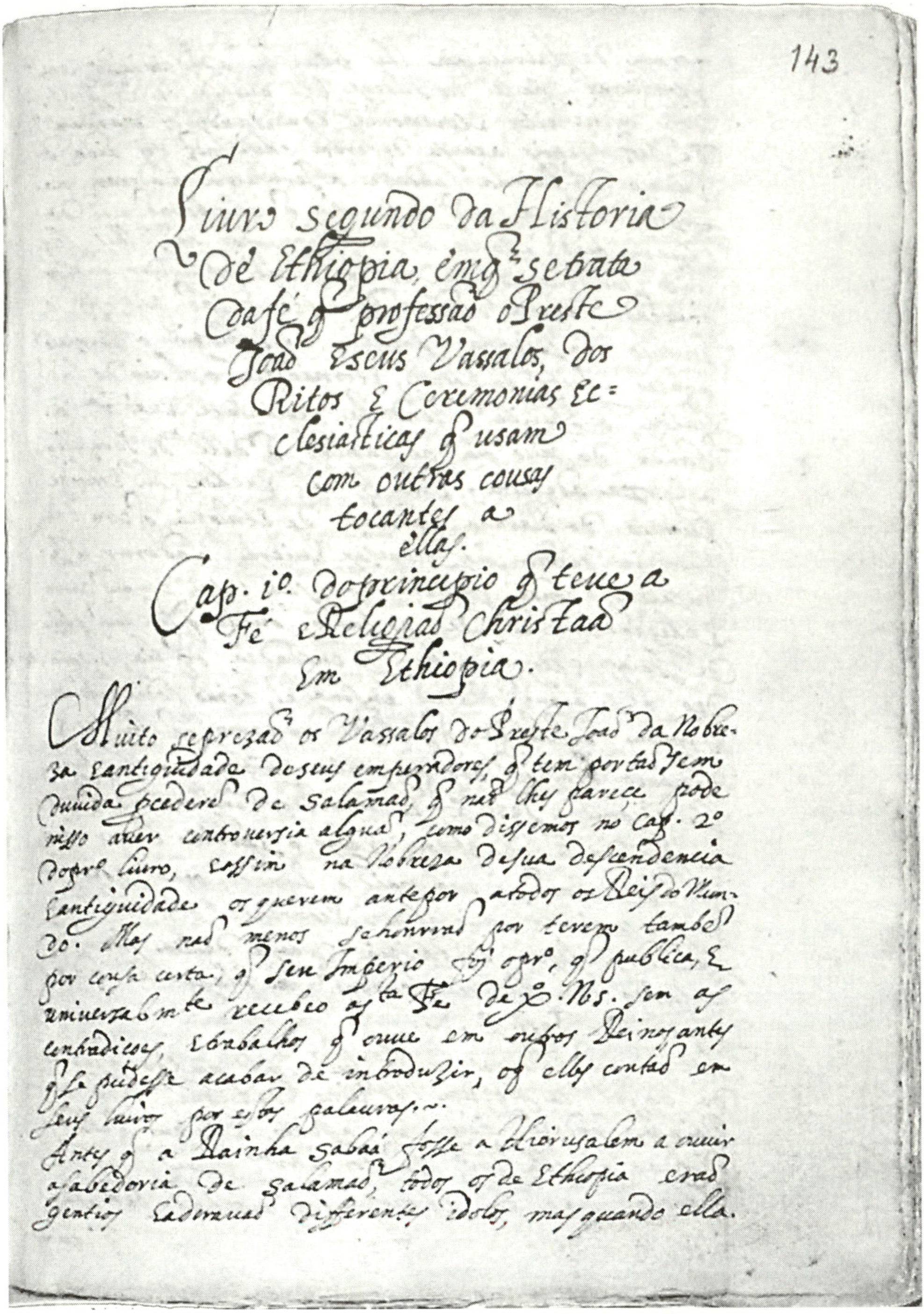
143

Liuro segundo da Historia de Ethiopia, em q̃ se trata da fé q̃ professão o Preste Joaõ e seus Vassalos, dos Ritos e Ceremonias Ecclesiasticas q̃ usam com outras cousas tocantes a ellas.

Cap. 1º. do principio q̃ teve a Fé e Religião Christãa em Ethiopia.

Figure 7. First folio of book II of Páez's *História da Etiópia*. Book II is written in a different hand from the remainder of the manuscript.
ARSI, MS Goa 42, f. 143.

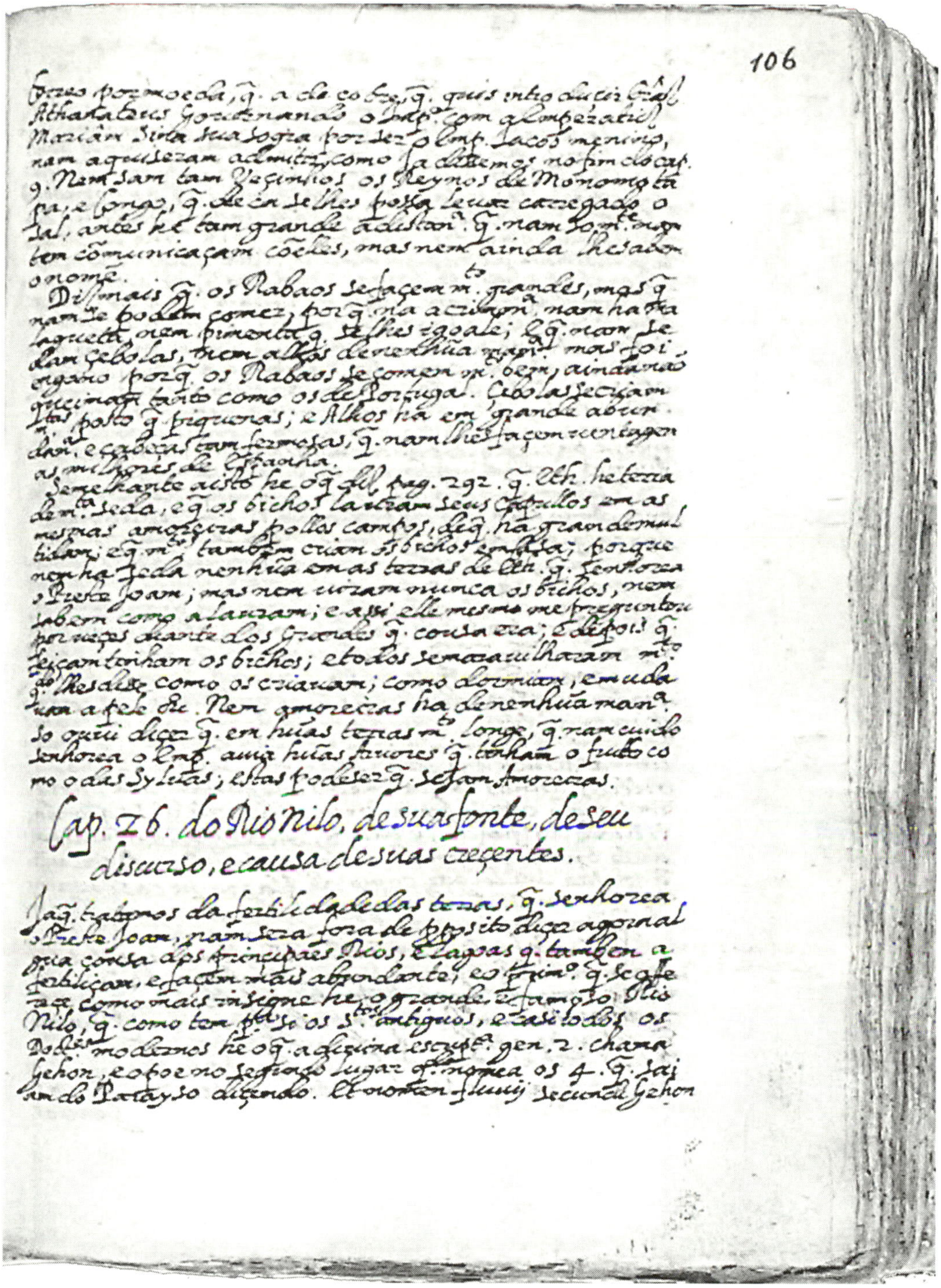

Figure 8. Autograph folio from book I of Páez's *História da Etiópia*.
ARSI, MS Goa 42, f. 106.

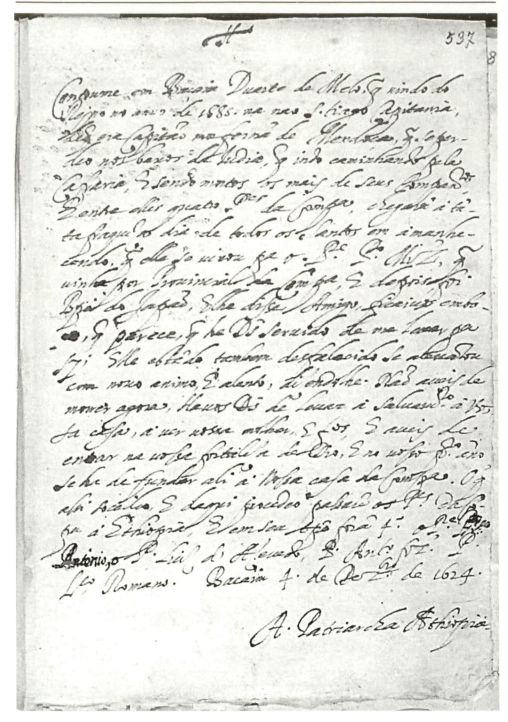

Figure 9. Annotation added by Father Afonso Mendes at the end of the *História da Etiópia*, dated 4 December 1624.
ARSI, MS Goa 42, f. 537.

content of the manuscript and merely proves that it was in India at that time. A letter sent by Mendes from Bandorá in Portuguese India, dated 26 December 1624, supports this. In it Mendes tells Father Francisco de Vergara, the Provincial of Goa at the time, that he had consulted Páez's writings in search of information on the best port through which to reach Ethiopia.[1]

The manuscript was therefore in India at the end of 1624 and, according to the above-mentioned documents, it was in the possession of Afonso Mendes, who had just arrived from Portugal with the title and powers of Patriarch of Ethiopia. He was to stay there until early April 1625, when he left for Ethiopia with a new contingent of missionaries.[2] Mendes knew of Manuel de Almeida's report urging that the *History of Ethiopia* should be printed and distributed in Europe, but he seems not to have been touched by Almeida's enthusiasm, since he considered the work unfit for publication. That decision marked the beginning of the second embargo on Páez's work and revealed the censorship at work within the Jesuit ranks both in India and in the Ethiopian mission itself. Afonso Mendes was most probably involved in this, as was the mission superior António Fernandes. The fact that the manuscript was taken back to Ethiopia, where Manuel de Almeida was called on to rewrite the *History of Ethiopia*, confirms the embargoes and censorship that were placed on Páez's work.

Father António Fernandes entrusted Almeida with the task of rewriting Páez's *History* towards the end of 1625. As the author of this new book, Almeida repeatedly acknowledged Páez's text as the source of his own, but in fact his *History of High Ethiopia or Abassia* was a complete recasting of the *History of Ethiopia*, since Almeida was extremely careful to suppress Páez's polemical arguments against Luis de Urreta. His opinion of the original work also appears to have changed, in that he now expressed certain reservations about it. He based these on linguistic grounds. Páez's text was drafted in a style of Portuguese riddled with Hispanicisms and therefore it demanded correction. 'Moreover, he was a Castillian [*sic*],' he wrote, 'and somewhat uncertain in the correct use of the Portuguese language in which he wrote, having already forgotten most of his Spanish, which he had not used for many years.'[3] Other missionaries in Ethiopia, such as Father Manuel Barradas (1572–1646), were of the same opinion and accused Páez of perverting the purity of the language with his broken Portuguese. This criticism of the text on linguistic grounds apparently held some weight in the decision not to publish Páez's work at that time.

The criticism was later reiterated by Afonso Mendes to justify a new commission to rewrite the work, this time addressed to the Jesuit provincial, Father Baltasar Teles. Páez had written in Portuguese although by nationality he was a Castilian, for whom 'the Portuguese language is usually very difficult', so that 'we all considered his command of the language poor', and, although Almeida had Portuguese as his mother tongue, 'he kept so close to Father Pedro Páez's disposition and words that to a great extent he absorbed their vices as well'.[4]

---

[1] Beccari, *RÆSOI*, 12, p. 110.

[2] Ibid., p. 143.

[3] Translation by E. Denison Ross (Ross, 'Almeida's "History of Ethiopia"', p. 786).

[4] Mendes, 'Carta'. This letter was included in Teles, *História geral de Etiópia-a-Alta do Preste Ioam*, but omitted from the English translation (Tellez, *Travels of the Jesuits in Ethiopia*).

It is unlikely that Páez had forgotten his Spanish during the long years he spent in Ethiopia,[1] as Almeida claimed, and it is also open to question whether his command of Portuguese was so poor that it meant his work could not be published, even after being revised by Manuel de Almeida. These linguistic justifications for Afonso Mendes's reservations about the work were probably readily accepted at the time, given the heightened political tensions between the Portuguese and Spanish associated with the restoration of Portuguese independence in 1640. They were, however, an excuse to avoid the problems that publishing the original text might cause, either because it was written by a Spaniard, or because it was too different from the Jesuit literary canons of the time, or even because in the meantime the Ethiopian mission, the success of which Páez sought to personify, had failed.

A number of factors must have led to the choice of Pedro Páez to write the refutation of Urreta's works: he was a missionary in those lands, he was the mission superior, and he was not Portuguese. The person who refuted Urreta clearly had to be of Spanish origin, to circumvent any accusation that the Jesuit province of Goa was attacking the Dominican friar from Valencia for nationalistic reasons. Nevertheless, his decision to write in Portuguese was only natural, in that he was a member of a mission sponsored by the Portuguese crown. Portuguese (together with Latin) was the lingua franca of the Jesuits in Ethiopia, who included fathers from Spain, Italy and Sicily as well as Portugal. Since bilingualism was extremely common in the Iberian context during the union of the Portuguese and Spanish crowns, the choice of the language used for writing was not necessarily based on concerns about nationality, although later this became important for determining the literary nationality of the works produced.[2] The decision to write in Portuguese was therefore due above all to strategies for the dissemination of knowledge, whether through publication or merely through the sharing and reading of material in manuscript form, which was particularly useful in preparing those priests who were setting out for the missions.

Although Páez's own words in the prologue that were later crossed out suggest that he intended eventually to have the work published, and although the changes made to the Braga manuscript could theoretically mean that it had been revised with a view to such publication, it should be borne in mind that the commission entrusted to him by the superior of the Goa province did not include publication among its aims. That is significant if we are to understand the nature of the work and the underlying reasons for the decision not to publish it. In one sense, Páez's work was not published at the time because, like many other examples of seventeenth-century missionary manuscripts, it was practically unpublishable.[3] While it had started out as an almost scholastic refutation, it gradually turned into a complex, heterogeneous object, an encyclopaedic compilation of the history and ethnography of Ethiopia, into which the narrator inserted an apologetic history of the Jesuit mission together with detailed and immodest self-glorification. Páez had taken the liberty of doing much more than he had been commissioned to do and, when at last it was finished, he decided too late – on his deathbed, as ill luck would have it

---

[1] See the letters Páez wrote in Spanish to Tomás de Iturén, the last of which was dated 6 July 1617, and to Muzio Vitelleschi, the general of the Society, on 16 and 23 June 1619 (Beccari, *RÆSOI*, 11, pp. 382–6 and 402–11).

[2] See Gruzinski, *Les Quatre Parties du monde*.

[3] See, for example, Girard, 'Les Descriptions qui fâchent'.

– to consider submitting the text to his superiors for their approval to publish it. They had asked him to write a refutation, but he was proposing a new formula: a refutation-*cum*-history. In other words this was an essentially polemical history, which had led him to examine a number of Ethiopian documents and to carry out veritable ethnographic fieldwork. This aspect made his work the opposite of Urreta's utopian vision: it was a dense and detailed portrait of a society that was certainly atypical, but also close to redemption because its sovereign had embraced the Catholic faith.

The subsequent rejection of Páez's work not only by Afonso Mendes but also by António Fernandes and Manuel de Almeida was also a reflection of the seventeenth-century notions of how history should be written. A 'history' was not a refutation. A 'history' should be written in more refined, correct and subtle language enriched with numerous references to the classics and the scriptures, and it should be coherent and well organized. In other words, it should be the kind of work that Manuel de Almeida to some extent sought to produce in his *History* and which would be more fully achieved by Baltasar Teles when his *Historia Geral de Ethiopia-a-Alta* was finally published in Coimbra in 1660 (Fig. 10).

Considering Manuel de Almeida's initial enthusiasm in his letter of 1624 where he recommended that his superiors publish Páez's work, it is important to determine whether his complaint about Páez's supposed lack of competence in the language, which he placed in the prologue of his own manuscript,[1] did in fact represent a change of heart about the Spaniard's work. We have seen that Almeida's original recommendation that the manuscript should be published, which he had made as visitor to the Ethiopian mission, had apparently been ignored, and Páez's work had never actually reached Europe. It had remained in India for a year and then returned to Ethiopia in the baggage of Patriarch Afonso Mendes and the missionaries who arrived there with him in early April 1625.[2] Consequently, it had only been disseminated among the members of the Society of Jesus who were in the province of Goa at the time. As Beccari notes, the decision for the manuscript to be returned to Ethiopia was made by Afonso Mendes, who, 'sailing from India to Ethiopia, took Páez's codex with him in order to use it to gain a more thorough understanding of the situation in the missions.'[3]

The fact that Almeida was commissioned a few years later to rewrite Páez's *History of Ethiopia* may be interpreted as a sign that the Society of Jesus was indirectly adopting the former visitor's recommendation. That would mean it recognized the impressive body of research that Páez had carried out and was interested in disseminating the content of his

[1] Probably written in 1643, after he had finished drafting his version of the *History*.

[2] 'Relatione et Epistolæ', in Beccari, *RAESOI*, 12, p. 143.

[3] Beccari, *RÆSOI*, 3, p. 508. The circumstances in which manuscript BPB, MS 778 was produced are obscure. It is clearly an copy of the autograph ARSI, MS Goa 42 and was made after 4 December 1624. The copyist included word for word the note added by Afonso Mendes on the last folio of the manuscript on that date, without differentiating between the end of the *History* and the patriarch's note. The copy may therefore have been made in India between December 1624 and March 1625 in order to revise the text with a view to publication or, at least, so as to safeguard the information it contained, given the risks of the journey from India to Ethiopia. If that was the case, we may speculate that the fact that Afonso Mendes took the autograph manuscript with him on that dangerous journey and left the copy behind meant that he valued the latter more highly, since it was a corrected and therefore improved version. It is also possible, however, that the copy was made in Ethiopia after the original had returned there (perhaps for the use of the missionaries in Tegray, a long way from the patriarch and the Ethiopian court), or that it was produced after the expulsion of the mission in 1633.

31

manuscript.[1] It would be senseless to suggest that, in the context of seventeenth-century missionary literary production, authorship of the work would have been valued in the same way as it is today. Admittedly, there are later signs of an attempt to erase Pedro Páez's name and even of censorship disguised by an inclination to hagiography on the part of those involved in publishing the work,[2] perhaps due to the fact that his nationality was a hindrance in the current mood of independence. Nevertheless, it is more likely that the work was so long in gestation because the Jesuits in charge of the Ethiopian mission wanted to revise and polish it, so that it could reach the European audience in a form that would enhance the mission's image and highlight the knowledge of Ethiopia that the mission was delivering.

The changing treatment afforded to the refutation of Urreta's works is an interesting sign of the different circumstances in which each of the texts was written. The refutation provided the structure for the first books of Páez's *History*, was placed in an appendix to Almeida's version, and was simply omitted from Teles's adaptation. In contrast to the later versions, Páez's restrained, realistic prose was produced in an environment relatively favourable to the acceptance of Catholicism in Ethiopia. In Almeida's case, he started his rewriting of the *History* in the land of the mission (in 1628), but drafted at least two thirds of his manuscript in Goa, after the expulsion of the Jesuit missionaries by the Ethiopian king in 1633. This episode, which he clearly describes as tragic in the prologue to his work, had a decisive influence on the form taken by the text, insofar as it is an historical interpretation of the abandonment of Catholicism by the Ethiopian court, together with an ethical explication[3] of the reasons for the mission's failure. Baltasar Teles's version was produced in the particular context of the separation of the Iberian crowns and the ideological preoccupation of Portuguese Jesuits with the restoration of Portuguese independence. The new *History* needed to help reassert Portugal's exclusive role in the Ethiopian missionary venture. The historiographic production of the following three and a half centuries suggests that it fully achieved this objective.

### 4.4. Bodies of Geographical Knowledge: Pedro Páez versus Luis de Urreta

Should the geographical knowledge brought to bear by Pedro Páez, especially in book I, chapter 1, but also throughout the rest of the text, be read or regarded as a new vulgate overturning the knowledge of the time? To some extent it should, but the impact of the information he provides is diminished by the double filter represented by the long sequence of revision and recasting of his *History* by Manuel de Almeida and Baltasar Teles. A question that needs to be addressed, however, concerns the type of dialogue that Páez intended to forge. The information he presented was substantially different from that given by the long line of European authors who had written about Ethiopia and the Horn of Africa before him, and it is worth remembering that he was not the only Jesuit to have done so, as we shall see. However, his intention was to use this body of geographical knowledge in direct response to that proposed by Luis de Urreta, who echoed the generally accepted view of Ethiopia's place in the wider African context as expressed in

---

[1] Pennec, *Des Jésuites au royaume du prêtre Jean*, pp. 264–7.

[2] See below, section 5.1.

[3] Beccari, *RÆSOI*, 7, p. 135. As King Susneyos got older he gave in to the temptations of the flesh and started worshipping the image of Solomon, leading Almeida to associate the end of Catholicism in Ethiopia with the king's sinfulness.

both the cartography and the cosmographic literature of early seventeenth-century Europe.

The bases from which Páez draws his information are presented systematically at the beginning of the *History*, where his aim is to counter the overall view expounded by Urreta by drawing on his own empirical knowledge of northern Ethiopia and, insofar as it coincides with the experience of other members of the Catholic mission, what might be termed Jesuit 'lore' on Ethiopia in general. His sources are also mentioned throughout the text, especially in his descriptions of the movements of the Christian court, the royal army and the various social, political and religious groups,[1] but also in his notes on journeys made through Ethiopia either by himself or by other missionaries,[2] and in historical or factual accounts derived from either Ethiopian or western sources.[3]

In Book I, chapter 1, Páez presents the main structure of his formal geographical knowledge of Ethiopia in the form of lists of the 'kingdoms' and 'provinces' ruled by the Prester John. The names and divisions he gives differ from those mentioned by his contemporary, Luis de Azevedo,[4] since he includes thirty-five 'kingdoms' and eighteen 'provinces'.[5] He does not use all the information contained in Azevedo's letter, although the version by Fernão Guerreiro did pass through his hands, as mentioned previously. Páez offers no explanation for the changes, additions and omissions he has made to this earlier list.[6]

Attempting to compile, check, correct and compare each piece of information in order to disentangle the 'true' from the 'false' cannot result in a satisfactory reading of Páez's work as a whole. A more productive approach is to examine the relations that the writer builds in responding to, questioning, contradicting or otherwise engaging with the various authorities whom he addresses. The same applies to the issue of the lands ruled by the Prester John. This discussion derives from a long-standing obsession with establishing a systematic administrative hierarchy for the kingdom that would reflect the traditions arising from the medieval *Prester John Letter*, in which this priest king with Christomimetic features is presented as the *Dominus Dominantium* controlling seventy-two kingdoms and provinces. Yet this chapter, in particular, needs to be compared and contrasted with Urreta.

The main thrust of Páez's enterprise, which took him from 1614 until his death to complete, as discussed above, was to thoroughly examine and systematically challenge a body of received opinion which he criticized as being Urreta's fabrication but in fact knew was widely held in Europe. Ironically, this view was partly based on the literature that had

---

[1] For example, see below p. 168 *et seq.*, on Páez's sources for his description of the manner in which the emperor travels.

[2] Particularly António Fernandes's travels in southern Ethiopia, described towards the end of book IV, see bk IV, chs 30–34, vol. II below.

[3] See below p. 270, for instance, regarding his sources for the history of Dom Christovão da Gama's military campaign

[4] Azevedo, 'Relationes et epistolae', vol. 11, pp. 130–33. The annual letter from Ethiopia of 22 July 1607 contains a detailed description of the 'kingdoms' and 'provinces' controlled by the Ethiopian king and of those associated with him. Azevedo had listed the names of twenty-seven 'kingdoms'. For each one he gave the religion of the inhabitants (Christians, Moors or 'gentiles'), together with the type of relationship of the 'kingdom' with the Ethiopian ruler, i.e. whether it paid him tribute or not. He then listed 14 'provinces', classed in the same way.

[5] See below p. 70.

[6] The differences in these two documents and also in the lists given by Almeida were pointed out by Beckingham and Huntingford in *Some Records of Ethiopia*, p. 11, but with little discussion of the missionaries' knowledge.

its roots in Portuguese contacts with the Abyssinian kingdom during the previous century, particularly Francisco Álvares's *Verdadeira Informação das Terras do Preste João* and Miguel de Castanhoso's *Historia [de] Dom Christouão da Gama (...) nos Reynos do Preste João*, copies of which were in Páez's possession. Páez firmly believed that the fact he was there *in situ* to look, ask, listen and observe gave him greater legitimacy to deny the propositions put forward by Urreta and, through him, the countless authorities on which the Dominican relied. His refutation was designed to deconstruct the second-hand information compiled in Urreta's two works and replace it with a detailed exposition of knowledge that he had both gained at first hand and structured on the basis of that empirical experience. This ultimately highlighted the primacy of 'being there' as the refuter's essential source of authority for affirming a 'truth' that was bound to be revolutionary in those times. It should be noted in passing that that procedure is not dissimilar to the discursive strategy of modern ethnographers, who regard 'being there' as an irreplaceable part of anthropological method, as upheld by Claude Lévi-Strauss, among others.[1] Not only does Páez use this procedure in setting down his geographical knowledge, but it also extends to his presentation of Ethiopian history, sociology, politics and religion.[2]

Páez counters Urreta's 'mere fictions' and 'great confusion'[3] with information gathered on the ground from local intermediaries, several of whom he names. As a confidant of King Susneyos (reigned 1607–32), whom he accompanied on his military campaigns, Páez made invaluable contacts among the court scholars, particularly the royal historiographer Tino, and the 'great men' in the royal camp, warriors who regularly patrolled recently conquered regions and areas that needed defending. Thus, when he presents his list of the kingdoms and provinces making up the Prester John's domains, he explains: 'The emperor's principal secretary listed all this for me and, afterwards, so that I could be more certain, in the presence of the emperor himself I asked a brother of his, named *Erâz* Cela Christôs,[4] and he told me likewise.'[5]

Páez gained his knowledge of the size of Ethiopia not with the aid of measuring instruments, since he had none, as he mentions,[6] but from the experience of his informants, who were used to calculating distances in terms of days of travel. The results therefore varied from one person to another, something that Páez is careful to point out for the sake of correctness. Thus he offers three estimates for travelling the length of the country from

---

[1] Lévi-Strauss, *Anthropologie structurale deux*, p. 25.

[2] By looking at Páez's work from this viewpoint, we can nuance Wendy James's overly harsh criticism of the methodological and epistemological weaknesses that she finds in her analysis of the Ethiopian studies tradition in comparison with that of Sudanese studies (James, 'Kings, commoners', pp. 102–11). Of course, the European scientific tradition's overemphasis on the connections between the northern Ethiopian ideological complex and the Semitic and Near Eastern world must be understood in terms of localizing strategies concerned with the Prester John legend (and also of the indigenous versions of the Queen of Sheba legend, a point missed by Wendy James; see Boavida and Ramos, 'Ambiguous Legitimacy', pp. 85–92). Nevertheless, a considerable proportion of such studies and the organization of the knowledge that they express depend to a great extent on the codification proposed in the ethnography of Páez and his correspondents, which deserves to be understood as intellectual procedures aimed at counterbalancing these localizing strategies rooted in the medieval European view of the eastern Christian king (Ramos, *Carta do Preste João*).

[3] See p. 69 below.

[4] See Glossary (Cela Christôs / Se'ela Krestos).

[5] See p. 71 below.

[6] 'I have no instruments or anything to help me' (p. 69 below).

north to south: two months, fifty days and forty-five days. Taking the distance travelled per day to be eight leagues, he calculates the median overall distance to be 400 leagues. He repeats the same procedure to calculate the distance from east to west and comes up with a result of between 240 and 300 leagues. His reason for wanting to circumscribe Ethiopia or, to be more accurate, what Ethiopia had been, was to deconstruct the data given by Urreta, which he quotes directly afterwards to show how wrong they were: 680 leagues north–south and 470 east–west.[1] He made use of his local sources to provide the necessary 'proof' because he would not have been able to produce his estimates without the aid of his informants, since he himself never visited the far reaches of the territories formerly ruled by the Prester John. He was not interested here in the area ruled by the Ethiopian king at the time of writing, as his purpose was another: to demonstrate that Urreta's claims were false. Even at a time when the area controlled by the Ethiopian kings was much larger (such claims by the Ethiopians were debatable, but it was not his intention to question them), its total extent was less than half that mentioned by Urreta, according to the information he gathered.

The information presented by Páez was not contemporary with the time when he wrote it down, as he was well aware. He did not fail to note the political changes that the 'Prester John's empire' had undergone in the mid-sixteenth century under pressure from the Oromo ('Gâlas'), which considerably reduced the area under Ethiopian control. In addition, this contextualization of Páez's writings also suggests why he did not use the geographical information given in Azevedo's letter. To take no account of the constant dialogue with and against Urreta would certainly result in a biased reading of the information Páez provided. It was not his primary intention to put forward this novel understanding of Ethiopia. All the information he supplied – on ethnography (habits and customs, ways of life and religious practices, ways of eating and dressing, rites of passage), geography (rivers, streams, lakes, mountains), history (royal chronicles and lists), and actual theology (matters of dogma and liturgy, hagiographies) – formed a weighty argument in the competition between the religious orders and contributed to a Jesuit 'library' of knowledge designed to modernize western scientific understanding of the world.

The importance of this information for the history of western geographical knowledge about Ethiopia and the Horn of Africa in general cannot be exaggerated. Páez's contribution was to compile information from local sources and to use the missionaries' empirical experience on the ground in order to rebut ideas about the Ethiopian context deriving from ancient and medieval world-views, both European and Arab, of which Urreta was the mouthpiece. By doing so, he greatly helped to resolve the disputes that had developed in the previous century among the proponents of various different theories about the status and extent of the Ethiopian kingdom, the location of the source of the Nile and the course taken by its waters to Egypt. These ideas had been put forward by European mapmakers and cosmographers forced to reassess the rediscovered Ptolemaic view of the world by the arrival of increasing volumes of first-hand information on the shape of the African coastline, which showed that the Indian Ocean was not a *mare clausum*.[2]

---

[1] See p. 70 below.
[2] For a recent discussion of this issue, see Relaño, *Shaping of Africa*, chs 8 and 10.

It should be remembered that Ptolemy's *Geography* proposed alternative names and routes for the course of the Nile and placed its source below the Equator, while Arab cartography introduced the idea of a large central African lake. These ideas clashed with medieval European views expressed in *mappae mundi*, which inherited both the ancient concept of two Africas (eastern, supra-Nilotic Africa and the western Hesperides) and the post-biblical view which associated the Nile with the River Ghion issuing from the earthly Paradise, and suggested an eastern source for this river. To reconcile these various hypotheses – which were clearly connected with the identification of the Ethiopian kingdom with the mythological complex of the Prester John of the Indies – the view developed that African hydrography was structured around the central lake, from which not only the Nile but also the major rivers of southern Africa flowed in different directions,[1] and that the kingdom of Ethiopia and its vassal states might cover up to a quarter of the continent.

The description of Ethiopia produced after 1540 by the chaplain Francisco Álvares during the long visit to the Abyssinian court by the Portuguese embassy under Dom Rodrigo de Lima had an unexpected result. It was not that cartographers reassessed the extent of the country but that, paradoxically, having redrawn Africa with a more 'realistic' outline, they adopted the place names and topography provided by Álvares in their obsession to fill its empty interior, thus expanding even further the 'extended' view of Ethiopia inherited from earlier centuries.[2]

The version of Ethiopian geography put forward by Páez formed the basis for the first 'realistic' map of Ethiopia, which was drawn to accompany the treatise by Manuel de Almeida (Fig. 12). It was also published by both Baltasar Teles in his recasting of the *History* and by Hiob Ludolf in the French edition of the *Historia Æthiopica*.[3] Through them, its influence spread throughout the European map-making world of the eighteenth century and it eventually toppled the 'extended' concept of Ethiopia. A few elements of the old symbolic cosmography did persist into the following century, particularly in the expeditions in search of the source of the Nile and the mythologizing on the central African lake, the Mountains of the Moon or King Solomon's mines. It is important, however, not to make a teleological reading of Páez's knowledge or to try to see in his motivation as a writer as anything other than a desire to refute the claims made by the Dominican monk Luis de Urreta.

## 5. Theologian, Translator, Author, Architect and Explorer

### 5.1. The 'Construction' of Páez's Reputation
An important question, in addition to the writing or rewriting of the *History of Ethiopia*, is the role that Pedro Páez himself, on one hand, and subsequent Jesuit writers, particularly Manuel de Almeida and Baltasar Teles, on the other, played in constructing the almost legendary reputation of Páez the missionary, which can still be glimpsed in popular

---

[1] Relaño, *Shaping of Africa*, pp. 201–11; see also Randles, 'South-east Africa', pp. 75, 80 *et seq.*

[2] See Relaño, *Shaping of Africa*, p. 216; and Hirsch, 'Cartographie et itinéraires', pp. 114–15.

[3] Ludolf, *Nouvelle histoire d'Abissinie ou d'Ethiopie*, 1684 (translation of *Historia Æthiopica*, 1681).

historical works even today.[1] The impression one forms from reading the book is that the author-narrator quite immodestly gave himself a leading role in the process by which the Jesuits gradually established themselves in Ethiopia and gained the royal ear. The history, geography, ethnography and religion of Ethiopia, which Páez makes us discover through constant reference to his own actions as investigator, explorer, translator and diplomat, appear interwoven with the history of the Jesuit presence in the country, which in turn centres on the figure of Páez himself. His autobiography sounds almost salvifical, as if he were destined to make a success of this mission, which had begun in 1557 and for decades had been neglected by the crown, the Society superiors and the authorities in Goa.[2] The Jesuit literature repeatedly mentions an episode that fosters the idea of Páez's predestination: it is said that while he was at prayer God said to him, 'Thou art the one who will reach Ethiopia, and not Father Montserrat.'[3]

The immediate pretext (the commission) for Páez to write his book was to denounce what he crudely described as the 'web of lies' spun in Luis de Urreta's books, and to tell Europe the 'truth' about the 'reality' of Ethiopia. Although his monumental work may possibly have influenced decisions on missionary policy (since it was designed to defend the Jesuit monopoly in Ethiopia against Dominican claims), it only indirectly and marginally served as a reference for subsequent European literary works on the country.

The *History of Ethiopia* in its original form remained entirely unpublished until the beginning of the twentieth century. Later writers – including of course Almeida and Teles, the rewriters of the *History*, who thus legitimized their intervention in the literary process – played a decisive part in establishing Pedro Páez's reputation. The reputation situated him not as a writer but as the multifaceted (re)builder of the Ethiopian mission, a man blessed with a variety of talents: from polyglot, architect and building contractor to explorer, theologian and converter.

It was probably Páez's obituary, written by Manuel de Almeida, that established this statutory view:

Father Pedro Páez was a truly apostolic man, chosen by God to be the apostle of Ethiopia ... . He was a Castilian by birth from near Toledo, of noble parents; he entered the Society and, with his theological studies complete, he came to India in 1588; he departed for the mission

---

[1] See the recent *Dios, el Diablo y la Aventura*, by Javier Reverte (2001), or the biography of Páez by Philip Caraman, *Lost Empire* (1985). Páez's role in the Jesuit mission in Ethiopia has also been highlighted in the specialist literature. Some historians have chosen to emphasize the supposed negative aspects of his work in the context of developing a 'black legend' (e.g. Aregay, 'El conocimiento de Pedro Páez de la Teología' and 'Legacy of Jesuit Missionary Activities'). Others have glossed the 'golden legend' constructed by Jesuit historiography since the 17th century, giving his biography an almost hagiographical tone (e.g. Marina Alfonso Mola and Carlos Martinez Shaw, 'Pedro Páez y la misión jesuítica en Etiopía').

[2] In this respect, it is interesting that the almost idolatrous panegyric on Patriarch Andrés de Oviedo (the 'martyr' of the first phase of the mission) that Páez includes in bk III, chs 5–11, of the *History of Ethiopia* functions in the text as a counterpoint to the successes of the later phase, which begins with and centres on Páez himself. Also of note is the fact that the role played by Páez's companion, António Fernandes, has been considerably cut down; the part he plays in the *History* is practically confined to the unsuccessful attempt to reach the East African coast via southern Ethiopia (bk IV, chs 30–35, vol. II below). On evidence for the rivalry between the two missionaries and the possibility that Fernandes blocked publication of Páez's work in favour of his own *Maqsafta Ḥasetāt*, published in Goa in 1642, see Pennec, *Des jésuites au royaume du prêtre Jean*, pp. 264–7.

[3] Guerreiro, *Relação annual*, pp. 362–3; Barradas, 'Tractatus Tres Historico-Geographici', p. 302; Teles, *História Geral de Etiópia-a-Alta do Preste Ioam*, p. 212.

in Ethiopia by very extraordinary routes, going to Muscat and Hormuz with the intention of from there making a great circuit to Grand Cairo and thence in the caravans that go overland to Ethiopia; in Muscat he set another course, leaving thence in a *tarada* for Zeila, but was captured off Dofar; he was taken to Xaer and Senan, where he was held captive for seven years; freed from captivity he returned to India, where he professed four vows, and he returned to his enterprise so to speak, as one who only in work found rest, in troubles enjoyment, and in the greatest hardships delight, pleasure and every contentment. He was tall and thin in stature, ruddy in complexion, quick witted, and so affable in nature that he would win over everyone he met; he fulfilled perfectly what the Apostle said: *Omnibus omnia factus sum ut omnes lucrifacerem*,[1] making himself not only a tutor and preacher of the true faith, but a doctor and nurse to the sick, architect, stonemason and carpenter to make churches for God and houses for the emperor, with such humility and sincerity that he captivated everyone by making himself the servant and captive of all.[2]

Almeida's obituary for Páez is particularly interesting as an example of historical construction. Páez's status as an author, which is readily acknowledged today, was entirely omitted by Almeida in favour of a fictitious status as an architect. A number of points have to be questioned:

*Pedro Páez's noble ancestry.*   Almeida was the first writer to provide this information, which is clearly repeated by subsequent authors such as Baltasar Teles. The Society's institutional documents, which exist for practically all the members of the order, make no mention of Páez's ancestors being of noble blood.

*His completion of his theological studies in Europe.*   This information from Almeida specifically contradicts the catalogues for the province of Goa. First, he began his theology course in Goa itself. Moreover, it was quite rare for Jesuits sent to India to have completed their studies. By claiming in this note that Páez had finished his course, Almeida was seeking to increase the prestige of someone whom he did not hesitate to call 'the apostle of Ethiopia'. Páez, however, never finished his studies. The catalogues (for 1599, 1605, 1614 and 1620)[3] mention at most two years of theology studies. Furthermore, he is known not to have completed either of these two years, in the first case because he left for Ethiopia, and in the second because of his lengthy illness on his return from captivity.

*Pedro Páez did take the four vows.*   The fourth vow promised particular obedience to the pope. According to Manuel de Almeida, Páez took this after his return from captivity. The highest level in the Society was that of professed priest, and this was generally conferred after four years of theological studies, not counting the time spent studying the humanities and arts. In some cases, however, years of missionary experience could count as years of study. That was the case with Páez, as the triennial catalogue of 1614 shows that he took his four vows on 24 June 1609, in other words six years after he had gone to Ethiopia. Once again, by making Páez a professed priest before he had left for Ethiopia the second time, Almeida was seeking to increase his prestige. He certainly was not unaware of the situation in India at the time: professed fathers were a rarity in the

---

[1] Slightly misquoted from 1 Corinthians 9:22: *Omnibus omnia factus sum ut omnes facerem salvos*; 'I became all things to all men, that I might save all.'

[2] Almeida, 'Historia de Ethiopia a alta', Beccari, *RÆSOI*, 6, p. 361.

[3] ARSI, MS Goa 24 II, *Catalogi breves a trienales 1595–1611*, ff. 286v and 396v; ARSI, MS Goa 25, *Catalogi triennales Goam. Malab., 1614–99*, ff. 17 and 29v.

province and, in terms of missionary policy, it would have been more appropriate to use such Jesuits in more 'profitable' missions than that of Ethiopia.

Almeida's aim with these details in the obituary was clearly to present Pedro Páez as belonging to the Jesuit élite in the province of India. What, then, of the last of Almeida's claims, where he describes Páez as a man of many talents – a good preacher of the Christian faith, certainly, but also a doctor and nurse to the sick and an architect, stone-mason and carpenter who made churches for God and houses for kings? Almeida later took his appreciation of Páez's architectural talents a stage further when describing how he built houses in the European style from 1614 onwards on Gorgorā peninsula (site of Susneyos's first royal camp and later a Jesuit residence in 1626).[1] He stated that Páez built a two-storey house for the king which became known as 'Babet Laybet, that is, *a House upon a House*'.[2] Almeida added that this building was regarded as a wonder of Ethiopia. The skills that Almeida attributed to his fellow Jesuit in the obituary were an invention, but one that was not inconsistent with his discourse.

The first point to consider was given by Páez himself in his *History*, when he discussed the towns and buildings of Ethiopia.[3] He described a palace located on the peninsula of Dambyā (he did not actually mention Gorgorā, but it can be identified from the highly detailed description he gave of it) and said that Emperor Seltān Sagad (Susneyos) had built it. There is no mention of Jesuit involvement or even his own. Might that be due to Páez's modesty? That appears most unlikely, since elsewhere in his account he never hesitated to mention his own role or that of other fathers. For instance, when describing his activities from the moment he arrived in Ethiopia in 1603, he stated that he threw himself into translating the *Cartilha* (catechism) into Amharic so as to teach the children in the Luso-Ethiopian community. We can be sure, however, that Páez would have been utterly incapable of producing such a translation without the aid of João Gabriel, the Portuguese captain. Even so, in the account he wrote ten years later, he had no qualms about claiming all the credit for the translation.

A second point that leads us to question whether Pedro Páez really had any architectural talent relates to the building of the first stone church in Old Gorgorā in 1618–19. When the king charged the Jesuits with doing this work, they confessed to him that they did not know how to, because 'it was not their trade' and they preferred to carry out more modest tasks.[4] None of the Jesuit fathers in Ethiopia between 1603 and 1622 really had the skills to take on the construction of churches or other buildings. Furthermore, just because the *Chronicle of Susneyos* mentions that 'There was a Frank who directed the building work[5] [of Gannata Iyāsus, in Azazo] by the name of Padry Pay',[6] it does not necessarily mean that he had any special talent as an architect. At most, it would seem he was in charge of the work, but in the end his building skills must have been limited.[7]

---

[1] Almeida, 'Historia de Ethiopia a alta', Beccari, *RÆSOI*, 6, pp. 293–5. The account was repeated by Teles, *História Geral de Ethiopia a Alta ou Preste Ioam*, pp. 334–5; Tellez, *Travels of the Jesuits in Ethiopia*, pp. 206–7.

[2] Tellez, *Travels of the Jesuits in Ethiopia*, p. 207.

[3] See bk I, ch. 20, pp. 201–3.

[4] Beccari, *RÆSOI*, 11, p. 413.

[5] *ḥenṣā*, structure, building, construction (Leslau, *Comparative Dictionary of Geʿez*, p. 238).

[6] Pereira *Crónica de Susenyos*, I, p. 259; II, p. 199.

[7] Páez states that Susneyos had the Catholic church built 'according to the plans that we had given him' (vol. II, p. 271). The ruins of various Catholic churches built while the Jesuits were in Ethiopia have standardized proportions, suggesting that architectural plans used in other Jesuit missionary areas had also been sent to Ethiopia.

Manuel de Almeida seems to have felt a need to replace Páez's talent as a writer with a different talent: that of architect or, in other words, the physical founder of the Jesuit mission. Pedro Páez, the apostle of Ethiopia, had changed the mission's status from temporary to permanent. The comment made by Luís de Azevedo in 1619, on the first stone church in Old Gorgorā, is significant: 'it was the material embodiment and the spiritual edifice of the Roman faith in this empire.'[1] A stone church is built to last. The Jesuit presence was now no longer provisional but definitive; the Catholic faith was putting down roots in Ethiopian soil and establishing its Church there.

### 5.2. The Discovery of the Source of the Blue Nile: a Case of Censorship?

One of the most widely publicized facts about Pedro Páez today is that he discovered the source of the Blue Nile (Ṭequr Abbāy). He visited it in 1618 during an expedition undertaken by King Susneyos to Giš Abbāy in Goǧǧām, and described it in the first book of the *History of Ethiopia*.[2] Most of the credit for making his discovery known in Europe must go to another Jesuit, the polymath Athanasius Kircher (1602–80), who had read Páez's manuscript in Rome. Aware of the significance of Páez's achievement, Kircher included the description of the source of the Nile (in Latin translation) in his monumental work on geophysics, *Mundus subterraneus*, ensuring that news of the discovery and the name of the discoverer reached a wide audience.[3] Kircher's authority was sufficient for the German scholar Hiob Ludolf (1624–1704) to attribute the discovery to Páez in his *Historia Æthiopica*, where he transcribed the passage from the *Mundus subterraneus* and added other accounts relating to the Nile.[4] The French historian Joachim Le Grand (1653–1733) did likewise in one of his dissertations on Ethiopian history, which he appended to his abridged translation of Jerônimo Lobo's *Itinerary*.[5] Le Grand's translation and dissertations were later rendered into English by Samuel Johnson (1709–84).[6] It should be noted, however, that none of the various known manuscripts and translations of Lobo's actual work associates Páez's name with the discovery of the source of the Blue Nile,[7] and this silence persists in the *History* as rewritten by Father Baltasar Teles. We may wonder whether this was a case of deliberate erasure as a result of internal censorship by the Society of Jesus, or whether the fathers were merely attempting to extend the glory of the discovery to the collective efforts of the Jesuits – or even the Portuguese, as suggested by Wyche in his dedication to *A Short Relation of the River Nile*.[8] This silence gave grounds for the Scottish explorer James Bruce, in his *Travels to Discover the Source of the Nile* (1790), to argue against the veracity of Páez's discovery as affirmed by Kircher. Since Páez was not even mentioned in this regard in the accounts left by his fellow Jesuits Afonso Mendes and Baltasar Teles, Bruce felt justified in claiming to be the first European

---

[1] Beccari, *RÆSOI*, 11, p. 417.

[2] Bk 1, ch. 26, pp. 244–5.

[3] Kircher, *Mundus Subterraneus*, I, pp. 72–4.

[4] Ludolf, *Historia Æthiopica*, bk 1, ch. 8, unpag.

[5] Le Grand, *Relation historique d'Abissinie*, pp. 209–11.

[6] Le Grand, *Voyage to Abyssinia*. 'Peter Pays' is credited with the discovery on p. 171.

[7] For example, in Lobo, *Short Relation of the River Nile*, translated by Sir Peter Wyche for the Royal Society and printed in 1669, which gained considerable literary fame and was translated into several European languages.

[8] '... these Discourses ... give the Portuguese their just and undoubted title of discovering daily to the West, the Wonders and Mysteries of the East' (in Lobo, *Short Relation of the River Nile*, pp. ix–x).

to have visited the mythical source.[1] Soon afterwards, however, his assertion was ironically refuted in the preface to a new edition of *A Short Relation of the River Nile*[2] and so never achieved the effect Bruce had intended. Indeed, several European travellers, including Henry Salt (1780–1827), Edmond Combes and Maurice Tamisier, Arnaud d'Abadie (1815–93) and Guillaume Lejean (1828–71) did not hesitate to credit Páez with the discovery and confirmed the accuracy of his observations as transcribed by Kircher.[3]

Nevertheless, Páez's name seems to have been deliberately erased from the descriptions of the source of the Nile by other Jesuits. Father Baltasar Teles, who rewrote the version of the *History of Ethiopia* left by Manuel de Almeida and published it in 1660, stressed the importance of the discovery in unravelling the age-old legend of the sources of the Nile and the origin of its floods. Yet he did not attribute it to Pedro Páez, who hardly gains a mention in his work, unlike the three Portuguese Jesuits Afonso Mendes, Manuel de Almeida and Jerónimo Lobo:

> Many treatises have been written by many of our religious men,[4] who have seen these secrets at close hand, and the best witnesses among them are our Patriarch of Ethiopia Dom Affonso Mendez, a man of the highest credit, and Father Manoel d'Almeyda, who recounts this at great length, and Father Ieronymo Lobo, who with great curiosity have seen with their own eyes and written about what in truth occurs there, and especially Father Ieronymo Lobo in the Commentaries on his long peregrination, which he communicated to me when he returned from Ethiopia to Portugal ... .[5]

As he did throughout his book, Baltasar Teles clearly plundered Páez's description of the Nile. It is curious to note that Jerónimo Lobo, who was himself a missionary in Ethiopia and gave an opinion approving Teles's manuscript in 1658, also described the sources of the Nile in a way that recalls Páez's original text, but again without ascribing the discovery to the Spanish-born missionary. A comparison of the descriptions left by the three authors clearly shows that Páez's text served as inspiration not only for Teles but for Lobo as well.

---

[1] Bruce, *Travels to Discover the Source of the Nile*, III, bk VI, chs 13–14. He develops his arguments against the idea that Páez had discovered the source on pp. 615–17, and even suggests that Kircher had 'invented' the episode. He also criticizes the description given by Lobo, insinuating that he had never visited the place.

[2] 'A late traveller, however, has, in various instances, asserted the ignorance of the Portuguese Missionaries, taxing them with wilful misrepresentation, and including them all under the polite appellation of Lying Jesuits!' (in Lobo, *Short Relation of the River Nile*, p. vi).

[3] Salt, *Voyage to Abyssinia*, p. 481, note; Combes and Tamisier, *Voyage en Abyssinie*, III, pp. 293 and 295; d'Abbadie, *Douze ans dans la Haute-Éthiopie*, p. 230; Lejean, *Voyage en Abyssinie exécuté de 1862 à 1864*, p. 18.

[4] Teles's use of 'our religious men' perhaps reflects nationalist feelings associated with the political situation of the time: when his *História* was published in 1660, Portugal was still at war with Spain. Charles II of Spain only recognized Portugal's independence in a treaty signed on 13 February 1668, after his defeat at the battle of Montes Claros.

[5] Teles, *História Geral de Ethiopia a Alta ou Preste Ioam*, bk I, ch. 5, p. 13, retranslated. The English translation of 1710 differs somewhat: 'It is now time to come to speak of what is certainly known at this Time, after being so long conceal'd, which we have from the Annual Letters and other Accounts, of several Fathers of the Society, who were Eye-Witnesses of what they Write, and more particularly among them the Patriarch of *Ethiopia*, Don *Alfonso Mendez*, F. *Emanuel de Almeyda*, and F. *Jerome Lobo*, who all curiously view'd those Springs, and writ the Truth of what they saw, and especially the last, who is most particular in these Affairs, in the Commentaries of his long Peregrination, which he communicated to me at his Return to *Portugal*, in the Year 1673' (Tellez, *Travels of the Jesuits in Ethiopia*, bk I, ch. 3, p. 13) [Translator's note].

Figure 10. Frontispiece of the *História Geral de Etiópia a Alta*, by Father Baltasar Teles, 1660.

Pedro Páez:

This source lies almost at the western edge of that kingdom, at the head of a little valley that
forms in a large plain. ... it appeared to be no more than two round pools four spans in
width. ... The water is clear and very light .... I had a lance thrust into one of the pools, ... and
it went down eleven spans and seemed to touch bottom on the roots of trees growing on the
edge of the bank.
The second pool of the source is lower down towards the east, about a stone's throw from
the first. ... A Portuguese had tied together two lances so that they were twenty spans long,
and when he put them in he did not find the bottom either. ... when they walk near those
pools, everything around shakes and trembles, [...] there is just water underneath and ... one
can only walk over it because the roots of the grasses are so intertwined together, with a little
soil. ... The surrounding area, which seems to be like a lake, is almost round, and one cannot
throw a stone from one side to the other, although it is easy with a sling.[1]

Jerónimo Lobo:

The source ... is discovered on a very gradual slope made by a certain mountain, seeming
more like a rather irregular field ... one discovers ... two circular pools or wells of water ...
separated from each other by a distance of a stone's throw ... in the shallower one, with a
lance eleven spans in length one could touch bottom, although some claimed this was not
the bottom but rather certain roots of some bushes which are in the bank .... The second one
lies to the east of the first in a lower place on the said slope or plain. It is so deep that with a
measure of more than twenty spans the bottom could not be found ... the part near the said
wells seems to be a subterranean lake, because the ground is so swollen and undermined with
water that it appears to bubble up when a person walks on it ... the roots are so intertwined
that, with the little soil that holds them together, they can support anyone who walks on the
field, which at its widest point can be crossed by a stone's throw, but only if shot by a sling.[2]

Baltasar Teles:

Among these Mountains is a spot of Plain ... and in the midst of it a little Lake, about a
Stones throw over. This Lake is full of a sort of little Trees, whose Roots are so interwoven,
that walking on them in the Summer, Men come to two Springs, almost a Stones throw
asunder, where the Water is clear and very deep, and from these two the Water gushes two
several ways into the Lake, from which it runs under Ground ... .[3]

The descriptions by Lobo and Teles clearly arrange Páez's information in different ways
in terms of the location of the source, the distance between the pools, the way their
depths were measured and the instability of the ground. In Le Grand's French translation
of Lobo's *Itinerário*, Lobo himself claims to have carried out the experiments with the
lances, which Páez ascribes to himself (with the aid of an anonymous Portuguese) in the
original text.[4]

---

[1] Bk I, ch. 26, pp. 244–5.
[2] *Itinerário of Jerónimo Lobo*, ch. 21, p. 228 (translated by Donald M. Lockhart).
[3] Tellez, *Travels of the Jesuits in Ethiopia*, bk I, ch. 3, p. 14 (translator unknown).
[4] Lobo's plain style made a deep impression on the young Samuel Johnson when he was translating Le Grand's
version of Lobo's *Itinerário* into English in 1735: 'He [Lobo] appears, by his modest and disaffected narration, to
have described things as he saw them; to have copied nature from the life; and to have consulted his senses, not
his imagination' (Samuel Johnson, 'Preface', in Le Grand, *Voyage to Abyssinia*, p. 1). He could not have suspected
that Lobo's description resulted from the censorship and appropriation of Páez's text.

Pedro Páez himself was aware of the significance of his discovery, and did not fail to mention it: 'I confess I was overjoyed to see that which in ancient times King Cyrus and his son Cambyses, the great Alexander and the famous Julius Caesar had so longed to see.'[1] The omission of his role in the discovery from subsequent Jesuit descriptions of the source of the Blue Nile may be seen as evidence that the recasting of his reputation was being closely controlled by the Portuguese fathers of the Society. However, in reconsideration of the position adopted in the introductions to the Portuguese and Spanish editions of the *History of Ethiopia* the editors now take into account the part played by Kircher in reporting and disseminating Páez's discovery within the context of Jesuit scientific production as a whole. Even though, as previously argued, Páez was a target of censorship at a local level, that attitude seems to have been confined to the province of Goa during a well-defined period. The fact that Kircher acknowledged his rightful place in the history of exploration is strong evidence for that.

In the nineteenth century, the focus of geographical discourse shifted away from the Blue Nile to the White Nile, not least due to the impact of expeditions organized by the geographical societies that had been founded during the colonial scramble for Africa. As a result, although the Jesuit's discovery had been widely mentioned in the geographical literature, it was to some extent pigeonholed with other writings on Ethiopia, which helps to explain why Father Páez's place in the general history of geographical discoveries gradually sank into oblivion.

### 5.3. *A Nationalized Missionary*

Although some writers, such as J.-B. Coulbeaux in 1929,[2] gave him credit for the discovery of the source of the Nile, Páez really only regained his status as a traveller and explorer after the publication of his biography, first by Philip Caraman (1985) and subsequently by George Bishop (1998) and Javier Reverte (2001).[3] The success of Reverte's book has in fact made Páez something of a media celebrity in Spain.

While the construction of the legend of 'Pedro Páez the architect' in the seventeenth century was, we might say, an exclusively Jesuit affair, his new fame as 'Pedro Páez the explorer' in the twentieth century and beyond began with Jesuit writers (Beccari, Caraman and Bishop) but has triggered a new Spanish discourse on Ethiopia during the last decade.[4] This discourse, which has nationalistic overtones and has arisen above all in the context of a historical revision of bilateral co-operation between Spain and Ethiopia, ignores Philip II's understanding of the union of the Iberian crowns, which entailed strict separation of Portuguese and Spanish affairs in the political and religious administration of their respective areas of imperial influence. That meant that the Ethiopian mission

---

[1] Bk I, ch. 26, pp. 244. Compare Teles's comment: 'But I confess that I truly do not know what diamond mines, what treasures of fine gold and what blessings those famous men Alexander, Caesar, Philadelphus, Sesostris or Cambyses imagined were to be found at the sources of the Nile' (Teles, *História Geral de Ethiopia a Alta ou Preste Ioam*, 1660, I, ch. 5, p. 12). This comment was omitted from the English translation of 1710 [Translator's note].

[2] Coulbeaux, *Histoire politique et religieuse de l'Abyssinie*, vol. 2, pp. 200–201.

[3] Caraman, *Lost Empire*; Bishop, *Lion to Judah*; Reverte, *Dios, el diablo y la aventura*.

[4] Books such as *Etiopía: hombres, lugares y mitos* (Madrid, 1990) by the Colombian priest J. González Núñez, *Dios, el diablo y la aventura* by Reverte, and the Spanish translation of *Lion to Judah* by G. Bishop were the main sources for material praising Pedro Páez as a 'Spanish missionary' in the Spanish-speaking media and on the Internet.

came under the Province of Goa, and the king of Spain had to correspond with his Ethiopian counterpart as king or emperor of Portugal. Since the late 1990s, Spanish diplomacy in Ethiopia has developed a new model for interpreting Hispano-Ethiopian relations based on the fiction of a diplomatic connection dating back four centuries. Pedro Páez – a Castilian, the mission superior from 1603 to 1622, the subject of biographies, and the author of one of the most widely cited books on the Jesuits in Ethiopia – very conveniently fits the bill as a leading figure in this connection, in the new legend combining hagiographic profiles that were previously considered contrary or incompatible: 'architect', 'explorer' and 'Spaniard'. Spain's political and diplomatic institutions have associated themselves both formally and informally with a series of initiatives[1] that reinforce Pedro Páez's posthumous revival and are not unrelated to his celebrity status in Spain and the promotion of Ethiopia as a tourist destination for a growing number of Spanish travellers in recent years.

## 6. The Sources of the *History of Ethiopia*

The stated purpose of the work – to refute Urreta's books – forced Páez to adopt a particular structure that would make the intertextual comparisons clear. Ignoring for the moment the rhetorical procedures he used, we see that the thirty-seven chapters of book I and many of the twenty-three chapters of book II include excerpts of varying lengths from the refuted books, transcribed in their original Spanish. That is not all, however. Páez had empirical knowledge of countless details of the nature, geography and customs of Ethiopia, and he gave an eye-witness account of his personal experiences from the time when he first left India for Ethiopia. He also transcribed verbal accounts given by several different personages. As a result, Páez was extremely well placed to support his arguments with his own assessment of the 'reality' of the country, since he was there *in situ* and could muster a substantial corps of oral and written sources, both European and Ethiopian.

The first set of source materials consisted of documents about Ethiopia written by European missionaries and travellers. Páez frequently quoted or paraphrased compilations of the annual letters by Father Fernão Guerreiro, particularly the previously mentioned 'Adição à Relação das coisas de Etiópia, com mais larga informação delas, mui certa e mui diferente das que seguiu o Pe. Frei Luis de Urreta no livro que imprimiu da história daquele império de Preste João' ['Addition to the Report on the affairs of Ethiopia, with more extensive information on them, very correct and very different from that which Father

---

[1] In 1998 the Spanish Embassy in Ethiopia invited the writer Javier Reverte to travel around Ethiopia and produce a biography of Pedro Páez; in 2003 it organized the 'Workshop commemorating the fourth centenary of the arrival of Father Pedro Páez in Ethiopia', the proceedings of which (*Conmemoración del IV centenario de la llegada del Padre Pedro Páez a Etiopía*) were published by the Spanish International Co-operation Agency in 2007; it promoted an exhibition of photographs on the architectural heritage associated with the presence of the Jesuit missionaries in Ethiopia, and received a delegation sponsored by the Real Sociedad de Geografía, which visited the source of the River Abbāy (Blue Nile) to lay a plaque there commemorating its 'discovery' by Pedro Páez; in 2004 it invited the archaeologist Víctor Fernández to visit the ruins of the Jesuit churches in the regions of Bāḥer Dār and Gondar and to develop an excavation project funded by the Ministry of Culture entitled 'Jesuits in the Kingdom of the Prester John (1555–1634): an ethno-archaeological survey in the region of Lake Ṭānā (Ethiopia)'.

Friar Luis de Urreta followed in the book that he printed on the History of that empire of the Prester John']. This was appended to the *Relação anual das coisas que fizeram os padres da Companhia de Jesus* (Lisbon, 1611). Páez began to collect drafts and copies of letters, once he had started work on the *History of Ethiopia*. He referred to the *Verdadeira informação das terras do Preste Joam das Indias* by Francisco Álvares,[1] in the Spanish translation by Friar Tomás de Padilla, OP. This was printed in Antwerp in 1557 under the title *Historia de las cosas de Etiopia, en la qual se cuenta muy copiosamente el estado y potencia del Emperador della, (que es el que muchos han pensado ser el Preste Juan) con otras infinitas particularidades, assi de religion de aquella gente, como de sus cerimonias* [*History of the affairs of Ethiopia, very copiously recounting the status and power of its Emperor (who is the one that many have believed to be the Prester John) with infinite other particularities, both of the religion of that people and of their ceremonies*]. This edition corresponds to the description given by Páez, whereas the Zaragoza edition of 1561 and the Toledo one of 1588 both have an index and retain the chapter divisions of the Portuguese edition. It should also be noted that Páez always referred to the work as *Historia etiopica* and never as *Verdadeira informação*, and the page references that he cited on several occasions correspond to those of the 1557 Spanish edition. Although Páez credits Guerreiro as his documentary source for his account of the Portuguese military expedition against the Muslim invaders of Ethiopia under Grāññ in 1542 in book I, chapters 31–37, in practice he quoted freely from Captain Miguel de Castanhoso's work, the *Historia das cousas que o muy esforçado capitão Dom Christouão da Gama fez nos Reynos do Preste João, com quatrocentos Portugueses que consigo leuou*, printed in Lisbon in 1564,[2] in chapters 31 to 37 of book I.[3]

Páez's second set of source works comprised the Ethiopian texts that were made available to him by various monks, courtiers and other individuals.[4] Examples of the religious texts mentioned are:

> *Hāymānot 'Abaw* ('Faith of the Patriarchs');
> *Maṣhafa Qedāsé* (missal);
> *Maṣhafa Senkesār* (synaxarion);
> *Gadla Takla Hāymānot* (hagiography of Takla Hāymānot);
> *Gadla Pānṭāléwon* (hagiography of Pānṭāléwon).

Texts relating to political power that are mentioned include:

> *Kebra Nagāst* ('Glory of the Kings');
> Catalogues of kings;
> Chronicles of kings.

Of the chronicles of kings prior to the Portuguese arrival in Ethiopia, Páez used the chronicles of 'Āmda Ṣeyon (book III, chapter 1) and Zar'a Yā'eqob (book I, chapter 5). He also had access to the chronicles of Lebna Dengel (book III, chapter 2), Galāwdéwos

---

[1] For the published English translation, see Álvares, *Prester John of the Indies*.

[2] For the published English translation, see Whiteway, ed., *The Portuguese Expedition to Abyssinia in 1541–3*. Whiteway translated the original title as 'A Discourse of the Deeds of the very valorous Captain Dom Christovão da Gama in the Kingdoms of the Preste John, with the four hundred Portuguese, his Companions'.

[3] See below p. 272 *et seq.*

[4] Beccari drew up an exhaustive list of the Ethiopian sources that Páez mentioned (see his 'Introductio', *RÆSOI*, 2, pp. xxxii–viii ).

(book III, chapter 3 and 5), Minās (book III, chapter 6) and Sarṣa Dengel (III, chapters 13–14), contemporaneous with the Portuguese presence and the first Jesuit mission, as well as that of Susneyos (IV, 16–20), contemporaneous with Catholicism in Ethiopia.

Páez seems to have categorized the Ethiopian royal chronicles in a similar fashion while he was organizing the parts of the *History* in which he drew on these sources, since he made use of them in two distinct ways. For the chronicles from the period prior to the arrival of the Portuguese[1] and those of the sixteenth-century kings[2] he included translated extracts and summaries of certain selected passages. In contrast, the translation he produced of the chronicle that was contemporaneous with Catholicism in Ethiopia – that of King Susneyos – was much less fragmentary.[3] This was the chronicle of a king who favoured the Jesuits and converted to Catholicism in 1622. Although it contained only rare and discreet references to that subject, this chronicle had an important role to play as an Ethiopian document that justified the Jesuits' presence and activities in Ethiopia. Páez incorporated his Portuguese translation of Susneyos's chronicle in chapters 16–20 of book IV. The method he used was first to translate the royal chronicle and then to comment on the events of the king's reign, particularly the progress made by Catholicism in Ethiopia, as he explained at the end of chapter 15:

> We shall now relate the latter's [Susneyos's] history so that the course of his life may be seen at length, and afterwards we shall add some points that are missing in it on how he proceeded and still proceeds in the matters of our faith; from that the reader will discern what we said above, that one could be sure that God wanted to give him the crown of the empire in order to make use of him in such important matters.[4]

---

[1] With the exception of the mythical origin of Ethiopian royalty (the union between the Queen of Sheba, or Saba, and King Solomon) taken from the medieval *Kebra Nagāst* (*Glory of the Kings*), the main pre-sixteenth-century episode translated by Páez was the conflict between King Amda Ṣeyon (1314–44) and the Muslims in 1332. He placed it in bk III, ch. 1 of the *History of Ethiopia*. Almeida used Páez's translation of the chronicle but placed it in bk II, ch. 24 of his 'História de Ethiopia a alta' (*RÆSOI*, 5, pp. 225–37). The chronicle of King Zar'a Yā'eqob (1438–68) was included by Páez in bk I, ch. 5 but by Almeida in bk II, ch. 25 (*RÆSOI*, 5, pp. 239–40).

[2] Páez included the chronicle of Lebna Dengel (1508–40) in bk III, ch. 2, whereas Almeida, who repeated Páez's translation, split the excerpt in two parts which he placed in two different chapters: bk III, ch. 3 (*RÆSOI*, 5, pp. 253–4), and bk III, ch. 6 (*RÆSOI*, 5, pp. 263–5). The chronicle of King Galāwdéwos (1540–59) is in Páez's bk III, chs 3 and 5, and Almeida's bk III, ch. 7 (*RÆSOI*, 5, pp. 269–70) and bk IV, ch. 9 (*RÆSOI*, 5, pp. 382–3). The chronicle was published with a French translation by W. E. Conzelman in 1895. For the chronicle of Minās (1559–63), Páez included his Portuguese translation in bk III, ch. 6, whereas Almeida placed it in his bk IV, ch. 10 (*RÆSOI*, 5, pp. 387–92). F. M. E. Pereira published the chronicle with a Portuguese translation in 1888, with an appendix containing Almeida's Portuguese version based on the British Museum manuscript (pp. 81–7). The fragment Páez translated from the chronicle of King Śarṣa Dengel (1563–97) takes up chs 13 and 14 of bk III in the *History of Ethiopia*, whereas Almeida placed it in his bk IV, ch. 26 (*RÆSOI*, 5, pp. 479–501). Conti Rossini published and translated this chronicle in 1907. In each case, Almeida copied the passages translated by Páez in full.

[3] In the case of Susneyos, Almeida did not directly repeat Páez's translation of the chronicle since he was able to work from an original version, as suggested by the copy of Almeida's manuscript (SOAS, MS 11966, ff. 483–543) containing the translation of the chronicle of Susneyos. He may have done so because Páez's translation contained a large number of errors that Almeida had to correct, or perhaps the chronicle itself had been changed between the time of Páez's death and the period before the Jesuits were expelled. Páez had seen a version produced before 1622, whereas Almeida may have had access to a later version, which could account for the differences found. The parts of Susneyos's chronicle that Páez translated into Portuguese are much longer in terms of the number of pages or folios they take up than the extracts he translated from the other chronicles.

[4] See p. 207 below.

The strategy Páez used for the first set of sources mentioned above, to justify his own positions, illustrate the 'truth' and contradict the 'lies' told by Urreta's informant, was either to give a direct transcription of selected excerpts in the language of the version he had in his possession (several missives are transcribed in full), giving the page reference where appropriate, or to paraphrase or summarize the text. This was the same procedure that he used for Urreta's works. Usually, he would introduce a direct quotation with the formula 'X, on page y, says:', and mark its end with 'Up to here are the words of the author'. He would provide a summary after having confuted a piece of information, generally from Urreta, with a source regarded as reliable. For example, he writes, 'From what we have said, it is easy to see how deceitful the information was that João Baltazar gave to Friar Luis de Urreta about these buildings, because he says on page 93 that they are two ancient temples that were built before Queen Saba, one in honour of the sun and the other in honour of the moon ...' .[1] Or similarly, 'Francisco Álvares was also very mistaken when he says, on f. 77 of his *Historia*, that these princes were held in a valley between two very rugged mountains, which was closed with two doors, and that the mountain was fifteen days' journey around and he had travelled along its foot for two days'.[2] He also used the technique of interspersing shorter direct quotations with summaries of the texts, sometimes with an explanation of what he was doing. Occasionally he made personal comments about the work in question, such as this complaint that '[Urreta] makes two chapters, 10 and 11, on this subject [the treasures] that are so long that it is no small penance for someone who has other things to do to be forced to read them'.[3]

The same strategy was used for the sources in the second set, once they had been translated into Portuguese. Páez translated them literally, keeping the repetition of conjunctions typical of Semitic texts. He also introduced words and phrases from Ethiopic languages into his own descriptions, giving their meanings in metalinguistic notes often marked with the Latin *scilicet* ('namely'). When describing the royal camp, for instance, he wrote: 'The most honoured [room] is called *ambaçâ bêit*, "house of the lion", and is the most intimate; the second, more to the outside, is called *zefân bêit*, "house of the bed"; the third, *farâz bêit*, "house of the horse".[4] Further on, when discussing the churches on 'Ambā Gešén, he remarked: 'One is called Egziabehêr Ab, *scilicet* "God the Father"'.[5] The examples given are paradigmatic. First, he translated *ambaçâ bêit*, *zefân bêit* and *farâz bêit* correctly, but his transcription of the latter two items is syntactically incorrect, since the determinative should be indicated by an affix represented by the first order character in the Ethiopic syllabary (*fidal*) or the letter 'a' in Latin transcription: *zefana bét* and *farāza bét*. The transliteration '*bêit*' perhaps shows the pronunciation current in the seventeenth century (it is now generally pronounced 'byét'), which may be an important finding for Amharic historical linguistics. Secondly, the name *Egzi'abehér*, which literally means 'Lord of the Earth', is a Ge'ez expression borrowed by the languages of the Christian Tigrayan and Amharic peoples to designate 'God', the translation chosen by Páez. Thirdly, Páez's concern with the phonetics of the language is shown by certain significant observations in the text, such as: 'I write *côi* with this letter "c", because I cannot find a better one, but

---

[1] See p. 125 below.
[2] See p. 122 below.
[3] See p. 132 below.
[4] See pp. 100–101 below.
[5] See p. 119 below.

it does not perfectly match the pronunciation of the Amharâs'.[1] The sound is in fact the glottal fricative [h], not used in Portuguese, and the word is pronounced '*hoy*'.

Páez's spelling of the place name 'Agçûm' seems to derive from assimilation of the phonetic values of the velar occlusives [g] and [k]. The correct form is 'Aksum'. The commonly found variant 'Axum' would be confusing to Portuguese speakers (for whom the letter 'x' generally represents the sound of English 'sh'), hence Manuel de Almeida's observation that the town should properly be called 'Acçum, not Axum, because that is the pronunciation used here by the Abyssinians.'[2]

Páez sometimes adapted Ethiopic words to Portuguese patterns, perhaps so as not to overload the text with unfamiliar elements. Thus, for instance, he treated the Amharic masculine word *ambā* as if it were a Portuguese feminine, since it appeared to end in the familiar feminine suffix '-a'. The form 'bataois' (hermit monks) results from adding the Portuguese plural '-s' to his transcription of the Ge'ez word *bāhtāwi*, the correct plural being *bāhtāwiyān*. Similarly, for the plurals of 'umbâr' and 'azâx' Páez wrote 'umbares' and 'azages' (Anglicized in this translation as 'umbars' and 'azaxes'), but only after first giving the more nearly correct forms 'umbarôch' and 'azaxôch' (for the Amharic plurals *umbarwočč* and *azažwočč*).

Although he wrote the *History of Ethiopia* in Portuguese, as required in the context of missionary work sponsored by the Portuguese crown, Pedro Páez's mother tongue was Castilian Spanish, in which he continued to write his personal correspondence. Since Latin was the principal language of his education and training, Portuguese must have been his third language, which he had learnt while immersed in a Portuguese cultural environment, first during his voyage to Goa and then in India itself. The learning process had not been without its troubles and interruptions: having spent only about a year (1588–9) in direct contact with Portuguese speakers, he was assigned to accompany the Catalan father Antonio de Montserrat on his first (unsuccessful) mission to Ethiopia. He then spent a second, longer period of six years and three months in Portuguese India (1596–1603), between his release from captivity in Yemen and his second departure for Ethiopia. This was followed by the third period, lasting nineteen years, which he spent in Ethiopia in contact with the community of Portuguese descent and his Portuguese-speaking fellow Jesuits. During all the journeys he made in the service of the Society of Jesus he must have learnt other languages – indeed language-learning was essential in the proselytizing strategy adopted by the Society. He made good use of this knowledge when writing the *History of Ethiopia* and, as we have seen, incorporated passages and individual words in Spanish, Latin, Ge'ez, Amharic and Arabic. Two of these languages, Spanish and Latin, were familiar to educated Portuguese readers and therefore required no translation.

Scattered throughout the text there is a dynamic mingling of Spanish and Portuguese, even though Páez clearly intended to write the *History* in Portuguese. This admixture of Spanish words, spellings and grammatical forms led his fellow priests to accuse him of writing in broken Portuguese, as mentioned previously. In BPB, MS 778, however, the copyist generally corrected such errors, thereby removing these traces of Páez's mother tongue. The predominant language of the text is unquestionably Portuguese, however, and the work therefore belongs in the corpus of seventeenth-century Portuguese

---

[1] See p. 111 below.
[2] Beckingham and Huntingford, *Some Records of Ethiopia*, p. 89.

historiography.[1] The literary nationality of the work is defined by the language and supported by Páez's working knowledge of it, which he had developed as a result of the common Latin basis shared by Portuguese and his native Spanish, and from his exposure to reading and listening to it in various contexts. Even so, the rhetorical abilities he displayed in the work do not reveal a strong command of Portuguese. A Spanish Jesuit yet a Portuguese author, Páez clearly expended considerable time and effort in writing the *History of Ethiopia* in his adoptive tongue, only to be criticized by his fellow Jesuits for his imperfect use of the language.

## 7. Editing Criteria

### 7.1. The Text

The codex held in the Archivum Romanum Societatis Iesu (ARSI), Rome, under reference Goa 42 is a thick quarto (22 cm × 16 cm) volume comprising sixty-eight quires mostly of eight leaves each, sewn together, making a total of 538 folios written on both sides. Numbering was added during the twentieth century[2] in the top right-hand corner of each recto; the first two folios have been left unnumbered. The paper – a scarce commodity at the time, but an essential one for the missionary programme – may have been put aside from a single shipment received from India.[3] The margins were marked with dry-point ruling to delineate a constant writing space, the upper and internal margins measuring approximately 1 cm, the lower margin 2.5 cm and the external margin 3 cm, except on the last two folios in the last quire (ff. 537 and 538), which were later used by Patriarch Afonso Mendes for two notes in his own hand. Wider margins appear to have been provided for subsequent annotations, additions or corrections to the manuscript. When the writer himself noticed a mistake, he would cross out the error and add the correction within the body of the text, whereas the marginal errata or notes seem to be the product of a later revision, with a cross inserted at the relevant point in the body of the text. The number of lines per page is not constant, indicating that the folios were not pricked or scored in advance. In the three autograph books (I, III and IV) the lines are more densely packed with very little space between them; the number of lines per full page ranges from forty to forty-nine, averaging forty-five in books I and III and just forty-one in book IV (in the last quire of which some folios are left blank). The writing is less dense in book II, which has fewer words per line and wider spaces between lines; the number of lines per page varies from twenty-nine to thirty-eight, with an average of thirty-three. Páez's apparent attempt to economize on paper was spoiled by the liberality of his fellow priest who penned the second book: book II took up 172 folios, compared with the 143 of book I (including the prologue and dedicatory letter), the 86 of book III and the 136 of book IV). The headings for books II, III and IV and the titles for each chapter were written in larger letters and centred on the line, with a blank line above and below. The

---

[1] Serrão, *A historiografia portuguesa*, vol. II, pp. 291–4.

[2] Beccari noted that when he found the codex it was not numbered ('Notizia e Saggi di opere e documenti inediti', p. 4).

[3] The known correspondence of the Ethiopian mission does not mention the arrival of any paper.

writer of book II also left a line space between most paragraphs. In addition to the last few folios, folios 400v and 531r–v were also left blank. No general title was included, perhaps because a separate title page was lost during the manuscript's travels between Ethiopia, India and Europe, before arriving in the archives in Rome. The codex is leather bound and in a satisfactory state of preservation.

For the present edition, this manuscript was considered authoritative, as it was almost entirely penned by the author. The gatherings corresponding to book II, which were written by another hand, stand up to comparative analysis of rhetorical markers, notably as regards the method of refutation. Several chapters in this book, which deals with the dogmatic debate, Ethiopian religious questions (sacraments, ceremonies and beliefs) and hagiography, are translations of texts which merely needed copying. In the other books, all the translations and often long quotations were patiently transcribed by the author. Subsequently at least one copy of the manuscript was made, now held in the public library in Braga, northern Portugal (BPB – Biblioteca Pública de Braga). This copy was also examined. Unfortunately, its poor state of preservation (oxidation of the ink and book-worm have damaged most of the folios: Fig. 11), which had already been noted some sixty years ago,[1] has since deteriorated to the point where parts of the text are now illegible. In such cases, therefore, we followed the palaeographical reading produced by Lopes Teixeira in the 1940s in order to compare the two known texts – autograph and copy – and record any variants. Beccari's reading of the ARSI codex was also consulted.

### 7.2. Formatting Conventions
The following conventions have been used in the text:

a) [f. 1] – manuscript folio number;

b) *text in italics* – extensive excerpts from other works or works transcribed from other languages;

c) ~~text struck through~~ – words or phrases that have been crossed out in the manuscript but which remain legible;

d) [text in square brackets] – words or phrases added in the margins or between the lines in the same or a different hand;

e) (text in parentheses) – comment interpolated by the author;

f) {text in braces} – variant (or folio number) in ARSI, MS Goa 42;

g) <text in angle brackets> – variant (or folio number) in BPB, MS 778;

h) «text in double angle brackets» – variant in SOAS, MS 11966 (Manuel de Almeida's version of the chronicle of Susneyos).

### 7.3. Critical Apparatus
Variant readings in the two Portuguese manuscripts are of three kinds: changes in construction (the most common kind), where the copyist has simplified the syntax by changing the order of elements in the sentence; omissions, either accidental or deliberate; and changes in gender, number, tense or spelling (sometimes resulting in a different meaning), either to correct an error or due to a misreading of the original. Where variants affect the translation, they have been indicated by means of the bracketing conventions described in 7.2 (f), (g) and (h) above. The critical apparatus also includes footnotes on

---

[1] Feio, 'Notícia biobibliográfica', p. xvii.

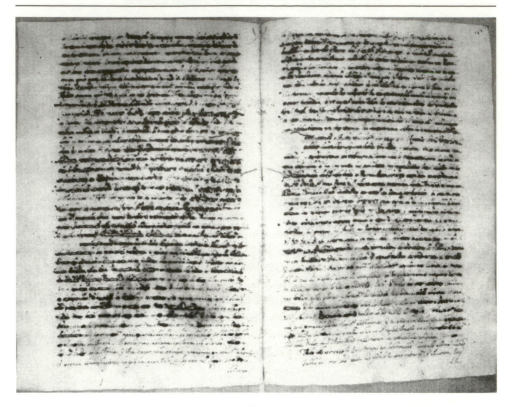

Figure 11. Damaged folios in BPB, MS 778.

philological, lexical, literary, geographical, historical, biographical and bibliographical points. These notes are intentionally brief and designed merely to provide information on an event or person, to supply references or to explain unfamiliar terms. The editors are particularly grateful for additional footnote information provided at various points by the translator, Dr Christopher Tribe.

Manuel de Almeida produced a translation of the chronicle of Susneyos, which was included in the manuscript of his *Historia da Ethiopia a Alta ou Abassia* now held at the School of Oriental and African Studies, London (SOAS, MS 11966, ff. 483–543). This translation is omitted from the other known manuscripts of Almeida's work: the British Library manuscript (BL, Add. MS 9861) and the nineteenth-century version held at the Biblioteca Nacional de Portugal (BNP, CUD 1769). Where Almeida's translation of the chronicle differs from that of Páez (in book IV of the *History of Ethiopia*), the variant reading is included here in English translation. Both the Páez and Almeida translations document an earlier version of the royal chronicle than the complete and possibly corrected version edited by F. M. Esteves Pereira in 1899–1900, and thus make an important contribution to the history of the chronicle's development and the censorship that it underwent in Ethiopia. The cross-referencing provided here not only allows for a comparative reading but may also illuminate the Jesuit fathers' production of translated texts.

A glossary is included which provides more extensive information on some of the persons, places, literary works, historical events and ethnographic topics mentioned in the *History of Ethiopia*. The glossary obviates the necessity for repetitive footnotes but does not seek to be complete. The choice of entries reflects the editing team's own interests, which may not coincide entirely with the reader's, and cannot claim to have provided a definitive account or explanation of any given subject. However, the glossary reflects the current state of research into the areas considered essential for an understanding of the work and of Páez's concerns in writing it.

## 8. Notes on the English Translation
by Christopher J. Tribe

The translation process is a search for equivalences, in the knowledge that perfect equivalence is elusive beyond the trivial level of particular words. How can the meaning of the original text best be put into a different language? The answer depends on how the translation is to be used. At one extreme lies the literal method, keeping as close as possible to the vocabulary and structures of the source text with scant regard for the fluency of the resulting translation; all the details are conveyed (and perhaps even supplemented in footnotes), but the reader has to be motivated to persevere. The opposite approach sacrifices word-for-word exactness so as to produce a natural-sounding piece in the target language; this will engage the reader more but may fail to render all the detail and nuances of the original text. Most translations, of course, fall somewhere between these two end-points. In translating the *History of Ethiopia*, I was aware that its significance as a historical document outweighs its literary value: Páez's style in Portuguese is rarely polished, usually unremarkable and sometimes plain clumsy. I therefore sought to put across the information it contains as completely as possible and, where I departed from the original structures, it was for the sake of clarity rather than elegance. I hope the resulting translation is readable yet close enough to the original text to be of use to historians unfamiliar with Portuguese.

My task was enormously facilitated by being able to work from the pre-publication manuscript of the new Portuguese edition of Páez's work (Lisbon: Assírio & Alvim, 2008), for which I am extremely grateful to the editors, Isabel Boavida, Hervé Pennec and Manuel João Ramos. In their edition the original Portuguese spelling has been brought up to date and palaeographical problems have been resolved. I compared their reading against Páez's manuscript (ARSI, MS Goa 42), folio by folio, using image files that they also generously supplied. The footnotes included in the Portuguese edition have been translated (except where they deal with purely Portuguese linguistic matters) and a few additional footnotes have been included where relevant for an English-speaking readership.

Most of the structural changes made to the text involved merely splitting up long sentences consisting of several consecutive main clauses marked off just by commas or 'and' or 'nor'. Very long, complex sentences containing digressions within digressions (over 200 words long, in some cases) required rather more drastic surgery to make them readable and intelligible while retaining all their meaning. It should be noted that the position of the manuscript folio number references in the translated text can only be approximate because of the different syntactical word order of English.

Quotations from the Bible have been taken from the Catholic Douay-Rheims version (1750–52 Challoner revision) rather than the more generally familiar King James Bible. The Douay-Rheims Bible is an English translation of the Latin Vulgate, the version that would have been used by Páez himself. It also differs somewhat from the King James Bible in the naming of the books and the numbering of the Psalms. The cross-reference to the King James version is provided in [ ] where there is a difference.

How to choose the best spelling for personal and geographical names in the translation was not immediately apparent: Páez's somewhat variable original spelling, the modernized Portuguese form, the local form current then or now, and the seventeenth-century or present-day English version might all be relevant in particular circumstances. The conventions adopted are as follows:

a) Páez's spelling (with his variants) is retained for names of Ethiopian people and places in the main text. As an exception, a simple 'c' has generally been used instead of 'ç' before 'e' or 'i'.

b) The spelling used for biblical personages and places is that of the Douay-Rheims Bible (e.g. Isaias, rather than Isaiah; (Queen of ) Saba, rather than Sheba; Sion instead of Zion). The spelling in the King James version is provided in the footnotes where it varies significantly.

c) Portuguese and other European names are presented as Páez spelt them with the exception of those of Popes and classical figures. Contracted forms have been expanded appropriately.

d) In editorial matter, names of persons have been spelt according to their nationality or in their standard English form. See below for a note on the transcription of Ethiopian names.

e) Geographical names outside Ethiopia and its neighbouring regions are generally given in their standard modern English forms where identification is certain (e.g. Mozambique), except when such places are mentioned strictly in relation to Ethiopian affairs, in which cases Páez's spellings are used (e.g. 'Melinde' for Malindi).

A brief note on Portuguese pronunciation is in order, since Páez's transcription of Ethiopic words and names follows Portuguese phonetic conventions of the time. As a very approximate guide, 'ç' is pronounced *ss*; 'nh' is like *ni* in the English word 'onion' (Spanish *ñ*); the 'u' in the groups 'gue', 'gui', 'que', 'qui' is generally silent; and 'x' represents English *sh*. In most cases 'j' has the sound of the *s* in 'pleasure' (French *j*) but, since Páez wrote initial capital 'I' and 'J' identically, an initial 'J' may represent an English *y* sound; the name transcribed as 'Jacob' could therefore equally well be 'Iacob' (Amharic 'Yā'eqob'). The circumflex (^) marks open vowels in Páez's transcriptions, and not necessarily the stressed syllable.

The scheme used for transliterating Ge'ez, Amharic and Tigrinya words in the footnotes, introduction, glossary and other editorial matter is the American Libraries Association/Library of Congress romanization system for Amharic.[1] This system has the advantage of avoiding digraphs (which can lead to ambiguity) and of not requiring

---

[1] Barry, ed., *ALA/LC Romanization Tables: Transliteration Schemes for Non-Roman Scripts*, pp. 8–9.

diacritics for two very common vowel sounds in Amharic (the first and sixth orders in the Ethiopic abugida or *fidal*). The seven orders of the *fidal* are romanized using the vowels: *a, u, i, ā, é, e, o*. Palatalized consonants bear a caron (ˇ) or tilde (˜) and ejectives a dot below or above (except in the case of *q*).

For the sake of simplicity and greater ease of recognition, the Amharic or Tigrinya versions of place names have been transliterated, although I acknowledge the fact that the current and/or historical inhabitants of some of these localities may be speakers of Oromo or other languages.

*History of Ethiopia*

# [DEDICATORY LETTER]

To [the very Reverend in Christ Our] Father
Mutio Vitelleschi[1] [Prepositus][2] General of the
Society of Jesus

After I arrived in this empire of Ethiopia[3] – which was in May 1603 – and began to see the things in it, I realized how little news one had of them in Europe, and thus I always wanted to send some to people in those parts. But my occupations were so many and so pressing that, {even though} in addition to this desire a number of fathers insistently asked me in letters to do so, I was never able to put it into practice. Now, however, I have been forced to rush through some tasks and also to use much of the time when I should have been resting from working on others, because the Father Provincial of India[4] has charged me with writing such news and, at the same time, responding to the allegations made against Father Patriarch Dom Joam Nunes Barreto[5] and the priests of the Society who came with him to Ethiopia by Father Friar Luis de Urreta of the holy religion of Saint Dominic, in a book which he published in Valencia in Aragón in the year 1610 on the political and ecclesiastical matters of this empire.[6] I have read it carefully and in the whole of it I have hardly found anything that bears any relation to what happens here, as will also be seen clearly by anyone who reads [this] *History* that I have produced on the same matters, in which I ordinarily speak from observation. And where I report things from the books of Ethiopia I have translated them faithfully, and where I write things from information I have tried to take them from the most reliable persons that there are here. And I am certain that there will be nothing in these things that can be criticized by anyone who has seen and experienced them, and even less in the other things that I write, as Your Paternity will be able to see, for every year you receive good information on what happens here in the letters from my companion fathers. And because of this, and {~~because of the obligation that I have~~} [because Your Paternity is so particularly the father of this mission],[7] it

---

[1] Vitelleschi was the sixth Superior General of the Society of Jesus, from 1615 to 1645.

[2] The words 'very Reverend in Christ Our' and 'Prepositus' [superior] were apparently added by another hand.

[3] See Glossary (Ethiopia).

[4] Francisco Vieira, Provincial of India from 1606 to 1615 (Beccari, *RÆSOI*, 10, p. xii).

[5] See Glossary (João Nunes Barreto).

[6] *Historia eclesiastica, politica, natural y moral, de los grandes y remotos Reynos de la Etiopia, monarchia del Emperador, llamado Preste Juan de las Indias. Compuesta por el Presentado Fray Luys de* Urreta, *de la sagrada Orden de Predicadores* [Ecclesiastical, political, natural and moral history of the great and remote Kingdoms of Ethiopia, monarchy of the Emperor called the Prester John of the Indies. Composed by the Presentee Friar Luys de Urreta, *of the holy Order of Preachers*], Valencia, 1610. See Introduction p. 11.

[7] Marginal note apparently written by another hand in ARSI, MS Goa 42; incorporated into the body of the text in BPB, MS 778.

seemed to me that I should offer Your Paternity {~~this work, so that, if it is such that it may be published, you may give permission for that, or if it is not then order it to be left; because my intention has been merely to comply with my obedience to the Father Provincial and to satisfy the desire of the fathers who have asked for it~~}[1] [this little work, in whose blessing and holy sacrifices and prayers I very much commend myself to the Lord.

From Dancas,[2] the emperor's court, 20 May 1622.

{Pº Paes]}[3] <PERO PAIS.>

---

[1] Passage omitted in BPB, MS 778; see Introduction pp. 23–4.

[2] See Glossary (Dancas/Dencâz/Danqaz).

[3] In ARSI, MS Goa 42 the passage in square brackets was written by the same hand that wrote the above-mentioned marginal note, to replace the passage in the original hand that has been crossed through; see Introduction pp. 23–4.

# {[f. 1]} PROLOGUE TO THE READER

One of the main reasons and causes why histories are written, my Christian reader, is so that, with time, things worthy of remembrance do not remain buried in oblivion, but serve as a reminder and an example to those coming after, as Quintilian says, *Institutiones oratoriae* book 10, chapter 1. And therefore Our Lord God ordered that chronicles be written about the memorable things that happened to the people of Israel, as may be seen in the holy scriptures, where not only the prosperous things but also the adverse ones, the good and the evil done by the kings, princes and monarchs of Israel are reported in detail; for that is the purpose of History, as Saint Augustine says in volume 2, Letter 131, *Ad memoriam episcopum*: to tell the whole truth about both the evil and the good of <[f. 1v]> him who has it. Histories are also written so that everyone may have news of the notable things that exist and the affairs that take place in very remote and distant lands, for that gives great pleasure, and it is very entertaining for people to take part even in such a manner in what they cannot see. But it is very important and indeed necessary that the historian should have correct information on what he is to write, because, as Lucian very properly noted in his book *Quo modo est scribenda Historia*, it is a great failure of a history when he who writes it is not well informed about the words, persons, incidents and places relating to it, and that is often lacking particularly in those who write based on information from others. And therefore one finds so many and such great errors in very renowned historians, as in Pliny and other ancient writers, and even in some modern ones who have written {of the things} of East India; but the greatest of all the errors that I have seen and heard are those of Father Friar Luis de Urreta of the Order of the glorious Father Saint Dominic, in a book that he printed in Valencia in Aragón in the year 1610, which he entitled *Ecclesiastical and political history of the great and remote kingdoms of Ethiopia, monarchy of the emperor called the Prester John of the Indies*, which has just come into my hands. And I find that, since he follows the information of a certain Joam Balthesar,[1] a native of the kingdom of Fatagâr in Ethiopia, there is hardly anything that bears any relation to the truth of what happens here. Not that that is very surprising because, in addition to the fact that long roads usually{[f. 1v]} make for big lies, he was unaware that this is the most common currency in Ethiopia, so much so that Emperor Malâc Çaguêd, who reigned for thirty-three years – and it will be twenty-three years since he died[2] – often quoted the proverb 'Lies of Ethiopia and greed of Egyptians'. I could include many examples of that here from the things that I have seen since 1603, when I arrived in Ethiopia, but suffice it to mention what happened when I was with Emperor Seltân Çaguêd,[3] who is the current one, on the terrace of some very tall palaces that he built

---

[1] João Baltazar.

[2] In 1597.

[3] See Chronology of Ethiopian Monarchs. Páez translates part of this king's chronicle in bk IV, chs 16–19, vol. II below.

recently. A servant of his came and told him that he had had some timber brought that he had ordered, measuring fifty spans[1] in length and three in width. The emperor told him to check carefully whether it was fully that size. He went off and soon came back, because the timber was already at the palace door, and stated that it was rather more than less. The emperor was so delighted to hear this that he went down to see it straight away with several of the grandees and myself with them and, on reaching it, he found that it was not even two spans in width, and so he turned away angrily and said, 'If from here to up there they bring me such a great lie, what will they do from the ends of my empire?'

Soon after that, he told me to choose a good piece of land and he would give it to me. And, when I named a piece of land that I had heard praised, he asked me if I had seen it and, when I answered that I had not but that I had heard it praised, he said, 'Your Reverence should not so readily trust what people tell you. Do not think that the people of our country are like those of yours. Look at the land first, and then say whether it is good or not.' With that he confirmed what many here say, that in Ethiopia one should only believe what one can see with one's own eyes. And thus I too found that that land was worthless, and so he gave me another piece <[f. 2]> that was very good. For if so many lies are told here in the land of Ethiopia, where one can easily prove whether something is a lie, it is hardly surprising that Joam Balthesar should have indulged in them so freely in a land so distant from here as Valencia, where nobody could contradict him. He went so far in that respect that one might say that nothing that Father Friar Luis de Urreta added to his information was more appropriate than the falsehoods he quotes from the poets, because the lies that Joam Balthesar assured him were great truths are no less false than theirs; indeed, their fancies were much less serious than all that this man invented without any scruples. Thus Friar Luis de Urreta was quite right when he said at the beginning of the prologue to his *Historia* that the things that he was writing were all new and had not been seen or read in all the writers and books in Europe, because, outside the books of chivalry, which {[[f. 2]} profess fictions, none is likely to include as many as Joam Balthesar told.

When I saw so many fables, then, I recounted some for amusement in the presence of the emperor and a number of grandees and, when I showed them the book, they were greatly surprised at how readily an unknown man had been given credence to print a book. And the principal secretary said, 'It seems that this Joam Balthesar is a buffoon, as he tells everything back to front.' The emperor replied, 'He is nothing but an evil spirit, because a buffoon could not invent so many lies.' And it would not have been so bad if he had done so just by aggrandizing the things of his land, but he tried so hard to belittle the affairs of the Portuguese (and everything that Friar Luis writes comes from him, as he states) and to criticize very worthy people of theirs that I felt that I had a duty to contradict his lies by declaring the truth. And, so that the reader may have some knowledge of them before reaching the places where he will see them refuted at length, I shall touch on some of them briefly here. He says then (as Friar Luis de Urreta mentions on page 207)[2] that, when Father Dom Joam came as patriarch of Ethiopia, he arrived in the country with

---

[1] See p. xix.

[2] Urreta, *Historia de la Etiopia*, bk I, ch. 21, entitled 'Of the Latin council that deals with business relating to Europe. A mission is described that thirteen priests of the Society of Jesus made, with a letter written by the Holy Father Ignatius to the Prester John Emperor of Ethiopia', pp. 192–219.

twelve companions from the Society and straight away caused turmoil, not only through-out the secular state of all the empire, but much more so among the clergy, since he ordered that thenceforth there should no longer be any married priests, but they should conform to the Latin Church in every way, and that secular folk should pay tithes to the Church on all that they produced, and other new things that had never been seen before in Ethiopia. And opposition grew so much that the patriarch and nearly all his compan-ions left Ethiopia and returned to Goa. The fact is that the Patriarch Dom Joam Barreto never came to Ethiopia in all his life, nor did he ever go beyond Goa, nor did any other father ever command such things.

On page 614[1] he says that in about 1555 more than 300 Portuguese Jews entered Ethiopia and, as the inquisitors wanted to seize them because they had been discovered as such, they fled, some to the Moors[2] and others to Goa, where <[f. 2v]> they told a thou-sand falsehoods so as to cover up their evil and apostasy, saying that the people of Ethiopia were schismatics and the Prester John was a cruel enemy of the Christian religion, and that Father Patriarch Andre de Oviedo was imprisoned and suffering great hardships in the gaols. And when this news reached King Dom Sebastiam, he was {[f. 2v] easily} <falsely> persuaded that what was nothing more than fable and malice was actually a true story. And he secured a brief from Pius V, which was subreptitious[3] because His Holiness was misinformed, in which he ordered Father Patriarch Andre de Oviedo to leave Ethiopia at the earliest opportunity he could find and to go and preach in China and Japan. All this too is very much beyond the bounds of truth, for {neither} <never> did <any such> Portuguese Jews {ever} enter Ethiopia, nor are there inquisitors, nor would such a Christian and prudent king as Dom Sebastiam have been easily persuaded that something untrue was so serious that he should inform His Holiness; rather, he was only persuaded on substantial grounds and consistent advice, and because he had very sound information that the Prester John was very much opposed to our holy faith and had imprisoned and dishonoured Father Patriarch Andre de Oviedo.[4]

Because of these and many other lies that we shall see later, this book may well suffer the fate that its own author mentions on page 343,[5] which in the Kingdom of Valencia befell the book by Joam Botero Benes,[6] which was banned by public proclamation for speaking little and falsely of the kingdoms and provinces of the world, Spain in particular; because it is not right to allow a book containing so many lies that affect the honour and repute of such a Catholic nation as the Portuguese, of whom even <the Moors> and Turks, despite being such great enemies of theirs, affirm that there is no more faithful and true nation than the Portuguese (as I heard many times in the seven years that they kept me captive in the Straits of Mecca); wherefore they could agree with Moses, Deut. 32:

---

[1] Urreta, *Historia de la Etiopia*, bk III, ch. 1, entitled 'Which includes a defence and apology of the Catholic faith and Christian religion that the Ethiopians have always held, and discusses the Christianity of the Christians of Asia, and of all the provinces of the world', pp. 571–623.

[2] Muslims other than Turks.

[3] Obtained by misrepresentation.

[4] See bk III, ch. 5 *et seq.*, vol. II below.

[5] Urreta, *Historia de la Etiopia*, bk I, ch. 32, entitled 'Of the great kingdoms, and lordships of the Prester John, of his many riches, tributes and incomes. The bitter wars that he has had with the Moorish and heathen kings, his neighbours, are discussed', pp. 341–66.

[6] Giovanni Botero Benisius. This may be a reference to the *Descripcion de todas las Provincias y Reynos del Mundo*, a Spanish translation printed in Barcelona in 1603.

'Inimici nostri sunt judices'.[1] Nor is it right that such a book should be dedicated to the Most Holy and Forever Virgin of the Rosary, the mother of truth itself. I do not say this to detract from the pious zeal with which one must presume Father Friar Luis de Urreta wrote, but to show what the great falsehoods with which Joam Balthesar deceived him really deserve.

What Father Friar Luis principally intends in all his work, and more particularly in Book 2,[2] is to show that the emperors of Ethiopia and their vassals have never been schismatic or disobedient to the Roman Church and are not so today; and that, even though for a long time they were unaware of many of the Church's ceremonies, yet in respect of the mystery of the Holy Trinity and of the fourteen articles[3] and of the sacraments they have always since the beginning of the Church kept themselves in all the purity and sincerity of the Catholic faith, without ever departing one iota from it or from the articles decreed and defined in the general councils. And as for {[f. 3]} circumcising themselves and keeping the Saturday Sabbath and other <[f. 3]> ceremonies of the Old Law, once they had dealings via Portuguese India with the Roman Church and understood that its Christians were scandalized that they kept circumcision and other ceremonies of the Law and that the popes ordered them not to do so, they desisted at once, without ever again circumcising themselves or keeping any Jewish ceremony at all or any other errors in which they previously used to dwell out of ignorance. And thus, on page 44,[4] he very severely reprehends those authors who have written the opposite, calling them presumptuous, calling them qualificators[5] just in name and not by office, saying that they speak badly and without grounds, and other similar things. That is the sum of his intention. And, in that respect, he says many other things that in the course of this *History* I shall show are false, without fearing the censure that he placed on those authors because, in the main, I shall speak as an eye-witness and from experience and not from information such as that given by Joam Balthesar, and for the rest I shall take my information from the most important people in this empire. And in all that I write, whether referring to the Portuguese or to the Ethiopians, I shall speak disinterestedly, with clarity and without exaggeration, for not only am I a cleric, whose duty it is simply to tell the truth of what I know, but flesh and blood shall not move me either to aggrandize the Portuguese or to belittle the Ethiopians, which would cause me particular displeasure; rather I owe them a great deal because ever since I arrived in their lands they have always done me many honours and favour upon favour, and not just the princes and grandees, but in particular three emperors that have reigned during this time.[6] Therefore, in accordance with the laws of good history and following the advice of Saint Augustine in the above-mentioned letter, I shall simply state the public good and evil of whoever has shown it, making no exceptions of anybody, but bowing above all to the judgement of those who charitably

---

[1] Deuteronomy 32:31: 'our enemies themselves are judges'.

[2] Urreta, *Historia de la Etiopia*, bk II, entitled 'Book two of the History of Ethiopia. The Faith, and Christian Religion, and holy ceremonies that are held in Ethiopia are discussed'.

[3] Presumably the 14 articles of faith as defined by an earlier Dominican, Thomas Aquinas (*Summa theologiae* III q. 1, a. 8).

[4] Urreta, *Historia de la Etiopia*, bk I, ch. 4, entitled 'In which the genealogy of the kings of Ethiopia is continued', pp. 35–45.

[5] A qualificator was a censor of the Inquisition who examined books.

[6] These were Yāʿeqob (1597–1603/1604–7), Za Dengel (1603–4) and Susneyos (1607–32).

wish to correct me, principally Father Mutio Vitelleschi, the General of our Society, to whom this *History* is addressed, because, not only does he have the power to remove what he pleases or to order that no one should see it, but no other person can correct it better than he, for every year he is kept faithfully informed of the things that happen by five other priests of the Society who reside here.[1]

---

[1] The author is referring to the annual letters from Ethiopia, or annual reports on missionary activities in that country (see *RÆSOI*, vols 10 and 11). The 'five other priests' that he mentions were António Fernandes, Francisco António de Angelis, Luís de Azevedo, Diogo de Matos and António Bruno. See Glossary (second Jesuit mission).

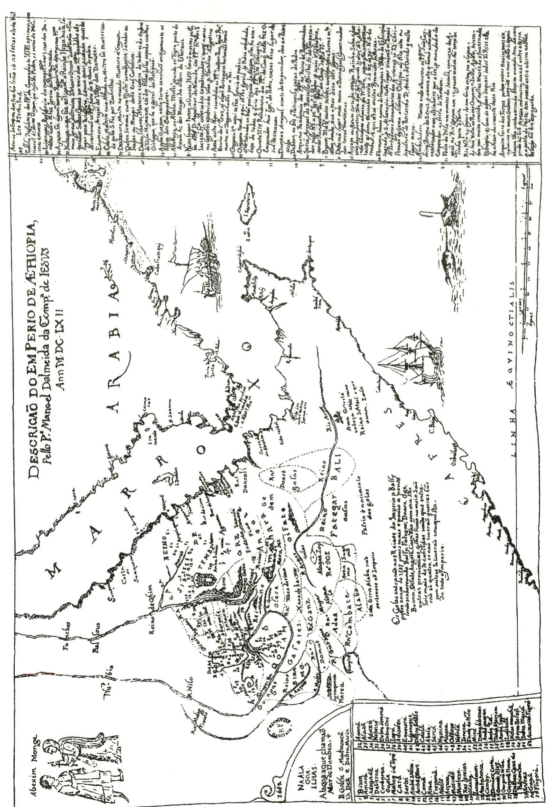

Figure 12. 'Description of the Empire of Ethiopia', by Father Manuel de Almeida of the Company of Jesus,' 1662. Courtesy of the ARSI archive.

# Book I[1]

# CHAPTER I

## Which deals with the situation, and with the number and names of the kingdoms and provinces of the part of Ethiopia ruled by the emperor whom they call the Prester John[1]

{[f. 3v]}There are many great differences among authors about the number of kingdoms and provinces included under this name Ethiopia and what they are called. But I shall not dwell on approving or condemning their opinions, because my intention is not to deal with it here in all its latitude but only with this part ruled by the emperor who is commonly called the Prester John.[2] And, even though many renowned authors, such as those cited in the prologue to the *Historia Ethiopica* by Francisco Alvarez,[3] and as Friar Luis de Urreta mentions in his chapter 18,[4] affirm that the Prester John is not this emperor but another very different king, on the borders with the Tartars, where <[f. 3v]> even now there are Christians, as I was told a short time ago by a young man from Tartary who happened to arrive in this land. Despite this, in the course of this *History* I shall call him the Prester John, as he is better known in Europe by this name than by any other. But before I name his kingdoms and provinces, it is worth remarking further that almost all the information that Joam Balthesar gave to Friar Luis de Urreta, not only with regard to the ecclesiastical matters of Ethiopia, but also on policies of peace and war, rites and customs, are mere fictions and prodigiously fabulous things. In his geographical descriptions, situation, ranking of lands, kingdoms, provinces, seas, rivers and lakes, he says nothing that makes sense but everything is so mixed up and in such great confusion that no one can understand it; and, on the proper names of things, one has to guess to know what he is talking about. Not even I, who live here, shall be able to talk about distances and positions of lands mathematically, both because I have no instruments or anything to help me, and because the people of this land have such little curiosity about these matters that they cannot say what is right, and they do not count in leagues but in days of travel, in which there may be great errors. But, by calculating more or less how far they commonly are accustomed to walk in one day, I shall derive the distances with the best probability that I can.

---

[1] See Fig. 12.

[2] See Glossary (Prester John).

[3] Pedro Páez used the 1557 Spanish edition of Francisco Álvares's *Verdadeira informação das terras do Preste João das Indias* [English translation published as *The Prester John of the Indies: True Relation of the Lands of the Prester John*, 1961]; see Introduction and Glossary (Francisco Álvares).

[4] Urreta, *Historia de la Etiopia*, bk I, ch. 18, entitled 'How all the first-born sons of the kings subject to the empire serve the emperor', pp. 174–7.

Dealing, then, with just this part over which the Prester John rules, its length runs from North to South, and it is all located within the tropics under the torrid zone. And it begins close to Çuaquem,[1] in a land called Focâi, and runs southwards to the land that they call Bahâr Gamô. I asked several people how many days' journey it would be and I found a great deal of variety among them; particularly, when I asked some grandees in the presence of Emperor {Seltân} Çaguêd, some said that it was a two-month journey, to which the emperor replied that it could not be so much and, adding it up with them, he made it forty-five {[f. 4]} days' journey; others said that it was fifty, which, at eight leagues that they might travel each day, makes 400 leagues, and if we wish to consider ten per day (which, from the way that they indicated the distance, was not the case) then it comes to 500. Its breadth, where it is greatest, begins at the far end of the province of Bur, in a land that is called Hazô, which is after one enters the gates of the Red Sea strait, and runs almost west-southwest to a land that they call Ombareâ. And they say that it must be thirty days' travel from one side to the other, which at eight leagues a day makes 240. And if we also want to calculate it at ten, then it will be 300 leagues.[2] And so, when some authors say that it was three months or more of travel from one end of the empire to the other, it seems that they were considering the day's marches made by the Prester John when he travels, which will be three or four leagues. Therefore, according to this, Friar Luis de Urreta in chapter 1, page 5,[3] extended himself greatly by saying that it is 680 leagues in length and 470 in breadth, and 260 where narrowest, and 2,000 in circuit. And he was much more mistaken, in the same place, in stating that this land is bounded in the west by the Black River,[4] Mount Atlas and the kingdom of Congo, in the south by the famous Mountains <[f. 4]> of the Moon and the Cape of Good Hope, and all the ocean coast from Mozambique to Cape Guardafui; for all these things are very far apart and preposterous, because the Black River (which he says is called Marâb here), when it leaves the lands of the Prester John, is very distant from the kingdom of Congo, and the mountains which he calls the Mountains of the Moon (if, as he claims on page 29, they are the sources of the Nile) are in the kingdom of Gojâm, well within this empire, and the Cape of Good Hope and Mozambique are many hundreds of leagues away from them. Nor has the Prester John ever held a hand's breadth of the ocean coast from Mozambique to Cape Guardafui, nor do his lands come anywhere near it, nor even on the Red Sea coast does he have any port today, for the Turks took them all from him now more than sixty years ago;[5] the principal ones of those are Çuaquên and Maçuâ,[6] which some call Dalêc, because this port was at first on an island called Dalêc but later was moved to Maçuâ. Both these ports are very small islands close to the mainland.

Leaving that aside, then, and looking at the lands ruled by the Prester John, I say that there are thirty-five kingdoms and eighteen provinces. {[f. 4v]} And, starting on the Red

---

[1] Suakin (Arabic Sawākin), a Sudanese Red Sea port.

[2] Manuel de Almeida counted 140 leagues from east to west ('Historia de Ethiopia a alta', in Beccari, *RÆSOI*, 5, bk I, ch. 2, p. 9).

[3] Urreta, *Historia de la Etiopia*, bk I, ch. 1, entitled 'Of the situation and cosmography of Ethiopia, and by another name Abassia', pp. 1–7.

[4] This may be a reference to the River Niger (literally 'Black River') in west Africa, in keeping with the classical use of the name 'Ethiopia' to refer to Africa as a whole (or at least the sub-Saharan part of it), rather than just the Empire of Ethiopia.

[5] In 1557.

[6] Massawa, or Meššewā, in Eritrea.

Sea side, the first kingdom is called Tigrê. Then there follow Dancalî, Angôt, Dobâ Seltân, Motâ, Auçâ, Amharâ, Olacâ, Xâoa, Ifât, Guedên, Ganh, Doarô, Fatagâr, Ôye, Bâli, Hadeâ, Alamalê, Oxelô, Ganz, Beteramorâ, Guraguê, Cuerâ, Buzanâ, Sufgamô, Bahargamô, Cambât, Boxâ, Gumâr, Zenyerô, Nareâ, Conch, Damôt, Gojâm, Begmêder, Dambiâ. These are held here to be kingdoms, although it may be that some do not deserve the name. The provinces are called Gadanchô, Arench, Orgâr, Cagmâ, Mergâi, Xarcâ, Gamarô, Abexgâi, Talaceôn, Oagrâ, Cemên, Çalâmt, Borâ, Abargalê, Salaoâ, Çagadê, Oalcaît, Maçagâ.[1]

The emperor's principal secretary listed all this for me and, afterwards, so that I could be more certain, in the presence of the emperor himself I asked a brother of his, named *Erâz* Cela Christôs,[2] and he told me likewise. But the emperor added that, even though his predecessors possessed all these kingdoms and provinces, he now had little control over some of them, since the greater part had been taken by some heathens that they call Gâla,[3] of whom we shall speak later. Hence we see that Friar Luis de Urreta was not well informed on this matter, for he says on page 5[4] that there are forty-two very large and well-populated kingdoms of Christians, and thirteen provinces of heathens and Moors, and that, as the people who live in them are not Christians, they are not given the names of kingdoms, even though in size they really are. Also where the lands of a single kingdom are governed by different lords, he names them distinct kingdoms, such as the lands of *Tigrê mohôn* and those of *Bahâr nagâx*, whom he calls Bernagaez,[5] which he says are kingdoms, whereas they are just lands of the kingdom of Tigrê. <[f. 4v]> And Bartholomeo Casaneo and Joam Boemo Aubano, whom he cites on page 343,[6] had even worse information, since the former (as he mentions there, *contra* Fathers Mafei and Ribadeneira) claims that seventy-four kings and almost an infinite number of princes obey the Prester John, and the latter says that he is one of the powerful princes of the world and the one with most kingdoms under his empire.[7]

The inhabitants of these kingdoms and provinces are commonly dark in colour, but there are some to be found that are almost as pale as Portuguese, among those they call Agôus and Gongâs in the kingdom of Gojâm, and among the Hadiâs. Others are very black. They ordinarily have good facial features and strong, sturdy bodies, and they suffer work, hunger, thirst, heat, cold and lack of sleep exceedingly well. The children of people {[f. 5]} of low birth, both girls and boys, go naked in the sun and the cold until they are well-grown and, at most, cover themselves with a goatskin or sheepskin. The children of great men, although they dress well, go barefoot and bare-headed until they are grown-up and, while they are still small, they wear very well styled forelocks and the hair on top of their heads long and braided into three or four plaits that hang down their backs. And as

---

[1] These names cannot all be securely identified or located. Some are discussed in Huntingford, *Historical Geography of Ethiopia*, the *Encyclopedia Ethiopica*, and Merid Wolde Aregay, *Southern Ethiopia and the Christian Kingdom, 1508–1708…*, unpubl. PhD thesis, SOAS, London, 1971.

[2] See Glossary (Cela Christôs/Seʿela Krestos).

[3] See Glossary (Gâla/Galâ/Galla/Oromo).

[4] Urreta, *Historia de la Etiopia*, bk I, ch. 1.

[5] See Glossary (Bernagaez/bahâr nagâx/*baḥr nagāš*).

[6] Urreta, *Historia de la Etiopia*, bk I, ch. 32.

[7] The French jurist Bartholomaeus Cassaneus (or Barthélemy de Chasseneuz, 1480–1541) and the German humanist Johannes Boemus Aubanus (or Johannes Böhm, c. 1485–1535) adhered to the medieval European view of the kingdom of the Prester John, based on the *Letter of the Prester John of the Indies*; see Glossary (Prester John; *Letter of the Prester John of the Indies*).

they are brought up in this way without being spoilt, they later become sturdy and healthy. And ordinarily they pass the age of eighty years with good strength and disposition, and they say that many aged a hundred are still thus. And I saw a monk who told me he was 131 years old and he could still walk, showing that he was quite strong.

In understanding, which is the best feature of man, they are commonly not outshone by the best of Europe, as we have often experienced with the nobles. And what surprises me {not a little} <little> is that they curb their natural passions, or rather, they hide them, in such a manner that, no matter how angry they may be with one another, they rarely show it, particularly the great men; rather, then, they are more courteous and gentle in their words, without for any reason there being the invective that occurs among other nations. But they also sometimes take revenge, although, once they have forgiven (which they do with ease when begged, however serious the matter), they consider it a great indignity and even a scruple to speak again about the matter over which they fell out, and so those that are reduced to our holy faith accuse themselves in confession of having spoken again (even if it were with friends) about what they had already forgiven.

It is a custom not only of great men but also of those of lesser condition never to deal with important business face to face. Everything is done through intermediaries and messages, no matter how close the parties, since they consider the time spent on these embassies to be a much smaller loss than the honour and correctness that might be forsaken through any show of passion or harshness of words, which are often not so measured when the spirit is disturbed.

<[f. 5]> The courtesies that they use with one another are to place the right hand on the chest and to bow the head, saying, '*Biçôn ayaoêl*', which means 'May evil not be in you.' And when one is an inferior, he lowers to his waist the cloth that he wears in place of a cloak and kisses the hand of the other and, on entering the house of a great man, he wraps the cloth round his waist and takes off his shoes. When great men go from one land to another and visit their kinsmen or equals, they kiss on the cheeks. And all of them, when they enter a church, take off their shoes and keep their heads covered, {[f. 5v]} in fulfilment of that which God ordered the prophet, Exodus 3,[1] that one should take off one's shoes out of reverence and respect and not uncover one's head.[2]

Great men's clothes are made of scarlet and other fine damask, velvet and brocade fabrics, which come to them from Cairo. The cut is the same as that of the Turks, but the inner caftan that they wear as a shirt has a high collar with buttons and ordinarily is made of white cotton fabric as fine as holland,[3] which they get from India. And their outer caftans are low-cut and long like those of the Turks, although this Emperor Seltân Çaguêd has begun to introduce cloaks like those of the Portuguese. Some wear turbans on their heads like Turks, others cloth caps, which are ordinarily red. Others have long hair, which they style in many ways. Low-born people dress as they can and ordinarily it is a white cotton cloth sewn as a sheet and with this they cover themselves, wearing nothing but breeches underneath. And some even wear no more than a cowhide, which they prepare like thick chamois. The dresses of noblewomen are long, loose chemises, low-cut, almost like those worn by women in our lands, finely worked, and over them something like a

[1] Exodus 3:5.
[2] ARSI, MS Goa 42 does not make a new paragraph here.
[3] Fine fabric from Holland.

basque[1] of silk or other material. Some cover themselves with damask or velvet shawls, or with rich silk cloths that serve as mantles for going out. And when they travel they wear burnouses and hats on their heads. They always wear a very well styled forelock and the rest of their hair done into many slender plaits, and they prefer black hair to fair. They wear beautiful gold earrings and the young women put on garlands with silver ornaments and other gold items with which they adorn their hair. Low-born women dress as they can: usually it is with a cotton cloth like a sheet or a hide like chamois.

The languages that exist in this empire are many and very different, even within a single kingdom. The most universal and courtly is the one they call *Amharâ*, a language that in eloquence greatly resembles Latin. The nations are also many and very different, but may be reduced to four: Christians, Moors, Jews and heathens. And in most kingdoms they are all found together. Hence the information that Friar Luis de Urreta had on this matter was very far off the mark, for he says, on pages 7[2] and 363,[3] that Prester John Alexandre III, on the advice of Father <[f. 5v]> Friar Daniel, prior of the monastery of Alleluia of the Order of Saint Dominic, in the 1570s, expelled the Moors and Jews from the whole of Ethiopia, even though they were numerous and the tribute they paid was very great. And any that {[f. 6]} dare enter the country without licence are condemned by law to be slaves. All that is very contrary to the truth, because in almost all the kingdoms and particularly in this one of Dambiâ where the court is now, there have long been many Moors and Jews, and the emperors have never been able to fully subjugate the Jews who are in the middle of their empire, three or four days' journey from their court, in the province of Cemên, even though they have tried to, sometimes by marching on them in person with large armies. And the emperor who is alive now, Seltân Çaguêd, because of an insurgent who joined them, bestowed many favours on them and gave them good lands elsewhere so that they would abandon those mountain strongholds, but they would not. And so he marched on them with a great army in October 1614 and, even though he killed many and seized the insurgent, he was unable to expel them from the mountains. And so today they remain there without wanting to obey him and therefore, in August 1616, he ordered all the Jews of Dambiâ and the others that were obedient to him to become Christians, and many obeyed. And others fled to the fastnesses, where there are Jews.

It is also false when he says that the Monastery of Alleluia is of Saint Dominic, because it is not and never has been, as I shall show later at the end of the second book, and the prior is not called Daniel, but Za Oald Madehên, which means 'Born the Saviour', and he was 131 years old in April 1616, when I went to visit him at his monastery to conclude certain things with him, and he told me that he had been the superior for forty years and that his predecessor, who was called Gâbra Maravî, *scilicet* 'Servant of the Husband', had been the superior for fifty-eight years. And never was there such an Alexandre III in Ethiopia, and the one who was reigning in the year 1570 was called Malâc Çaguêd and his baptismal name was Zar Za Denguîl, *scilicet* 'Proceeded from the Virgin', and he reigned for thirty-three years. And when he died in '96, his son Iacob succeeded him and took the name Malâc Çaguêd.[4]

---

[1] A short, tightly fitting bodice.

[2] Urreta, *Historia de la Etiopia*, bk I, ch. 1.

[3] Urreta, *Historia de la Etiopia*, bk I, ch. 32.

[4] In ARSI, MS Goa 42 there is a paragraph here that was not mentioned by previous editors.

One could deduce from this just how fabulous the things are that Friar Luis de Urreta attributes to this Alexandre III in the course of this *Historia* of his, because they are so false. However, because he makes mention of him in many places, since he began here, it is worth revealing how there was no such Prester John in the times that he claims, and how often he contradicts himself when talking of him, so that one may understand what credence should be given to the rest of the things in his book. Thus, on page {88} <617>,[1] he says that this Alexandre III succeeded Emperor Paphnucio who succeeded Naum. And later, on page {617} <88>,[2] he says that this Alexandre III succeeded Pres<[f. 6]>ter John {[f. 6v]} Mena. Firstly, there was no such Emperor Paphnucio, and the one that he calls Naum (who was actually called Naôd) was succeeded by his son Lebena Denguîl, *scilicet* 'Incense of the Virgin', and when he was made emperor he took the name David. And that is what he was called when Francisco Alvarez, chaplain to King Dom Manuel of Portugal, arrived in Ethiopia in the year 1520,[3] and later he changed his name and called himself Onâg Çaguêd. He was succeeded by his son Glaudeos *scilicet* 'Claudio', and he called himself Atanâf Çaguêd, and he was emperor when Dom Christovão da Gama[4] entered Ethiopia with 400 Portuguese, which was in the year 1541. And later he was killed in battle by the Moors in March 1559. He was succeeded by Minâs, his brother, whom Friar Luis calls Mena, and who called himself Adamâs Çaguêd, and he died in 1563. Therefore Friar Luis was very mistaken in saying that Alexandre III succeeded Paphnucio and later that he succeeded Mena, for this Minâs did not succeed Onâg Çaguêd, whom he calls Paphnucio, but his son Atanâf Çaguêd.

He also says, on page 616,[5] that this Emperor Mena wrote to Pope Pius V that Father Andre de Oviedo was the president of the Latin Council, and that they revered him as a saint. And, on pages 192 and 193,[6] he says that Emperor Alexandre III instituted this Latin Council at the request of Father Andre de Oviedo and made this priest its president. One can clearly see the contradiction in this because, while I shall leave it until its proper place to show that there never was such a Latin Council in Ethiopia, if Alexandre III instituted the Latin Council, how could Emperor Mena, who was before him (as it says on page 617), write to Pius V that Father Andre de Oviedo was the president of this Council? Moreover, he says on page 91 that, when this Alexandre III was a prince and was at Mount Amharâ,[7] Joam Balthesar served him there a great deal. Since the last one whom they took from there to be emperor was Naôd, who, as everyone in Ethiopia says and as can be seen in the catalogue of emperors, had left there 118 years before Friar Luis's book was printed, which was in 1610 when, as he says on page 7,[8] Joam Balthesar was approaching seventy years of age, therefore by that account fifty years or so before Joam Balthesar was born he

---

[1] The page number given in ARSI, MS Goa 42 (p. 88) is the correct one. Urreta, *Historia de la Etiopia*, bk I, ch. 7, entitled 'Of the name of the emperor of Ethiopia Beldichian, and it is explained why he is called the Prester John of the Indies', pp. 80–88.

[2] The page number given in ARSI, MS Goa 42 (p. 617) is the correct one. Urreta, *Historia de la Etiopia*, bk III, ch. 1.

[3] See Glossary (Francisco Álvares, Father).

[4] See Glossary (Christoval da Gama).

[5] Urreta, *Historia de la Etiopia*, bk III, ch. 1.

[6] Urreta, *Historia de la Etiopia*, bk I, ch. 21.

[7] See Glossary (Mount Amharâ/*Ambā* Gešan).

[8] Urreta, *Historia de la Etiopia*, bk I, ch. 1.

was already serving Alexandre III on Mount Amhârâ. He also says, on pages 7, 118[1] and 139,[2] that Alexandre III died in the year 1606 and in his place they elected a prince of the line of David who was called Zarac Haureat, and he was alive in 1608. All this is false, because I arrived in Ethiopia in May 1603 and did not find any such Alexandre, but Iacob, the son of Emperor Malâc Çaguêd, who also called himself Malâc Çaguêd, and in the following September they removed him and, sending him captive to the end of the empire to a kingdom they call Nareâ, they raised a cousin of his called Za Denguîl, *scilicet* 'Of the Virgin', and on 13th October 1604 they themselves killed him and brought back Iacob. But on 10th March 1607 a cousin of his {[f. 7]} called Suzeneôs gave battle and killed him and thus <[f. 6v]> became emperor and called himself Malâc Çaguêd. Later, as there were so many with this name, he changed it and now calls himself Seltân Çaguêd, which means 'Power Worships'[3] or 'Power Bows'. All this we shall declare later at length and, to conclude this matter, I say that it is quite certain that there was never an Alexandre III in Ethiopia, because nobody knows anything about him and in the catalogue of emperors there is only one Alexandre, whom they call Escander, and he was long before the Portuguese discovered Ethiopia, and so Francisco Alvares was also mistaken in what he says, on folio 128,[4] that while Alexandre was the emperor Pêro de Covilham, a Portuguese because he travelled from Portugal, as it says in the prologue to his *Historia*, entered Ethiopia in 1487, but Emperor Alexandre had died before in 1475, whence it is certain that he mistook the name of the emperor.[5] That will be enough for now for the reader to know how fabulous are the things that Friar Luis de Urreta says about this emperor in the course of his *Historia*.

Returning, then, to the inhabitants of the lands of the Prester John, the most courtly, noble and powerful, generally speaking, are what they call *Amharâs*. The rest have many different names according to their families and the provinces where they live, and therefore in a single kingdom there are peoples of very different names. However, there is one almost general name for all the land and its inhabitants which is '*Habêx*', because they call the land '*Habêx*' and its inhabitants too, whether one or many.[6] This is not only among themselves, one to another, but principally the Moors and Turks call the land and the inhabitants '*Habêx*', although ordinarily when talking just about the land everyone calls it Ethiopia, and this name is more correct, and thus the local people only use this name in the letters and books that they write; for many people believe that the name '*Habêx*' was invented by the Moors, and none of the many people whom I asked could tell me what it means. But Friar Luis de Urreta, on page 4,[7] corrupts the name, as other authors do as well,

---

[1] Urreta, *Historia de la Etiopia*, bk I, ch. 11, entitled 'Of the jewels and precious stones that the Prester John has at Mount Amara', pp. 118–28.

[2] Urreta, *Historia de la Etiopia*, bk I, ch. 12, entitled 'How the sons of the emperors of Ethiopia are kept at Mount Amara, on their upbringing and education, and on the guarding of said mountain', pp. 129–39.

[3] Páez has misspelt '*adora*' ('worships') as '*adoura*' ('gilds') here, producing an ambiguous reading; the ambiguity is resolved on f. 439 of ARSI, MS Goa 42, where he gives the correct spelling in an identical context. The misspelling is found again on f. 25 in the same context, and on f. 62 in a context that requires the meaning 'worships'.

[4] Alvares, *Prester John of the Indies*, 1943, bk I, ch. 104, 'How Pêro da Covilhã, a Portuguese, is in this land of the Prester John and how he came there and why he was sent', p. 375.

[5] Eskender died in 1494, apparently after Pêro da Covilhã arrived at the Ethiopian royal encampment.

[6] See Glossary (*Abexim/Habexim/Habexi*).

[7] Urreta, *Historia de la Etiopia*, bk I, ch. 1.

and calls the land '*Abassia*' and the inhabitants '*Abissinios*',[1] and he derives an apparently imaginary etymology, because I have never been able to find it either among the Moors or among the people of Ethiopia, even though he says that in the Arabic or Turkish language and in that of the Ethiopians it means a free and independent people who have never served a foreign master or a recognized foreign king, and that such is the land of Ethiopia. Therefore, on page 7[2] and pages 16 and 17,[3] he claims that even though low-lying Lower Ethiopia, which runs from next to Egypt as far as the island of Meroe, has had foreign masters and obeyed foreign emperors, the greater Upper Ethiopia, which runs {[f. 7v]} from Meroe to the Mountains of the Moon and lakes of the Nile, has never been conquered and has never obeyed a foreign master; always [for many years] up until the emperor who governs today, both Lower and Upper Ethiopia have obeyed the same master, who is the Prester John.

But leaving aside the etymology that Friar Luis gives to the name '*Abissinios*' and the fact that he errs greatly in the bounds that he places on the lands of the Prester John, he was given very false information when he says <[f. 7]> that they have never been conquered and that they have always been governed, as they are today, by their legitimate children and native emperors. Because in 1528 or thereabouts there came with a great army a captain of the king of Adel, a Moor who was called Mahamed and, because he was left-handed, they commonly call him Granh[4] (for that is how they call left-handed people in the language of the country), and on entering these lands of the Prester John he seized almost all of them and he ruled them for twelve years, or as some say fifteen, so that no more than very few lands were left, which were very insecure, because the emperor and the people from there were always fleeing from one place to another. And if Dom Christovão da Gama had not come to help them with the 400 Portuguese that we have already mentioned, there would not have remained a hand's breadth of land that the Moor did not control, as we shall say later when we deal with Dom Christovão's arrival in Ethiopia.[5]

In addition, at the time of Emperor Onâg Çaguêd, there came from the south some black heathens, whom they call Gâlas, cattle herdsmen, very cruel and wild people who, as soon as their women have given birth, whether to boys or girls, throw them out into the fields and there they die or are eaten by animals, some for the space of six years, others for ten, and if someone steals a child that they have thrown out so that he does not die and he is found out, they punish him severely and consider him a cursed man. They do not till the fields and ordinarily sustain themselves only on milk and butter and raw meat, although they sometimes roast and eat it. They have no king, but every eight years they elect captains who govern them in peace and war. These people, coming almost naked and armed with nothing but two assegais[6] and a shield and a wooden club, moved into this

---

[1] '*Abissinos*' in ARSI, MS Goa 42.

[2] Urreta, *Historia de la Etiopia*, bk I, ch. 1.

[3] Urreta, *Historia de la Etiopia*, bk I, ch. 2, entitled 'In which are declared how many provinces there are that are called Ethiopia, for an understanding of the work, and of many places in the Holy Scriptures', pp. 8–17.

[4] See Glossary (Granh/Grāññ/Aḥmad ibn Ibrāhīm al-Ghāzi).

[5] See bk I, chs 31–6.

[6] Throwing spears.

empire so that today they control a great part of it, and in the remaining part they make many incursions and carry out great attacks almost every year, nearly always taking plenty of booty, particularly cattle, women and children. They kill all the men since they do not trust them, although sometimes, after they have seized their booty, the captains of the empire attack them and force them to leave it behind, and kill some of them. But if they want to go to where they are, they rarely catch them, since they flee {[f. 8]} with their cattle. And as the lands are all barren, since they do not sow them, they cannot follow them very far as they cannot find anything to eat. But in the last two years they made some incursions and, coming upon them suddenly, they killed many and brought back plenty of booty, as we shall say in the fourth book. This plague of Ethiopia they say was foretold by the Patriarch Dom Joam Bermudez,[1] who arrived with Dom Christovão da Gama and, as they did not give their obedience to the Roman Church as they had promised, he later returned to India, cursing the lands through which he passed and saying that he could see some black ants entering Ethiopia which would destroy it, and all the lands that he cursed are now destroyed and in the possession of the Gâlas.

When Friar Luis says that Ethiopia has always been governed by legitimate emperors he is also far from the truth, because not only do the books of Ethiopia recount it, but it is very well known here that, on his death, Emperor Armâh or, as another catalogue <[f. 7v]> says, Delnaôd, left a very young son, and the person who remained as his tutor and governor of the empire was a very powerful lord called Zagoê, who was married to a woman of royal blood. And when the boy died soon afterwards, he went on governing the empire as before without proclaiming himself emperor and without wanting to elevate any member of the line of Solomon, to whom the empire belonged, until he died. And a son of his remained, who proclaimed himself emperor and killed all those that he could find of the line of Israel to whom the empire might belong, so that no competitor should be left. And the descendants of this Zagoê ruled over the whole of Ethiopia for 340 years, for, although the catalogue of emperors shows no more than 143, they say that many are missing and that this is the true count. And at the end of that time there rose up one of the line of legitimate emperors who had escaped by hiding in distant lands and, although he had few supporters, he knew that the leaders of his opponent's army would welcome him, and so he went against him confidently; and when he drew near, they told the emperor that that son of Israel (which is how they called those of the royal caste that were descended from Solomon) was coming against him and that he should leave. He replied that it was not necessary and that one captain would be enough to deal with him, and so he sent the one who was in the vanguard. But as the captain was secretly with the other, he straight away joined those who were rising up. When the emperor heard this, he sent two other captains, whom {[f. 8v]} he considered loyal. But they too did as the first one had, and all together they turned against their lord; when he saw that, he fled on his horse and, as he could not escape, he took shelter in a church, saying that he was taking as his protector a saint that was in there, whom they called Charcôs. But the son of Israel, who was pursuing him, soon arrived and said, 'Lord, do not protect him, for he took the empire which did not belong to him', and, striking him with his lance, he killed him and thus became emperor by common assent and they called him Icuno Amlâc, which means 'God Be With Him'. And since this emperor the line of Solomon has continued until now,

[1] See Glossary (João Bermudes).

which is more than 350 years. {~~Since that emperor the line of Solomon has continued until now, which is more than 350 years. He had five sons or, as others say, nine, and when he was about to die he begged them dearly to be very united and to have great love for one another and that each one should reign for one year, starting with the eldest. And so they did, but when the empire came to the second or, as others claim, the seventh, the youngest lost his patience, because when he had to eat with his two brothers, who were the new emperor and the eldest, who used to eat together, they would make the others leave the room to wash their hands, and then they would come in to eat. Annoyed with this, he said to his friends, 'I shall not act in this way, but when the empire comes to me I shall seize all these brothers of mine and put them in a place from which they will never escape.' Somebody of course told the one who was emperor, and so he immediately ordered all his brothers to be seized and taken to Mount Amharâ, which they call Guixên, which is very strong, as we shall say later, and after that it became the custom to put the emperors' sons there, until Emperor Naôd, who ended this custom, so that only those who had been there before remained; and on the mountain there are still the descendants of Frê Heçân, who was the cause of their beginning to put people there, as I was told by Emperor Seltân Çaguêd.~~} Hence the information that they gave to Friar Luis de Urreta, that Ethiopia had never been governed by a foreign master but only by native and legitimate emperors, was very much contrary to the truth, for it is recorded that the line of the emperors was cut for a period of 340 years and that, even though that Zagoê was married to a woman of the royal caste, his children could not inherit the empire because it was not the custom for the sons of women to inherit, even if the women were daughters of the preceding emperor, unless their husbands were of royal caste through the male line.

# {[f. 9]} CHAPTER II

## Which deals with the line of the Emperors of Ethiopia, beginning with Queen Saba[1]

It is a very certain and confirmed fact among the Ethiopians, to the extent that they feel that there can be no controversy of any kind, that their emperors descend from Solomon through Queen Saba, because all their books are full of that, and they have always boasted of it and today take great pride in calling themselves Israelites and sons of David; therefore, since we have to discuss <[f. 8]> them, we must first talk about the mother through whom they have received such a great honour as being sons of David. And moreover, this is the style of the Holy Scriptures, to talk first about the mother when they wish to discuss the son, and so, when the holy scribe wished to tell of the great deeds of some king, he would first say who his mother was and what she was called; as he did when, wishing to discuss Jeroboam, he first said that his mother's name was Sarua, a widow woman: *Cuius mater erat nomine Serva, mulier vidua* (3 Kings 11).[2] He did the same again when wanting to talk of King Joas in 4 Kings 12, and of King Ezechias in 4 Kings 18, first declaring who their mothers were and what they were called;[3] which the glorious evangelist Saint Matthew imitated in his chapter 1, where, in order to write about the marvels and greatness of Christ Our Lord, he first tells who his mother was and what her name was. Since I have to discuss the first emperor of Ethiopia, who was of the line of Solomon and his other descendants, I say that his mother was Queen Saba. And, as those who have more news of the histories of Ethiopia claim, she was born in the kingdom of Tigrê in a village that is still called Sabba today, a quarter of a league west of a town called Agçûm,[4] where she later had her court. And from the port of Maçuâ to there must be twenty-five leagues more or less, going almost due south. She was also called Negesta Azêb, which means 'Queen of the South', and these two names are very often found in the books of Ethiopia. In 3 Kings 10 and 2 Paralipomenon 9 they call her Saba,[5] and in Saint Matthew 12, where our version says *Regina Austri*,[6] the Ethiopian version says *Negesta Azêb*.

Another name is also sometimes found in their books, which is Maquedâ, but they say that this name is {[f. 9v]} Arabian and means Amharâ. Therefore *Negêsta Maquedâ* is 'Queen Amharâ', and a book from Agçûm, talking about Queen Azêb, says that she built

---

[1] See Glossary (Queen Saba/Queen of Sheba; and *Kebra Nagaśt*).

[2] 3 Kings [1 Kings] 11:26: 'whose mother was named Sarua, a widow woman'.

[3] 4 Kings [2 Kings] 12:1 and 18:2.

[4] See Glossary (Agçûm/Aksum).

[5] 3 Kings [1 Kings] 10:1–13 and 2 Paralipomenon [2 Chronicles] 9:1–12: 'queen of Saba' (Holy Bible, Douay-Rheims version); 'queen of Sheba' (Holy Bible, King James version).

[6] Matthew 12:42; 'queen of the south'. 'Our version' means the Latin Vulgate.

a capital city of Ethiopia which was called Dâbra Maqueda. And I do not think it would be wrong to say that this city of Maqueda is the one they now call Agçûm, for in the book where they place the catalogue of the emperors it says that Queen Azêb began her reign in Agçûm, and the ruins of the buildings, which can still be seen, clearly show that it was the most sumptuous city that there was in Ethiopia, although it is now a small town. But, while leaving room for everyone to say what he thinks {best} about this, for there is so little, we shall go on to recount the journey she made to Jerusalem, desiring to see the greatness and marvels that fame made known about Solomon; because, in the course of it, it will be seen on what the emperors of Ethiopia base their claim that they are descendants of the royal house of David. And so that this story shall bear neither more nor less embellishment than it is given in the books of Agçûm from which I have taken it, I shall tell it in the same words in which they recount it, which are as follows:

<[f. 8v]> *When King Solomon determined to build the Temple, he sent a message to all the merchants in the world for them to bring him rich goods and he would give them gold and silver. And, having particularly had news of a rich merchant of Queen Azêb's Ethiopia, who was called Tamerîn and had 520 camels and seventy-three ships, he sent word to him that he should take him the richest things that he could find and fine gold from Arabia and black wood; which he did and, gathering all the things that he could, he came to Solomon with them. And he took what seemed good to him and gave him much more than it was worth. This merchant was a discreet man of good understanding and, marvelling at Solomon's wisdom, he carefully noted the sweetness of his words, his justice, the modesty in his bearing and his way of life and the loving way in which he treated everybody, the magnificence of his table and the orderliness of his servants, the wisdom with which he governed his household, forgiving those who erred and, when he punished, it was with clemency. He spoke in parables, and his words were sweeter than honey. And so those who came close to him did not want to go away when they saw his wisdom and the sweetness of his words, which were like water to those who are thirsty and bread to those who are hungry and medicine to the sick, and he passed judgement with the truth without making any distinction among people. And God gave him much honour and wealth, gold and silver and precious stones, rich garments, so much so that gold was like silver, and silver like lead, and iron like straws of the field.*

*Having been there for a long time, he asked Solomon for permission to return to his land, saying, 'Lord, I should very gladly have stayed {[f. 10]} in your house as the least of your servants, because happy and blessed are those who hear your words and perform your commands, but I have already lingered a long time. It is now time to return to my lady, according to the promise that I made her, {and to deliver her property to her} for I am also her servant.' Solomon made him many honours and gave him much property and with this he sent him away in peace for the land of Ethiopia. And, on coming to his lady, he delivered to her the property that he was bringing and told her how he had come to Solomon and all the things that he had seen and heard, and she was so delighted with this that every day she would ask him again what he had seen, and she burned with desire to go and see him, to the extent that she would weep with love and the great desire she had to see those things. And so she determined in her heart to go, and God gave her firmness in this purpose. And so she began to organize her household and ready herself for the journey and the things that she had to {present} <give> to Solomon. And she commanded the princes and great men to ready themselves, because the journey was long, and to gather together pack animals, camels, mules* and ships. And she addressed them, saying, 'Listen to my words and consider my reasons. What I desire is to seek wisdom, because the love of it has closed my heart and pulls me with very strong cords, because wisdom is better than treasure of gold <[f. 9]> or silver and better even than everything that has been created on earth. With what under the sun may wisdom be {bought} <compared>? It is sweeter than honey, and gladdens more than wine, and is more resplendent than the sun.' And, having uttered many praises to wisdom, she finished her speech by saying that, from the news that she had had of Solomon, she loved him without having seen him, and all the things that she had heard of him were to her like water to the thirsty.

On hearing this, the princes and members of her household answered, 'Lady, since you desire wisdom so much, you shall not want for it. As for us, we are ready to accompany you if you go and to stay if you stay and to live and die with you anywhere.' And so she made ready with great abundance, honour and majesty. And they loaded 697 pack animals and countless mules, with which she departed. And she went on her way with great trust in God in her heart. And, on arriving in Jerusalem, she was received by Solomon with great honour. And he lodged her near his house, sending her dinner and supper in great abundance, fifteen corê[1] of wheat flour, many sweetmeats, and thirty corê of flour made into bread. Five cows, fifty capons, fifty sheep, {[f. 10v]} apart from goats, chickens, and wild cattle and deer, sixty large measures of new wine, thirty of old, and twenty-five things that Solomon liked most. And, when Solomon went to see her, he always gave her fifteen of his new robes that were so splendid that they drew all eyes towards them. And she too would visit him and converse in his house, and she saw and heard his wisdom and justice, his honour and majesty, the sweetness of his words and how he gave commands with gravity and answered with the fear of God. Seeing all this, she marvelled at his great wisdom and how there was nothing wanting in his words but all that he said was perfect, and how he gave orders and measurements for everything that the craftsmen who were building the temple had to do, regarding both the timber and the stone, and everything else. And, just as light shines in the darkness, so did the wisdom in his heart shine in all things. Thus he did everything with the great wisdom that God gave him when he begged Him not for victory over his enemies or for riches or honour, but for wisdom to govern His people and to build His house.

On seeing all these things, the queen said to Solomon, 'Blessed are you, Lord, for you have been given such great wisdom {and understanding}. I wish I could be as one of the least of your maidservants and wash your feet and hear your wisdom. How good have your answers and the sweetness of your words seemed to me! Your wisdom is immeasurable and your understanding endless, like {my} <the morning> star among the other stars, and like the sun when it rises. I give many thanks to Him that made me come to you and see you, and to Him that made me enter through your doors and made me hear your words.' King Solomon replied, 'What wisdom and understanding <[f. 9v]> have sprung from you! For I have that which the God of Israel gave me, as I asked of Him and sought in Him, but you, without knowing the God of Israel, have so much wisdom in your heart that you have come to see me and to be humble like a slave of my God and to stand at the door of His house where I serve my Lady, the Ark of the Law of the God of Israel, the holy heavenly Sion. I am His servant and not free. Nor was it by my will, but by His, nor is this word mine, but I say that which He has made me say

---

[1] *Qoros*, a unit of weight in the duodecimal system, equal to twelve loads; see Pankhurst, 'A Preliminary History of Ethiopian Measures, Weights and Values – Part 3', p. 47.

*and I do that which He has ordered me to do and I receive the wisdom that He gives me. When I was bread He made me flesh, when water He curdled me and made me in His image and likeness.' He said many other things to her, with which he exhorted her to be humble and to love God; on hearing that, she said, 'How useful is all this conversation of yours to me! Tell me whom I should worship, because we worship the Sun as our fathers taught us and we say that he is king of all the gods, because he ripens our crops and lightens the darkness and dispels fear and therefore we say that he is our creator {[f. 11]} and we worship him as God. But of you Israelites we have heard that you have another God, Whom we do not know, and that He has given you the Tablets of the Law by the hand of Moses, His prophet. And they say that He Himself comes down to you and speaks to you, and makes you understand His justice and His commandments.'*

*To this King Solomon replied, 'In truth it is right to worship God, Who created the heavens, earth, sea, sun, moon and the stars together with all the other things that are in them. He alone deserves worship with fear and trembling, with joy and contentment. It is He Who kills and gives life, punishes and forgives, raises the poor man from the ground, gives sadness and joy, and there is no one who can say to Him, "Why did You do that?" To Him are due glory and praise from angels and from men. As for what you said, that he has given us the Tablets of the Law, in truth they were given to us by the hand of the God of Israel, so that we should understand His commandments, His justice and punishment that He has ordered in His temple.' The queen replied, 'Then henceforth I shall not worship the Sun, but its creator, the God of Israel. These tablets of His Law shall rule over me and my generation and all my vassals; for because of this I have found honour before you and before the God of Israel, my creator, Who made me come to you and hear your words, see your face and understand your commandment.' With that she took her leave and rested in her house. Afterwards she used to visit him often and hear his wisdom, keeping it in her heart. He too would visit her and declare to her whatever she asked him.*

*After seven months had passed, the queen wished to return to her land and said to Solomon, 'I wish I could be with you always, but because of my people I need to return. All this that I have heard, may God make it bear fruit in my heart, and in the hearts of all those who have come with me.' On hearing this, Solomon said in his heart, 'Who knows if of this woman of such beauty, who has come from the ends of the earth, <[f. 10]> God may give me fruit.' And he answered her, 'Now that you have come to such a distant land, why do you have to return without seeing the organization of my kingdom and the manner in which the great men are dealt with? Come to my house so that I may show you.' She replied, 'Willingly shall I do so, so that you may increase wisdom and honour in me.' Solomon was delighted with the answer and commanded that rich robes be given to the principal ones among those accompanying the queen. And he ordered that in his house there should be great splendour and double the customary amount of delicacies on his table, so that never before had there been seen such great splendour as on that day. And, as the king's table was made ready, the queen entered, not by the main door but by another small door, and she sat down {[f. 11v]} in a place that the king had prepared very richly with many precious stones and other beautiful things, and with many fragrances, and done with so much art and wisdom, that she could see everything that was happening without being seen by anyone, and she marvelled greatly and praised the God of Israel in her heart. The king having sat down at his table, he sent to the queen the delicacies from it that might make her most thirsty. And, when the meal was finished, the princes and* *great men of the kingdom went in, and the king, rising, went to where the queen was and said that she should take her ease and rest there until the following day. She answered that she would do so, but that he must swear to her by the God of Israel that he would do her no wrong. Solomon said that he would swear, but that she too must swear that she would take nothing from his house. She answered, smiling, 'Lord, as you are so wise, how do you speak in this way? Perchance am I to steal from the king's house that which he has not given me? Do not think, Lord, that I have come for love of goods, because my kingdom, by your grace, is also rich and I lack for nothing that I desire. I have come only to seek your wisdom.' They both swore and the king left to rest on his bed opposite hers. And he ordered a page to bring water and to put it in a carafe in sight of the queen and to leave, closing the doors behind him.*

*When the queen had slept her first sleep, she awoke with a great thirst and desired greatly to drink of the water that she had seen. And, as it seemed to her that {Solomon} <the king> was asleep, she arose and went very quietly to take the water, but Solomon, who guilefully was still awake, seized her by the hand and said to her, 'Why have you broken your oath?' Afraid, she answered, 'Is drinking water breaking my oath, perchance?' The king said, 'Have you seen a greater thing under the sun than water?' She answered, 'I have sinned on my head. You have kept your oath.' Then the king took her to him and, when he was asleep, it appeared to him in a dream that a very resplendent sun was coming down from the sky and that it shone brightly on Israel and that after a while it went to the land of Ethiopia and shone brightly on it for ever, because it wished to be there. Solomon awoke <[f. 10v]> astonished at this vision and, rising, he told the queen what he had seen. She begged him dearly to let her go to her land, and so he went into his treasure house and gave her many riches and precious robes, loading many animals and 7,000 wagons. Then he took a ring from his finger and gave it to her, saying, 'Send me this as a sign, if God should grant me some fruit, and if it is a son, then let him come.' And with that he bade her farewell in peace and advised her to remember well what he had taught her: {[f. 12]} to worship but one God and always to do His will, so that her land might be blessed through her.*

*Departing with all this honour and splendour, the queen came to her land of Bala, which is Disanâ, and nine months and five days after she had left Solomon she gave birth to a son and gave him to be nursed with great honour. And, forty days later, she entered her city with great pomp and majesty and the princes and great men of the kingdom rejoiced at her entry and brought her many presents. She too gave them very rich robes, gold, silver and objects of great beauty, and she governed her kingdom in such a way that there was no one that disobeyed her.*[1]

I have taken this from a very old book that is kept in the church at Agçûm, in which one can see that that merchant Tamerîn, a servant of Queen Saba, having left Solomon, came to Ethiopia where his lady was and, when she heard the marvels that he told of Solomon, she determined to go and see him; therefore, according to this and to what everyone in Ethiopia states without controversy, it is quite certain that Queen Saba departed from Ethiopia when she went to Jerusalem, but from which land of hers the

---

[1] The author has translated part of the *Kebra Nagaśt* (*The Glory of the Kings*), the myth of origin of the Ethiopian Solomonic dynasty. The full text has been published by Bezold with a German translation, and by Budge, *Queen of Sheba* with an English translation. Manuel de Almeida used the translation produced by Pedro Páez ('Historia de Ethiopia a alta', in Beccari, *RÆSOI*, 5, bk II, ch. 2, pp. 93–8). See Glossary (*Kebra Nagaśt*).

books do not mention, and the local people do not know for sure. Some say she departed from a land that they call Fazcolô, where the finest gold in Ethiopia is found, and it lies to the west of the kingdom of Gojâm, not very far from it. Others claim that she departed from Agçûm, where they say she had her throne and, at that time, it was a very large city even though it is now a small town; and this is what they think is more likely. The land to which she came when she returned from Jerusalem, which the story calls Bala, they say is in the province of Amacên, not very far from [the port of] Maçuâ.

# CHAPTER III

## In which it is declared how Menilehêc, the son of Queen Saba, went to Jerusalem to see his father Solomon

Before we continue the history of Queen Saba's son, it must be pointed out that the books kept in the church of Agçûm give him various names, *scilicet*: Bainalehequêm, Ebna Elehaquêm, Ebnehaquêm, Menilehêc, and not Melilec, as Friar Luis de Urreta says on page 46;[1] but it is this last, Menilehêc, that the people of Ethiopia commonly use and it means in the ancient language 'Looks Like Him', because he looked very much like Solomon. But Solomon, when he made him king, gave him the name {[f. 12v]} David like his father. This is the origin of the custom that the emperors of Ethiopia change their baptismal name when they are given the empire. The other names mean 'Wise Man's Son'. Having explained that, so that the reader will not be confused by the {variety} <novelty> of the names, <[f. 11]> we shall continue with the history of Menilehêc, which we began in the previous chapter, in the same manner as the book tells it. And it says:

*The boy grew and she gave him the name Bainalehequêm. And, when he was twelve years old, he asked those who cared for him who his father was, and they told him it was King Solomon. He also asked the queen, and she answered him with vexation, 'Why do you ask me about your father, and not about your mother?' He went away without saying anything and, returning three days later with the same question, she answered him, 'His land is far away and the road is hard. Do not wish to go there.' Thus he remained until he was twenty-two years old, when he learnt all kinds of horsemanship and hunting. And then he begged the queen most insistently to let him go and see his father. On seeing the great desire that he had, she called for her merchant Tamerîn and told him to take him to {the king} his father, because he was continually importuning her night and day; but that he should try to return quickly and safely, if the God of Israel so wished. And, readying what was necessary for his journey, in accordance with his honour, and the items that he was to present to the king, she sent him off with a great retinue, recommending to them all that they should not leave him there, but that they should bring him back and that they should ask <King> Solomon to make him king of Ethiopia, with an order that thenceforth all his successors should be men of his line, because it was a custom for maiden women to reign, without ever marrying; and that he should send her a piece of the covering of the Ark, before which they might pray. And, taking her son aside by himself, she gave him the ring that Solomon had given her from his finger, as a sign by*

---

[1] Urreta, *Historia de la Etiopia*, bk I, ch. 5, entitled 'Of Queen Saba, who from Ethiopia went to visit King Solomon, of whom she conceived a son who was called Melilech, from whom descend all the Abyssinian emperors; the tablets of the Law are discussed', pp. 46–65.

*which he might know that that was his son and to remind him of the oath that she had made to worship none but the God of Israel, and that all her vassals did the same. And with this she bade him farewell in peace.*

*During his journey, he came to the land Gazâ which Solomon had given to his mother, where he was received with great honour, for it seemed to them that he was Solomon himself, because he differed from him in nothing and, as if to their king, each one presented him with what he could according to his station. But later some said that he could not be Solomon, who was in Jerusalem; others affirmed that he was Solomon himself, the son of David. {[f. 13]} And, with this doubt, they sent people on horseback to Jerusalem where, on finding Solomon, they told him that all his land was troubled by the arrival there of a merchant who was like him in every way without there being any difference at all. The king asked where he was going. And they answered that they had never dared ask him, because of the great majesty that he had, but that his people said that he was coming to him. On hearing this, Solomon was disturbed in his heart but joyful in his spirit, understanding what it could be, for until then he had no more than one son who was called Jeroboam.[1] And he commanded a servant of his, on whom he relied, to go and {receive} <wait for> him, taking many presents and a large<[f. 11v]> number of wagons, and to bring him back with as much speed as there could be.*

*Solomon's servant set off with great pomp and, on arriving where Bainalehequêm was, he gave him the presents and said that he should go with him {straight away}, because the king's heart was burning with love and desire to see him: 'As for me, I do not know whether you are his son or his brother, but I do not think you are anything else, because you resemble him in every way.' To which he replied, 'I give many praises to the God of Israel, because I have found honour before my lord the king, without seeing his face; he has made me rejoice with his words. Now too I have hope in this same God Who will make me come to see him and return in peace to the queen my mother and to my land of Ethiopia.' Solomon's servant replied, 'Much more that that which you desire shall you find in my lord and in our land.' Then Bainalehequêm gave rich robes to Solomon's servants and departed with them for Jerusalem. And, on his arrival in the city, when they saw him, it seemed to them that he was Solomon himself, at which they marvelled greatly. And when he went in to the king, he rose from his chair and embraced him. And he said, 'Here is my {father} David raised from the dead and renewed in his youth. You all told me that he was like me; he is nothing but the face of my father David when he was a young man.' And, placing him in his chamber, he gave him rich robes and put rings on his hands and a crown on his head and he made him sit on a chair equally with him. And the princes and great men of Israel made reverence to him and blessed him, saying, 'Blessed be the mother who bore you, because there has sprung for us from the root of Jesse an enlightened man to be king for us and for our children.' And everybody, each according to his station, brought him their presents, and he secretly gave Solomon his mother's ring, telling him to remember what he had told her. Solomon replied, 'Why do you give me this ring{?} As a sign<?> In your face I see in truth that you are my son.'*

---

[1] The name of Solomon's son as given in the manuscript of the *Kebra Nagaśt* used by Budge for his English translation (London, BL, Oriental MS. 818) may be transcribed as 'Iyorbe'âm' (Budge uses 'Îyôrbe'âm [Rehoboam]'; *Queen of Sheba*, pp. 42, 50 and 69). Páez's latinized transcription ('Ieroboam') suggests that the manuscript he consulted in Aksum similarly confused the name of Solomon's son and heir Roboam (or Reheboam in the King James version) with that of his political adversary Jeroboam. Páez keeps the reading of the original Ethiopian manuscript without comment or correction.

{[f. 13v]} *After Solomon had finished talking to his son in secret, Tamerín entered and said to him, 'Hear, Lord, what your servant the queen has commanded me to tell you: she begs you to anoint this your son king of our land and to command that henceforth no woman shall reign there, and to send him back to her in peace to gladden her heart.' The king replied, 'What has the woman over the son apart from giving birth with pain and caring for him? The daughter for the mother and the son for the father. Therefore I shall not send him to the queen, but make him king of Israel, because he is the firstborn of my line whom God has given me.' And sending him every day rich foods and precious robes, gold and silver, he said that it was better to stay where the house of God and the Ark and Tablets of the Law were and where God Himself dwelt. But he replied, 'So much gold, {and} silver and rich robes are not lacking in our land. I came only to see your face, to hear your wisdom and to subject myself to your <[f. 12]> empire and then to return to my land and my mother, because everybody loves the land where he is born. And so, no matter how much you give me, I shall not be happy to stay here, because my flesh pulls me to where I was born and where I was brought up and, if from there I worship the Ark of the God of Israel, He will honour me. It will be enough if you give me a piece of the covering of the Ark of Sion so that I, with, my mother and everyone in my kingdom, can worship; for my lady has already destroyed all the idols and converted our people to the God of Sion, because that is what she heard and learnt from you and, as you commanded her, so she has done.' Solomon sought to persuade him to stay with many reasons and promises and that he would be king of Israel and he would possess the land that God had given to His people and the Ark of the Covenant. And, being unable to reach agreement with him, he gathered together his counsellors and the princes and great men of his kingdom. And he told them that, as he could not reach agreement with his son that he should stay, for he wanted to go by any means, therefore they all should make ready to anoint him king of the land of Ethiopia; and that, just as they were here at his right and his left hand, so their first-born would be there with him; and they would send priests to teach the Law so that they should serve the God of Israel. They all answered, 'As the king orders so shall it be done. Who can defy the commandment of God and of the king?'*

*Straight away they made ready the sweetest fragrances and oil. And, with musicians with joyful voices playing all kinds of instruments, they put him in the* Sancta Sanctorum *and he was appointed by the mouth of the priests Sadoc and Ioas. And he was anointed by the hand of the prince of Solomon and they gave him the name* {[f. 14]} *David, because he found the name of a king in the Law. And, going out, he mounted King Solomon's mule and they took him around the whole city saying, 'Long live the king! May the God of Israel be your guide and the Ark of the Law of God, and, wherever you may go, may all serve you and may your enemies fall before <you>.' Then his father blessed him, saying, 'The blessing of Heaven and of earth be with you.' And everyone answered 'Amen.' Solomon then said to Sadoc the priest, 'Declare to him the justice and punishment of God, so that he may keep it there.' Sadoc the priest replied, 'Listen well to what I tell you because, if you do, you will live in God. And, if not, he will punish you severely and you will be less than those of your people and defeated by the multitude of your enemies. Listen to the word of God and obey it. Do not depart from His Law, neither to the right nor to the left.' And he made him a very long speech, declaring to him the punishments that God would mete out to him if he did not keep His Law, and the mercies that He would do {to him} if he kept it.*[1]

---

[1] Páez has here summarized a longer passage from the source text.

*All the land rejoiced greatly because Solomon had raised up his son as king, but they were saddened because he had commanded them to give up their firstborn, even though he was to do them the honours that Solomon did to them themselves. And Solomon commanded <[f. 12v]> his son that, just as he had organized his household and shared out the offices, so should he do in his, and for that purpose he gave him the firstborn, who were called Azarias, the son of Sadoc the priest, and he indicated him as chief of the priests, Jeremias, grandson of Nathan the prophet, Maquîr, Aarâm, Finquinâ, Acmihêl, Somnîas, Facarôs, Leoandôs, Carmi, Zarâneos, Adarêz, Leguîm, Adeireôs, Aztarân, Macarî, Abiz, Licandeôs, Carmî, Zerâneos. All these were given to David, King of Ethiopia, the son of King Solomon, and to them he shared out all the offices and commands of his household. He also gave him horses, wagons, gold, silver, precious {stones} <items> and people to accompany him with many other necessary things for the journey.*

*The princes of Ethiopia then made ready to depart with great joy and happiness. But those of Israel were very sad because they were taking away their firstborn, and the weeping of their parents, kinsfolk and friends for them at the time of their departure was very great. But, while they were getting ready, these firstborn gathered together and said to each other, 'Now that we are leaving our land and our kinsfolk, let us all swear to keep {[f. 14v]} love and unity among ourselves always in the lands to which we go.' Azarias and Jeremias, the sons of the priests, replied, 'Let us not suffer at leaving our kinsfolk, but at being made to leave Sion, our Lady and our hope. How can we leave our Lady Sion? If we say that we do not want to go, the king will have us killed. We cannot fail to obey his command and the word of our fathers. So what shall we do for love of Sion our Lady?' 'I shall give you counsel', said Azarias, the son of Sadoc, 'if you swear to me that you will not tell anyone. If we <all> die, we will die together, and if we live, it shall also be together.' Then they all swore in the name of God of Israel and of the Ark of God, and then he said to them, 'Let us take our Lady Sion, for we can certainly take her, God willing. If they find us and we die, let us not suffer, for we die for love of her.' They all rose and kissed his head because of the pleasure and great consolation that they felt, and they said <to him> that they would do all that he commanded. Zacharias, the son of Ioab, said: 'I cannot contain myself with pleasure. Tell me in truth if you will do this? I know very well that you can do it, for you are in your father's place and have the keys to the house of God in your power: consider well what we must do and do not sleep so that we can take her and go with her, and it will be joy to us, but sadness to our parents.' He then had a box made of pieces of wood, of those that were left over from building the temple, of the length, breadth and height of the Ark of God, in which to carry it, and he said that they should not reveal it, not even to the king, until after they had departed and were very far away.*

*While Azarias was asleep at night, the angel of God appeared to him and told him to take four yearling goats for his sins and those of Elmias, Abizô and Maquîr, <[f. 13]> and four clean yearling sheep and a cow that had not been yoked, and to sacrifice them to the East, half of the sheep to the right hand of the cow and the other half to the <right>[1] left: 'And your lord King David shall say to King Solomon that he wishes to sacrifice in[2] Jerusalem and the Lady Ark of God, and that the son of the priest shall also sacrifice for him in the manner that*

---

[1] Apparently an error by the copyist of BPB, MS 778.

[2] The original text says that he wishes to offer a sacrifice to the holy city of Jerusalem and to the Lady Sion, the holy celestial Ark of God's Law. Páez's translation confuses the location with the purpose of the sacrifice and is syntactically questionable. (See Budge, *Queen of Sheba*, p. 69).

*he knows. Then King Solomon shall command you to sacrifice and you shall take the Ark of God. And I shall tell you how you must take it, because God is angry with Israel and wishes to take His Ark away from them.' When Azarias awoke, he was very joyful because of the dream that he had had and the words that the angel <had> said to him. And, gathering together his companions, he told them everything and said that they should go with him to King David their lord to inform him of this, and so they went and told him, {[f. 15]} at which he rejoiced greatly. And he summoned Joab the son of Jodahe and sent him to Solomon with a message saying, 'Lord, let me go to my land with your goodwill and may your prayer follow me wherever I arrive. One thing I very much beg of you, that because of this you will never diminish the love that you have for me. I also wish to sacrifice sacrifices to Sion, the Ark of God, in this holy land of Jerusalem for my sins.' Joab went to Solomon {and on hearing} <with> this message he rejoiced greatly and commanded great sacrifices to be made ready for his son to sacrifice. And he was given 10,000 oxen and cows, 10,000 sheep, 10,000 goats and other wild animals that are eaten, and ten of each species of clean bird, one zal[1] of wheat flour, twelve shekels of silver,[2] and forty* memesrehâ abaioâ.[3] *All this King Solomon gave to his son and then the king sent word to Azarias, the priest's son, to sacrifice for him. At which Azarias rejoiced greatly and brought from his house a cow that had not been yoked and four yearling sheep and four goats, also yearlings, and he put his sacrifice together with the king's sacrifice, just as the angel had told him.*

*The angel appeared again to Azarias and said to him, 'Rouse your brothers Elmiâs and Abizô and Maquîr.' And, when he aroused them, the angel said {to them}, 'I shall open the temple door for you, and you shall take the Ark of God and without any harm you shall take it, because God has commanded me to be with it always.' They went to the temple straight away and found the doors open until they arrived at the place where the Ark of God, Sion, rested. And it raised itself straight away in an instant, because the angel of God was controlling it. And they took hold of it and took it to the house of Azarias and placed it on silk cloths and lit candles to it and sacrificed a clean sheep and offered incense and it was there for seven days.*

[4]*Then King David, very joyful to be going to his land, went to his father {King} Solomon and, making reverence to him, asked for his blessing. The king made him rise and, taking him by the head, said, 'May God, who blessed my father David, be with you always and bless your seed, as he blessed Jacob.' And he gave him many other blessings. With this he departed and they put the Ark on a wagon, and they loaded many riches and robes that they had received from King Solomon and others {on} <100> wagons. And the priests rose and played many instruments and the whole land was in a tumult of voices. The firstborn who were going wept with their parents. And all the people also wept, as if their hearts told them that <[f. 13v]> the Ark was being taken. {[f. 15v]} The sadness and wailing was so great that even the animals seemed to weep, and everyone put ash on their heads. Even Solomon, on hearing the voices and seeing the weeping of the people and the honour of those who were going, wept and said, 'Now henceforth our happiness and our kingdom have gone to the strange people that does not know God.' And, summoning Sadoc, he told him to bring one of the coverings of the Ark and to take it to his son David, because the queen had asked it of him, through Tamerín*

---

[1] *Ṣāhl*, a Ge'ez word meaning goblet, here used as a unit of capacity.

[2] Hebrew coins and units of weight.

[3] 'Baskets of bread' (see Budge, *Queen of Sheba*, p. 70).

[4] The new paragraph made by the previous editors has been retained.

89

*her servant, so that she could pray before it with all her people, and to tell him that Sion the Ark of God was his guide and that he should always keep that covering in his encampment; and that, when he or his people had to swear, it should be by it, so that they should no longer remember other gods. Sadoc went and did all that Solomon commanded, at which David rejoiced greatly and said, 'May this be my lady.' Sadoc replied, 'Then swear to me that this covering shall always be in the hands of my son Azarias and of his sons, and that you will {also} <always> give him the tithes of your kingdom. And he shall always teach God's Law to you and your people, and shall anoint your sons kings.' And thus he swore. And Azarias received from the hand of his father Sadoc the covering of the Ark and they took it on a wagon and went their way directly, their guide being Saint Michael, who made them march so fast it was as if they flew so that the wagons were raised a cubit above the ground and the animals a span, and they were covered from the sun by a cloud that accompanied them, and through the sea he took them as the sons of Israel were taken through the Red Sea.*

*The first day that they set off, they came to Gazâ, the land that King Solomon gave to Queen Saba, and they passed into Mazrîn, the land of the Egyptians. And all this journey they did in one day; and, when the princes of Israel saw that they had done a journey of thirteen days in one, without tiring or feeling thirst or hunger, neither man nor beast, they understood that this was a thing from God. And, when they saw that they had arrived in the land of the Egyptians, they said, 'Let us rest here, since we have arrived in the land of Ethiopia, for the water of Tacaçê comes and reaches here.' And, pitching their tents, they rested. Then Azarias said to King David, 'Here, lord, are the marvels of God, which have been accomplished in you. Here you have the Ark of God, only by His will and not yours. And thus she will also be where she wishes, for nobody can take that from her. Now, if you keep God's commandments, she will be {[f. 16]} with you and will defend you.' Then King David, in awe at so many marvels, gave thanks to God, he and all his encampment. And everyone's joy was so great that, marvelling, they raised their hands to Heaven, giving thanks to God, and the king leapt about with pleasure. Like a lamb and like a kid when it is full of milk, that is how David rejoiced before the Ark of the Covenant. And, entering the tent where the Ark was, he bowed to it and kissed it and said, 'Holy God of Israel, glory be to You, because You do Your will and not that of men.' And he said a very long prayer, giving Him thanks for the mercy that He had done him. And they played many instruments and they all made <very> great celebrations, and all the heathens' idols, made by their hands, fell down. And <on> the next day, they placed the Ark on the wagon, <[f. 14]> covered with rich cloths, and began to march with loud music. And the wagons were raised about a cubit off the ground. And they arrived at the sea of seas, the Sea of Erterâ,[1] which was opened by the hand of Moses and the children of Israel marched across and, because God had not yet given Moses the Tablets of the Law, therefore the water remained like a wall on one side and on the other and they passed across the bottom with their women and children and animals. But, when they arrived with the Ark, playing many instruments, the sea received them as if it were rejoicing and celebrating with its waves, for even though they rose like mountains, the wagons went across raised almost three cubits above them. And the fish and monsters of the sea and the birds of the air worshipped the Ark. And, when they left the sea, they rejoiced greatly, just as the children of Israel did when they came out of Egypt, and they arrived opposite Mount Sinai and made camp there with loud music.*

---

[1] The Erythraean Sea or Red Sea.

*While they were making this journey, Sadoc the priest entered the temple and, not finding the Ark but some timbers that Azarias had made in its likeness and placed there, he fell on his face on the ground as if dead in pain and terror and, as he was long in coming out, Josias entered and found him fallen and, on making him rise, he too saw that the Ark was missing and threw ash on his head and began to shout so loudly from the door of the temple that he was heard in {[f. 16v]} King Solomon's house. And when he learnt what had happened, he rose in great terror and commanded that a proclamation be issued for everyone to gather together in order to go and seek the people of Ethiopia and to bring back his son and to put all the rest to the sword, for they deserved to die. And when the princes and the great and powerful of Israel had gathered, Solomon went forth with great wrath to pursue them. And the elders, {the} widows and maidens gathered in the temple and wept greatly because the Ark of God's Law had been taken from them. Solomon went along the road to Ethiopia and sent out people to the right hand and to the left, in case they had left the road out of fear of what they had stolen, and sent them ahead on horseback at full speed and those that found them should return to tell him where they were. And later, knowing for sure, both from some of these horsemen who had returned, and also from the people of Gazâ where he arrived, that he could not catch them because their wagons were travelling raised off the ground in the air with as much speed as birds, he wept greatly. And he said, 'Lord, while I live, have You taken the Ark from me? I would rather You had taken my life.' And he uttered many other words that showed the great sadness and anguish of his heart. Then he returned to Jerusalem and, with its elders, wept again. And, when the great men saw that he was shedding so many tears, they consoled him saying that {he} <they> should not suffer so, for he knew that Sion could be nowhere but where she wished to be and that nothing could be done but the will of God. 'His will was done when first the Philistines took it and then He had it returned; so now, by His will, it has been taken to Ethiopia and He will make it return, if He so wishes. And, if not, here too you have the house that you have built for God, with which you can console yourself.' Solomon replied, 'If He had taken me and us, or had had them possess our land – what is impossible to God? There is nobody in heaven or on earth that can withstand <[f. 14v]> His will or disobey his command. He is the King whose kingdom shall not be taken away for all eternity. Let us go to His house and give thanks to Him for everything.' And, on entering the temple, they all wept bitterly, until Solomon told them to cease, so that they should not give the heathens pleasure and joy at the news of their loss. They all answered, 'May the will of God and your will be done.'*

*King David continued his journey and arrived at Balentos, the limit of the lands of Ethiopia, and he entered with great joy and contentment and with many kinds of music and celebration, rushing forward in his wagons and they sent people with great haste to give {[f. 17]} news to Maquedâ, the queen of Ethiopia, that her son was coming and how he reigned and that they were bringing the heavenly Sion. When this message arrived, the queen rejoiced greatly and straight away ordered a proclamation to be issued throughout her land that they should go and welcome her son and principally the heavenly Sion, the Ark of the God of Israel. And before her they played many instruments, making great celebration and rejoicing greatly, both great and lesser folk, and they went to the land of her power, which is the capital of the kingdom of Ethiopia in which in later times the people of Ethiopia were made Christians, and they prepared countless perfumes in Baltê as far as Galtêt and Alçafâ. And her son came on the road from Azêb and Ûaquirôn and went out through Mocêz and arrived at Bûr and the land of power which is the capital of Ethiopia, which she herself built in her name* *and was called the land of Debrâ Maquedâ. And King David entered the land of his mother with great celebration and rejoicing. And when the queen from afar saw the Ark, which was shining like the sun, she gave thanks to the God of Israel with such great joy and contentment that she could not contain her pleasure, and dressing herself richly, she made great celebration and everyone, both great and lesser folk, rejoiced exceedingly and, placing the Ark in the temple of the land of Maquedâ, they put 300 men on guard with their swords and the princes and great men of Sion <and> the powerful men of Israel, 300 with swords in their hands. And to her son she also gave 300 guards and her kingdom bowed to him, from the Sea of Alibâ to Acêfa, and he had more honour and wealth than anyone was to have, either before or after him. Because at that time there was nobody like King Solomon in Jerusalem and like Queen Maquedâ in Ethiopia, for both were given wisdom, honour and wealth and a great heart.*

*On the third day, the queen offered her son 7,700 chosen {horses} <camels> and 7,600 mares that were with foal and 300 she-mules and as many males and many very rich robes and a great sum of gold and silver. And she gave him the throne of her kingdom and said to him, 'I have given you your kingdom and I have made king him whom God has made king and I have chosen him whom God has chosen.' Then King David rose and {bowing} <bowed> to the queen <and> said to her, 'You are my queen and my lady. Anything that you command me, I shall do, whether for life or for death. And wherever you send me, I shall go, because you are the head and I the feet, you the lady and I the slave.' And with many other words of humility he offered himself to her. And, when he finished, many instruments were played and great celebration was made. Afterwards, {[f. 17v]} Elmîas and Azarias took out the book that was written before God and King <[f. 15]> Solomon and they read it before Maquedâ and the great men of Israel. And, when they heard the words, all those who were present, both great and small, worshipped God and gave Him many thanks. Finally, the queen said to her son, 'May God give you truth, my son. Go by it, do not stray to the right hand or to the left. Love your God, because He is merciful and His goodness is understood in His things.' And, turning to speak with the priests and people of Israel, she made them many offers and promised to have them always as fathers and masters, because they were the ones who kept the Law and taught the commandments of the God of Israel. They too gave her many thanks and Azarias, particularly, many praises. And he said that everything that they had seen seemed good to them, apart from their being black in the face. Then Azarias said, 'Let us go before the Ark of Sion and let us renew the kingdom of our lord David.' And, taking his horn full of oil, he anointed him and thus was renewed {his} <the> kingdom of King David, the son of King Solomon, in the land of the power of Maquedâ, in the house of Sion. And, gathering together the great men of the kingdom, the queen made them swear by heavenly Sion that thenceforth they would not admit a woman as queen on the throne of the kingdom of Ethiopia, but only sons that descended from David. And Azarias and Elmîas received the oath from all the princes, great men and governors, and the sons of the force of Israel with their King David renewed the kingdom. And the people of Ethiopia left their idols and worshipped the God that made them.*

Up to here are words from a book that is kept in the church of Agçûm,[1] and it does not continue the story further. Nor can the people there give any certainty about the lands of

---

[1] Continuation of the account of the *Kebra Nagaśt* (*The Glory of the Kings*). Manuel de Almeida used the translation made by Pedro Páez ('Historia de Ethiopia a alta', Beccari, *RÆSOI*, 5, bk II, ch. 3, pp. 99–109). Baltasar Teles summarized this episode in bk I, ch. 25 of his *Historia Geral de Ethiopia a Alta ou Preste Ioam*, 1660 (translated into English as Tellez, *The Travels of the Jesuits in Ethiopia*, 1710), and criticized it in the following chapter.

Ûaquirôm, Baltê, Galtêt and Alçafâ. Only Bur is known, which is a province of the kingdom of Tigrê, one day's journey from the port of Maçuâ. As for the name Debrâ Maquedâ, for the city that the queen built, *dêber* actually means 'mount'. But, because they {very ordinarily} {actually} build temples and monasteries on mountains, they also call the temple or monastery *dêber* and, when another name is added to this name *dêber*, they {say} <will say> *debrâ*. Therefore Debrâ Maquedâ means 'Mount or Temple of Maquedâ'. And if, as we said in the preceding chapter and as can be gathered from what is mentioned in this one, Maquedâ was the city of Agçûm, it will mean {Mount or} 'Temple of Agçûm', for in it {there was} <she had> a very sumptuous temple.

Regarding what it says, that the angel appeared to Azarias in dreams {[f. 18]} and commanded him to take the Ark of the Covenant and {that they brought} <to bring> it to Ethiopia, it is all an apocryphal and fabulous story, because the Holy Scripture teaches the contrary <in the> second <book of> Machabees, <chapter> 2, where it says that the prophet Jeremias hid the Tabernacle and the Ark and altar of incense in a cave on the mountain of Nebo, which Moses climbed and whence he saw the promised land, Deut. 34, which is in Arabia, as Saint Jerome says in *De Locis Hebraicis*. The words of the holy text are these: *Tabernaculum, et Arcam iussit propheta, divino responso ad se facto, comitari secum, usque quo exiit in montem, in quo Moyses ascendit, et* <[f. 15v]> *vidit Dei haereditatem. Et veniens ibi Hieremias invenit locum speluncae, et Tabernaculum, et Arcam, et altare incensi intulit illuc, et ostium obstruxit. Et accesserunt {quidam} simul <quidam> qui sequebantur, ut notarent sibi locum, et non potuerunt invenire. Ut autem cognovit Hieremias, culpans illos, dixit: 'Quod ignotus erit locus, donec congreget Deus congregationem populi.'*[1] That will be at the end of days, shortly before the Day of Judgement, according to Saint Epiphanius in his life of the Prophet Jeremias.[2] Many people in Ethiopia {also} consider this {story} <story> to be false, even though the monks of Agçûm always affirm that this Ark is in their church. But when a brother of Emperor Seltân Çaguêd, who is called Cela Christôs, *scilicet* 'Image of Christ', went to the kingdom of Tigrê as viceroy in the year 1608, on his journey he arrived in Agçûm, as the viceroys customarily do because of the great name that the church there has, and he told the monks to show him the Ark of the Covenant.[3] And they answered that they could not do so, because it was not shown even to the emperors, nor had they ever forced them to do so, on account of the great reverence in which the holy Ark must be held. He said, 'Why did they go on with those inventions?' and left them. <And> later, when I went to visit him, because our residence is about two leagues from Agçûm, he spoke to me about this affair of the Ark, and I told him that what the monks claimed was a fable, because Scripture

---

[1] 'The prophet, being warned by God, commanded that the tabernacle and the ark should accompany him, till he came forth to the mountain where Moses went up, and saw the inheritance of God. And when Jeremias came thither he found a hollow cave: and he carried in thither the tabernacle, and the ark, and the altar of incense, and so stopped the door. Then some of them that followed him, came up to mark the place: but they could not find it. And when Jeremias perceived it, he blamed them, saying: 'The place shall be unknown, till God gather together the congregation of the people' (2 Machabees [Apocrypha, Maccabees] 2:4–7).

[2] The passage from the point where he condemns the story as being apocryphal up to here was copied by Páez from Luís de Urreta's critical commentary with only very slight changes (the Spanish text has been translated into Portuguese, but not the Latin quotation); he appropriated it without giving credit (see Urreta, *Historia de la Etiopia*, bk I, 5, p. 54).

[3] A letter from Father Azevedo confirmed that Se'ela Krestos was in Tegray in 1608 (Beccari, *RÆSOI*, 11, p. 165).

taught the contrary and, bringing to him the passage that I have just mentioned, he too said that everything they said was false. The following year, the emperor went to Tigrê with an army, because someone there was rising up and claiming the empire, and on the way he was crowned in Agçûm and he asked the monks to show him the Ark of the Covenant, but they gave so many excuses that the emperor desisted. And, later, he recounted to me the arguments that he had had with them, deriding the way that they put that into the heads of ignorant people.

Although Ethiopia has not and never could have had the Ark of the Covenant, another very precious relic worthy of great {[f. 18v]} veneration is attributed to it by Friar Luis de Urreta, p. [54 and] 55, in these words:

*Something widely received {in} <of> all Ethiopia is that, among many other splendid objects and jewels of great value that Solomon gave to his son {Melilec} <Maliec>, one was very precious and regarded as such by all the emperors, for he gave him a piece of the tablets that were written by God's finger, and Moses broke them at the foot of the mountain when filled with holy zeal against the people's idolatry. And Don {Juan} <Joan> is an eye-witness, because he has seen it and held it in his hands many times. And he says that {it is} two fingers in thickness, as large as a quarter-sheet of paper. On it there are carved some whole letters and other half ones very different from those that the Hebrews now use. They keep it within an Ark of fine gold, which is in a room of the library. It is continuously guarded day and night by the soldiers that are on Mount Amarâ. And a little further on he confirms this, saying: And even all the Jews in Africa and Asia are of this opinion, and they revere this holy relic with great demonstrations, not because they have seen it, nor are they given such an opportunity, but because when they come <[f. 16]> with goods in their caravans from Persia, from Mecca and Arabia and pass on to Libya, Nubia, Borno and other kingdoms, when they arrive at the famous Alleluia monastery, which is of friars of the glorious Saint Dominic, for from there one can see the famous Mount Amarâ, where said relic is kept, they prostrate themselves on the ground and remove their turbans. And making great bows, their hands raised, they cry out saying, 'Adonay, Adonay, geis Adonai', 'Lord God, Lord God, Lord of all lords.' And they say it with such warmth that there are some that weep with great tenderness. And when the monks ask them the cause of those ceremonies, they answer that on that mountain are the marvellous works of the great God; that the Prester John is very beloved of God, for He has given him such a relic that with it he will be king of the world, he will defeat his enemies, God will give him the dew of heaven, and the fat of the land, and He will gather up his soul as Abraham gave a welcome to the angels.*

Continuing this story, the author says on page 57: *We have said that there are on this piece of the Tablets some carved and open letters, some whole and others half letters. And although some are Hebrew like those that they use now, the others, however, are very different, and there is nobody who knows how to read them. And when Don {Juan} <Joan> de Baltazar {[f. 19]} went as the Prester John's ambassador to the king of Persia, he was commanded to bring back a Jew, the most famous rabbi of all those in Asia, who was in Mecca, called Rabbi Sedechias, to see if he could read the letters. This man went with great pleasure, just to see that fragment of the Tablets of the Law. On arriving where the relic was, having performed many salaams and ceremonies with much ado, although he recognized some letters, he said of the others that he did not recognize them and that they were not Chaldean, or Greek, or Arabic, or Persian, or Indian, or Chinese. Because if they had been, he*

*would have read them, as he was learned in them all.* And further on, on page 61, he says:
*Finally, so that this history may be well-prepared and defended on all sides, I shall reply
briefly to anyone who might doubt that that piece of stone is from the tablets that Moses broke.
In the first place, a fully sufficient argument is the universal tradition that is more than 3,000
years old, in which time nobody has ever cast doubt or even less contradicted it. Secondly, all
the other surrounding nations grant it this glory, and concede to them the greatness of this
relic without contention. Those who, it seems, ought to contradict it are the Jews, and they
admit it without any discussion whatever and they worship the stone as a piece of the Tablets
of Moses. And the final proof will be taken from the authentic scriptures that have been kept
since those ancient times of King Solomon, which are on Mount Amara in the monastery of
the Holy Cross of the Order of Saint Anthony the Abbot, where they hold the above-
mentioned relic.*[1]

Friar Luis Urreta wrote all this, {as he affirms, from the information and testimony}
<from the information (as he affirms)> of Joam Balthesar. But they are such fabulous
things, as are many others that he has told, because neither is there <[f. 16v]> such a
piece of the Tablets of the Law on Mount Amhará, nor has there ever been in Ethiopia.
And, thus, when I very deliberately asked kinsmen of the emperor, who had spent a
long time on that mountain, and the oldest and most learned monks of the court if
they had any news that there was a piece of the Tablets of the Law on Mount Amhará
or anywhere else in Ethiopia, they all answered that they had never read such a thing
in any book, nor had they heard it said; rather, they were sure that there was no
memory of what had become of those pieces of the Tablets, which Moses broke. And
to be even more certain of the truth, I asked the emperor, in the presence of {many}
<some> great men and {some} <many> monks, saying that Joam Balthesar had
asserted it in Spain, and they all laughed heartily at how he had gone there {[f. 19v]}
to put such a great falsehood into people's heads, because never had there been such a
thing in Ethiopia. What I find amazing is how a man born in Ethiopia, even though a
liar, could say such a great absurdity as that from the famous Alleluia monastery one
can make out Mount Amhará, because it is not less than saying that from the riverside
in Lisbon in Portugal one can make out Coimbra, or, to speak of lands that I have seen
better, that from Segovia one can make out the Alhambra in Granada; because the
distance from the Alleluia monastery to Mount Amhará is no less, nor are the
mountains lower than the passes of Segovia and those of Andalusia, but rather
incomparably higher; nor can the merchants that he mentions pass by the Alleluia
monastery, because it is very much out of the way, and the forest so thick that, when I
went there taking with me people of that land to guide me, I could not pass without a
great effort, and the woods still tore my clothes, although the merchants {from
Dambiá} <of Ambiá>, who are no more than Christians and Moors, when they go to
the port of Maçuá, sometimes pass not far from that monastery; nor is it of friars of
Saint Dominic, as I said in chapter 1 and will show in the second book; nor can one
say that there is another Alleluia monastery from which one can make out Mount
Amhará and where merchants pass, because there is no other Alleluia monastery in
Ethiopia, and he is speaking of this same one, because he puts it in the land of Tigrê

---

[1] Urreta, *Historia de la Etiopia*, bk I, excerpts from ch. 5, pp. 46–65. Páez quotes these passages in Spanish.

Mohôn, on page 311;[1] nor has this empire any trade with Persia for merchants to come from there.

It also seems to be a fable where Joam Balthesar says that he went as an ambassador to the king of Persia, because I have never been able to find anyone who had heard tell of such an embassy, nor do these emperors have any friendship or dealings with those kings, nor do people come here from the region of Persia. As for saying that he brought the Jew who was in Mecca to read the letters on the piece of the Tablets, it is mere fiction because, as well as being such a nonsensical thing to pass through Mecca in order to go from here to Persia, no Christian or Jew or heathen may enter Mecca on pain of death, or he must become a Moor, as I was told by many Turks when I was a captive in the Strait of Mecca. If he had said that he had brought him from Mocâ, he would have gilded his lie more, because they can easily go there. But, if there <[f. 17]> {was no such piece} <were no such pieces> of the Tablets, why should the Jew come to Mount Amharâ to read the letters? However, just as they often blend lies in with some truths, this lie may be blended in with what Emperor Malâc Çaguêd did in the kingdom of Tigrê, because, when he was going to be crowned in Agçûm, where the emperors are crowned, and when he saw many very ancient letters that are written there on very large columns and stones, {[f. 20]} he wished to know what they said.[2] And, as he did not find anyone who {could} <knew how to> read them, he sent for a Jew who knew many languages and who it seems must have been in the same kingdom, and he did not know how to read them. I too wished very much to know what they said, and I went there with two priests who know Greek and a Greek man who knew his books very well, and they could not read them. Nor are they Latin, or Arabic, or Hebrew although some letters resemble them, because if they had been I should have read them.

It may also be that Joam Balthesar based the lie that he had held the piece of the Tablets of the Law in his hand on Mount Amharâ on having held some piece of ancient altar stone, which some monk wished to baptize as a piece of the Tablets of the Law, because the books of Ethiopia and all the people call the Ark of the Covenant and the Tablets of the Law and the altar stone by the same name, which is *tabôt*, and they carve deep letters on all the altar stones in which they put at least the name of the saint to whom the church is dedicated.[3] And there is no lack there of very white transparent stone from which they make altar stones; for, just a short time ago, Cela Christôs, the emperor's brother, sent me a very beautiful altar stone of transparent white stone, which he had had made for our church and in their fashion they put on it the beginning of the Gospel of Saint John in very deep letters. And he wrote to me that at the end of the kingdom of Gojâm, where he is viceroy, there were so many stones of that kind that they could make houses and that they could be worked very well. Wherefore {I say} that on Mount Amharâ they might have some piece of old altar stone with the letters that were used at that time. And as the altar stone is called *tabôt*, as are the Tablets of the Law, if Joam Balthesar were told that

---

[1] Urreta, *Historia de la Etiopia*, bk I, ch. 29, entitled 'Of the famous black river, of its course and path, of the great riches that are found in it. Concerning amber, and whether the river Phison is one of the rivers of Paradise', pp. 310–20. Däbrä Halleluya or Hallelo was in fact in Tegray.

[2] See bk I, ch. 20; Beccari, *RÆSOI*, 4, pp. 229 and 233–6; *RÆSOI*, 5, pp. 83–5; *RÆSOI*, 11, p. 107 (letter from Azevedo to the provincial of Goa, 22 July 1607) and p. 260 (letter from Pedro Páez to Tomás de Ituren, 14 September 1612).

[3] See Glossary (altar stone/*tābot*).

that was a piece of the *tabôt*, he would understand that it was from the Tablets of the Law; or it may be that some monk, to ennoble the things of his church, told him that it was a piece of the Tablets of the Law, as those in Agçûm do now when they say that they have the Ark of the Covenant itself, but when he says that that {piece} <small> of stone is kept in an ark of fine gold and that the room is guarded {night and} day <and night>, it is false, because there is no ark of gold, nor any such guards, nor a monastery of the Holy Cross where the authentic scriptures are kept, as he says; because on Mount Amharâ there are no more than two <[f. 17v]> churches: one is called Egziabehêr Ab,[1] *scilicet* 'God the Father', and the other is of Our Lady. And there never have been any others, as we shall say later in its proper place.

---

[1] See Glossary (Egziabehêr Ab/Egzi'ābeḥ ér Ab (*Ambā* Gešan)).

## Concerning the officials that King Solomon gave to his son David to serve his household and those that the Prester John now has

We have already said how, when King Solomon in Jerusalem had his son Menilehêc crowned, he ordered that they should give him the name David, both in memory of King David, and because he greatly resembled him, and that not only did he give him the priests to teach the Law, but some of the firstborn sons of the princes and great men of Israel, in order that they should accompany him and wait on his presence. In addition to these, he gave him other less important people to serve in his household and for the good government and order of his republic, wishing that he should as far as possible keep all things in the same manner and style, principally the majesty of his household, the order and harmony of his servants, the excellence of his service, the magnificence and great courtliness, with all the other rites and ceremonies that were used in his house and kingdom. But to refer to these I shall not only say what is in the books of Ethiopia, but also jointly I shall put what those people say who are now the heads of these offices, because it is very much mixed up and changed, even though some of the offices are served today by the descendants of those {same men that} <to whom> Solomon gave <them>.

First, until a short time ago, there was one who was called *behêt ûadêd*,[1] which means 'only beloved'. This man dwelt on the right of the palace and, in the field,[2] he always placed his tent to the right of the emperor's, and another with the same title pitched on the left, and both governed everything under the emperor. When he did not go to war, one of these would go forth {in his place} as the general of the whole army and the other would accompany the emperor. But, as they had such great power and command, they grew so arrogant that they did not bend their opinions to that of the emperor, so that, as he could not tolerate them, Emperor Atanâf Çaguêd, or it may be (as some believe) that he feared that they might rebel since they were so powerful, stripped them of their titles and commands and reserved them for himself. But, later, Emperor Malâc Çaguêd reintroduced just one with the name of *erâz*, which means 'head'. And Emperor {Seltân} <Seltâm> Çagêd, who is now alive, gave this title and position in the year 1611 to a brother of his called Emâna Christôs, *scilicet* 'Christ's Right Hand', and he stripped him of it in 1615 because he would not obey him properly. And when I spoke to him about him, he told me that he was determined not to make anyone else *erâz*, because they grew very {[f. 21]} arrogant; for, if that one who was his brother could <[f. 18]> be so arrogant,

---

[1] See Glossary (Behêt uâdêd/behêt oadêd/*beḥt waddad*).
[2] In the royal encampment or *katamā*.

what would the others do? But later some kinswomen of his and the great men at court begged him very much and so he gave him back his command.

There were also two who were called *hedûg erâz*. These remained in the place of the other two chiefs when they were absent. Two more were called *gueitâ*, *scilicet* 'lord', and took the place of the *hedûgs*. There are two *uzta azâx* and two *jânderebôch azaxôch*. The main office of all these ten is to judge, particularly in serious matters, and to go to war as chiefs. There is another very great title that they call *acabe eçât*,[1] which means 'keeper of the fire'. This is always some great monk or priest, who ordinarily accompanies the emperor and comes in to him when he wishes without anyone being able to stop him, and he knows all the secrets and advises him on everything for the good of his soul and body. Even in eating and drinking he tells him, 'That is enough.' But he is not his confessor or teacher, because they call this one *quêz hacê*, *scilicet* 'priest as of the emperor', for I have not found anyone who can tell me exactly what *hacê* means. And they call the emperor 'fire', because they say that he should be like fire, which has three things: it lights, it heats and it burns. Thus the emperor should light others with his good works and examples for life, which alludes to what Saint Gregory says in Homily 13, *Lucernas quippe ardentes in manibus tenemus, cum per bona opera proximis nostris lucis exempla mostramus*.[2] He should heat with his fervour for goodness and with his liberality to everyone. Finally, he should burn with his justice, when he has to purify in the republic. Others affirm that it should be pronounced *acabeçaât*, which means 'keeper of the hours', because it was his task to declare the hours when the emperor was to dispatch his business and was to do other things.

The other offices are: *erâz balderabâ* (there were two of these servants loyal to the emperor, whom they always accompanied indoors, and apart from them two *behêt ûadêd* or *erâz*, like guards, so that nobody should do or say anything against the emperor); *hedûg erâz balderabâ*, these were also servants that the emperor trusted and they supervised the *hedûgs*, as the former did the *erâzes*, or *behêt {ûadedôch} <uodedôch>*; *gueitâ balderabâ*, these likewise supervised the two that are called *gueitâ*, *scilicet* 'lord'. Others {[f. 21v]} were called *manguêst bêit*, *scilicet* 'house of the kingdom', these collect and have in their charge all the emperor's chattels and baggage, and they are governors of the prisons; *marêd bêit*, *scilicet* 'house of tremor', these are in charge of the emperor's wardrobe and all his arms; *janbelêu*, who is in charge of receiving the horses that are brought for the emperor and seeing that they are stabled; *aicenfô*, who receive and stable the mules that are brought in tribute for the emperor, and they take one in ten of them; *êguer {zaconê} <iaconê>* have the office of giving possession of the lands that the emperor bestows on someone <[f. 18v]> for ever, and they walk around them playing *atabales*[3] and marking the boundaries, where they bury a goat's head, and if somebody removes it, they receive a great punishment; *janaçanâ umbarôch* are magistrates, and when the emperor is travelling in a deserted area, if they find some cliff or deep thing in the path, they throw holy water before the emperor arrives, reciting Psalm 67, *Exurgat Deus et dissipentur inimici eius*, etc.;[4] *{jantacâl} <jautacâl>*, these carry the emperor's flags and move people aside along

---

[1] See Glossary (Acabe eçât/acabeçaât/acabiçât/*aqqābé saʿāt*).

[2] 'We should keep our lights burning, that is, by good works should give a good example to our neighbour.' The last word in Latin should read '*monstramus*'.

[3] An Arabic loan word for drums. The equivalent instrument in Ethiopia is called *nagārit*.

[4] 'Let God arise, and let his enemies be scattered' (Psalms 67:2 [68:1]).

the road; *janderabâ*, when the emperor travels, they carry the books in which he prays, which are ordinarily the Psalms, and they also keep the people out of the emperor's way; *janxalamî, scilicet* 'adorners of the emperor', are his goldsmiths and armourers; *tecâcanâch*, these are sons of the emperor's kinswomen and they carry sticks on which they put a cloth like a canopy to shade the emperor, when he dismounts, if the tents are not erected; *balde-banâ*, when someone begs a favour of the emperor to give him someone who will remind him of the business that he has with him and who will be like his proxy, he indicates one of these; *balê taguaçaguçâ*, palace doormen; *balê mecahâf* are also doormen; *uzt magûoz, taraçambâ, {curâ çacalâ} <curâ çacabâ>*, these three houses[1] are also palace doormen; *begâ mâch* erect the emperor's tents and always keep watch that the stakes are not pulled out when it rains or is very windy and, at the end of the summer, they keep the tents for themselves and make new ones for the next summer, for tents older than one {single} summer are of no use to the emperor.

*Dêb ambeçâ* play {the} *atabales*; *derâ moâmoaî* carry the tents and baggage of the church of Saint Michael when the emperor goes to war; *bêit ançâ* carry the tents and baggage of the church of Our Lady;[2] *beztegrê* carry the tents and baggage of the church of Jesus; *botragêt* carry the bed on which the emperor sleeps and always keep close to him because, ordinarily, when he dismounts he sits on it; *zâyeyahâx* carry the wine for the emperor, which is made from honey; *beita guêber, scilicet* 'house of the office', this means the cooks and those who take the food to the doorway of the room where the emperor's table is; *cuamôch*, there are many of these and it is mainly their duty to take the food to that doorway and some of them enter and put it on the table, and then go out, {[f. 22]} because nobody stays where the emperor eats except the steward and the overseer and four pages who serve; *bâla çêm* take care of bringing the torches used at night in the palace; *bêita hâiz* clear the roads and tracks along which the emperor is to pass; *ite agrôd* is a woman who has the office of punishing those who flee in war before the field is lost, because, when someone is proved to have fled as a coward, he is not punished by a man but by this woman, to his greater dishonour. And the punishment that she gives him is this: she gathers many people together <[f. 19]> and dances in front of him, mocking and insulting him, and from time to time she hits him and passes a stick with some viscera impaled on it across his mouth.

A short time ago, two more offices were added. One is called *talahâc balatinôch gueitâ*,[3] which means 'lord of the emperor's great servants'. *Gueitâ* is 'lord'. This one has very great command, because not only is he placed over all the servants in the palace, but also over all those in the encampment, even if they are captains. Even the viceroys depend on him greatly, and no command is given and no lands are bestowed on anybody without his advice. And all the letters that are sent out, after the secretary has shown them to the emperor, are seen by him, and if he thinks that he has to propose something on them to the emperor, he does so and, if not, he sets the emperor's seal, which is in his hand, and sends them. The other is called *tecacân balatinôch gueitâ*, 'lord of the lesser servants', *scilicet* 'the emperor's pages'. These pages are now split among three rooms which were formerly all one-storey houses. The most honoured one is called *ambaçâ bêit*, 'house of the lion',

---

[1] Hereditary positions.

[2] See Almeida, 'Historia de Ethiopia a alta', Beccari, *RÆSOI*, 7, bk 6, ch. 11, p. 156.

[3] See Glossary (Balatinôch gueitâ/*blātténoččgétà*).

and is the most intimate; the second, more to the outside, is called *zefân bêit*, 'house of the bed'; the third, *farâz bêit*, 'house of the horse'. In all, there are 150, and most of them are slaves, the children of Gâla and Agôu and Kafir heathens. And of the others there are very few who are not the children of ordinary men and those of one house cannot pass to another without the emperor's permission, because that is to go up to greater honour. And in each one there is a head page who tells the others what they have to do in their offices, and those who have to take out messages from the emperor, if he does not summon one of them in particular. They also go out alone when they want to, which was formerly not permitted, because they only rarely went out and only with a loyal guard who brought them back, and there was such great strictness in this that (as their books say) if anyone went outside the palace to eat or drink or talk, they would kill him and the one who invited him. {[f. 22v]} There were formerly thirty of these boys, all slaves, and they could not cut their hair without the emperor's permission, and this number was not increased, because when they put in young ones, they removed older ones. Now there is no set number except as the emperor sees fit. And no other emperor had as many as this one. And in past years he had many more still, but he removed those aged twenty and gave them lands and horses so that they could accompany him to war.[1] The reason for liking to have such a crowd I think is what he gave me to understand when he was talking to me alone about some great men who did not show such a willing heart towards his affairs, because he said, 'Father, those whom I bring up and honour will serve me with a willing heart; but as for these, they are hardly to be trusted.'[2]

The most intimate chamber, as we have said, is called 'house of the lion' because, as if it were guarded by a lion, nobody enters it when the emperor is there, not even his son, except for someone who is summoned, which he seldom does. And so, when he enters the 'house of the lion', nobody comes to the door; the only ones to enter are the pages assigned to that retreat. In the room that they call *zefân bêit*, 'house <[f. 19v]> of the bed', because he has his bed there, he gives audience to everyone. But there is a bed not just in one house but in many, because they serve him as a throne, and thus there is no distinction in the name. Not even among the pages, as all these are called *zefân bêit*. The room that they call *farâz bêit*, 'house of the horse', is the one of least honour and is always low down, because there is at least one horse in it. Formerly there used to be many horses there all the time, day and night, throughout the watches, with bridles and saddles and, on the pommels, helmets, mail and swords. But that is no longer the custom, although there is always one horse; nor do the pages of this house take care of it but of the bed that is there, since the emperor often goes in there to see the horse and sits on the bed, and if the weather is cold those pages make him a fire there and serve him in any other way that is necessary, because the pages of one house are not allowed to go and serve the emperor in another, and not even when he goes out will one group of pages allow others to enter the house that is in their charge.

In the past the emperor used to stay in his palace with those thirty boys without any man seeing him, which was not a small penance. Only the *behêt ûaded* of the right hand and of the left would enter, and *acabê eçât* to render him an account of the affairs of the empire and to learn how he wanted them to be dispatched. And these three alone declared

---

[1] ARSI, MS Goa 42 has a new paragraph here; BPB, MS 778 does not.
[2] BPB, MS 778 has a new paragraph here; ARSI, MS Goa 42 does not.

his wishes and decisions to the people regarding everything that occurred. When he wanted to do a great favour to someone, who could only be a brother-in-law or son-in-law or some other great man, {[f. 23]} he ordered him to be summoned at night and, all the candles having been removed, he would speak to him in the darkness, and thus the one who {entered} <was there> could only hear his voice but could not see anything. And even this was regarded as a very great favour, because he rarely did so. And, when his food is[1] brought to him, those pages would go out to the door and receive it there, and everything that was left over from the delicacies that he touched and the bread that he broke was buried by them, for nobody had permission to be able to eat it. And as his book says, they used to bring 126 delicacies, and 180 dainty breads, and 120 others of lesser kind, and 20 small and 100 large *calões*[2] of honey wine. These things were partly being abandoned in the time of Emperor David (who sent a monk called Çagâ Za Ab,[3] which means 'Grace of the Father', as an ambassador to Portugal, and later gave up the name David and called himself Onâg Çaguêd), and therefore people could enter there more easily and see him. Later, in the time of his son Glaudiôs, who called himself {Atanâf} <Ahanâf> Çaguêd when they gave him the empire, they stopped burying the food and all the great men could enter, but they would wrap around their waists the cloths that they were wearing and would be left naked from the waist up, as a sign of submission and humility. This custom began to be given up twenty-four years ago, for as Emperor <[f. 20]> Iacob was a boy, some great men would enter clothed and would only wrap around their waists the cloths they wore over their robe in place of a cloak. But now they all enter very well dressed, and they only wrap their cloths at their waists out of courtesy. And at times, when speaking of this, this emperor told me that he thought the old custom of entering the palace naked in that way was very bad. And thus he even commands the enslaved pages to be dressed, particularly during celebrations, in velvet and other silks.

From what we have said, it can be seen how false the information was that Joam Balthesar gave to Friar Luis de Urreta on this subject, if it was on that basis that he wrote what he says on page 11,[4] where, refuting Francisco Alvares, because in his *Historia Ethiopica* he said that the officials that the emperor has in his house as valets, doormen, etc., are descendants of the Jews that Solomon gave to his son Menilehêc for these offices, he puts these words:

*The true story is that Abyssinian gentlemen are very pure in their lineages and very noble without any Jewish admixture, and the emperor's officials are not Jews and never have been, but the most noble gentlemen of the empire, because they are the firstborn of the kings who are subject to the empire, {[f. 23v]} who have never been Jews, nor do they regard themselves as such. Those Jews who came to Ethiopia from Jerusalem lived there while Melilec was alive, and so they were respected and honoured by everyone for many years. When Melilec – David – died, he was succeeded by his only son Josue, who was also called David, and he had nine sons. He and another, Juliano the apostate, returned to heathenry and wanted to bring back idolatry throughout his kingdom, and taking from the sad Jews the temple that he had given them on Mount {Amarâ} <Amzô>, he threw them all out of the whole land of Ethiopia, and*

---

[1] The sequence of tenses would require 'was'.
[2] Large jug (from the Tamil *kalam*); unit of capacity equivalent to one *almude* (c. 16.8 litres).
[3] See Glossary (Çagâ Za Ab/Ṣaggā Za 'Āb).
[4] Actually on p. 51.

*the Ethiopians returned to the old rites and superstitions. Some of these miserable Hebrews stayed in the far reaches of Africa, at the Cape of Good Hope and in other deserted and uninhabitable lands at that time, others returned to Jerusalem, and others in many provinces of Africa.*[1]

Up to here are the words of Friar Luis de Urreta. And first of all, as I have already pointed out, Solomon's son was not called Melilec but Menilehêc, and he wrote all this for want of true information, because the Jews who came from Jerusalem with Menilehêc have never been thrown out of Ethiopia; rather, this empire has until now been full of their descendants, living freely in their Judaism, although some have become Christians, particularly since the year 1616, because <[f. 20v]> of the proclamation that the emperor sent out, as we said in chapter 1, and with all that many remained in some strongholds, where they took shelter, and many more in the province of Cemên, where they have their main chief (whom the people of the land call Guedon, meaning Gedeon), and as the mountains are very strong they have defended themselves in them until now. As for the emperor's officials, they are all Christian, but many of them are descendants of the Jews that Solomon gave to his son Menilehêc for these offices, and this is such a well-known and obvious thing in Ethiopia that, when I asked some great men of the court in order to be more certain, an old monk, a friend of mine, laughed loudly that such an indisputable matter should be questioned, and said to me, 'Your Reverence should look here at so-and-so and at so-and-so, for they are such', and he indicated two of those who were there. I did not content myself with this, but also asked the emperor, and he replied that it was most definitely so. And speaking particularly about those whom we mentioned above, *azaxôch* and *umbarôch*, who are judges and magistrates, he said that they did not allow these offices to be filled at all even by the sons of their daughters, but only by the sons who descended by the male line from those {[f. 24]} Jews that Solomon gave to his son Menilehêc for these offices, for they say that, if the sons of their daughters were to fill them, since the husbands are ordinarily from different families (for they cannot marry kin of less than the seventh degree, according to the custom of Ethiopia, although some do not keep to that), the direct line from those ancestors of theirs would soon be cut.

Friar Luis de Urreta says something else that is also very contrary to what has always been the custom of the emperors of Ethiopia in their palace, when he says that they are served by the firstborn of the kings subject to the empire; he deals with this very vaguely in chapter 18, where, among many other things, he says this:

*When one of these princes comes to the court, on his arrival at the imperial palace two of the oldest members of the council come out to receive him and take him into the presence of the emperor, who orders them to put him in the first chamber, one of the five that there are before the imperial room, where the emperor ordinarily lives. In this first chamber the firstborn serves for five years, and from there to the second where he serves for five more, and thus he goes from one to the next as far as the fifth and last chamber, which not all of them reach, because it may happen to one that, when he is more or less thirty years old, the emperor gives him a wife, because they cannot marry without the emperor's permission, and when he marries he sends him back to his kingdom, even if his father is still alive, because if the father*

[1] Urreta, *Historia de la Etiopia*, excerpt from bk I, ch. 5, p. 51. Páez quotes this passage in Spanish.

103

*dies, he straight away crowns the firstborn king and with a great retinue sends him to govern*
<[f. 21]> *his estates. But however he goes, whether married or {to govern} on the death of his*
*father, his place is always taken by his younger brother, if he has one, and if not then the*
*closest kinsman comes to serve provided that he is of the royal lineage, and in such a case if this*
*gentleman is only a kinsman of the firstborn, on whose behalf he serves in court, he only*
*remains there until the other has sons able to fulfil the obligation for him.*[1]

All this that the author says is imaginary, because the emperors of Ethiopia have never
had this form of service in their palace, but rather that which we said above, nor have there
ever been such kings' sons, but rather those thirty slave boys. And even now that this has
been opened up for some freeborn boys to enter, they are not the sons of great men. Nor is
there such a distinction of five chambers, but rather the three that we have mentioned,
*ambaçâ bêit, zefân bêit, farâz bêit, scilicet* 'house of the lion', 'house of the bed', 'house of the
horse'. And in these things {[f. 24v]} there is no doubt at all, because I have heard them
from the main heads of these offices and from the boys themselves, whom I know and see
almost every day. And I know when many of those who are now there were brought as
captives. And some of them even came to me, because the emperor gave me twelve of them
who arrived before being baptized. These, then, are the firstborn of the kings subject to
the empire that Joam Balthesar fabricated, these the pages of royal blood that serve the
emperor of Ethiopia, the sons of Gâla, Agôu and Kafir heathens, although very similar.
And of those who are not slaves, there is hardly one that is not the son of a very common
man. No, {because} <for> if the emperor wished to be served by the sons of great men
within his house, they would not have wanted for much and would have held it to be a
great honour, but he wants only to follow the style and manner of his ancestors.

[1] Urreta, *Historia de la Etiopia*, excerpt from bk I, ch. 18, p. 176. Páez quotes this passage in Spanish.

# CHAPTER V

## In which two catalogues of the Emperors of Ethiopia are presented and the common names that they have are discussed

In the books kept in the church in Agçûm and one that Emperor Seltân Çaguêd lent to me, from which I took what I said above about Queen Saba and Menilehêc her son, there are two catalogues of emperors, their descendants, that are very different both in the number of them and in their names. And, as for one being shorter, it may be the fault of the person who copied the book that he left out the names that are missing, for, as all the books are hand-written, a great many mistakes can be found in them, and they do not entirely have the names of those of the family of one who was called <[f. 21v]> Zaguê, who held the empire in tyranny for 143 years, as is stated in one of the catalogues; but those who know the histories well have assured me that it is wrong, because many of this Zaguê's family are missing, and that the true count of these years is 340. As for the difference in the emperors' names, many say that it comes from the fact that sometimes they put in one catalogue the names that the emperors had before becoming emperors, and in another the names that they took when they were given the empire; because, ordinarily, they change their name in imitation (as they say) of Menilehêc, whom they called David when they crowned him. And some even change their name twice, as did Emperor Naôd's son, who was baptized with the name Lebenâ Denguil, *scilicet* 'Incense of the Virgin', and, when they gave him the empire, he called himself David, for after the {[f. 25]} death of his father the Empress Elena[1] had governed for many years, and she, as some old monks and Emperor Seltân Çaguêd told me, was not his mother because he was a bastard and, for want of a legitimate son, they made him emperor. And some years later he gave up the name David and titled himself Onâg Çaguêd. The one who is now emperor did the same, for, having the baptismal name of Sûseneôs, which they say is the name of a martyr, when they swore him in as emperor he called himself Malâc Çaguêd and now he is called Seltân Çaguêd, which means 'Power Worships'[2] or 'Power Bows'. And because it may be that in some Portuguese books that talk of the same emperors one finds different names because of the variety of these catalogues, in order that this does not cause confusion, but rather one may know whence it comes, I shall put them both here, starting with the one that recounts many of the names that the emperors had before they were given the empire, which says:

[1] See Glossary (Helena/Elena).
[2] See n. 3 on p. 75 above.

105

*David the king begat Solomon; Solomon begat Menilehêc who reigned in Ethiopia in the land of Agçûm.*[1] *And after him reigned his son Zagdûr, and then in succession those that follow:*[2]

| | | |
|---|---|---|
| Zabaceô. | Zafeleâ. | Guermâ Calêr. |
| Taoceâ. | Elguebúl. | Guermâ Azferê. |
| Aderiâ. | Baoaúl. | Zaradô. |
| Uareçâ. | Baoarêz. | Cululeaceôn. |
| Auceô. | [18][3] | Zarguaê. |
| Maceô. | Aoenâ. | Zaraî. |
| Zaûa. | Mahacê. | Zarrâ Azguêd. |
| Baceô. | [20] | Zeôn Haguêz. |
| Autêt. | Malcuê. | Mala Agnâ. |
| Bahaçâ. | Bacên. | Zaf Arâd. |
| Zaoadâ. | *In the eighth year of his reign, Christ Our* | Agdêr. |
| Adenâ. | *Lord was born.* | Abrâ and Azbâ, brothers. |
| Calêz. | Zenfâ Azguêd. | |
| Gotoleâ. | Bahâr Azguêd. | |

*These were great friends and reigned together and, in their time, Bishop Fremenatôs came from Jerusalem and preached baptism and the doctrine of the Holy Gospel,*
[16]
*and they believed his doctrine and called him Abba Çalamâ (scilicet 'Father of Peace').*[4] *Then there reigned:*

Azfâ.
{Arfêd} <Ardêd>.
{Amçî} <Anci>.

*These were brothers and reigned together and divided the day into three parts to rule. They were succeeded by:*

Aradô.
Aladobâ.
Amiamîd.

*In his time there came many holy religious men from Rum*[5] *and they spread throughout the empire. And nine stayed in the kingdom of Tigrê, where they built many churches that today have the names that the people of the land gave them. Only one proper name <[f. 22]> has been preserved, which is Pantaleam.*
[8]
{[f. 25v]} *They called the others Abbâ Arogaoî, Abbâ Guerimâ, Abbâ Alêf, Cehemâ, Afcê, Abbâ Licanôs, Adimatâ, Abbâ Oz. (Later they called him Abbâ Gubâ, scilicet*

---

[1] See Glossary (Agçûm/Aksum).

[2] The following lists are arranged in three columns in the MSS.

[3] The numbers given in square brackets in these lists are Páez's column totals.

[4] See Glossary (*Abba* Çalamâ/*Abba* Salamá/*Abbā* Salāmā I/Fremonatôs/Frémenãṭos/Saint Frumentius).

[5] Rome, or Byzantium.

'Puffed Up', because he made a church on a hill and stayed by himself, and so they said, 'Who is this puffed up monk, who makes a church by himself?', and he was left with this name Gubâ.)

*These performed many miracles through which they succeeded in converting the people of the land. And among these miracles they recount one of a terrible serpent, which was near the city of Agçûm, to which they would give two sheep and some* calões *of milk every day because, if it did not find that, it would come to the villages and kill many people. They also gave it a maiden on certain days in the year. When those holy men learnt that, they were very sorrowful, and one of them went with many people and, on coming within sight of the serpent, he knelt down with his hands raised to heaven begging Our Lord to deliver those people from such a terrible monster. And straight away it burst and fell dead, at which everyone marvelled greatly. And they said that those men were sent by God for the good of their souls and bodies, and so they held them in great veneration and now honour them as saints, making great celebrations to them on their days.*

*After Amiamîd there reigned:*

| | | |
|---|---|---|
| Tacenâ. | Freçanâi. | Degnâ Michael. |
| Calêb. | Adoraâz. | Badagâz. |
| Grabrâ Mazcâl. | Oaiçâr. | Armâ. |
| Constantinôs. | Madâi. | Hezbinanî. |
| Bazgâr. | Calaudên. | Degnaxân. |
| Azfê. | Guermâ Azfarê. | Ambaçâ Udm. |
| Jan Azguêd. | Ite Zargâz. | Delnaôd. |

*After this one, God gave his kingdoms to another people, who were not of the seed of David nor of the house of Israel, who were called Zaguê. And, when many years had passed, God returned the kingdom to those of Israel and there reigned:*

| | | |
|---|---|---|
| Iconû Amlâc, scilicet 'God Be With Him'. | Theodôroz. | Onâg Çaguêd. |
| Agbaceôn. | Isaac. | Atanâf Çaguêd. |
| Bahâr Azgâd. | Andreas. | Adamâs Çaguêd. |
| Hezb Arâd. | Hezb {Inânh} <Imânh>. | Malâc Çaguêd. |
| Cadmâ Azguêd. | Amd Iesu. | Iacob, who later called himself Malac Çaguêd like his father. |
| Udm Arâd. | Badel Inânh. | Za Denguîl. He called himself Atanâf Çaguêd. |
| [25] | Zara Iacob. This one gave the command to keep the Sabbath. | |
| Amd Ceôn. | Bêda Mariâm. | Suseneôs. He calls himself Seltân Çaguêd. |
| Zeifa Arâd. | Escandêr. | [22] |
| Udm. | Amd Ceôn. | |
| David. | Naôd. | |

{[f. 26]} <[f. 22v.]> The catalogue (which, as they say) commonly has the names that the emperors took when they were given the empire is as follows:

*Queen Azêb began to reign in Agçûm in the 37th year of the reign of Saul. And in the fourth year of the reign of Solomon she went to Jerusalem and, after returning, she reigned for 25 years. And the son that she had by Solomon, Ebnâ Elehaquîm, reigned for 29 years.*

Handodeâ: 1 year.

Auceô: 3.

Zaoê: 34.

Gaceô: half a day.

Maoât: 8 years and 1 month.

Bahâz: 9 years.

Caudâ: 2.

Canêz: 10.

Hadinâ: 9.

Oezhô: 1.

Hadinâ: 2.

Calaz: 6.

Çateô: 17.

Fileâ: 27.

Aguelbû: 3.

Aucinâ: 1.

Zebuoâs: 29.

Mahecî: 1.

Bacên: 17.

In the eighth year of his reign, Christ Our Lord was born.

Certû: 27.

Leâz: 10.

Macenêh: 7.

Ceteîo: 9.

Adguelâ: 10 years and 2 months.

Agueba: 7 months.

Melîz: 4 years.

Haquelê: 13.

[29]

Demahê: 10.

Autêt: 2.

Elaudâ: 30.

Zeguên and Zaremâ: 8 years.

Gafalê: 1.

Becêçarê: 4.

Those of Azguaguâ: 77.

Those of Hercâ: 21.

Beecê Zaueçâ: 1.

Oecanâ: 2 days.

Hadaûz: 4 months.

Those of Zaguêl: 3 years.

Those of Azfahâ: 14.

Those of Zegâb: 23.

Those of Çamerâ: 3.

Those of Aibâ: 17.

Those of Escandî: 37.

Those of Zahâm: 9.

Those of Zan: 13.

Those of Aigâ: 18.

Alamida: 30 and 8 months.

Those of Aheyeoâ: 3 years.

Those of Abraha and Azebehâ, guides of light: 27 years and 7 months.

Azbehâ: 12 years.

Those of Azfahâ: 7.

[Those of Çahêl: 14.

Those of Adehena: 14.]

Those of Rête: 1.

[28]

Azfehê: 1.

Azbahâ: 5.

Those of Amidâ: 17.

Those of Abrahâ: 7 months.

Those of Çahêl: 2 months.

Those of Gabêz: 2 years.

Those of Zehûl: 1.

Those of Izbah: 3.

Those of Abrê and those of Adahanâ together: 16.

Those of Zahâm: 28.

Those of Amidâ: 12.

Those of Zahêl: 2.

Those of Zebâh: 2.

Those of Zahâm: 15.

Those of Gabêz: 21.

Of Agabê and of Levî together: 2.

Those of Amidâ: 11.

Of Iacob and of David together: 3.

Armâ: 14 years, 6 months and 8 days.

Zitanâ: 2 years.

Iacob: 9.

Constantinôs: 28.

Gabrâ Mazcâl: 14.

<[f. 23]> Nacuê.

Bacên: 17.

In his time the church in Agçûm was founded.

[31]

{[f. 26v]} Zenfa Azguêd.[1]

{Bahâr} <Bahôr> Azguêd.

Guermâ Azfarê.

Culule Ceôn.

Cergâi.

Zerâi.

Begamâi.

Jan Azguêd.

Zeôn Hegz.

Moaelguehâ.

Zaf Arâd.

Agdêr.

Abrahâ and Azbaha, brothers.

Azfehê.

Arfêd and Amcî, brothers.

Arâd.

Cel Adobâ.

Alamidâ.

Amiamîd.

Tacenâ.

Calêb.

Gâbra Mazcâl.

Constantinôs.

Bezgâr.

Azfêh.

Armâh.

Jan Azfêh.

Jan Azguêd.

Freçanâi.

Aderâz.

Aiçôr.

Delnaôd.

Maadâi.

After these there reigned in Amharâ a woman of the generation of Jews, whom they called Eçatô (*scilicet* 'Fire'). And in the kingdom of Tigrê another woman Gudît (*scilicet* 'Monstrous') *ruled for 40 years, and destroyed all the churches. After her there reigned:*

---

[1] Páez does not include any column totals on f. 26v, nor the number of years reigned for the emperors listed in the first column and a half.

| | | |
|---|---|---|
| *Ambaçâ Udm.* | *Zergâz.* | *Badgâz.* |
| *Hualâ Udêm.* | *Degnâ Michael.* | *Armâh.* |
| *Guerma Azfarê.* | | |

*After him the direct line of the kings of Israel was cut and Mararî, of the family of Zagoê, reigned for 15 years.*

| | | |
|---|---|---|
| Imrâh: 40. <(Anno Domini 1210.)> | *Nacutolâb: 40.* | *Harbâi: 8.* |
| Lalibelâ: 40. | | |

(These alone are in the book, but they say that many others of this family are missing, and that altogether they reigned for 340 years.) *Then God returned the kingdom to those of the line of David, and there reigned:*

| | | |
|---|---|---|
| Icûnu Amlâc (*scilicet* 'God Be With Him'): *15 years.* | *Tedrôs: 9 months.* | *Lebena Denguîl: 33 years.* |
| Agba Ceôn: 9. | Isaac, with his son: 16 years. | Glaudeôs: 18 and 7 months. |
| Two sons of his: 3. | Hezbnânh: 4. | Minâs: 4 years. |
| Three sons of these: 2. | Two sons of his: 1. | Zer Za Denguîl: {33} <1>. |
| Udm Eraâd: 13. | Zarâ Iacob: 34. | {Iacob: 10.} |
| Amd Ceôn: 30. | Beda {Mariâm} <mauâm>: | {Za Denguîl: 1.} |
| Ceif Arâd: 28. | 10 and 2 months. | Seltân Çaguêd: 16 (until this |
| Udm Azfarê: 10. | {Escandêr: 15 and 6 months.} | year of 1622).[1] |
| David: 33. | {Amd Ceôn: 6 months.} | |
| | Naôd: 13 years and 9 months. | |

{[f. 27]} <[f. 23v]> Up to here I have taken it from their books.[2] But it must be pointed out that not only is Lebenâ Denguîl a baptismal name, as we said at the beginning of this chapter, but Glaudeôs is as well. And the latter called himself Atanâf Çaguêd when they gave him the empire; Minâs called himself Adamâs Çaguêd; Zer Za Denguîl called himself Malâc Çaguêd; Iacob, Malâc Çaguêd as well; and Za Denguîl, Atanâf Çaguêd.

From these catalogues one can see how wrong are the names of most of the emperors whom Francisco Alvares and Friar Luis de Urreta and others who have written about things of Ethiopia have mentioned in their histories. And, leaving aside many others, the one that Francisco Alvares, on f. 127,[3] calls Zeriaco is actually called Zara Iacob, *scilicet* 'Seed of Jacob', and they say that, when they gave him the empire, he called himself Constantinôs. They speak very badly of him in Ethiopia and they {affirm} <say> that, after he had issued a command to keep the Sabbath, because a superior of Dêbra Libanôs, *scilicet* 'Monastery of Lebanon', which was the most noble that there was in Ethiopia, did not want to keep it, saying that it was Judaizing, he commanded that he should be slain

---

[1] See Chronology of Ethiopian Monarchs.

[2] Manuel de Almeida copied Páez's lists ('Historia de Ethiopia a alta', Beccari, V, bk II, ch. 5, pp. 115–17). Baltazar Teles recompiled the data, crediting Almeida with the research and transcription of the Ethiopian catalogues (Teles, *Historia geral de Ethiopia a Alta ou Preste Ioam*, bk I, ch. 27, pp. 67–9; Tellez, *The Travels of the Jesuits in Ethiopia*, bk I, ch. 14, pp. 74–6), possibly believing the note in which Almeida discounted Páez's previous work and attributed to himself alone the 'many investigations' done in relation to the catalogues (bk II, ch. 1, p. 91). Almeida did, however, contribute a comparative analysis of the two lists (*ibid.*, chs 6–7, pp. 119–29).

[3] Álvares, *Prester John of the Indies*, ch. 99: 'How long the land of the Prester John was without an Abima and for what cause and where they go to seek them and of the state of the Abima and how he goes when he rides', p. 356. 'Abima' is a misreading for 'Abuna' ('patriarch').

along with many others; and that he also ordered the goldsmiths and blacksmiths to be slain, because he said that they were all sorcerers, and he had many gathered together in a field and slain. And a short time ago, when Emperor Seltân Çaguêd was talking about this in front of me and some great men, he said, 'Zara Iacob did such evil deeds! He is burning in Hell.' An old monk replied, 'Your Majesty should not say that, for he was an anointed king.' The emperor said, 'Perchance, just because he is an anointed king, can he not be in Hell? His works {are} <must be> what must save or condemn him.' And, calling for a book, he said to me, 'If you will look at this book, Your Reverence, you will find the things of Zara Iacob.' I took the book and, where it began to speak of him, it said as follows:

*In the time of our King Zara Iacob there was great fear and terror in all the people of Ethiopia at the severity of his justice and strength, principally against those who worshipped idols. And when some came {to say} <and said> that others had worshipped them, he would give them no other oath than to say, 'Their blood be upon you.' And with that he commanded those against whom they bore witness to be killed, so zealous was he of the honour of God. He did not pardon even his children. He killed Glaodeôs, Amd Mariam, Zara Abraham, Betiâ Ceôn, {[f. 27v]} and his daughters Delcemarâ, Eronguenelâ, Adelmengueçâ and many others. And then he ordered a proclamation to be issued saying, 'Let the Christian people hear what the Devil has done. We commanded that the people should not worship idols, and {he} <the Devil> entered our house and led our children astray.' And he showed everyone the wounds from the lashings that he had given them in punishment, and they were so great that some died there and then and others shortly afterwards; when the people saw that, they wept bitterly. Then he commanded that all should write upon their foreheads:* Za Ab, oa Ûald, oa Manfâz quedûz (which means 'Of the Father, the Son and the Holy Spirit'); *and on their right arms:* Quehêd queûo la Diabolôs regûm âna guebrâ la Mariâm emûla fetarê cûlu Alem (which means 'I have denied the accursed Devil I the slave of Mary, mother of the Creator of all the world'); *and on their left arms:* Quehêd queûo la Diabolôs {Dazcbâc} <Dezcbâc>, oa ba Christôs amalêc <[f. 24]> (*scilicet* 'I have denied the dirty, deceitful Devil, and I worship Christ'[1]), *and he commanded throughout his empire that anyone who did not do so would have his possessions seized and would be slain.*[2] And, a little further on, the book says that if one of the palace pages (of whom there were thirty, all slaves, as we said in the previous chapter) went outside to eat, {or to} drink, or {to} speak, they would kill him together with the one who took him and the one who invited him. And fearing that a wife of his, called Ceôn Mogueçâ, might raise up his son Beda Mariâm, he commanded that she be given so many blows and torments that she died and they buried her secretly. But her son learnt of it anyway and he took incense and candles to the church; when Zara Iacob, his father, heard of that, he had him seized and nearly killed him.

This book recounts many other things of great severity, which I shall leave out for the sake of brevity. It also says that there was a path with a fence on either side from the palace to the church, along which he would go without anyone seeing him. And only the superiors of some great monasteries could enter the church to sing. And, when he wanted to enter the chapel to take communion, everyone would go out, leaving only the *acabê eçât*

---

[1] Páez's translation deserves some qualification: the attributes of the Devil have been added and the last words do not form a separate clause, but should be translated 'in Christ the Lord' (the particle *'oa/wa'* is not found in the original Ethiopic text).

[2] Excerpts from the chronicle of Zar'a Yã'eqob (published by Perruchon as *Les Chroniques de Zar'a Ya'eqob*, 1893; see pp. 4–6).

and four other priests. And, when he was going to the church and when he was returning, one of the pages had the job of making a sign with his hand from inside to the musicians, who were waiting outside with many instruments, to play and make celebration. And, in one of the houses that he had inside his fence, there were many priests singing psalms {[f. 28]} of David throughout the watches, without ceasing day or night. And they continually sprinkled holy water on the walls inside the house, because sorcerers were casting spells on him out of envy of his faith. He also had an enclosed area made near the church and had it filled with water and there he baptized himself for many years until he died. And he ordered that near {all} the churches they should make tanks in which to be baptized and that everybody should always keep the Saturday Sabbath as well as Sunday, because his captains had won a victory on a Saturday over an enemy of his called Bedelâi Aurê. Up to here are the words of that book.[1] But where it says that he killed his children because they worshipped idols, Emperor Seltân Çaguêd does not believe it because, when I was talking to him about this, he told me, 'Who knows whether he had them killed for another reason? He was a very strong man. He even wanted to kill Beda Mariâm so that no other son would be left to him.'

In addition to the specific names that the emperors have in these catalogues, they are given other general ones, as is the custom in other kingdoms with all kings. The first is *negûz*, which means king. And they say that he can use only this name until he is crowned. Afterwards he is titled *neguça nagâzt za Ethiopia*, *scilicet* 'king of kings of Ethiopia', that is, 'emperor of Ethiopia'. But this is not kept, because I knew King Iacob of Ethiopia and King Za Denguîl, who both died before they were crowned, and even so they put on their letters *neguçâ nagâzt*, 'emperor'. They also call him *aceguê*. I asked many people the meaning of this name, and some said that it meant 'king' and others that it did not, but something <[f. 24v]> of greatness. It seems to correspond to 'majesty', and everyone uses this name most commonly, particularly when speaking to him or to others in his presence. They do not say '*negûz*' but '*aceguê* commanded such-and-such a thing', as one might say 'Your Majesty or His Majesty commanded.' Ordinary people, who cannot come to the emperor, shout from afar, each in his own tongue, in order to be noticed. And then the emperor sends a page or a great man to ask what they want, and he dispatches them. But they say neither *negûz* nor *aceguê*, for these words are not apt then. The Portuguese say 'Lord, Lord', the Christian Gongâs say: '*Donzô, donzô*', *scilicet* 'Lord, Lord'; the Agôus say '*Jadarâ, jadarâ*', which is the same thing; the Moors '*Cidi, cidi*', 'My Lord, my Lord.' And others according to their tongues use the same word; but the Amhârâs shout many different words, {[f. 28v]} saying '*Jan côi, jan côi*', which means 'My king, my king'; *jan* in the ancient language means 'elephant', although in the common tongue of nowadays it is not called that, but *zohôn*. And, because the elephant is so powerful and generous, they formerly called the emperor *jan* and they still use this name today. The word *côi* is a diminutive and means 'my', and so *jan côi* is now the same as saying 'my king' or 'my emperor'. I write *côi* with this letter 'c', because I cannot find a better one, but it does not perfectly match the pronunciation of the Amhârâs.[2] They also say '*dêlbe jân, dêlbe jân*',

---

[1] The excerpt summarizes a number of fragments from the Ethiopian chronicle; see Perruchon, *Les Chroniques de Zar'a Ya'eqob*, pp. 9, 105–6, 27, 35, 40–41, 75 (in the order referred to in the text). The excerpts were copied in full by Almeida ('Historia de Ethiopia a alta', Beccari, V, bk II, ch. 25, pp. 239–40; this fragment was published by Perruchon, pp. 199–205).

[2] ARSI, MS Goa 42 has a new paragraph here.

111

which means 'victory in the emperor', because *del* means 'victory', *be* 'in', and *jân* 'emperor', as we have said. They also make use of another word, {which} <and it> is *belûl côi, scilicet* 'my emperor', not because *belûl* primarily means 'emperor', but rather a certain gold ring that they used to put in the right ear of the prince whom they chose to be emperor, but because that was a sure sign of having been chosen to be emperor and his specific insignia, so *belûl* is taken to mean 'emperor', and they very often say '*Jan côi, Belûl côi*' together.

Friar Luis de Urreta, on page 81,[1] says that the emperors of Ethiopia, apart from their specific names, have a common name and appellative associated with their imperial dignity, which is {Beldigian} <Beldigran>. And, giving the reason why people in Europe have called the emperor of Ethiopia the Prester John, he says thus, on page 88: *Why are many of the emperors priests ordained to say Mass? Because (as we shall say) when the princes guarded on Mount Amara, who are successors of the emperors, are many in number, they oblige the one elected to be ordained a priest, so that in this way he will not have children and thus* <[f. 25]> *the number of {sons} princes will not increase, but rather diminish. Those who have been priests now in our times are Emperor Daniel II and Emperor Paphnucio, who succeeded Naum, and Alexandre III, who succeeded him, a most valiant and warlike prince. All these have been priests, not to mention many other ancient ones, because this custom has been kept in Ethiopia since the beginning of Christianity, the emperor being ordained a priest when there are many heirs. And, as the Ethiopians adhered to the patriarchate of Alexandria, which, because it followed Greek ceremonies, used Greek terms, also calling priests presbyters, thus the Ethiopians made use of many Greek names, calling their priests presbyters. And, when the emperor was a priest {[f. 29]} they named him Prester Beldigian. And, since the merchants who dealt in Cairo, in Alexandria, and <since> the pilgrims who went to visit the holy city of Jerusalem heard it said that the emperor {of Ethiopia} was a priest and that his vassals called him Prester Beldigian, when they came back to these provinces, corrupting and violating the word – since they spoke in their own fashion – they named him the Prester John of the Indies, that is the Emperor of Ethiopia, whom they call the Prester Beldigian. And that was the reason why they title that most powerful prince the Prester John, not usurping the name of the other prince of Asia called Unchian, but using his own name, Prester Beldigian, abbreviated and syncopated through being poorly understood and difficult for Latin people to pronounce.*[2] Up to here were the words of Friar Luis.

When I saw this name Beldigian, which I had never heard or found in many books that I have seen in Ethiopia, I did a good deal of research to find out whether it existed by asking learned men and noble kinsmen of the emperor. And they all said that they had never seen such a name in a book or heard it. And if they had said *belûl jan* here, I might have thought that Friar Luis de Urreta had not properly understood Joam Balthesar's pronunciation when he said *belûl jan*, and had understood 'beldigian'; but these two words *belûl* and *jân* do not go together, because they only say *jan côi, belûl côi*. Hence it seems that this name Beldigian is imaginary and that there never was such a name, because it is not possible that not one of all those learned men and lords that I asked would have heard of it. And it is no less fictitious when he says that, when the successors of the emperors are many in number, they oblige the one they elect to be ordained to say Mass

---

[1] Urreta, *Historia de la Etiopia*, bk I, ch. 7, entitled 'Of the name of the emperor of Ethiopia Beldichian, and the reason is given why he is called the Prester John of the Indies', pp. 80–88.

[2] Urreta, *Historia de la Etiopia*, excerpt from bk I, ch. 7, p. 88. Páez quotes this passage in Spanish.

<[f. 25v]> so that he has no children; and that in our times the three emperors that he names were priests, because, apart from there not having been such a Paphnucio, as can be seen from the catalogues of the emperors, nor Alexandre III, but rather just one Alexandre, whom they call Escander, nor is the other one called Naum, but rather Naôd, the emperors were never ordained to say Mass, nor were they obliged to be, because that would be to oblige them not to marry but to remain forever celibate; for, as they all say, nobody may marry after he has been ordained to say Mass. Joam Balthesar would say (and it is correct) {the emp} that many of the emperors receive orders as deacons, but later marry; that they only do that to be able to enter the chapel of the church to hear Mass {[f. 29v]} and take communion, because those who are not ordained cannot enter there, nor pass beyond some curtains that they have in front in some long churches. And in the others, which are round, they do not go inside but stay on the veranda that runs around it, and communion is brought out to them there.

As for the reason why people in Europe call the Emperor of Ethiopia the Prester {John}, it may be because, as ordinarily he is a deacon, some Greeks would call him *presbyter*, and then, adding the name *jan* which (as we have already said) they give to the emperor, they would come to say *Preste Jân*. And foreigners, who often corrupt names in accommodating them to their own tongues, would call him the Prester John. This name *jan* is very old in Ethiopia, because they always use it in referring to some of the officials that the emperor used to have and still has, descendants of those that Solomon gave to his son Menilehêc, saying 'such-and-such officials of *jan*' instead of saying 'such-and-such officials of the emperor', as we have seen in chapter 4, where they are named. And so they would call the one who was like the chief groom *jan belêu*, 'groom of *jan*', *scilicet* 'of the emperor'. And even today they call the goldsmith and the emperor's armourer *jan xalamî*, 'decorator of *jan*', *scilicet* 'of the emperor'.

It may also be, and I think it is a highly likely reason, that people in Europe called this emperor of Ethiopia the Prester John for the reason that Father Friar Thomas de Padilha gives in the prologue that he added to the *Historia Ethiopica* by Francisco Alvares, when he translated it from Portuguese to Spanish, where he says that King Dom Joam II of Portugal received news that in the East there was a very powerful Christian king who, as well as being king, was also priest to his Christian subjects, and his vassals called him the Prester John. And he sent two Portuguese, Pêro de Covilham and Afonso de Paiva, via Cairo, <[f. 26]> in the year 1487, to learn whether it was possible for his ships to go from the Cape of Good Hope (which had already been discovered) to India where the spice was found that they used to take up the Red Sea to Egypt, and to find out very much on purpose where the kingdoms of the renowned Prester John were. And so they went to Cairo and then down the Red Sea, where they separated. And Pêro de Covilham went to India to find out about the navigation and the spices it had, and Afonso de Paiva went to Ethiopia where, as they had been assured, they were all Christians and had a very powerful emperor, to see whether this was the Prester John that they were seeking, and they agreed to meet again {[f. 30]} in Cairo at a certain time. But when Pêro de Covilham returned to the appointed place, he learnt that his companion Afonso de Paiva had died. And he found letters there from his king, in which he commanded them to finish what they had begun as swiftly as possible and, if they had news of the Prester John, to try to take him a letter that he was writing and to visit him on his behalf, asking him for every friendship as is required between two Christian princes. He replied, telling him of what he had seen in India and that it was quite possible to sail there via the Cape of Good Hope and, additionally, that in Ethiopia there was a Christian emperor, who he thought was the Prester John that His Highness had commanded him to seek; and therefore, since his companion was dead, he would go and carry out the embassy as commanded.[1]

When this news reached King Dom Joam, he was justifiably delighted, and it was made known in Spain that the Prester John reigned in Ethiopia and that is why the emperor of Ethiopia was always given the name Prester John, although it really belonged to the emperor of Cathay. And for that I cite Marco Polo and others. And Friar Luis de Urreta, in chapter 7 of his *Historia*, quotes Jacobo Nabarcho and Gerardo Mercator and many others in confirmation of the same opinion.[2] What is certain is that no mention can be found of this name Prester John in the books of Ethiopia, because one of the learned men whom I asked would have known of it.

---

[1] The details given in the prologue justify Tomás de Padilla's decision to use the title 'emperor' in his translation in place of Álvares's 'Preste Joam'.
[2] Urreta, *Historia de la Etiopia*, bk I, ch. 7, p. 87.

# CHAPTER VI

## Of Guixên Ambâ, where the descendants of the former emperors are held

The marvels that Friar Luis de Urreta recounts in chapter {8} <3>[1] about this Guixên Ambâ, which he calls Mount Amarâ, are so many and so great that, while it is a very long way from this kingdom of Dambiâ, where I ordinarily live, I very much desired to go there, and I should have done so, even though the route is difficult, if the danger of robbers had not been so great because of the Gâlas who are waging war in those parts. Not because I am not <[f. 26v]> very well aware of how fabulous the information is that he has been given on this, but in order to speak from sight. However, everything that I say on this subject will be from reports by two of those descendants of the emperors, who are called *Abeitahûm* Memenô and *Abeitahûm* {[f. 30v]} {Taquelâ} <Zaquelâ> Haimanôt, who lived there for a long time and now reside at court, and by another great friend of mine, who is called *Abeitahûm* Orcô, who is at present in that fortress but sometimes comes to court with the emperor's permission, because he does not fear him, and by others that have been in there and know what there is there. But, so that one can better understand the name of this fortress, it must be pointed out that in the language of Ethiopia every mountain and rock on top of which the people can defend themselves from their enemies is called an *ambâ*. There are many of these in Ethiopia, and very strong ones; hence the proper name of that place where they hold the descendants of the former emperors is not *ambâ*, which in general belongs to all strongholds, but *Guixên*, which means 'Was Found'.

Having said that, I shall first of all refer to what Friar Luis says in the above-mentioned chapter where he describes this fortress, placing it above {all} the strongest in the world with so much praise, as if nature had done a perfect job on every aspect of it, wanting to produce something exceedingly prodigious in fertility, beauty and loveliness in order to show the world its great excellence and perfection. And so that nobody may think that I have added words to his, I shall report his own, which are these:

*All these rocks and mountains* (he had spoken of some rocks that seemed impregnable, which were taken by Alexander the Great)[2] *and all the others that the world has may keep silent, and admiration for them will cease if they are placed in parallel and comparison with the famous Mount Amarâ which is in Ethiopia, where the princes of the empire are held. Because those mountains of India, although apparently impregnable and strong, were finally entered, their heights scaled, their difficulties overcome, and reduced to Alexander's power. But*

---

[1] The chapter number given in ARSI, MS Goa 42 is the correct one (Urreta, *Historia de la Etiopia*, bk I, ch. 8).
[2] Interpolation by Páez.

*the fortress of Mount Amarâ is such that there is no way to enter it by any of said means. It is such a prodigious fortress that it seems that nature did a perfect job in forming it and revealing to the world a stronghold without the aid of any human artifice. And not only is it a well-defended place, but it is one of the sites best endowed with the greatest comfort and sport that there is in the whole world. And it is so to such an extreme that Philo the Jew says that if there is an earthly paradise it is on this mountain; and that it is so peregrine[1] and singular that as a fortress it is the largest and most impregnable that there is or has ever been in the universe; and of all the {[f. 31]} flowery gardens, delightful orchards and pleasant arbours, it is the most perfect of them all: in short, paradise. Hebrew, Latin, Greek and also Turkish and Arabic historians have described and mentioned it in their writings.*

<[f. 27]> *A little further on, he says: Mount Amarâ is located in the middle of Ethiopia as the centre of all the empire of the Abyssinians, below the equinoctial line. Nature set it in such flat country, on such even and prolonged plains {and} in such an extensive, unoccupied and open land that no mountain or hill may be found for more than thirty leagues around that might trouble or obstruct it. It is higher than and stands astride the whole country. Its shape is round and circular, and so one can easily reach any part of it. Its height is so great that it is about a day's climb from the foot to the summit. All around it is sheer rock from top to bottom, so smooth and even that it seems to have been made with a {square} <charcoal> and trowel, without there being any overhanging or unequal crags or rocks, but rather it is like such a high wall that, when one stands at its foot, it soars so high that it seems to prop up the sky and act as an abutment and pier for it. At the top of all that wall of sheer rock, the crags and rocks become irregular, projecting out from the wall for the space of 1,000 paces, and they form a lip and vamplate[2] in the shape of a mushroom – a rare work of nature and one so unique that no other can be found in the world – which makes it impossible to scale it on the outside. And so there is no reason to fear being scaled. And as it is so high nobody can make earthworks or ravelins to match it. In circuit, it must be more than twenty leagues around. It is surrounded at the top by a very graceful and finely made wall, to prevent the wild beasts and game that live there from falling off, and men too, for it was made for that purpose alone and not for defence, because there is no need for that, since there is no harquebus or musket that could reach the top of the mountain. The summit and field that is on top of this mountain is all very flat and even. Towards the south a hillock rises gently, which graces all that field and serves as a lookout from where the human eye can enjoy the most agreeable views that one can imagine. From that hillock emerges a perennial, most abundant and clear spring with {[f. 31v]} so much water that by means of a number of channels it runs through the whole field, watering the gardens and making the earth fruitful, finally plunging down from the top of the moun-tain. At its foot it makes a small pool and lake, from which there comes a river that flows into the Nile. To climb to the top there is no path or track anywhere, and in this Francisco Alvarez was mistaken, because it is like a straight tower. And therefore they have mined and dug into the living rock, making a stairway by dint of picks, <[f. 27v]> hammers and axes, which is a spiral without steps or stairs, but which little by little creeps upward, so broad, so open and well made that one can ride a horse up it with great ease. And to light this stairway its loop-holes and skylights are made broad on the outside and inside and narrow in the middle, and very tall and deeply rent, of the kind and style of the stairway of the great tower in the City of*

---

[1] Meaning 'foreign' or 'outlandish.'
[2] Circular thin plate.

*Seville. At the foot of this stairway there is a very beautiful but extremely strong gate, with its guards, and along its course there are landings and level areas for resting. Half-way up the stairway there is a large, spacious hall, cut and carved out of the rock itself, with three windows, and I call them that because the higher the stairway rises, the larger are the windows. Here too there is a guard. The height of the stairway, I mean from floor to ceiling, is more than a lance and a half, and in this way it goes up to the top of the mountain, where it also has its gate and guard.*

*The air that blows at the top of this mountain is so delicate, pure and healthy that it never corrupts or contaminates. And so ordinarily those who dwell there live very long and remarkable lives, and very healthy and wholesome old ages, without the diseases and ailments that usually accompany them. On the top there is no city or village at all, just many royal palaces, each one by itself, and there are thirty-four of them. And they are like great castles: sumptuous, tall, elegant, beautiful, very spacious buildings, where the princes of the empire reside with their people and servants. The other people, who are soldiers and guards of the mountain, live in tents and pavilions. There are two temples, so ancient that they were built before the time of Queen Saba, one in honour of the sun and the other in honour of the moon, the most sumptuous and magnificent that exist in all Ethiopia. When Queen Candace was converted by the {[f. 32]} Eunuch's preaching and was baptized, she consecrated these temples in honour of the Holy Spirit and the Cross. They were also consecrated later by the glorious apostle and evangelist Saint Matthew, when he went to preach in Ethiopia, which land fell to his lot, with the same dedication. On this mountain there are many beautiful gardens and orchards of great freshness, delight and curiosity, filled and populated with all kinds of fruit trees both native of the land and brought from Europe: pear trees, pippin trees and many others; {there are} <and> all types of citrus fruit, oranges, citrons, bitter oranges, limes and the rest. There are gardeners who have the job of filling its conduits and beds with cheerful greenery. Such rare and peregrine trees are found on this mountain that they are found nowhere else in the world. One of them is the tree they call* cubayo; *its fruit is the colour and size <[f. 28]> of a quince and, when it is ripe, as soft as a sorb-apple; its rind is yellow, the flesh inside white and so sweet and tender that it resembles nothing more than very well made blancmange. They suck this fruit like someone eating very ripe sorb-apples. It is the most substantial and healthy food to be found among all the fruits in the world, of which the great physician Amato Lusitano said that there is no food that so preserves a man's health and comfort and helps his nature. And it is no surprise that those who dwell on that mountain live so long, because they live on this fruit. And, apart from this tree, there are many others that are only found on this mountain, particularly balsams, of which there are many.*

*There are artificial fountains made with great skill and artifice with many spouts, whose waters end up in many large and small pools, thronged with a thousand kinds of fish for the pleasure and amusement of those princes. And just as there are some fruits that are only found on this mountain, so there are such singular birds that they only live and move on this mountain without ever having been seen elsewhere in the world. There is one like a canary,[1] whose song is extremely sweet and its music so delicate that it seems to transport. There is another bird the size of a thrush with its neck raised and erect, its plumage of various pretty colours, with a comb and wattle like a cock, and from the comb there rise five or six largish plumes like {[f. 32v]} aigrettes, tinged with various pretty colours, and the whole plume is so*

---

[1] Canary. Páez does not transcribe the supposed local name of the bird given by Urreta ('*mihinihi*').

*beautiful that the emperor of Ethiopia presents them as a precious gift to other kings. There are also many meadows and woods and pastures, where a large number of cattle of all kinds, large and small, graze, for the very sufficient and very plentiful sustenance of the people of the mountain. And in the open lands and forests there is a good deal of game of all kinds – fallow deer, roe deer, red deer, wild goats, wild boar – for they have them there enclosed as in a chase, and there is plenty of room for them all, because, as I have said, the area is twenty leagues in circumference and around. In short, on top of the mountain there are many forests full of a variety of game for all kinds of hunting for their amusement. And they have the means for all that, with pointers, greyhounds and bloodhounds, catching partridges at feeding or drinking places with nets, nooses or decoys. There are no venomous animals or savage beasts but just game animals for sport and recreation. There is also plenty of cleared land for all kinds of grain and vegetable crops, and the land is fruitful and productive. Finally, this mountain is a place of so much pleasure and delight that I am not surprised that the doctors call it Paradise, because this name suits it and fits it perfectly and naturally.*

Continuing with this, he gives many reasons to prove how the name of Paradise suits it perfectly, and he concludes the chapter by saying: *This may be verified on Mount Amarâ, because all year there is fruit plucked fresh from the tree, figs, melons, freshly gathered, beans* <[f. 28v]> *and green peas are there all year. And they sow three times a year. The reason is because the weather is constantly like the autumn or spring. And there are trees that produce fruit two or three times a year, half of the tree in one half year and the other half in the other half year. Because when the sun moves and turns on the Tropic of Capricorn, the part of the tree that faces south to the noonday sun produces and is full of fruit, the other half remaining as if it were winter. And when the sun goes towards the Tropic of Cancer, the other half, which is towards the north and the Arctic Pole, produces fruit, the other half remaining leafless and as if dead. And when the sun is at the equinox, the crown of the tree has fruit, the other branches, which are at the sides and the lower ones* {[f. 33]} *remaining without fruit or leaves. So that every year in December, March, June and September there is fruit on the trees, some branches and some fruits succeeding others. Whence it may be inferred that we may give this mountain, for its fertility and largesse, the name of Paradise.*[1]

Up to here are the words of Friar Luis de Urreta, not continuous as he has them, because in some parts there are long digressions that he makes and I have only taken the parts that refer to what he calls Mount Amarâ, which is Guixên Ambâ. But one will clearly see the extent to which the information that he has had on this subject is apocryphal and fabulous from what I shall say now, not diverging one iota from what I have been told by the princes that I have mentioned above and other men of great credibility who have seen this fortress. So I say that, among the *ambâs* in Ethiopia that are no less strong than Guixên Ambâ, this one has a very great name because of its strength and because the descendants of the former emperors are held there, to whom the empire will belong if the one who has it has no heir, as we shall state later. It stands on the edge of a kingdom that they call Amharâ, which formerly was {almost} the middle of the empire, but is now almost its southern extreme, because some heathens that they call Gâlas gradually took over some very large extents of land to the south just a short time ago, as the emperors

---

[1] Urreta, *Historia de la Etiopia*, bk I, selected excerpts from ch. 8, pp. 90–100. Páez quotes these passages in Spanish.

were occupied in wars with their own captains who had risen up in the kingdom of Tigrê, in Dambiâ and other places. The location of this *ambâ* is in country that is not very flat, because it has plenty of hills and valleys and, towards the east, some two gunshots away, some very high mountains, which are called Habelâ, and others further away called Açêl Ambâ. On the other sides there are no mountains except very far away. Its shape is almost like a cross and, on top, it must be half a league in length, more or less, but at its foot it is a long way around. Its height is so great that it would be difficult to reach it with a slingshot, all sheer rock and in some parts, near the top, the rock itself turns outwards, so that it is impossible to climb up there, but people used to climb up on another side, as we shall say later. There is only one entrance, which is called Macaraquer. And at the bottom, at the beginning, the path is broad and it rises a little thus until it reaches a small platform, {[f. 33v]} and thereafter <[f. 29]> it is so narrow and steep that one can only climb with great difficulty. And so, when they want to take a cow up to slaughter on the top (which they seldom do, because they slaughter them at the bottom), they tie it with ropes and drag it up almost as a dead weight. At the top, there is a gate and a house where the guards live. Inside, there are many houses, some like long, broad halls, others round, but all one storey and poor, roofed with straw. In the middle, there is a large tank of fresh water where they wash their clothes and, a short distance away, another small one from which they drink. And, as some people say, it is water that rises there but does not flow away, and there is no other water there on the top, nor fish. Near the large tank, almost to the east, the land rises a little more and forms a kind of small hill on which two straw-roofed churches are built. One is called Egziabehêr Ab, *scilicet* 'God the Father', and it is made of timber; the other is dedicated to Our Lady and made of very good stone and is to the south, the other almost to the north, which we shall discuss in the next chapter. Near them, on one side, live the monks and the *debteras*,[1] who are like canons, but married, and on the other side, those who descend from the former emperors, with their wives and children, whom they call Israelites.

On the whole of this *ambâ* there are no fruit trees at all, just one kind that they call *coçô*[2] and it only grows in very cold lands. They are usually not very tall trees, with many branches and a good crown; the leaf is long and not very broad and has some white hairs at the base. There is nothing in Portugal with which to compare its fruit, but it is rather like the spike of the {dock} <gourd>, but much longer and thicker. Its bitterness is so extraordinary that it greatly exceeds that of wormwood. And despite all that, every two months they all drink it dissolved in water for a serious ailment that the natives of Ethiopia {generally} have, caused by creatures like worms, but very long, that grow in their stomachs, apparently from the raw meat that they eat, because foreigners do not have such a thing. And it is such strong medicine that some die from it in a few days, spitting blood. But if they do not take it at the time that I said, they get very thin, and those creatures begin to come out through their noses. There are other very tall trees that they call *zeguebâs*, {[f. 34]} but they do not bear fruit; it is white wood and good for buildings.[3] There are also cedars, not like those of Spain, but wild ones with little crown and very tall, and only a few of all these trees, because the area is small. They also sow some barley and beans just

---

[1] See Glossary (Debtera/dabterâ/*dabtarâ*).

[2] Kosso (*Hagenia abyssinica*), a vermifugal plant commonly used to expel tapeworms.

[3] African fern pine (*Podocarpus falcatus*).

once a year. And apart from that there are no other seed crops or trees at all, but something like jasmine, which they call *endôd*, climbs up some of them. Its fruit is like bunches of pepper and they use it as soap to wash their cotton cloths.[1]

There are no wild animals except monkeys and rabbits, and these do not have long ears like those of Spain, and the toes on their feet and hands are also different from the domestic ones.[2] There are few sheep and goats, as there is no pasture for them. They haul some oxen up on ropes to plough the land where they sow the little barley and beans that I mentioned, and then they take them down by means of the same ropes because they have little grass up there to give them, for here they do not eat <[f. 29v]> meal or grain, but just dry grass or straw from the field or something very tiny, finer than mustard seed, which they sow and call *têf*.[3] There are no mules or horses or other animals apart from these, and some venomous snakes.

This is all that great multitude and variety of animals that Friar Luis de Urreta places on this rock. These are the meadows, {the} forests and pastures full of different sorts of game for all kinds of hunting and amusement. This is <all> that perfection of {all the} flowery gardens. These are the artificial fountains made with great skill {with many spouts} and threads of water pleasing to the eye. This is that crystalline spring that emerges from the hill and waters all this paradise – the two tanks that I mentioned from which the water flows nowhere. As for the tree of life that he places in this paradise, the fruit of which is as sweet and tender as very well made blancmange, and greatly helps man's nature, and those who eat it live many years without the diseases and ailments that accompany old age, it must be the one they call *coçô*, because those who have lived there for many years say that there is no other tree there that bears fruit. But he was wrong in what he says about its sweetness, because there is nothing more bitter in the world. And although, as I have said, they take it as medicine, if they are a little careless and increase {[f. 34v]} the measure, it cuts out their livers and they die within a few days, spitting blood, as I have seen. Nor is there anybody who can give any news of the other mysterious tree that he mentions, saying that, when the sun is to the south, the half of the tree that falls to that side has leaves and bears fruit, and the other half is as if dead; and when the sun passes to the north, the half of the tree on that side, which was previously as if dead, produces leaves and bears fruit and the other half is as if dead; and when the sun is at the equinox, the crown of the tree has fruit, and the branches on its flanks remain leafless. I did not find a single one of the many people whom I questioned because they had entered Guixên Ambâ, or of those who had lived there for many years, who had seen this marvellous tree or ever heard tell of it; rather, some laughed heartily, as if they had been asked something very absurd. Therefore, since it is not to be found in the paradise of Guixên Ambâ, where the author places it, it is certain that it {is not to} <will not> be found anywhere in the world. The royal palaces, which he makes like great castles, high and sumptuous, I have already said are miserable one-storey houses roofed with straw. Nor is there up there that handsome wall that he depicts, nor even one of dry stone, let alone that ingenious stairway for climbing up inside, for the path and entrance are outside and as rough as we have said. Nor do the soldiers live in tents, nor could they at least in the winters, which are very harsh.

[1] Endod or African soapberry (*Phytolacca dodecandra*), the berries of which are used as a detergent and a molluscicide.

[2] The 'rabbits' are probably hyraxes.

[3] *Têf* 'teff' (*Eragrostis tef*), an indigenous cereal of Ethiopia.

He gives one to understand, on page 91,[1] that he wrote all these things from the reports given by Joam Balthesar, who he says had been in Guixên Ambâ for a long time serving Alexandre before he was emperor, and later went up there many times at his command. But I cannot convince myself that Joam Balthesar (although a liar) told him that all those things were in Guixên Ambâ, but rather he was telling him about the whole kingdom of Amharâ, but he understood him to mean just Guixên Ambâ; because, although some things are fabulous, such as that there are those two trees <[f. 30]> and pears, pippins, palms, balsams, artificial fountains and gardens like the ones he paints, many other things that he mentions are found in that kingdom, which is very fertile in fruit and provisions, and there are many of the animals that he names, both domestic and wild. In addition, the bird that he says is like a thrush with a comb and wattle like a cock is found, not in Guixên Ambâ, but close by, in the hot country. But the feathers that he mentions do not come out of its comb but from behind, and they curl over it, and {[f. 35]} they are not valued as much as he claims, although they are beautiful. And the author himself shows that he understood Joam Balthesar to mean just Guixên Ambâ, when he was telling him about [the things] of the kingdom, because the title of chapter 8, where he discusses this subject, says 'Of Mount Amara and its strength and <its> fertility', and this name does not belong to that mountain alone, but to the whole kingdom. And, <on> page 97, he says that even the name that theologians give to the earthly paradise, which is *hortus delitiarum*, belongs to this mountain, because in the language of Ethiopia the word *Amarâ* means just that: 'garden of pleasures, delights and recreations', and therefore it is certain that he was mistaken, taking what he was told about the whole kingdom to refer just to that mountain, although one should not write '*Amarâ*' or even less '*Zahamahahrâ*', as he amends it, but '*Amharâ*', for that is what that kingdom is called; and, if in all rigour we pronounce this word '*Amharâ*', it means 'appeared good' or 'beautiful'; but it is used for a beautiful thing, and that is why they gave this name to that kingdom, which is very fertile and beautiful.

Nonetheless, although the author was mistaken with this word *Amharâ*, he should have taken good note of one point that he makes here so as not to contradict himself later. And it is what he says on page 96, that the princes held in Guixên Ambâ have pointers, greyhounds and bloodhounds for their hunting and amusement. And, on page 254,[2] he states that in all Ethiopia there are no dogs and that if they bring some in, as happens when ships arrive from Europe and leave some dogs from Ireland and England, within a month they become weak and die. But the truth is that there are so many dogs everywhere in Ethiopia that they are beyond count, as we shall say later. It is also false when he says here that Joam Balthesar served Alexandre for a long time in this fortress of Guixên, before he became emperor, because, as we have already noted in chapter 1, the last prince that they took from there to be emperor was Naôd, who, as shown in the catalogues of the emperors that we put in the previous chapter, had left there 118 years before Friar Luis de Urreta printed his *Historia*, which was in the year 1610, and Joam Balthesar was approaching seventy then, as he says on page 7;[3] and therefore they took this prince out of Guixên Ambâ to be emperor some fifty years before Joam Balthesar was born, and never since has any other left there for that reason.

[1] Urreta, *Historia de la Etiopia*, bk I, ch. 8.
[2] Urreta, *Historia de la Etiopia*, bk I, ch. 25, entitled 'Of the animals, both wild and domestic, that there are in Ethiopia, different from the ones that Spain and Europe have', pp. 241–60.
[3] Urreta, *Historia de la Etiopia*, bk I, ch. 1.

Francisco Alvares was also very mistaken when he says, on f. 77[1] {[f. 35v]} of his *Historia*, that these princes were held in a valley between two very rugged mountains, which was closed with two doors, and that the mountain was fifteen days' journey around and he had travelled along its foot for two days. But the princes are not in a valley but on top of Guixên Ambâ, and the mountains that he saw must be some very high ones that are not very far away and are called Habelâ, and they have very rugged, narrow passes where many of those who are obliged to guard <[f. 30v]> Guixên Ambâ live, because that is where they have their lands. And as they told him that nobody could go from there onwards on pain of death, and as Guixên Ambâ could not be seen from that side, he would have understood that the princes were held in the valley that lies between those mountains, which could easily have happened to him, because he did not know the language of the country.

---

[1] Álvares, *Prester John of the Indies*, ch. 60, 'Of the size of the mountain in which they put the sons of the Prester John and of its guards and how his kingdoms are inherited', pp. 243–4.

# CHAPTER VII

## Concerning the two churches and monasteries at Guixên Ambâ

So that we can better state whence these churches had their origin and how old they are, it is worth recalling something that usually everyone knows, that it was always the custom of benighted heathens to worship their false idols and offer them sacrifices on high mountains and beneath cool and shady trees; this was mentioned by the prophet Jeremias when, reprehending the people of Israel for having fallen into the same darkness, he said to them with great pain and feeling, '*In omni colle sublimi et sub omni ligno frondoso tu prosternabaris meritrix*',[1] chapter 2; it has always been deeply rooted in Ethiopia, as the mother of idolatry, if it is true that its King Menno invented it, as Diodorus thought, in books 1 and 4, as Friar Luis de Urreta reports on page 29.[2] And if Ethiopia was not the inventor, it is certain that many {diabolical} kinds of idolatry have entered the country, and are even now so entrenched in many lands of Christians where there are heathens that it is impossible to completely stop them worshipping snakes and other animals or offering many sorts of sacrifices to the devil in the sources of the Nile and on the highest mountains that they can find. The devil has no lack of ministers to deceive these barbarous people, for rather there are many sorcerers among them who with devilish arts make them believe their falsehoods and lies, particularly with one art used by those they call *Agôus* of the kingdom of Gojâm, and it is that in one of the ceremonies that they perform to their idols, in which they sacrifice {[f. 36]} many cows, they gather plenty of firewood at the command of their sorcerer and, when the sacrifice ends, he covers himself with the layer of tallow from one or two cows and, sitting on an iron chair in the middle of all that firewood, he has it set alight and he remains amid those flames until all the wood is burnt but without the tallow that covers him melting, and by that means that those miserable people are deceived.

When a heathen, a man of rank, recounted these things to a cleric in order to aggrandize his accursed sect, the cleric replied that if he would take him there safely on the day of that ceremony, he would clearly show how that was all deceit and falsehood by that sorcerer, who had a pact with the devil. The heathen accepted, confident that the cleric had no power over his sorcerer, and promised to protect him so <[f. 31]> that no one should do him harm. And when the day came, he went with the heathen to the place of the sacrifice, carrying a little horn of holy water concealed on him. And when the fire was lit, as was customary, he saw that no matter how high the flames rose, they caused no

---

[1] 'For on every high hill, and under every green tree thou didst prostitute thyself' (Jeremias [Jeremiah] 2:20).

[2] Urreta, *Historia de la Etiopia*, bk I, ch. 3, entitled 'Of the first settlers of Ethiopia, and of some Kings and emperors, until Queen Candace at the time of Christ', pp. 18–34.

{damage} <harm> to the sorcerer. Therefore, taking out the holy water, he threw it on the fire, saying these words from Psalm 67: *Exurgat Deus, et dissipentur inimici eius et fugiant qui oderunt eum a facie eius. Sicut deficit fumus deficiant, sicut fluit cera a facie ignis, sic pereant peccatores a facie Dei.*[1] Hardly had he said this when the sorcerer started burning and, without those around him being able to help him, in a short time he was turned to ashes, which shocked everybody. But instead of converting when they say that marvel, they flew into such a great rage and ire that they would have torn the good cleric limb from limb if the heathen, who was powerful, had not protected him as he had promised.

This infernal fire of heresy has always burned in Ethiopia without the emperors ever having been able to extinguish it, however much they have tried with arms and with doctrine, although by the grace of the Lord it is now dying out among the Agôus of the kingdom of Gojâm through the efforts of two fathers, companions of mine, who are working there,[2] as we shall say at the end of this *History*. And they have built churches in the main places where they used to practise their sorcery in order to [remove the memory of them,] which is the means that the emperors also used for the same purpose, building them on the mountains where they used to offer sacrifices to their idols; they did that particularly on Guixên Ambâ where, because {[f. 36v]} it is such a noteworthy mountain in height and strength, as we said in the previous chapter, the heathens formerly made great sacrifices to a famous idol that they had there, which they called Darhê, not inside sumptuous buildings, as Friar Luis de Urreta says in chapter 9,[3] but beneath a very large bush that they call *endôd* which, as we have already said, does not make a tree but, if it finds some support, climbs up like jasmine or ivy and makes good, cool shade. But to remove the memory of this accursed idol, Emperor Lalibelâ, who reigned in about 1210, built a church for Ethiopia the great and beautiful in the same place, and dedicated it to God the Father. And so he gave it the name Egziabehêr Ab, *scilicet* 'God the Father'. And because they did not allow women to enter this one to take communion, the people of the land made another, smaller one not very far away, dedicated to Our Lady.

These were the first churches built on Guixên Ambâ. Later, <[f. 31v]> Emperor Naôd[4] prayed in the Church of Our Lady while still a prince, and promised to make a large church there if the Virgin would gain the empire for him. And a year later they took him away to be emperor, and so he had that church pulled down and had another large one built, but before it was finished he died, and later his son Onâg Çaguêd, who was first called David,[5] completed it. It is round, like a half-orange, made of very beautiful white stone, and has two orders of stone columns around it. Above the inner ones, a dome of the same stone, and in the middle is an altar, which one approaches up seven steps. The altarpiece consists of four painted panels, which are not very large: one of Our Lady, one of

---

[1] 'Let God arise, and let his enemies be scattered: and let them that hate him flee from before his face. As smoke vanisheth, so let them vanish away: as wax melteth before the fire, so let the wicked perish at the presence of God' (Psalms 67:2–3 [68:1–2]).

[2] Father Francisco de Angelis and Father Luís de Azevedo; in 1620 the latter was sent to the Jesuit residence of Qwālala in Goǧǧām, founded in 1612 ('Historia de Ethiopia a alta', VI, p. 237).

[3] Urreta, *Historia de la Etiopia*, bk I, ch. 9, entitled 'Of the two monasteries that are on Mount Amara, and of the famous library that the Prester John has in one of them', pp. 101–10.

[4] Nā'od, throne name of Anbassā Badār; see Chronology of Ethiopian Monarchs.

[5] The two names given by the author are the throne names (Wanāg Sagad/Dāwit) of King Lebna Dengel; see Chronology of Ethiopian Monarchs.

Christ Our Lord crucified, one of Saint Michael, and the last of Saint George. They can all be removed and replaced when needed. The second order of columns also makes a circle, but it does not have a dome, but rather timber. Between one order and the other there is a distance of seven cubits. Then, seven cubits further out, there is a wall around with its doors, and no one may go inside it apart from those who are ordained deacons, for the *abunas*[1] never confer subdeacon's orders separately; rather, many people think that they only confer deacon's orders, as we shall see in the second book. The other men and women remain outside, on a veranda that runs around it. And the whole church is roofed with straw, which makes it so dark inside that one cannot read without a candle. They say that a captain of the king of Adêl, who was called Granh, climbed up there and wanted to burn down this church, as we shall say later, but he did not succeed even though he set fire {{[f. 37]}} to the timber of the veranda roof, and today one can see where it started to burn, for they have left it so on purpose as a reminder that Our Lady delivered her house from the Moors' fire. But the Church of God the Father, which Lalibelâ made, was entirely burnt down and later they made another small one of timber roofed with straw.

These two churches are in the charge of monks and clerics; the latter are married. Formerly, there were (as they say) fourteen monks at most in them, and they lived close to them in little one-storey houses roofed with straw. Now there are six and, at regular intervals, these leave and others come up from the monasteries that are down there in the countryside. There are thirty clerics and their superior is called *lica* {*cahenât*} <*lahenât*>,[2] *scilicet* '*lica* of the clerics', which seems to correspond to prior. They ordinarily stay up there, and they live with their wives in little houses like those of the monks, whose superior is called *memehêr*, *scilicet* 'master'. All the people that live on top, men and women, must total 200, but formerly there were many of them, as we shall say later in chapter 10.

<[f. 32]> From what we have said, it is easy to see how deceitful the information was that Joam Balthesar gave to Friar Luis de Urreta about these buildings, because he says on page 93[3] that they are two ancient temples that were built before Queen Saba, one in honour of the sun and the other in honour of the moon, the most sumptuous and magnificent that exist in all Ethiopia, which Queen Candace, when she was converted and baptized by the Eunuch's preaching, consecrated in honour of the Holy Spirit and the Cross, because, when she climbed up there to baptize those of the imperial line and lineage of David, who were held there as they are now, when she was engaged in this holy exercise, baptizing the princes, she saw a most beautiful dove flying there, all burning in flames and giving off rays of light, similar to the form taken by the Holy Spirit appearing to the apostles. And after it had flown a good distance through the air in sight of everybody, it came to rest on the very top of the temple of the sun. That is why the queen consecrated that temple to the Holy Spirit and the moon temple to the Most Holy Cross. And later the Evangelist Saint Matthew consecrated them with the same dedications when he went to preach in Ethiopia. And later, on page 101, where he deals with this specifically, he says:

*These two Churches, one of which is named after the Holy Spirit and the other after the Holy Cross, are the most sumptuous and magnificent that there are in all Ethiopia, the tallest,*

---

[1] See Glossary (*abuna*/metropolitan).

[2] The title referred to is *liqa kâhenât*, and therefore the variant that appears in BPB, MS 778 is a copyist's error. *Liq* translates as 'elder'.

[3] Urreta, *Historia de la Etiopia*, bk I, ch. 8.

*finest and most handsome buildings, with the best design, artifice and architecture, and the richest. Because, as the ancient peoples made them in honour of the Sun and the Moon, which were their greatest gods, the ancient emperors used the rest of {[f. 37v]} their riches for their adornment and beauty. And they have been continually perfected ever since. Each of these two churches must in greatness and size be equal to the holy and magnificent cathedral in Seville. They only differ in that they have but three naves, roofed with stone vaults bearing on very thick, strong walls and on many very beautiful and richly worked columns. The stones are all precious: jaspers, alabasters, marbles, porphyries, and many of fine garnet, for in those times they were not known. Large pieces are found in the Black River, as well as many other stones of great beauty and value which, when placed in order, create a work of art and greatly adorn the building. There are many highly gilded chapels with their cornices, carvings, artfully battered walls and architecture, with their brush-painted altars. And together with these two temples, two monasteries of monks of Saint Anthony have been built, which are among the most beautiful and splendid that said order possesses, and it has many very magnificent ones. In each of them there are military knights commanders of the Cross of Saint Anthony, and there are priest monks, who are also knights of the same order. And they also have lay brothers and attendants, who wear the whole Tau of Saint Anthony without the little flowers that the knights and priest monks wear. In each monastery there must be about 1,500 overall, comprising these three estates. So that in the two monasteries <[f. 32v]> there must be 3,000 religious members, who are always on the top of the mountain attending to the service of their churches and monasteries and to that of those most illustrious princes. In each monastery there are two abbots, one spiritual, whom they call* abbas *in their tongue, and the other a military abbot just for the knights, whom they call* abbas coloham, *and the greater is the spiritual one.*[1]

Up to here are the words of the author, which, if they are compared with what we have said above, will show how great the fiction and lie is that Joam Balthesar put into Friar Luis's head here. For, not only before Queen Saba but also afterwards, there never were any temples of idols, nor churches either, until Emperor Lalibelâ began to build them a little over 400 years ago. So Queen Candace could hardly have dedicated them to the Holy Spirit and the Holy Cross because, in addition to the fact that they do not have and have never had such names, but rather *Egziabehêr Ab, scilicet* 'God the Father', and 'Our Lady', the Queen lived more than 1,000 years earlier, in the time of the apostles, because Saint Philip baptized the Eunuch who converted her; nor could she have baptized those of the imperial line and lineage of David on that Mount of Amharâ, because the first who began {[f. 38]} to put them there was Udm Arâd, who put his brothers there for the reason that we gave at the end of chapter 1, and that was in about 1295; nor could Saint Matthew have consecrated those churches, because they were made such a long time after his death; rather, many old monks who know the histories of Ethiopia have sometimes told me that Saint Matthew did not reach those lands of the kingdom of Amharâ. As for what he says about the military knights commanders of the Cross of Saint Anthony and the priest monks, who are also knights of the same Order, we shall see at the end of the second book how fabulous a fable that is, because there is not and there never has been in Ethiopia such a form of religion.

---

[1] Excerpt (with omissions) from bk I, ch. 9, pp. 101–2. Páez quotes this passage in Spanish.

# CHAPTER VIII

## Concerning the library of Guixên Ambâ

The fables and lies told by Joam Balthesar [(if they are all his)] that led Friar Luis de Urreta to write a very long chapter about this subject have forced me to write this one. It could all have been stated in the previous one, together with what we said about the churches (where he claims the library is and the emperor's treasures are kept), and not much writing would have been needed if the truth of what happens were to be told plainly; but because he says many things that are so far from the truth, and it is not good that they remain uncorrected, I am making this a distinct chapter, in which I shall put first what he says as briefly as I can, and then what is actually the case regarding this subject.

Having, then, talked about the library in Alexandria, in which he says there were 700,000 volumes of books, and about the library in Constantinople, in which there were 120,000 books, the author says on page 103:

*These {famous} <beautiful> libraries and all those that have had name and fame are insignificant and will lose their fame and glory if they are compared <[f. 33]> with the library that the Prester John has in the monastery of the Holy Cross on Mount Amara; because the books that it has are innumerable and countless. Suffice it to say that Queen Saba began to collect books from many parts, and put in it many books given to her by Solomon and others who continually sent them to her. And ever since those times the emperors have gone on adding books with great care and curiosity. There are three extremely large rooms, each more than 200 paces long, where there are books of all sciences, all on parchment, very fine, slim and burnished, with much curiosity of golden letters and other handiwork and decoration; some are richly bound with their boards, others are loose, like court rolls, and placed inside some {[f. 38v]} taffeta bags and sacks; there are very few on paper, and it is a modern thing and very new among those of Ethiopia. The list which was brought to His Holiness Pope Gregory XIII is as follows.*[1]

Here he includes a very long catalogue of books, which I have felt it unnecessary to copy, because few of those he indicates will be found throughout Ethiopia, for there is no science for which he does not include many authors. And he says that there are more than 500 books just of hieroglyphs and symbols. And at the end of the catalogue, on page 107, he says:

*This table that I have put in this chapter is part of an index and list that was made of all of them by Antonio Grico and Lorenço Cremones, who were sent by Pope Gregory XIII at the*

---

[1] Urreta, *Historia de la Etiopia*, excerpt from bk I, ch. 9, p. 103. Páez quotes this passage in Spanish.

request of Cardinal Zarleto, and they went to Ethiopia solely to examine the library in the company of others who were sent for the same thing, and they came back astonished at seeing so many books, for they had never in their lives seen so many all together and all handwritten, and on parchment, and all very large because they are like choir books made of whole parchment, on very curious cedar shelves and in such different tongues.

The reason why there are so many books is the curiosity and diligence that the emperors have always had in collecting them since the time of Queen Saba. And in all the travails that the Jews suffered at the hands of the Babylonians, Assyrians and Romans, the emperors of Ethiopia have always sought to see the books. Their care has been so great that when the emperor of Ethiopia called Mena heard that Emperor Carlos V had won the city of Tunis, on receiving news that King Mulea kept a copious and rich library, he sent word to the merchants of Egypt, Rome, Venice, Sicily and other places that they should at his expense buy the books that the soldiers were carrying off, for, as they were in Arabic, they were almost giving them away. And in that way he collected more than 3,000 books on astrology, medicine, herbs, mathematics and other curiosities. And with this diligence continuing for so many thousand years, since the times of Queen Saba until today, it should be no surprise if I say that there are more than a million books, and I think that even that falls short, or even very short.

Very great care is taken of this library, because it is the most precious thing that the empire has. And of the monks of the Abbey of the Cross, more than 200 monks are appointed as librarians and take care of the cleanliness, care and inconvenience[1] of the books. And every Monday they make 300 or 400 soldiers of the guard <[f. 33v]> that live at the foot of Mount Amará come up, and they sweep the {rooms} <houses>, clean the books and shake off the dust, and do all that they are commanded. These monks are librarians in accordance with the languages that they know, because they are all very learned in them; they take care of {[f. 39]} the books that are written in the language of which they are informed, which they see are not eaten by bookworms, check that the letters do not smudge, because, as they are on parchment, it easily happens, and do whatever is necessary. When they crown the emperors, they give them the keys to the treasury and also the key to the library, and the emperor gives it to the spiritual abbot of the monastery of the Holy Cross, where the library is, and sternly entrusts him with the care, custody, vigilance and curiosity of the books, saying that he values them more than all his treasures, for the empire has treasures even though there are no mines, but the books of that library are unique in the world.[2]

Up to here are the words of Friar Luis de Urreta, in which there are very few that tell the truth of what happens, because firstly all this enormous, beautiful library that Joam Balthesar, or whoever informed the author, has depicted formerly came down to a matter of 200 books, which the emperors had been putting there, because it is a custom that has lasted until today that, when an emperor takes the throne, he has his predecessor's books transferred and, keeping the new ones, he gives the others to whichever church he likes. And from these and some others that have come from elsewhere, although I have not found anyone who might explain that to me, they collected those books there, almost all

---

[1] There is a copyist's error here, with '*incomodidad*' ('inconvenience') in place of the word '*incolumidad*' ('safety') that appears in Urreta's original text.

[2] Urreta, *Historia de la Etiopia*, excerpt from bk I, ch. 9, pp. 107–10 (with omissions, including a long passage about the possibility that there might be copies of the Cabbala and Talmud in this library). Páez quotes this passage in Spanish.

on parchment; for Ethiopia it is a large number, because there is no printing and they take a long time to write a book, for their script is slow and the letters do not join together; it is almost in the style of the Hebrew script, but they do not write towards the left as the Hebrews and Arabs do, but towards the right as we do. But in about 1528, a Moor named Mahamed came out of the kingdom of Adêl and, as he was left-handed, in Ethiopia they commonly call him Granh, *scilicet* 'Left-handed' and, at the time, he was the vizier of the king of those lands, which is like a governor, and he entered these lands with an army and took them until he came to Guixên Ambâ. And a captain of his climbed up on a side that the people of the land showed him and burnt down the church of God the Father, where many books were lost, and others were taken by the soldiers to sell to the people of the land that had bowed to them. Therefore, if Joam Balthesar, as Friar Luis says, was approaching the age of seventy in 1610, he could hardly have described this library from sight, but would have heard tell that it was very large, for small things {[f. 39v]} are made much larger in Ethiopia, and would therefore have spoken with such exaggeration, whereas now there are no more than twenty books, more or less, in both churches. And four of them, which are the largest, are not made of whole parchment but half, but one, which deals with the *Miracles of Our Lady*,[1] has many gold letters. The remainder are not as Friar Luis depicts them, but very ordinarily crafted.

Regarding the part where he says that Queen Saba began to collect books from many parts there and included the ones that King Solomon gave her, we have already said in the previous chapter that on Guixên Ambâ there were never any temples of idols or any building where the books might be kept, <[f. 34]> and the queen had no need to keep up there the books that Solomon gave her or any others that she might want to keep, since she held her empire so unopposed, as we have seen in chapter 3, and since she lived in such a strong city with such sumptuous and noble buildings, as the ruins of Agçûm now show well. And if she did not want to have them with her (which seems unlikely, since Solomon's were so precious), she should have put them at Ambâ Damô,[2] a day's journey from Agçûm, which is much stronger than Guixên Ambâ, which is fourteen days' journey away, and it may be that at that time nobody had any report of it, but rather it was dense forest. The churches, as we have already said before, were begun in about 1210 at the time of Emperor Lalibelâ, and neither of them was dedicated to the Holy Cross but to God the Father and Our Lady. Nor have I ever been able to find anyone who had heard that the emperors used to have books brought from other kingdoms to collect there. And Minâs, whom he calls Mena, was much less likely than others to have done so because, in addition to having little curiosity about books and not having any trade with the other lands mentioned by the author, during the four years that his reign lasted he had enough to do defending himself from the Turks, who defeated him in the kingdom of Tigrê, and from his own captains, who rebelled against him in many parts because he was so severe and intractable. Nor would Emperor Carlos V's soldiers have carried off so many books in Arabic from Tunis, for they would have been totally useless to them, and if they took some, they would already have thrown them away or scattered them so that they could not be collected when Minâs, who was then called Adamâs Çaguêd, began to reign, because he became

---

[1] See Glossary (*Miracles of Our Lady/The Miracles of Mary/Ta'āmra Māryām*).

[2] A mountain in Tegray famed for its inaccessibility. It has been occupied since the 6th century by the monastery of Dabra Dāmo (see also bk I, ch. 31; bk II, ch. 16; Beccari, *RÆSOI*, 4, pp. 279–82).

emperor in March 1559 and Tunis had been taken twenty-four years earlier, in 1535. And if, as the author claims on page 106,[1] {[f. 40]} all the books that are in those three rooms are in Greek, Arabic, Egyptian, Syrian, Chaldean, Hebrew and Abyssinian, most of them should be on paper and also many should be printed, because these foreign nations hardly ever write on parchment, and yet he claims that there are very few on paper. And the emperor's kinsfolk whom I have asked say the same.

As for that huge number of 3,000 books on astrology, medicine, herbs and mathematics that he says are there, even if he was not speaking about now, when there are so few, but about the ones there initially, that could not have been the case, for there were no more than some 200 in all, and nobody has been able to tell me what the books in Arabic that were there then or are there now were about. But what I have found is that even the most learned men know little more than nothing about these sciences, to the extent that, when I talked to them about very ordinary things like meteors and the course of the Sun, it was all completely new to them. And some would say that the Sun did not go round under the Earth, but that when it set on our horizon it travelled around it, and the fact that the Earth was in shadow was because of some high mountains that were there, until I told them how it could not be so. And they marvelled much more because, when I was talking to the emperor about the effects of the Moon, I said to him, 'In fifteen days' time there will be an eclipse of the whole Moon. And it will start here two and three-quarter hours after midnight, more or less, and in Portugal at two minutes past twelve' <[f. 34v]> (which was the eclipse of 26th August 1616). They all asked how one could know what was to come and tell not only the day but the time as well. I answered that many years beforehand people used to write down the eclipses that were to happen to the Sun and the Moon without making the tiniest mistake, because of the knowledge that they have of their course, and that they should watch out for this one and they would see if it was right or not. They did so with so much care that even the emperor rose a long time before and, when the Moon began to darken, he went out onto the terrace in front of the door to the palace and stood there looking for a long time. Afterwards he told me that I should write down for him in his language when there should be others. And when I also gave him a drawing of what would happen to the Moon, he was very pleased to see it and said that his people knew nothing about that. Nor do they know anything at all about medicine. And so, when they fall ill, not only poor people but also the rich and great lords, {[f. 40v]} they die without making any remedy even if the sickness is a long one. And when a short time ago the emperor found a book of surgery in Spanish, which Dom Christovão da Gama brought when he came with the Portuguese to help this empire, he asked me to translate into his tongue some things that are now used. Therefore I think that there are no books of medicine on Guixên Ambâ, because it is not possible that they would not have translated them, or at least have learnt something from them.

What the author claims – that the catalogue of books that he mentions was made by Antonio Grico and Lourenço Cremones, who came to Ethiopia sent by His Holiness Pope Gregory XIII solely to examine this library – will be better known in Rome, where the papers are, because there is no recollection of that here; rather, when I asked many old monks and people of this land and some Portuguese as well as a Venetian, who is called Joam Antonio and has been here for many years, they all said that such men had never

---

[1] Urreta, *Historia de la Etiopia*, bk I, ch. 9.

come, except for one called Claudio, who died here, and two others, Jeronimo and Contarino, who left for India in about 1596, more or less. But whatever the case may be with Antonio Grico and Lourenço Cremones, there is one thing for which I have no answer, which is that, if there were more than a million books in this library in the time of Gregory XIII (as the author says), there are now so few, as we said above, when it is certain and well known by everyone in Ethiopia that since then no books have been removed or lost, as testified principally by those who have lived there since long before that time. In addition, the number of over 200 monks of the Abbey of the Cross who, he says, are appointed as librarians is very large, for, as we have already said in chapter 7, there have never been more than fourteen monks up there in both churches, nor more than thirty clerics, and there never has been such an Abbey of the Cross.

# CHAPTER IX

## In which it is shown that the Prester John never kept any treasure on Guixên Ambâ

If Friar Luis de Urreta was long-winded in talking about the library of Guixên Ambâ, he is much more so when dealing with the treasures that he imagined – or the idea was put into his head – that the Prester John kept there, {[f. 41]} because he makes two chapters, 10 and 11,[1] on this subject that are so long that it is no small <[f. 35]> penance for someone who has other things to do to be forced to read them, principally if he knows just how fabulous all the things he says in them are. Therefore, even though I shall report his words, I shall include no more than the ones that are most relevant in putting across his intention, in short, which is to place the treasures and riches of the emperor of Ethiopia above those of all the kings that there are and ever have been in the world. And so, after mentioning that he does not wish to speak of the many mines in which Ethiopia is so abundant and rich, he says, on page 112:

*I only intend to describe the treasure that is kept on Mount Amarâ in the monastery of the Cross, together with the library, which is of such immense wealth that I dare say, and say with confidence, that no king in the world, neither ancient nor present, no empire or monarchy, even though this account may include the four renowned empires on earth: Babylonians, Persians, Greeks and Romans, with all their victories, triumphs and rich spoils, ever had so much gold together nor precious stones as are gathered on Mount Amarâ.* And further on, on page 114: *The treasure that is on this mountain, according to tradition throughout Ethiopia, began to be gathered together at the time of Queen Saba. And ever since those so ancient times, every year the emperors of Ethiopia add and hoard up as much income and wealth as they have, and they never take anything at all out, because the Prester John has no need of it, because the cities of the empire, according to ancient custom, pay for all the warriors, the guards of his person and pavilions and Mount Amarâ. And the income from three powerful kingdoms, Saba, Zambra and Gafatê, is allocated for his court and household expenses, and they contribute far more than enough for {these} <the> expenses. And the income from the other kingdoms, of which there are fifty-nine, is free and left over, and as it is so plentiful, because all the kingdoms are rich in gold and silver mines and highly populated, and as it has been collected in the treasury on Mount Amarâ for the space of 3,000 years, let the reader*

---

[1] Urreta, *Historia de la Etiopia*, bk I, ch. 10, entitled 'Of the huge treasure that the Prester John has kept since ancient times on Mount Amara', pp. 111–17; bk I, ch. 11, entitled 'Of the jewels and precious stones that the Prester John has on Mount Amara', pp. 118–28.

*consider how much gold will have been collected and stored, for it will surely exceed every measure and account.*

*For if in the time of Queen Saba* (he says on page 115) *there was so much wealth of gold and silver, and from then until today the income has been collected and stored, how many millions will the gold and silver have amounted to? The empire's treasurers and accountants themselves can put no value on it, but always speak in admiration and appreciation. The treasure is kept in four very large, spacious rooms. Formerly the gold was stored in these rooms* {[f. 41v]} *in the form in which it was extracted from the mines, with all its dross. The purest was the gold they extracted from the Black River and other rivers in nuggets, which were sometimes really big. This custom lasted until Emperor David, whom a Portuguese named Miguel de Silva advised to melt all that gold down into roundels and bars so that it could be stored more conveniently. The emperor did so and filled all those four houses from the floor to the ceiling with piles of square gold blocks, one span long and wide and three finger-breadths thick. The gold is extremely pure, because there are blocks that bend and curl as if they were made of dough, for the gold of Arabia and Ethiopia is already famous for being very pure and precious. In each* <[f. 35v]> *room, judging from the size of the piles, according to some Venetians and Portuguese who have seen them, there must be more than 300 million, and as there are four rooms, that makes more than twelve times 100 million.*

He says more on page 118: *Emperor Alexandre III, who died in 1606, seeing that all Christian princes struck coins, engraving their images and arms on them, determined to strike coins on the advice of the great Council and all the clergy and priests of Ethiopia, who saw that it was a very good policy and at the same time highly beneficial and convenient for those doing business, so he left the Council determined and resolute that coins should be struck throughout the empire, but that their shape should not be round but long like an oval, and on one side is engraved the image of the glorious apostle and evangelist Saint Matthew, the patron of Ethiopia, and on the reverse of the coin the figure of a lion with a cross held in its hands, which are the arms of the emperors. The writing around the edge on the lion side is: Vicit Leo de tribu Juda,[1] and on the side with the likeness of Saint Matthew: Ethiopia præueniet manus eius Deo.[2] If silver has been mentioned little in this chapter, it is because there is little in comparison with gold, and formerly they did not know how to work it nor did they care much about it. Now it is worked and serves as coinage and they use it to deal with merchants from other nations, because gold may not be taken out of the empire, but just silver.*[3]

On the same page, where he starts dealing with the precious stones in the treasury, he says this: *I want to become a lapidary one day without actually being one, since this chapter is our motivation and the flow of this history, taking us by the hand, has led us into the room of jewels and precious stones that the Prester John has next to the rooms of gold on Mount Amarâ, in the monastery of the Cross. This room is lined with very large chests, some of cedar, others of* {[f. 42]} *ebony, well reinforced and with strong locks: on each of the coffers is the number of stones inside it. The room is very large and, as it is full of precious stones, the value and price of it is inestimable. Nobody knows when the emperors of Ethiopia began to collect*

---

[1] Apocalypse [Revelation] 5:5: 'the lion of the tribe of Juda ... hath prevailed.'

[2] Psalms 67:32 [68:31], 'Ethiopia shall soon stretch out her hands to God'. Urreta wrongly ascribes this passage to St Matthew.

[3] Urreta, *Historia de la Etiopia*, bk I, excerpts from ch. 10, pp. 112–18. Páez quotes these passages in Spanish.

*precious stones, because those that Queen Saba had are today kept in the city of Saba in the church of the Holy Spirit, where she was buried. On entering the room, one straight away finds some very large chests filled with very fine emeralds; these stones are of great value as they are resplendently green, so much so that there is nothing created that is as green as they are, or that gladdens and delights the eye so much. There are extremely large pieces in these coffers, because, of all the different precious stones, the emerald is the one of which the largest stones have been found.*[1]

A little further on, he says that a king of Babylonia presented a king of Egypt with an emerald that was four cubits in length and three in width, and that in the city of Tyre, in the temple of the god Hercules, there was a very large column made entirely <[f. 36]> of one emerald, and another in Egypt, in the temple of the god Jupiter, which was forty cubits in length and four in width at one end and two at the other, made of just four emeralds, and in one of the labyrinths of Egypt there was a statue that was nine cubits in height made of a single emerald; and that it is a tradition in Ethiopia, and they are certain of it, that these imposing emeralds were taken from Ethiopia. And enormous pieces of emeralds are found and stored among the other jewels even today, and the Prester John has dishes, bowls and jars made of emeralds and other precious stones. Then he talks about all the names that there are for precious stones, and how great coffers are full of each kind, saying:

*There are other chests, some of very precious diamonds, others of the best rubies in the world, and some as large as one's thumb. The stones of which there is very great abundance in this room are turquoises, sapphires, topazes, and balas rubies. There are jacinths and some amethysts. There are also chests of chrysolites, although they do not hold them in such esteem. There is a mine of chalcedonies. And there are many of agate stone, but they used not to know how to use it until some craftsmen sent by Francisco de Medeçis, the Duke of Florence, fashioned some very fine cameos. There are many chests full of pearls, some from the East Indies, others from Hormuz and some from the Black River.*[2] *There are such large pearls that, when Bernardo Vecheti, the famous {[f. 42v]} lapidary who was sent by Duke Francisco de Medeçis, saw them, he said that he was sure that the renowned pearls that served as earrings for Queen Cleopatra could not have been larger than the ones kept there.*

He continues, on page 127: *Among the many fine and priceless stones that the Prester John has that one might recall here, there is a boulder and lump of rock of pebble stone that was found in the Black River (which is the river that produces more precious stones than any other in the world), in the making of which it seems that industrious nature gave up and threw off her necessary obligations and, with her fingers polishing and her hands burnishing, she crafted a starry sky and wished to put together all the precious stones that she normally produces scattered around different parts of the world. This square rock is two and a half spans by about three spans square, and one span thick at the thickest part and four finger-breadths at the thinnest. The stone is coarse and rough,* <[f. 36v]> *like that of a reef pounded by the ocean waves, and in it nature encrusted 1,000 different kinds of precious stones. There*

---

[1] Urreta, *Historia de la Etiopia*, bk I, excerpts from ch. 10, pp. 118–21. Páez quotes these passages in Spanish.
[2] Up to here the author has summarized the content of pp. 122–5 of Urreta's text, instead of transcribing it as he claims.

*are more than {160} <150> diamonds, some as big as the palm of one's hand, others two or three spans in width, others like a thumb in length, and the smallest must be like a fat hazelnut, all of them extremely fine and weighing many carats. There are more than 300 emeralds, large and small; there are more than fifty of the largest rubies in the world, some like one's index finger. There are sapphires, turquoises, balas rubies, amethysts, spinels, topazes, jacinths, chrysolites: in short, every kind of precious stone. Apart from that, some very beautiful little stones, whose name is not known, are encrusted in it. In short, it is a miracle and prodigy of nature. When placed in the sun, it has so much brilliance and beauty that there is no sight or loveliness in the world to equal it. When Bernardo Vecheti, sent by Duke Francisco de Medeçis of Florence, saw it, although he was a man who knew a great deal about stones, he was amazed and said that it was priceless and exceeded any estimate. The emperor has had it set in gold and covered with a tablet of pure gold and, at the urging of said Bernardo, he has had two gold desks made and has encrusted them with thousands of precious stones, having chosen the finest and most beautiful from the jewel collection, and he uses them {for} when ambassadors from the kings of Europe come, whom he receives beside and leaning on one of these desks.*[1]

Up to here are the words of Friar Luis de Urreta, to which {[f. 43]} we can easily reply that this so rich and <so> priceless treasure was like those treasures that people pretend were enchanted and could not be seen. Moreover, his exaggerations and way of telling the story are very similar to those used by people who deal in such fictions, for he claims that there are four {large and spacious} rooms filled from floor to ceiling with gold blocks three finger-breadths in thickness, and so pure that they bend like dough. It is a <very> marvellous thing, in addition to there being such a great hoard of gold, that blocks three finger-breadths thick should bend and curl as if they were {made of} dough. Nor should we find it any less amazing if we were allowed to enter that room of precious stones into which the flow of his history led the author by the hand, for on one side and the other it is lined with those very large, well reinforced chests, full of such beautiful and fine stones. But, above all, we should be astonished and awestruck if they raised for us that tablet of pure gold <[f. 37]> covering the boulder on which industrious nature, throwing off her necessary obligations, worked so perfectly that she put together in it all the precious stones that she normally produces scattered around different parts of the world. There is no doubt that, if we saw the beauty and brilliance of such varied and priceless stones, we should be forced to confess that our mind could never have imagined anything like what our eyes could see, and we should recognize a great marvel in this miracle and prodigy of nature. And the problem is that a rock two and a half spans square, or a little more, can be encrusted with all those gems that he names as well as those that he says have no name, some the size of the palm of one's hand and others two or three finger-breadths, unless someone were to say that these stones had the property of angels and occupied no space; although that cannot be true of corporeal things, I should readily concede that these did not occupy any space, for in truth they are nothing more than imaginary and fabulous. Nonetheless, since he claims to have what he says are eye-witnesses, it is worth describing the great investigation that I have made to find out the truth.

[1] Urreta, *Historia de la Etiopia*, bk I, excerpts (with some passages omitted) from ch. 11, pp. 127–8. Páez quotes these passages in Spanish.

First of all, it is quite certain that for many years, because of the wars with the Turks, Moors and Gâlas and the civil wars, which until a short time ago inflamed this empire, the emperors' income has been so diminished that they have not had any excess to hoard away, and very often they have not even found {[f. 43v]} a source from which they could draw enough for the needs facing them. So when Emperor Claudio – whom they call Glaudeôs in Ethiopia, and when he was given the empire he titled himself Atanâf Çaguêd – wished to send some Portuguese from Dom Christovão da Gama's company away content and to remunerate them in some way for the great services that they had rendered him, for after having recovered his empire for him they wanted to go to India, he had nothing to offer them but the jewels belonging to the empress his mother and some of his own that he was able to add, and so he begged their forgiveness for not having anything else with which he could settle the obligation that he had towards them but that, if they wished to stay, he would give them very extensive lands. The Portuguese, however, thanked him very much for the good will with which he offered them those jewels, {but} they would not take anything from him. Nor in the end did they go to India. I have also been told, as something quite certain, that Emperor Seltan Çaguêd, who is alive now, reached such a point in 1614 that he had some of his personal gold chains cut up in order to pay for certain things <[f. 37v]> that he needed; I can easily believe that because, apart from being very liberal with everybody, he had great expenses in the wars. Not because he is forced by justice, in accordance with the old custom of Ethiopia, to incur such expenses with the soldiers, because he divides up the crown lands among them and, so long as they eat from them, they are obliged to serve in the war, and not because the towns give them their pay, as Friar Luis de Urreta said through lack of information. Nevertheless, to keep them content and to honour those who most distinguish themselves, he always gives the captains and great men in particular brocade, velvet and damask robes and other items, which they buy from the Turks for much more than they are worth, together with gold daggers like those of the Turks, or gold bangles, which are commonly worth 200 or 300 *cruzados*. And sometimes he gives two together for greater honour, in addition to bribes and other expenses that occur.

But, to get to the details concerning the treasure on Mount Amharâ, which, as I have already said many times, is called Guixên Ambâ, I asked many elders and especially those two noble kinsmen of the emperor, *Abeitahûm* Memenô and *Abeitahûm* Taquelâ Haimanôt, whom I named above, and one of them must be close to seventy years old and the other close to sixty, who lived up there for a long time, although they now reside at court with the emperor's permission. And they told me that the emperors have never kept gold {[f. 44]} or precious stones on Guixen Ambâ; and that even in the old days, when the princes who were there {had more possessions}, 10,000 *cruzados* of gold would not have been found among all of them together; because, even though the emperors had promised to given them one third of the empire's income, this was never fulfilled. At most, what they were given consisted of cotton cloths, honey and provisions. I did not content myself with this but asked the emperor himself, telling him as if it were a joke that there were said to be a great many houses full of gold bricks and chests of precious stones on Guixen Ambâ. And he answered with a laugh, 'Just one would be enough for me, even if it were no bigger than this bed', which was a curtained bed on which he was reclining at the time. 'That man really exaggerated the riches of my empire, but the truth is that none of that has ever been kept on Guixên Ambâ.' It is so off-course and far from any truth to say that the emperor has a treasure of precious stones, for he could not even find enough for an emperor's crown, which he wanted to make in our fashion, except for a few very bad fake stones that the Moors bring here, perhaps from India, and so he greatly entreated me to have some brought for him. And even though the ones that they sent me were fake as well, yet he was very pleased because they were more sparkling. And some seed pearls came too, which he had requested for decorating the top of the crown, for not even these did he find here, let alone chests full <[f. 38]> of pearls as large as the ones Queen Cleopatra put in her ears; indeed, the emperor showed me two rings set with two seed pearls as if they were something special, but together they would not be worth six *cruzados* in India.

As for the dishes, bowls and jars of emeralds and other precious stones that he says the Prester John has, I can give a good account, because not only have I asked about them, but I have at times seen all his tableware and often eaten off his own dishes and table, because, when he rose from it (for nobody may eat with him or even be at his table, except for the officials that I mentioned above), he summoned me in from the room outside to sit with two or three lords, his kinsmen, to whom he sometimes does this favour and mercy. And, apart from the brass and copper service that he has, consisting of dishes and ewers – for there is no lack of this and {moreover} very well crafted, although in the style of the Turks – all the rest is some pottery from China, dishes and fine porcelains, and many local items, which are as black as jet. And that is the sum of all the emperor's tableware, since he does not eat off silver or gold. He has no lack of glassware, which the Egyptians and Moors who come from Cairo bring. But he has no dishes or jars made of emerald or {[f. 44v]} other precious stones, and nobody can say that there have ever been any in Ethiopia, or that such emerald and chalcedony mines have ever been discovered, as the author was made to believe. Nor is there any recollection of Queen Saba's precious stones, which he says are kept in the city of Saba, nor is there even any such city, but just a very miserable village of this name in the kingdom of Tigrê, where she was born; had they been there, they would not have been concealed from the emperor and, therefore, as he had such rich jewels in his land, he would not have needed to work to have fake stones brought from India for his crown.

From what we have said, it can clearly be seen how great a fable it is to say that Bernardo Vecheti and the other lapidaries that the author claims were sent by Francisco de Medeçis, Duke of Florence, came to this empire. For Joam Antonio the Venetian, who has been here for many years, and the old Portuguese men and local people all affirm that no others have come here apart from those that we have mentioned above. In addition, if, as the author himself claims on page 91,[1] it is true that the foreigner who came closest to the mountain where he says the treasury and library were only saw it from afar, for people are not allowed to come close to it, it follows that none of the foreigners who {he claims} came to see the treasury and library actually entered <[f. 38v]> there. Nor is any further proof needed of this than to know that there never has been such a treasure of pearls and precious stones in Ethiopia as they said. Even the emperor told me that there was no recollection that his predecessors had ever had any communication with the Dukes of Florence, when I gave him a letter from Duke Cosme de Medeçis, which the fathers of our Society sent me from India in July 1616, because a *Habexi*[2] monk who was bringing it remained there, and it

---

[1] Urreta, *Historia de la Etiopia*, bk I, ch. 8.
[2] See Glossary (*Abexim/Habexim/Habexi*).

was dated 7th April 1611 and said that the Most Serene Grand Duke Ferdinando his father was a great friend and servant of His Majesty and had a great affection for his nation; and that he, as his son, heir and successor, had the same will and affection, together with many other words of love and benevolence, in which he showed his desire to renew their friendship. At which the emperor was very pleased and told his secretary what he should reply, and the secretary added that he was pleased that he was being offered such a good opportunity to renew the friendship that his {ancestors} <predecessors> had had with the grand duke's {predecessors} <ancestors>. And, when he took the letter to the emperor, the latter told him in my presence to remove that, because he had never heard it said that his ancestors had ever had any communication with the Dukes of Florence. The secretary replied that, since the duke wrote in that manner out of friendship, {[f. 45]} it was unimportant and could well be left in, and therefore he let it pass.

Nor is there any force at all in what the author alleges, on page 114,[1] that the Portuguese Pêro de Covilham told Francisco Alvares, as the latter mentions on f. 167 of his *Historia*,[2] that the emperor of Ethiopia had such great treasure that he could buy a world with it, because they never took out any of what they hoarded away. It is easy to see that this is exaggeration and a way of speaking, and that we may call it very great hyperbole with more justification than he has when, taking too great a liberty, on page 113,[3] he terms hyperbole what the Holy Scripture says of Solomon's riches, because they were not the greatest in the world. And yet, in {42} <2> Paralipomenos 1, God promised to give him so many riches that no king before or after {him} would be like him: *Sapientia et scientia data sunt tibi. Diuitias autem et substantiam, et gloriam dabo tibi ita ut nullus in regibus, nec ante nec postea fuerit simili tui*;[4] and in 3 Kings 10 the Holy Scripture shows that this promise was kept, saying: *Magnificatus est ergo Salomon super omnes reges terrae divitiis, et sapientia*.[5] And, above the riches of Solomon and of all the kings that have ever been and are now on earth, Friar Luis places the treasures that the Prester John has on Guixên Ambâ, which he calls Mount Amarâ, which is all as fabulous as we have shown above. Nor did Francisco Alvares say that that treasure was <[f. 39]> on Guixên Ambâ in the rooms that the author depicts, but rather far from there in a cave, near which Pêro de Covilham had his houses. Nor did it contain the treasure that he imagined, but rather caftans of velvet brocade and damask, and other fine items that had been brought to the emperors from Mecca and Cairo, and some coffins, as Emperor Seltân Çaguêd assured me, when I asked him about this. And he said that everything was burnt when that Moor from Adêl, whom they call Granh, came. Nor has the income in gold ever been so great that the emperors might hoard much, as we shall see later when we deal with this.

There was also great exaggeration in what Empress Elena[6] said at the end of the letter that she wrote to King Dom Manoel of Portugal: that if he would raise 1,000 ships, she would give the provisions and would supply in abundance everything that was needed for

---

[1] Urreta, *Historia de la Etiopia*, bk I, ch. 10.

[2] Álvares, *Prester John of the Indies*, 1943, ch. 128, 'Of the way in which they carry the Prester's property when he travels and of the brocades and silks which he sent to Jerusalem and of the great treasury', p. 448.

[3] Urreta, *Historia de la Etiopia*, bk I, ch. 10, actually on p. 115.

[4] 'Wisdom and knowledge are granted to thee: and I will give thee riches, and wealth, and glory, so that none of the kings before thee, nor after thee, shall be like thee' (2 Paralipomenon [2 Chronicles] 1:12).

[5] 'And king Solomon exceeded all the kings of the earth in riches, and wisdom' (3 [1] Kings 10:23).

[6] See Glossary (Helena/Elena).

the fleet. And Friar Luis adds for as long as the war lasted. And he says that she was Emperor David's grandmother, but he was mistaken, because she was the wife of Emperor Naôd, whose son was David, but a bastard, as the emperor told me recently. And there was even greater exaggeration in what this David, who later was called Onâg Çaguêd, wrote in the letter that he sent to King Dom Joam, that he had gold, men and provisions like the sands of the sea and the stars of the sky. He wanted to aggrandize the things of his land, which, although very fertile, far from deserves {[f. 45v]} such words. And that great multitude of people of which he spoke was of little use to him afterwards, because when that Moor Grânh arrived with an army he took nearly all his lands. And he fled from place to place until he died in the kingdom of Tigrê. And if Dom Christovão da Gama had not come with 400 Portuguese to help, the Moors would have taken over the empire without anyone being able to stop them.

Regarding what Friar Luis de Urreta said, that Emperor Alexandre III, who died in the year 1606, struck oval coins with the image of Saint Matthew on one side and a lion with a cross in its hand on the other, etc., the information that he was given was all false, because, firstly, I have already said many times that there was never an Alexandre III in Ethiopia, and that when I arrived in May 1603 the Emperor was called Iacob. This was his baptismal name, and his throne name was Malâc Çaguêd, like his father. And, while he was a child, Empress Mariâm Cinâ governed together with her son-in-law *Erâz* Athanatêus, who persuaded all the great men that it was a good idea to strike coins, for they had not been used before then, and they began with copper. The shape was round and as large as a Venetian; on one side was engraved the image of Emperor Iacob from the waist up, with a crown on his head, and on the other side his name, without anything else. I was told this by people who had seen the coin and by one of those who had made the dies and opened them: a Greek goldsmith who is still alive. And they were so far from engraving Saint Matthew's image on the coins in Ethiopia that they found it very strange that Saint Mark's was engraved on Venetian coins. The people did not want to take this coin <[f. 39v]> since it was made of copper, and so they only struck 3,000 pounds in weight of copper, as this Greek told me, who had it weighed, and all that was lost. Then they returned to their old ways, which is to exchange some things for others, or to buy things with weighed gold.

The author was no less mistaken in saying that silver was worked and served as coinage to trade with merchants from other nations, because gold could not be taken out of the empire, but just silver. He should have said that only gold left the empire, because they traded with merchants of other nations only in gold, and there is no silver that might leave, rather they always buy it in from the Turks' port. And in recent years here they have been giving one pataca's[1] weight in gold for five patacas, although the usual rate is seven. Not because there are no silver mines, but because they do not seem to know how to extract it, because they have already tried a few times since I came here. And some that they showed me was very good, but they desisted because it was costing them a lot of work to extract very little.

[1] Silver coin of the Portuguese empire.

139

Which explains why the emperors' sons started to be put on
Guixên Ambâ, until which emperor this custom lasted, and how the
descendants of those first ones are held today

The main reason and cause for Guixên Ambâ to be so renowned and to have been so famous for a very long time, not only among foreigners but also among people native to Ethiopia, when there are other stronger places in the country that are no less suitable for habitation, is that this mountain or stronghold (not made by artifice but by nature herself), which lies in the kingdom of Amharâ, was chosen by the ancient emperors in order to hold in custody upon it not malefactors and enemies, but their own sons and brothers, for even these kinsmen's desire to reign is to be feared. But to understand this better, one must realise that Emperor Icûnu Amlâc, whom we mentioned {at the end of} <in> chapter 1, had five sons or, as others say, nine, and when he was about to die he implored them most earnestly to love one another dearly and to remain united, and said that each one should reign for one year, starting with the eldest. And so they did, but when the empire passed to the second brother – or, as those who say there were nine brothers claim, when it passed to the seventh – the youngest, who was called Freheçân, lost his patience, because the emperor and the one who had already been emperor always used to eat together at a table and, when they had finished, the remaining brothers would sit at it, but they would not let them wash their hands in front of them, but made them leave the room to wash, and then they would come in to eat. Annoyed with this, Freheçân said to his friends, 'I shall not act in this way, <[f. 40]> but when {the} <my> empire comes to me I shall seize all these brothers of mine and put them in a place from which they can never escape.' Somebody of course told the one who was then emperor, and so he immediately ordered all his brothers to be seized and, knowing that Guixên Ambâ was very strong and suitable for holding them, because the inhabitants were already Christian and had had churches since the time of Emperor Lalibelâ, some seventy years before, he commanded that they be taken there and given everything necessary in abundance and kept under good guard so that they might not escape. And there are still descendants of Freheçân on Guixên Ambâ today, as I was told by Emperor Seltân Çaguêd, who was one of those who told me this story.

From then until the time of Emperor Naôd, which must be about 212 years, it remained the custom to put the princes on Guixên Ambâ, and they would take them there when they reached the age of {[f. 46v]} eight. And over time they multiplied so much that they came to number more than 500, with wives and children, because they always married and kept their wives and sons up there, as those who are left still do today.

But their daughters have never been forbidden to leave and marry at will wherever they wish, because their daughters' sons cannot inherit the empire, and nor can the sons of even the emperor's daughters, because, if the emperor does not have male children, after his death they have to seek the one to whom the empire will belong via the male line among the princes who are outside Guixên Ambâ, and if there are not any, they have to bring out one of those who are held there. They say that these princes had been promised a third of the empire's revenue for their expenses, but they were given very little gold, although they had plenty of provisions, cotton cloths, butter, and honey for eating and for making wine, because they ruled over many lands around Guixên Ambâ, whose inhabitants supplied them with all these things in abundance. And these people were also obliged to build their houses and compounds, albeit of one storey and roofed with straw, as we have already said, and also to sweep them and clean whatever was necessary. The other people whose services they ordinarily used were slaves, and they could not have any other servants at all, for not only were they forbidden to have the sons of great men but also those of lesser rank, to prevent them from plotting to further their claims by availing themselves of these servants and their parents to influence those outside.

A very large watch and guard was posted, so that neither could the princes come down off that *ambâ*, nor could anybody go up without the emperor's express permission. These guards lived at the top in a house by the entrance gate (as we said in chapter 6), and they were changed from time to time, with some coming down <[f. 40v]> and others going up; these did not live at the foot of the *ambâ*, because there is no village there and there never has been, but some two gunshots away, along some mountains, called Habelâ, where they had been given some land to support them. Apart from these, there were {some} <other> noblemen who, on account of their offices, were called *acahâ ambâ*, *xobhêr* and *jan cirâr*, who were in charge of taking care of the princes' possessions, ensuring that the income from their lands was collected, and that they were provided with everything necessary at the right time, so that nothing should be lacking in their service. All messages and letters that came for the princes were given to these men and, after they had seen them, they would either deliver them or not, as they saw fit. They would also see the letters that the princes wrote and, if they found them acceptable, they would send them on, and if not they would tear them up. These men controlled the princes to such an extent that they would not even let them make changes to their everyday clothes. And so, when one of them saw a prince more strangely dressed than was customary, he gave him a slap and reprimanded him sharply, saying that that clearly showed that his {[f. 47]} heart was restless and wanted to reign, and he made him take off the clothes. Yet it happened that the emperor died soon afterwards, and the prince chosen was that one. When the man who had slapped him saw that, he kept away out of fear and shame at what he had done and never again dared appear before him. But once the emperor was enthroned, he summoned him; the man came in great fear and threw himself at his feet, begging his forgiveness for what he had so very rashly done. The emperor ordered him to rise and had rich robes and a gold bangle brought, and with gentle words told him not to be afraid, for he had served his lord very well by doing that, and that he should put on the robes and that bangle and return to his command, because he hoped that he would serve him with the same loyalty with which he had always served his predecessor.

The matter of the princes remained thus until the empire came to Zâra Iacob. I do not know why he grew angry with the members of Emperor Hezb Inânh's family, but he commanded that they should be taken from that *ambâ* to some very hot and disease-ridden lowlands called *colâ*, *scilicet* 'hot land', where only peasants lived. And he said that they would be Israelites of Colâ, which was tantamount to saying that he was taking away their nobility as Israelites who descended from the emperors and was making them peasants. They greatly resented this insult and the discomfort and hard work of their dwelling-place but, as they were under good guard, none of them could escape. And they were held there until, on the death of Zâra Iacob, his son Bêda Mariâm became emperor. He sent word to them thus: 'Perchance will the son not pardon that which angered his father? Return to your former dwelling-place of Guixên Ambâ and be not wrathful, for I shall <[f. 41]> be good to you.' And after they had returned to the *ambâ*, he sent three servants to ask them to see what they wanted, for he would please them in everything and offer them favours. But as they still held a bitter memory of the insult they had suffered and an even greater desire for revenge, they took no heed of what he offered them but instead seized all three servants and killed them and then took over the mountain top. The guards were unable to stop them because they were unprepared, as they had never expected such a thing and there were many of them. When he learnt of this, the emperor was furious and, burning with rage, determined to destroy and put an end to the descendants of that house. With that intention, he set off for there straight away with many men and, on arriving, tried hard to get his men up the mountain. But those on top, who were quite aware that his intention was to seek revenge, defended the very narrow and rough path to the top with rocks, so {[f. 47v]} that all the emperor's men found it impossible to get in. And so, albeit very reluctantly, he decided to turn back. But just then some local people came and told the emperor that they would show him a way up. He promised them great rewards, and they showed an entrance that they call *mestanquêr*, for the usual entrance is called *macaraquêr*. And, even though the rock on that side is so steep that none of those on top feared that anyone could get in that way, nonetheless they scaled it at night, holding on to little trees and roots sticking out from the cracks in the rocks. Shortly before dawn they suddenly came upon those on top, who, as they were unarmed and were not expecting such an attack, were soon overcome and taken to the emperor. He then commanded that eighty of them be beheaded, placed good guards on the *ambâ* and returned.

The third emperor after this Bêda Mariâm was called Naôd, and he was the last of the princes on Guixên Ambâ to be elected. The reason for this is said to have been that, when one day a son of his came before him, he remarked, 'Has this boy grown up already?' He replied, 'I have grown up enough for Guixên Ambâ.' That hurt the emperor so much that he swore that he would not put anyone else there, and he made the great men swear on pain of excommunication that even after his death they would not put any of his children there, but that they should continue to hold all those of the house of Israel who were already there. And that is what they have done until today. Even though, when Emperor Malâc Çaguêd died, which was in about 1596, they seized his nephew Za Denguîl, they did not take him to Guixên Ambâ but to an island called Dec, which is in the Lake of Dambiâ,[1] and they gave the empire to Iacob, the bastard son of Emperor Malâc Çaguêd. And later, in 1603, they seized Iacob and sent him under guard to the kingdom of Nareâ, not to Guixên Ambâ, and gave the empire to Za Denguîl. And Emperor Seltân Çaguêd,

---

[1] See Glossary (Dec/Daq; and Lake of Dambiâ/Lake Ṭānā).

who is alive today, had a son who died on 24th December 1616,[1] aged twenty, and now he has one of eighteen and another of seventeen and two younger ones, and none of them has ever been sent to Guixên Ambâ. They have always been at court with the emperor and are there now, because that custom ended with Emperor Naôd, who died 114 years ago before this year of 1622.[2]

<[f. 41v]> However, even though they have not put the emperors' sons on Guixên Ambâ ever since that time, they still kept a close guard on those who were already there until the time of Emperor Atanâf Çaguêd, who was first called Glaudeôs, *scilicet* 'Claudio', and who began to reign in about 1540. He paid little heed to them and did not care that some of them came down off the *ambâ* and stayed in {[f. 48]} some villages where they had their pastures. Afterwards this happened more and more, so they now only forbid fifteen remaining members of Emperor Hezb Inânh's family to come down, since they are afraid of them. All the others ordinarily come down in winter and stay in their villages, because in the rainy season the ascent is very difficult for the serving folk who take them firewood and provisions, etc. But in summer they go back up for fear of the heathen Gâlas, of whom we spoke in chapter 1, {who} <and> make many incursions particularly in that area, stealing and capturing women and children, for they kill all the men and {sometimes} <often> even the women, with great cruelty. All those who gather on Guixên Ambâ in summer must number 200, counting women and children. But they say that formerly there were more than 500.

This, briefly, is the situation with regard to what we proposed in the title to this chapter, according to the information I have been given by princes who have spent a long time on Guixên Ambâ and other lords of the court, and by Emperor Seltân Çaguêd; I asked him on purpose about the main things, saying that I wanted to write them down, in order to check the facts, as I have more confidence in talking to him. He told them in the manner that I have written them down here, agreeing with what the other lords had told me. Therefore, what Friar Luis de Urreta wrote in chapter 12[3] on this matter is all very much contrary to the truth, since there was none in the information that he followed. And to give the reader a better idea of what he says, I shall mention some of the {many} things that he recounts there, starting on page 132, where he says that putting the emperors' sons on Mount Amharâ is such an ancient tradition that it was instituted by King Josué, the grandson of Solomon and son of Menilehêc, in order to remove any opportunity for ambition, factions and civil wars; and that later some emperors, moved by love for their sons and forced by the supplications of the mothers, stopped doing it for a short time. But Emperor Abraham had a revelation from God to restore the ancient custom and once again place and imprison the crown princes on that mountain if he wanted to perpetuate the sceptre and monarchy in his generation and lineage of David.

It is easy to see how contrary this is to what we have said, because the emperors' sons began to be put on Guixên Ambâ, which he calls Mount Amharâ, many centuries after {the sons of} Menilehêc. Nor did Menilehêc have a son called Josué, as can be seen in the catalogues of the emperors that we put in chapter 5,[4] nor in any of them can one find an

---

[1] See bk IV, ch. 19 (ARSI, MS Goa 42), vol. II below.
[2] See Glossary (sons of Susneyos).
[3] Urreta, *Historia de la Etiopia*, bk I, ch. 12, pp. 129–39.
[4] See pp. 106–9 above.

emperor by the name of Abraham, nor is there anyone who knows of him, unless they mean that Abrahâ and Abraham are one and the same, but even if that were so this Abrahâ was also many hundreds of years before the son of {[f. 48v]} Emperor Icûnu Amlâc, who began to put the princes on Guixên Ambâ. I am well aware that Francisco Alvares <[f. 42]> in his *Historia Ethiopica*, ff. 66 and 73,[1] says that it was revealed to an Emperor Abraham that he should put all the princes on a mountain range, except the one who was to inherit the empire, and, as he did not know which mountain range that could be, it was revealed to him again that he should have his men look at the highest ranges and, where wild goats were seen to go as if they would fall off, that was the one where the princes of Ethiopia should be held. And, when he commanded his men to look for the mountain, he found it to be that one, which is so large that a man would take a good two days to climb it from foot to summit, all of it sheer rock and so steep and high that, when a man stands at its foot and looks up, it seems that the sky is resting on it. Up to here according to Francisco Alvares. And later, on f. 77,[2] he says that on top of that mountain range there are other ranges and hills that form some valleys; one of these valleys, between two exceedingly rugged mountains, is such that one cannot escape from it by any means, because it is closed with two gates. And in this valley they put those who are closest to the emperor, such as brothers, uncles, nephews and others, and they have been shut in recently, so that they may remain there more securely.

All this story is apocryphal, because neither was there such an Emperor Abraham, nor were the princes put on that mountain range because of a revelation, but for the reason that we have already stated. Nor did they put there at first just the princes who were not going to inherit, but also the heir, nor were they ever in a valley, but on top of Guixên Ambâ, which is not a mountain range as he describes, but as we described it in chapter 6. But it is no wonder that he made a mistake because, as he was a foreigner and was travelling along those roads in such a hurry and with such difficulty, as he says, he was unable to inform himself in any detail about things or to examine with all due care the reports he was given; even though some of these reports were taken from local books, they would demand careful examination since almost all of them were full of untruths.

Friar Luis de Urreta continues, on page 133:

*These princes gather whenever they please to play, hunt, fish and entertain themselves with whatever they like best. But they are all obliged to gather to hear Mass on feast days and the other holy offices; they must not be absent from such gatherings unless ill, and the order that they keep in this matter is as follows: there is a hall kept for this gathering which is very spacious and richly adorned with the most precious cloths and hangings of great value, and once all the princes are gathered there, they leave in order, making a procession in this manner. Four mace-bearers go in front, wearing black damask cloaks all highly pleated {[f. 49]} at the neck and so long that they drag on the ground in great skirts and trains, with long sleeves, which they call pointed sleeves, that reach the ground, and bearing their gold maces on their shoulders. Then there follows a young man dressed in damask made with whirls of black and yellow; his clothes reach down to his <[f. 42v]> calves and he holds a little*

---

[1] Álvares, *Prester John of the Indies*, ch. 59, 'Of the mountain in which they put the sons of the Prester John, and how they stoned us near it', pp. 237–8.

[2] Álvares, *Prester John of the Indies*, ch. 60, pp. 243–4.

*cushion in his hands, and on it a gold crown lined with blue satin, so as to make it clear with these insignia that all those princes are of the lineage and descent of David and suitable to be elected emperors. Then there follow the princes, two by two, the oldest taking the best position, which is on the right, dressed in black, each with his blue cross on his chest, fringed with gold thread at the edges – the cross is Saint Anthony's Tau with some little flowers – and a cleric's four-cornered biretta on his head, which has been worn since Paul III, who ordered it, for previously they wore round ones, which is the habit of the Knights of Saint Anthony. Behind them follow all the pages and servants, who are all nobles, the sons of kings, and after them all the other people. In this order they walk to the Church of the Holy Spirit, at the door of which the spiritual abbot of that abbey is waiting, dressed in pontificals, with the pastoral staff in his hand, and a military knight next to him holding a drawn sword, for this manner of attendance is customary for spiritual abbots. And sprinkling all the princes with holy water, they enter the church, the abbot placing himself at the left hand of the oldest of the princes, to whom he performs the same ceremonies in the course of the Mass as are customarily performed to the emperor.*[1]

Further on, he says that the monks of that abbey, of whom there are 1,500, take charge of teaching the princes and governing their palaces and servants, whom they take on and dismiss at will, and, in order to perform this ministry better, they appoint four of the monks each week to take charge of assisting and helping in the princes' service by commanding what has to be done. He also says that each of the princes has ten servants for the ordinary service of his person, and they are the sons or descendants of the vassal kings of the empire. They have a duty to serve there for one year and are chosen by the spiritual abbot, and, when the year is over, they return to their abbeys where they used to live and where they {[f. 49v]} were given the cross, but each one takes with him a very good jewel which the spiritual and military abbots {of the Holy Cross}, together with the prince whom they served, choose from the treasury of precious stones, according to the services performed by each one. And, as these go down from the mountaintop, ten others go up to serve the prince. Apart from these servants, his company includes some personal assistants distinguished in counsel, letters and virtue, sent by the emperor and his council, for the prince to make use of their discretion and virtue.

The author says these and many other things which, if they were true, would show great polity and governance, given that they had to have the princes there. But it is all mere fiction invented by the person who informed him because, firstly, as we said in chapter 6,[2] up there on the mountain there are no animals to hunt, except some that we call rabbits, since they look like the ones in Portugal, but nobody eats them, and also monkeys, but there are no fish; hence the princes cannot gather in order to hunt or fish, <[f. 43]> nor even do they gather to hear Mass in that hall that he portrays as being so ornate with rich cloths, because there is no such hall. At most, two of those princes may go to Mass together, if they are friends. And, if they do not want to hear Mass, nobody will ask them why, as they are far from being obliged to go to Mass. In that well-ordered procession that Joam Balthesar made up, neither do they wear a blue cross on their chests, nor does it appear that a four-cornered biretta has ever been seen in Ethiopia, let alone worn by them

---

[1] Urreta, *Historia de la Etiopia*, bk I, ch. 12, p. 133. Páez quotes this passage in Spanish.
[2] See bk I, ch. 6, above.

on their heads. Some wear turbans, others a round or pointed cap, in whatever colour they find. Most commonly they go bare-headed and wear their hair long. Their clothes are commonly white {cotton}, and they are not served by kings' sons, but by slaves, as I said above. Nor do I know where they would find so many kings' sons or descendants, if each prince had to have ten and they had to give him new ones every year. That shows how great a {fable} <falsehood> it is that, when the year is over, the spiritual and military abbots of the Abbey of the Holy Cross get together with the prince whom they served and go to the treasury of precious stones and give each one his own, according to his merits. For there are no such servants, nor has there ever been any treasure there, or an Abbey of the Holy Spirit or of the Holy Cross, nor is there such a religion of religious and military knights of Saint Anthony, {[f. 50]} nor have there ever been more than fourteen other monks up there, at most, and thirty clerics, as was stated in chapters {6} <5>,[1] 7 and 9.

At the end of chapter 12, on page 139,[2] the author says furthermore that it is forbidden, on pain of very severe punishment, for any woman to climb this mountain, whatever her status or rank, and that none has climbed up since Queen Candace, who lived at the time of Christ, who went up to baptize the princes who were there. And he refutes Francisco Alvares's claim that the princes up there on the mountain were married with children, who also married, because Joam Balthesar spoke as an eye-witness, as he had been a servant of Emperor Alexandre III, who died in 1606, when he was on the mountain as a prince, and later he often went up and lived on it. Francisco Alvares, however, wrote the truth of what happened then and still happens today, because it is patent and well-known by everyone in Ethiopia that the princes who were held on Guixên Ambâ used to marry and that their descendants always married and kept their wives and children up there, and still do, as <[f. 43v]> we have already said. He also stated what Joam Balthesar wanted when he said that he had served Emperor Alexandre III, who died in 1606, when he was on the mountain as a prince, because there has never been more than one emperor in Ethiopia with that name, whom they call Escander, and this one died in about 1475,[3] so a long time before Joam Balthesar was born, for the author says on page 7[4] that, when he arrived in Europe and gave him this information, he was nearly seventy, and the last prince that they took off that mountain to be emperor, who was called Naôd, left there some fifty years before Joam Balthesar was born; so from then until 1610, when Friar Luis's book was printed, it is 118 years. In addition, I arrived in Ethiopia in 1603 and did not find that Alexandre, as I stated in chapter 1, which shows how often he contradicts himself when he mentions Alexandre III in the course of his *Historia*. Nor could the princes there be served by {men} pages like Joam Balthesar, but rather by slaves, as was stated in chapter […].[5] Nor do I need to waste time refuting what he says about Queen Candace climbing up to baptize the princes, because I have shown at the end of chapters 1 and 7 that the first one who began to put them on that mountain was Udm Arâd in about 1295.[6]

---

[1] The chapter number in ARSI, MS Goa 42 is correct (ch. 6).
[2] Urreta, *Historia de la Etiopia*, bk I, ch. 12.
[3] King Eskender actually reigned 1478 to 1494.
[4] Urreta, *Historia de la Etiopia*, bk I, ch. 1.
[5] Páez leaves a space here in ARSI, MS Goa 42 to fill in the chapter number later.
[6] See, 'Historia de Ethiopia a alta', in Beccari, *RÆSOI*, 5, pp. 213–19.

Which describes how they used to elect an emperor in Ethiopia by choosing one of the princes from Guixên Ambâ, and how they do it now

The customs that Friar Luis de Urreta said were kept in the upbringing of the princes on Guixên Ambâ and in teaching them their letters and how to behave were very important and well ordered, as we saw in the previous chapter. But even more important and no less well arranged are the ceremonies that, as he claims in chapter 13, are held in the election of the Prester John, Emperor of Ethiopia, because, as he says on page 141:

*Among the people of Ethiopia, the title of emperor is handed down by succession and also by election, which is done with so much Christianity and virtue that it seems more like the election of a prelate among monks than the election of an emperor among lay folk; its style, observance and ceremony will be seen by those who accompany me in this chapter.*

*On conclusion of the obsequies for the previous emperor, his soul having been committed <[f. 44]> to God and his body to the ground,[1] the order is then given for the future election of the emperor, for which a fast is proclaimed throughout the empire for thirty successive days; not only are the clergy obliged to observe it by custom, but also all lay people of whatever status and rank. These fast days begin on the day when the death of the emperor is announced, and throughout these thirty days the Mass of the Holy Spirit is sung in all the countless churches of the empire. Meanwhile, the Grand Council, which stands in for the emperor and holds absolute power over all the empire while the vacancy lasts, orders that four of the subject kings of the empire go to Mount Amharâ, where, together with three patriarchs, three archbishops and three bishops and the ambassadors of the other kings, they must attend the election; they cannot lodge in any town or village at all, but only in their pavilions and tents, although the surrounding towns send them all they need to feed them and the people who accompany them in great abundance and plenty. On arriving at Mount {Amharâ} <Amaharâ>, they stay in their pavilions and wait until all those who are needed and have an office to perform in said election have gathered together. Meanwhile the two {[f. 51]} spiritual abbots from the two abbeys on the mountain, who are the electors of the emperor, come down to receive, visit and regale the members of the Grand Council, kings and prelates who are at the foot of the mountain and have come there for the forthcoming election. Once all those who are obliged to attend are gathered, the ambassador of the grand abbot or master of the Order of Saint Anthony indicates the proper day for the election of the emperor. Meanwhile all the prelates, archbishops and bishops sing Masses of the Holy Spirit in the pavilions, giving communion not*

---

[1] The author omits Luís de Urreta's reflections on the equality of all men in death.

*only to the electors, but also to any of the people who so desire. Every morning and evening they preach, exhorting and admonishing everyone to ask God, with tears and prayers, to grant the electors His spirit, favour and grace and wisdom, so that they may elect the right person for the spiritual and temporal benefit of the whole empire. And this manner of communing and preaching is maintained throughout Ethiopia until news arrives of the election of the emperor.*

*When the appointed day arrives on which the election is to take place, the princes of the lineage and house of David from whom the choice of emperor will be made confess and take communion in the Abbey of the Holy Spirit. <[f. 44v]> After communion, they take each of them to his own palace and shut them up there as in a conclave, in such a way that nobody may speak to them or see them and they may neither receive nor send any message. And there is a very diligent and vigilant guard to ensure that this is so. Once the princes have been shut up, the four kings, the abbots and ambassadors, the prelates and members of the Grand Council, who were in the pavilions at the foot of the mountain, climb up to the Abbey of the Holy Spirit. Inside the church, the four kings put on long, blue habits reaching to the ground, with gold chains, which is the figure of Saint Matthew the Apostle, and, wearing their crowns, they sit on a raised area that has been prepared for this purpose on the gospel side. A patriarch, an archbishop and a bishop, dressed in pontificals, sit on the epistle side, with a table in front of them on which is a book of the Gospels. Next to them are the members of the Grand Council with the other prelates, and behind them the ambassadors of the {[f. 51v]} other kings, according to the dignity and seniority of each one. This same order is kept by the four kings, who are assigned their places according to their seniority. This care is the duty of the spiritual abbots of the two abbeys on the mountain, and these two abbots, who are the electors, sit on their seats in the middle of the church in the company of the two military abbots and twelve councillors from the abbeys.*

*When all this has been done and all are seated in their places, the ambassador of the grand abbot enters and, sitting on a chair raised on two steps among the prelates and kings, he makes a brief speech to them all about the election. After the speech, the patriarch, who is on the epistle side next to the altar, has a hymn sung in the Chaldean[1] language, which is almost the same as the hymn the Latin Church sings for the Holy Spirit,* Veni, Creator Spiritus. *After the hymn, he calls the two spiritual abbots of the mountain and, making them swear on the book of the Gospels, which they have open on the table, to answer according to their conscience and, in voting for the emperor, to have regard only for the service of God and the welfare of the kingdom, without self-interest, passion or bias, he asks them how many princes of the house and lineage of David there are on the mountain and the age of each one and what their inclinations are, in which virtues they excel most, and what the defects of each one are that might most offend the commonweal of the empire; and having answered everything, the spiritual abbots kneel on the ground and the patriarch, raising his voice, says to them, 'Fathers, you who as confessors, as tutors and masters have held <[f. 45]> the office of spiritual and temporal fathers, governing and teaching these princes, you who know and recognize their natural inclinations and habits and understand the present needs of the empire, you who together want to remedy them, nominate among them the one who appears to you to be the most proper and apt for the government of the empire and for the greater service of God and the good of us all.' After this speech, the abbot of the Holy Spirit says: 'So-and-so has these*

---

[1] The name used by writers in the 16th–17th centuries for Ge'ez, perhaps because they associated Ethiopian Christianity with the Syrian Church.

*qualities and excels in such-and-such a virtue, and thus he appears to me to be worthy of such a dignity and deserving of the crown and sceptre of all Ethiopia, and as such I nominate him to be emperor.' And if the abbot beside him, who is from the {[f. 52]} Abbey of the Cross, is of the same opinion,* ipso facto *the nominated prince is elected. And if perchance these two abbots do not agree (which has never happened), the election passes to the other two military abbots of the abbeys on the mountain, with the twelve knights of their council.*[1]

Up to here are the words of the author. And, a little further on, he says that they have such Christianity and so much virtue and religion in their elections that there have never been factions, pretenders, schisms or partisanship; and that, since the emperors are so virtuous, the people of Ethiopia are so obedient to them that there have never been traitors or murderers or attackers of princes among them. On page 146[2] he says that, when the choice has been made and the prince who is to be emperor has been nominated, the two elector abbots go to where the prince is in reclusion and dress him in the habit of the knights of Saint Anthony and take him to the Church of the Holy Spirit, where the other electors are, and after many ceremonies they place a fine gold crown on his head and the sceptre, which is a gold cross, in his hand; of all the kings and monarchs in the world, not one holds a cross as a sceptre except the emperor of Ethiopia. And he goes on recounting so many things that, if I were to mention them all, it would add a great deal of writing and tire the reader with things that are very alien and very different from the way they are in Ethiopia. Nonetheless, he puts some things at the end of the chapter, on page 151, which, if true, would do much for his principal intention in his *Historia*, which is to prove that the people of Ethiopia have always been and still are highly obedient to the Holy Roman Church and have never accepted any doctrine contrary to its own, and therefore I shall mention them in his own words, which are as follows:

*Having spoken, the patriarch approaches the emperor and takes his oath, saying, 'Do you swear to keep all the divine laws and to ensure that they are kept throughout your empire? Do you swear to keep the four General Councils of Nicaea, Ephesus, Chalcedon and Constantinople? And do you swear to keep the Council of Florence celebrated by Eugene IV? Do you swear to keep observance and obedience {[f. 52v]} to the Holy Roman Church <[f. 45v]> of Saint Peter and Saint Paul the Apostles? And do you swear to keep the constitutions and statutes of our Emperor and Lord Juan the Holy and Phelipe VII? To all of which the emperor swears as requested.*[3]

After he has given this oath, the author says that they all rise and take the emperor {in procession} around the cloister,[4] singing hymns and psalms; when they re-enter the church, the emperor sits on his throne and all the others in their places in the same order as before. And the six men of the magistracy, together with the abbots and their council, go to fetch the other princes from the palaces where they have been shut up, and they

---

[1] Urreta, *Historia de la Etiopia*, bk I, ch. 13, entitled 'Of the election of the Prester John and Emperor of Ethiopia, and of the ceremonies performed at his coronation, and at the taking of the oaths', pp. 141–3. Páez quotes this passage in Spanish.

[2] Urreta, *Historia de la Etiopia*, bk I, ch. 13.

[3] Urreta, *Historia de la Etiopia*, bk I, ch. 13, p. 151. Páez quotes this passage in Spanish.

[4] Here, the ambulatory veranda that runs round the church, like an external cloister.

149

come to the church dressed in the habit of the knights of Saint Anthony. When they enter, everyone rises and bows to them, and they go two by two to where the emperor is and kiss his hand and swear loyalty and obedience to him. Then the four kings do the same and, after them, all the prelates and ambassadors according to the dignity and seniority of each one. And, this oath being concluded, the emperor retires to the rooms of the abbot of that abbey, and he is brought food and he rests for the remainder of that day and sleeps there that night.

With this, the author concludes his chapter {13} <12>,[1] in which, as we have seen, he says so many things about the election, oath and coronation of the emperor. But hardly any of them correspond to or have anything to do with what is customary in Ethiopia. Because, in the first place, the people have never gathered at Guixên Ambâ for the election of the emperor, nor have they sworn or crowned him there or had any other ceremonies than those that we shall mention later. Nor do they proclaim the thirty days of fasting that he mentions, nor do they preach, nor is there any subject king of the empire other than the King of Dancalî, who is a Moor and has never come to the court except once, a short time ago, to ask the emperor for help, because another kinsman of his had defeated him in battle and taken over the kingdom, but the emperor gave him men with whom he returned to recover it. In addition, formerly (as they say) the King of Dequîn, a Moor, used to be a subject, but he is no longer; he is just on friendly terms. And these kings would not be involved in the election, because they are Moors, nor would any heathens, nor can the king who is still alive today in the kingdom called Zenyerô take part, because he is a heathen. And Friar Luis de Urreta also shows that the kings of whom he speaks are Christian, because on page 161[2] he says that the men who bring each king before {[f. 53]} the emperor to swear say, 'Lord, here is the king of such-and-such a kingdom who has come to swear loyalty and obedience to you. He says he has lived in a Catholic manner and has devoutly kept the holy Council of Florence,[3] etc.' He says that they all swear in that way. But now there is no Christian king other than the ruler of the kingdom of Nareâ, for about thirty-two years ago [this year being 1622] Emperor Malâc Çaguêd went there with an army and made it Christian, and this king does not come. If there used to be some formerly, they know nothing about them. The author was mistaken in thinking – or was told by Joam Balthesar – that mere viceroys were actually kings. Thus he says on page 162 that those that Francisco Alvares called viceroys in his *Historia* <[f. 46]> he himself refers to as kings, because they are true kings, and therefore the kingdom is passed down from fathers to sons and, if the emperor deprives someone of the kingdom, his son or closest kinsman succeeds him. But there is no such thing, because the emperor removes anybody whenever he likes, often before they have been there for three years, and he puts in others who are not their sons or kinsmen, as I have seen on many occasions. Nor have I found anyone who said that kings ever took part; not even in the very ancient book that they have about the ceremonies that must be held and about those that have to gather to crown

---

[1] Urreta, *Historia de la Etiopia*, bk I, ch. 13, pp. 140–52. The chapter number (13) given in ARSI, MS Goa 42 is the correct one.

[2] Urreta, *Historia de la Etiopia*, bk I, ch. 15, entitled 'Como los Reyes de los Reynos de la Etiopia sujetos al imperio, dan la obediencia al emperador quando le juran por tal, y despues de siete en siete años' ['How the kings of the kingdoms of Ethiopia who are subject to the empire give obedience to the emperor when they swear him in and every seven years thereafter'], pp. 156–62.

[3] See Glossary (Council of Florence).

the emperor is there any mention at all of any king or of patriarchs, archbishops or bishops, because in Ethiopia there are none, except the prelate that the Patriarch of Alexandria sends to them, whom they call *abuna*, which is an Arabic name that means 'our father'. Not even he is a patriarch, as I was told by *Abuna* [Simam],[1] whom they killed a short time ago, as we shall say below; I asked him whether he was a patriarch (among other things), and he answered that he was not, but a bishop, and that his predecessors had never had such a title, either.

This *abuna* is <not>[2] the {only} one who confers orders. But in 1615 he was challenged by a monk, who is like the general of the religion that they call *Taquelâ Haimanôt, scilicet* 'Plant of the Faith', and whose title is *icheguê*,[3] saying that he had the right to confer orders and the *abuna* had the right to bless the oils. After each of them had stated his case at length, the judges appointed by the emperor ruled that only the *abuna* could confer orders, as we shall describe further in book 2, where we shall deal with the way in which he confers orders and with the archbishops and bishops that somebody put into Frei Luis de Urreta's head as existing in Ethiopia.[4] As for the spiritual and military abbots {[f. 53v]} of the Order of Saint Anthony, I said at the end of the previous chapter and of chapter 7 that there has never been such a kind of religion in Ethiopia, and we shall see that at greater length at the end of the second book. As for where he says that in the {elections} <election> of the emperors there have never been factions, schisms, partisanship, traitors, murderers, or attackers of their princes, we have already seen in chapter 5 how the Zaguê family usurped the empire for 340 years. And later we shall see how many revolts, partisan rebellions and uprisings there have been in Ethiopia, particularly in the last sixty years. Where he says that, of all the kings and monarchs in the world, not one holds a cross as a sceptre except the emperor of Ethiopia, he is also much mistaken, because they do not bear a cross as a sceptre (nor do I think that they have ever known what a sceptre is), but rather to show that they are deacons, for deacons and priests ordinarily hold crosses <[f. 46v]> in their hands that are about a span and a half long and are usually made of iron. Deacons' orders are taken by the emperors and great men just so that they can {go in and} take communion and hear Mass where it is said, because all those who have not taken orders remain outside on the veranda that they have around the church, without being able to see what is happening inside, because there are curtains in front, and communion is brought out to them there.

But to come to the most essential thing that the author mentions in this chapter, regarding the oath that the patriarch gives the emperor to swear, that he will keep the four General Councils and the Council of Florence and obedience to the Holy Roman Church, I say that it would please Divine Mercy if the emperors did so and kept them, because they would have saved all the many thousands of souls that, through lack of such obedience, have already been lost and will be lost in future, unless His Divine Majesty calms His wrath and gives them particular grace to submit to His Holy Roman Church and the doctrine that it teaches. However, such an oath is not given to the emperor at all,

---

[1] See Glossary (Simam/Simão).

[2] The 'not' here does not make sense, since the *abuna*, or metropolitan, conferred orders on members of the secular clergy.

[3] See Glossary (*icheguê/icheguê/eččagê*).

[4] See bk II, ch. 13, below.

and in the book that contains the ceremonies that they use at the emperor's coronation there is no mention of such an oath. Since this is something of such great moment, I was not content with asking many elders and great lords, but I asked Emperor Seltân Çaguêd himself, who is alive now; he told me that such an oath was not given to the emperors to swear, and he was not given any oath at all to swear, but that, when there were two competitors for the empire, the winner had to swear to fulfil the conditions that he conceded to his competitor. Furthermore, how could they make the emperor swear that he would keep the Council of Chalcedon[1] if they themselves do not accept it? {[f. 54]} In fact, they speak of it in terms so alien to Christians that they call it the 'Council of Jews'. And a book that they entitle *Mazaguêbt Haimanôt*,[2] which means 'Treasury of the Faith', speaks of this council and says: 'There gathered together 630 foolish masters, with vanity and pride, wishing to be double the number of the 318 just men of the faith.' And {a little} <therefore> further on it says:

*They took a word out of the faith of Nestorius, who put two persons in Christ, one of the son of Mary and the other of the son of God, and they said that by their union they formed one person. They said this because of the Patriarch Cyril's excommunication[3] and composed it from the words of the Patriarch Cyril and the words of Nestorius, and so they said {Christ one} person, two wills, two natures, two intents, of the Godhead and of the manhood. They said that the Godhead performs works of Godhead, and the manhood works of manhood, by two paths: one works wonders and the other suffers infirmities, and therefore the manhood is less than the Godhead.*[4]

<[f. 47]> Up to here are words from that book, in which they want to show that many men came together on purpose at the Chalcedonian Council in order to undo by force what the fathers at the Nicene Council had determined, as if there they had dealt with the two natures, two wills and two operations in Christ, and as if that had been an error in faith, which they claim it is. And, for that reason, they speak of Saint Leo the Pope in very base terms, saying that he was like Lucifer. And, in a book that they call *Haimanôt Abbô*, *scilicet* 'Faith of the Fathers', Theodosius, the patriarch of Alexandria, says these words in chapter 2: 'We do not separate, like that accursed enemy Leo, who separated Him who was not separated and said two natures, two intents, and two works to one Christ.' And a little further on he says: 'This accursed and treacherous Leo said two natures and two works and, in saying one person, in this the accursed wished [to conceal][5] his error {in saying one person.' In other words, to conceal his error} of the two natures, etc., Saint Leo put one person.[6]

Regarding what they feel about the Council of Ephesus, I shall include the words of a letter signed by the Fathers Manoel Fernandez and his companions of our Society, who came to Ethiopia with the Father Bishop Andre de Oviedo, which was reported by Father

---

[1] See Glossary (Council of Chalcedon).
[2] See Glossary (*Mazaguêbt Haimanôt*/*Mazgaba Hāymānot*).
[3] See Glossary (Nestor/Nestorius; and Cyril of Alexandria).
[4] See Cerulli, *Scritti teologici etiopici*, p. 77.
[5] Words added in the translation to complete the meaning (see bk II, ch. 3, p. 321 below).
[6] See Glossary (*Haimanôt Abbô*/*Hāymānot Abaw*; and Leo I, Pope).

Fernão Guerreiro in chapter 5, folio 296, of the addendum[1] that he makes to the matters of Ethiopia, in the report for the years 1607 and 1608. Their words are as follows:

*And although by divine grace the bishop* {[f. 54v]} *always had the last word with him* (that is, Emperor Claudio) *and all the others, they however would jeer and shout that they had won, so that everything he said was in vain. Therefore, as the father bishop could see how little progress he was making in this matter, he took all the main subjects and points of their errors and set out to write upon them, and later he presented these documents to him, to which the king replied by writing other documents on these, resolving at the same time that he would not obey Rome. And, after he had stated this abundantly and shown his displeasure with the bishop and said publicly that he would not accept the First Council of Ephesus, which the bishop was urging him to embrace, but instead only the customs and faith of his forefathers, the bishop took his leave of him determined* (saltem ad tempus[2]) *to make room for his displeasure. The king gave these very clear indications of his real feelings at the end of December '58.*[3]

As for the fact that Friar Luis de Urreta says that he swears to keep the constitutions of Emperor Joam the Holy and Phelipe VII, I reply that not only are there no such constitutions, but that there have never been such emperors in Ethiopia, as we shall show later.

We have already seen how fabulous the information was that Friar Luis de Urreta followed about the election of the emperor. Let us now see what some of the princes of Guixên Ambâ, with whom I have spoken, have to say, as well as some other very old men, both great lords and monks, particularly one who is called *Abba* Marcâ, who must be over eighty years old, a learned man who has a good deal of knowledge about ancient things; Emperor Seltân Çaguêd made him *quêz acê*, which means 'the emperor's priest' and seems to correspond to chaplain of the royal chapel. I obtained my information from these people, since I could not find <[f. 47v]> a book dealing with this subject. They said that when an emperor died, the electors of the prince to whom the empire was to be given would ordinarily meet at court straight away; these electors were some of those who had the same titles as the officials that Solomon gave to his son Menilehêc for the government of his empire and service of his household, whom we named in chapter 4. And they are: *behêt oadêd*, of the right hand and of the left hand; *uzta azâx*, of the right hand and of the left hand; *hedúg erâz*, of the right hand and of the left hand;{ *goitâ*, of the right hand and of the left hand; *acabiçât*}. These were the electors of the one who was to be emperor, but they always included as advisers some important religious men and doctors whom they call *debterôch*, and all together they would discuss among themselves which of the princes of Guixên Ambâ would be most suitable for the good {[f. 55]} government of the empire and most useful and worthwhile for its vassals. And, after each one had answered according to the information that he had about the princes, the electors would make their decision and name the prince who appeared best to them. Then they would call in a great lord, whose office it was to summon the elected prince and, because of his charge, he was titled

[1] Páez is referring to Guerreiro's 'Adição à Relação das coisas de Etiópia', which was published with the *Relação annual,*1611 ( 942, pp. 287–380).
[2] Latin: 'at least for the time being'.
[3] Guerreiro, 'Adição à Relação das coisas de Etiópia', p. 324.

*jân çarâr*, 'summoner of the emperor', and they would tell him to go to Guixên Ambâ and call said prince. And *Tigrê* {*mohôn*} <*mahôn*>, who used to have much greater power and command than he has now, would go with him, taking a great company of armed men. Having climbed the mountain, they would enter the house of the elected prince and *jân çarâr* would say to him, 'The governors summon you', because the electors were the governors of the whole empire while the throne remained vacant. And they would straight away put in his right ear a gold ring, which they call *belûl*, which was the insignia of having been chosen emperor, as we said in chapter 5. Afterwards, all the princes on the mountain would gather and congratulate him on his good fortune. Taking his leave of them with great demonstrations of love, he would go down to the plain, where there was a fine tent erected with all that was needed in the way of mules and horses for the journey, on which they set out the following day.

While the prince was on his way, the governors would prepare the reception that they would give him and, when he drew near, they would go out to the road with great accompaniment and splendour, all dressed for the celebration. Dismounting from their mules and horses, they would bow before him, and he would then gesture with his hand for them to ride on, and they would surround him and take him with much music and dancing to a field tent that they had erected, which was very large and round, rather like ours, which they call *debanâ*.[1] And nobody can have a tent of this kind except the emperor; other people's tents are not round, but long and much smaller. And he would only dismount inside the tent. Then *quêz acê*, *lîca debterôch*, *lîca memerân*, *cerâi maçarê*,[2] who are ecclesiastical dignitaries like priors, and many priests would gather round him and sing psalms. Then *cerâi maçarê* anoints him with sweet-smelling oil and they dress him in a rich robe that they call *lebzaçahâi*, which means 'robe of the sun', and they place on his head {[f. 55v]} a <[f. 48]> gold crown topped with a cross and in his hand an unsheathed sword to signify that, in matters of justice, he has to cut straight, without heeding kinship or friendship, however great it might be, or being swayed by any other human respect. And then *quêz acê* and the other dignitaries take him by the hand and seat him on the imperial throne, which they have richly adorned, and there they give him many blessings.

After this, *quêz acê* climbs on a high chair and, like one making a proclamation, says, 'We have brought so-and-so to reign.' And then those around shout in a certain manner, which they employ as a sign of great celebration and joy, and they play many instruments. Then the electors and other magistrates come to kiss his hand and give him their obedience; *quêz acê*, *lîca debterôch*, *lîca memerân* and all the priests who are present do the same. And great celebrations begin, which last for many days. But the coronation ceremonies do not end with that, for rather they do not consider it a coronation and he cannot be called emperor, but only king (so they say), until he is anointed and crowned in the church of Agçûm in the kingdom of Tigrê with the ceremonies that we shall see in the next chapter, or, at least, in a church in the kingdom of Amharâ that is called Garangarêdaz.[3]

---

[1] See also bk I, ch. 14, and bk III, ch. 13, vol. II below.

[2] See Glossary (*lîca memerân*/*liqa mamhérān*; and *cerâi maçarê*/*şerāg ma'asaré*)

[3] See bk I, ch. 12. See also, 'Historia de Ethiopia a alta', in *RÆSOI*, 5, pp. 221–3. Baltazar Teles summarizes this description (Teles, *Historia geral de Ethiopia a Alta ou Preste Ioam*, bk I, ch. 18, pp. 48–9; Tellez, *The Travels of the Jesuits in Ethiopia*, bk I, ch. 9, pp. 49–50).

This is what used to happen, when they chose one of the princes in Guixên Ambâ to be emperor. But ever since Emperor Naôd they have not taken any from there; they have always given the empire to the eldest son of the emperor who has died. And Emperor Athanâf Çaguêd, who had no son, was succeeded by Adamâs Çaguêd, his brother, and he was succeeded by Malâc Çaguêd, the eldest of his four sons. But when the latter died far from his court, on his way back from war, not only the great men who were in the encampment but also the captains and all the heads of families of the soldiers, who are many, gathered together to elect an emperor, and they appointed Iacob, the bastard son of the deceased emperor, because he had no other.

# CHAPTER XII

## Of the ceremonies that they perform in Ethiopia at the emperor's coronation

When the ceremonies and celebrations that we described in the previous chapter are over, {[f. 56]} they set the time that they consider most appropriate for anointing and crowning the emperor in the church of Agçûm in the kingdom of Tigrê, because, although sometimes they were crowned in Garangarêdaz church in the kingdom of Amharâ, they considered it a greater honour to be crowned in the one in Agçûm, as it had been the capital of Queen Saba and her son Menilehêc and a very sumptuous city, although now it is a very small village. And they thought it less inconvenient to put off the coronation for a long time than to hold it elsewhere, and many of them did so, <[f. 48v]> particularly Emperor Malâc Çaguêd, who only went to be crowned in Agçûm after holding the empire for many years, although he could easily have been crowned in the kingdom of Amharâ, had he so wished. And his son Iacob, whom I met, was never crowned, despite holding the empire for ten years or a little less after being elected, counting six or nearly seven years while he was young when the empire was governed by Empress Mariâm Cinâ, his father's wife, since he was illegitimate.

[1]When the time arrives for the emperor to be crowned, he travels with great splendour to Agçûm, where the book of the ceremonies[2] that have to be performed at the coronation of the {emperors} <emperor> is always kept. It also contains the names of the officials who are obliged to attend, but in the manner that they used to be named, and I shall put them thus here:

Elahaquetât, scilicet *'head of the people or chief steward'*; quelebâs, scilicet *'counsellor',* *and he bears a small box;* ceraimacarê, *this one bears oil to anoint the king in a gold box, and holy water;* quezagabêz, scilicet *'church treasurer';* lîca diaconât, scilicet *'archdeacon';* arnês *who is* maçarê, *who goes in front, keeping the people back with a long, thick rope of silk yarn tied to a short stick;* arnês *who bears the parasol or sunshade;* ceoâcergôi, scilicet *'godfather';* delcamoâ, *and* negûz hezbâi,[3] scilicet *'governors of the king's household';* râcmacerâ, *and* deccâf, scilicet *'groom of the horses' and 'groom of the mules'. All these attend the coronation ceremonies and offices and stand when they anoint him [with the objects of their charge in*

---

[1] New paragraph made by the editors.

[2] This is the *Śerʿâta Qwerhat* (ceremony of royal consecration), which Páez has partly translated and partly summarized from a Geʿez manuscript.

[3] *Dalkamay waneguś hezbay.* Manuel de Almeida, in his 'Historia de Ethiopia a alta', proposes a different reading: 'De Lamoâ ye Negus Hezbâj' (see Beccari, *RÆSOI,* 5, p. 88).

*their hands], six on the right-hand side and six on the left-hand side, and no one else takes part in this duty;* elahaquetât *brings wild and domestic animals and birds that can be eaten;* quelabâz *brings flowers from the field and fruit and all kinds of seeds that are eaten;* ceoâcergôi *brings milk and grape wine; the 'maidens of Sion' bring water and honey wine and sweet-smelling leaves;* {[f. 56v]} *the one bearing the box brings musk in it, which is an unguent of the kingdom; the* quezagabêz *and the* lîca diaconât *stand holding the altar stone;*[1] râcmacerâ *holds the horse by the bridle and* deccâf *the mule.*

{*Those who bring the presents from Belenê, which is*}

*The king rides his horse to Agçûm from the east, and outside in a designated place there wait, as people always wait for their kings, all the great men and the people, each in his own place, all the clergy with their vestments and splendour, and three maidens in the middle, one on the right hand and another on the left, some distance apart, and the third between the other two. The two at the sides hold a rope of silk yarn by its ends, so that it is held across the road along which the king must pass. And when the king draws near, the one in the middle says to him, 'Who are you?' He replies, 'I, the King.' She says, 'You are not.' She asks a second time, 'Of whom are you king?' and he answers, 'I am King of Israel.' She says, 'You are not king.' She asks a third time, 'Of whom are you king?' Then the king pulls out his sword and cuts the rope, saying, 'I am King of Sion.' She says, 'Truly, truly, you are King of Sion.' And then all <[f. 49]> those present, great and small, utter the same words and fill the air with cries of joy and they all play their instruments. The king goes past, scattering gold on the ground, which is picked up only by those who are accustomed, and, on reaching the gate to the church compound, where many carpets are laid on the ground, he again scatters gold on them and this is collected for the church as it is a present for Sion.*

*Those who bring the presents are: from Belenê, which is the land of* {Amacên} <Amacê>, *they bring* torâ, *scilicet wild cow; from Zalamt and Zagadê,* gox, *scilicet buffalo; from Cemên,* hayêl, *which is like a deer but with different horns; from* {Açâ} <Açê> *they bring* agacên, *which is also like a deer, but with twisted horns; from Torât they bring* iabedû, *which is wild goat;* Tigrê mohôn *brings* ambaçâ, *scilicet lion, and other fierce animals. King* {Grâbra} <Gâbra> Mazcâl, *on the advice of Iarêd, a priest, added to this the ceremony that is performed on Palm Sunday, commanding the people to bring palm fronds and olive branches with fruit. The priests stand with the cross and thurible and the singers sing* Benedictus qui venit in nomine Domini,[2] *etc., and* {[f. 57]} *other songs with various tunes, and two particularly praising the king. All this they sing while walking round and round the place where they hold the ceremonies, and then they bring out the Old and the New Testaments and read the parts that deal with kings and priests as well as the Psalms of David and the Song of Solomon and other songs. And then the people who are present go as if in a procession once round the place where the royal chair is and they throw flowers and scents onto it and, if there is someone in the place of the ceremonies who is not one of those appointed, they throw him out. And, close by, a lion and a buffalo are tied to columns, and the king wounds the lion with his spear, and then they release the other tame and wild animals and all the birds, and the people of the encampment kill those they can catch in celebration.*

*As the king enters the place where his chair is, he scatters gold over the carpets placed on the ground. He sits on the chair, and they bring two gold dishes and two silver: in the two gold*

---

[1] See Glossary (altar stone/*tābot*).

[2] 'Blessed is he that cometh in the name of the Lord' (Matthew 21:9, 23:39; Mark 11:9; Luke 13:35; John 12:13).

*dishes, milk and honey wine, and in the silver ones, water and grape wine. Then they anoint the king in accordance with the custom and sprinkle all the ceremonial objects with water that they have from the River Jordan, and they cut the hair on the king's head like that of clergy having their first tonsure, and the clergy take the hair, and the deacons the altar stone and lit candles. And they go away singing, and the clergy censing with thuribles. And after walking round the place where the royal chair is, as in a procession, they go to a stone that is at the door of the church {of Sion}, which is called* meidanita negestât, *scilicet 'protector of kings', and place the hair on it <[f. 49v]> and set light to it with the thuribles and then all the clergy commend the king to God and Our Lady. When they return, they tell the king everything that they have done. Then they begin to sound all the instruments in the encampment, and the people shout with joy. Then the king goes to the church and, coming close to the altar, he commends his soul to God and Our Lady, and then he returns to the place where he was anointed. There he stands in the midst of the twelve officials, six on his right hand and six on his left as before, and the abuna arrives with the priors of the churches, clergy and deacons, and each one separately gives him his blessing. Then come the great men and likewise each* {[f. 57v]} *gives his blessing and, when they have finished, the king also gives his blessing to them all and then goes to his house accompanied as he came.*[1]

[2] Up to here are words from the book, and it says nothing else about the emperor's coronation, from which it may be seen that, as it names those who are obliged to attend it, it makes no mention of kings, patriarchs, archbishops or bishops. It certainly would not fail to mention such personages if they took part in this act and, if there were any in Ethiopia, at least some would not fail to take part; that confirms what we said in the previous chapter, that the information that Friar Luis de Urreta had on this matter was very fanciful.

I could have provided first-hand confirmation of all these ceremonies if Emperor Seltân Çaguêd had not unintentionally prevented me. A tyrant had risen up in the kingdom of Tigrê, pretending to be Emperor Iacob (who had died in battle the previous year but there was a rumour that he had escaped), and so many people joined him that the emperor was forced to go there from Dambiâ with an army in March 1608, and he decided to be crowned in Agçûm while passing through. I was very pleased at that, as I wanted to see that celebration, for I was in Tigrê at that time. And so I went with another father to welcome him a day's journey away, for which he thanked us greatly and did us many honours. He had pitched his main tent among some trees beside a stream. And the whole plain, though very large, was filled with tents and a great multitude of people, but it seemed to me that the pure fighting force numbered no more than 25,000 men. From there he went on to Agçûm and arrived on a Saturday morning and, as they said that he was to be crowned that very day, I went ahead and took a place where I could see everything. But he did not want <[f. 50]> to enter the town; he remained about a quarter of a league away on a very flat plain and, before noon, he summoned me and said that he would only be there on the Sunday, and on Monday he wanted to go and hear Mass and the sermon at our church, which is some two leagues from there, along the road that he

---

[1] This passage is also to be found in Almeida ('Historia de Ethiopia a alta', in Beccari, *RÆSOI*, 5, pp. 88–90, and Beckingham and Huntingford, *Some Records of Ethiopia*, pp. 93–6). There are slight differences in translation and a completely different arrangement.

[2] New paragraph made by the editors.

had to take. And so I went off straight away so as to be able to arrange the church and prepare everything necessary, but the captain of the Portuguese, who is called Joam Gabriel,[1] who was coming with him, told me later that, that afternoon, some monks went to the emperor's tent together with the abbot of the monastery that there is in Agçûm, in the church of which he was to be crowned, and they took the book where {[f. 58]} the ceremonies that we mentioned above are written, and they read them all out loud to him so that he should know what he had to do. He listened attentively without disapproving of anything. But, after they had left, he said to the captain, 'As for me, I will not do all the things that these monks said, because some appear to me like heathen superstitions.' The captain replied, 'Lord, I did not notice anything against the faith, so in that case, if Your Majesty refuses to do them, it will be widely noticed, because the monks will complain, and others will say that Your Majesty scorns and disapproves of what all emperors have done and learned men have approved.' The emperor said that he had not noticed anything against the faith either, but that some of those things seemed highly impertinent to him.

On Sunday morning, the emperor came out richly dressed in brocade and crimson satin, with a gold chain round his neck, from which hung a very fine cross; he was riding a powerful horse that was very well decked out, and because he was one of the best endowed of his court in stature, of dark complexion, with a long face, large and handsome eyes, a slender nose, thin lips and a well-proportioned, long black beard, he looked very majestic. He was then thirty-two years old.[2] He was preceded by all his captains, each with his troop drawn up in order with men on foot in the vanguard and then those on horseback, all dressed for celebration with many banners and playing their drums, trumpets, shawms and flutes, which they have in their own fashion, and firing many guns so that the whole of that broad plain echoed. Lastly came the emperor with many lords on horseback. The *abuna* was waiting about a crossbow-shot away from the village, together with many monks and clerics bearing crosses and thuribles, and a great throng of people. They had placed many carpets on the ground along a stone that was not very tall, two cubits {wide} <high> and less than two spans thick, flat on both sides, <[f. 50v]> and written all over with such ancient letters that there is nobody now who can read them. As the captains arrived, they arranged themselves on either side of the road and they all dismounted. The emperor passed through the middle of them and dismounted just before he reached the place where the priests were, and he walked on alone until he reached the rope of silk yarn that two maidens were holding by the ends, as we said above is ordained in the book of ceremonies. And the other one in the middle asked him, {[f. 58v]} 'Who are you?' He answered, 'I, the King.' She said, 'You are not.' Then he turned round, walked back five or six paces, turned round again towards her (even though this is not in the book, the monks told him that he had to do so) and, as he reached the rope, she again asked, 'Of whom are you king?' He replied, 'I am King of Israel.' She said, 'You are not our king.' He turned round as before and, as this was one of the things he thought were impertinent, he could not help giving a hint of a smile, although few noticed it. The third time that the maiden asked him, he took hold of a very fine broad sword that he was wearing slung over his shoulder and cut the rope, saying, 'I am King of Sion.' And, sheathing his sword again, he

---

[1] See Glossary (João Gabriel).

[2] This portrait of Susneyos is of great interest for reconstructing an image of the king, since such descriptions were not at all common and nothing similar can be found in Ethiopian accounts.

159

started scattering little pieces of gold over the carpets. The maiden said twice, 'Truly, you are King of Sion. Enter.' And then everyone shouted, 'Hail, hail the King of Sion.' And they began to sound all the musical instruments that they had and to fire their guns in great celebration.

When this was over, they went in procession to the monastery, the monks and clerics singing *Benedictus qui venit in nomine Domini*,[1] etc., and other things, until they entered the first enclosure, where there is a large courtyard and, under some trees, twelve finely carved stone seats placed in a row and, a short distance away, four stone columns with well-made capitals – it seems that they formerly supported a dome – and between them two more stone seats. They say that on these and the other twelve there used to be very finely carved stone chairs and that when the emperor was crowned they were all covered with silks and brocades. Francisco Alvares also says on folio 45[2] of his *Historia* that they were there and that they were made out of a single stone and fashioned so naturally that they seemed to be made of wood, and that those twelve were for the twelve magistrates that the emperor brought in his court. But now there are no such chairs, although one can see the slots in the stone where it seems they used to fit. And the book of ceremonies also suggests that, when it says that the royal chair was in the place where the ceremonies were performed, because <[f. 51]> they always used to crown the emperors who lived in Agçûm where those columns are. They just covered these two seats between the columns with silk cloths and the ground with very beautiful carpets. And the emperor sat on the right-hand seat and the *abuna* on the left-hand one. The monks and clerics remained outside {[f. 59]} a low stone parapet that they had made anew around the columns, and they sang and read from the books for a long time. At certain points, the *abuna* would rise and perform his ceremonies. At times he anointed the emperor on the head and at others he cut off his hair where the oil had touched it; and the priests took it, singing and censing with their thuribles, and burnt it by the door of the church and put the ashes into a stone that they keep for that, and closed it with another and returned to the others who had remained singing close to the emperor.

At the end of the ceremonies, which lasted a long time, the emperor and the *abuna* rose and, preceded by the monks and clerics with their crosses and thuribles, singing, they went in procession to the church, which is inside the second cloister, and entered. After praying, the emperor sat on a throne made for him, with silk curtains round it, and they said a solemn Mass during which the emperor took communion. And when he had finished, he went outside with a great retinue, wearing a dark blue, wide-brimmed velvet hat on his head, its crown covered all round with gold plaques like fleurs-de-lis and surmounted with an ornament encrusted with some small stones, for this is the kind of crown that the emperors used to wear until the present one, who, in September 1616, had a gold crown made like those that our kings wear, on a model that {came} <they sent> to him from India. And, mounting his horse, he went back to the tents with the same order as he had come. And even though he had told me that he would come the following day, he stayed there for three days with many celebrations.

---

[1] 'Blessed is he that cometh in the name of the Lord.'

[2] Álvares, *Prester John of the Indies*, ch. 38, 'How St Philip declared a prophecy of Isaiah to the eunuch of Queen Candace through which she and all her kingdom were converted and of the buildings of the town called Aquaxumo', pp. 154–5.

On the Wednesday at ten o'clock he arrived in our village, which is called Fremonâ,[1] where we three priests were waiting with the church very neat and tidy, ready to say Mass and give a sermon. But as he was hot from the journey, he said we should leave it until the following day. So he entered our house with a few great men and stayed there talking to us about various subjects with as much familiarity as if he were one of the most devout lords that we have here, until sunset, without eating or drinking since it was Lent (for they do not eat or drink during Lent until the sun has gone down), and then he went to the tents, which were nearby, where we sent him a few delicacies. And, although there were not many, he appreciated them <[f. 51v]> greatly because they were seasoned in our manner. That night he received news about which he needed to take {[f. 59v]} counsel. And so the next morning he commanded the army to move off and he remained in the tent with the captains, and he sent word to us that the baggage train <would go ahead> and the people on foot would leave before the sun went down much, but that he would hear Mass. The council meeting only finished shortly before noon, however, and so he left with all the cavalry, which was large, and sent word to us that he regretted that time did not allow him to hear Mass. And he gave us the weight of 300 *cruzados* in gold, because (as I have already stated) there is no coinage here. And he added to the lands that we already held a much more extensive area that was continuous with them.

After travelling for two days, he received news that the rebel had gone into some very rough, mountainous country near the sea. And so he determined to spend Easter there, partly because it is not their custom to travel during the eight days, but especially because he wanted to find out where the rebel had gone, so as to know which way he should go after him. And he sent word to me {on Palm Saturday} that, because he had not been able to hear Mass before, I should go and give a sermon to him during Holy Week. I was very pleased, because in Ethiopia they hardly ever give sermons. But on the Monday, as I was about to set off, another message arrived that I should not trouble myself to go, because he had been forced to march in a great hurry before the rebel could flee to a land of heathens, where they said he wanted to go. He set off straight away and had all the passes secured, so that the rebel had no option for escape other than to leave all the men he had gathered and to hide in the thickest part of the woods with just four trusted companions. And it also happened that, no matter how hard the emperor tried, he was never able to find him, because he was hiding in a cave and living on the milk of a few goats that he had taken with him. When the emperor saw that winter was coming, which begins in June here, he returned to Dambiâ without doing anything. But after the winter, when the rebel went into other lands with some 600 men, they killed him, as we shall see later.

It can clearly be seen from what we have said that the things that Friar Luis de Urreta mentions in chapter 13[2] about the coronation of the emperor of Ethiopia are very different from what actually happens. Furthermore, in chapter 14[3] he relates how, after they have crowned him, they hand over the treasures of Guixên Ambâ to him with great solemnity and he shares them liberally with those present. Then he goes down the mountain

---

[1] See Glossary (Fremona/Fremoná/Fremonâ/Mãy Gwãgwã).

[2] Urreta, *Historia de la Etiopia*, bk I, ch. 13, pp. 140–52.

[3] Urreta, *Historia de la Etiopia*, bk I, ch. 14, entitled 'How they hand over the treasures to the emperor, and he goes down the mountain, and travels to the city of Zambra, which is the Court, and to the city of Saba where they swear him in as emperor', pp. 153–5.

accompanied by the lords of the Grand Council, the kings, ambassadors and prelates and all the others who went up to the election, and he goes to the city of Zambra, where they <[f. 52]> give him a great {[f. 60]} welcome, and he enters the city with great splendour on a richly bedecked elephant. And after fifteen days spent in celebration, he sets off for the city of Saba. And in chapter 15[1] he says that all the kings subject to the empire come to the city of Saba to give obedience to the emperor, and each of them arrives on an elephant. And they do the same thing again every seven years after that. But all these things are fables and mere fictions because, as we said in chapter 9, on Guixên Ambâ (which he calls Mount Amara) there neither are nor ever have been any treasures; and they have never gathered there, nor do they gather there, to elect or to swear allegiance to the emperor; nor are there any such kings, as we have seen in the previous two chapters. Even less are there tame elephants, nor have there ever been any in Ethiopia, nor those cities of Zambra and Saba, as we shall say below.

---

[1] Urreta, *Historia de la Etiopia*, bk I, ch. 15, pp. 156–62.

# CHAPTER XIII

## Which deals with the way in which the emperor of Ethiopia hears the divine offices

In the old days, when the emperors of Ethiopia did not allow themselves to be seen by anybody, except by thirty boys who lived within the palace, by their wives, by the *behêt oadêd* of the right and left, and by the *acabiçât* – if any other great man, even a brother-in-law or son-in-law, was given permission to speak to the emperor, it had to be at night and with all the candles removed so that he could not see his face, as we said in chapter 4 – when the emperors bore themselves in this manner with their vassals, they also took great care not to be seen when they went to Mass. So Emperor Zara Iacob had a path made with a very high fence on both sides from the palace to the church (as is told in the book of his history) and he would walk along it without being seen. And when he entered the church, only the superiors of certain large monasteries could be there, to sing, and then he would go behind his curtains and hear Mass from there. And when he wanted to enter the chapel to take communion, everyone would go out, leaving only the *acabiçât* and four other priests. And then he would return to the palace by the same route. But on both his way out and his way back, a pageboy would gesture from inside the palace to the musicians, who were waiting outside with many instruments, for them to play and celebrate, and the people outside knew from that when he was going to and coming from Mass, as we said in chapter 5. But later emperors gradually gave up this superstition and began to show themselves {[f. 60v]} to the people and go to Mass with great splendour, as Francisco Alvares states in his *Historia Ethiopica*, f. 147, speaking of Emperor David, who later called himself Onâg Çaguêd. I give him much more credence in this respect than I give to the information from people of this country, because he says that he saw this on Easter Resurrection Day before dawn. I shall therefore quote his words, which are as follows:

<[f. 52v]> *After midnight we were summoned and, on reaching the main entrance to his great tent, we saw that from there to the Church of the Holy Cross (which was a harquebus shot away) there were more than 6,000 candles alight along the sides, arranged in careful order with one line some forty or fifty paces from the other. Behind them there were countless people, so that the ones holding them had to shield them, because they had canes tied together in a line in front of them, on which they placed the candles in a rhythmical movement. In front of the emperor's tent there were four lords on horseback, and they put us close to them. And then the emperor emerged on a fine reddish-black mule, as large as a large horse, which he held in great esteem and always took with him. The emperor came out wearing very long brocade robes that reached the ground, and the mule was also caparisoned in the same material. On his head he wore his crown and in his hand he bore a cross. Behind him they brought two*

*powerful horses harnessed and caparisoned in brocade, and in the candlelight they appeared to be all made of fine gold, and each of them had a very long diadem with large plumes on its head. As soon as the emperor came out, those four horsemen moved off and put us behind him, in order that we should go there without anybody else following him, save twenty or thirty lords who walked in front of him. In this manner we arrived at the Church of the Holy Cross, which the emperor then entered behind his curtains. The clergy from inside had come out and joined many others who were outside, as they did not all fit inside the church, and a very solemn procession was formed, with us at the front of it among the most honoured dignitaries that there were. Having returned to the church, they performed Mass and, when it was over and they wanted to give communion, they told us to go and say our Mass, for we already had our tent erected for the purpose next to the emperor's tents. We went straight away, and, when we saw that they had put up a black tent for us, we thought[1] that they were mocking us and so we left it and went to our own tents beside the river.[2]*

{[f. 61]} Up to here are the words of Francisco Alvares, which reveal the splendour with which the emperor went to Mass. But on that occasion they would have wanted to make it even more splendid than was customary, because there were foreigners at his court. Now the emperor rarely goes to church at night, nor does he need to do so to hear Mass, because, although the offices always begin two hours or more before dawn in all churches, on feast days they are so long that they do not finish before the sun is up. And then Mass begins, or sometimes much later, but at whatever time Mass is due to begin, the two churches that the emperor has nearby, outside his palace compound, are obliged to give a signal in case he wants to go and hear Mass, not with bells, because there are none, as we shall say in the second book,[3] but with a drum for each <[f. 53]> church, similar to ours. And they beat it a few times with their hands near the palace door and the emperor then sends them a message as to whether he will go or not. But when he wants to hear Mass, he ordinarily sends a message well before it begins and they place his chair there in time. The one he has now is like ours, of crimson damask with fringes of crimson silk yarn and gold thread, the nails with large heads, very well made and gilded, and on top two {copper} finials, also gilded. He has other chairs from China, gilded, with seats of green and crimson velvet. He always goes to church on foot, because it is very close to the palace. And, when he leaves the palace, he is preceded by many richly dressed lords and followed by some young pages, also very well dressed. And, ordinarily, both sides of the path are crowded with people. And in front of those lords go many palace doormen with short sticks to which are tied some very long straps, with which they move the people back to make way. And, once the emperor is in the church, he sits on his chair, which is surrounded by very beautiful silk curtains, and from there he hears Mass, and he returns in the same way as he came. But in the palace he does not ordinarily sit on these chairs but on a gilded chest with four columns as tall as a man, with much lacework, and the back almost as high as the columns, with some figures,

---

[1] Páez has changed the word 'said' to 'thought', and does not transcribe a short dialogue between the ambassador and Francisco Álvares.

[2] See Álvares, *Prester John of the Indies* ch. 112, 'How we kept a Lent at the court of the Prester, and we kept in in the country of the Gorage, and they ordered us to say mass, and how we did not say it', pp. 401–2. Páez quotes this passage in Spanish from Padilla's translation of Álvares, which varies somewhat from the published English translation.

[3] See bk II, ch. 15, p. 413 below.

shells and foliage, which make it look magnificent, and a very beautiful silk canopy, all very well decorated with silk covers and brocade valances with fine gold fringes.

{[f. 61v]} This is what I have seen many times, when Emperor Seltân Çaguêd goes to Mass. Emperor Atanâf Çaguêd, too, who was first called Za Denguîl, in June 1604, after I had spent many days disputing before him with his learned men on the things in which they go against our holy faith, and after he had understood the truth very well and had decided to give his obedience to the Holy Roman Church, told me that he very much desired to hear {our} Mass and to hear the sermon. I replied that I had no wine, for I had sent it to a land where the Portuguese were, two days' journey away, as I thought I should be going there soon so that they could confess and take communion. He commanded that I should be given raisins, {saying} that, for want of wine, I should at least give it the right taste, as he thought that we said Mass with wine made from raisins as his priests did. I answered that I would have the wine brought back as quickly as possible, as Mass could not be said with raisin wine. When the wine arrived, he had a very large, three-pole tent erected within the palace compound, which was very spacious, where I arranged an altar as well as I could, with some images. And to the gospel side, a short distance away, they put another small, very beautiful tent, and on the ground {many} fine carpets and on them his chair with two crimson velvet cushions in front. Later, when it was time, the emperor came dressed in crimson satin robes cut in the same manner as the Turks down to his feet, but with an undershirt with a high collar like ours. In front of him came many doormen, who cleared the way with straps like those I mentioned above, because there were so many people that it was difficult to make way. Behind the doormen followed many richly dressed lords, and lastly the emperor with the governor of the empire and his steward and, behind him, some pages. When he arrived he sat down on his chair, and all those <[f. 53v]> lords remained beside the small tent, sitting on the ground on carpets, so that they could not see him. Just two young pages, dressed in *bofetá*[1] and tunics of *taficira*[2] of crimson silk, with turbans on their heads and swords in their hands, not drawn but in their sheaths, stood at the entrance to the tent, one on each side. And thus they heard Mass and sermon amid complete silence from everyone. And when it was over, he went in the same manner as he had come. Later, when I deal with this emperor, I shall report in more detail the things that occurred on this and another occasion when he heard Mass, because for now I merely intend {[f. 62]} to show the way in which the emperors go to church and remain there.

Friar Luis de Urreta deals with this {subject} <mystery> in chapter 16[3] and mentions some of the main feast days, on which he says that the emperor of Ethiopia goes to church with pomp and splendour. The first is that of the Invention of the Most Holy Cross, on the eve of which he claims that they place a fine tent outside the city and, inside it, the priests set up a strange altar and place on it a cedar cross in memory of the one that the Empress {Saint} Helena[4] found. And the following day the emperor comes out on an elephant accompanied by all his court and, on reaching the tent, he enters, kneels before the cross and worships with great devotion, and the others do the same and remove their clothes

---

[1] Very fine cotton fabric from Asia.

[2] Or *tafecira*: Indian coarse cotton fabric, similar to calico.

[3] Urreta, *Historia de la Etiopia*, bk I, ch. 16, entitled 'Of the ceremonies that the Prester John performs in the divine offices', pp. 163–7.

[4] Saint Helena of Constantinople.

and put on black garments, as the emperor does as well; he then goes to the altar and, picking up the cross with great reverence, carries it to the city on foot in the company of those knights and prelates, who go in procession in due order. When he reaches the palace, he places it decently in the imperial chapel, where they remain kneeling for about a quarter of an hour. And then each one goes to his home. This is what Friar Luis says, but, first of all, as we have already said and as the emperor himself has told me, no tame elephant has ever been seen in his lands, nor is the feast of the Invention of the Most Holy Cross held at all. And when I asked an old monk who might know better than the others if they used to hold this feast before, he told me that they used to, but he did not know whether it was with these ceremonies. And even if they did hold it thus, they would not have taken the cross to the palace, because there was never any chapel inside, but to one of the two churches that the emperor ordinarily has a good stone's throw away; one is the Church of Jesus and the other of Our Lady. Nor would they have knelt, as he says, because it is the custom here to pray only standing up or sitting on the ground. However, on the day of the Exaltation of the Holy Cross[1] they hold a very great festival and dance the whole night. And in some lands, such as the kingdom of Tigrê, they even start dancing in the streets every night a month before. And, on the day itself, before dawn, the young men and boys go around with very long burning torches made of very dry thin sticks, shouting and joyfully begging God to let them reach the next year. And when dawn comes, they light the piles of firewood that they have gathered. On this day the emperor goes to Mass {[f. 62v]} accompanied in the manner that we have mentioned above, but he does not perform any of the ceremonies that Friar Luis refers to. And when he returns, many young men go and dance at the palace door, and he orders that they be given eight or ten cows. Then they go dancing round the lords' houses, and they too give them cows <[f. 54]> or goods with which to buy some. They do this for eight days. Even the heathens, who do not obey the emperor, hold this festival by lighting great bonfires and killing lots of cows.

The second festival that he mentions is Palm Sunday, when he says that the emperor goes to church with his customary pomp and, from his throne, he hears the offices until the Passion begins, when he descends from his throne and, removing his imperial robe, puts on what he wore on the mountain. And those around do the same and, having removed their rich clothes, put on other black garments which they wear throughout Holy Week, during which he does no business nor is he accompanied by anyone but the ambassadors from Portugal and from the viceroy of Goa, and the consul of the merchants from Italy. And he eats with them on that {Friday} <Thursday>, and on Easter Day he goes to church accompanied by the same people and those of his court. And, when *Gloria in excelsis Deo* begins, the emperor and the knights accompanying him change from their ordinary clothes into rich ones. When they have finished hearing Mass, taking communion and giving thanks, the emperor returns to his palace on foot. And the next day, after Mass, they put out three large tables with three rich side tables, one with gold tableware, one with silver, and the third with porcelain and fine earthenware. The emperor eats at the first table with two priests, the ambassadors and knights of Roman lands at the second, and at the third the kings' sons with the members of the emperor's Grand Council. And when the tables are cleared, he offers each of them a curious item such as a dish of crystal or something similar.

---

[1] See Glossary (Exaltation of the Holy Cross/*Masqal*).

Everything that Friar Luis says here is also very contrary to the customs of this country, because the emperor and those who accompany him on Palm Sunday do not change their clothes in the church, nor has there ever been a consul of the merchants from Italy, nor has any ambassador come from Portugal or from the viceroy of India ever since father Bishop Dom Andre de Oviedo arrived in Ethiopia, which was in March 1557; and we shall describe later how he was received. Nor does anyone ever eat with the emperor at all, not even priests, nor are there such side tables with gold and silver tableware {[f. 63]}, but just fine black earthenware, porcelain and copper, as we said in chapter 9. As for the ceremonies that the clergy and lay people keep in Holy Week, we shall deal with them in the second book.

The third festival that Friar Luis mentions is that of the Most Holy Sacrament. And he says that Pope Paul III, who was elected in 1534, commanded that it be celebrated in Ethiopia. And as his *Breve* arrived at the time of Prester John David, two years before he died, he obeyed as an obedient son of the Roman Church and immediately commanded that it be celebrated throughout Ethiopia. And he says that they make a solemn procession through the city with the Most Holy Sacrament, and behind it goes the emperor, and that the candles they carry are innumerable, and that nearly all of them dance along the way. And it is their custom that, while the procession is passing down a street, the people must not stand at the windows or on their roof terraces, but they must all go out into the street bare-headed and kneel down in great devotion and humility. <[f. 54v]> And they adhere to this so strictly, for they think that seeing the Most Holy Sacrament from a window or high place is an act of irreverence, that it is a very common custom that nuns, whose convents happen to be in the streets along which the procession passes and who cannot help seeing it from their corridors, all go down to the church door and arrange themselves in two choirs covered with their veils and, with candles in their hands, they kneel while the procession passes.

All this that the author says was also invented by the one who informed him, because such a procession is not and never has been held in Ethiopia, because they never remove the Sacrament from the church for any reason. They only bring it to the door, where the women and men who do not have holy orders take communion, for without holy orders they cannot take communion or hear Mass inside. If Pope Paul III had commanded that such a festival should be held here, it would not have been implemented. And the buildings here are not like those in Europe for people to be able to stand at the windows, but, as I have said several times, they are single-storey houses, some like long cabins and others that are round and very low, all covered with thatch reaching down very low, except in the province that they call Hamacên, where they usually have flat roofs, but no houses have upper storeys and they are all very low. The current emperor, Seltân Çagûêd, recently made some two-storey palaces with roof terraces and a building on top {[f. 63v]} to serve as a lookout, [and] sixty spans tall from the ground to the top.[1] Nuns too live in these thatched huts, not together, but each one where she pleases. And she goes wherever she pleases, without anyone questioning it, because, when the monks give them the veil, they return to their parents' or kinsfolk's houses, or to their own, if they already had a separate one. And if some of them want to stay next to the monastery of the monks who gave them the veil, each one lives apart in her own little hut and goes where she pleases, but they say that, formerly, there used to be some who lived in communities.

[1] The author gives more precise details in bk I, ch. 20.

# CHAPTER XIV

## Of the splendour in which the emperor travels and of the order in which he arranges his tents[1]

Just as in former times the emperor of Ethiopia, when he was in his palace, did not allow himself to be seen {by anybody} other than by those whom we mentioned in the previous chapter, so also when he travelled nobody could see him, because, as it says in an Ethiopian book that deals with the affairs of Emperor Zara Iacob, everyone would keep a great distance, except three who would keep the sun off him and shelter him with three large silk parasols and some who would fan the flies away. And another book that deals with the emperor's officials says that, if the tents had not been erected when he dismounted, they would put up a cloth as a canopy, fixed to poles, with which they would keep the sun off him, and he would be sheltered by some sons and kinsmen of his who always took charge of this, as we mentioned in chapter 4. But later, they used curtains instead of those parasols, as <[f. 55]> Francisco Alvares, on folio 117 of his *Historia*, says was done in the time of Emperor David. And because he speaks from personal experience, I shall quote his own words:

*The next day we were told to travel according to the order that we were given. The reason was that the emperor no longer wanted to travel in secret, as on the previous days, when he stayed behind or went in front, but now he began to travel in the sight of everyone, as I shall tell. He was riding a mule, with his crown on his head, amid some red curtains covered with a canopy of the same, so that these curtains covered his sides and back. They were very high and long, and those that carried them walked along on the outside {[f. 64]} supporting them with long poles in their hands. The mule was wearing very ornate headstalls over the bridle, with its plaques or points. And on either side of it walked two pages, who seemed to be guiding the mule by the bit. Two others then followed, one on each side {as well}, with one hand on the mule's neck. And behind them came two others with their hands on its flanks near the cantle. These pages are called in their language* legamoveos, *which means 'pages of the bridle'. In front of these, there were twenty more pages on foot, and in front of them six very powerful, very richly caparisoned horses were led: four main people went with each of them, two beside the bridle like those with the emperor, and two more beside the saddle with their hands on it. In front of these horses four more mules were led, each with four men as well, neither more nor less, beside them as with the others. Further in front still were twenty of the principal lords on mules, wearing their burnouses. And just in front of them was where we went, because that was*

[1] See Fig. 13.

Figure 13. Engraving by Pieter van der Aa, *La Galerie agréable du Monde*, Leiden [1769]. Palácio Nacional de Mafra, Inv. 136.

*the place shown to us, and no one else was allowed to go either in front of or beside us, except for some men on horseback who went galloping past to keep the rest of the people away. The* betudetes *kept guard of the emperor's person, and each one marched to one side with over 6,000 guardsmen. They usually kept a distance of about a harquebus shot to the sides of the emperor, sometimes rather more or less, depending on what the road allowed. If it happened that there was no more than a narrow pass at some point through which everyone had to pass, then the* betudete *of the right hand went forward with his soldiers and afterwards the other one went through as in the rearguard, the two corps being separated by as much as half a league. Apart from this, they also {take} <took> the four lions with their strong chains, as I have already said, and the churches with all due reverence.*[1]

Up to here are the words of Francisco Alvares, in which it should be noted that those that keep their hands on the neck and flank of the emperor's mule, which they ordinarily do when they are travelling along difficult trails so that he does not fall off, are called {*dagafôch*} <*degabôch*>, and not '*legamoveos*,' <[f. 55v]> because there is no such name, and {[f. 64v]} if he meant to say '*leguamôch*', these cannot come close to the emperor, because they are stable boys. In addition, the word is not '*betudete*' but '*behêt oadêd*',[2] which means 'I am loved'. On the order and manner in which the emperor travels, he is right, because they used to travel in that way at that time, but the emperors stopped using curtains a long time ago and would just wear a wide-brimmed hat, commonly of blue velvet with some gold plates and precious stones on top, because it was their crown. That is what Emperor Seltân Çaguêd wore until recently; a short while ago he put a crown like ours on a narrow-brimmed hat of crimson satin just like those in Portugal, because he very much likes all our fashion and he has had hats made for his crown in the colours that he usually wears, so that his hat always matches his clothes.

[3]As for the manner in which he travels, I shall mention what I have seen many times, although I shall not deal with the first days after he leaves the court, because he only travels a short distance and so many people stay at home, and the ones that go ahead of him (who are always in great numbers) keep little order, although not the ones accompanying his person, who are his officials and bodyguards as well as plenty of other cavalry. I shall just talk about when all the people have gathered to him and {he is passing through lands} where more order is required. But for a better understanding of this, it should be noted that all the fighting men in the emperor's encampment (not counting those brought by the viceroys who accompany him, because they follow their viceroys) are divided into four parts: one, consisting of the emperor's officials and bodyguards with some great lords, always accompany his person; another part follows the captain of the vanguard, whom they call *fit aorarî*;[4] another goes with the captain of the right hand, whom they call *cânhe azmâch*;[5] and the last goes with the captain of the left hand, whom they call *guerâ azmâch*.[6]

---

[1] Álvares, *Prester John of the Indies*, ch. 93, 'Of the travelling of the Prester John and on the manner of his state when he is on the road', pp. 335–7. Páez quotes this passage in Spanish from Padilla's translation of Álvares, which varies somewhat from the published English translation.

[2] See Glossary (behêt ûaded/behêt oadêd/*beḥt waddad*).

[3] New paragraph made by the editors.

[4] See Glossary (fit aorarî/*fit awrāri*).

[5] See Glossary (cânhe azmâch/*qaññazmāč*).

[6] See Glossary (guerâ azmâch/*gerāzmāč*).

In view of this, when the emperor has to travel, the captain of the vanguard always gives a signal with his drums at daybreak or a little after, and then they all strike camp and load their equipment. Shortly afterwards he sets off with his banner to the sound of the drums, of which there are ordinarily four on two mules, some of red copper and others of wood covered with cowhide, and {[f. 65]} he is followed by all those whose duty it is to do so. Then the chief groom rides in front of the emperor's tent, something that no other man may do, however great he be. And he rides a horse or a mule, as he wishes, but ordinarily they all ride mules with the horses in reserve in front. Next the captains of the right and the left hand set out with their banners and drums, and each one waits in his place with his men, until the emperor leaves. He mounts inside his tent, and the under-groom holds the stirrup; others hold the mule by the bridle; {and} others cover {it} <him> all around with curtains, so that even if the entrance to the tent is open nobody outside can see him mount. The mule's bit <[f. 56]> always has a good deal of silver worked in points, which makes it look very handsome, and the saddle is covered with brocade on which, on the outside of the cantle, they lay gilded silver in which they fashion roses and fleurs-de-lis. The emperor sometimes goes out wearing brocade, but not often, because it is heavy. More commonly it is crimson satin or damask, because he likes this colour. And his robes reach down below mid-calf level, with rather tight breeches of the same fabric covering his legs right down to his shoes, for he never wears boots. Over everything he wears a crimson velvet burnous with a large hood and plenty of trimmings of gold thread and thick gold buttons; a hat like ours made of silk, which he puts on; and, on top of it, the crown, which is of very fine gold with some stones set into it, with pearls on all the points of the fleurs-de-lis, and on the very top [of the hat], to finish it off, a beautiful stone set into the tip of a gold finial, because the top of the hat goes inside the crown. On his head, under his hat, he sometimes wears a very fine, white turban, the points of which hang down below his chin and go round so that they cover his mouth and nose because of the dust. Other times, he wears only his hat and a pageboy carries his crown in front. When the emperor leaves his tent, they begin to play their shawms, which, although they are not like ours, make good music. And then the captains of the right and the left hand and all the rest march off in order, keeping a good distance from the emperor. And, if they are close to where they will have to fight, or if there is some threat on the road, the captain of the left hand takes his men and goes up near to the captain of the vanguard. Then the captain of the right hand follows and, with him, strictly speaking, the captain of the Portuguese ought to go with his men. But, ordinarily, he stays close to the {[f. 65v]} emperor, because he likes having the Portuguese there.

The viceroys' men, who come to accompany the emperor from the neighbouring kingdoms, travel in the places assigned to them. Some priests usually come next, bearing the altar stones of four churches,[1] which the emperor always has with him in his encampment. Francisco Alvares, on <folio> 112 of his *Historia*,[2] says that there are thirteen, but it seems that that was the custom in those days, but for many years now it has not been the custom to take more than four (as everybody says). They carry them on their heads or shoulders, and they are covered with silk or brocade cloths. In front of each one go two acolytes, one

---

[1] See bk I, ch. 4, p. 100 above. There, however, the author only mentions three churches.
[2] Álvares, *Prester John of the Indies*, ch. 89, 'Of the churches at court, and how they travel and how the altar stones are revered and how the Prester John shows himself to the people each year', p. 323.

with a cross and thurible in his hands and the other ringing a hand bell. And they are all given such great respect and reverence that, if these priests hurry forwards (which they may do, as they do not have an appointed place but can go where they please, except to stay behind the emperor), everyone moves aside off the road until they have passed. Some distance behind the priests come the emperor's banners, of which there are ordinarily three made of crimson damask, not as large or as square as the field banners <[f. 56v]> that are usual amongst us, but like guidons. And to cap the pole they have a gilded copper ball and on top of it a cross of the same material. The drums follow next, usually eight very large copper ones, their mouths covered with cow hide, and he sometimes takes more loaded on mules, two on each, and the players ride on the mules' hindquarters. Near them go the palace judges with their servants.

After all these comes the emperor's foot guard, which now consists of 800 young men with white shields, whom they call *characâ, scilicet* 'light', and the same number with black shields, {all} made of buffalo hide. The latter are called *cocâb, scilicet* 'star', although they do not shine so much, but are as black as their shields. Each of them carries two spears and a club made of very hard, heavy wood: they throw this club first and then one of the spears, which has a head like that of a short lance, while keeping hold of the second, which has a broad head two spans in length. Apart from them, there are many men with guns and a good many of these are young men of very pale complexion, because they are the sons of Turks who became Christians here. They ordinarily march together in squadrons, those with white shields in one, those with black shields in another, and those with guns in another, although sometimes they form two columns. In the middle they lead by the bridle {[f. 66]} two, or sometimes four, of the emperor's mules, with very ornate bits and saddles. Behind them come six, or sometimes eight, very large and richly caparisoned spare horses; on their bits they have a great deal of gilded silver, and other trappings on their necks of the same material like those that the Grand Turk has, because they were made a short time ago by a craftsman who came from there; their blankets and saddles are made of crimson velvet and others of brocade. The horse closest to the emperor has a very finely worked, gilded silver saddle-bow, and a cantle of the same metal on the outside, but fretted and with silk of various colours in the openings to set off the gold better. Next to this horse walks the page of the lance and others who bear the emperor's arms. Then follow twelve well-trained young men, the sons of Turks as I have just said, six on each side, dressed in red cloth with quivers decorated with gold over their shoulders and Turkish bows in their hands and plumed, gilded copper helmets on their heads. Then comes the emperor. And if the *erâz* – which means 'head', and he has the same office that the one who used to be called *behêt oadêd* had – is there, he takes the right-hand side, keeping a little behind the emperor's shoulder. And the one who is like the chief steward, whom they call *balatinôch gueitâ*, goes on the left, and others of the emperor's officials, the viceroys and great lords go nearby. And, when the emperor speaks to one of them, if he is wearing a cape or a rich silk cloth which they customarily wear over their robes, he lowers it to his waist. Behind these men, they bring the emperor's bed covered with a silk cloth because, when <[f. 57]> he dismounts, he ordinarily sits or lies on it. At the sides and behind come a great many horsemen, but a good distance away.

Behind the emperor and the lords who travel with him comes the empress, about a gunshot away, and she is ordinarily accompanied by many other ladies and they bring a great crowd of maidservants and menservants. Behind them comes the baggage train, which is like another army, because apart from the tents and provisions and camp equipment, which they bring loaded on mules, oxen and asses, there are a great many taverners and merchants. Lastly, in the rearguard, there is always a captain with a large number of warriors. But this captain is changed every day and another is put in his place. And two or three days before {[f. 66v]} they get to where they are going to fight, if they fear that the battle will be hard, the empress, all the ladies and the baggage remain in a safe place with men to guard them, and the emperor goes on with his army.

This is the order that they keep when they march through perilous lands, but otherwise the emperor does not take banners or any captains at all, but just drums and shawms. And the empress and other ladies go ahead very early, if they wish. And the captains keep little order because their men travel at a distance from each other so as to travel more at ease, and as there are so many of them whenever the emperor sets out, they cover the countryside in such a way that the wild animals that are flushed out among them can rarely escape – since partridges and some other birds do not fly very much at all – unless they succeed in hiding where they cannot be seen.

[1]I have often wanted to find out how many actual warriors would ordinarily travel with the emperor (for it would be difficult to count all the others) and they have never been able to tell me. So once, when the emperor commanded his captains to show him their men, I asked him directly how many men he should have, and he answered that he did not know for sure. The time that I saw most, I do not think there were more than 40,000. But if he wants to gather all his men (which he can easily do, since in summer there is no river that can prevent him from doing so), it seems that they will come to well over 100,000 men, with whom he can not only recover the lands that the heathens called Gâlas have been taking from him, but also subjugate many others, if they fight in a united way; but they keep very little military order and, if the ones in front start to turn back, all the rest soon turn as well; although they used to consider it a great dishonour to flee, and anyone who did run away was punished with the insults that we mentioned in chapter 4, they no longer have this quality and point of honour, since they are much more imposing and better armed than their enemies, because the latter are naked from the waist up and only carry a shield and two spears and a wooden club, and their horses are very small and poor, whereas the emperor's men have very good mail and helmets and large, fine horses, and many lances, bows and arrows <[f. 57v]> and guns. And so, when I saw them one day drawn up in order, as when they intend to give battle, the foot soldiers in front in squadrons and the cavalry behind, I said to the emperor that I was amazed that they did not always defeat their enemies, since they were such a large and impressive force and had such good weapons and horses. And he answered, 'Your Reverence should not think that these men of mine fight with their hearts or with order, because some throw themselves in while {[f. 67]} others stand and watch; so, as they do not hold together, they are easily beaten by the Gâlas, who always stand shoulder to shoulder and determined to fight. But when we keep our order, we rarely fail to achieve a victory.'

Regarding the manner and order in which they arrange their tents:

[2]The captain of the vanguard has the task of choosing the place where they will pitch camp and always tries to ensure that it is a large area where there is plenty of water for the

---

[1] New paragraph made by the editors.
[2] New paragraph made by the editors.

173

army and grass for the mules and horses and pack-asses. And in the middle, if it is flat, or on some higher spot they then put up a white flag as a sign that that is where the emperor's tents are to be erected, so that each person will know which place he is to occupy. Then they erect there at least two very large, three-pole tents, not round but long, with their entrances to the west. They also bring a very large, round tent, which they call *debanâ*, and nobody is allowed to put up a tent like this except the emperor, but they do not always erect it. They surround these tents at a certain distance with curtains of cotton fabric woven in black and white, supported on poles taller than a man, and around them they leave an open space forty lances wide, each lance being fifteen spans in length. No tents may be erected within this ring except the ones that serve as the Church of Our Lady, which is placed on the right towards the north, and the Church of Jesus, on the left towards the south, behind the emperor's tents. Outside the boundaries of that area are the empress's tents, surrounded by curtains in the same fashion. All round on either side continue the tents of the emperor's kinsmen and women, together with those of their servants. And all these lords' and ladies' tents have curtains round them. Behind these tents they put those of the emperor's kitchen, some on the right and others on the left. Near those of the empress are erected those of the *balatinôch gueitâ*, who is like the emperor's chief steward. And then come those of the first secretary, treasurer and many others of the emperor's officials, with many guardsmen. On the right, near the tents of the emperor's kinswomen, are those of twenty-two lords, and on the left the same number, with many men that they call *jan bêit tabacôch*, which means 'guards of the emperor's house', because although *jân* strictly speaking means 'elephant' in the ancient language, it is now taken to mean 'emperor', as we said in chapter 5. Near these, on the {[f. 67v] right, are placed the tents of the *erâz* with those of their people, of whom there are many, because they hold the highest honour and command of the empire. <[f. 58]> Behind these are the tents of the captain of the right hand with those of all his troops, and likewise those of the captain of the left hand. In front, towards the west, near the tents of the emperor's kinsmen, are those of the palace judges, who are called *azaxôch, scilicet* 'commanders'. Between these tents they always leave a very wide street, and the chief ones are on the right-hand side of the road and the others on the left. On the latter side are the tents of the captain of the vanguard and his men. Here there is a Church of Saint Michael. Then, on either side of the street, there follow the tents of those who are like magistrates, whom they call *umbarôch, scilicet* 'chairs', because these judges almost always sit on chairs to pass judgement. Further on, a great crowd of tents is put up by taverners, who sell wine made from honey[1] and another kind made from barley and maize and other seeds that they call *çâoa*,[2] and they take in people from outside for a small fee. Then follow the tents of the goldsmiths, and next to these come those of the blacksmiths, of whom there are also a great many.

This is the order that those who are obliged to travel with the emperor's encampment always adhere to when pitching their tents, and people cannot go from one part to another, such as from the left{-hand side} to the right, but each person must stay in his place unless the emperor orders otherwise or gives him permission. And so they all pitch

---

[1] *Ṭaǧǧ*, mead.
[2] *Ṭallā*, a beer made from fermented grain.

their tents very quickly, usually without any disputes, because the neighbours know each other. And if there is some dispute on the right{-hand} side about the width of a plot or about some street, it is soon settled by the magistrates and the captain of that side, who are in charge of it. And the magistrates and captain of the left hand do the same if something happens on that side. Apart from these people who ordinarily follow the emperor, there are many more with the viceroys of the neighbouring kingdoms who come to accompany him. And these too have their places on the right or left, as the emperor commands, but their tents are erected at the edge of the encampment, or sometimes a short distance away in peaceful lands, so that each of these viceroys makes his own encampment, which means they occupy a very large area. And on the forward side, a short distance from the encampment, they hold a market every day (except on Sundays and feast days), to which countless people come and where all kinds of clothing, provisions and other necessities may be found.

In which it is stated whether the Prester John always enters into marriage with one of the families of the Three Magi or with the lady that he thinks is the best in his empire

In chapter 17 of book I of his *Historia*, Friar Luis de Urreta considers it a very certain and established fact that the Prester John always marries a woman from one of the families of the three <[f. 58v]> Magi who worshipped Baby Jesus. So he says on page 170:

*The emperors of Ethiopia have sought to enter into marriage with women of holy, noble and illustrious lineage. And as they believe that in {all} their kingdoms and states there is no better lineage than that of the holy Magi, presuming – and most probably correctly – that the heroic virtues, that fervent devotion, that unique holiness, in the end like the first fruits of the Holy Church, would shine in their offspring, a statute was made that whenever they were to take a woman to wife, she should be from one of these three lineages, which are to be found today in Ethiopia. And it is received wisdom throughout the country that one of these Kings was from Ethiopia and the others from Arabia. These two had lived Christian lives with their families in their kingdoms for a long time, but the great persecution by the Aryans forced them – both Melchior's descendants, who were kings in Arabia, and Balthazar's, who were kings in Persia – to escape to Ethiopia, as it was a land of Christians. Emperor Juan the Holy, who lived at the time of Saint Basil, gave Balthazar's descendants the kingdom of Fatagâr and Melchior's that of Soa, but for Caspar's descendants, he exchanged the kingdom of Saba, which they then held, for that of Bernagasso, which they hold today. Thus these three families have come to be together in Ethiopia. And it is a miraculous fact that in all of them legitimate sons are born with a star marked on one side of their bodies. And this is so true that, in 1575, which was the Jubilee year in the time of Pope Gregory XIII, three gentlemen of all three families were found in Rome with this birthmark. And when His Holiness Cardinal Farnesio, glory be to him, the protector of Ethiopia, was informed of this, he wished to see it and, in the presence of many princes and cardinals, he found that they all had it. But while we may find this amazing, it is even more amazing to see {[f. 68v]} that not only are the Christian sons of these families born with this mark, but the Muslims too, if they are legitimate, for if Don Juan[1] had not sworn to me that he had seen it in Persia and Arabia, I would not have dared mention it. To honour these families, Juan the Holy and Philippe VII ruled that the emperors who were going to marry (for not all of them marry) should take a wife from one of these families.*

*For the wedding to take place, the bride leaves the kingdom of her parents accompanied by her mother, brothers and kinsfolk, and by all the nobility of her kingdom, and she travels to*

---

[1] Joam Balthesar.

*the city of Saba, where the emperor awaits. She always travels in a litter and, on arriving at
a boundary shrine more than a league from the city, she finds many pavilions erected and
rests there that night. The following morning she has a {fine} elephant prepared with rich
trappings, and on its back is a tall <reclining> seat {of respect} on which they seat the empress,
<[f. 59]> and some of the ladies who accompany her go on elephants, others on horses and
others on mules, and they are all richly dressed. As she travels thus, four queens, who have
been called by the emperor to perform this duty, ride out of the city on elephants to receive her
and, placing themselves on both sides of her, they accompany her to a certain place where the
emperor is waiting, wearing his usual clothes, on horseback, and accompanied by the kings'
first-born sons, the Grand Council and all the court. And when the empress arrives, they pay
each other many compliments and courtesies and, leaving all the court to accompany her, he
returns just with four kings' sons and the ambassador of the grand abbot and goes to the church
where weddings are performed, and there he puts on his imperial attire and, on a chair and
royal throne outside the church door, he sits in majesty and greatness awaiting the empress.
At his side is a plain chair. After the empress has passed along the streets indicated for these
festivals, which are richly decorated and full of courtiers wearing expensive clothes and
everyone in a festive and joyful mood, when she arrives at the Prester John's throne, she
dismounts from the elephant and the emperor takes her by the hand and bids her sit on the
plain chair. Then the most senior archbishop, who acts as the supreme pontiff, comes out
dressed in pontificals, accompanied by two bishops, and stands at the church door. Rising from
his throne, the emperor takes the empress by the hand, and they go to the archbishop and
kneel before him; he marries them {[f. 69]} with the ceremonies used by the Roman Church.
When the wedding is over, the emperor takes off his imperial attire and, taking the empress
by the hand, they walk to the palace accompanied by all the court. The people in the streets
throw flowers and scented waters over them and follow them with a thousand blessings.*[1]

Up to here are the words of Friar Luis de Urreta. And he deals at length with the same
subject, as regards the three Magi, in the third book, from page 628[2] onwards. But everything he says about them that happens in the lands of the Prester John are fables and mere
fictions, because not only is there no statute saying that the Prester John must always
marry a woman from one of the families of these holy kings, but there is no such family in
all his empire, nor any memory that there ever has been one. And, to confirm this truth, I
did not content myself with asking many people who might know of this – and they said
that they had never seen such a thing in books or heard tell of it – but I even spoke to the
emperor himself. In short, when I mentioned {all} these things to him, he laughed heartily
at the idea that they should have given credence to an unknown man so readily that they
authorized and printed them. And he said that there was no such statute, and that none of
his predecessors had been called Joam, and that in his lands there had never been any
family of the three <[f. 59v]> Magi, and that he knew nothing about them other than

[1] Urreta, *Historia de la Etiopia*, excerpt (with some passages omitted) from bk I, ch. 17, entitled 'How the
Prester John always enters into marriage with one of the families of the three Magi who worshipped the newborn
baby Jesus. On the clothes of the women of Ethiopia', pp. 170–72. Páez quotes this passage in Spanish. This
chapter may be compared with ff. 1–2 of the 'Relatione dei Grã regno deglo Abissini/ouero d'Ethiopia/datta da
don Baldassari Abissinio Caualero dell'Ordine di Sant. Antonio' (BM, MSS. Italiani cl. 6, n° 332).
[2] Urreta, *Historia de la Etiopia*, bk III, ch. 2, entitled 'In which are written some lives of saints, of the many that
in Ethiopia have shone in holiness and virtues', pp. 623–72.

what the Holy Gospels said. He told me that the emperors always married the woman that they thought best and that, if they so wished, they could even marry Moorish women, if they became Christian. That is what Emperor Seltân Çaguêd told me. And I know that Emperor Iacob did indeed bring a Moorish woman from the Moorish Hadeas in the year 1605 in order to marry her, as I was told then by a great captain who was very close to him. And that was quite clear from what the emperor did and the way I saw him treat her; but before he could get married, they killed him.

I also met and had many dealings with Empress Mariâm Cinâ, who was the wife of Emperor Malâc Çaguêd, and she was not of royal blood, despite being a great lady from the province of Sirêi. And even less so was the lady whom Emperor Za Denguîl married, after I arrived here, and the empress to whom Emperor Seltân Çaguêd is now married is not of very high blood. Although they marry daughters of the lords of their empire, since they are surrounded by Moors and heathens and {[f. 69v]} women from other Christian kingdoms cannot come to them, even so they are more concerned that they should be good-looking than that they should be the daughters of the greatest lords, because, even if they are of lesser rank, they need only marry the emperor to have as much honour as they could wish for. And so, even if the empress is the daughter of the greatest lord in Ethiopia, when they speak of her in histories or private conversations, they do not call her by her own name if they wish to honour her, saying 'Empress So-and-so', but they add the word *mogoçâ*, which means 'supreme honour', to the name of the emperor, so as to declare that all the honour of the emperor whom she married has come to her. Thus they call Emperor Adamâs Çaguêd's wife Adamâs Mogoçâ, and his son Emperor Malâc Çaguêd's wife Malâc Mogoçâ, although her own name is Mariâm Cinâ. And this Emperor Seltân Çaguêd's wife, who is called Oadeçalâ,[1] they call Seltân Mogoçâ.

[2]As for the author's claim that all the men who descend in a direct line from those three families are born with a star on one side, and that in the time of Pope Gregory XIII three gentlemen of all three families were found in Rome with this birthmark, we have nothing to say: they will know about that there. But if it is true that they were seen, it is also true that they were not from the lands of the Prester John, for there are no such families here. What I know and have seen many times is that in these lands and over in Cairo the people make many marks for the sake of adornment: some prick with needles and rub indigo and other things into the blood and the mark turns blue; others <[f. 60]> make the mark that they want with a blade and, without adding dye, the mark is left on them, so that it almost appears natural. Even the *abuna* who was killed a few years ago[3] had a very well-marked cross on his left arm with some sort of stars around it, which I saw sometimes when I was talking to him, because he ordinarily wore a shirt with wide sleeves in the Turkish fashion and thus exposed his arm.

Regarding his claim that the emperor's wife comes from her lands in a litter and then, to enter the city where the emperor is waiting, she mounts a fine elephant and four queens come out to receive her on elephants, and other ladies also accompany her on these animals and on horses, and that the most senior archbishop, accompanied by two bishops, marries them, I have already said several times that there is no archbishop or bishop other

---

[1] See Glossary (Oadeçalâ/Walda Sa'âlâ).

[2] New paragraph made by the editors.

[3] The *abuna* referred to here is undoubtedly Seme'on, who was killed in 1617. His death is narrated in bk II, ch. 5, below.

than the *abuna*, nor are there queens; and many people including Emperor Seltân Çaguêd himself have told me that in the whole of his empire there is no tame elephant {[f. 70]} nor any recollection that there ever has been one; nor do the ladies mount horses at all, nor have they ever seen a litter or know what one is: they all ride mules with rather broad saddles, covered with silk or other more ordinary cloths according to the person's rank. And each one is accompanied by two men close to the saddle-bow, one on one side and the other on the other, each with his hand on the mule's neck, and she often leans on them, putting her hand on the shoulder of whichever she pleases; two others go behind in the same way with a hand on the cantle, both for honour's sake and so that there is no risk of her falling off. However, those that cannot afford so much have just one man on the right-hand side.

[1]The manner and ceremonies that are customary at their weddings are as follows. Before the emperor announces whom he has decided to marry, he very carefully finds out whether that lady descends from people who at some time had some contagious disease, such as leprosy or something similar. And if he finds that she does not, and if she is not at court, he sends for her to come accompanied by a great retinue and entrusts her to a kinswoman of his on whom he relies to have her in her house and to pay close attention to her nature, whether she is harsh or gentle in character, and to teach her the ceremonies of the palace and how she must behave towards the princes and great men, {or} <and> with those of lesser rank. Once they find that she is of good character and has been well taught, the emperor sets the day when he is to receive her and, in the morning, they both go to church. The emperor leaves the palace on foot, richly attired and accompanied by the great courtiers, and she comes from the house where she has been staying, also very {expensively} <richly> dressed and accompanied by the most noble ladies of the court, and they both hear Mass and confess and take communion. Then they go <[f. 60v]> to the palace with all that retinue and there the *abuna*, ordinarily accompanied by many monks and clerics, blesses them, reciting that which has been ordained for this in Ethiopia, which is some prayers and psalms. When he has finished, they play the emperor's shawms and other musical instruments at the palace door. Then they set the table for the emperor and he eats alone, as he always does; the empress eats at another table with {some} <other> great ladies who are the emperor's kin. All the priests and the great men of the empire who have gathered there are given a splendid banquet in another house. When they have finished, they go into the room where the emperor, the empress and the other ladies are, and they spend all that day and many others in celebrations and great banquets are held.

{[f. 70v]} In addition to these celebrations, others are held later on a day set by the emperor, at which the empress is given a certain name of honour, which is *iteguê*, because ordinarily she is not given it on the day that she marries, so that it can be done with new splendour. All the great courtiers go to the palace richly dressed for this purpose and, when they are standing in the emperor's hall in order, each according to his status, and with the emperor sitting on his throne, the empress enters accompanied by many great ladies. Drawing near to the emperor, they bow to him and he then commands that they dress the empress in imperial robes, which they do there in front of the emperor. After that she sits on the bench that they have prepared for her near the emperor, and then one of

---

[1] New paragraph made by the editors; in the MS the new paragraph comes after this sentence.

the greatest courtiers, accompanied by others, goes out to the palace compound, where there is a great multitude of people waiting, and, climbing onto a tall iron chair, he announces in a loud voice on behalf of the emperor, '*Anegueçanâ danguecerachên*', which means 'We have made our servant reign.' And then all those around raise their voices in joy and people begin playing instruments and celebrating. And thereafter everyone calls the empress *ituguê*, which seems to be a name of majesty because, although I asked many people, they were unable to tell me its actual meaning, just as they are unable to give the meaning of another name that the emperor has, which is *azeguê*. But not even when they give the empress the name *ituguê* or at any other time do they put a crown on her head.[1]

[2] We shall speak about the ceremonies that they perform and the celebrations they hold at other people's weddings in the second book, when we deal with the errors that they have in the holy sacrament of marriage.

---

[1] See, *História de Etiópia a alta*, in Beccari, *RÆSOI*, 5, pp. 61–4.
[2] New paragraph made by the editors.

<[f. 61]> CHAPTER XVI

## Which deals with the judges that the Prester John has, the manner of proceeding in justice and the punishment that they give to offenders

All the judges that the Prester John has in his empire – who are called *azaxôch*, which means 'commanders', and *umbarôch*, *scilicet* 'chairs' (because they ordinarily sit on chairs to hear the parties and to pass judgement) – descend in a direct line from those judges that Solomon gave to his son Menilehêc, as they affirm as a very certain and established fact and testify in their books, and they are very proud of that. They try so hard to preserve this line of descent in the office of judge that they will not appoint anybody to it at all except {[f. 71]} men who descend from those ancient judges in the male line. Therefore, if their daughters marry men who are not from those families, their children are not allowed into such offices, because they say that that will then cut the direct line of their forefathers, as we stated at the end of chapter 4, according to the testimony of many people and of the emperor himself. And even if he gives this title of *azâx* to certain men who are not members of those families, it does not mean that they become judges like them, for the title is given merely as an honour. These *azaxes* are like supreme judges, but they cannot hand down death, loss of a limb or exile without the emperor confirming the sentence. One of them is called *farâ cembâ* and is like the court magistrate. The *umbars* are like lesser magistrates, and the viceroys always have these in their councils. The court judges always live opposite the emperor's palace, which ordinarily is always towards the west. When the emperor travels round the country, they pitch their tents in front of the emperor's, as we said in chapter 14, and they always leave a very broad street in the middle. The *azaxes* [are all members of the royal council and make a single tribunal], but the *umbars* on the right-hand side of the street make a higher tribunal than those on the left. Near the palace enclosure, on both sides of the street, they have houses or shades[1] where they hear the parties and pass judgement, although they often do so inside their own houses. The *azaxes* are drawn with the emperor's sanction and approval from the *umbars* who most distinguish themselves in performing their duties. In each tribunal of *umbars*, one acts as the president, and the same happens in the tribunal of *azaxes*. These presidents have the task of assigning a judge to anyone who comes and asks for one for whatever affair it may be, but a person is not obliged to ask the presidents of the lower tribunals but whomever he pleases, since he may even ask the president of the *azaxes* or even the emperor himself, who then assigns whomever <[f. 61v]> he likes, because it is not necessary for these judges to be from the families of the *umbars* and *azaxes*, although when it is an important matter an *umbar* ordinarily goes, or if it is very important, an *azâx*.

---

[1] Shady trees under which assemblies were traditionally held and justice administered.

Once the judge has been selected, if the complaint is within the court, he just hears the parties and what the witnesses that they produce have to say without writing anything down, because they never write {[f. 71v]} anything, no matter how serious the affair. But if the complaint is to be heard elsewhere, the judge, even when sent by the emperor, is obliged to go to the lord of the place (for all lands have lords, although they do not pass down from father to son, because the emperor changes them whenever he pleases) and ask him to assign him a man (whom they call *barcafâch*) to sit with him to hear that case. If the lord of the place has some privilege from the emperor (which he is accustomed to give to certain people, as he has to us), he will not allow that judge to enter, but commands the one he has appointed there to hear the case. And, if he has no privilege, he assigns a man to sit with the judge and they both hear the parties. If the respondent asks for time to seek an attorney, they give him three days, unless it is a matter of inheritance, adultery, treason or death, because then they give him ten. Meanwhile the judge eats at the expense of the one who brought him there. The other one is held prisoner unless he gives a surety that he will face justice, and if he is accused of one of those serious matters, they do not accept a surety, but hold him prisoner and often by both hands. His restraint is an iron ring on his right arm, tightened so that he cannot remove his hand, with a short chain, and another ring at the other end of the chain attached to the left arm of somebody whom they trust to guard him, who is called *corânha*. And if they hold him prisoner by both hands, they attach two people to him, one on one side and one on the other.

When the time granted to find an attorney is over, both judges sit on chairs or on the ground on {some} carpets or something else, and the parties with their attorneys stand before them. The plaintiff starts to speak first, or his attorney speaks for him, and he speaks for as long as he pleases, without anyone interrupting him. Then the defendant or his attorney responds, also saying what he pleases without being interrupted. When he finishes, if the plaintiff needs to reply he does so, and if they ask for time to bring witnesses, they grant it as they see fit. From then on the judges eat at the expense of the accused, but if he is later found not to be at fault the accuser has to pay him back in full. When they produce their witnesses, the other party has to say whether they have some suspicion to put forward, and they have to prove it; if not, the witnesses swear an oath and testify {[f. 72]} before the parties, who then claim justice if they are in the right. Then the man that the lord of the place appointed as a companion passes judgement, saying, '*Fêtna negûz* <[f. 62]> *aiatafa* {*egziabehêr*} <*egziabehêz*>',[1] which means, 'Justice and the king may God not lose', *scilicet* 'May God not allow them to lose'; and then he gives the ruling that he thinks appropriate. And the other judge also says the same words and passes judgement. If the parties are satisfied with that, the case ends there, and if not, they appeal to the tribunal that appointed the judge, and if the emperor appointed him, they are forced to go to the lowest tribunal, which is that of the *umbars* of the left hand. Just because they went first to a high tribunal that appointed the judge, the party is not deprived of the right, after the magistrates in that tribunal have passed judgement, to appeal against the ruling if they wish by petitioning the magistrates of the lower tribunal to pass judgement as well. Although in the past the higher courts complained a good deal about that, even so the emperors ordered that it should not be prohibited, saying that they wanted everybody's

---

[1] ARSI, MS Goa 42 is correct here ('*egziabehêr*').

opinion to be heard, so that they could more effectively give justice to the one who was in the right.

Supposing, then, that they take the {ruling} <case> to the *umbars* of the left hand, these sit on their chairs and, ordinarily, there are three or four of them, and the two judges with the parties and their attorneys remain standing. The one appointed by the lord of the land where the complaint was made speaks first, reporting everything that the parties and witnesses said and what judgement he made. Then the other judge repeats the same things and says what judgement he made. If the judges have left something out, the parties or their attorneys add it, and again they argue everything that they think is for the good of their case without interrupting one another. Then, if some new inquiry is necessary, the *umbars* allot time for it, and if not, the lowest-ranking one passes judgement while remaining seated on his chair. I am aware that Francisco Alvares said, on folio 164[1] of his *Historia*, that the magistrates rise to pass judgement, but he was mistaken, confusing them with people who are not magistrates, because sometimes the magistrates out of courtesy ask some of those present to deliver judgement, and those people stand up to pass judgement, but the magistrates do not rise, nor should they, for they are acting on behalf of the emperor, and that is why nobody else there may sit on a chair except them. Next, the magistrates pass judgement one by one, the lowest-ranking one beginning with those words: 'Justice and the king may God not lose.' And all the rest do the same, the president {[f. 72v]} always delivering his judgement last. If the convicted party so wishes, he can appeal to the *umbars* of the right hand, and then the president of those of the left hand goes with the parties and reports everything as it happened and what judgement was delivered in his tribunal, stating whether different rulings were given or not. And then those *umbars* deliver their judgements in the same way as the previous ones. If they confirm the ruling and the convicted party wishes to accept it, believing that they have judged well {~~or because of his expenses (for they always take a long time ...)~~}},[2] it ends there. If not, he appeals to the *azaxes* {~~... to go when~~}, and the two presidents {of the *umbars*} go with the parties and report everything in order and what judgements they have delivered. And then the *azaxes* pass judgement, the president always remaining until last; ...[3] And there the complaint ends, <[f. 62v]> unless it concerns treason against the emperor, adultery, death or inheritance or some other very serious matter, because the *azaxes* cannot conclude these without going to the emperor, nor do they judge them before the parties: they just hear what the witnesses have said and what judgement the judges have delivered, and then they go to the emperor and report everything to him in order and deliver their judgements, one by one, beginning with those on the left hand, and lastly the emperor passes judgement.

In the past, when the emperor had to judge something, the president of the *azaxes* would go with six of the most senior members and the *behêt oadêd* of the left hand and of the right hand. While the parties and their attorneys remained outside the palace, they would go in and, standing before the emperor, one of them would report the whole process of the affair and what judgement was delivered in each tribunal and whether there

---

[1] Álvares, *Prester John of the Indies*, ch. 122, 'Of the tent of justice and its methods, and how they hear the parties', p. 440.

[2] The last two words crossed out are illegible, but the general meaning is clear.

[3] There are nearly three lines of text here that are crossed out and illegible.

were different rulings, and, if he forgot something, another would remind him of it. Then they would pass judgement, one by one, beginning with the least senior, and the last one would be the *behêt oadêd* of the right-hand side: although he and his companion were not of the family of the *azaxes*, nevertheless, as they were the supreme heads of the empire, they passed judgement together with them in serious matters. Then the *acabiçât*, whose dignity and office we mentioned in chapter 4, seated near the emperor, would deliver his judgement, and lastly the emperor. His ruling would then be enforced, without further appeal. Nowadays, ordinarily (as I have seen many times), only the president and two of the most senior *azaxes* enter and, once they have reported the affair {and delivered their judgements} in the order {[[f. 73]]} that we have mentioned, the emperor delivers his judgement without the *acabiçât* being present, although in the most serious matters the emperor always summons other *azaxes* and the *erâz*, if he is at court, and the *balatinôch gueitâ*. They always do this on Wednesdays and Fridays, which are the most convenient days, because they fast and do not eat until six o'clock in the evening, more or less. I mean during the year, because in Lent they do not eat until the sun has set. But if some affair cannot be put off, the emperor will also hear it on a different day. It may be the case that, without passing through these tribunals, they order the offender to argue his case right at the end, as I have seen twice with some rebels that they brought within the first palace enclosure. The emperor sent many *azaxes* with the *balatinôch gueitâ*, and they asked them many questions and came back to the emperor with their answers and then went back to ask them again, and in this way they spent a good part of the day in comings and goings, until they handed down the verdict to cut off their heads. And it was done straight away.

[1] The viceroys also have *umbars* like these in their councils, where they act almost in the same way as those of the court. When the viceroy delivers his judgement it ends there, even if he gives a death sentence, because he acts in place of the emperor, but sometimes he refers certain cases to the emperor, particularly concerning inheritance and treason.

Apart from these <[f. 63]> *azaxes* and *umbars* who are in the tribunals of the emperor and {his} <the> viceroys, there is one that they call *xum* in each town and village, who is appointed by its lord. This man is not a member of the *umbar* families, but some other person that the lord of the place wants. This judge hears all the complaints of that place, unless the plaintiff brings a judge from the court of the emperor or the viceroy of that land, because if he brings one the *xum* does not hear the case except as the companion appointed by the lord of the place, as we said above, and then he receives one third of what the judge who comes from outside gets. But if no other judge is brought in, he sits in a public place, ordinarily together with the elders and most respected men of the place, although that is not obligatory. He hears the parties and the witnesses and, when they have finished pleading, he tells one of those seated to pass judgement. This man stands up and reports what the parties have alleged and then he passes judgement as he sees fit. The others do the same in turn, although the most respected ones do not stand to {[[f. 73v]]} deliver their judgements. Lastly, he delivers his own judgement. If the convicted party wishes to abide by the sentence, it ends there and he pays little by way of costs. If not, he appeals to the *umbars* of the court, if the place lies in their district, or to those of the viceroy to whom the land belongs. This judge then goes with the parties and, in front of them, reports to the *umbars* everything that they have alleged and proven and what

---

[1] New paragraph made by the editors.

judgement he has delivered. From that point on, the case runs as we described above, and the *umbars* to whom the case went first receive a certain fee according to the complaint, which the convicted party pays. But even if he appeals to other tribunals, they do not add further costs to those he has to pay to the first one, for all of them are given their livings by the emperor.

The most common punishments that they give to offenders, even {for} <in> serious cases that affect the emperor, are exile or imprisonment on an island that they call Dec in Lake Dambiâ,[1] which they call a sea, or in some mountain fastness. And there they remain under guard until they are pardoned, which is usually not for very long. In the past they used to throw some off cliffs, as Emperor Adamâs Çaguêd commanded, but now they only cut off their heads or feet or hands, or hang them. Thieves, if the theft was not very great, are whipped the first time with long straps, and the second time they have their ears or noses cut off, and sometimes a hand or foot, and the third time they are hanged. The theft may be such <[f. 63v]> that they are hanged the first time. Hanging is also used for other crimes, such as killing someone, if the person is low-born; and sometimes, when one person has killed another, after he has been sentenced to death and the emperor has confirmed the sentence, they hand him over to the kinsfolk of the deceased for them to do with him what they please. Some will pardon him because of entreaties or goods; others will take him to the countryside and spear or hack him to death. Sometimes, however, because the people that gather round there shout out in pity at seeing that, the kinsfolk run off {quickly} leaving him for dead when he is not, as happened to someone in 1614: after inflicting many wounds, including two that went right through him, they left him, thinking that he was dead; when his kinsfolk took him away to bury him, they found he was still alive and so hid him and cured him, and they came to me to ask me to obtain a pardon and protection from the emperor, because his opponents would kill him wherever they found him. I asked the emperor for this protection, and he answered that he would give it willingly, because they had already {[f. 74]} left him, considering themselves avenged for the evil thing that he had done to them. He immediately commanded the president of the *azaxes*, who was there, to issue a proclamation that nobody should do harm to that man, on pain of death. He said that that was nothing new, because that case had already been settled in that way on other occasions. On this occasion, I said to the emperor that it would be good to command that the judges should not hand over murderers in that way, because they were killed cruelly and not without hatred. He answered that they had that custom because, when they were handed over, they were ordinarily pardoned, but that it did not seem right to him either. I never heard of that being done again from that time forward. They also say that formerly they used to throw traitors to the emperor to the lions, but that is not the custom now and it has not been done for a long time, except in the case of a very noble woman who, because she had adopted our holy faith, was ordered to be thrown to the lions by Emperor Adamâs Çaguêd, but they did not harm her, as we shall see later. A person who is going to be executed for some crime does not confess, nor is there anyone to remind him how he should prepare for that step, and I also pointed that out to the emperor and told him what happens in our lands. He thought it was very good and said that he would command that they give the person time to prepare himself, and the *azaxes* thought it was very good.

[1] See bk I, ch. 10, p. 40 above.

Adultery is never punished with death, but with a fine. If the husband {asks for justice} <makes an accusation>, they rule that the adulterer should pay him in goods according to his person and that the adulteress should shave her head and leave the possessions she had to her husband; and having done that she may go and marry whomever she pleases. Moreover, anybody who wants to may leave his adulterous wife and freely marry another woman, because they say that Christ Our Lord gave permission for this in the Gospel. But, from the continual conversations and disputations that we have had with them and their lawyers on this subject, many now understand that neither did Christ Our Lord mean such a thing, nor should it be done, as we shall declare in the second book.

<[f. 64]> From what we have said, it is clear to see how false the information was that Friar Luis de Urreta was given on this subject, since he says in chapter 19 that the Prester John's Grand Council, which knows about all the affairs of the empire, both civil and criminal, because it has supreme authority over everything, consists of thirty councillors, six patriarchs, six archbishops, six bishops, six abbots of the Order of Saint Anthony and six lay gentlemen, all persons of great prudence, learning {[f. 74v]} and virtue chosen from among the nobles. That is very different from what happens here, because none of the emperor's tribunals or councils contains anyone other than those we have mentioned above, and from *umbars* they rise to *azaxes*, and they are all married men. And in Ethiopia there are no patriarchs, archbishops or bishops, as we have already stated, but only the one that they call *abuna, scilicet* 'our father', and he is always sent to them by the patriarch of Alexandria.

A little further on, on page 179, he says that they have no need of lawyers or jurists because they do not have written laws, apart from 127 statutes that the former emperors Joam the Holy and Phelipe VII made, which are posted in public in the main square of any city, and rulings are handed down according to them. Anything else is judged by good men. On this subject, he tells a story of some learned men from Portugal in these words:

*In the time of the Prester John who was called Panusio, many doctors in law arrived in Ethiopia, sent by the King of Portugal with great libraries of their Baldos and Bartolos, with the aim of introducing the doctrine of their laws. On seeing so many books, the emperor asked which science they dealt with, and he received the reply that they were books of imperial, civil and canon law, and that they were doctors in law, whose office it was to assist in the good government of cities, provinces and kingdoms, to decide suits, prosecute causes and find in favour of those in the right, and they had brought those books for that purpose. The emperor replied as if spitting on an empty stomach, 'In the end, what we gather from all that you have said is that you call yourselves Doctors, <and> I know of no other Doctors than those of the Church – Saint Augustine, Saint Athanasius, Saint Jerome and Saint Basil – and in my lands it is not permitted for anyone to be called a doctor except the holy theologians. These are books of laws. I do not know that there is any other law than that of Jesus Christ, and we should be very wise if we knew this law, for we do not call the rest laws but constitutions. And since your office is to prosecute causes and inform about justice, I have no need of lawsuits in my kingdom. And so it serves the peace of my empire for you to return to Portugal, and for you all to depart from all my lands within so many days, taking all these books with you, because I shall throw them all into the Nile, without recourse. And if you argue, you will go in after them.' When they saw the Prester John's determination and that he spoke to them with an angry look, a severe expression <[f. 64v]> and a complaining tone, threatening them, they* *considered it best to embark for Goa, without awaiting further replies or deferrals according to the law.*[1]

{[f. 75]} Up to here are fables by Joam Balthesar or the person who informed the author, because, in the first place, there have never been such emperors in Ethiopia as Joam the Holy, Phelipe VII or Panusio, nor have such Portuguese lawyers ever come here, because the first Portuguese to discover this Ethiopia and enter it was Pêro de Covilham, who had been sent by the king of Portugal, Dom Joam II, on 7th May 1487; and next came another Portuguese called Joam Gomes with a cleric sent by Tristam de Acunha, as Francisco Alvares says on folio 94[2] of his *History*. Ambassador Dom Rodrigo de Lima arrived here in 1520, sent by King Dom Manoel, with Francisco Alvares, his chaplain, and others who accompanied them, and they stayed in Ethiopia for six years. Then, in 1541, Dom Christovam da Gama came with 400 soldiers and recovered the empire, almost all of which was already under Moorish rule. In 1555, Ambassador Diogo Dias arrived, who had been sent by the viceroy of India, and Father Master Gonçalo Rodriguez with him as his companion.[3] In March 1557, Father Bishop Dom Andre de Oviedo came with five members of the Society[4] and a few Portuguese. Lastly, we seven fathers[5] have been here since 1603 until this year of 1622, and I do not think any other Portuguese have entered Ethiopia to this day. However that may be, it is quite certain that the lawyers that the author mentions never came to Ethiopia. If they had come, the emperors are not so unrefined that they would have treated in such a manner the lawyers that such a great prince as the King of Portugal had sent to their land; on the contrary, they welcome even the Moors and heathens that come from other parts and treat them very well, as I have seen in many cases. Rather, one of the things that they would have liked most is the laws of Portugal, as I have always noticed, because the emperor that they elected shortly after I arrived, who was called Za Denguîl and who later titled himself Atâf Çaguêd, wrote to me, before I met him, asking me to bring him the *Book of Justice of the Kings of Portugal*, because he very much wanted to see it. And *Erâz* Athanatêus,[6] the son-in-law of Emperor Malâc Çaguêd, who on the latter's death governed the empire with Empress Mariâm Cinâ for seven years because {Prince Iacob} <the prince> was still small, sometimes begged me to send for the *Book of Ordinances of Portugal*, because the judges did not know how to judge and the emperors even less, so that when rulings were brought to them they ordinarily confirmed {[f. 75v]} the judgements delivered by the judges. And Emperor Seltân Çaguêd, who is alive now, has often told me to try to have these books sent to him.[7]

---

[1] Urreta, *Historia de la Etiopia*, excerpt (with omissions) from bk I, ch. 19, entitled 'Of the Prester John's Grand Council, of the manner of proceeding in justice, and of the punishments that they give to offenders', pp. 177–86. Páez quotes this passage in Spanish.

[2] Álvares, *Prester John of the Indies*, ch. 74, 'How they told the Ambassador that the grandees of the Court were advising the Prester not to let him return, and how he ordered him to move his tent, and asked for a cross, and how he sent to summon the Ambassador', p. 278.

[3] Páez narrates this episode in greater detail in bk III, ch. 4, vol. II below.

[4] See Glossary (first Jesuit mission). The episode is narrated in bk III, ch. 5, vol. II below, and Manuel de Almeida repeats it ('Historia de Ethiopia a Alta', in Beccari, *RÆSOI*, 5, pp. 369–70.

[5] See Glossary (second Jesuit mission).

[6] See Glossary (Athanatêus/Atenâtéwos).

[7] Páez apparently did not fulfil the request. At that time, he might have received the *Ordenações, e leis do Reino de Portugal, recopiladas per mandado do muito alto catholico e poderoso Rei Dom Philippe o Primeiro* (Lisbon, 1603), and the *Repertório das ordenações do Reino de Portugal*, by M. Mendes de Castro (Lisbon, 1604).

<[f. 65]> He says something else, on page 183,[1] that he might well have dispensed with, even if it were true, concerning some Italians that he claims were persuaded by the evil sin, which had never been heard of in the land of the Prester John. Thus the scandal and agitation that it caused among the *Abexins* was so great that the Grand Council was confused, not knowing what punishment to give them. Therefore, at the emperor's command, they referred them to the Latin Council for judgement under the laws of Europe, and the councillors, considering the seriousness of the crime and the scandal that they had caused, judged that they should be burnt, but the Grand Council did not want that to be done in Ethiopia, but that they should be taken to Mozambique and the sentence carried out there. The emperor, however, commanded that they be taken as prisoners to Goa, where they were publicly burnt on arrival. All this is mere fiction, because there never has been a Latin Council in Ethiopia (as we shall say later), nor is there any recollection of such a case, and, had it happened, the old Portuguese here would have heard of it, and they all affirm that they have never heard of such a thing and that the people of the country would not have forgotten it. Moreover, those who are against our holy faith would be throwing it in our faces every day, because they even invent other falsehoods in order to discredit Saint Leo and those of the Catholic faith, and therefore it is certain that such a thing never happened. In addition, to say that they sent them as prisoners to Mozambique is ridiculous, since they would have had to go overland, through countless deserts and kinds of people that lie in between; nor by sea does any ship go there, nor could they have sent them as prisoners to Goa, except with great difficulty.

What he says {a little} further on is also a fable, that they throw heretics and apostates to the lions, and that the Prester John has agreements with all the neighbouring Moorish kings, such as the King of Borno, the Pasha of Egypt and the Kings of Arabia, that, if anyone from Ethiopia renounces his faith and becomes a Moor, they will hand him back and they throw him alive to the lions; or if he becomes Catholic or is stubborn in his apostasy, he must certainly die; and the Prester John is also obliged to hand over to the Moorish kings any Moor who becomes a Christian so that they may deal with him. But there is an advantage for the Christians that the Moors granted, which is that if some infidel becomes a Christian, they deliver him straight away to the friars of Saint Dominic, who catechize him and put a small scapular on him with a certain seal {[f. 76]} of the prior; when he is wearing that, nobody can say anything and the Prester John is not obliged to hand him over to his king. And, when the Moors find out that the new convert is wearing the insignia of Saint Dominic, they fall silent and waive their claim, because they hold the monks of the Alleluia in such high regard that they consider it a good outcome, thinking that as he is in the power of those monks they can only be absolutely right.

<[f. 65v]> That is what Friar Luis de Urreta says. But nothing happens in that way, because there is no such agreement between the Prester John and the Moorish kings – neither the Kings of Arabia nor the Pasha of Egypt, who are so far away to hand over anyone who became a Moor. Not even the Turks in {Alquîco} <Alguîco>,[2] which they call Adecono, which is on Ethiopian soil, will hand over a Christian who becomes a Moor.

---

[1] Urreta, *Historia de la Etiopia*, bk I, ch. 19.
[2] Arqiqo (Ḥergigo), a Red Sea port on the mainland opposite the island of Massawa (Mešŝewā' – Páez's Maçuâ).

Even less will the emperor hand over a Moor who becomes a Christian. Rather, when a young Moorish man of royal caste fled here from the lands that Friar Luis here apparently calls Borno (which they actually call Dequîn), and when the king of those lands asked the emperor to send him back if he wanted the horse contract to continue (because the emperor gets many very good horses from there) since the young man was a Moor, the emperor replied in my presence, 'That Moor is very foolish if he thinks that I will hand over those who come and ask for my protection, something that not even the heathens do.' And he commanded that he be given good lands straight away, and later he became a Christian. Nor do they throw heretics and apostates to the lions, but if someone who became a Moor or heathen comes and says that he was wrong and wants to become a Christian, they baptize him again and, at most, they give him some penitence. And in Ethiopia there are no friars of Saint Dominic, as we shall see in the second book, nor do the Moors take the monks that are here, or indeed Christians, into any account; rather, they regard us all as men without law or knowledge of God.

Furthermore, he says on page 185[1] that they wall up witches {for ever} and they punish a blasphemer the first time with a verbal reprimand, the second by putting him half-naked at the church door on a feast day with a candle in his hand, and the third time, considering him an irrational beast, they dress him in yellow and put a halter round his neck and in his mouth and lead him around the whole city and then exile him to a desert island in the Red Sea or down near the Cape of Good Hope, where he dies of hunger. But no such thing happens, because they neither wall up witches nor know {[f. 76v]} what that means, and they do not send blasphemers to such islands; nor could the emperor do so even if he wished, because he does not govern anything in the Red Sea, let alone the Cape of Good Hope. And it would be very good if they did punish them, but blasphemies are often heard without anyone taking notice of them to punish them.

---

[1] Urreta, *Historia de la Etiopia*, bk I, ch. 19.

189

# CHAPTER XVII

## Of the investigation that they conduct into the emperor's and the viceroys' magistrates

It would not have been necessary to make a special chapter to deal with the investigations that they conduct into the emperor's judges and magistrates and into those of the viceroys, because everything that there is to say on this subject could have been said in a few words if Friar Luis de Urreta had not forced me to refer to some things in chapter 20 of his first book, because, if I were to pass over them without mentioning <[f. 66]> them, people might think that there was some truth in them, although they are nothing more than mere fiction invented and sketched out in the mind of the one who informed him. This is what he says:

*Of all the nations in the world, one of those that most abhor gifts and donations are the Ethiopians, so much so that, when Emperor Phelipe IX learnt that they had received a present during the vacancy left by his predecessor, he commanded that every seven years half of the Grand Council should go to Mount Amara to be investigated for the way they governed and administered justice, and that custom is maintained today in the form and manner that will be described. When the emperor is with all the Council members in a hall, he commands the fifteen of them to go to Mount Amara with one of the kings' firstborn sons who serve him, accompanied by 1,000 horsemen of his bodyguard, and, as soon as they have taken their leave of the emperor, they set off, with a horseman going before them bearing his standard of yellow taffeta with the arms of the empire on it. On arriving at the mountain (where they are received by the military abbots), the councillors dismount from their horses and the firstborn son, remaining on his, says these words to the abbots: 'My lords, I deliver to you the fifteen of the Grand Council who are here by order and command of the emperor, the greatest king over all the Abyssinian kings, Emperor of Ethiopia, forever David my lord.' And after saying this he returns to the court, where he reports the course of his journey to the emperor. Then the emperor makes it known to all the cities of the empire, through his attorneys, {[f. 77]} who constantly reside at court, that anyone who feels aggrieved by those councillors should state his grievance and ask for satisfaction for it, so that justice may be done. When this command arrives in the cities, the nobles there gather with some of their clergy and have it proclaimed in public, commanding that those who have received some grievance should write it down in a report with their name and that of the councillor by whom they feel aggrieved, and the circumstances and the time when it happened. They do that and cast the papers with their complaints into a securely locked chest, which is put in a public place for a {continuous} period of eight days, with a narrow opening, like a trap, through which the papers and reports can be inserted but cannot be removed by any means. When the allotted eight days are over, each city*

190

sends its chest as it is, without opening it (because only the emperor has the key), to the court with a good guard of soldiers, and a citizen goes as a guide bearing a standard with the arms of that city. On arriving at the court, they go straight to the palace, and the emperor gives a key to his manservant (who is the one of the firstborn who has served him most), commanding him to use it to open a large room where they put these boxes, and when the gentleman has placed it in there he gives the soldiers and the people who brought it permission to return to their city. And this style and manner of proceeding is kept with all the chests that the cities bring.

<[f. 66v]> After all the chests have been collected in the room, the emperor enters it when he sees fit, accompanied by all the firstborn of his vassal kings and by twenty other gentlemen of his household, and commands them to open said chests; they take out the papers and, keeping those of each city separate, they make them into a book and volume and on it they write the name of the city that sent {it} <them>, and they place them all together in another large box, which he sends with the ambassador of the chief abbot of the military Order of Saint Anthony, whom we call the Grand Master, accompanied by 300 horsemen, to the priests of Saba, who will be the judges, on a litter covered with black satin. When it reaches the city, they come out to receive it with great pomp and place it under good guard in the Consistory, which is the place where the nobility gather, and the ambassador returns to the court with all his company. Then the priests of Saba come out of the church where they have been, accompanied by many people, their faces covered according to the custom of Abyssinian priests. On reaching the consistory they sit at a round table and, having sent out everyone else, {[f. 77v]} they open the box and take out all the papers. Reading the grievances written there one by one, the priests of Saba write them down and send them under guard to the priests and nobles of the city whence the petition or complaint came, so that, after investigating the case, they may send them a report on it. If it seems that the councillor is at fault, the priests of Saba advise him of it so that, if he has a justification for what he is accused of, he may issue it within a certain time, in which he explains himself to a gentleman of the mountain, and if evidence is needed for his defence, the priests send the gentleman himself to find it wherever necessary. And if they find the councillor innocent of the charges brought, they command the priests of the city whence the complaints and accusations came to punish those who sent them straight away with a like-for-like penalty, depending on the seriousness of the crime, as an example to everyone. Having done this and everything else that is needed to conclude the investigation, the priests of Saba shut the councillors' charges and justifications together with their ruling or opinion in a cedar box, which they send to the emperor with the priests whom they appoint as deputies for this task; these priests take it to the court and, before arriving, they spend the night in pavilions. And then the emperor sends a firstborn, who goes out to receive them accompanied by 100 horsemen of his guard, and the firstborn, having received and welcomed them courteously, accompanies them with his men to the palace; they go with their faces covered by their veils and, once they have dismounted from their horses and climbed the stairs, the emperor <[f. 67]> receives them with much show of love. After the deputies have given him the chest, he has it put away in his chamber and gives them permission to return, which they do in the same way as they came.

When the emperor has seen the opinion of the priests of Saba, he sends a letter and writ to the oldest of the princes of the empire who live on Mount Amara, to send the councillors back to their places. And if any one of them is excluded by the letter, he is seen thereby to be have been removed from the Grand Council for ever, without recourse. After that, the councillors

*return to the court accompanied by the gentleman who took the letter and by 12,000 horsemen
of the emperor's guard, and when the councillors come close to the city of Zambra, they spend
that night in pavilions and tents. The next morning, the nobles and citizens of the court come
out to accompany them with much celebration of trumpets and other musical instruments.
With this celebration and applause they take them to the palace, where they find {[f. 78]}
the emperor seated on a high throne with twelve steps, covered with rich carpets and rugs,
dressed with imperial majesty, and with all the firstborn sons of his vassal kings around him.
When the councillors come before the emperor, he raises a cross that he holds in his hand as a
sceptre, and they kneel on the ground, leaning against some long benches. Meanwhile the
ambassador of the grand abbot climbs up to a pulpit and, speaking to the emperor, says to
him, 'You see here, lord, those who counsel <you> for the benefit of your peoples and subjects,
and, while they have been on Mount Amara by your command under investigation, nothing
at all has been found against them. And now, by your order, they have returned to your Grand
Council to serve you on it as they used to do.' Then all those present shout out as one, 'Long
live the emperor who preserves the constitutions of his empire for the glory of God and of the
princes of the Apostles, in observance of the laws instituted by Juan the Holy and Philipe VII.'
To all of that the emperor, with a joyful and smiling countenance, shows that he acquiesces in
what they say and that he is pleased to accept what his peoples have shown. And with that the
investigation is brought to an end.*[1]

Up to here are the words of the author, in which, apart from what he says at the beginning about bribes (although he overstates this as well), there is nothing that resembles the
truth of what happens here, as I have seen in the eighteen years since I arrived in this
empire,[2] and I have spent most of this time at the court. In order to inform myself further
about the facts, I asked the president of the Supreme Council and two other colleagues of
his about them {in great detail} <on many occasions>. They assured me that none of
those who are <[f. 67v]> now members of this and the other tribunals (and some of them
are very old) have been to Mount Amharâ[3] in order to be investigated, nor have they heard
it said that their predecessors ever went there for that purpose, nor has there been such a
statute, nor a limited time to conduct the investigation, nor were they all investigated
together, but instead, whenever somebody complained about one or more of them, the
emperor would give him a judge straight away and he would put forward his grievances to
him and make his complaint and the judge would give his ruling. If one of the parties was
not satisfied and wished to appeal, they would come to his tribunal and the judge would
report the whole course of the complaint and what judgement he had made, and the
parties, who are present with their attorneys, add anything that the judge may have forgotten {[f. 78v]} that relates to their case, and they put forward again anything else that they
please; and then the *azaxes* go to the emperor and report everything to him and deliver
their judgements before him as they each see fit; and lastly it is the emperor's turn. And
then his ruling is made public and put into practice.

---

[1] Urreta, *Historia de la Etiopia*, excerpt (with minor omissions) from bk I, ch. 20, entitled 'Of the investigation
that they conduct into the Grand Council, and how they greatly abhor bribery and corruption', pp. 188–91.

[2] From this information, the writing of this particular chapter may be dated to about 1621/22, since Páez
arrived in Ethiopia in May 1603.

[3] See bk I, chs 6–9, above, and the Glossary (Mount Amharâ /*Ambā* Gešan).

If the emperor has had bad reports about that magistrate against whom he has been asked to provide a judge, not only does he provide one, but sometimes (though rarely) he orders a proclamation to be issued just in the town or district where he is, for everyone who has a grievance against that magistrate to enter a complaint. And those who so desire do so and, even without this proclamation, they often accuse him of having taken bribes, although the emperor has commanded that they must not take bribes on pain of excommunication. But they hardly ever succeed in having the emperor judge these complaints about bribes, because, even if the party can prove it, he gives up before then, either because he comes to an agreement through the entreaties of others, or for fear that he might later fall into his hands on some occasion. Not long ago they complained that one of the Supreme Council members had taken bribes, and there was no lack of evidence, because it was clear that he had taken many. Even so, the affair did not reach the point where the emperor's judge would issue a verdict; so it was covered up because of entreaties or some goods that he handed over in secret.

Complaints are made against the viceroys' magistrates in the same way: when someone is aggrieved, he asks the viceroy for a judge. He makes his complaint before the one that the viceroy appoints and, if necessary, the viceroy delivers his judgement as well. But, if the party wishes, he may appeal to the emperor. And that concludes all the mysteries that Friar Luis de Urreta makes about the investigations into the members of the Grand Council. And there never have been such emperors as Joam and Philippe VII, or even Philippe I, in Ethiopia, as Emperor Seltân Çaguêd assured me and as may be seen in the catalogues of the emperors, which we put in chapter 5.

# CHAPTER XVIII

In which it is declared whether there is or has been a Latin council in
Ethiopia to deal with matters concerning Europe

In chapter 21 of his first book, Friar Luis de Urreta recounts many and varied things about
the Latin Council that he claims exists in Ethiopia for matters that concern people from
Europe that live in this country. We may briefly reply to that that they are all fables
invented by {[f. 79]} Joam Balthesar <[f. 68]> or imagined by the person who gave the
author the information. {But since they redound to the discredit of very important
persons who are worthy of veneration, as are the most Christian defender of the august-
ness of the Holy Roman Church, the King of Portugal, Joam III, the Most Reverend Dom
Joam Nunes Barreto, patriarch of Ethiopia, Father Bishop Melchior Carneiro and other
fathers of our Society, it behoves me to state them in greater detail, so that the truth of
what happened may be made clear and not rendered obscure before those who do not
realize that in such important matters credence should not be given to information from
an unknown man to print and publish it to the world as if it were true; for even when I
mentioned other, much less important things that the book says, Emperor Seltân Çaguêd
was astounded that they should so readily give credence to a man that they did not know
to authenticate his lies by printing them.} But so that what we are to say {here} may be
better understood, I shall {first} mention some {word} thing of what the author {begin-
ning with what} says about the Latin Council, for the rest is not relevant to us here. He
says, then, in chapter 21:

*Having written about the order of the Grand Council, it is appropriate to deal with the
other lesser Council that the emperor has in his court, called the Latin Council, which was
founded by Alexandre III, because, on seeing that many nations and merchants had been
arriving in his states from Latin lands every day since their discovery, it seemed to him not
only useful but also very necessary for the sake of good government to make and found a council
for the Latin people, and it was named the Latin Council after them. He assigned large
stipends and very substantial salaries to the councillors and, from each nation that arrived in
the empire, he selected two experienced and God-fearing persons of wisdom and conscience,
who were two Venetians, two Florentines and two Portuguese. The Venetians and Florentines
come mainly via Cairo, and the Portuguese from Goa, and some from Portugal. These six
councillors make up the Latin Council, which serves to inform the emperor about the affairs
of Europe, especially when some arrive from those parts to do business or to see Ethiopia with
letters from certain princes, or from the Abyssinians who live in Rome. In such a case, one or
two of the councillors appointed by the council go to the emperor to inform him in detail not
only of the stranger's purpose and motive in entering the empire, but also of his land, rank*

{{f. 79v}} *and position, because the emperor treats the strangers according to the report from this council, and sometimes he indulges and regales them, if their rank so requires. It is also this council's responsibility to interpret the letters that go to the emperor from Latin lands and to answer them in the appropriate language. This council was set up on the insistence and persuasion of the Very Reverend Father Andres de Oviedo, a priest of the Society of Jesus, who, because he was so learned and exemplary, was sent by the Apostolic See with the title of patriarch, and he lived for many years in this dignity, setting the Abyssinians a very good example to their spiritual benefit, and the Prester John honoured him very highly and gave him the position of president of this council, and the good Father fulfilled his role with as much satisfaction, contentment and applause from the Abyssinians as they could desire.*[1]

Up to here are the words of Friar Luis de Urreta, but nothing in them <[f. 68v]> corresponds to the truth, because, in the first place, nobody knows of this Alexandre III, and in the catalogues of the emperors that we put in chapter 5 there is only one Alexandre, whom they call Escander, and he lived long before the Portuguese discovered Ethiopia, because, as we said in chapter 16, the first Portuguese who discovered Ethiopia and entered it was Pêro de Covilham, who left Portugal on 7th May 1487, and Emperor Alexandre had already died in 1475.[2] And when the author speaks of this same Alexandre III on pages 118[3] and 139,[4] he says that he died in 1606, and I arrived in Ethiopia in May 1603 and did not find any such Alexandre, but Iacob, the son of Emperor Malâc Çaguêd, who had died seven years previously having reigned for thirty-three years, and nobody has been called Alexandre since then. If we accept that there was such an Alexandre III, what he says about him here, that he founded the Latin Council on the insistence of the Father Patriarch Andre de Oviedo, to whom he gave the post of president of this Latin Council, does not agree with what he says later, on page 615,[5] that Emperor Mena (who was actually called Minas) wrote to Pope Pius V that Father Andre de Oviedo was the president of the Latin Council and that he was revered as a saint, because then, on page 617,[6] he claims that Alexandre III succeeded Mena. Therefore there is a very obvious contradiction, because if Alexandre III founded the Latin Council, how could Mena, who came before him, have written to Pius V that Father Patriarch Andre de Oviedo was the president of the Latin Council, which had not yet been set up? {{f. 80}} The author contradicts himself many more times when talking about this Alexandre III, as we showed in chapter 1; had he noticed them, they would have been enough for him not to give credence to the information from Joam Balthesar, however much he insisted that they were authentic papers, as he says on page 211.[7]

However, leaving aside the contradictions and Alexandre III, it is quite certain that there is not and never has been a Latin Council in Ethiopia, and a Venetian called Joam Antonio, who says he arrived here thirty-two years ago, says the same. And[8] [the

---

[1] Urreta, *Historia de la Etiopia*, excerpt from bk I, ch. 21, pp. 192–3.
[2] Eskender in fact died in 1494.
[3] Urreta, *Historia de la Etiopia*, bk I, ch. 11.
[4] Urreta, *Historia de la Etiopia*, bk I, ch. 12.
[5] Urreta, *Historia de la Etiopia*, bk III, ch. 1.
[6] Urreta, *Historia de la Etiopia*, bk III, ch. 1.
[7] Urreta, *Historia de la Etiopia*, bk I, ch. 21.
[8] Several words have been crossed out and are illegible.

Portuguese captain], Joam Gabriel by name, a man aged sixty-six who as a boy was brought up by Father Patriarch Andre de Oviedo, says that he has never seen or heard of such a Council in Ethiopia. The same testimony is given by many old men, the sons of Portuguese, who were also brought up in the patriarch's household, and by others of this land whom I have asked. And I am an eye-witness to the fact that there has not been such a thing between 1603 and now. Yet the author states, on page 210,[1] that it was still in existence when he was writing, which must have been in about 1608, hence everything he says about the Latin <[f. 69]> Council is false. And equally far from the truth are almost all the things that he then tells about the mission that thirteen fathers of the Society made to Ethiopia, taking the opportunity of having said that Father Andre de Oviedo had been the president of the Latin Council to show how he had arrived in Ethiopia, and principally to refute Nicolao Sandeiro, Father Pêro Mafei and other fathers of the Society who have written on this subject.[2] But we shall see how unjustified he was in book 3, where he also deals specifically with Father Patriarch Andre de Oviedo.

[1] Urreta, *Historia de la Etiopia*, bk I, ch. 21.

[2] Urreta only mentions the authors that Páez names, commenting that they had been ill informed about Ethiopian Christianity (Giovanni Pietro Maffei, *Societate Iesu Historiarum Indicarum libri XVI*, with various editions after 1588; Nicolau Sandero, *Monarchia*). See Urreta, *Historia de la Etiopia*, bk I, ch. 21, p. 211.

# CHAPTER XIX

## On whether the Prester John visits the cities of his empire
in person

After Friar Luis de Urreta, in chapter 22 of his first book, has described the great splendour and pomp with which he says the Prester John goes to visit the cities of his empire one year after being crowned in Saba and every seven years thereafter, he continues his *Historia* on page 221 with these words:

*When the emperor reaches a city, he sets up his pavilion nearby and rests in it that night, and, early the next day, dressed in his imperial attire and riding an elephant, he makes his way to the city with all the majesty and greatness with which he went to Saba to be sworn in. The king may not remain in the city {[f. 80v]} or be in residence there: instead they make him go away somewhere for the duration of the visit. When the emperor enters, the six aldermen and jurors on whom the government of the city depends stand at the gate, wearing robes of black damask, together with a horseman with a standard bearing the city's arms, and likewise all the priests, one of whom holds a missal in his hand, and the mayor of the city with a short staff and a black cowl like that of a collegian on his shoulders, except that this kind is worn around the neck and hangs down in front like a stole, and it is finished with gold tassels and the emperor's arms. The emperor dismounts from his elephant and, placing his hand on the missal, swears to uphold the constitutions of the Florentine Council and of all the Apostolic See together with those of Juan the Holy and Phelippe VII. After that, the priests come two by two to make reverence, and behind them the mayor and aldermen, who, having sworn him obedience, promise to give him one out of every three sons for the defence of the empire, as we shall say in due course. Then the emperor enters the city on foot accompanied only by the forty-two kings' sons, the fifteen members of his Grand Council, the ambassador of the grand abbot and a few gentlemen from Latin lands. With this retinue he goes to visit the four parish churches and the Abbey of Saint Anthony, and then the consistory of the nobility, where he makes a speech to them about observing the statutes of the empire, concluding by offering them his help and imperial sponsorship for whatever is necessary, which he does indeed provide in those matters that he considers appropriate. After that he arrives at the convent of maidens (of which there is one in every city), <[f. 69v]> where with much beneficence he supplies them with what they need, and he does the same in the young people's seminaries, as we shall describe below. And if in the convent of maidens there is one who is about to marry, he gives permission for that, for otherwise she could not do so without going against the custom that they have that no king's child can marry without the emperor's licence, nor a noble without that of the king, nor a citizen without that of the nobles, nor a plebeian without that of the* *citizens, except where the emperor gives licence, as we have said. The emperor continues his visit to the rest of the cities in the manner that we have described.*[1]

Up to here are the author's words, in which there is hardly anything that is not a fable. To start with the customs of former years, so far were the emperors from {[f. 81]} visiting the cities of their empire that they did not even allow themselves to be seen inside their palace, except by their wives and thirty young slaves who served them and three great men who governed the empire. If someone else needed to speak to them, even if he were a son-in-law or brother-in-law, he would have to enter at night and, with all the candles out, he would speak without seeing anything but just hearing the emperor's voice. Even that was considered a very great favour, because it was rarely granted, as we said in chapter 4. But, when they had to pass judgement on a matter of importance, the president and six of the most senior *azâxes* would come in together with the three who governed, as we stated in chapter 16. Even after that superstition had been abandoned, that kind of visit was not customary [as everyone affirms]. As for the years from 1603 until now, I am an eye-witness since I have almost always been at court, and the emperor has never done such a thing. Nor are there cities as Friar Luis imagines: even the places where the viceroys or a few local governors live are just large villages. When people are aggrieved at them or their magistrates and want to ask the emperor for a judge, he sends one there straight away to carry out justice. And if the matters are serious and the people think that justice will not be done properly if it is done there, they ask the emperor to send for the culprit or wait for him to come to court, because the viceroys who do not live very far away come quite often, and then they bring suit against them before the emperor's magistrates, who then relate everything to the emperor for him to pass judgement.

As for when he says that the emperor goes to the city on an elephant, not only does he never ride one, but a tame elephant has never been seen in Ethiopia, although there are plenty of wild ones. And even if the emperor did go and visit the cities, they would hardly have him swear at the entrance gate on the missal that he would keep the constitutions of the Florentine Council and of all the Apostolic See together with those of Joam the Holy and Phelippe VII, because they do not obey the Roman Church, as we have already said, and as we shall see at length in the second book; nor has there ever been an emperor in Ethiopia called Joam or Phelippe VII, nor the custom of giving the emperor one out of every three sons for the defence of the empire, because everyone goes to war when necessary, except the {old men} <serfs>, who work the land. Nor do those forty kings' sons accompanying the emperor exist, or the ambassador of the Grand {[f. 81v]} Abbot. And there is not even one convent of maidens in the whole empire, let alone one in every city; nor is permission from the emperor [for there are no kings, as <[f. 70]> we have already said] necessary for noble maidens to marry, nor permission from the nobles for the citizens, or from these for the plebeians; because without any of that everyone marries when he likes and {with} <in> the best possible {person} <way>. There is, however, a custom by which, if the young man or woman who is about to marry is related to the emperor, they inform him, not because his permission is necessary, because they can marry without it if they wish, but so that he can bestow certain honours on them, which involve

---

[1] Urreta, *Historia de la Etiopia*, excerpt from bk I, ch. 22, entitled 'Of the manner and style that the Prester John adopts in disputes, and visits to the cities of his empire' pp. 221–2. Páez quotes this passage in Spanish.

going to the palace on the afternoon before the marriage as night is falling, accompanied by the principal lords of the court in the case of a young man or, in the case of a maiden, ladies, beneath a silk cloth, or at least a cotton cloth with various painted designs, which they get from India. It is held up by the corners in the manner of a canopy by four maidens, but it is much longer than it is wide. And so other maidens walk beside the lady, holding the cloth up with their hands so that it does not touch her head, and it hangs down the sides and behind so that even the ones holding it by the corners can hardly be seen at all from the outside. This kind of cloth is used by all the emperor's kinswomen, and by them alone, when they go from one house to another on foot, but not when riding a mule. And when the young man or the maiden comes to the emperor, they kiss his hand and then he has them go into another chamber and put on very rich robes that he has had prepared for them. When they come out, they kiss the emperor's hand again and he gives his blessing with kind words, sending them on their way accompanied by many of the emperor's pages with torches, who go in front playing their drums and shawms. Thus they are taken back home, where the wedding feast begins with much music and dancing, which goes on for many days.

# CHAPTER XX

## Which deals with Ethiopia's cities and government buildings, distinction of inhabitants and costume

In Ethiopia there are no cities other than the emperor's court and where the viceroys or certain great governors have their seats, and we might even call some of these just small towns. When the viceroys move somewhere else (which they do frequently, and the emperors do sometimes) those cities are left as small towns or tiny hamlets, because they care little about the buildings since they are of a kind that we shall describe below. The other settlements are small towns with few inhabitants, and villages of no more than fifty houses, and many have fewer because ordinarily a few people get together {[f. 82]} where they grow their crops and they build their houses there. Therefore, apart from a few mountain ranges and deserts which are not inhabited, the remainder is {commonly} full of these little settlements, particularly now, because ever since some heathens that they call Gâlas came through <[f. 70v]> the land and took a lot of it, as we said in chapter 1, the people who lived there have retreated to these lands, and so they are very full.

The buildings are very poor, as we have said on other occasions: little houses made of stone and mud or round poles, comprising just one storey and very low, covered with timber and long straw. Some are wide and have a {wooden} column or post in the middle on which the timber frame is supported. Others are long with wooden posts in a line down the middle that support all the timber; these too are roofed with straw and are single-storey, and they are called *çacalâ*, and the emperors ordinarily used to live in them. And so, when they said, 'he is going to the *çacalâ*', or 'he is in the *çacalâ*', it was like saying

Figure 14. Ruins of the Catholic church at Gorgora Nova.
Ugo Nanni, *Che cosa e l'Etiopia*, 3rd ed., Milan, 1935.

Figure 15. Ruins of the palace at Gorgora Nova.
Courtesy of Architect Sérgio Infante.

'he is going to the {palace} <*çacalâ*>', or 'he is in the palace'; however, it is not just the emperor who uses this kind of house, but also the lords and anyone else who so wishes. In some parts, principally where it does not rain much, they make houses with flat roofs, not from *chunambo*,[1] but from well-beaten earth. All houses used to be just one storey high: for a long time they rarely used to make any two-storey buildings, and they did not last long, because they did not know how to make them. But on a peninsula in Lake Dambiâ, which they call a sea, Emperor Seltân Çaguêd, {who is now alive,} is making some fine palaces of well-cut white stone, with his private rooms and halls. The upper house is fifty spans in length, twenty-eight in width and twenty in height; as the winter wind blows very hard there, and as the lower house is also tall, they did not raise it any higher. Above the main door there is a fine, large veranda and two smaller ones at the sides with very good views. The timberwork is nearly all very fine cedar, and the halls and one private room upstairs where the emperor sleeps have many paintings in various colours. It has a flat roof made of *chunambo*, and the parapet around it has very fine stone columns with large balls of the same stone on their capitals, except for the four corner columns, which have balls of gilt copper with fine decoration. Above the staircase leading up to the roof there is another small house with three large windows which he uses as a lookout, because not only is the house located on the highest part of the peninsula, which is large, but it is sixty spans in height.[2] And so the whole city, {[f. 82v]} which he also built anew, lies below it and it has views over large tracts of land and almost the whole lake, which must be some twenty-five leagues in length and fifteen or more in width, with very good fresh water.

[1] Or *chuna*, an Indo-Portuguese term for a concrete-like mix containing straw and lime from crushed oyster shells. See also Yule and Burnell, *Hobson-Jobson*, s.v. *chunám*.
[2] See Glossary (Gorgora Velha and Gorgora Nova/Old Gorgorā and New Gorgorā).

201

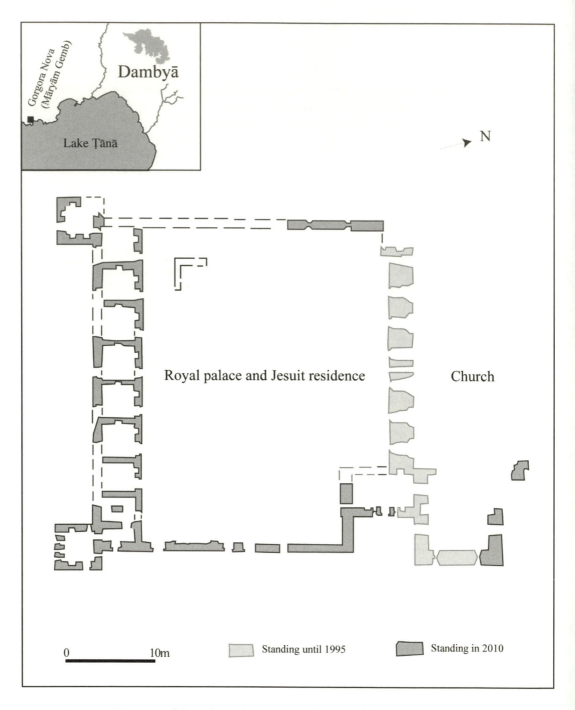

Figure 16. Layout of the palace, the Jesuit residence and the church built in 1626 at Gorgora Nova (Māryām Gemb).
S. Angelini, *Ethiopia: The Historic Route*, 48, 1971.

This lookout too is covered with a flat roof with stone columns around it like the ones below and gilt copper balls in the four corners. One of the emperor's brothers, *Erâz* Cela Christôs by name, later made other palaces similar to these in the kingdom of Gojâm, where he is the viceroy, but they are not so large. These two buildings are the largest that exist in the empire <[f. 71]> (not counting churches). All the other houses are poor, as I have said, and they ordinarily make a thorn fence around them, so that if the fence or the house happens to catch fire, it is difficult to put it out without everything burning down. Where people make houses with flat roofs, sometimes ten or fifteen get together and build one house joined to the next in a circle with the doors towards the middle, where they leave enough open space for their cattle and other animals, with just one door to the street, which they close at night and remain safe from wild animals and fire. The lords of the settlements rarely build their houses with their own materials, because the peasants build them at their own expense. And when the emperor takes away their lands and gives them to another (which he often does), if the peasants built the houses, they are left for the new lord, but if the previous lord built them with his own materials, he takes the timber with him.

The government of the cities is the same as we described in chapter 16, when dealing with the Prester John's judges and the tribunals that he has in his court and those of the viceroys of the kingdoms of his empire. Apart from these, there is a judge called *lebadîm* in each province, whose duty it is to investigate the thieves of that land and to send them captive to the viceroy to whom the land belongs, or to the magistrates at the emperor's court, together with a person to report the crimes of which he has found them guilty if he cannot go himself, although he will conclude certain cases. There is also another judge to whom they take everything that has been lost when the owner is not known, such as slaves, mules and other animals. And if the person who finds it does not take it within a certain time, he is punished, and the judge keeps it and make use of it until the owner is found, and he cannot sell it; and so a person who has lost something like that can easily find it at this judge's house. In every town and village there is a judge called *xum*, appointed by the lord of the land, but as both this and their manner of proceeding in justice have been dealt with at length in chapter 16 it will not be necessary to repeat it again.

The distinction of the inhabitants of the court is also the same {[f. 83]} as the order they keep when putting up their tents in the emperor's camp, as we stated at the end of chapter 14. So when the emperor wanted to build the city that I mentioned above, on the Lake Dambiâ peninsula, he issued a proclamation that everyone should go there with him on a certain day and put up their tents as they were accustomed to do in the field, so that each one should know the location of his house without any disputes; nevertheless there was no lack of argument over how much space each should have around his house. To spare me and my companions of all that, he told me to go <[f. 71v]> first and take whichever place I thought best, which was no small privilege, both because that was never done, not even for his mother, and because the Portuguese had an obligation to set themselves up on the right-hand side. That part proved to be a poor site, in fact, so we chose a very good one in front. Thus they all have their dwellings according to their nobility or office, either closer to the palace or further away, on the right or on the left, in front or behind. And not only does the emperor give the site of the houses free, but he ensures that land all round the city is left uncultivated so that their animals can eat. In the viceroys' cities there is not so much order, and in the small towns and villages hardly any, although the lord of the land tells whoever is going to build a new house where to build.[1]

Regarding costume, in former times it was poor, because even the great lords did not wear shirts, at least when they went around court and entered the palace, but loose black or red cotton breeches almost down to their feet and a long cotton or silk cloth instead of a cape. When they entered the palace, they would gird the cloth to their waist so that it would hang down almost to their feet and the rest of their body would be naked or, at most, they would wear a lion skin over their shoulders, or the skin of another animal that they call *guecelâ*,[2] which has very soft black fur. But to talk about what the great lords and nobles wear now, it is a long white shirt made of fine boffeta[3] from India, like holland,[4] reaching almost down to their feet, with a high, tight collar and buttons of alternating crimson and green taffeta, or sometimes silver or gold, that fasten with cords of silk yarn in the same colours, and tight sleeves down to the hand, but so long that when worn they gather into many folds and look good. They gird these with an Indian sash edged in gold thread or in red, or with a silk belt with many gilded silver adornments. Over this shirt they sometimes wear {[f. 83v]} another, also made of boffeta, which is open in front like a gown and the same length as the first one but without a collar, like a Moorish caftan, and with long, pointed sleeves to the elbow with buttons as before, but they do not fasten and are just for decoration. Other times they wear caftans in the same style but made of damask, satin, velvet, brocade – very fine fabric of all colours that comes from Cairo. These caftans sometimes have very long, narrow sleeves; they do not use these but put their arms out through slits, as in a gown. Some wear loose breeches to below mid-calf level, made of red bertangil,[5] but most often they wear tight breeches down to the ankle, where they fasten with buttons; often the part that shows is made of damask, velvet or brocade, and then the buttons are gold or silver. Their shoes are red or other colours and are sometimes made of velvet, but they do not wear boots or buskins.[6] Round their necks they wear many-looped gold chains that reach almost to their waists; <[f. 72]> on the chain hangs a cross of the kind that the knights-commander of Saint John wear, and the cross alone ordinarily weighs 100 *cruzados*, while the chains are commonly 400. Some of them have a certain kind of gold ornament at the top, from which the same loops of the gold chain also hang down at the back as much as they do in front, and some long, bell-like objects are set into the ends.

Those who cannot wear <gold> chains wear crosses made of gold or enamelled silver, or of delicately carved black wood, half a span in length or less, hanging from many slender, commonly black, cords of silk yarn. At their waists they wear large daggers with gilded silver handles and sheaths, some set with stones that sparkle, even though they are false. This emperor, Seltân Çaguêd, began to wear ruffs like those of Spain, but later he stopped because of the heat. On their heads, some wear turbans like Moors, others round and relatively tall caps of red or other coloured cloth. When travelling they wear hats like ours, but

---

[1] See , 'Historia de Ethiopia a Alta', in Beccari, *RÆSOI*, 5, pp. 75–7. Almeida includes a brief description of Danqaz on p. 77.

[2] Amharic *gessella*, black panther (*Panthera pardus*).

[3] Very fine cotton fabric.

[4] See above, p. 165, n. 1.

[5] Cotton cloth used in Africa and Asia.

[6] Laced, calf-length boots.

not as fine, and burnouses, or {*ferreruelos*} <*farragoulos*>[1] like the Portuguese, from whom they took them. Others have long hair, with which they do many innovative things, twisting it in such a way that their head is covered in many little cords, not going past their ears; others curl it in many ways, and they ordinarily keep it greased with {[f. 84]} butter. Boys have a long topknot reaching from one ear to the other, and they shave their heads higher up with a razor almost to the crown, from where three plaits of long hair hang down behind, and they also leave a little hair on the nape, which makes them look charming.[2]

Women, principally ladies, also have a very tall topknot, and above it maidens wear a garland of little flowers of gold with plenty of silver decoration; with the rest of their hair they make many slender plaits that hang down their backs decorated with other gold adornments. Married women seldom put gold in their hair, but with a razor they shave a finger's breadth near the topknot and the plaits of hair start from there, and the blacker their hair the more they like it, and so they have a certain oil mixture that makes it very dark. They do not use preparations of whiting and rouge, although some of them are almost as pale as Portuguese women, but certain sweet-smelling liquors that leave their faces very lustrous. Their dress is a very long, loose chemise that reaches their feet and drags some distance behind, with loose sleeves that are narrow at the wrist, and a long neck opening so that they can put it on without spoiling their hair; even so it covers their shoulders, and it is well embroidered around the edges with silk yarn or gold thread. On feast days they wear crimson damask or other silks, and on other days fine cotton fabric like holland, which comes from India. They gird this chemise with a fine sash or silk veil, and sometimes they put another over it, like a basque, with many pleats at the waist, but coloured rather than white. <[f. 72v]> They wear tight breeches that reach down to their feet, and shoes. Over everything, instead of a mantle, they wear a large cloth, either white like the shirt material or made of silk and edged all round with fringes of gold thread. Around their necks they wear very beautiful necklaces made of gold, or sometimes of glass beads interspersed with gold purl. In their ears maidens wear large gold or silver discs with enamelled adornments on them, instead of pearls, while most married women enlarge these holes by gradually inserting thicker items, and afterwards they put in tubes of gold or gilded silver that are closed up and well ornamented. Less fortunate women put in a piece of black wood covered with a little silk. When they travel, over everything else they wear {[f. 84v]} burnouses with many gold buttons and cover their heads and faces with a turban, so that only their eyes can be seen, and on top they wear a hat like those in Portugal, made of some silk, and long points of the veil fall over their shoulders.

In the past, men who were not nobles used to dress in just a coarse, white, cotton cloth and, at most, they would wear calf-length white cotton breeches and go barefoot and bare-headed. And they could not put on any other kind of clothes without permission from those who governed their land. Now, if they have them, they can wear not just white shirts but cloth {and} <or> silk caftans, and a turban or cap on their heads, but only if they are not in the place where the lord of those lands is. And if they come from elsewhere to talk to him, the first time they enter they must not wear cloth or silk caftans, but just a white shirt or one made of *taficira*[3] or no shirt at all, and they gird to their waist the cloth

---

[1] *Ferreruelo* (Spanish), *farragoulo* or *ferragoulo* (Portuguese): short cloak with a collar.
[2] The tuft of hair left on children's shaven heads is believed to protect them from evil spirits.
[3] Or *tafecira*, Indian coarse cotton cloth, similar to calico.

that they wear instead of a cape, so that it covers them almost down to their feet. After that, they can wear what they like. The same applies to great lords in relation to the emperor the first time they go in to see him when they come from another land, though they always wear a shirt, ordinarily made of *tafîcira*. The peasants who work the land wear cow hides even today – they prepare it like chamois – without breeches or anything else at all. Some have a little piece of coarse cotton cloth tied at the waist which reaches down to the knee or a little further, and a sheepskin with wool on their back, with one hind foot and one forefoot tied in front on their chest. But on Sundays and feast days those that have them wear large cotton cloths. If they were to put on shirts and wear turbans or caps, they would not be punished for it and nobody would say anything to them, although in the kingdom of Nareâ (as they say) they still keep to the old custom of not being able to vary their dress without permission from the governor.

Peasant women wear skins like their husbands and, in some areas, some woollen cloths five or six cubits long and three wide that they call *mahâc*, and they could quite fairly call it haircloth because it is much rougher than what Capuchin monks wear, for in Ethiopia they do not know how to make cloth, and the wool is not suitable for it <[f. 73]> as it is very coarse. They all go barefoot and often naked from the breasts up, with tiny glass beads of various colours strung so as to make a band two fingers in breadth around their necks. They wear their hair in many little plaits, as we said above, but in some lands {[f. 85]} these plaits are very thin and they cut them so that they only cover their ears.[1]

Friar Luis de Urreta deals with most of these matters in chapter 23 of his first book. Speaking about the government of the cities, he says:

> *In each city they elect six aldermen, different ones each year: two nobles, two citizens and two plebeians. Their job is not only to look after the public good, but they also have ordinary jurisdiction to examine cases relating to their rank. So the two nobles do not interfere in judging the citizens or plebeians, and vice-versa, provided that none of them pass judgement without the agreement of the city's mayor, who is elected every year from among the nobles, one year from one family and the next from another, so that they all equally enjoy the honour and take part in the work. To prevent the mayor too from being biased, he cannot judge cases without two priests from the defendant's parish being present. A citizen is always present in the plebeians' assembly, and one of the nobles attends the citizens', in order to report the proceedings to his own gathering, so that the nobles can inform the emperor or the king. The same custom is observed by private individuals, in that they do not sell their chattels without the permission of those of higher rank. To prevent layabouts, vagabonds and idlers, nobody may go from one town to another without taking letters patent from the judges in the city from which he is setting out, and anyone caught without them is arrested and the city from which he has come is informed, and if he is found to be a ne'er-do-well or vagabond, he is severely punished.*[2]

This is what Friar Luis says, but it was for lack of information, because none of these things are done or ever have been done, because neither have there been nor are there any

---

[1] See , 'Historia de Ethiopia a alta', in Beccari, *RÆSOI*, 5, pp. 50–52.

[2] Urreta, *Historia de la Etiopia*, excerpt (with omissions and interpolations) from bk I, ch. 23, entitled 'Of the government and rule of the cities, and the distinction of the inhabitants among themselves, and something of the customs of Ethiopia', pp. 223–4. Páez quotes this passage in Spanish.

such aldermen or mayor who are elected every year, nor such a mode of government, other than what we have said above; nor is it necessary for people travelling from their city to other places to carry letters patent from the city's judges. Anyone can go where he wishes without anybody asking him anything, and they do not question vagabonds. There is just one thing: if some inhabitant of the place is found to eat and dress well without having a farm or a position from which to earn it, then the judge of that place, who is called the *xum*, asks him who gave it to him. And if the *xum* believes that he steals or others give him stolen goods to keep, he arrests him and hands him over to the person who should examine the case.

<[f. 73v]> In addition, in the last chapter of his first book, on page 368, the author deals with two cities that he claims the Prester John has, {[f. 85v]} and he makes them so different from what I have said here that he equates them with the finest that there are in Europe, and so I shall quote his very words:

*Although the cities in Ethiopia have no more than 3,000 houses, the two famous cities of Saba and Zambra are exceptions, for they are magnificent and populous with a great many houses, and have public buildings, towers, porticoes, spires, arches, obelisks, pyramids, exchanges, squares, temples, palaces, walls and monuments, and among the finest and most well-endowed in the world. The city of Saba was the greatest in all Ethiopia, with the most houses and largest number of inhabitants, and the capital of all that great empire. It was founded by Queen Saba when she returned from visiting the holy temple in Jerusalem, and it took her name and has also given it to the kingdom in which it stands, because it is called the Kingdom of Saba. It is a very rich city, endowed with the many assets that nature and the finest art have given it. It has famous temples, tall, elegant buildings, sumptuous palaces, harmonious portals and graceful façades of extraordinary, wonderful architecture. Its large and magnificent houses number 15,000; its streets are very broad and spacious, and all of them have arcades and vaulted roofs so that one can walk all round the city under them without being troubled by the sun. The walls are made of mortar and are quite tall and so thick that an ox-cart could be driven on top with plenty of room to spare. It is beautified with many fountains, basins and spouts of water.*

*Near this city there are many gold mines and veins and lodes of silver. There are many vegetable and flower gardens for great sport and recreation, full of a thousand roses and various other flowers, where the industrious hand of nature, aided by the artifice of the gardener, has so distinguished itself that it seems it wished to compete with the hand of God in making a second paradise on earth to counterbalance the first. The trees bear fruit three times a year. The emperors, on being elected, take possession of the empire in the city of Zambra, which is currently the court, and then they leave for the city of Saba, where all the cities, towns and subject kings swear allegiance.*

*The {beautiful} <formidable> city of Zambra is the largest in Ethiopia in terms of houses and buildings. It has 30,000 houses. Its inhabitants are many and form a countless throng of people. {[f. 86]} It is built in the kingdom of Çafates next to the great Lake Çafates, which is usually called the Lake of Zambra after this city. This city is the court of the Prester Johns, who, giving up their former customary roving and peregrination, living in the field under pavilions and tents, set their imperial seat and court in this city, since it is extremely well provisioned and its fields are fertile and highly agreeable. Its streets are broad and spacious, and it has strong, high walls, <[f. 74]> stately palaces, sumptuous and magnificent temples.*

*The imperial palace is of great majesty and beauty; in it lives the Prester John with the first-born of the kings, and the empress and the forty-two daughters of kings with their ladies-in-waiting, and the members of the Grand Council together with those of the Latin Council. This city was built in about 1570 by the officials and architects sent by the Duke of Florence at the time of Prester John Alexandre III. It is built in the modern style, with a thousand exquisite and beautiful details, on the layout of the city of Florence. It has a very good and spacious port on Lake Çafates.*[1]

Up to here are the words of Friar Luis de Urreta. But everything he says in them is a fable and mere poetic fiction, painted according to the idea that whoever informed him, or whoever wrote the book from which he took it, wished to form in his imagination. First of all, in all the lands over which the Prester John rules there are no such names of cities as Saba and Zambra. But from what he says about the one he calls Saba, that it was built by Queen Saba when she returned from Jerusalem, it seems to be the town that they now call Agçûm, which is in the Kingdom of Tigrê, because I read in a book that they keep as an antiquity in the monastery in this place that Queen Azêb (who is the same person as Saba, as books in Ethiopia give her both names, as we stated in chapter 2) built a capital city of Ethiopia which was called Dêbra Maquedâ. And it says in the book containing the catalogue of the emperors of Ethiopia that Queen Azêb began her reign in Agçûm. But now one can hardly call it a city because it has at most 150 or 200 houses, all one storey, very small and sad and roofed with straw, and each inhabitant has his little thorn fence around, although a few make their houses of stone and mud, and their streets are very narrow and {[f. 86v]} without any order or arrangement. And in them there are no fountains or other waters apart from a small tank and a few wells and, a good distance away from the town, two streams that are not used for watering anything. There is no trace of gardens or groves; some people just have vines within the enclosures round their houses, but very few.

The inhabitants of those lands say that it is a very well-established tradition of theirs that the city was formerly very illustrious and the largest that there has ever been in Ethiopia, and the ruins of the buildings that can still be seen now clearly show that they were sumptuous. And on a site within the town, thirteen finely carved stones are standing today, some about thirty spans tall, and there is one with many frames which is five spans thick on each side and twelve across the front, and it must be a hundred tall, even though it is all a single piece of stone, and at the top it seems to be four or five spans across with a decoration like a half-moon with the points downwards. Many others have fallen down, two of which are well carved with frames, and one is ten spans thick on each side and sixteen across the front, and 135 in length, and it looks as though it used to be much longer, because it is lacking a large part of the tip and it is also buried deep at its foot. It is a brownish stone. There are other <[f. 74v]> small ones with very ancient letters that nobody can read today.[2] There was a very sumptuous monastery with many monks and a very fine church, but since we shall deal with

---

[1] Urreta, *Historia de la Etiopia*, excerpt (with several omissions) from bk I, ch. 33, entitled 'Of the feasts and rejoicings that happen in Ethiopia with lions, tigers and other wild animals, and of the famous cities of Sabâ and of Zambra', pp. 368–72. Páez quotes this passage in Spanish.

[2] See bk I, ch. 3 above. This brief description of Aksum's obelisks reveals careful observation.

that and the other churches in Ethiopia in the second book, I shall not take the time here to speak of its grandeur and architecture.

As for the city that the author calls Zambra, it can be none other than the one they call Gubâi,[1] because it was built in about 1574 near the great Lake of Dambiâ, but not by Alexandre III, since there has never been an Alexandre III in Ethiopia, as we said in chapter 1, but by Malâc Çaguêd; even though his father, Adamâs Çaguêd, spent a winter there a long time previously, it did not take the form of a city until Emperor Malâc Çaguêd made it his seat on purpose. And it was not built by architects from Florence, because, again as we have already said, there is no recollection that they ever came to Ethiopia, nor were the buildings as sumptuous and magnificent as the author depicts them, but low, single-storey little houses roofed with straw, like our description of Ethiopian houses at the beginning of this chapter. And the walls were not made of mortar, since they did not have *chunambo* or even stone that could be worked, unless they brought it from a great distance away. So {[f. 87]} they planted thick stakes on both sides of the fence and filled the middle with stones and mud, and they did not build it very high but made it wide enough for two men on horseback to ride on it shoulder to shoulder with ease; however, as the mud was poor and it rains there a lot, it began to fall down before they had finished enclosing the whole town, and so they abandoned the work and everything they had built fell down in little more than two years. Only a small stone enclosure was left which they had built around the emperor's houses, and that too eventually collapsed. Today nobody can say how many inhabitants there used to be in that city, but it seems unlikely that there were any more than the number that live in Emperor Seltân Çaguêd's city today, which I do not think come to 15,000. Emperor Malâc Çaguêd stayed there for a few {months} <years> and then moved on to a cool country that they call Aibâ,[2] a day's journey from there, and it was then gradually deserted until not a single house was left on that site, because in winter there was a great deal of mud. I went to see it on purpose a short time ago and it is in a land that they call Anfaraz, about two leagues from the edge of Dambiâ to the east.[3] A small stream flowed the length of the city, and two larger ones not far away, and the Lake of Dambiâ, which also extends into those parts, was little more than half a league to the south. Round it there were very broad, fine pastures, where there are now extensive fields of crops. When I arrived in Ethiopia, which was in May 1603, Emperor Iacob, the son of Emperor Malâc Çaguêd, had already brought the court back to a higher site half a league from there called Cogâ, which is much better than Gubâi. <[f. 75]> Some people call it New Gubâi, because it is so close. But since Emperor Seltân Çaguêd, his successor, moved to the peninsula that we mentioned previously, only about 150 houses have remained there. And this peninsula in turn has now been left almost deserted because the emperor has made another new city in a cooler land that they call Dencâz,[4] a little over a day's journey away. As we said at the beginning of this chapter, when the emperor moves his court somewhere else, few people stay behind.

The author was no less poorly informed when he says that, having given up their former peregrinations living in the field under tents, {[f. 87v]} the Prester Johns placed their seat

---

[1] See Glossary (Gubâi/Gubâ'é).
[2] Conti Rossini, 'Historia Regis Sarsa Dengel', p. 137; Basset, *Études sur l'histoire de l'Éthiopie*, p. 112.
[3] The now ruined palace of Enfrâz probably dates from after the time when Páez was writing.
[4] See Glossary (Dancas/Dencâz/Danqaz).

and court in this city, because, even though the emperor ordinarily stayed in it in the winter, every summer he would go out to war and live in tents, as those who have come after him have continued to do until today. And as for the delightful and joyful festivals that, as he says on page 373,[1] used to be held near that city, to which the empress and her ladies would go on richly caparisoned elephants, and where people would run many fierce and wild beasts, and make lions and tigers fight elephants, and lions and tigers fight each other, and wild horses together, ostriches and monkeys, cats and leopards, and more recently bulls – such festivals have never been held in Ethiopia, nor have tame elephants been seen, as we have already said. {[If appropriate, this part of the contradiction can stay, since it is only a little.]} Furthermore, a few lines later in the same place, he contradicts himself because, when dealing with the order in which they would go to these festivals, he says that on a certain day the Prester John would leave the city of Zambra accompanied by 1,000 magnificent horsemen, and behind them they would take 100 richly caparisoned spare horses, and then many elephants, dromedaries and richly adorned mules, and that everything was brought after the emperor just for the sake of grandeur and majesty. Then followed the captain of the imperial guard and, behind him, the firstborn of the kings on fine horses. Behind these came the magistrates of the Grand Council, and, after all this cavalry and retinue had passed, there came all the ladies of the court on elephants and among them the empress and, on her left hand, the emperor. If, as he says, the emperor went in front and then he was followed {in order} by such a large retinue, with the empress right at the back, the emperor could hardly be at her left hand if he was so far away from her at the front. But whatever the truth about this contradiction may be, the fact is that everything that he says about the festivals and the splendour with which they went to them is merely a fable, because there has never been such a thing in Ethiopia.

[1] Urreta, *Historia de la Etiopia*, bk I, ch. 33, pp. 366–77.

# CHAPTER XXI

## Which explains something of the nature and customs of the Prester John's vassals

The people of Ethiopia commonly have faces with fine features, their bodies are strong and robust, and they suffer hard work, hunger, thirst, heat, cold and lack of sleep exceedingly well. <[f. 75v]> In understanding, which is the best part of man, the people of Europe do not outdo them. They are gentle and kind by nature {[f. 88]} and, although there exist ruthless, hard-hearted men as elsewhere in the world, there are fewer of them; the remainder are very well inclined and thus readily forgive any insults or injuries, no matter how great, even the death of parents, children, brothers or sisters, as I have often seen and experienced in some of these pardons in which they have involved me, for, although I sometimes did not know the people whom I was to entreat, I easily obtained the pardons. If the one they ask to mediate refuses to do so, they are highly aggrieved, and the others notice that as well, most especially if they ask him for Our Lord's or Our Lady the Virgin's sake, because they rarely ask for something in that way that is not granted. Once something has been forgiven, they consider it extremely poor manners or even churlish to speak of it again, so that those who are reduced to our holy faith accuse themselves in confession that they have spoken again (even if it was to a friend of theirs) of something that they had already forgiven.

They are also very charitable and generous towards the poor, and so, as the poor begin to beg some three hours before dawn, they give them plenty of alms at that time, as they think that some of them did not dare beg by day. After daybreak, the poor sit {near} <beside> a church or in a street where more people pass or at the entrance to the town, and there they beg for alms until the great men eat, which is ordinarily before ten o'clock in the morning and at five in the afternoon. At those times they gather at their doors, and as soon as the great men have finished eating, they give them what is left over. They do not come to the palace door, because it is not the custom to give alms there, but the emperor makes many very large donations because, apart from what he generously gives to the churches and monasteries, he abundantly supports those who he knows are in need, particularly if they are honourable. In addition, he has a person of confidence called the 'father of orphans', who every year distributes among the widows and orphans related to the emperors (even if only distantly) a large quantity of grain from the revenue that the peasants pay to the emperor. They call it *colô*,[1] meaning 'toasted': this revenue is very large but, since it is in the form of grain for the emperor, they have given it this name as if it were some trifle that they were offering him to toast.

[1] Toasted grain (generally wheat or rye).

211

They are also highly devout, so {[f. 88v]} the offices begin in the churches as soon as the cock crows, which must be three hours after midnight (because cocks never crow at midnight here), when they give the signal, which in the parish churches is a number of beats on some instruments <[f. 76]> like drums, while in the monasteries they use three little boards tied at the edges that make a loud noise, or some long, thin stones that are not very wide. From afar it sounds as if they are ringing bells, but there are no bells in Ethiopia: I have only seen one small one and another that I have had brought from India for our church. When the signal is given, men and women rise and go to the church where they can enter (because not all churches allow women inside, and even men cannot go beyond a certain curtain unless they are ordained, as we shall say below). And they hear the offices and pray, most of the time standing up, although they also sit down. They must not enter wearing shoes, although they keep their heads covered, in fulfilment of God's command to the Prophet in Exodus 3, that he should take off his shoes out of reverence and respect and not that he should bare his head. They do not spit on the floor inside, but in their handkerchiefs, out of reverence for their churches. And for the same reason, if they come on horseback, they dismount before reaching a church and do not remount until they are well past it. Of those who remain in their houses, many say prayers until dawn or recite Psalms of David or read from Saint Paul or the Gospel, and then they go about their business. It is very common when they travel, either alone or when going to war, that every honourable man takes a servant with a prayer book and a light, folding iron stand covered with red leather. Once the tents are erected, when they have to rest from the labours of the journey, they immediately sit down to pray, not because they are obliged to do so, but out of devotion and because it is already a common custom. In some churches in the empire there are tombs of men that they hold to be saints, to which they come on pilgrimage with great devotion from very far away. Many men and women even go to Jerusalem, which is a very long and difficult journey, not only because of the great harshness but also the great heat of the lands through which they pass. All monks and nuns and those who have deacons' orders, even if they are married men, carry a cross in their hand made of silver or iron or black wood, about a span in length.

Above all, they are very inclined to fasting and penances. They fast every Wednesday and Friday in the year, except those that fall after {[f. 89]} Easter and until Pentecost. They eat in the afternoon when the shadow is eight feet long, for there are no clocks here, but it must be at about five o'clock. They do not eat eggs, milk or butter, but really badly seasoned herbs, grains, lentils, beans and other seeds that they have, and fish for those that can find it, for there is very little of it, except in the Lake of Dambiâ and in some rivers. Many people do not eat things that have no scales, because of the habit that they have inherited from the Jews. They also fast on some days before Christmas and fifteen days before the Assumption of Our Lady, but not everyone does so, because that is done out of devotion. During Lent, everyone fasts and they do not eat until the sun has set, nor do they drink a drop of water, even many of those who are sick, and some, particularly monks, go for two days or more without eating. On Saturdays they do not fast, but instead they fast for seven days before our <[f. 76v]> Lent begins, starting on the Monday after Sexagesima. To increase their penance, some people eat certain bitter seeds and also aloes. Their Easter sometimes falls on the same day as ours, other times a week later and, sometimes, a month later, as happened in 1617, when our Easter was on 26th March and theirs on the following moon.

Monks make many other penances during Lent, one of which is to stand for a long time praying (they do not kneel to pray), at most leaning against the wall or on a stick if they become too weary. History tells of one monk, who was called Taquelâ Haimanôt, whom we shall put in book 2,[1] who stood for many years inside a hut without leaning on anything, seven years of which on one leg. They also claim that in former times some of the monks that lived in the deserts (of whom there were many then) used to climb up some trees that are very thick and smooth to a great height, which they call *demâ*.[2] They would do so as follows: they would fix pegs into the trunk one above the other (which was easy to do, since this tree is soft inside) and would climb up them to a height where they would be safe from wild beasts, and there they would carve out a hole like a little cell the size of a man, and a monk would get inside and never come out again; others would feed him until that little cell closed up (because it fills up again inside very quickly) and so it would squeeze him until he remained there dead and buried.

Even though the penances given to lay people in confession {[f. 89v]} may be very severe for minor wrongs, they accept them and willingly fulfil them, although many people do not know how to confess, because they do not specify their sins but just say, 'I have sinned, I have strayed.' At most they tell some things and leave all the rest that they have done, but it is because they are not taught that they should confess all sins very well, as other people do. Yet some desire so strongly to be saved that they publicly confess their sins, no matter how great they may be, as I was told by some Portuguese, who saw the penultimate *abuna* who came here sitting on his chair with many people standing on either side of him, and others would come down the middle, one by one, and on getting close to him would recount their sins in a loud voice. If there was a serious sin, the *abuna* would say, 'Did you do that?' and, raising his staff, he would strike the person hard on the back three or four times, and then he would command two men that were standing there with long straps to lash the person thirty or forty times, as he saw fit. Once they had started the lashing, the others would beg him to pardon the sinner, and so he would command that the lashing stop. But if the sins were not serious, he would give another penance.

As for their customs, I shall only mention a few, so as not to tire the reader with many things that they have of little importance. The courtesies that they use when great men meet are to bow their heads and also, sometimes, to place their right hands on their breasts, without uncovering their heads at all, even if they are wearing caps or hats. The first one to speak says '*Chêr âlu*', which properly <[f. 77]> means 'Are ye well?' for they always address someone in the plural out of courtesy, even if there is only one person. He replies, '*Chêr cebahât la egziabehêr*', 'Well, glory be to God.' And then he also asks the other if he is well {with the same words}, or by saying, '*Mininhâ âlu*', *scilicet* 'How are ye?' And sometimes, the first speaker says, '*Bicôn ayaûl*', 'May your opponent not endure.' This word 'opponent' means not only enemy but all kinds of evil, because *biz* means 'bad'. This plural form of address must be used by someone who is not as noble as the person addressed, but equals, even if they are great men, often address each other in the singular, particularly if they are close friends. And the less noble one not only has to speak in the

---

[1] See bk II, ch. 19, below, where Páez gives an abridged translation of the hagiography of the Ethiopian monk Takla Hāymānot (c. 1214–1313).

[2] Baobabs. See bk I, ch. 25, p. 241 below.

plural, but he has to lower the cloth that he wears instead of a cape, so that it leaves at least one shoulder uncovered. And the lord that he addresses may be such that he is obliged to uncover both shoulders and even gird {[f. 90]} the cloth at his waist. The more noble one replies, '*Chêr alêc?*' 'Art thou well?' When they go and visit one another, they ordinarily remove their shoes at the entrance to the house, and if the lord or lady of the house is the emperor's kin, they also gird their cloths at their waists, as we have said they do in the emperor's palace. When they leave, they say, '*Bafeçâ yauleô*', 'Remain in happiness.' They also say, '*Baheioât carû*', 'Stay with life.' They also have other manners of speaking, but these are the most common. Lords and ladies say nothing to the emperor when they come before him, and they are always accustomed on entering (unless it is a very close and trusted kinswoman, particularly an elderly one, who will say to him, '*Biçôn ayaûl*', 'May your opponent not endure') just to bow their heads and remain standing in their rightful place according to their nobility – both ladies and lords – until the emperor commands them to sit. He ordinarily keeps ladies standing only for a very short time, but in the case of the lords, no matter how great they may be, he takes his time to command them to sit, and never on chairs, but on the floor, on carpets. This too used not to be the custom in former times, because no lord would sit before the emperor, but it began to be introduced in about 1597, because Emperor Iacob was still little.

Additionally, when some lord comes from outside the court, whether summoned or not, he arrives at the palace gate and sends a message by the head doorman or a friend of his (for he may not enter without permission) as follows: 'So-and-so says to the *Aceguê*: *Biçôn ayaûl*, may your opponent not endure'; and, if the emperor commands him to enter, they call him. When he comes in, he kisses the emperor's hand {or knee} <and kneels> without saying anything and moves back a little or a good deal, depending on his nobility. Then the emperor asks him something or, after waiting a little, he approaches the emperor again and says his business, if he has any. If, however, the emperor does not reply when they tell him that that lord is there (for he ordinarily feigns not to have heard for a good while), the lord will remain waiting at the gate until given permission. If he is the viceroy (who does not usually come unless he is summoned), he stays by the gate <[f. 77v]> in the first fence and sends a message to the emperor, who then sends at least two and sometimes four great men, and they say to him, 'The emperor says that you are welcome and that you are to enter.' They also salute him and go back, and he follows them and waits again at the gate in the second fence (the palace always has two fences) until others come and tell him to enter, and he goes with them and kisses the emperor's hand and stands talking until the emperor dismisses him or commands him to sit. When the emperor sends a message by word of mouth or letter out of the court, the one to whom it is sent, however noble he may be, comes {[f. 90v]} out of the door to his house and girds his cloth to listen to the message and take the letter.[1]

The emperor is ordinarily seated on a chest coloured crimson or gilded, like the one the current emperor has, sometimes with fine curtains or a canopy made of silk, or other times without them. It always has four or six covers: the edge of one reaches nearly to the floor, the next a little higher, and so on with the rest, so that just a little of each one shows, and the last one is always made of very fine silk; and there are one or two brocade or velvet

---

[1] Almeida touched on the same subject very briefly (see 'Historia de Ethiopia a alta', in Beccari, *RÆSOI*, 5, p. 49).

cushions on which he leans. On the gilded chest, however, the covers are ordinarily on top and hardly fall down the sides at all, because they have a brocade or velvet border with a fringe of gold thread. This is his throne, although he also sometimes sits on a high chair with a damask or velvet back, with fringes of gold thread and gilded nails, as we have already mentioned. All the lords sit on the floor on carpets, even in their own homes, because they rarely sit on chairs. And so they always eat on the floor on some round boards with a rim two fingerbreadths high and, although they are made of a single piece of wood, some of them are eight spans across. They call this table {gabêta} <gahêta> and they put neither tablecloth nor napkin on it, but just some very thin, round cakes[1] of wheat or other seeds that grow here and, on top of them, the dishes with the food, and bread like ours made of wheat. They eat all kinds of meat – cows, sheep, goats, chickens and partridges – except for pigs, which many people do not eat, and hares and rabbits, which nobody eats. One of the greatest delicacies for some people is raw beef: when the cow has just been slaughtered, they put it on the table and, striking it a few times, they put its own bile on top, and then they slice pieces off and eat them. They say that it tastes very good, so much so that most of them would not stop eating it for anything, even though they pay a high price for it, because they develop thin creatures like long worms in their stomachs which do them great harm, unless they take every two months <beforehand> the fruit of a tree that they call coçô,[2] the bitterest thing that {it seems} there can be, and so strong that, if they are not careful but exceed the dose, many of them die, some spitting blood. These creatures come from eating this raw meat, as they themselves say. It is quite clear, because the descendants of the old Portuguese, the Moors and Jews who eat it also have this disease, and if they do not eat it or stop eating it after some time, they do not have these creatures, <[f. 78]> nor do they take the medicine. This emperor, Seltân Çaguêd, who stopped eating this raw meat, {[f. 91]} was cured of this disease many years ago, and the eldest prince, who is called Faciladâz, has never had it because, as the emperor told me, he has never even wanted to try raw meat.

There are no butcher's shops. Only at the emperor's court they kill a few cows every day outside the city, in the countryside, and the ordinary people go there to buy some, not by weight but by eye, by sharing it out. Those who can will slaughter the cows or sheep that they need at home, and there they also bake the bread that they are to eat, because there are no baker's shops, but just some poor women who take some bread to market, but honourable men do not buy it. Their drink is wine, which they make from honey,[3] and some of it is as strong as wine made from grapes, but it does not last long – a month at most and then it goes sour. There is also another kind of wine {or beer} which they make from maize and barley and other seeds,[4] which is not found in Spain, and this is commonly drunk by those who cannot afford honey wine, because they hardly ever see any grape wine, as we shall say later. Thus there are many taverners who sell it, not in small quantities but by the jugful, because it costs very little. When they travel, it is to be found every step of the way, since the places are very close to each other, but honey wine is seldom found except in the towns. Thus when lords travel, they take mules or oxen laden with very large

---

[1] The author is referring to injera (enḡḡarā), a kind of large pancake that is the staple food in the Ethiopian highlands and is usually made from the native cereal ṭéf.

[2] For kosso, see above p. 119, n. 2.

[3] Mead, or ṭaḡḡ.

[4] Ṭallā, a local, beer-like fermented drink.

horns full of this wine, and honey to make it with. If it is to be a long journey, wherever they arrive to shelter for the night they have to be given lodging and everything they need to eat free of charge, depending on the people's rank, for even low-born men are sheltered in this manner, which is a great burden for the peasants, for it is they who have this obligation. But this is not the custom in the cities, where everyone eats at his own expense.[1] Their journeys are {usually} short, but when necessary they make no less extensive ones than in Spain. And they do not talk in leagues, because they do not divide journeys up in such a way, but rather in days.

The manner they usually have of buying and selling is to exchange some things for others, such as grain for butter or cotton cloths or blocks of salt, each one of which is roughly eight fingerbreadths long and two and a half wide. With these blocks they can find what they want better than with gold in many places, and they are worth more or less according to the greater or lesser distance from the area where they are cut (for they are extracted from only one land, even though there are smaller amounts of salt in other places). Here at court, where it is a sixteen- or eighteen- <[f. 78v]> day journey to bring them, thirty-two are worth one *cruzado*, sometimes more, <and> {[f. 91v]} sometimes less, and they are used as coinage, because no coins are struck here. Gold is given by weight in little pieces, and the usual weight is called an *oquêa*, which is exactly eight Venetian coins in weight, and a half *oquêa*, after which they gradually go down to a very small weight. Cotton, too, has its own weight, and they measure the cloths made of it and the silks and clothes that come from abroad in cubits. Grain, honey and butter have certain measures. They do not work the fields in any way except with oxen, and they put a yoke on their necks in the same way as they yoke mules in Spain, and so they tire quickly and plough little. They do not use carts, nor is the land suitable for them, as there are many rugged mountains and in summer the plains are usually covered with huge cracks and openings. The weapons they use are bows and arrows, often poisoned,[2] swords, long lances and shorter ones, which they hurl, and small {clubs} <axes> made of very hard wood, which they throw from a distance. They now have many guns, which they did not have before, but they often burst since they do not know how to harden iron properly. They do not know how to cast artillery or even how to make use of eight *cameletes*[3] that they first took from the Turks. They also have defensive arms, such as helmets, skirts of mail and very strong black and white shields made of buffalo hide. Their kettledrums are made of copper or sometimes wood covered with cowhide, and others are like side drums. They have trumpets, shawms (although not as good as ours), fiddles and other instruments like harps, with which they make reasonable music.

Regarding the manner of their weddings and the ceremonies that they perform in them, we touched on that above in chapter 15 and we shall deal with it at greater length in book 2. We shall only mention briefly here the custom that they have in their inheritances, when the husband or wife dies. If, when a man married, it was with the condition that on his death his wife would take one third of his property or less, she takes that and certain other things that they rule should be hers, depending on how much property there is, and she shaves her head for it. And the dead man's father and mother inherit all the rest, if he

---

[1] See M de Almeida, 'Historia de Ethiopia a alta', in Beccari, *RÆSOI,* 5, pp. 53–5.

[2] With plant poisons.

[3] Small-bore cannon.

had no children. If they did not make an agreement, the dead man's parents take everything, apart from what is judged to be hers for shaving her head and what she brought into
the marriage. But if the husband no longer had a father or mother, she takes everything
even if he had brothers or sisters. If he leaves children, the mother takes two parts of the
property, the firstborn son two more, and the other children one part each, so if <[f. 79]>
a man died leaving three children and property worth 600 *cruzados*, then the wife takes
200, the first child the same again, and the other two children 100 each.

{[f. 92]} Before the estate is divided up, they take from the total sum not only what
was spent on the day of the burial in alms, which they give according to their possessions,
but also what is to be given later, because after seven and ten days they give something to
the prior of the monastery or church where the man is buried and to the monks that they
appoint to recite the Psalms of David and other prayers for thirty days, and on the last day
they slaughter cattle if he was a rich man, and they feed them and all the poor people who
come. On the fortieth day they take many candles and incense to the church, and slaughter
many more cattle and give large amounts of alms; they also give some after eighty days and
when a year is up, but not so much. They call this *tascâr*,[1] which means 'reminder'. And
even though they remember the dead so much, even so many of them deny Purgatory, as
we shall say in book 2.[2]

The sign of mourning that they use for a father or mother, husband or wife, is to shave
their heads, even the servants of the house. The wife and maidservants tie on their foreheads a long strip of very fine, white cotton cloth, which they get from India, a little more
than two fingerbreadths wide, with the two ends hanging down their backs. The dress is
black, and they wear it for a year. Kinsfolk wear blue, although some who want to show
greater feeling also wear black for a few days and shave their heads, but it is not obligatory.
They ordinarily make great shows of feeling, throwing themselves on the ground all of a
sudden, and they suffer such falls that I know one person who nearly died and another
who was crippled for the rest of his life. The women tear out their hair and scratch their
faces until the blood runs. Some people in the kingdom of Gojâm, who are called *gafates*,
even cut their heads and arms with knives. They wail loudly from a little before dawn until
eight or nine o'clock, and this goes on for many days. Most of the time they stand beating
with their hands and sometimes beating their chests, and they take a piece of the dead
mans clothing or weapons and brandish it, saying so many things that those who hear
cannot help weeping. I once went to one of these lamentations, since I was in great debt to
the dead man, who was a great defender of our holy faith and was called *Abeitahûm* Bêla
Christôs, a cousin of the emperor, who therefore commanded that his imperial tent,
which is very large, be erected in the palace yard, and all the lords and ladies of the court
gathered there and brought the dead man's weapons and caparisoned horse {[f. 92v]}
covered with a mourning cloth, and they put it in front of the tent and some of his clothes
inside. Then the emperor came {covered} <dressed> in mourning and sat on the ground
on carpets, with black curtains around him. When the emperor came in, the dead man's
wife began to wail loudly and everyone wept for a long time, but seated. Then an elderly
woman stood up and, taking in her {left} hand a cap belonging to the dead man, she held
it up, saying amidst her tears, 'Where now is that prince who wore this cap on his head?

---

[1] See Glossary (*tascâr/tazkār*).
[2] Particularly in ch. 16.

What has become of that great and valorous captain, whom nobody surpassed in war and who had no equal in letters?' And in this way she went on saying so many things that she moved every heart, no matter how hard it might be. And so everybody, including the emperor, shed many tears, and that lasted almost until midday.

<[f. 79v]> A short time later, I found myself at the death of a prince, the son of this emperor. He was already twenty years old, and I was at his bedside, helping him as well as I could at that time and for a long time before, since the emperor had asked me to do so. When he passed away, which was late at night, they put up the tent and placed the body on a high place in the middle of it, with torches all around. Shortly after midnight the emperor arrived, covered in mourning, with all the great men, and they made an extraordinary lament until morning came, when they took him to be buried in a monastery on an island in the Lake of Dambiâ, where the emperors are now buried.[1] They all went covered in mourning with the emperor's banners and drums going in front, playing on a sad note. They wept at court for many days and kept displaying things belonging to the dead prince, as that woman had done. But the emperor did not go out in public except on that night, although he wept bitterly in his chambers, because he had loved the prince dearly. And once, when a <great> man who was {very much} his confidant and I were alone with him, he said, 'I wish, my son, that I had died rather than you', and other things in which he clearly showed the great pain and sadness in his heart.

We {shall} conclude this subject, leaving aside many other customs, such as one that certain Christians have, which is that when a man or woman of that caste has just died, before the body is cold, they break the arm and leg bones and make the body into a ball and wrap it in a shroud and bury it, and they laugh a lot and make fun of the others, saying that they bury their dead as they are, when they die stretched out, as if they were logs.

{[f. 93]} From what we have said, it can be seen that Friar Luis de Urreta was misinformed about some of these things, since he says, in chapter 23 of his book 1,[2] where he deals with them, that in each city the emperor has many lands for wheat and grain, which are ploughed and sown at his expense, and that he commands that everything that is harvested should be distributed among the poor, the monasteries and churches, without keeping anything for himself. This does not happen in this way, because the grain that is distributed among the poor, who ordinarily have to be widows and orphans related to the emperors, and which may sometimes be given to monasteries and churches (which will rarely happen because they have their own lands) is merely taken from the revenue that the peasants pay to the emperor, which they call *colô, scilicet* 'toasted', as we said above, and not even a tenth of this revenue is distributed. All the rest the emperor spends on the ambassadors that come from abroad, because he commands that some of it be given to them and their people and saddle animals, and on some soldiers who do not have enough land, and on whatever else he wishes. Furthermore, the colour yellow is not dishonourable (as he says it is) because, even though the lords commonly like other colours more, they sometimes wear this colour, and many monks and nuns also wear yellow. He also says that men of lower rank remove their caps out of courtesy to their superiors, such as the emperor and great men, and whereas in Spain they say '*merced*' (favour), here they say '*quisquis*'. But nobody takes off his cap to anyone, however great he may be,

---

[1] See also bk II, ch. 16, below.
[2] Urreta, *Historia de la Etiopia*, bk I, ch. 23.

<[f. 90/80]>[3] and no such word as *quisquis* exists in any of the manners of speaking. Nor do they eat at high tables, as he says, and people who said that they eat raw meat here were not mistaken, as he claimed they were, because they do like it a lot. The cow is slaughtered for the lord only a short time before he will eat it, and they do not even finish flaying it properly before they take the meat to the table, because if it is cold they do not like it so much. This is not exaggeration or hearsay, but something that I have often seen. He also says that at first they did not know what glass was, but that since Francisco the Duke of Florence sent them glassmakers, among other craftsmen, they now make use of it; and that they have craftsmen who arrange wool and weave very good corduroy, serge and other things that are customarily made of wool. However, there are no such glassmakers here or any other glass than what comes from Cairo and from the region of Arabia, which is very little, and they did not know of what it was made, so that some great men asked me, in front of the emperor, what it was. Nor do they know how to make the woollen cloths that he mentions, but only those that we described in the previous chapter, which some poor women wear and which might rather be called cilice than cloth. He also says that the firstborn sons {[f. 93v]} in all families inherit all their parents' property, with the obligation of feeding their younger brothers and sisters in the judgement of their parish vicar and two kinsmen, but it does not happen like that, because they all take their portions as we described above.

---

[1] BPB, MS 778 has a mistake in the folio numbering here, as f. 79 is followed by f. 90.

# CHAPTER XXII

## Which explains whether in Ethiopia there are seminaries and colleges to teach boys and girls, and universities where the sciences are read

Very large and well-ordered colleges and seminaries for the teaching of boys and girls, and universities where the sciences are read, are depicted in Ethiopia by Friar Luis de Urreta, in chapter 24 of his book 1, and he places the Ethiopians among the nations that have best cared for the upbringing of their youth, with the following words:

*The Ethiopians are among those nations that have most distinguished themselves in the upbringing and education of their children. For not only did they have colleges and seminaries for the teaching of their youth during the times of pagans and the early Church, but even nowadays they keep this custom more strictly than ever. Thus in all the cities of the empire there are established seminaries and colleges, each with three different rooms: one for the nobles, one for the citizens and the other for the plebeians. One of these seminaries is for the teaching of boys and the other for the teaching of girls. The latter is located inside the city, and the boys' one is outside by a quarter of a league. The latter is called the place of the virgins and the former <[f. 90v/80v]> the place of knowledge. In the latter live all the daughters of the townspeople from the age of ten up to twenty, and in the former all the boys from the age of eight to sixteen. From the latter emerge maidens, some to be nuns and others to marry and others to serve in houses, and from the former the young men, some to enter the Church and others to serve the emperor or king in the court or in war, according to the rank and obligation of each one. And in the end, both of them teach the Christian doctrine and whatever else they need, such as letters for the boys as well as the other arts to which they are inclined and which their rank requires, and needlework and other exercises for the girls, according to the custom of the land. To this end, both boys and girls have their tutors and masters, although the masters for the nobles are different from those that teach the citizens, and all these live apart from the masters for the plebeians, so that each kind is governed by those of their rank, without one kind interfering with {[f. 94]} the others, except that among the nobles there are four gentlemen and four matrons who supervise, the former in the seminary of knowledge and the latter in the seminary of the virgins, and they have absolute power over the citizens and plebeians.*

*Doctors are highly esteemed throughout Ethiopia, and enjoy the most privileges in the whole empire, because while everyone is obliged to give one of every three sons to go to war, which obligation even the kings have, only doctors are exempt from this strict obligation. They may also pass through the city riding on elephants, although only emperors, prelates, priests and virgins may ride such mounts. They may wear sashes {round their necks}, which is a custom restricted to magistrates. They are free from all taxes, tributes and duties of the empire. Lastly, they are the people with the most freedom and liberty, and the most esteemed by all.*

*The reason is that no science is {studied} <taught> in public other than medicine, and there are seven general Universities in Ethiopia to teach it. Being a student does not depend on the individual's desire, but on appointment, because the aldermen of each city and town appoint three young men, those with the greatest understanding and ability who are inclined to letters, and who must come from the nobility, and they alone go to the Universities and study for many years, because they learn not only medicine, but also surgery and the art of the apothecary, and so each one is a physician, an apothecary and a surgeon. Since they are so esteemed and so honoured, and students are appointed, they study hard, because if they do not they are removed and others are sent in their place. They are supported at the expense of the cities that send them. In this way they come out as highly renowned doctors and in particular great herbalists, because of the many very medicinal herbs that there are there.*

*Once the students have finished their courses in order to graduate as doctors (which they call becoming <[f. 91/81]> philosophers), the doctors that are appointed in the Universities examine them and, if they pass, they give them the letter of examination. They take it to the monasteries of Alleluia and of Plurimanos of the Order of Saint Dominic where, accompanied by <their> kinsfolk in the monastery churches the friars come out and the prior dresses him in a black cowl with {[f. 94v]} sleeves like that of a Benedictine monk. And then he makes him swear obedience to the Roman Church and the <Florentine> Council {of Florence}, at the time of Eugene IV. After the oath, they put round his neck a kind of stole made of cloth of gold with just one lappet, like a scapular, which falls in front over his chest with the emperor's arms on it, and in this way he becomes a doctor.*

*Holy theology is not read in the universities, but in the monasteries of Dominican monks and monks of Saint Anthony, and in the churches of the clergy. Only ecclesiastics study it. The manner of reading is in their {native} Ethiopian tongue, and the text that they gloss – like Saint Thomas or the Master of the Sentences for us – is the four General Councils, which the doctors usually call four more Gospels, which are the Nicene Council, the Constantinopolitan Council, the First Ephesian Council and the Chalcedonian Council. And just as we might say, 'This Doctor is reading the first part of Saint Thomas or the second question on such-and-such, or the first or second of the Sentences,* distinctio *number so-and-so', they say, 'That master is reading the Nicene or Ephesian Council, canon number so-and-so.' The Dominican fathers have the parts of Saint Thomas, translated into their language with the book* Contra Gentes, *and they study them, although their normal manner of reading is from the Councils. They read the Holy Scripture, which is in the Chaldean language, which men of the Church learn, as here we learn Latin, and they find more grounding in the Scripture.*[1]

Up to here are the words of that author, but he was as poorly informed about almost all of these matters as he was about the other matters that we have seen so far. First of all, in the lands of Ethiopia over which the Prester John rules there are not and never have been any such seminaries of boys and girls, for although many have their sons and daughters taught to read and some also to write, it is not in that way, but each one as he wishes gives his child to some monk to be taught and pays him very well, and the monk ordinarily collects six or {eight} <seven> and keeps them in his home, because the monks do not live

---

[1] Urreta, *Historia de la Etiopia*, excerpt (with several omissions) from bk I, ch. 24, entitled 'Of the seminaries and colleges that there are in all the cities for teaching boys and girls. Of the Universities where the sciences are read, and of the whores' brothels', pp. 232–40. Páez quotes this passage in Spanish.

in closed monasteries like those in our lands, but each one lives in his own house near the church, usually, and some also far away, since formerly many lived within a compound, in huts separate from one another, and there are still traces of that even now. The boys stay there with the monk all the time, and their parents give them all they need, and the monk teaches them to read and sometimes to write, and he makes them learn the Psalms of David by heart, <[f. 91v/81v]> and to do that they get up before dawn. When he sees fit, he gives them leave to go and enjoy themselves {[f. 95]} at their parents' home, and as they have just learnt the Psalms by heart and can read well and, perhaps, write too, they pay what was agreed and go home; and if one of them is to recite Saint Paul or another book, they have to make another agreement with a different payment.

The sons of great lords often do not stay like that in the monk's house to learn, because the monk whom the lord has chosen to be his son's tutor is taken to his house instead. He eats and lives there almost permanently, the better to be able to teach the child. And they do the same with their daughters, for most lords have them learn not just to read but also to understand Saint Paul and the Gospel, because all the Scripture is in a very different language from the common one.[1] So even if they can read it, they do not understand it and cannot recite it, as is the case of Latin with us. So they have monks in their houses to teach them, because they do not take much notice of the clergy. Ordinarily, the monks who teach these boys and girls, unless they die first, accompany them after they get married and bless their water and their table like chaplains, and even though the blessing is very long, they all remain standing until it is finished. When one of these lords is made a viceroy or is given another command, the monk who was his tutor goes with him to find wealth, and the woman's tutor goes with her, and they eat and drink together. The truth is that if they taught as they should they would produce plenty of fruit, but they do not seek what is good for the soul so much as honour and wealth. So they do not say anything that might displease their lords: they just tell them what they want to hear and what they think is best for their own interests. When we asked some of them in private why they did not explain the truth of the faith and everything else that they are obliged to, they answered that they dared not do so, because they would lose their living and harm would come to them. Some of the lords understand very well that all they want is honour and wealth; thus one of the foremost lords in the whole empire, who is called *Erâz* Athanatêus, the son-in-law of Emperor Malâc Çaguêd, once told me this: 'Father, we have no tutors. These monks of ours are like Pharisees; all they want is honour and wealth; they do not know anything. And if they do understand something, they do not dare say so. Does Your Reverence see that one over there?' (There was a very modest monk opposite us, some distance away.) 'Well, he is my tutor, and he is as much a Pharisee as the others.'

In this passage, Friar Luis de Urreta includes many passages about prostitutes,[2] but they are all fables without any basis in fact. I point this out because, if we were to pass over them in {[f. 95v]} silence, somebody might take them to be true, and even if they were, one might well dispense with dealing with this matter. No less apocryphal <[f. 92/82]> is his story that those who are converted are sent to Goa to the nunnery of the Converted Women and that their children and any other bastard or illegitimate children are sent to

---

[1] The language of the Scriptures is Ge'ez.
[2] Urreta, *Historia de la Etiopia*, bk I, ch. 24, pp. 232–3. See the *Relatione dei Grã Regno degli Abissini* (Venice, BM, MSS. Italiani cl. 6, n° 332, ff. 11v–12).

Goa or to Hormuz, Ceylon or Mozambique, where they are fed at the expense of the priests, because they cannot live in Ethiopia. But neither the women nor the children are sent to any of those places, nor do I know what reason there might be for obliging priests in India to support the bastard and illegitimate children of Ethiopia, because not even the priests in Ethiopia give them anything – and there are many of them in the land – unless it is to their own.

As for the seven universities that he mentions, where they read medicine and study with all the curiosity that he depicts, they too are mere fiction, for there are no such universities in Ethiopia and there never have been any, nor any such examinations or graduations of students. And even if there had been, the prior of the monastery of Alleluia and of Plurimanos (which is in fact called Dêbra Libanôs) could hardly make them swear to obey the Roman Church, because they themselves do not obey it. And these doctors were not privileged {by being exempted} from giving one out of every three children to go to war, because nobody does so, and there never has been such a custom, because when it is necessary and the emperor summons, everyone is forced to go, and only the peasants stay behind to till the land. And they could not ride {through the city on} elephants because, as we have said several times, no tame elephant has ever been seen in Ethiopia. The doctors that live in Ethiopia are some people who know about herbs and cure with them, but they know very little even about herbs. What usually happens is that when they fall ill they do not make any remedy at all, but go on a very severe diet, until either nature prevails or they die. One remedy that they {take} <took> at least every two months is called *coço*, which we mentioned in the previous chapter. It seems to protect them from many diseases because, as well as killing the creatures that are born in their stomachs from eating raw meat, for which they take it, it serves as a very effective purge, but if they take too much they die as well.

There is another tree from which they make great use of the bark, the root and the milk of its leaves. It is a singular remedy for resolving swellings, before {they begin to make} <to create> pus, as well as anthrax or carbuncle, which is so dangerous; it infallibly cures it if they apply it straight away. They call this tree *corpâ*, and some people call it {[f. 96]} *guindâ*.[1] Its leaves are broad and not very long and grey in colour, although they are green above. Its fruit is rather like a reasonably sized quince, and it turns yellow later, but inside it is hollow and it only has a very thin skin; it only grows in very hot lands. If I remember correctly, I saw one on Goa island, near Santa Ana. From the leaves of this tree <[f. 92v/82v]> (which is ordinarily not very big) they take the milk on wheat or barley flour, but those who want to do better take the rind of the root and, when it is dry, they grind it and take the milk on this flour, and they take it wherever they want, because it keeps well for a long time; but the rind of the root is enough, although the milk is better. They apply it as follows: they grind the rind very well once it is dry and mix the flour with fresh cow's butter and spread it on the swelling twice a day, and it does not hurt and cannot be felt. But for anthrax or carbuncle they have to spread it all round but not on the top or head that forms, and they have to drink some of that rind – about two wheat grains in size or a little more – dissolved in water. They rarely drink the milk, because it is very strong. They also put it on swellings on horses, mules and cattle, but any hair that it touches falls out and then grows again, but that does not happen on men.

---

[1] Unidentified tree. *Qarafâ* is cinnamon; *gend* now means 'trunk'.

Since I have talked about remedies, I shall not fail to mention what I also saw when I was imprisoned in the Strait of Mecca. Two of my fellow captives were very ill, their faces swollen and yellow, and they could not eat anything. They were told to take every morning on an empty stomach, in a lightly poached egg, about half a nutshell of powdered lily root, not a Madonna lily bulb, but the other kind, which has a blue flower. After that they were ruddy and felt very well again; they just said that they felt a little nauseous until they had had the runs once or twice. They also told me that it was a certain and proven fact that taking about half an eggshell of the juice of this lily root with a little diluted vinegar and ground spikenard for two weeks on an empty stomach will cure dropsy.

Friar Luis de Urreta says, on page 237,[1] that in Ethiopia there is a leaf like ivy which, when crushed and placed on wounds, cures them within a few hours, but I have not been able to find anyone who knows of it, or of the new mummy[2] – more excellent than ours – that he claims has been invented by Ethiopian doctors.

As for the manner that he says they have of reading the holy theology, {[f. 96v]} by glossing the {four} General Councils, again he was mistaken, because they do not read in that manner, nor do they accept the Chalcedonian Council, but rather they revile it, because it declared as{ a matter of faith} <established> the doctrine of Saint Leo on the two natures, [whence there follow also two] wills and operations in Christ Our Lord, which they deny, and it condemned Dioscorus, whom they venerate as a saint. Thus, in a book that they call *Mazaguêbta Haimanôt, scilicet* 'Treasure of the Faith', which might better be called 'Treasure of Lies', and in another that they entitle *Haimanôta Abbô, scilicet* 'Faith of the Fathers', they say that the fathers of that holy council were foolish and proud, and Saint Leo was accursed and treacherous, as we saw in chapter 11 and will state at greater length in book 2.

What they say about the councils that they have is not, ordinarily, any more than what the language in which they are written means to those <[f. 93/83]> who do not know it, because it is different from the common tongue. They have some interpreters of the Holy Scripture that are very weak and full of mistakes, and even they reach few people. And a monk who succeeds in understanding something only teaches it to those who pay him very well, and so he shuts himself up in some house with them to explain what he has read to them, without letting anyone else in. Lastly, much of what they teach is fables and lies, as did one monk who prided himself on being a great scribe and, as he was so famous, the present Emperor Seltân Çaguêd took him to be his teacher, but shortly afterwards he died. Later, when I was talking to the emperor about certain things in the Scripture, he told me that when that monk who taught him came to explain that part of Genesis 6 that says *'Videntes filii Dei filias hominum quod essent pulchrae',*[3] etc., he had told him that those that the Scripture here calls sons of God were angels, and that when they saw that the women were fair, they joined with them and they gave birth to giant sons of such great and extraordinary stature that they would plunge their arms right down to the bottom of the ocean sea and, standing up, they would roast the fish that they had taken from there in the region of fire. And when they had destroyed all the fish that were in the sea, they started on the animals. When these were finished, they started to eat the men who were

---

[1] Urreta, *Historia de la Etiopia*, bk I, ch. 24.

[2] Balm, such as is used in mummification.

[3] 'The sons of God seeing the daughters of men, that they were fair' (Genesis 6:2).

not of their race. And when God saw such shamelessness, he sent the waters of the deluge, {with} which {he} punished them. To that I replied that it was all fable, because those whom the Scripture here calls sons of God were not angels but sons of Seth, whom it wanted to distinguish with this honourable name from those of the reprobate generation of Cain, whose descendants {[f. 97]} were so bad that they delivered themselves in every way into the hands of their appetites. The daughters of these miserable creatures were very fair, and when the sons of Seth saw them they were taken by their great beauty and fairness and broke with the tradition and custom that they had of not admitting to their conversation and dealings people of such a perverse stock. And when they married them, they also received the perverse customs that they brought with them, and with that the religion and divine cult in general became perverted and the evils of men reached the utmost peak of dissolution that could exist in creatures of the earth, so much so that the Holy Scripture did not wish to enter into detail about such nefarious offences, but contented itself with saying that in all their sins they changed the style and natural order that reason teaches: *Omnis quippe caro corruperat viam suam super terram*[1] (Genesis 6). 'That, my lord, was the reason why God Our Father sent the waters of the deluge, not because the giants had eaten <[f. 93v/83v]> the fish of the sea and the animals of the earth.' The emperor said, 'Indeed, his explanation appeared to me to be well off the path, like another one that he gave me, when I asked him how the sons of Israel had multiplied so much during the time they were in Egypt. Because he replied that the first time that the women gave birth, each one came with two, and the second time four, the third time eight and the fourth sixteen, and thus they always went on doubling.' I said, 'The poor things were certainly forced to bear a very large burden for several months. And anyway, after they gave birth, how much milk and how many breasts would they need to nurse such a great multitude of children as over time would come to be born together?' The emperor laughed heartily and said, 'Your Reverence will see from that what our teachers are like, and this one was even one of the most renowned that we have.'

As their interpreters of the Scripture and their teachers are so weak and even so sell the little they know so dearly, they are greatly amazed and edified to see that we teach everything free of charge, and even more so at how well our fathers explain the Scriptures, because we have given them, translated into the language of their books, the Epistle to the Romans, as explained by Father Toledo, the Epistle to the Hebrews by Father Ribeira, the Apocalypse by Father Bras Viegas, and the Gospels of Saint Matthew and Saint John by Father Maldonado.[2] We are now translating the Gospel of Saint Luke and the remainder of Saint Paul by Father Benedito Justiniano, and the beginning of Genesis by Father Benedito Pereira, as well as a treatise on all the errors of Ethiopia,[3] demonstrating the truth of our holy faith with the doctrine of many saints, with the Holy Scripture and holy Councils, with reasons and with authorities of their {[f. 97v]} own books, and answering all their objections and arguments. And everything that they have so far been given in writing has been so well received, by the grace of God, that almost everybody praises and

---

[1] 'All flesh had corrupted its way upon the earth' (Genesis 6:12).

[2] The translation of the works of exegesis into Ge'ez began in 1612 and was performed by Fathers António de Angelis, Luís de Azevedo and António Fernandes, with Ethiopian collaborators (Se'ela Krestos and Fequra Egzi'e took part in this work).

[3] See Glossary (religious controversy; and *Tratado sobre todos os erros de Etiópia* (*Treatise on all the errors of Ethiopia*)).

exalts this doctrine so much that they say it can only have been the Holy Spirit that dictated it to those fathers, because it does not seem that human understanding could achieve something so lofty. The emperor and *Erâz* Cêla Christôs, his brother, are extremely pleased to see that in every way the people believe what we say, and they ask us very insistently to send for the comments[1] on the rest of the Holy Scripture and to clean up their books, which are full of mistakes.

[1] Commentaries.

# <[f. 94/84]> CHAPTER XXIII

## Which deals with the animals, both domestic and wild, that are found in Ethiopia

I have travelled through many and varied lands of Christians, heathens, Moors and Turks and in some of them I have stayed for a long time. I have passed through many thick woods and long deserts, in which there were many and varied animals. But nowhere have I seen or heard say that there are so many animals or such different kinds of them as they say there are in Ethiopia and that I in part have seen, because first of all there are all the races of domestic animals that there are in Europe, such as very good horses in the kingdom of Tigrê and even better ones that come from the kingdom of Dequîn, which belongs to the Moors called *Balôus*, opposite Çuaquên, but they do not last long in this land, because they develop sores on their feet, from which they die. The other horses in the empire are commonly small but strong and run fast. There are many mules and they are good for riding, although they are ordinarily smaller than those of Europe. The emperor told me that two mules in the kingdom of Gojâm gave birth and then died with their foals; but reliable people have told me that a mule gave birth in the kingdom of Tigrê a short while ago and that until ...[1] the dam and the foal. They never shoe either mules or horses, and so they often go lame. There are many camels, domestic donkeys and wild donkeys. But the *chatins*[2] and those who are going to war usually only carry loads on oxen. There is a great multitude of cows, and in some parts of the kingdom of Tigrê, such as the provinces of Amacên, Bur and others, they give birth more often than those in Europe, because they enjoy {[variety of winters in the Red Sea and kingdom of Tigrê]}[3] two winters, when they find long grass that is full of flavour. Because when in the region of the Red Sea it is winter, which begins there at the end of October and lasts until February {or} <and> March, here inland it is summer; and when here it is winter, which begins at the {[f. 98]} end of May and lasts until October, there it is summer. And it is a marvellous thing that certain mountains are always the limits of winter and summer. So they always take the cattle to the side where it is winter, because they find plenty of grass, and even though it rains a lot, it is not cold. They have some very large oxen that they call *guêch*,[4]

---

[1] A blank space has been left at this point in both manuscripts.

[2] Traders. *Chatim* was an Indo-Portuguese term for a merchant from Coromandel (Dalgado, *Glossário Luso-Asiático*, pp. 265–7), which only later acquired its pejorative meaning of 'trafficker'. See also Yule and Burnell, *Hobson-Jobson*, s.v. *chetty*.

[3] A marginal note written in a different hand in ARSI, MS Goa 42. The handwriting is similar to that used in the whole of bk II.

[4] Amharic *goŝŝ*, buffalo, here presumably a domesticated form.

and they raise them from the time they are very small on the milk of two cows. They do not plough with them: ordinarily they are only used for the lords to eat. Their horns are so long and thick that people use them for carrying honey wine when going to war or making long journeys. There are not many goats and sheep, and their meat is not good, but in some areas the rams are good, and some have four large horns; as for small horns, <[f. 94v/84v]> I once saw an ox with eleven, two like a goat's and the others all around, the length and thickness of a little finger or a little more, which they exhibited as a {very} extraordinary thing. Some rams have a tail a span or more in length, and almost as much across. Others, even though they are very tall, have tails that almost reach the ground and are a span or more in thickness and, as they are very heavy, they walk slowly; these are commonly white. There are many dogs, come very strong, but those they use for hunting are not as good as the greyhounds of Spain; most are like podengos.[1] There are also wild dogs, and I saw one once that had been captured young, and they are hardly any different from domestic dogs, except in their muzzle which is much longer, and they call them *taculâ*,[2] and say that they are found in very thick forests. And they say that, when they hunt, some hide in the places where the prey ordinarily passes, and the others search for it until they raise it and then pursue it, trying to drive it to where the others are, and when these leap out it rarely escapes from them. And they also attack people. There are also many fine cats.

There are many more differences among wild animals than in Europe. Some sons of Portuguese have told me that in the kingdom of Gojâm, in a land called Naninâ, when they were going hunting, they saw in a valley a fine horse with a very long mane and a tail that reached the ground, and many animals, like wild goats, gazelles and *merus*,[3] accompanying it. On seeing them, it fled at high speed into some very dense woods, and all those animals followed it. And even though they could not make out whether it had a horn on its forehead or not, they thought it could only be a unicorn. There are other animals which, according to what I have been told about them, seem to be rhinoceroses or *abadas*,[4] because they say they have a body as fat as or fatter {[f. 98v]} than a cow, very small eyes and a skin so hard that it would be difficult for a spear to pass through it. I just wonder whether they are *abadas*, because they have two horns, one on the nose and one on the forehead, while I do not remember whether the *abada* that I saw in Madrid in 1587 had more than one, sawn off.[5] The ones here have two, and a short time ago they brought some to Emperor Seltân Çaguêd, still attached to the skin, which he showed me and he gave me one of them. The one on the forehead was black and thick at the root; a little higher up it was nearly three fingerbreadths wide and less than one thick, and about three spans long, and its tip was not sharp. It

---

[1] An ancient Portuguese breed of dog used for hunting rabbits.

[2] Amharic *takwelā*, African wild dog (*Lycaon pictus*).

[3] From the Konkani (Goan) word *merum*, deer. Deer are not found in sub-Saharan Africa, so the writer may be referring to some kind of antelope.

[4] Term adopted in Portuguese from the Malay *badaq*, rhinoceros.

[5] Both African species of rhinoceros (the black rhino, *Diceros bicornis*, Amharic *awrāris*, formerly widespread in Ethiopia, and the white rhino, *Ceratotherium simum*, not historically found in Ethiopia) have two horns, the Indian species, *Rhinoceros unicornis*, only one. An Indian rhino was shipped to Lisbon in 1579 and then transferred with Philip II's court to Madrid in 1583, where Páez saw it four years later. See Rookmaaker, *Rhinoceros in Captivity*, pp. 80 and 91.

looked like a piece of a scimitar with its black scabbard, for it curved in a similar bow-shape towards the top of the head. The other horn on top of the nose was not black but the same colour as cow horns normally are, and round like them, thick at the root, and four fingerbreadths higher up it began to taper considerably and, at the tip, it was very sharp and curved up, almost like the other one, and it was the same <[f. 95/85]> length as that one, and both were solid and about half a span apart. But it seemed that they would be much farther apart, because the skin was already very dry and shrivelled and was more than one span from one end to the other. They call this animal *aurarêz*.

There is another animal that they call *jerâtacachên*, which means 'thin tail', of misshapen height.[1] The emperor showed me one, and had me called specially when they brought it; even though it was still young, from the ground to the top of its head it measured nineteen spans, and they said that the old ones are even taller. Its head is very small and like a camel's, but on its forehead, almost on the very top, it has two points, one next to the other, which are thin and four fingerbreadths in length, and it seems that they are made of bone, because they are covered with skin and hair; its neck is slender, long and held straight up; its body is the size of an ox, but longer; its forelegs are very thick and disproportionately tall, while the hindlegs are very short in comparison; its hooves are cloven like a cow's; its colour is light brown, and the whole body is covered with very red rings, as large as the palm of one's hand, which make it very attractive. It does not bite or do any other kind of harm at all. In the woods, it runs faster than a horse and, if it is captured young, it becomes very tame, but they do not ride it because, as the hindlegs are short and the forelegs comparatively very long, it would easily throw off anyone who mounted it.

Wild asses are plentiful, and they say that they are not different from the domestic ones, apart from being very lively and fast. But there are others, which they also call wild asses, of extreme {[f. 99]} beauty, because it seems that they had been painting them with a brush. Their ears are just rather large, like those of {asses} <others>, but they are also beautiful, because they are covered with thin stripes in circles, some very black and others white and all uniform. Around their eyes they also have other circles like those. And from the tops of their heads, other stripes come straight down to their nostrils, but there the white stripes are not as white as elsewhere, because they tend to be reddish. The whole neck is covered all round with those black and white stripes. From the withers along its back to the tip of its tail runs a very black stripe more than two fingerbreadths wide and, from it, other narrower but very uniform black and white stripes run down on either side. On its forelegs and hindlegs, from the top to the hooves, it has stripes in circles, as on its ears. Its hooves are like an ass's, and its coat is short and very soft.[2] The emperor has two of these, and I saw another kept by his brother, *Erâz* Cela Christôs, which was like these from the head to just over halfway along its body, but from there backwards the stripes did not go downwards but turned straight towards the haunches, creating a different

---

[1] Amharic *qaččené*, giraffe (*Giraffa camelopardalis*). Páez gives the meaning in Portuguese as '*cabo delgado*', '*cabo*' meaning the end part of something (and by extension a handle, hilt, headland, rope, cable, etc.), although not specifically an animal's tail ('*rabo*'), which is the sense of the Amharic word *žerāt* incorporated in the name given here.

[2] The description matches Grevy's zebra (*Equus grevyi*), found in the Ethiopian highlands, which has narrow, vertical stripes on its flanks.

beauty.[1] These animals are only found in very hot lands and are few in number and therefore highly prized. In body size they are like the largest asses found in Spain.

There are also many wild cattle, which they call *torâ*,[2] buffalos, elephants, <[f. 95v/85v]> but no tame ones, lions, tigers,[3] leopards, but not as fierce as those they bring from Africa to Spain. There is {however} <also> another animal which they call *guecelâ*,[4] the size of a lion, and they say that it is very wild and fierce; I have seen its skin, and the fur is very soft and black. There are tame pigs and three kinds of wild ones, and many porcupines, and some animals like foxes, but a little larger, which they call *cabarô*.[5] There are countless wolves, which are so savage that they attack people by day in the bush and at night they often enter compounds, and they even sometimes got into the compound of our house in Dambiâ, even though it was made of stone and thorns and we had many good dogs. A short time ago, when *Erâz* Cela Christôs, the emperor's brother, had camped his army in a land that they call Çarcâ, in the kingdom of Gojâm, the wolves came at night and dragged off a young man who was sleeping at the edge of the camp and, even though he shouted out, when people reached him the wolves had already torn him apart.[6]

Civet cats are plentiful, and they call both them and their oil {*tirinh*}<*tirênh*>.[7] They are almost twice as big as cats, and look similar. They keep them in cages and there they feed and water them, because they are so shy that they never become tame. If they escape, it is difficult to capture them again. They have {[[f. 99v]]} the civet oil in a little bag that nature has placed between their legs, and people are careful to extract it in time, not only because of the profit that there is in it, but because of the harm it causes to the cat, which becomes sick with a fever if they leave it there too long. So the cats that run wild in the bush rub themselves against the tips of dry sticks to get rid of it, and as people know about this, they look for them along their runs. In the kingdom of Nareâ, where they are plentiful, they set short sticks with pointed tips in the ground on purpose (so they say), and there they find a lot. There is also musk, which they call *mesque*.[8] There are many wild cats, and they and {two} other kinds of animals, which are like ferrets, do great damage to chickens.

There are countless monkeys of many kinds: some are very small with long tails; others are larger and beautiful with white under their arms and on parts of their neck and head. These ordinarily stay in the tops of trees. There are other larger ones that are ugly like the small ones, and others like large dogs which are much uglier than any other; from the breast up to the head these have longer manes than lions, and they bite a lot. They all cause considerable damage to crops and, if people did not watch over them as much as they do, monkeys would destroy all the crops sown near the woods and rocks where they live. Yet

---

[1] The more horizontal stripes on the hindquarters identify this animal as a plains zebra (*Equus quagga boehmi*), found in southern Ethiopia.

[2] Perhaps feral zebu (*ţor* means 'war' in Amharic).

[3] An error by Páez, since there are no tigers in Africa.

[4] Amharic *gessellā*, black panther, a melanistic variety of leopard (*Panthera pardus*).

[5] Amharic *qabaro*, a generic term for jackals and foxes.

[6] The Ethiopian wolf (*Canis simensis*, Amharic *qay qabaro*, 'red jackal') feeds mainly on small prey such as rodents. Páez may be confusing wolves with more powerful spotted hyaenas (*Crocuta crocuta*, Amharic *ğebe*).

[7] Amharic *ţereňň*, African civet cat (*Viverra civetta*), which produces a strong, musk-like scent.

[8] From the Arabic *al-misk*. Scent produced by musk deer from the mountainous regions of Asia.

they do steal a lot because, while the person on guard goes one way, they come out some-where else. Once I was in a valley and raised my eyes on hearing a man shouting to keep them out of some grain that he was guarding, and one of them ran out in front to the edge <[f. 96/86]> of the grain, grabbed in both hands as much as would fit in its mouth and retreated before the owner could get to it. Even though they are so large, they climb up such steep rocks that it would seem only birds could go there. The people call them *zenyerô*[1] and the ones with white on them *gureçâ*.[2] They keep both kinds chained in their houses as pets, though only rarely.

There is another very great plague in all these lands of Ethiopia that I have seen, such as the kingdom of Tigrê, Begmêder, Gojâm, Dambiâ and others, particularly in the province of Oagrâ, consisting of mice without count, which do great damage to the crops. Not even inside houses do they leave people in peace, no matter how many cats there are or how many traps are set for them. There are venomous snakes, although not many, and very large serpents, and they say that the breath of some of them is enough to make cattle swell up and die if they are not given medicine straight away. There are many other animals that I shall not mention, either because they are well known, or because they are of very little importance.[3]

What we have said shows how false the information was {[f. 100]} that they gave to Friar Luis de Urreta on some of these things, for he claims in chapter 25 of his first book that the Prester John can put 500 castled elephants into war, although there is no tame elephant in all his lands or even a recollection that there ever were any, as everyone says and as the emperor himself told me. He also says that in Ethiopia there are neither wolves nor dogs, whereas both are very common, and that caused great amusement to everyone who heard it. I was no less amused by something else that he claims, that there are no dogs even in Arabia, because if he is speaking (as it appears) of the part of Arabia that runs from the fortress of Muscat, which belongs to the Portuguese, to well within the gates of the Strait of Mecca, then I have passed through a large part of it and always found plenty of dogs. And if he had remembered what he had said on page 96,[4] that the princes who live on Mount {Amharâ} <Ambarâ> keep pointers, greyhounds and bloodhounds for hunting, he would not have stated here, on page 254,[5] that there are no dogs in the whole of Ethiopia and that, if ships arrive from Europe and leave some from Ireland and England, they die within a month.

He also says about civet cats that each one knows its home like other domestic animals and that they go off into the bush to catch their prey, because they do not live on anything else; and when they eat more bush meat, their civet is better. When the little bag where it collects is full, they return to their homes, running and jumping as if rabid; and the first person to see them when they come in picks up a stick and starts hitting the floor and walls as if trying to hit the animal, <[f. 96v/86v]> which jumps from one side to the other until it tires {and sweats}. Then they open its wooden cage and it runs in and there they remove the civet from it with a spoon. Then it sleeps for two or three days and, when it wakes up, it goes off into the bush again. Everyone found this very ridiculous, because they

---

[1] Amharic *zenğaro*, baboon (genus *Papio*).
[2] Amharic *gurézā*, colobus monkey (*Colobus guereza*).
[3] Almeida dealt with the Ethiopian fauna in his 'Historia de Ethiopia a Alta', in Beccari, *RÆSOI*, 5, pp. 41–2.
[4] Urreta, *Historia de la Etiopia*, bk I, ch. 8.
[5] Urreta, *Historia de la Etiopia*, bk I, ch. 25.

always keep them in cages and feed them in there, and if one gets out it is very difficult for them to catch it again. What caused them most amusement, however, was another fable that he tells about monkeys or baboons, on page 252, in the following words:

*monkeys are used in Ethiopia as servants for all duties, for there is no other difference than speaking or being silent. They scrub, draw water, sweep and turn the spit to roast meat. There are men who have thirty or forty who work for them in their fields like labourers. They give them lunch in the morning and they give each one its little spade and hoe and send them off to the field, where they dig the beds, hoe them, remove the weeds and stones and leave them very clean. They do it as neatly as a man, and when they finish they return to the house, where they are fed. And they send them to buy meat and wine and a thousand other things that seem incredible. Soldiers who are on enemy borders, {[f. 100v]} in strongholds and fortresses, use monkeys as guards and lookouts, and they climb onto the finial of the tent or the lookout tower on the wall and keep watch all night long much better than a soldier, because they have keener ears and as soon as they hear a sound half a league away they wake all the soldiers with their screams.*[1]

That is what the author says about monkeys, and he does not consider it incredible because he writes as if it is true. Nonetheless, not only have the people of Ethiopia never seen such things in their land, but they had not even heard of them until now, when I told them, and they consider them so fantastic that they think they could never occur anywhere. That is enough for me justifiably to condemn the one who told him that such things existed in this land and the fact that he gave them so much credence as to write them as the truth, while I do not reprove what he took from Father Joseph de Acosta,[2] of whom he says that, when dealing with the natural things of Peru, he mentions similar things about monkeys. There was one that was sent to the inn for wine, and if the boys said anything to it, it would put the jug by some doorway and rush after them throwing stones; when they had fled, it would pick it up again and go on its way. I have nothing to comment on this, because I know very well that that father would not write anything as true if it were not very much so.

No less novel did he find the manner in which he says the people here kill rhinoceroses <[f. 97/87]> or *abadas*, which he tells as follows, on page 246:

*They live in the Province of Gojama, at the feet of the Mountains of the Moon, where the River Nile starts, and they are only found in this of all the lands of Africa. When people hear news of one, they load their guns and take a monkey, which they have trained for this kind of hunt, and send it into the field. It straight away starts to look for the rhinoceros, and when it sees it, it goes up to it and starts leaping and dancing about, doing a thousand monkey tricks, and the rhino is very happy to see the fuss it is making. The monkey jumps up one of its legs and onto its back, where it scratches and strokes its hide, which gives it great pleasure and delight. Jumping to the ground, the monkey starts to rub its belly, and the rhinoceros drops to the ground in gratification and stretches out on the earth. Then the hunters, who are hiding*

---

[1] Urreta, *Historia de la Etiopia*, excerpt (with some passages omitted) from bk I, ch. 25, pp. 252–3. Páez quotes this passage in Spanish.

[2] Acosta, *Historia natural y moral de las Indias*, p. 280.

*somewhere safe, shoot their crossbows and guns at its navel, which is very delicate and soft with the hide of its belly, and once they wound it there it dies straight away, as that is where its pulse is. When it is dead, many people approach, tie its hind legs together and hang it from a tree, its head hanging down so that all the blood and humours will drain down to it, and it remains thus for some four days, and then they cut off its horn, which is what they want of it, and thus it has more virtue against any poison. And for the horn to be even finer, they wait for certain {[f. 101]} moons of the year, for they do not kill them at just any time.[1]*

Up to here are the words of Friar Luis de Urreta. Since I wished to know the truth in them, for this is such an amusing way to hunt such a fierce animal, I asked Emperor Seltân Çaguêd, from whom I had first heard that he used to kill them when he was a young man, and I also mentioned what he says here. And he was much amused by the fuss that the author says the monkey makes of the rhinoceros. He said that there was no such method of hunting in Ethiopia and that they did not know what a crossbow was, but that they would go with their horses and short spears which they throw from a distance, and they would kill the rhinoceros with them, and that quite often it would kill their horses as well. Pointing to a son-in-law of his, a very great horseman, who was there, he said, 'This man has already had two very fine horses killed. I often used to go hunting like that. Once, I threw my spear at one and hit it in the flank and the whole spearhead went in, and my servants finished it off.' His steward then said, 'So-and-so here has killed five with his own hands. But for that we do not wait for certain moons, nor do we believe that the horn has more virtue in some moons than in others. When we kill them, we cut off their horns.'

---

[1] Urreta, *Historia de la Etiopia*, excerpt from bk I, ch. 25, p. 246. Páez quotes this passage in Spanish.

## Of the birds that there are in Ethiopia

Just as there is a great multitude of animals in Ethiopia, one can also find many differences and various sorts of birds, because it has almost all the ones that are common in Europe as well as many more that have never been seen there. There are farmyard chickens and others in the bush that are the same size, with blueish feathers speckled with many well-arranged white dots smaller than a lentil; and when they are fat, which is when the grain is harvested, they are very good to eat. There are so many of them that they cannot be counted. If they are caught when small, or their eggs are put under farmyard chickens, they become very tame, and they say that some are reared in the house, and they are called {*zegrâ*} <*zagrâ*>.[1] There are tame pigeons and wild ones, of three or four kinds. There are other, very white birds that they call *sabisâ*,[2] and they live in very large flocks and from a distance look like pigeons, but they are not used for eating because their flesh is very black and bad; they have much longer necks, beaks and legs than pigeons. There are three kinds of doves: some are very small, others are like those of Europe, and others are larger; I have seen a completely white one of these. Partridges are also found in three kinds: some are much larger than those of Europe, but in their plumage, feet and beak they are very similar to them; the other two kinds are the same size as ours and have similar beaks and feet to them, but their plumage is very different. And none of them is as good to eat as those of Europe, but rather their meat {[f. 101v]} is very dry and unpleasant. I do not think there are any francolins, because I have never seen any or found anyone who knows of them, but on the Arabian side of the Strait of Mecca there is no lack of them: in the house where I was held captive, two used to run around with the chickens, but their wings were clipped. They only differ from European partridges in having a very black area from below the beak to near the eyes and in calling differently.[3] There is a great multitude of quail in summer and, when winter comes, it seems that they go to other lands where summer is then beginning, because within the same lands that are governed by the Prester John there is always winter and summer together: when it is winter towards the coast, further inland it is summer, and vice versa.

There are many parrots little larger than thrushes, and they say that larger ones are found in some places, and they are commonly green, although some have a little red in their tails. There are orioles; starlings; <[f. 98/88]> sparrows; others, no less harmful, that are the same size with yellow bodies and brown wings; other smaller, blue ones; others jet

---

[1] Amharic *ǧegrā* or *žegrā*, helmeted guinea fowl (*Numida meleagris*).

[2] The Amharic word *sābisā* is used for birds such as herons and egrets.

[3] Black francolin (*Francolinus francolinus*).

black; others like crimson velvet with feathers also like velvet hair; others painted black and white with comb and wattles like cocks and beautiful feathers emerging from behind the comb that curl over it;[1] and there are many other beautiful birds, different from those of Europe. Of those that sing well, there are solitary canaries and many other kinds of songbirds that make very good music. There are others, as big as a pigeon, striped in brown and white, which sing very badly; their bill is half a span long and curved; and others the same size that are green with a yellow breast, and when they sing it sounds just like a dog barking; others scream to burst one's eardrums: they are as large as chickens, some brown and others very white, and they have a thin, curved bill almost a span in length and are called *anân*.[2] There are other birds almost as large as a swan, but white only on their breasts and wingtips, the rest tending towards black; they have long legs and tail, a short beak and some long, delicate golden feathers on their heads that look like crowns.[3] They always gather in flocks, particularly in Dambiâ, whose viceroy is called the *cantîba* and these birds are called *cantîba mecercâna*, or 'the *cantîba's* shawms', because their cries sound like the shawms that always precede him and make rather poor music.

Since we are talking of such good singers, it would not be right to leave out the ravens, of which there are two or three kinds: some are very large with a white patch {[f. 102]} on the nape; others are all black, the size of those in Europe; others have a white breast and neck, although these look more like crows than ravens. There are also many forms of vultures: some white, with yellow bill and feet; others black, with a partly white breast; others brown, with very large bodies and with a very extraordinary sense of smell, because when some animal dies, they come immediately from very far away and gather in large flocks. There are others which, in the size of their bodies and their tail, look like turkeys from Peru, but they are black with only their wingtips white, and on their heads, near their large beak, there is a little horn three fingerbreadths long and two thick, but all hollow and open at the tip, and they say that it is a counterpoison and works against plague and that, if lepers eat its flesh <[f. 98v/88v]> in the early stages of the disease, they get well; it is called *hercûm*.[4] There is another bird as large as this one which they call *eceitân farâz*, 'the Devil's horse', because it is very ugly and very long from neck to tail and runs very badly, though fast; it is brown and has a yellow beak and feet and, on its nape, some long feathers sticking straight back which could be used as reins.[5] In the company of this one we could put the emu or ostrich, if it should really be counted among the birds, because it too is quite ugly; but even though some people see its feet as being similar to those of a camel, they do not look at all like them, because they have two toes on each foot like a bird's toes, but gross and ill-formed: the inner one is long and the other shorter. I do not know how with those toes they can pick up stones and throw them backwards at those pursuing them, as they also say, because they are not made for picking them up. I have often seen them run in the emperor's compound, with the servant boys playing behind them, and I have never seen them throw a stone. It seems that people might see them fleeing among rocks and, as they run very hard, when they put their feet on some

---

[1] Possibly wattled ibis (*Bostrychia carunculata*), endemic to Ethiopia.

[2] Unidentified name, possibly referring to a species of wader.

[3] Black crowned cranes (*Balearica pavonina*).

[4] Amharic *erkum* means stork or pelican, but the description matches the Abyssinian ground hornbill (*Bucorvus abyssinicus*).

[5] Amharic *yasayṭân faras*, secretary bird (*Sagittarius serpentarius*).

stones the stones might be kicked back, and they might think that the ostriches were picking them up and throwing them. They are plentiful in this land, and they say that they run so fast that a horse would have great difficulty catching them.

There are many birds of prey of different species, such as sparrowhawks, falcons and goshawks, which kill many partridges and wild chickens, and sometimes they attack farm-yard chickens, but the people do not know how to hunt with them. There are others that take quail and other small birds. They say that there are some golden eagles, but I have not seen one yet. There are many, of several kinds, that prey on rats. There are also many black kites, and storks of many forms: some smaller than those of Europe and the same colour, which they call *hebâb oât*,[1] {[f. 102v]} 'snake swallower', for they call a snake *hebâb*; others are large, but they have a white breast and the rest is black, and of these there are two or three different kinds. There are many cranes in the summer, particularly in Dambiâ. And it is a noteworthy thing, and one that the inhabitants of this land have observed, that they arrive at the same time every year, with no more than three or four days' difference, at most, from one year to the next. When the time comes for them to return to their land (which they also have fixed), the ones in Dambiâ all fly up every morning so high that they can hardly be seen, on eight or ten successive days, and they call out until nearly midday, as if calling those that are <[f. 99/89]> in neighbouring lands to come and travel all together. And indeed, many others come to Dambiâ on those days and they all depart together.

There are many more kinds of birds that live on rivers and lakes than of any other kind, and there are so many that they cannot be counted. Apart from herons, which are well known, and cormorants, there are ducks of many kinds and some that are like large shel-ducks with meat that tastes the same, but they are black with a white breast; they call them *uyçâ*;[2] others are a little smaller and brown and are called *ibrôch*, or *ibrâ* if there is just one.[3] There are many of these, and they cause serious damage to crops, so when there is fruit it has to be guarded, otherwise they and the cranes would destroy it. There are also other birds the size of bustards which are all white and have yellow bills a span in length and three fingerbreadths in width. I shall not dwell on the lake birds, for were I to deal with just those that live along this lake of Dambiâ, where I am most of the time, it would take a very long time, because they are beyond number.

There are also many night birds, like eagle owls, little owls, barn owls and bats, and the latter are quite a nuisance in churches, where they gather in large numbers because they are dark, high places, and so they infect them with their bad smell, together with the fact that there are ordinarily many swallows in them, which also make them very dirty because they breed inside.[4]

Friar Luis de Urreta deals with this matter of the differences of the birds in Ethiopia in chapter 26 of his first book. In certain things, however, he did not have correct informa-tion, as when he says on page 268 that there are no night birds, or sparrowhawks, or goshawks, or other birds for falconry, save those that they bring from Persia as presents for the kings and princes. He also says that since chickens lay they cannot be eaten; and that to hatch eggs they put 1,000–2,000 together in the sand and, covering them with manure, they put more sand on top and, as it is a land where it hardly ever rains and the sun is very

---

[1] Amharic *ebâb wăč̣*, an unidentified species of stork.

[2] Amharic *wăssâ*, possibly referring to the spur-winged goose (*Plectropterus gambensis*).

[3] Unidentified species (Amharic *yebrâ* now means 'duck' in general).

[4] See , 'Historia de Ethiopia a alta', in Beccari, *RÆSOI*, 5, p. 43.

strong, they hatch and the chicks come out; and then they take a turkey, pluck its breast and lash it with nettles, and in that way they teach it to brood the chicks, and the 2,000 run after it. That, they say, {[f. 103]} is the custom down in Cairo, where there is little or no rain, but in the lands of the Prester John there is no such thing, nor have they ever seen turkeys, or is there any recollection of anyone ever bringing sparrowhawks or falcons from Persia, nor do they know how to hunt with them here, for if they did they would have no lack of them in their own land.

<[f. 99v/89v]> Something more fabulous and ridiculous than all these things in Ethiopia is what he says about a bird at the end of his chapter, in the following words:

*The other bird, which I have kept for the end of this chapter, is the one that here they call the bird of Paradise, or as they call it in Ethiopia,* camenios, *which means 'chameleon of the air'. The body of this little bird together with its head is about a finger joint in length, much smaller than the body of a nightingale. Its beak is longer than the whole of its body, and it opens its mouth much wider than one would suppose for such a small body. Its feathers are very large, more than three spans long, the finest of the brightest colours, most beautiful hues and different enamels that nature has produced, such that neither the parrot, the peacock nor any other bird can match it. It has no feet and it flies through the air day and night, and in the air it lives on little flies and on the air itself, and it sleeps in the air, without ever landing on a tree or bush, rather it dies as soon as it touches the ground. And it is so delicate that sometimes boys put bird lime on a long rod and, on seeing these little birds, try to touch them so as to catch them, and while they are bringing down the rod the bird is already dead. One might ask, if they die on touching the ground, how do they multiply? How do they lay their eggs and sit on them? Industrious nature came in support of all this with a strange artifice, so that in considering these marvels we should praise God in His works: nature gave it a sinew in the place of its feet, as long as its feathers and as thin as a guitar string. And when the time comes when the male's nature inclines him to multiply, he seeks out the female and seizes her with that little cord and attaches himself to her, flying all the while. When the female wants to lay her eggs, she seeks out the male and, on seeing him, grasps him and ties herself to him with that little sinew and lays her eggs on top of the male's wings, between which nature formed a seat and hollow like a nest, and the female sits there and incubates here eggs until the young have hatched. And they fly all the time while brooding, living on little flies and air. Once the chicks have hatched, the female flies off and the male carries his pleasant load on his back until their feathers grow and they start flying. There are many of these birds in Arabia and in many parts of Ethiopia, especially on Mount Amara, because they are regions where it seldom rains and the air is not disturbed.[1]*

{[f. 103v]} All this is mere fiction, for no such bird exists in Ethiopia or, it would seem, anywhere in the world. Thus, when I asked some very great lords, [who] had spent a long time in the kingdom of Amharâ, about it, in the presence of the emperor, they all laughed heartily at this tall tale, and the emperor with much merriment related other things to them that I had told him, <[f. 100/90]> such as the great treasures that the same book

---

[1] Urreta, *Historia de la Etiopia,* excerpt (with omissions) from bk I, ch. 26, entitled 'Of the many birds that there are in Ethiopia, and in particular the ones called birds of Paradise', pp. 275–6. Páez quotes this passage in Spanish.

says there are on Guixên Ambâ, which he calls Mount Amharâ, and that there were ants as big as dogs. They were amazed that anyone should take the trouble to invent so many lies, because, in addition to the very great lies about the treasures and ants and that there was such a bird in Ethiopia, it rains a lot throughout the kingdom of Amharâ and it often hails so hard that it damages the crops, so such birds could hardly live there if they did exist. And even if it never rained, the winds, which are often so strong that they break trees, would be enough to dash those birds against rocks or woods, and they would not be able to withstand the great force of the wind as their bodies are so small and their feathers so long. As for his claim that there are also many of these birds in Arabia, if he means the part bordering the Red Sea, then I visited a large area of it inland during the seven years that the Turks held me captive there, and I never saw such a bird or heard tell that it might exist.

# CHAPTER XXV

## Which deals with the climate, minerals and fertility of the lands of the Prester John

Almost all the lands governed by the Prester John have good airs and are very temperate and healthy, to the extent that there are many 100-year-old men in very good shape, and I have even seen some aged 120 and 130 who are still strong. There are, however, some lowlands where it gets very hot at the end of summer when it begins to rain, and there are many sicknesses there and people die, and so people there ordinarily live in high places; but, however hot it may be, if they go into the shade they find it cooler. There are also very cold lands, as in the kingdom of Begmêder, in the province of Oagrâ, and above all in the province they call Cemen, which is freezing cold. The waters in both the hot and the cold lands are generally good and healthy. There is great variety in the weather, because from April to August the days are longer than in Spain. If one faces east, the shadows move to the right. Then the days become shorter, so that in November and December they are very short and the shadows move to the left.[1]

{As regards the fertility of the lands, it is very great because, even though there are some that are less fruitful}

There are some goldmines, particularly in the kingdom of {[f. 104]} Nareâ, but the best is the gold they take from a large river that they call Bebêr by washing sand from the banks. Some people dive into the deepest parts holding wooden bowls tied to ropes. When they have filled them with sand from the bottom, others standing on the bank pull them out with the ropes and there they often find large pieces. In another land called Fazcolô, not far from this one, they say there is a lot, if they knew how to get it, because, when they set fire to the bush, which they often do – and they are stands of bamboo – the bamboo shoots that emerge bear pieces of gold on their tips, and this is the finest <[f. 100v/90v]> in Ethiopia. In another land as well, which was recently subjugated by *Erâz* Cela Christôs, the emperor's brother, and is called Ombareâ, near Gojâm to the west, there is good gold, but they do not know how to extract it there, either, because they are ignorant, coarse Kafirs. They say that a gold mine was once found in the kingdom of Tigrê, in the province that they call Tambên, and that Emperor Malâc Çaguêd commanded that they cover it up and not speak of it so that the Turks should not try to take that land. In Agçûm too, which is in the same kingdom, they say that lots of little pieces of gold can be found on the land when it rains a lot.

There are also silver mines in the province of Tambên and that of Zalâmt and, when I arrived in Ethiopia in May 1603, some Greeks were extracting it by order of Emperor Iacob.

[1] See , 'Historia de Ethiopia a alta', Beccari, *RÆSOI*, 5, pp. 17–18.

They showed me some and it was very good and soft, but soon afterwards they stopped extracting it. When I recently asked Emperor Seltân Çaguêd (who was buying some that came from the Turks) why he did not have it mined, since he had some in those provinces, he answered that it was too much work for too little gain. There is iron in many places and lead in some, but so little of the latter that it is barely enough to make balls for their guns, and so when they go to war the captains share it out very carefully among the soldiers.[1]

As regards the fertility of the lands, it is very great because, even though there are some that are less fruitful, there are few that are not sown every year without ever resting. In some of them they harvest two crops every year, not just in the valleys where they can be irrigated, but on the plains. With all that, for some seeds which they call *daguçâ*[2] and *tef*,[3] which are not found in Europe – and they are as fine as mustard seed – they often harvest 100 or 150 measures for one measure sown. From it they make bread that the ordinary people eat, but it is black and has little substance. Maize also produces well. There is wheat of many kinds, barley, grains, {[f. 104v]} broad beans, lentils, common beans and other seeds in abundance, but they do not produce as much as the first ones: at most, they yield twenty or thirty to one. They sow a good deal of flax and even in fields where it is not irrigated, it grows as tall as in Spain, but they do now know how to use it to make cloth, because they throw the stems away and collect the seed for a certain food that they make from it. They have sesame and another seed that they call *nug*,[4] like linseed but black, from which they make a lot of oil, because there is no olive oil. They sow plenty of garlic {and} onions, cabbages (but they are bad), radishes, and other things like turnips that do not exist in Spain, which they call *xux* and *denîch*,[5] which the poor people turn to at times of famine. There is sugar cane, ginger, cardamom, black cumin, dill, fennel, coriander, cress and some bad kinds of lettuce, but just two years ago some lettuce, cabbage and chicory seed arrived for us from India, and everything is beginning to grow very well. Some chilli seed came at the same time and there is now plenty, and the people like it very much.

<[f. 101/91]> There are not so many different kinds of fruit trees as in Spain, but there are many peach trees, pomegranates, figs like those of Portugal and India, and another kind, which in its leaves hardly differs from Indian fig trees and, although it does not produce fruit to eat, it is more provident than those because they eat the stem or midrib of the leaf and from the same leaf they make ropes and [very fine mats], and spin thread with which they make cloths that the poor wear; and the root, which is ordinarily more than two spans across, is eaten cooked, and from it they make very fine, white flour, which they eat cooked in milk, but bread made from it is not very good. And if they cut it right down to the ground, it sends out suckers all around, which they plant elsewhere and they soon take; it is called *encêt*.[6] There are orange trees, citrons, limes and others that give very large fruit, tamarinds, jambolans,[7] jujubes,[8] some large trees which are called *xe*,[9] like their fruit

---

[1] On Ethiopia's mineral wealth, see Almeida, 'Historia de Ethiopia a alta', Beccari, *RÆSOI*, 5, pp. 35–6.
[2] Amharic *dāgussā*, finger millet (*Eleusine coracana*).
[3] Amharic *ṭéf*, teff (*Eragrostis tef*), an indigenous cereal of Ethiopia.
[4] Amharic *nug*, niger seed (*Guizotia abyssinica*).
[5] Root vegetables, perhaps yam and sweet potato (Amharic *denneč* is today used for 'potato' in general).
[6] Enset, or false banana (*Ensete ventricosum*).
[7] An Indian fruit tree (*Syzygium cumini*).
[8] A fruit tree of the Middle East and Asia (*Ziziphus zizyphus*).
[9] Red milkwood (*Mimusops kummel*), a tree used for fruit and shade.

– in taste, colour and appearance they resemble dates, but they are more slender at the tip. They have also recently planted coconut palms and they are now bearing fruit, and there are a few small date palms, but in the kingdom of Dancali there are many.

There are no grapevines like those in Spain; they are all grown on trellises, and there are few of these. They plant eight or ten canes together and never prune them, and so a single vine takes up a lot of room and needs a large trellis, but even so they bear many grapes and large bunches. They are now planting the main ones, because the emperor is very curious. On one of the enclosures of some palaces that he built just a few years ago, he planted 150 vines in September and at Christmas he ate some twenty ripe bunches, although it was not even four months since they had been planted, for I saw it all myself. Later, he had 5,000 planted in a field, and since they space them well apart, because {{f. 105}} they are not going to prune them, they take up a lot of land. Since he really wants everyone to plant them, he had it proclaimed that anyone who planted vines or any fruit trees would never lose their land, not even for treason to the crown, although it is a custom for the emperor to take lands away from some and give them to others whenever he likes, except lands that they have bought from the crown. Now they have sown papayas again, which came from India, and they do very well. There is a lot of cotton, with which they make some very good cloths, but they are ordinarily not like Indian cloths either because the cotton is not so good or because they do not know how to make it. However, they make another sort of cloth, very long and strong, which they use on their beds like a mattress and thick blanket, and it is very warm, because it has a pile four fingerbreadths long; they call it *becêt* and some are so good that they cost ten *cruzados*. It seems that anything that is sown or planted in this land will grow, particularly olive trees, because there are many wild olives and some have fruit almost as large as cultivated olives, not because they have ever been grafted, <[f. 101v/91v]> because they do not know how to do that, but because the land is suitable for them.

The wild trees are commonly thorny, and some are very tall and thick. There are also many tall cedars, but their crowns are not like those of Spain, but their branches are spread out, as Dioscorides[1] depicts and describes them, and their wood is sweet-smelling and very good for houses. There is very good angelim, blackwood, and some trees that they call *zeguebâ*, which are very tall, handsome and thick, with fine white wood,[2] as well as many other kinds of trees that do not grow in Spain or Europe, particularly one that they call *demâ*.[3] This tree grows so fat that four men could not reach round it and, ordinarily, even though they are very tall, they only put out branches near the top. The trunk is smooth inside; although it is not hollow, it is very soft. Certain monks who live in the desert put pegs in it one above the other up to a great height; climbing up on them, they easily carve into it and make a cell inside, where they sleep at night for fear of lions. They also claim that in former times some monks would get inside and others would feed them until the cell closed up, because it fills up again inside very quickly. And so they would be left there

---

[1] Dioscorides of Anazarbus, Greek physician, 1st century AD. This reference seems to indicate that the fathers had a version of his standard pharmacopeia, which described some uses of cedar. It is usually known as the *De materia medica*, but was also published in vernacular languages in several illustrated editions in the 16th century.

[2] Amharic *zegbā*, East African yellowwood (*Podocarpus falcatus*).

[3] Amharic *dimā*, baobab (*Adansonia digitata*).

dead and buried, as we have said before.[1] Along the streams there are many jasmines, which also grow in the woods with many other scented flowers.[2]

Although these lands of Ethiopia are so fertile and abundant in crops, as we have said, for all that there has often been a great lack of them in many parts, because of the {innumerable} <many> locusts that generally come from the east: a plague so great that, wherever it comes, it leaves the fields like dust, the plants destroyed {[f. 105v]} and the trees without a single green leaf. They often land in such great numbers together that stout branches break under their weight. If this plague happened everywhere every year, there is no doubt that the lands would be abandoned and left totally deserted, but they do not come to the same parts every year. They say that it is thirty years now since they came to the kingdoms of Gojâm, Begmêder, Dambiâ and others, and in the kingdom of Tigrê, where they used to cause great damage almost every year, they have not been seen for twelve years, except in very small numbers.

Friar Luis de Urreta deals with this matter of the minerals and fertility {of the land} of Ethiopia in chapter 27 of his first book.[3] But he was badly informed in many of the things that he says, such as that in the kingdom of Damôt there are many gold mines of the finest and highest-carat gold in all of Africa, which he seems to have taken from Francisco Alvares, on f. 170 of his *Historia Ethiopica*.[4] But he was mistaken, because in Damôt there are no gold mines or, if there are, they do not know of them, unless he uses this name Damôt with so much latitude that it also includes the kingdom of Nareâ, <[f. 102/92]> as the common people do. Even so, it is certain fact, as everyone says and Emperor Seltân Çaguêd has told me, that the finest gold in all his lands is from the kingdom of Fazcolô, which is a long way from Damôt. Nor does he appear to be right when he says that Pêro de Covilham said to Francisco Alvares that in the kingdom of Begmêder there is a huge mountain all made of silver and that the Ethiopians did not know how to extract it, but that they made a pit and laid a fire in it, as if it were a lead oven, and the silver ran out in torrents. That was not just exaggeration but a lie because, if there really were such a rich mountain and so much silver could be extracted so easily, the memory of it would not have been lost so quickly, for now there is nobody who knows or has heard tell of such a thing. Nor would they have taken the trouble to extract silver from rock in the province of Zalâmt and Tambên, as some Greeks were doing at the emperor's command when I arrived in Ethiopia, and even though the silver was very good, they later stopped extracting it because it was too much work for too little reward.

No less a lie is what he says right there on page 252,[5] that now they know how to extract the silver there is so much that they value it little, because there was never so much silver in the lands of the Prester John or he would not have needed to buy it from the Turks, even though they sold it very dear. In years past, for five patacas they used to give one ounce of gold, which is the weight of one. He also says in the same place that salt is no longer used as currency as it used to be in the past, but that they take it as merchandise to

---

[1] The *demâ* was mentioned before in ch. 21, p. 213 above.

[2] Almeida dealt with the Ethiopian flora in his 'Historia de Ethiopia a alta', Beccari, *RÆSOI, 5,* pp. 37–9.

[3] Urreta, *Historia de la Etiopia*, bk I, ch. 27, entitled 'Of the wealth of minerals, fertility of trees and plants, abundance of fruits that there are in the land of Ethiopia', pp. 276–93.

[4] Álvares, *Prester John of the Indies*, ch. 134, 'Of the kingdom of Damute, and of the great quantity of gold there is in it, and how it is collected; and to the south of this are the Amazons, if they are there', p. 457.

[5] Urreta, *Historia de la Etiopia*, bk I, ch. 25.

Monomotapa and Congo. But that is not right, because until today it has always {[f. 106]} been used as currency, because when *Erâz* Athanateus, who was governing the empire with Empress Mariâm Sinâ, his mother-in-law, since Emperor Iacob was still a boy, tried to introduce copper coins, the people would not accept them, as we said at the end of chapter 9. Nor are the kingdoms of Monomotapa and Congo so close that salt could be transported to them from here; rather, the distance is so great that not only have they no communication with them, but they do not even know their names.

He also says that radishes grow very large but cannot be eaten because there is no chilli or pepper to equal them in bitterness, and that onions and garlic do not grow at all. But he was mistaken, because the radishes are very good to eat, and they are not as hot as those in Portugal. Onions are grown a lot, although they are small, and there is garlic in abundance with heads so fine that they are not outshone by the best garlic in Spain.

Similarly, he says on page 292[1] that Ethiopia is a land of abundant silk and that the silk-worms spin their cocoons in the mulberry trees themselves, of which there are vast numbers in the fields, and that many people also keep silkworms at home; but there is no silk at all in the lands of Ethiopia ruled by the Prester John, and they have never seen silk-worms or how they make silk. Thus the emperor himself sometimes asked me in the pres-ence <[f. 102v/92v]> of the lords what it was and, later, what silkworms looked like, and everybody was greatly amazed when I told them how they were kept, how they {slept} <ate> and shed their skin, etc. And there are no mulberries here at all. I have only heard that in some far-off lands that I do not think are ruled by the emperor there are some trees that have fruit like blackberries; they could be mulberry trees.

---

[1] Urreta, *Historia de la Etiopia*, bk I, ch. 27.

# CHAPTER XXVI

## Of the river Nile, its source and its course, and causes of its floods

Since we are dealing with the fertility of the lands ruled by the Prester John, it will not be out of place now to say something about the main rivers and lakes, which also fertilize it and make it more abundant. The first of them, which stands out as the most notable of all, is the great and famous River Nile, which the holy men of old and almost all modern scholars consider to be that which the Holy Scripture, in Genesis 2, calls {Gehon} <Gehan>. It puts it in second place when it names the four that issue out of Paradise, saying: *Et nomen fluvii secundi Gehon.* {[f. 106v]} *Ipse est qui circuit omnem terram Ethiopiae.*[1] The people of this empire call it the Abaoi. It has its source in the kingdom of Gojâm, in a land called Çahalâ, the inhabitants of which are called Agôus. They are Christians, but they have many heathen superstitions through their dealings and proximity with other heathen Agôus, their relations, of whom there are many. This source lies almost at the western edge of that kingdom, at the head of a little valley that forms in a large plain. On 21st April 1618, when I came to see it, it appeared to be no more than two round pools four spans in width. I confess I was overjoyed to see that which in ancient times King Cyrus and his son Cambyses, the great Alexander and the famous Julius Caesar had so longed to see. The water is clear and very light, in my opinion, since I drank some, but it does not run over the ground, although it comes up to the edge of it. I had a lance thrust into one of the pools, which lies {against} <at the foot of> a small bank where this spring first appears, and it went down eleven spans and seemed to touch bottom on the roots of trees growing on the edge of the bank.

The second pool of the source is lower down towards the east, about a stone's throw from the first. When the lance, which was twelve spans long, was put into it, it did not touch bottom. A Portuguese had tied together two lances so that they were twenty spans long, and when he put them in he did not find the bottom either. Those that live there say that it has no bottom and, when they walk near those pools, everything around shakes and trembles, so it is clear to see that there is just water underneath and that one can only walk over it because the roots of the grasses are so intertwined together, with a little soil. And I was told by <[f. 103/93]> many people, including the emperor himself, who was nearby with his army, that it was not trembling much because the summer had been very dry; in other years they were very afraid to approach the place, because when one stepped on the grass it seemed that one would sink to the bottom. And even eight or ten steps ahead it would shake up and down. The surrounding area, which seems to be like a lake, is

---

[1] 'And the name of the second river is Gehon: the same is it that compasseth all the land of Ethiopia' (Genesis 2:13).

almost round, and one cannot throw a stone from one side to the other, although it is easy with a sling.

Near the upper spring there live some people. And from there one climbs up little by little until one reaches a hill about half a league from the source to the west, which the inhabitants call Guix. And even though on this side it seems that the top is within gunshot range from the foot, on the other sides it is very high. But one can climb to the top from all sides, and on the summit there rises a mound, where the {[f. 107]} heathens sacrifice many cattle. In former times, on a certain day in the year, their sorcerer, whom they held as a priest, would come here and sacrifice a cow near the spring, and he would throw the head in and make it sink to the bottom. Then he would go up to that mound, where he would make a solemn sacrifice, killing many cows that the heathens brought to him. After that he would cover himself all over in their tallow and sit down on an iron chair that he had placed in the middle of a pile of dry wood, which he would order to be set alight, and he would sit in the middle of it until the wood was consumed, without being burned himself or the tallow even melting. Sometimes he would go in after the fire had been lit and would sit on his chair. And he deceived those people with his sorcery, so that they held him to be a great holy man and gave him whatever goods he wanted.

From the foot of that hill as far as the source they sow a good deal of wheat and barley, and around it from the southern side to the east and north there is a large area of low shrubs that look like tamarisk, and beyond that many lands that they sow. All together, it makes about a league of countryside. But from whatever direction they wish to approach the hill (except from that mound), they have to climb up, and they can do so from all sides, although the climb is higher and more difficult on the eastern and western sides. It is easy to pass from north to south and, on the southern side, about a {league} <lake> from the spring, there is a deep, broad valley, where there rises a very large stream which will flow into the Nile, and it may even come from the upper spring itself. The trickle of water that flows underground after leaving that round area at the spring runs eastwards as a rather narrow stream for the distance of a gunshot, as shown by the grasses and the appearance of the land, which is lower in that direction, and then it turns gently northwards. Having gone about a quarter of a league, the water can be seen among some stones and it forms a brook which, when I saw it, was not as broad as a man, although at other times it is larger, they say. A little further on it is joined by two small streams from the eastern side, and later on it collects many more, with which it gets <[f. 103v/93v]> larger and larger. Having gone a little more than a day's journey it receives a large river called the Jamâ. Then, with many twists and turns, it turns westwards, and having gone twenty or twenty-five leagues it is now a large river and begins to turn northwards [twisting all the way], so that after roughly thirty-five leagues of its course it flows east again and enters a flank of a great lake which lies between the province called Bed in the kingdom of Gojâm and the kingdom of Dambiâ. I reached the place where it enters the lake and then I went {[f. 107v]} a good way ahead and, looking out from a high spot on the edge of the lake, it seemed to me that the river flows within it for about half a league. The thread of its current can be picked out very easily when the lake is calm, as it was then, because some green plants, which the river brings with it before reaching the lake, are gently borne along on the current while the rushes and other things that lie on the lake waters on either side do not stir. Although I did not reach the place where the river flows out of the lake, from what they showed me from that spot and the time that they said it would take a man to walk from where it enters to where it leaves, it must be more or less six leagues. But when it leaves the lake, it takes with it much more water than it brought when it entered and, even though it is a very large river, in summer it can still be crossed on foot in some places where it spreads out.

As it leaves the lake, it very gradually turns southwards. After flowing some five leagues, it reaches a land called Alatâ, where it plunges vertically over some rocks, which must be fourteen fathoms high, and a sling would be needed to throw a stone from one side to the other. In winter, from the impact it makes at the bottom, the water rises into the air like smoke, so much so that it can be seen from very far off, as I have seen many times. A little further on, it narrows so much between two rocks that people easily put poles across from one to the other and make a bridge, over which the Emperor sometimes passes with all his army. Near there, the rock itself makes an arch, over which some more daring people cross, even though it is very narrow at the top. Here the river has the kingdom of Begmêder to the east, and it runs for several days between that kingdom and Gojâm; then the kingdom of Amharâ, after that Olacâ, and then the kingdom of Xaoâ; and after that, the kingdom of Damôt, all the time flowing round the kingdom of Gojâm. On reaching a land called Bizân on the Damôt side and another called Gumâr Çancâ on the Gojâm side, the river is so close to its source that one can reach it in one day. When, in the presence of Emperor Seltân Çaguêd, I asked his brother, *Erâz* Cela Christôs, how many days' journey it would be from Gumâr Çancâ along the river upstream as far as its source, he started counting, together with some great men who were present, and they found it to be twenty-nine, if I remember rightly. From Gumâr Çancâ onwards it continues to run <[f. 104/94]> around Gojâm for a few days, and then it passes between the kingdom of Fazcolô and that of Ombareâ, inhabited by very black heathens, which *Erâz* Cela Christôs conquered with a large army in the year 1615. As it was such a large and little known land, they called it Ayez Alêm,[1] which means 'New World'. From that point on, {[f. 108]} the emperor does not rule, nor do they know the names of the lands or the course of the river, beyond saying that it passes through the land of heathen kafirs towards Cairo.

We shall therefore stop following the course of this great river and {give} <tell> the reason for its annual flood. The fact that it is always at the same time of year, from July onwards, when elsewhere the rivers are shrinking and drying up, gave Saint Irenaeus so much difficulty in his Book 2, *Adversus haereses*, chapter 47 (as mentioned by Friar Luis de Urreta on p. 303),[2] that, after gathering many opinions, he did not venture to consider any one of them correct but said that only God knew the truth. Lucanus and Abulensis say that it is a well-concealed secret of nature, and Theodoretus confesses that he does not understand it. Others who, guided only by its course, have tried to give the reason have offered a thousand absurd explanations, saying, for instance, that the winds blowing against the Nile's current held back the waters, which thus grew in height. Others have said that the great amount of sand carried by the Nile settles in the mouths through which it enters the sea and blocks its course and, as the waters are held back, they cause Egypt to

---

[1] Addis Alam; Páez's mistake was repeated by the copyist.

[2] Urreta, *Historia de la Etiopia*, bk I, ch. 28, entitled 'Of the River Nile, of its sources and springs, its course and causes of its floods, and other strange curiosities. Concerning crocodiles', pp. 294–310. On pp. 303–4, Urreta summarizes the opinions of the ancient writers mentioned by Páez.

flood. Even Aristotle, the prince of philosophers, in a book that he wrote, *De Inundatione Nili*, said that along the Nile there are many springs that are closed in winter, but when the soil expands with the heat of the sun in summer they pour out and the Nile rises. Friar Luis de Urreta too, in his Book 1, p. 305,[1] philosophizes in his own manner and attributes these floods to the waters of the ocean {sea} which, pounded at that time by furious winds, enter along secret channels and aquifers as far as the lake where the Nile rises, and make it swell, and hence the river swells as well.

That is all very different from that which experience – which cannot lie, as the discourse of men can – has shown not only to the people of Ethiopia, but to all of us from Europe who live in this country. The fact is that winter ordinarily begins in these lands in early June and it rains so hard until September, and sometimes for the whole of that month and part of October, that not just the rivers but also the tiny streams become so swollen that they cannot be crossed except in boats; they make these from a reed-like straw which, although it is four fingerbreadths thick, is very light when it dries, and the boats never sink even if they overturn. There are many of these streams in the kingdom of Gojâm, which in winter resemble great rivers, and they all flow into the Nile, and many others join it from other parts, including mighty rivers which, having passed through <[f. 104v/94v]> many lands and received enormous {[f. 108v]} volumes of water in winter, empty into the Nile. Lake Dambiâ too, through which (as we said above) this river passes, fills up by mid-August, more or less, with all the waters that flow into it, and thereafter it empties into the Nile even more furiously without being diverted elsewhere, because no other river or even a stream runs out of it, although many very large ones flow in, particularly in winter. This, then, is the real cause of the annual flooding of the River Nile: the many waters that join it, because it is winter here at that time and it rains a great deal. All the other causes that people give are fables and mere imagination. At the end of September, the waters here in Lake Dambiâ ordinarily begin to diminish and the streams to fall since there is less rain, and consequently the Nile does so as well. But it does not stop so quickly that it carries no more water than usual until Christmas.[2]

Along some parts of its course, it has no trees at all on its banks. Along others, it supports very tall ones, such as wild cedars and other trees that are not found in Spain. In the river there are sea horses that people here call *gumarî*.[3] The people that pass by in boats are very wary of them, because sometimes they charge and, placing their forefeet on the boats, they overturn them with their great strength and weight and they kill those they can catch with their teeth, which are very{ long} <large>. There is a great abundance of many kinds of fish, which are fat since they find plenty to eat, and among them the one that we call 'torpedo' in Latin and the people in this land call *adenguêz*,[4] which means 'fright', because, as they say, anyone who holds one in his hand gets a fright if it wriggles, and he feels as if all his bones have been dislocated. This happened to some Portuguese

---

[1] Urreta, *Historia de la Etiopia*, bk I, ch. 28.

[2] See , 'Historia de Ethiopia a alta', Beccari, *RÆSOI*, 5, pp. 19–22. Manuel de Almeida wrote about the Blue Nile 'as an eye-witness' (p. 19), but he makes no mention of the earlier expedition by his fellow Jesuit Pedro Páez.

[3] Amharic *gumãré*, hippopotamus (*Hippopotamus amphibius*).

[4] Amharic *adangez asâ* ('stun fish'), electric catfish (*Malapterurus electricus*), a freshwater species. The electric ray or torpedo (genus *Torpedo*) to which Páez refers is a marine fish found in the Mediterranean but not in Ethiopia.

who told me about it, and principally their captain, Joam Gabriel, who was relaxing one day on the river bank with some others when with his rod he pulled out a fish more than a span in length, without scales, which looked rather like a dogfish, and it came up without wriggling. When he took hold of it to remove the hook, it wriggled and he dropped it straight away because he felt as if all his bones and even his teeth had been shaken and that he had been stunned; he would have collapsed had he not been sitting down. He soon came round and realized what the fish was. To play a trick on one of his servants, he called him over and told him to take that fish off the hook. When the man took hold of it, it wriggled and he fell to the ground dazed, without knowing what had happened to him. Getting up again, he said, 'What have I done to you, master, for you to give me such a fright?' The captain and the others roared with laughter to see that he had been so stunned that he did not know what had happened. They waited for the fish to die before taking it off the hook. <[f. 105/95]> The captain told me that he personally believed {[f. 109]} that if it does not wriggle it does not cause that effect, because he did not feel anything until it wriggled; and that another Portuguese had caught another of these fish that was a cubit long.

From what we have said, it is clear to see how poorly informed Friar Luis de Urreta was on the matters of the River Nile, since, when speaking of its sources, which he places among some inaccessible mountains, he says these words on p. 298 of his first book:

*They are very rugged mountains and so high that the Alps and Pyrenees are mere huts in comparison. The native people call them the Gafates Mountains. It is so difficult to climb these mountains that it is humanly impossible to climb to the top of them, because of all the waters that constantly run down them, because they are covered with marshes, springs, streams, gorges and even mighty rivers. All these waters collect in a great lake, which they call by the name of the Gafates Mountains, and the Zaire as another name, and Lake Zambra; as it is so large and extensive, they give it the names of the various provinces that it bathes. It is one of the great lakes that the world must possess, because it must be about 150 leagues long from north to south and more than eighty leagues wide in the middle. Three famous rivers flow out of it: the Zaire and the Aquilunda westwards, and the Nile, which flows ever northwards.*[1]

All this is very different from what in fact happens, because the source of the Nile is nowhere but in that plain that we have said lies on top of the mountains, and the only lake there is that little area surrounding the springs, where in summer one can walk in the manner described. Nor will any lake one third as big as he says be found in all the lands ruled by the Prester John, nor does any more water issue from the mountains than a few very small streams, nor are they so high that they can be compared with the Alps and Pyrenees, let alone say that these are mere huts in comparison. Nor are they called the Gafates, but the principal one is Guix, as we have already said, nor is the climb so difficult that one cannot reach the top from all sides, and very easily from two sides. Thus it was that Emperor Malâc Çaguêd crossed over there once with a large army and pitched his tents around that same spring, and some of the Portuguese who accompanied him then

[1] Urreta, *Historia de la Etiopia*, excerpt from bk I, ch. 28, p. 298. Páez quotes this passage in Spanish.

are with me today. And Emperor Seltân Çaguêd passed beside the spring with a large army at the end of April 1618.

{[f. 109v]} No less mistaken is what he says later, on page 300,[1] that the River Nile enters the kingdom of *Tigrê Mohôn* and further on splits into two great branches and makes the famous island of Meroé, which is 100 leagues long and thirty-four wide, and that the eastern branch divides the island from the kingdom of Lacca and Barnagasso. Because, first of all, the lands governed by *Tigrê Mohôn* are not a kingdom, but a certain part of the kingdom of Tigrê, but they are extensive lands, and that is why Francisco Alvares, in his *Historia Ethiopica*, folio 40,[2] says that it is a large kingdom. And if by 'Bernagasso' he means *Bahâr Nagâx*,[3] as he does in other parts of his book, <[f. 105v/95v]> this lord governs other lands of the kingdom of Tigrê towards the Red Sea, up to near Arquico. And therefore, in the area where the Nile flows closest to the lands of *Tigrê Mohôn* and those of *Bahâr Nagâx*, there are three very large provinces and the kingdom of Dambiâ in between. And there is no such island of Meroé while the Nile passes through the lands of the Prester John, as many have informed me, and the emperor himself told me that they had never heard of such an island, nor did they know that the Nile had any inhabited island, and that those that it formed in their land were so small that one could not live on them.

On this occasion, in the presence of many great men, I told them what Friar Luis recounts later, on pages 303 and 307,[4] that near that island the emperor had posted many people to wait for news from those who elsewhere were watching certain stone wells, where the height of the flood that was necessary for Egypt's fertility was marked with numbers. When the water reached the mark they had made on the stone, they left for the post on camels and, on giving the message to those who were near the island of Meroé, they diverted the Nile floodwater to the Red Sea along some great channels that they had made so that it would not flood too much in Egypt. And so that they would not divert the river entirely, leaving the people bereft there, every year the Turk, whose land it is, paid him 300,000 gold sequins,[5] each of which is worth sixteen reales. They all roared with laughter at the tale, even the emperor himself. He told me that he has no such people posted on the river, and nor had his forefathers, nor is the floodwater diverted anywhere, nor does the Turk pay him such tribute, nor has he ever done so. There is thus very little value in what Friar Luis claims at the end of Doctor Luis de Bania's third book, where he says that the Turk pays tribute to the Prester John.

I am not greatly surprised at these tales if they are information given by Joam Balthesar, because even that which he has sworn to be true is, I find, very far from it. For example, Friar Luis says, on page 305,[6] that he swore to him that in the year 1606, when he left Ethiopia, it had not rained for ten years, whereas when I arrived in the country in May 1603 I found very heavy rains for the next four months in the kingdom of Tigrê, where I was. And later they told me that they had been much heavier in

---

[1] Urreta, *Historia de la Etiopia*, bk I, ch. 28.

[2] Álvares, *Prester John of the Indies*, ch. 34, 'How we arrived at Temei, and the Ambassador went in search of Tigrimahon and sent to call us', p. 138.

[3] See Glossary (Bernagaez/bahâr nagâx/*baḥr nagāš*).

[4] Urreta, *Historia de la Etiopia*, bk I, ch. 28.

[5] Turkish gold coins introduced in 1478.

[6] Urreta, *Historia de la Etiopia*, bk I, ch. 28.

the kingdom of Gojâm. And in 1604 {I} <he> spent {[f. 110]} July, August and September in Gojâm, a day's journey from the very source of the Nile, and the rains were so heavy and the streams so swollen that I could not reach it; indeed, I could hardly leave the house. Later, when I was forced to go somewhere else, I found so much mud in October that I could not travel by mule save with great difficulty. I also asked respected men aged sixty and sixty-five if they had ever seen a year when it had not rained in these lands, and they assured me that they had never seen such a thing in all their lives, nor had they ever heard of it happening. That shows what credence can be given to Joam Balthesar's information.

# CHAPTER XXVII

## Of the rivers Marâb and Tacaçê, and of the course of their currents

In chapter 29 of his first book, Friar Luis de Urreta calls the River Marâb the 'Black River', not because its waters are not clear and transparent, but because it always runs through lands of black people; and that this is the river of which he is speaking there is shown by the description he gives, saying that it rises near Alleluia monastery in the kingdom of *Tigrê Mohôn*, in Ethiopia, and divides the kingdom of Dambiâ from the kingdom of Medra, although nobody knows of that name in Ethiopia. He tells so many marvels of this river, placing it above all the rivers in the world in riches, that he has obliged me to leave until later other large rivers that are closer to the Nile and to go back to near the Red Sea to deal with it, not because it deserves to be compared with them, but because, as Friar Luis gives it pride of place after the Nile, it would not be fitting to talk of another river before telling the reader how true the things he describes about it are. For that it will be necessary to give at least a brief summary of all that he recounts at length.

In that chapter, then, he speaks about the Black River in the following words:

*Its source, as the Ethiopians believe, is in some vast marshes, bogs and pools that lie near the Alleluia Monastery, which is of the Order of Preachers, in the kingdom of Tigrê Mohôn in Ethiopia. Its waters, taking a path towards the equinoctial line, disappear underground and re-emerge in a large lake that they call the Black Lake, which is rather more than forty leagues long from north to south and about twenty wide. Out of this lake flows the Black River, serving as the border and limit {[f. 110v]} of all Ethiopia to the land of black people. It divides the kingdom of Ambian Cantiba (he should say Dambiâ, because that is the name of the kingdom, and they call any viceroy 'cantiba'), which belongs to Ethiopia itself, from the kingdom of Medra. On leaving Ethiopia it divides the great kingdom of Nubia from the kingdom of Biafara, and when it reaches some large mountains it disappears underground and, flowing unseen for more than thirty leagues, it gushes out with great force in the kingdom of Zafara, forming a large lake running east–west, which is fifty leagues long from east to west and thirty wide. Further on, on leaving the kingdom of Mandiga and the kingdom of Cano, it makes a large lake where it spreads out over a breadth of many leagues. The lake is triangular, and each side is about forty-six leagues long, so that it must be 138 leagues around. It is called Lake Guarda. From this great lake issues the Black River, taking its course to the west. As it runs between the kingdom of Tombotu to the north and the kingdom of Melli to the south, it is joined by a river of that name. Here it spreads out again, making a lake thirty leagues long and seventeen wide, from which issue four very mighty rivers into which the Black River splits. One of them runs <[f. 106v/96v]> northwards between the kingdom of Caragoli and the kingdom of Genchoa and, entering the kingdom of Arguim, it flows into the*

251

*southern ocean at nineteen degrees of latitude. This river is named after Saint John and forms a good harbour in its mouth which they call Tofia, and it is little more than thirty leagues below Cape Blanco. The other river into which the Black River splits flows due west through the kingdom of Senega and reaches the ocean above Cape Verde. The third river into which the Black River splits flows due west and divides into two arms, reaching the ocean sea about thirty leagues beyond Cape Verde towards the equinoctial line. The last branch of the Black River divides straight away into two: they call one of them the River of Saint Dominic, and it discharges its waters into the sea near the city of Stacara, at thirteen degrees; the other arm, turning towards the equinoctial line, makes a large bay where it enters the sea on the other side of Cape Roxo and they call this arm the River Grande.*

*This is the course taken by the Black River, which is the richest that there must be in the whole world because not only are vast quantities of very fine gold found in great abundance in its sands, but many valuable precious stones are also found. Rubies are found, the largest and best that may be found in all Africa. Sapphires, emeralds and topazes, and very fine ones, are found. Such is the wealth of this river that most of the precious stones {[f. 111]} in the treasury on Mount Amara, as described above, were taken from this river. Large pieces of garnet stone are found, and in such abundance that they used to use them in former times for stonework in temple buildings, because they did not know their value and price. But since the Duke of Florence, Don Francisco de Medeçis, sent many lapidaries and craftsmen to the Prester John to cut stones, they have taught them the value of garnet and of many others, and the Abyssinians have learnt from the Italians how to work precious stones, and they make thousands of kinds of rare jars, ewers and vessels, especially from garnets.*

*On its banks there are a thousand kinds of leafy, branching trees that line its margins, agreeable to the sight and, particularly where it sinks below ground for the whole extent of more than thirty leagues, the land is the most fruitful and abundant in the whole of Ethiopia or even Africa. Many heathens from the kingdom of Beafrix, the kingdom of Zafe and other parts come to this deck over the river to enjoy the cool of the trees and meadows, where they hold their feasts at the waxing moon, which they worship. There are great pastures for cattle, and so countless numbers graze on this deck, both from Ethiopia and from the kingdom of Borno. Many pearls are gathered from this river, like the good ones found throughout India. The artifice to gather the pearls is as follows: they throw some timbers and large logs into the mouth of the Black River, in the ocean that they call the River Grande, and there the oysters attach for some time to the logs, <[f. 107/97]> which they hold firm with their fasteners, and thus without any danger or hard work they collect the oysters and remove the pearls. The Prester John has his guards for this fishery, and the guards are also used to collect the ambergris that whales disgorge in the Black River.*[1]

Up to here are the words of Friar Luis de Urreta, but almost all the things he says are such fabulous fables that I do not know how whoever who put them into his head to write them down invented them. The reason is, first of all, that the source of the River Marâb, which he calls the Black River, is not in the marshes and pools that he places near the

---

[1] Urreta, *Historia de la Etiopia*, excerpt (with several omissions) from bk I, ch. 29, pp. 311–14. Throughout this passage (as in his ch. 1, reported by Páez in ch. 1 above), Urreta confuses a river in Ethiopia with the River Niger (literally 'Black River') of West Africa and its supposed connections with rivers flowing west into the Atlantic between Mauritania and Guinea Bissau. Páez quotes this passage in Spanish.

Alleluia monastery, for there is no more than a very small pool there, which dries up in summer, nor is the monastery of the Friars of Saint Dominic, because there are none in the Prester John's empire, as we have already said and as we shall show at the end of the second book. And even though the river disappears underground, when it re-emerges it does not form the forty-league lake that he mentions, nor further on does it serve as the border of all Ethiopia, as we shall soon state, when we speak of its course. It certainly does not then divide Dambiâ from the kingdom of Medra, because, as he says, the river has then already left {[f. 111v]} the lands ruled by the Prester John, and there are large provinces between it and Dambiâ. Nor is it possible that it should enter the ocean near Cape Verde, because, apart from that being absurd, in the middle lies the River Nile, which on leaving the kingdom of Gojâm flows on as we described in the previous chapter, and after passing Cairo flows into the Mediterranean Sea, as everyone knows and Friar Luis himself says on page 301.[1] And Alleluia monastery is in the kingdom of Tigrê, six days' journey from Arquico or Adeconô, as they say here, on the Red Sea coast. And from Alleluia monastery it turns west and, a few day's journey later, some say, it joins a large river called the Tacacê, about which we shall speak later, although others claim that it does not, but that it ends in the kingdom of Dequîn. But even if it went beyond, it would be impossible to reach the ocean sea, because it would inevitably have to encounter the Nile.

As for his saying that it is the richest river in gold and precious stones that there must be in the world, he is very much mistaken, because no gold is found in it, or the rubies, sapphires, emeralds and very fine topazes that he mentions. Rather, there are very fine toe-bruisers, for there is no lack of rocks that break the feet of those who do not take care when crossing it, for it is not such a large river than it cannot be crossed on foot even in winter. As for the garnet stones that he puts there in such abundance that they used to build temples with them, neither do they exist, nor do people know what they are. Nor is there any recollection that the Duke of Florence ever sent <[f. 107v/97v]> lapidaries or other craftsmen to the Prester John. The part where he says that, particularly from where the river goes underground to where it reappears, the land is the most fruitful and abundant in the whole of Ethiopia, with great pastures for cattle, is a fable like the rest, because it is just barren land with very little grass, as it is sandy, although there are some cool trees, but not fruit trees. It is no less fable and groundless imagination to say that they gather pearls and collect ambergris from this river, because neither of these things is to be found in it, nor in any other of the rivers ruled by the Prester John. And when we consider such a great absurdity and impossibility as that it flows into the ocean near Cape Verde, it is impossible for the Prester John to put men there on guard to collect the pearls and ambergris, because of the many large kingdoms and unknown provinces that have never been heard of in Ethiopia which lie between it and Cape Verde. Therefore, leaving aside these fables, we shall say something briefly about the source and course of this River Marâb.

The source of the River Marâb is some two leagues to the west of a town that they call Debaroâ, if we had to name it as it is written in the books of Ethiopia, for many of the common people just call it Baroâ. This is the usual residence of the governor of those lands, whom they call *Bahâr Nagâx*, because this is where {[f. 112]} duty is paid on the goods that Ethiopian merchants bring from the island of Maçuâ, on the Red Sea, where ships arrive from India, which is three days' journey from Debaroâ. So two leagues from

---

[1] Urreta, *Historia de la Etiopia*, bk I, ch. 28.

this town the river has its source, which I went to see so that I could talk about it better. It lies between two rocks about sixteen cubits apart and twenty high. As the water comes out from between them, it runs across a flat rock for thirty-six paces and then falls straight down a high cliff of the same rock. As it was the end of summer at that time, there was so little water that after reaching the bottom it only ran a very short distance without drying up. I was told that it is like that most years at that time, but that when it flows it runs directly eastwards and, leaving Debaroâ on the right, it very soon receives a reasonable-sized stream and it starts turning south. Then other streams join it, but it continues with the name of Marâb and flows round a province that they call {Zaraoê} <Zaraoî>, on its right, and on its left another that is called Zamâ and a third, Guelâ. Then continue <[f. 108/98]> the lands of *Tigrê Mohôn*, Açâ, Haricê and {Torât} <Forât>, which are large provinces. With all that, it is Zaraoê alone that lies along the right bank of the river, while the others succeed each other on the left. After three days' journey, it turns north and reaches Alleluia monastery, which lies to its left on a high mountain, about a gunshot away. Two small streams reach it from either side of the mountain, and it makes its way between high hills covered with thick forest. As far as I could see from a high point at the monastery, there was nothing but land that was hardly worked at all. A few leagues further on, the river disappears underground and emerges thirteen days' journey later. There they call the river Tacâ, which means 'Spread Water'.

They say that all this land that serves as a deck over the river is barren, because most of it is loose sand. The captain of the Portuguese, Joam Gabriel, told me that he had jour-neyed over it for three days in the company of a viceroy of Tigrê called *Azmâch* Dargôt,[1] and they had found very little grass, but there were cool trees, the shade of which they enjoyed greatly because of the very hot weather there. To drink, they had to dig down eight or sometimes twelve spans in the sand, and they found plenty of running water and fish that they could catch on a hook, and he ate two large ones. The inhabitants of that land are heathens and obey the emperor, although only just. {[f. 112v]} A little further on begins a large kingdom called Dequîn: it is a land of very black Moors whom they call *Balôus*, and they do not obey the Prester John, but they are on friendly terms, and they bring him many fine horses for sale, and some they present to him, but they do not last long because of a certain disease that they catch in this land.

In this kingdom of Dequîn the river waters many lands, for as soon as it emerges from under the ground the Moors share out the water over many parts, which is why it is called Tacâ, *scilicet* 'Spread Water'. People who live there have told me that all the lands it irri-gates are the coolest and most fertile and beautiful that exist in Ethiopia. Some Christians say that after watering those lands it goes on and joins a large river that they call the Tacacê, which then flows into the Nile. But the Moors of that land told me that it does not go beyond their kingdom of Dequîn and all its water is used up in those lands that it irrigates. And it is not even enough, because it disappears into the sand some ten leagues before reaching the end of the kingdom.

Since we have mentioned the Tacacê, which is an incomparably much larger river than the Marâb – and I have crossed it many times when going from Dambiâ to Tigrê and back again, for one cannot go from one of these kingdoms to the other without crossing it – it would be appropriate to say something briefly about it. It has its sources very close

---

[1] See Glossary (Dargôt/Dahāragot Azmač).

to the borders of the kingdom of Angôt, in a land called Axguaguâ, at the foot of a high mountain that rises to the east. They are <[f. 108v/98v]> three large springs that gush up with great fury, as if boiling, about twenty paces apart. A little more than a stone's throw away all three join together and form a large stream, flowing westwards for a few days between the provinces of Dacanâ and Oâg to the north and Ebenât and Quinfâz to the south. Then, with many twists and turns, it veers northwards, leaving on the right the province of Bargalê and on the left that of Cemên, which has the highest and most rugged mountains in almost all the lands ruled by the Prester John, and they are extremely cold. Further on, now flowing due north, it leaves on the right the provinces of Tambên, Adêt and Zanâ of the kingdom of Tigrê, and on the left {Zalâmt, which} <Zazâmt, and it> is very large. I forded it here in summer with very great difficulty, because it carries a lot of water and it does not spread out much. Continuing on its course towards the north, it leaves on the right the province of Sirêi of the kingdom of Tigrê and, on the left, the Desert of Aldubâ, which is a monastery of monks, to whom the emperors granted that the land extending almost three days' journey towards Dambiâ and much more towards the west should not be populated, because they like to be alone so that they can more easily give themselves to prayer and do their penances. Up to here, the river has flowed between very high, rugged mountains, but in this area, although the mountains are still high, there are good crossing-places in the summer because the river spreads out and so, even in the {[f. 113]} deepest part of the channel, the water does not come above one's waist. The water is very clear, but in early winter, when it begins to get muddy, it is dangerous to cross because of the lizards that live in it, which bite people and animals and even sometimes carry them off. At that time of year, therefore, people do not cross without slapping the water with sticks, and one cannot cross at all in winter except on a certain kind of raft that they make. Along its banks there are no fruit trees, apart from some tamarinds, and they do not even know how to use these. A little further on, a province that they call Oalcaoît lies on the left and, beyond it, they say that it flows through very hot lands until it reaches the River Nile, according to what some great men told me in the emperor's presence. When I found that unlikely, as it seemed to me that its course was very different from that of the Nile, the emperor told me that there was no doubt about it, because it was a very well known fact. Later, the inhabitants of a land called Berbêr told me that it joined the Nile close to their land. It is a river with plenty of very good fish. And they say that there are also sea horses in it.[1]

---

[1] See , 'Historia de Ethiopia a alta', Beccari, *RÆSOI* 5, pp. 24–5.

# CHAPTER XXVIII

## Which deals with the rivers Zebê and Haoâx

Among many other rivers that there are in the lands ruled by the Prester John, two very powerful and well-known ones, after the Nile (which they call the Abaoi, as we have said), are the Zebê, <[f. 109/99]> which some people in Ethiopia say is even larger than the Nile [although it is not], and the Haoâx, which they also say compares well in size with it.

[1] The Zebê has its source in a land that they call Boxâ, in the kingdom of Nareâ, which are the last lands in that [southward] direction ruled by the Prester John. Beginning its course towards the west, it soon turns north and starts flowing round a small kingdom that they call Zenyerô, which means 'monkey'. And that is how the king of the land shows himself to his people, as a monkey, because near his house he has built a high mound of earth like a little tower, and on top there is a tent with carpets inside, to which he alone climbs from behind, without being seen. When he appears on top, all those who are down below prostrate themselves on the ground on seeing him until they come to the front of the mound, and then they kiss it and, standing up, they perform other ceremonies that we shall report in the fourth book, when we deal with the journey made by Father Antonio Fernandez of our Society to that kingdom that the Zebê flows around, so that it almost becomes an island. On leaving it, the river turns south and enters a land that they call Coratâ. And they say that later, not many days' journey away, it flows into the ocean sea. Some people think that its mouth is at Mombaça, or {[f. 113v]} near the coast of Melinde. A man from a land adjacent to the kingdom of Zenyerô said that a servant of his had recently travelled along near this river until he reached some white men who had a fortress beside the sea, and their books had golden leaves on the outside and other red ones. It cannot be Mozambique, because he said he had travelled only a few days, and Mozambique is a long way from that land, and in between, so they say, there are so many deserts and peoples so unknown that not only do they not trade with Mozambique, but it seems that they cannot, even if they wanted to. Other people say that the river that comes out at Mombaça is not the Zebê but another that is no smaller than it.

The second very well-known river in Ethiopia after the Zebê is the Haoâx. It rises at the foot of a mountain called Gecualâ and flows between the kingdoms of Fatagâr and Ôye to the south and the kingdom of Xâoa to the north, and its course runs almost northwards. It is soon joined by another river, which is called the Machî, and it flows out of a lake that they call Zoâi, in the kingdom of Ôye. Then, on entering Ançâguralê, a province in the kingdom of Adêl, which is Moorish, it waters all those lands and many others in the same kingdom, where it rains very little or not at all, and so with great diligence they share

---

[1] New paragraph made by the editors.

out the river water to irrigate all the lands that it can reach and it makes them very fertile. But I could not find anyone who could tell me for certain whether it ended there or if it continued to the sea, although many believe that it does continue.[1]

Friar Luis de Urreta, in chapter 30 of his first book, also deals with the two great rivers that he says are in Ethiopia, which he calls the Rivers Zaire and Aquilonda, and he claims that they flow out of the same lake as the River Nile. Starting with the Nile, <[f. 109v/99v]> he says these words:

*Its current is short compared with that of the Nile, because it only waters two kingdoms: one is that of Gojame in Ethiopia to the east and, on entering the kingdom of Congo to the west, it crosses it, running through it for the space of 125 leagues, and although it is such a short course, even so it is a mighty and extremely deep river, with a very broad, extensive bed, so that large, seagoing ships can sail up it. There is only one drawback, which is that at a certain point there are some shoals and cliffs through which the river is squeezed in such a way that they prevent navigation and ships cannot sail up from the sea to the lake nor down from there to the sea. But the Prester John who is alive now has set many workmen and people to remove the reefs from the river together with some engineers that the Duke of Florence sent to him for this purpose, to make navigation easy. Once this is done, ships will be able to sail from the lake and the city of Zambra, the Prester John's court, which lies on its shores, follow the river to the ocean and come to Lisbon and Seville, without entering any other domain than that of King Dom Phelippe III, so that {[f. 114]} the two kings can communicate with each other through their own lands.*

*Two other rivers flow out of the same Lake Gafates, beyond the Zaire towards the Antarctic Pole: one is called the Prata, some thirty leagues from the River Zaire and, sixteen leagues from the River Prata, the lake is the source of the famous River Aquilonda, which flows from east to west in the kingdom of Malemba, in Ethiopia. They run through it for some 150 leagues, and both discharge their waters in Lake Aquilonda, which takes the name of the river. All these rivers swell at the same times as the Nile swells, because, as they all have their origin and source in Lake Gafates, when the lake swells on account of the ocean winds, which is the reason given, it is clear that they too must swell.[2]*

Up to here are the words of Friar Luis de Urreta, all very different from what in truth occurs, because in all the lands ruled by the Prester John there are no such names of rivers as Zaire or Aquilonda or Prata, nor such a Lake Gafates, nor does any other river at all flow out of the lake through which the Nile passes, as we said in chapter 26. Nor do these rivers, even if they existed, flood because the lake rises with the winds from the ocean sea, as he also says on page 305,[3] where he dealt with this at length, because this is a fable. The rivers in Ethiopia swell from June to the end of September, more or less, only because at that time it is winter and it rains heavily, as we have said. He also seems to place the kingdom of Gojâm next to that of Congo, because he says that the River Zaire only waters two

---

[1] See, 'Historia de Ethiopia a alta', Beccari, *RÆSOI*, 5, p. 23. The River Awās flows into Lake Abbe in the Danakil desert.

[2] Urreta, *Historia de la Etiopia*, excerpt (with several omissions) from bk I, ch. 30, entitled 'Of the Rivers Zayre and Aquilonda, and of Lake Cafates. Hippopotamuses, or sea horses, are described', pp. 321–3. Páez quotes this passage in Spanish.

[3] Urreta, *Historia de la Etiopia*, bk I, ch. 28.

kingdoms: that of Gojâm in Ethiopia to the east and Congo to the west. But that is very far off the path because, apart from there being many kingdoms and provinces between one and the other, if it <[f. 110/100]> flowed out of Gojâm, it would be impossible for it not to join the Nile, because the latter river, as we have already said, flows all round Gojâm [leaving only a small part in the west], and the River Tacacê, of which we also spoke above, which is six or eight days' journey from Gojâm to the north, goes and joins the Nile well below in the kingdom of Dequîn. It is also mere fiction that the Prester John who was alive when he was writing this – which, as he says elsewhere, was in the year of 1608 – was busy removing the rocks from the middle of the River Zaire with many workmen and some engineers that the Duke of Florence sent to him for this purpose, because I arrived in Ethiopia in May 1603 and I was almost regularly with three emperors who reigned until 1608 and I know very well that such a thing did not happen at that time. They could not have occupied themselves with that even if they had wanted to, because everything was ablaze in wars and uprisings until then. Two of these emperors were killed in battle by the rebels themselves, and the emperor who took over the empire in 1607, who is alive now and is called Seltân Çaguêd, {[f. 114v]} has also had many wars and uprisings until today that have given him a great deal of trouble; he had to worry more about how to defend himself than about removing rocks from the river, and he does not know of any such rocks and has never heard of them. I asked some great men who were nearly sixty years old and had always been at court, and they said that they had never heard of such rocks or that the Duke of Florence had sent workmen. Even if all that had been true, it would not be true that ships could go from the Prester John's court to Lisbon and Seville without entering any other domain than his and that of King Dom Phelippe III, because between the ocean sea and the lands ruled by the Prester John there are many lands that do not obey him and never have done.

# CHAPTER XXIX

## Which deals with the principal lakes that there are in Ethiopia

There are so many lakes in the lands rules by the emperor of Ethiopia that it would take a very long time and might tire the reader if we spoke of all of them, and so I shall only name some of the largest, leaving the principal one until last, since it has particular things that it will be appropriate to mention. The first that offers itself is the one that they call Zoâi, and it lies in the kingdom of Ôye, some six or seven leagues from Zêfbâr, where Emperor Atanâf Çaguêd had his court for fifteen years. This lake runs from north to south, such that to go right round it they say takes almost a whole day, walking fast, and it is almost as broad as it is long. It has an island in the middle and on it a monastery in which <[f. 110v/100v]> a few monks live; they have no lack of fish, because there is fish in abundance there. A river called the Machê flows out of it to the north, and soon afterwards it joins the great River Haoâx, as we said in the previous chapter. Some three leagues from this lake, in the same kingdom, there is another called Xacalâ, which one could walk round in rather less than half a day, and it is much longer than it is wide.

In the kingdom of Angôt, near the kingdom of Amharâ, there is another lake that they call Hâic, and it could be walked around in half a day or less. It has an island on which there is a monastery and some monks and the church is of Saint Stephen.[1] I know that Francisco Alvares, in his *Historia Ethiopica*, f. 80,[2] places this lake in the kingdom of Amharâ, but he was mistaken, as it is less than a league from the border of Amharâ, as I was told by people who spent a long time there and by Emperor Seltân Çaguêd.

The principal lake of all those that exist in Ethiopia lies between the kingdom of Gojâm, to the south, and that of Dambiâ, to the north, which they call Dambiâ Bahâr, which means 'Sea of Dambiâ'. {[f. 115]} It runs from north-west to south-east, as sailors would say. Its length, if one goes along the shore, is twenty-five leagues or more and its width more or less sixteen as it seemed to me on three occasions when I went right round it and many other times when I went from one end to the other on the Dambiâ side, where there are large fields of crops, for the land is very flat, and the people could make delightful gardens there if they were curious enough, but they are not given to that. Only this emperor has begun one, in which he has planted fig trees like those of Portugal and India, papayas, grapevines, peach trees, pomegranates and many thorn trees, and they are

---

[1] See Glossary (Hâic/Ḥayq; and Saint Stephen's/Dabra Esṭifânos).

[2] Álvares, *Prester John of the Indies*, ch. 63, 'Of the end of the kingdom of Angote, and the beginning of the kingdom of Amara, and of a lake and the things there are in it, and how the monk wished to take the Ambassador to a mountain, and how we went to Acel, and of its fertility', p. 249.

growing very well. And he brings up water with a water wheel, and it seems that it is the first one that has been seen in this land of Ethiopia; at least, people alive now have never heard of one. On the Gojâm side there are also many beautiful cultivated lands along the lake, but not so many as in Dambiâ, because in parts there are forests of wild cedars and other kinds of very tall trees that are not found in Spain.

This lake has many islands with lots of trees, some deserted and others settled, and on twenty-one of them there are monasteries with many monks. The principal ones, starting from the western side, are called:[1]

– Gâlilâ:[2] this one is opposite a high, spacious peninsula, where (as we have already said in chapter)[3] Emperor Seltân Çaguêd made a city where he placed his court, although later he moved it to another land, which they call Dencâz, rather more than a day's journey away. The island is a league and a half or more from the Dambiâ shore.

– Another island is called Dec and is much flatter than the others, and so large that its governor told me that 400 pairs of oxen work it. Here the emperor customarily places certain great men that he has had seized, when he wants them to be held more securely. This island <[f. 111/101]> has two churches and is closer to the kingdom of Gojâm than to that of Dambiâ.

– Near this one is another smaller and higher island called Remâ,[4] with a famous monastery where the emperors have been buried in recent years.

– Near this one is another large island called Çaanâ,[5] with a monastery and good church, as people say.

– Further on is another high island that they call Quêbrân,[6] with many monks. They do not allow women in here under any circumstances.

– About three-quarters of a league from this one is another high island called Debra Antonz,[7] where monks and nuns live. I have been to this one, and it is so strong that four men would suffice to defend the entrance against a very {[f. 115v]} large force of people, if they had no guns.

The remaining islands are not so renowned and therefore I shall not mention them.

The boats in which the monks go from island to island and come to the mainland, and which everyone else uses, are, as we said above, made of reed-like straw which grows in abundance in certain areas along the lake, and although it is very thick it is very light when dried.[8] To make these boats, they take a pole, rather thicker than a man's leg and as long as they want the boat to be, which is ordinarily short and narrow, but with its own kind of stern and prow. They base the boat on the pole, tying that straw on either side not with ropes, but with something that climbs up trees like ivy but

---

[1] The main islands in Lake Ṭānā are listed here in separate indents, for ease of reading. The manuscripts put them in a single paragraph.

[2] See Glossary (Gâlilâ/Galilā).

[3] The chapter number is missing in the manuscripts. The author may mean bk 1, ch. 20.

[4] See Glossary (Remâ/Rémā).

[5] See Glossary (Canâ/Çaanâ/Çana/Ṭānā Qirqos).

[6] See Glossary (Quêbrân/Kebrān).

[7] See Glossary (Debra Antonz/Dabra Entons).

[8] These papyrus-reed boats are known as *tankwā*.

is very thin and strong and, although it grows very long, it is always uniform like rope. Then they put that straw all tied together inside the boat and on top of it they put the load and people sit. It has no sail, and the oars are not like ours, but are long, thin poles. Holding them in the middle, they dip the ends in the water on both sides. They do not withstand large waves or the people sitting too much to one side, because they easily capsize, but they do not sink and so anyone who knows how to swim can climb back on straight away. Nonetheless, although their patriarch[1] could swim well, he was so afraid of these vessels that, to get to his island, he had a ship-like boat built in 1613. However, because the wood was heavy and they loaded it with too much cargo, it sank while he was on it, and he swam off, even with another person on his back, although they were a long way from land. But he would have done better to drown than later, as was to happen, be the cause of many deaths and be speared to death himself on 11th May 1617, as we shall say in the second book.

In this lake there is a very great abundance of fish of different sorts, both with and without scales. Of the latter type there is one kind that looks very much like a dogfish, except in its head, which is large and ugly like a toad. In winter, when the lake is high, at the time when it rains a lot, so many come out onto the fields <[f. 111v/101v]> along the shore (for in some areas they are covered with water for some distance) that people kill a great number just with sticks, and they are very tasty at that time of year because they are fat. There is another sort of scaly fish, about the size of a bream or a little larger, with a large mouth; when she lays her eggs she remains there until the fry hatch and then she stays with them; and if she senses something to fear, she opens her mouth and they all jostle to get inside; then she closes her mouth and swims off with them and, when she feels safe again, she opens it and lets them out. Once, when I was on the lake shore at the western end, where the emperor has given us lands, a fisherman cast {[f. 116]} his net and caught one of these, among others. When he opened its mouth in front of me, six little fish wriggled out. As it seemed to me that it had caught them to eat, I said to the fisherman, 'You caught it before it had swallowed its prey.' He answered that it had not taken them into its mouth to do them harm, but to protect them, because they were its young. And he told me what I have just recounted and put the little fish back in the water. Afterwards, other people also told me that that was correct and a well-known fact.

The fiercest and most monstrous thing in this lake is an animal that the people of the land call *gumarî* and the Portuguese who came with Christovão da Gama called a 'sea horse';[2] that is what it appears to be, according to what I heard in India from people who had seen sea horses. It is a four-footed animal and as large as a cow, but its legs are very short. On each foot it has four hooves: the front two are large and long, one other is smaller and the last is smaller still, and they are not joined together but separate. Its body is broad and not very long. It has short ears like a horse and a blunt snout. Two top teeth are four fingerbreadths thick and a span and a half long, more or less, and curved like a wild boar's. I measured some of the smaller teeth and they were eight fingerbreadths long and almost three thick. When it opens its mouth it shows some that must be three spans

---

[1] Páez's use of the term patriarch is surprising, because he is often at pains to explain that the Egyptian monk appointed by the patriarch of Alexandria was merely a bishop or metropolitan and that the Ethiopians called him *abuna*. It is clear from the context that he is referring to *Abuna* Seme'on and not to a Catholic patriarch, because none had been appointed at that time.

[2] Hippopotamus.

or more long. Its neigh is somewhat like that of a horse. Its neck is short, and it cannot bend it much. It has very sparse hair, like a pig's, and its tail is very short with a few bristles on the end. Its skin is so soft that any arrow or spear that they throw at it will pierce it, although it is very thick, but when it dries it is difficult for a gunshot to go through it. Its fat is like pork fat and its meat is like beef.

There are many of these animals in the lake. They stay in the water by day and come out at night onto the fields, where they cause great damage to crops if the people do not enclose them, but if they lay out a few stones a couple of spans high the animals do not enter, as their legs are very short; if fires are set at the edge of the <[f. 112/102]> fields, they do not come close either. Ten or a dozen live together and they are ordinarily found near the shore where the water is shallow, for they rarely go further out into deep water. Animals of one company do not come to where others have their home – which is always where they can find ground to be able to come out and feed – or they will have very serious fights. Even if there are a large number together, people say that there will only be one male among them, and those who hunt them also claim that when one of those females gives birth to a male calf, she immediately flees a long way away with him, otherwise the father will kill him. The two of them stay there until the youngster is big and then the mother bites {[f. 116v]} and fights him to test whether he is strong enough to do battle with his father. When she thinks he can, she takes him back to the place from which they fled. The father attacks the son straight away, and if he does not kill him but the son is beaten, he flees to a place where he waits until he feels bigger or stronger, and then he fights his father again. And he challenges him time after time until he kills him or defeats him and makes him flee from that place; with that he becomes the lord of that company and of his own mother. However, if she gives birth to a female calf, the mother does not run off and the father does her no harm, but rather protects her with {great} <so much> love that, if people pass close by, even on the boats that I mentioned above, he attacks like a lion. Putting his forefeet on the boat, he overturns it and tears anyone he finds to pieces with his teeth. Even if they do not have young, they are so wild – particularly in winter, when they are fat – that they charge like bulls. I know a fisherman who had a leg bitten off when he was on his boat, and he escaped with great difficulty. A Portuguese nearly died when he came close to water where there was one of these *gumarís*; it rushed out so ferociously that the Portuguese could not get away and it caught one of his arms with its teeth and tore it to pieces and he was thrown a long way by the blow it gave him with its snout; if other people had not rushed up, it would have torn him apart.[1]

This lake, as I have said, is the largest in all the lands ruled by the Prester John. Therefore, Friar Luis de Urreta was very mistaken in placing in the kingdom of Gojâm - as he says on page 298 of his first book[2] – a lake which is almost 150 leagues from north to south and more than eighty wide. Moreover, on page 322,[3] he says that on the borders of Ethiopia there is another lake that they call Aquilonda, which is thirty-five leagues from north to south and twenty from east to west, but there is no lake with such a name here,

---

[1] See, 'Historia de Ethiopia a alta', Beccari, *RÆSOI*, 5, p. 27. Almeida only described Lake Ṭānā, which he called 'Lake Dambeâ'.

[2] Urreta, *Historia de la Etiopia*, bk I, ch. 28.

[3] Urreta, *Historia de la Etiopia*, bk I, ch. 30.

nor anyone who knows of another as large as this one of Dambiâ. I have often seen water-spouts like whirlwinds come down from the clouds onto the lake and draw so much water up high and with so much fury that, had I not seen it, I could not have believed it. They say that when one catches a boat with people, it overturns it and nobody can be saved, and I believe that to be <[f. 112v/102v]> quite true, for such was the fury and destruction that I saw caused to the houses at court by a waterspout that left the lake and passed through one flank of it.

# CHAPTER XXX

## Which deals with the revenue and tributes paid to the Prester John by his vassals

As we have already seen how very fertile the lands ruled by the Prester John are and dealt with the principal rivers and lakes that make them even more remarkable, it is <also> appropriate now to speak of the revenue and tributes that his vassals pay him every year. Starting with the gold from the kingdom of Nareâ, where more is found than in any of the other lands, every year he receives the weight of 15,000 *cruzados* of very good gold. {[f. 117]} At first they paid him 30,000, and once, it is said, they sent him 50,000; but now, with the constant wars that that kingdom has with some heathens that they call Gâlas, it is so short of funds that the emperor does not oblige it to give more. The kingdom of Gojâm pays 11,500 *cruzados*, but the gold is not as fine as that from Nareâ. Gold used to be extracted in other places as well, but only a small amount, and they paid some revenue from it. However, they have now been so destroyed by the Gâlas that they cannot pay anything. For the commands that the emperor bestows, such as viceroys and governors, they also give him some gold, horses, mules, silks and other things. The viceroy of Begmêder gives 4,000 *cruzados* in gold, and the viceroy of the kingdom of Tigrê gave 5,000 a short while ago; *Bahâr Nagâx* 5,000; *Sirêi xûm* 4,000; *xûm Tambên*[1] 4,000; *abargalê* 3,000; *xum Xahârt* 1,000; {*Ambaçanet* 2,000; *Emderta* 300; *Agâmia* 1,000;} *Zamâ* 300; all these are lands of the kingdom of Tigrê, and therefore 25,600 *cruzados* are ordinarily taken from this kingdom; *Çagade* 1,000 *cruzados*; *Dambiâ cantiba* 1,000; *Bed xûm* 1,000; *Colâ xûm* 1,000; *Alafâ xûm* 1,000. This is the usual amount, but sometimes they give more, sometimes less. At times the emperor waives much of that which they promise him, and when he gives these commands to his sons-in-law he takes nothing from them.

Apart from this gold, which is paid by the lands where it is extracted and the lords on whom he bestows commands, the emperor has other revenue: from cotton cloths, honey, cows' butter, and grain; these amounts that each kingdom has to pay are certain and fixed. I was told by *Erâz* Cela Christôs, the emperor's brother, who is now viceroy there, that every year the kingdom of Gojâm gives 3,000 cotton cloths, which ordinarily are worth one *cruzado* each, though few of them end up in the emperor's hands, because he often leaves them for the lords to whom he has given many of those lands for a living, for very few of the empire's lands belong to private individuals rather than the emperor. And so he takes them from some and gives them <[f. 113/103]> to others whenever he likes. Gojâm also pays 200 cotton cloths of another kind, which they call *bezêt*; these are very broad but

---

[1] The copyist of BPB, MS 778 misread 'Tambên' (a province) as '*também*' ('also').

not very long, napped and closely woven, and the lords use them on their beds instead of mattresses, because they are soft and warm, and some are so good that they are worth ten *cruzados* each. It pays very little honey, because only one province in that kingdom has this tribute, and it gives 500 *calões*, and one *calão* must be rather less than the measure called an *arroba* in Castile. It pays no grain at all, because this viceroy has waived it and ordered, with the emperor's blessing, that it should no longer be paid, although it would be worth 10,700 *cruzados*. It also used to pay many mules {[f. 117v]} and, they say, 3,000 horses, which run fast and work hard, although they are as small as {*quartagos*} <*quartãos*>.[1] Emperor Malâc Çaguêd stopped collecting this revenue years ago so that the people of the land could used these same horses to fight the Gâlas, who often invade those parts. Likewise, the lord who was given the command of *Bahâr Nagâx* in the kingdom of Tigrê used to pay 150 horses, and better ones than those of Gojâm, and now gives no more than forty. Other lords of that kingdom also used to pay horses and now give very few.

In the other kingdoms they do not pay so many cloths, because some peasants give grain, honey and other cloths. Each of the peasants who do not pay cloths gives a certain amount of grain, which they call 'the emperor's *colô*', which means 'toasted', to show that it is merely an acknowledgment and something so trifling that it does not deserve a better name than toasted, but even so it is four Castilian {*hanegas*} <*fanegas*>[2] or a little less, and they call this quantity *handchân*, 'a load'. Since there are so many peasants that it would be difficult to count them, this revenue turns out to be very large. Apart from that, the peasant pays rent for the lands that he works, although this is not general, because in some places they give cloths instead. This rent was formerly one third of everything they harvested from the lands, but later, because those who sowed them used to hide a lot and, when the time came to take one third of the grain, they found little, Emperor Malâc Çaguêd ordered that they should not do it that way but, when the grain was ready for reaping, the judge of the land should go with the owner and two or three others and they should decide from the grain how much its owner {should} <could> pay. But they never decide on one third, but one fifth, more or less. This rent is for the lord to whom the Emperor has given the lands for a living, and the peasant also pays him two jars of honey every year, one at Easter and the other at the Exaltation of the Holy Cross, and on each of these days he also gives a chicken. The remaining lands that the emperor has chosen for himself, which are numerous, and those that he takes whenever he likes provide all this for his stewards. Every shepherd – they come from known families – <[f. 113v/103v]> pays a jar of butter, and every weaver a cloth if he is a Christian, or a certain weight of gold, which must be worth a *cruzado*, if he is a Moor. The emperor's stewards also collect all this.

In addition to these revenues, he has the duties that are paid at the markets, of which there are many, but he ordinarily gives these to the viceroys and other lords. There are also many ports {[f. 118]} in the land, where they pay one tenth of all the goods that arrive from overseas, but they do not take so much on goods from the land itself. However, as there is plenty of trade in slaves, ivory, salt, wax and other things, the duties are considerable. The emperor either rents these ports to lords or gives them for a certain time in return for gifts that they present to him.

---

[1] A *quartão* is a small, stout horse used in Portugal for transporting goods.
[2] Unit of dry measure, equivalent to 55.5 litres.

265

Apart from these revenues and tributes that they pay to the Prester John every year, they have another of cattle, which is collected every three years and is very large, because the kingdom of Gojâm pays 12,000, Olaçâ 5,000, Damôt 2,000, Amharâ 2,000, Begmêder 6,000 and Darâ 5,000. I could not find out the right number for Dambiâ, Oagrâ, Çalâmt and many other provinces that also pay, and so I shall leave them out. But the kingdom of Tigrê pays 15,900, and Çagadê and {Oalcaît} <Oalcaêt> 3,000.[1]

Friar Luis de Urreta, in chapter 32 of his first book, makes the Prester John so much richer and more powerful than I have said that, with the exception of King Dom Phelippe, he places him above all the kings and monarchs of the world, on page 342, in the following words:

*He is greater than all the kings of the world in wealth of gold and silver and precious stones and in men, for in ten days he can gather 200,000–300,000 soldiers, and in a month he will gather a million men, and I do not know if there is a prince in the world who can do that. Although the emperors of Ethiopia were extremely powerful in former times, as the histories tell us, they have never been so much as they are now, because Alexandre III, who died in 1606, and Zerascaureat, who governs today, have all the domains and kingdoms that their predecessors had as well as many more that have been conquered.[2]*

That is what the author says, but all those things are as fabulous as those that he ordinarily has in his book, as can be clearly seen from what is said in chapter 9 about the treasures that he put on Guixên Ambâ and what we have reported here of the principal revenues that the emperor has today, all of which I was informed by *Erâz* Cela Christôs, the emperor's brother, and by the treasurer, who would not have deceived me by saying that it was less than it really is, because not only are they very serious and excellent men, but they confess with me, and I told them that I was asking in order to write about it. Since they were not sure about the number of cattle paid every three years, the emperor's chief secretary gave me a list that he had taken from a book in which the revenues of the empire are written down, which I could not have. But when I was speaking <[f. 114/104]> to *Erâz* Cela Christôs, in the emperor's presence, about the revenue in gold, the emperor told me that his predecessors were formerly not paid so much gold {[f. 118v]} as they have been since Emperor Malâc Çaguêd, who died twenty-six years ago. As for the number of warriors that the emperor has, I do not think they number 200,000 fighting men, even if he gathers all his power. Speaking of the armies that I have seen of the three emperors that there have been since I arrived in Ethiopia, I doubt if any of them had 50,000 men, even though they sometimes tried to gather a large force, although the number of other people following the army was large. He is also wrong in saying that the emperors nowadays are more powerful and have more kingdoms than their predecessors, because they have neither as much power nor as many kingdoms as the emperors of old, even though they have a lot of both. Moreover, there has never been more than one emperor called Alexandre, and he died many years ago, as I have already said several times, and there is no such Zerascaureat, because I arrived in Ethiopia in 1603, and the emperor at that time was called Iacob<e>, and soon afterwards he was succeeded by another, who was called Za

[1] See, 'Historia de Ethiopia a alta', in Beccari, *RÆSOI*, 5, pp. 79–82.

[2] Urreta, *Historia de la Etiopia*, excerpt (with one passage omitted) from bk I, ch. 32, p. 342. Páez quotes this passage in Spanish.

Denguîl, who was killed in October 1604, and Iacob, whom he had exiled, returned; Iacob too was killed in 1607, as we have said and will describe in the fourth book, and was replaced by the one who is now alive, who was called Suzeneôs and titled himself Malâc Çaguêd, but later gave up this name and is called Seltân Çaguêd.

No less of a fable is what he says in the same chapter, on page 344,[1] that every year on Epiphany day the kings who are subject to him each give him an elephant laden with gold, silk and brocade, together with the things that their kingdoms produce, because there is no such tribute, nor has a tame elephant ever been seen in Ethiopia, nor has the kingdom of Gojâm ever paid in tribute 330,000 *cruzados* of gold, as he says on the following page. I am well aware that he took this claim about Gojâm and everything else he tells about the tributes from that kingdom and the way they have of delivering it to the emperor from Francisco Alvares, although he does not cite him, because folio 157 of his *Historia Ethiopica*[2] says it in almost the same words that he uses. But although Francisco Alvares claims that he saw the arrival of 3,000 mules, 3,000 horses, 3,000 *becêt*, cotton cloths, and 30,000 cloths of another, much cheaper kind, and the gold with the order and lengthy ceremonies that he recounts there, I say that they must have wanted to show more splendour than they commonly do, since there were foreigners at their court, and that they misled him in the amount of gold so as to make him think that they had great wealth, because never was 330,000 *cruzados* of gold revenue paid by the kingdom of Gojâm.

He also says, on page 346,[3] that in Gojâm there are ants the size of large dogs and the earth that they dig{[f. 119]} out at the mouth of the ants' nest comes with lumps of gold and silver. The people go very quietly to collect them when the heat is <[f. 114v/104v]> at its greatest, when the ants go to the deepest parts to escape from it. The people do not linger there long but go back very quickly because, if the ants sense them, an incredible multitude rushes out straight away and there is no way to escape from them by running, because they are very fast and so strong, fierce and savage that they tear anyone they find apart and eat them. Although he reports this from certain authors, he says that this should not make the reader laugh, because it is not unknown for there to be such ants in the world. Despite this warning, however, the emperor could not contain himself when I told him and, breaking with all his restraint and gravitas, he laughed long and loud at this tall tale, since it seemed to him that such ants could not exist not only in Gojâm but anywhere in the world.

Similar to this is what he says later, on page 348,[4] that the Prester John has a coastline of more than 800 leagues along the ocean to the east of the Cape of Good Hope. Starting at Cape Guardafui, he names many kingdoms as far as the mouth of the River Cuama,[5] which he says all belong to the Prester John: conquered by him, and a great many Moors thrown out. In addition to all these great kingdoms, many extremely powerful heathen kings pay him some kind of tribute and allegiance, not just because they have been conquered by the Prester John David, but because they see him as such a great and powerful prince and wish to have him as a friend and protector, to be safe from the other heathen kings, who do not

[1] Urreta, *Historia de la Etiopia*, bk I, ch. 32.
[2] Álvares, *Prester John of the Indies*, ch. 118, 'How, after the death of Queen Elena, the great Betudete went to collect the dues of the Kingdom, and what they were, and how the Queen of Adea came to ask assistance and what people came with her on mules', pp. 425–6.
[3] Urreta, *Historia de la Etiopia*, bk I, ch. 32.
[4] Urreta, *Historia de la Etiopia*, bk I, ch. 32.
[5] In other words, from Somalia to the Zambezi.

dare wage war on those who are the Prester John's friends, for fear of his power. Among those kings who, he says, flatter him with presents and pay him tribute like vassals, he names the kings of Biafara and of Gelofos, Tungubutu (which is the metropolis and capital of the kingdom of the Folos), together with others of the Guinea coast and that lie on the mainland that runs from before Cape Verde to Sierra Leone; and also the kings of Congo and of Monomotapa, who he says is the lord of all the land that ends at the Cape of Good Hope; and, finally, all the kings of the Island of Saint Lawrence[1] pay allegiance to the Prester John, sending him presents and donations, because they are close to his lands, which is the kingdom of Titut and Sibit.

That is what the author says, but it is all a long way off the mark and shows well how little he knows of the bounds of the Prester John's lands, because he does not hold {even} a span of the ocean coastline and certainly does not rule {[f. 119v]} the kingdoms that Friar Luis mentions towards the Cape of Good Hope, because the last kingdom of his empire in the direction of Mozambique is that of Nareâ and one can reach the end of it from Gojâm {in eighteen days}, as I have been told by people who have lived there for a long time, and from there to Mozambique there are such great deserts and so many lands of kafirs unknown to the Prester John's vassals that not only have they no dealings with them but, as they themselves say, they have never heard of their names. When I was talking to the emperor about this matter on purpose a few days ago, he said that his people did not go past Nareâ <[f. 115/105]> and that there was no recollection that his predecessors had ever ruled beyond there, nor did they now know what kind of lands they were. Therefore, if any of them reached Mozambique or the coast of Melinde, it would have been on board the *gelbas*[2] which come from that coast with slaves to Mocâ, as I saw when I was being held captive there.

Hence one can clearly see how fabulous the things are that he says on page 354[3] about the victories that he claims Emperor David had over the Troglodites, whom he places near Mozambique, opposite the Island of Saint Lawrence, and about a captain who {he says} rebelled against his lady, Queen Betfaga, the lady of all the land that ends at the Cape of Good Hope, which they call Monomotapa. She asked Prester John David for aid, promising him submission and a certain tribute, and he himself went to her aid by giving battle to the rebel captain and he defeated him, cut off his head and sent it to Queen Betfaga. To show her gratitude, she always gave the Prester John great presents and tributes, a custom that all her successors continued. However, as today's Prester John affirms, they have never heard of such a queen or had any trade with those lands, which should suffice to show how much credence one should give to all that Friar Luis says on this matter. Nonetheless, for greater confirmation, I shall report in his own words what he says about Emperor David's third victory: *The third victory and notable triumph was the one he had over the powerful king of Monicongo, whom he defeated in open battle, in which there were a million or more men. But the king of Monicongo was fortunate to be defeated by the Prester John, because it was God's will that by that means he should come into the knowledge of the Christian law and be converted. And he and all the others in his kingdom were baptized, with the Prester John as his godfather. There have been many Christians {[f. 120]} in that kingdom ever since.*[4]

---

[1] Madagascar.
[2] Small boats used in the Red Sea.
[3] Urreta, *Historia de la Etiopia*, bk I, ch. 32.
[4] Urreta, *Historia de la Etiopia*, bk I, ch. 32, p. 355. Páez quotes this passage in Spanish.

Nothing more apocryphal could be portrayed than that, for it is so well known, since many histories have told it, that the king of Congo and {a great many of} his vassals were baptized in the year 1491, when the king of Portugal was Dom Joam II, who, driven by the {great} zeal that he had for our holy faith and the conversion of heathens, sent Rodrigo de Sousa to that kingdom as his ambassador together with three friars of the holy Order of the glorious Saint Dominic, and they were the first in that kingdom to preach the Holy Gospel, with very great zeal for the good of the souls there, and they baptized the king and queen, together with most of the lords <[f. 115v/105v]> of their court. Then, from that time on, they baptized most of the people, so that that kingdom became wholly Christian because of Portugal and the zeal of King Dom Joam II, and not through the Prester John. Nor would he have been able to reach there, even if he had tried with all his might, on account of the great distance from his lands to the kingdom of Congo, for it borders the ocean sea from the Cape of Good Hope towards Portugal.

A little further on, on page 356,[1] he says that when {Emperor} <King> David died he was succeeded in the empire by his son Abraham and that he was wounded in a battle that he had with the king of Adel and, even though he had fought from morning till night with many deaths on both sides, they separated without knowing who had gained victory; with all that, his feelings were so extreme to see that the Moor had defended himself so valiantly that he burnt in a great fever, with which his wound worsened, so that within a few days he died and afterwards his men fled, so the Moor considered himself victorious. Later, they elected Claudio, his brother, in his place.

That was misinformation, because, firstly, this son of the first Emperor David, also called Onâg Çaguêd, was not called Abraham but Fiquitôr; and he did not die after his father but before. Because, after the emperor had been defeated by a Moor from Adel, who was called Ahamêd – and they commonly call him Granh, because he was left-handed, for *granh* means that in the language of Ethiopia – and he was fleeing from the Moor from one place to another, his son Fiquitôr, who was very courageous although not very old, said to him, 'How long must we flee, my lord? Would it not be better for us to die fighting?' On seeing the courage and determination of his son, he gave him the empire. Gathering together {[f. 120v]} his army, he went out to meet the Moor and they fought in the kingdom of Xâoa, and he was defeated and killed. And because his father was still alive, he was not counted among the emperors, as everyone says, and it seems to be so, because he is not found in the catalogues of emperors that we put in chapter 5, which were taken from the very books as they are listed there. In addition, he states there that the Moor climbed on an ass when he wanted to celebrate that victory, in order to show it had not been gained through his own efforts but with divine assistance, but it was not this Moor that did so, but another that they called Nur, who killed Emperor Claudio, as we shall see in the third book, when we recount his history. He says many other things in that chapter 32 that are much less than he exaggerates them to be, but what he has added to Emperor David he has taken away, at the end of the same chapter, from the things that Dom Christovão da Gama and his soldiers did in Ethiopia. Therefore, it will not be right to go on without declaring how mistaken he is in what he says about them.

---

[1] Urreta, *Historia de la Etiopia*, bk I, ch. 32, pp. 358–62.

Which begins to report some of the things that Dom Christovão da
Gama did in Ethiopia

As it is my intention to give some news of the principal things of this part of Ethiopia
that is ruled by the Prester John and of the most noteworthy things that have
happened in it, such as those performed by that valiant and courageous captain, Dom
Christovão da Gama, well known in Portugal for his great nobility and high birth, and
much more in Ethiopia for the wonders that Our Lord God saw fit to work through
him against the Moors in defence of His holy faith, it seemed to me that I would not
be fulfilling my duty if I did not mention some of them. In addition, had I passed over
them in silence, it might seem as though I approved of all that Friar Luis de Urreta
says of them in his first book, chapter 32,[1] where, for lack of information, he recounts
them very differently from the way in which they actually happened, as told by the
the old men of Ethiopia, and one of them in particular who, as a boy, accompanied
Dom Christovão from when he arrived until the day he was defeated, and that which
Father Fernam Guerreiro of our Society wrote at the end of the 'Addition' that he
made to the Report on Ethiopia in the book for the years 1607 and 1608,[2] taken (as
he says) from Miguel de Castanhoso, one of the Portuguese who arrived in Ethiopia
with Dom Christovão da Gama,[3] to whom all credence should be given since he was
an eye-witness.

Friar Luis de Urreta thus says on page 358:

*Meanwhile, the Moor* {[f. 121]} (that is, Granh) *was in the kingdoms bordering
Ethiopia, doing a thousand ill deeds and committing unheard-of cruelties against the
unfortunate Christians. The Prester John's mother, who was called Elisabeta, sent a letter
to the viceroy of Goa, who was called Don Estevan de Gama, asking him for help. And he
sent 400 soldiers and to captain them Don Christoval de Gama, his brother. They left Goa
fully armed in the month of June 1541 by ship and arrived, not without difficulty, in*

---

[1] Urreta, *Historia de la Etiopia*, bk I, ch. 32, pp. 358–62.

[2] F. Guerreiro, 'Adição à Relação das coisas de Etiópia', ch. 13, entitled 'Of what he says regarding that
which Dom Cristóvão da Gama did in Ethiopia. The truth about everything is told', pp. 370–80 (account of
the expedition).

[3] See Miguel de Castanhoso, *Dos feitos de D. Christovam da Gama* (1898, facsimile ed. 1983). This account
had been published in 1564 with the title *Historia das cousas que o muy esforçado capitão Dom Christovão da
Gama fez nos Reynos do Preste João com quatrocentos Portugueses que consigo levou* (reprinted 1855), but with
some passages cut and with variants in relation to the manuscript edited by Esteves Pereira at the end of the
19th century.

*Ethiopia, making port in the kingdom of Bernagasso, where many people flocked to them. The empress, having understood that help was on its way to her, came out of hiding and went to visit the captain, who received her with a great salvo of artillery and many festivities. She supplied him with plenty or even an excess of provisions and, since Don Christoval de Gama considered that there was no time to tarry, he set off with his 400 soldiers and many thousands of Ethiopians on long marches, travelling day and night, in order to catch the enemy unawares. It happened as he wished, because he found the Moors so unaware that they had the enemy so close that they were unarmed and not drawn up for war, as if they were not in enemy lands. <[f. 116v/106v]> So they fell upon them suddenly and took them with their bare hands before they could <come at them. And before they could> defend themselves, they gave them such a beating that they were not rid of the pain so soon. They were easily defeated and, turning tail, they all fled as fast as they could. And since fleeing is like flying, they stopped running and flew. A great many died in the attacks, and King Gradahametes, wounded by a musketeer[1] which went through his leg and killed his horse, was thrown to the ground, although his men carried him to safety, and he recovered from the wound. The good captain enjoyed very rich spoils, including countless weapons and harquebuses, with which he armed his men. And, marching in pursuit of his enemy, rowing and sailing the sea of his victories as the triumphant victor, he entered the kingdom of Adel, burning and ravaging and destroying and turning everything to fire and blood, as far as a mountain which King Gradahametes had make his stronghold. And there Captain Gama surrounded him, with the intention of not leaving until he had taken him dead or alive and sent him to the Prester John.[2]*

Almost everything that the author says here happened very differently, because neither did Dom Christovão da Gama leave Goa with the purpose of coming to Ethiopia, nor could he have left in the month of June, {[f. 121v]} because there it is the depths of winter and one cannot sail the sea, let alone cross the gulf to Ethiopia. And when he arrived in Ethiopia, he was not joined by thousands of Ethiopians as he says, nor did he defeat the Moors because he found them unprepared and unarmed. And after his victory he certainly did not enter the kingdom of Adel ravaging and burning everything, because he never went there, since it is many leagues away, as we shall see below. It should be noted in passing that this Moor was not the king of Adel but the {*guazîr*} <*guazêr*>,[3] as the Moors say, which is like governor of the kingdom under the king. He was not called Gradamartes, either; his proper name was Ahamêd, as we have already said, but the people of Ethiopia call him Granh, because he was left-handed, which is what *granh* means. The author seems to have joined these two names Granh and Ahamêd together, thinking that they were one, and by corrupting both (as he does with many others) he made Gradahametes. Because he is usually given this name Granh, I too shall call him that from now on. And the empress, the Prester John's mother, was not called Elisabeta but Zabelô Oanguêl.

---

[1] Páez mistakenly puts '*mosquetero*', musketeer, where Urreta's original text has '*mosquetazo*', musket shot.

[2] Urreta, *Historia de la Etiopia*, excerpt from bk I, ch. 32, pp. 358–60. Páez quotes this passage in Spanish.

[3] Arabic *wazîr*, vizir, a councillor or minister.

Having said that, we shall now report the exact truth of this history as briefly as we can. It happened as follows:[1] In 1541, when the Governor of India was Dom Estevam da Gama, the second son of Admiral Count Vasco da Gama, who was the first person to discover it, he put together a large <[f. 117/107]> fleet with the intention of going to the Strait of Mecca and up the Red Sea to Suez in order to burn the Turkish galleys and fleet, which was being fitted out in that port in order to sail to India. Although he was unable to burn it, since by the time he arrived they had beached it, having had news of his fleet, nevertheless on his return he caused great damage in many places in Arabia, sacking and burning everything and taking any ships that he found. On reaching the island of Maçuâ, he was met by a lord from the house of Adeganâ, whose name was Isaac and at the time was *bahâr nagâx*, which means 'governor of the sea', because he governs all those maritime lands. With him there was another great lord called {Robêl} <Rohêl> with letters from Empress Zabelô Oanguêl, mother of Emperor Claudio, who was now reigning after the death of Emperor David, his father, in which she begged him dearly to come to the aid of this Christian empire, most of which Granh the Moor had conquered fourteen years previously, killing and capturing an infinite number of people and burning and destroying many churches and renowned monasteries. On hearing this, the governor took counsel with the captains and {[f. 122]} nobles in the fleet and they all agreed that it would not only be a great service to Our Lord to attend to that most urgent need, but it would also be to the king of Portugal, their lord, for many reasons. And many very noble captains and lords very fervently and zealously offered to take part in this enterprise, including Dom Christovão da Gama, to whom the governor, his brother, quite properly entrusted it, after careful consideration, and he gave him 400 soldiers for the purpose. They say that he offered 1,000, but that *Bahâr Nagâx* Isaac did not dare to take so many, since the land was so devastated that he thought it could not support them.

With this magnificent, well-equipped force, doubly armed and with some artillery pieces, Dom Christovam left the island of Maçuâ on 9th July 1541, taking with him in his company the Patriarch Dom Joam Bermudez and a priest, and I do not know whether there were any more. According to what they say here, the governor brought him on purpose to see whether he could get him into Ethiopia, where he had already been, and they had promised him that if he brought some men to aid the country they would receive him as patriarch and accept the faith of the Holy Roman Church and would give the king of Portugal one-third of the empire. Accompanied by the *bahâr nagâx*, they marched inland into Ethiopia with great difficulty, since that land was very hot and rugged and they were almost all on foot, for they could scarcely find enough camels and mules to carry their baggage, munitions and artillery. In many places they had to unload everything and

---

[1] The episode that begins here was repeated in full by Manuel de Almeida: 'Up to here I have copied word for word what I found written by Father Paes, without reducing or augmenting, taking away or adding, or making any change whatsoever' ('Historia de Ethiopia a alta', Beccari, *RÆSOI*, 5, pp. 271–316). Baltazar Teles did the same, giving his word that he was relating 'this history as it was found written in the papers of this good Father' (*Historia geral de Ethiopia a Alta ou Preste Ioam*, 1660, bk II, ch. 7, p. 116; narrative in bk II, chs 8–16, pp. 117–37). [The English translation of Teles states 'How the Emperor was reliev'd by the *Portugueses* in this Distress, we will now deliver out of *F. Peter Pays* his Account of the Affairs of *Ethiopia*, he having liv'd 19 Years in that Country ...' (Tellez, *Travels of the Jesuits in Ethiopia*, p. 120).] Pedro Páez transcribes several passages from Guerreiro's 'Adição à Relação das coisas de Etiópia', but discontinuously and with frequent interpolations, so we have chosen not to place them in italics.

carry it on their backs for a good distance. Dom Christovam very gladly and enthusiast-ically was the first to take what he could on his own back, at which the soldiers took heart to do the same, even though they were very tired.

<[f. 117v/107v]> They marched thus for six days until they left the mountains, and there they rested for two days. The next day they arrived at a town called Debaroâ, where (as we have already said) the *bahâr nagâx* ordinarily resides. Many people and many monks in procession with their crosses came out to receive Dom Christovão; on hearing that he was coming, they had left the strongholds in the mountains where they had taken refuge for fear of the Moors. They came up to Dom Christovão and thanked him profusely for coming to their aid at a time of such great need, and they said to him that, since the Lord in his infinite mercy had brought him for that purpose, he should seek to avenge the dishonour and damage that those accursed and sacrilegious Moors had done to the holy churches by destroying and profaning them, and the cruelties that they had meted out on the priests and monks, and the affronts that they had {[f. 122v]} committed against married women, widows and maidens.

When they had finished, they all began to call out to Our Lord to be merciful and to give Dom Christovão strength against his enemies, with such devotion and tears that the Portuguese could not help shedding some as well. Dom Christovão consoled them, saying that he had only come to this land to do his best to throw out the Moors, and that he trusted in divine mercy that they would soon be free of the adversities in which they found themselves. They then all returned in the same order as they had come, and all the Portuguese went with them to pray in the church and, from there, to the tents that the *bahâr nagâx* had already had put up for them near the town, where he received them with many festivities.

The next day, Dom Christovão divided up his men among his six captains – Joam de Fonseca, Manoel da Cunha, Viçente de Acunha (his brother), Inofre d'Abreu, Francisco d'Abreu (his brother), and Francisco Velho – giving each of the five fifty soldiers and ordering the rest to guard the royal flag. He then sent Manoel da Cunha and Francisco Velho with their men on his behalf to visit and to bring back Empress Zabelâ Oanguêl, Emperor Claudio's mother, who was a day's march away on a very high rock that they call Damô,[1] to which one climbs up by rope. When they arrived, she commanded that the two captains should come up, and they were raised in some baskets tied with very strong straps. On reaching the top, they were received by the empress, who shed many tears of pleasure, giving thanks to God for having sent her such succour and for releasing her from that prison-like place where she had been for so long. After asking about Dom Christovão and his men in great detail, she commanded that they should be given shelter that night with great honour and splendour. The following day, the empress was lowered down in those baskets, together with many handmaidens and servants, because from the top of that mountain there is no other way in or out, as it is very high, sheer rock all round. On top it has good land where they sow, and many wells like cisterns that collect a large amount of water in winter.

<[f. 118/108]> Once they had all descended, the empress came on a fine mule covered with silk almost down to the ground, and she was dressed in very fine white cloths from

---

[1] Däbrä Damo monastery, to the east of Aksum, founded in the 6th century by the Ethiopian saint *Abuna* Aragāwi, according to Ethiopian Orthodox tradition. It is more than one day's journey from Debārwā.

India, over which she wore a brown satin burnous with fringes of gold thread and her face was covered with a very fine veil showing only her eyes, as is the custom of ladies that travel. Some men bore a silk canopy, with which she was covered {[f. 123]} so that she could not be seen except from the front. When she arrived near Dom Christovão's camp, he came out to receive her richly dressed in satin and cloth of gold, with all his men drawn up in order looking magnificent. They saluted her twice with all their artillery and firearms. As Dom Christovão approached, the empress stopped and, to honour him and as a gesture of love, she commanded that the canopy be removed and she uncovered her face a little. Then Dom Christovão greeted her and told her how he and all those men had come at the governor's orders to aid and serve her, and that he knew for sure that they were all determined to die for the holy faith of Christ and the defence of her empire. The empress thanked him profusely for the zeal that he displayed and the willingness with which he and the other Portuguese were offering to face such great dangers and adversity, saying that mighty God would reward the king of Portugal and the governor and them for everything, because neither she nor her son nor any prince on earth had the power to recompense such a great act, and that she did not consider this empire to belong to her, but to the king of Portugal. After her speech, the Portuguese took in their midst the empress and the ladies and maidens who were accompanying her on very fine mules, and with the *bahâr nagâx* leading the empress's mule by the reins, they took her to her tents.

Two days later, Dom Christovão and the Portuguese, all richly attired and with the most magnificent arms that they had, went to visit the empress and, in front of her tent, they showed her their method of fighting, at which she was greatly amazed to see something so new and extraordinary in her land, and no less joyful and content, for it appeared that there was no doubt that they would free her empire from the tyranny of the Moors. Dom Christovão, the *bahâr nagâx* and some great lords entered her tent and agreed with the empress that they would remain there until the end of October, when winter ends in this land. And Dom Christovão sent news of his arrival to Prester John Claudio, who now called himself Atanâf Çaguêd, who was very far away, having withdrawn to some mountain strongholds without daring to leave, since Granh the Moor had defeated him and killed many men. Dom Christovão began at once to make war engines and gun carriages for the artillery pieces, which were six half-stocks and two stocks. And he always kept a very good lookout in his camp, because Granh constantly sent out spies to find out <[f. 118v/108v]> how many Portuguese there were, what weapons they had and what they were doing: they discovered this from two spies that were captured dressed as *Abexins*, whom Dom Christovão later had torn asunder on the gun carriages that they had made, at which the Moors were so afraid that thenceforth {[f. 123v]} they never again dared to put themselves in such danger. They also made two sorties at this time at the empress's command, and they attacked some neighbouring lands whose inhabitants did not wish to obey, since they were very strong; they killed many people and brought back large numbers of mules, cattle and oxen, with which they equipped themselves for the march, for they had no mounts.

At the end of winter, letters arrived from the Prester John in which, with many courteous and loving words, he congratulated Dom Christovão and the other Portuguese on their arrival and made them many offers and asked that they should make their way to him as fast as they could, and he would also come to join them. Everyone rejoiced at the news and they hastened to do all that remained to prepare for their journey. When everything was finished, they left Debaroâ on 5th December, taking with them the empress and just 200 *Abexins* who accompanied them. Dom Christovão went in front, with 250 well-equipped Portuguese. Then came the baggage train, guarded by two captains and their men, and a little further back the empress and her ladies and maidens, and fifty Portuguese and some of those *Habexins*. They marched thus for a few days, with great difficulty, since they came across such rugged mountains that it seemed impossible to carry the artillery and munitions over them. But with Dom Christovão's industry and hard work, everything was made easy, so that the empress was amazed and often said that there were no men like the Portuguese, because no others could overcome such arduous and difficult conditions. Dom Christovão also remained very watchful, always having men in front to scout out the land and constantly sending spies to Granh. He would personally ride up and down the whole company twice a day to see if they were marching in order and to provide whatever was needed. To do so he would use mules that rode well, for so far they had no horses at all. And wherever he passed, the Moors that Granh had posted there to collect the revenue from the land would flee and the inhabitants, who had obeyed them out of fear, would come out with great joy to see the Portuguese and to subject themselves to the empress.

On the first day of February 1542, as Dom Christovão continued his journey, he reached a very strong mountain that Granh had taken with deceit and treachery and on which he had posted a captain with 1,500 soldiers. He had taken so long on the journey, not because it was <[f. 119/109]> very far from Debarôa, for it could easily be reached in three days by a direct route, but because he had taken a very large detour through other lands to reduce and pacify them. He decided to attack, {[f. 124]} because, if he went ahead and left those Moors there, all those lands would go back to obeying them, and the Moors could also do them great harm by cutting off their supplies and raiding them. But the empress said that he should not try such a thing, because there was no way that he could succeed in it, and when the Moors saw him fail they would be heartened and encouraged to attack him. Dom Christovão replied that he was forced to try to take that mountain, and gave so many reasons for it that the empress acquiesced, albeit against her will. This mountain has about a league of land on top, though not much of it flat, and enough water for many people. Although there are three ways up, they are so difficult that, even with very few guards, it would seem impossible to get in by force of arms. The rest is very high, sheer rock all around, as I have seen many times. The main way in is called Ambâ Çanêt, and they give the same name to the mountain. At the foot of this entrance there was a very strong wall with a door, and from there one climbs for a while up a very steep and narrow path and at the top there is another door in the rock itself. The second entrance is called Ambâ Xambût and is not so strong, although still very difficult. The third one is called Ambâ Gadabût; it is even stronger than the others because there is no path, but just holes carved in the rock, up which people can climb barefoot with difficulty, and the rock is exposed so that the entrance can easily be defended from above just with stones. The entrances are about a gunshot apart, and at each of them there was a captain with 500 Moors armed with bows and arrows, spears and shields.

Dom Christovão had informed himself well about all this, but before attacking he wanted to go and see where he could best place his artillery and make the Moors waste their arrows and the boulders they had prepared, so that they would not cause him so much damage later. To do so, he entrusted the first entrance to Captains Francisco Velho

275

and Manoel da Cunha, with their men, and he gave them three artillery pieces. He gave the second to Joam de Fonseca and Francisco d'Abreu, with their men, and three more pieces of artillery. Since the third was the most dangerous, he took it for himself with the rest of the Portuguese, except for fifty with harquebuses whom he left guarding the empress. And he said to the captains that, with all their men drawn up, they should make it look as though they wanted to get in though those entrances, but that they should not get too close, and that when he withdrew, they should all do the same. So they started their approach that afternoon. The number of arrows {[f. 124v]} and stones that the Moors shot down from above was beyond count, and they cast such enormous boulders down the rock that just <[f. 119v/109v]> the noise they made was enough to frighten anyone who was not so valiant and courageous as those Portuguese. They also fired off their harquebuses, so as to disguise what they were trying to do. After a long time, once Dom Christovão had seen as much as he wanted, he withdrew with all the others. On seeing this, the Moors thought that victory was theirs and, feeling quite safe, they celebrated with a great tumult and then spent the whole night sounding trumpets and drums. The empress, who was within sight of it all, was very sad and disconsolate, because it appeared to her as it appeared to the Moors that the Portuguese had no more heart than that which they had shown there. On realizing that, Dom Christovão sent word to her explaining why they had advanced and withdrawn, and that the following morning Her Majesty would see how the Portuguese fought and what men they were.

At dawn the following day, a priest took a crucifix in his hands and Dom Christovão and the other Portuguese knelt before it and, with much devotion, begged Our Lord for courage and strength against His enemies and offered Him their souls and lives with great fervour and desire to end them in defence of His holy faith. And the Patriarch Dom Joam Bermudez, who was present, gave them his blessing. Thereupon they were put in order for the mountain and they took their positions opposite the entrances, as they had done the previous afternoon. When Dom Christovão gave the signal, they all attacked with great spirit, and they began to fire their artillery and firearms, which made the Moors so afraid that they did not dare expose themselves much. However, they cast down large boulders, with which they did great damage and killed two Portuguese before they could properly reach the rock. Dom Christovão saw this and realized that they needed to finish this quickly, so he attacked with all his might and all the others followed. They leant their lances against the rock and started climbing up them, but many were wounded and they were twice toppled off. Even so, they continued climbing with great courage, with Dom Christovão among those in front, and a fierce battle was joined with the Moors. As it was already hand to hand, however, they could not withstand the thrust of the Portuguese for very long and so those 500 men turned tail, and Dom Christovão kept striking at them. By then, Francisco Velho and Manoel da Cunha had also fought their way in, though with great difficulty, because many of their soldiers were wounded at the first entrance door and two were killed just beyond. Although the Moors retreated, they did not want to close the upper door {[f. 125]} as they thought that the Portuguese attack would end there, since that was the strongest point, and so they closed ranks waiting for them. <[f. 120/110]> The Portuguese, however, attacked vigorously and, thrusting and slashing at first, they entered the mêlée. The Moorish captain was fighting with great valour and courage; pulling out a short lance that he carried, he thrust it into the chest of a Portuguese with such force that it went straight through him even though he was wearing a very good coat of mail. Then, raising his sabre, he struck another's helmet such a blow that he smashed it and the man fell to the ground, stunned, but another Portuguese came to his aid and killed the Moor, and they soon forced the rest to retreat.

While events were unfolding thus at that entrance and at Dom Christovão's, Joam de Fonseca and Francisco d'Abreu also got through theirs, although with great difficulty and the loss of three Portuguese, because the Moors fought hard, but when they saw that they had got in, they started withdrawing up the mountain. Each group was unaware of the rout of the others until they all reached the same place together, where they tried to hold out. As Dom Christovão and his men and the other captains arrived from different directions, they caught them in the middle and killed them, leaving not one of those who were there alive. Some who had fled previously to the houses they had on the highest parts were also put to the sword and those of them who threw themselves off the cliff, thinking that they would be saved, were dashed to pieces. They found a large number of captive Christian women here, and many other Moorish women, together with some booty, nine horses and ten very fine mules. When the Portuguese had gathered up there, they saw that they had lost eight men, who had died at the entrance, and that more than forty were wounded. Dom Christovão had the wounded tended diligently and the dead brought up; he commanded that the mosque be cleared of Moors so that the patriarch could bless it and the men could be buried in it.

When that was finished, Dom Christovão sent word to the empress, telling her of the favour that Our Lord God had done them and that if she wished to see her mountain Ambâ Çanêt and what the Moors had done with it she could do so in safety, because they were now all dead. She was very happy and joyful at this news, and so amazed that she could hardly believe that all those Moors had been killed in so short a time. When her servants assured her that it was indeed so, she praised the Lord, who had given the Portuguese such great courage and strength, and she said very tenderly that they truly were men sent by God for the salvation of this empire, and that now {[f. 125v]} she would think that nothing was impossible for them. Sending Dom Christovão her thanks at such good news, she said that she did not dare go up there, because not only was the climb too hard, but she was told that it was all covered with dead Moors, which she would find very loathsome.

When he heard that the empress was not going to come up, Dom Christovam asked <[f. 120v/110v]> the patriarch to bless the mosque, which he did solemnly, giving it the name of Our Lady of Victory, and they then buried the eight Portuguese in it. The following morning he said Mass with great rejoicing. They all gave thanks to the Lord for granting them such a remarkable victory and for turning that house, which had formerly been a house of abomination where Mohammed was worshipped, into a temple where they could offer such a sublime and holy sacrifice. When Mass was finished, Dom Christovão left the wounded installed there, because they could not climb down, and went with the rest to the empress, who received him with the love and benevolence due to one who had served her with such valour and courage. She then delivered the mountain to a captain of hers, whose forefathers had been lords of it. And they remained there for the whole month of February because of the wounded. As news spread that the mountain had been taken, a feat that the local people had little expected, they were well supplied not only by them but by people from further away, who brought them an abundance of provisions and other necessary things.

During that time, two Portuguese arrived there from the sea, with some local people guiding them, bringing a message from Manoel de Vasconcelos, the captain-general of five *fustas*[1] that Governor Estevam da Gama had sent to find out about the Turkish galleys and the success of Dom Christovão's expedition to this land and whether he needed any assistance. Not only were Dom Christovão and the Portuguese joyful and pleased at this, but so was the empress and all her people, believing that the remedy of her empire was assured. Dom Christovão then sent Francisco Velho with forty well-equipped Portuguese and some very good mules to make all haste to Maçuâ, where Manoel de Vasconcelos was, to give him letters for the governor and a report about what had happened and the current state of affairs, and to bring back some munitions of gunpowder, cannon balls and other necessaries from the *fustas*. When they had left, Dom Christovão decided with the empress to move on to some very good lands where there was a Christian captain who of necessity obeyed the Moors but had sent word that they should go there straight away, for they would not find any resistance at all.

[1] Single-masted galley.

## How, as Dom Christovão continued his journey, Granh came in search of him with a large army, and what happened to him

A few days' journey after Dom Christovam had left Ambâ Çanêt mountain, a messenger reached him with letters from the Prester John, telling him that he was coming with the utmost speed, that Dom Christovam too should hasten his journey as much as he could, because Granh was going in search of him with a large army, and that if they did not meet before <[f. 121/111]> Granh arrived it would be very dangerous to give battle. Because this was what Dom Christovam wanted, he pressed on with long days' marches. When he arrived in the lands of the captain who had called him, the captain came out to receive him and presented him with eight very fine horses and said that he should equip himself very well, because his spies had assured him that Granh was coming for him with many men and that he was already so close that he could not pass through without encountering him. Dom Christovam thanked him for the warning and asked him to send out spies again to find out precisely where he was coming from and how many men he had with him. And he continued his march concerned that, if Granh was as close as they said, the Portuguese he had sent to the coast would not be able to return in time and he would not be able to join forces with the Prester John before fighting. Two days later, as he came onto a flat plain which they call Çart, at the end of the kingdom of Tigrê, the spies came back to say that Granh was already so close that he was less than a day's journey away, and that he had countless men with him. On hearing this, Dom Christovam decided to fight, telling his soldiers that they could do nothing else, since it was impossible to go on to join forces with the Prester John as all the lands were held by Moors, who would not only cut off their supplies so that they would starve to death, but would hold them back with raids until Granh arrived with his army. He said they would have the same problem of supplies if they turned back, because the people would not dare give them any when they knew that the enemy was so close behind with such a powerful army, and that victory was in the hands of the Lord, who could give it just as well to the few as to the many, and that, if it were not to be that they should have it, they would die fighting for His holy faith. The captains and soldiers agreed with his opinion and they all placed themselves with great confidence in the hands of God.

{[f. 126v]} The following day, which was Palm Saturday, as they marched across that flat plain, two scouts that Dom Christovam had sent ahead on horseback to spy out the land came back and said that Granh was approaching just a league away. Therefore Dom Christovam commanded his army at once to pitch camp on a hill that rose in the middle of the plain, which was very suitable for what he was intending, close to a pleasant stream called Algôl. Putting the empress in the best place, for since she was a woman she was rather afraid, they kept very careful watch all that night. On Sunday morning, on a far-off hill there appeared five Moors on horseback, who had come to spy out the land; when they saw the encampment they very hastily turned back. Dom Christovam then sent two Portuguese on two horses to ride to that same hill and find out <[f. 121v/111v]> how large the enemy camp was and where it they were pitching it. They returned, saying that the enemy's men covered the plain and were pitching camp right up to that hillock. While the tents were being erected, Granh went up the hill with some 300 horsemen and three large standards, two white with red crescents and one red with a white crescent, and there he stayed watching Dom Christovão's camp. Afterwards he commanded his men to fall in and march, and they bore so many standards and such a host of trumpets and drums and they marched with so much shouting and tumult that there seemed to be many more men than there were. Dom Christovam thought that they were about to attack and got ready to fight, but they only meant to surround the camp and, when they had done so, they kept watch all night with many fires and loud shouting. The Portuguese were also ready all the time with powder pans in their hands and fuses lit for their guns. Now and then they fired off some mortars, which stopped the enemy from daring to come any closer, and the camp appeared to be so menacing that they could not be persuaded that there were so few Portuguese as there had seemed to be by day.

Once the night had passed with such great adversities and the sun was rising, Granh sent an ambassador to Dom Christovam to tell him that he was greatly amazed that he had dared enter that land and appear before him with such a small force; he really appeared to be as youthful as he had been told, as well as naïve and inexperienced; but in view of his tender age, and knowing that that woman and the people of the land had brought him there under false pretences, for those people were so false that they had no loyalty even for their own king, {[f. 127]} he felt sorry for him and was resolved to use his greatness and accustomed clemency by pardoning his poorly considered rashness on condition that he went over to him together with all the Portuguese; and if he did not wish to join his company he should return to his land and he would give him safe passage so that no harm should come to him; and he should do what he commanded straight away, for he could see so clearly the false pretences under which they had brought him; and he should accept what the ambassador would give him, which was a monk's cowl and a rosary, showing that he did not regard him as a captain but as a monk, because they gave this same name to all the Portuguese who were there.

After Dom Christovam had heard the embassy, he treated the one who had brought it with every honour and gave him a robe of purple satin and a cap of scarlet, with his expensive medal, and said that he should go, for he would send a reply to his lord. And he had him accompanied until he left the camp. Then Dom Christovam, taking counsel with his officers, ordered that the reply should be taken not by a Portuguese, <[f. 122/112]> for Moors were not to be trusted, but by a {fair-skinned} slave of the Portuguese. They dressed him very well and gave him a mule to ride and what he was to say, written in Arabic so that Granh could read it. It said that he had arrived there at the command of the Great Lion of the Sea and Mighty Lord of the Land, whose custom it was to come to the aid of those who can do little, and so, having received news that the most Christian emperor of Ethiopia, his brother in arms, was defeated and dispossessed of his kingdoms by infidel enemies of the holy Catholic faith, he was sending the assistance that he could see there, which, although small, was a match for all his multitude, for they were so evil and had taken that land without any right or justice, not by their own strength, but because the true God had permitted it be so in order to punish the *Abexins* for their sins; but he trusted in His divine mercy and that His wrath would be appeased by what they had already suffered and that He would return them to their former freedom and possession of their lands by means of the Portuguese; and even though there were few of them, he would see on another day how they fought and how much they were worth, because they had not come in order to turn back, but to seek him out. And he sent him a large mirror and some small tweezers of the kind that women use for their eyebrows, making him out to be a woman. When the slave came to Granh with this reply, he fell into a rage; even so, he said that men of such great heart who, even though they were so few, dared to fight with him, who had such a large {[f. 127v]} force, deserved to have all the kings give them many honours and favours. And with that the slave returned.

The Moor was determined to keep them there surrounded without allowing any supplies to get through, so that he could starve them out. That was something he could do easily, because he had 15,000 foot soldiers, all with shields and spears, bows and arrows, 1,500 horsemen and 200 Turkish harquebusiers, whereas there were no more than 350 Portuguese, because eight were dead and the rest were away. And the Turks were so daring that, not content with having the Portuguese surrounded at a distance, they came very close and built some dry stone walls from which they fired and caused so much damage that Dom Christovam had to send Manoel da Cunha and Inofre d'Abreu with sixty Portuguese to throw them out of there, which they did with great valour and courage. However, as Moors on horseback came in support of the Turks, a very fierce battle was waged in which some Portuguese were wounded and they killed many Moors, aided by those in the camp with the artillery. When Dom Christovam saw that a large number of Moors were charging, he sounded the retreat, which the Portuguese did straight away in very good order, and the Moors went back {as well} <at once>, as they did not dare get close to the camp, but they still remained all around just as they had surrounded it before.

Dom Christovam realized that the Moors intended to starve him out, so he resolved to give battle before reaching such an end. Therefore, on the following day, which was <[f. 122v/112v]> 4th April 1542, at cock crow, he ordered the tents and other baggage to be loaded. Posting the captains and their men to the right and the left, he placed the empress in the middle with her women and 200 *Habexins* who accompanied her, and he took the rearguard, because they were surrounded on all sides. As day broke, his camp began to move in that order. When the Moors saw that, they were overjoyed, since it seemed to them that as they were leaving that hill it would be easy to defeat them, so they went at them right away, sounding so many trumpets and drums and shouting so loudly that it seemed that the plain was melting. The Portuguese began to shoot their harquebuses and fire artillery rounds everywhere, which made the foot soldiers keep back and give them an open field. When the Turks saw that, they rushed forward and came so close that they caused great damage with their guns. At that, Granh himself stirred, with the three standards that he always {[f. 128]} kept in front of him and 500 more horsemen and, on reaching the side where the Turks were, he gave battle so fiercely that the Portuguese found themselves in great difficulty. Dom Christovam therefore told them not to move so far away but to let the artillery do the fighting; the ones in charge of it did so with such spirit and fired rounds so fast that they kept the horsemen at bay and killed many of them. But the Turks were fighting hard and getting very close, so Dom Christovam was forced to send Manoel da Cunha with fifty Portuguese to strike at them; they attacked and there was such a mêlée that the Turks seized their standard, killed the standard-bearer and three other Portuguese and shot Manoel da Cunha in the leg, so he withdrew, leaving many Turks dead and wounded.

All this time, Dom Christovam was encouraging his men, for many of them were wounded. He always put himself where the danger was greatest, and so he was shot in the leg, which was a great blow to all his men but a much greater honour to him because, despite being wounded, he was coming to everyone's assistance, urging on his soldiers and fighting with even more valour and skill than perhaps the most notable and famous captains celebrated by the histories had ever done in such difficulties. While the battle was raging fiercely, and it was already past noon, it seemed to Granh (who was watching it from the side) that his men were weakening. As he came to help with the men who accompanied him, he approached so near that he was hit by a gunshot that went through his leg and into his horse, which fell dead. When his men saw that and realized that he was losing <[f. 123/113]> a lot of blood, they dipped their standards three times, giving the signal to retreat, and then they carried him off in their arms. Dom Christovam knew very well that it was he who was being carried off wounded, so he ordered his trumpets and drums to be sounded in rejoicing and attacked with the Portuguese and 200 *Habexins* with such momentum that he soon made all the Moors turn tail. Leaving the field covered with the enemy dead, he continued the chase until the Portuguese were very weary. As they had no horses, Dom Christovam feared that if they went any further the Moors on horseback might see how tired they were and turn on them, so he sounded the retreat. When they got back to the camp, they found the empress with her servants in a tent tying wounds with their own hands, using their own headdresses, without wanting to wait for other cloths.

{[f. 128v]} When Dom Christovam arrived, he sent men to search the field and bring back the Portuguese who had died to be buried, and they found eleven. The *Abexins* also recognised four of Granh's chief captains and thirty Turks, all dead. When they had finished burying the Portuguese, and Dom Christovam should have been resting from all the excessively hard labour he had done, he set to treating the wounded with his own hands, because the surgeon they had was wounded in his right hand. After treating everybody else, he treated himself, since he was more concerned about his soldiers' wounds than his own. That night, he secretly sent a man to the Portuguese who had gone to Maçuâ to give them news of the victory that they had had and of how Granh had been wounded, and to say that they should come as fast as they could, because he trusted in the Lord that with their arrival they could complete the conquest. They remained there for a few days, waiting for the wounded to be able to bear arms again and for the other Portuguese to arrive. Seeing, however, that they were taking a long time and fearing that the Moor would recover and attack them again (as in fact he had already commanded those captains of his who were scattered around to come {with the utmost haste}, and many men were joining him every day), Dom Christovam decided to give him another battle straight away, having great hope in the mercy of the Lord, for Whom they were all fighting and in Whose hands they had placed their lives, so that, even though the enemy horde was so great, He would give them victory as He had done before.

# CHAPTER XXXIII

## How Dom Christovão gave battle to Granh a second time

Twelve days after Dom Christovam had defeated Granh, when the wounded already felt that they could bear arms, they all confessed and, on Low Sunday, before dawn, they struck camp and marched in formation to the Moors, who were close by. As it grew light and the Moors saw them, they rushed out shouting as usual and no less proudly than the first time, because a great many people had joined them. The one who urged them on most of all was a very arrogant captain named Garâd Amâr, <[f. 123v/113v]> and he had come back again with 500 horsemen and 3,000 foot soldiers. As he said to the captains of the army, how could so few Portuguese last so long against them, and how could such a great multitude not turn them to dust straight away? Taking the lead himself, he attacked {[f. 129]} {with his men} so boldly as if he was not in the least concerned about the Portuguese. In fact, if all his 500 horse had been as resolute as he, they would have put them in serious difficulties, but they did not dare to break through united for fear of the artillery, which killed many of them. Only the captain and five very courageous {Moors} <men> on horseback threw themselves into the Portuguese lances and died fighting valiantly. At this moment, Granh, whom some men brought along on a litter borne on their shoulders since he was wounded, commanded that all the rest of the {horse} <men> should attack at several points, which they did with great force. Fierce battle was joined, both sides fighting valiantly for a long time. The ones who distinguished themselves most of all were eight Portuguese who had horses, who attacked with great spirit where the Moors were strongest, and they always broke through and killed many wherever they went. As their group was very small, however, they did not dare chase them very far. Had they all had horses, they would have done wonders that day and Granh would not have been able to escape. The Portuguese on foot did not fail to do wonders in their positions either, because they too made their sorties, killing many of the Turks and so many Moors that the whole plain around the camp was strewn with them.

While the battle was raging fiercely and the Moors on horseback were charging at the part where they could see Dom Christovam was weakest, the gunpowder they had there accidentally caught fire and killed two Portuguese and burnt others, who were severely injured. Such was the explosion it made and the blaze that rose up that all the Portuguese thought they were finished there and then, but the Moors' horses turned away with such fury that they would not obey the bit at all and bolted with their riders across the plain. They retreated a fair distance like that, leaving the area free of attackers. Therefore, even though the gunpowder catching fire was a great disaster since all those Portuguese were burnt, it was very helpful in securing victory. That is not only because the Moors had been seriously threatening that area, but also because, when they retreated so far away without being able to turn their horses back again quickly, the Portuguese were left freer to attack the Turks on foot, and that is what they did, so that even the Turks, who were the ones fighting hardest, had to retreat. From then on, neither they nor the horsemen dared to close in, and Dom Christovam realized from that that they were now weakening. Therefore, {[f. 129v]} he attacked with great force <[f. 124/114]> and the Moors, who could not withstand the onslaught, gradually fell back fighting until they found themselves so pressed that their only remedy was to turn their backs and flee as fast as they could. Those who escaped with their lives considered themselves very lucky and fortunate, because the Portuguese came after them fiercely, slaughtering them like sheep. They chased them for something like half a league, but were so tired from all the running and fighting that they could go no further, even though they wanted to, since they could see Granh in the distance being carried away on his litter and everyone fleeing as fast as they could. If they had had horses, he would not have escaped them, and his capture would have put a stop to the fighting.

As Dom Christovam saw that his men were exhausted, he turned back, sounding the retreat. On arriving at the Moors' camp, they found the tents erected and plenty of goods inside them, which they had not been able to take with them in their haste to flee. After gathering their booty the Portuguese assembled and found that fourteen were missing. They then searched the field very carefully for them and brought them all back dead and buried them with great sadness, but at the same time giving many thanks to the Lord for such a notable victory. Since the area had been ruined for grazing for the cattle and it was none too comfortable for the wounded, of whom there were more than seventy, four of whom later died, they moved on to another part where there was a cool stream. As they came close, they saw many Moors sitting along it, with Granh among them, as he had decided to rest there that night since it was already very late and he thought the Portuguese would not be able to come so far, even if they wanted to. Therefore, when he saw them, he said furiously (as a *Habexim* who was with him later reported), 'Those friars' (for that was how he always referred to the Portuguese) 'really do not want to leave me alone.' They all leapt up {in great haste} and fled for eight days, not considering themselves safe until they had reached some impregnable mountains. Many died on the way, both because they could not find enough provisions, for the local people saw them in disarray and refused to give them any, and because they had many wounded and were travelling with them very fast.

Dom Christovam remained beside that stream, resting and tending the wounded, since he realized that he could not carry on the chase for the time being. Two days later, the Portuguese who had gone {[f. 130]} to Maçuâ and the *bahâr nagâx* arrived with thirty horsemen and 500 foot soldiers, and they were welcomed with great celebration and joy. But they were extraordinarily sad not to have taken part in those battles and to have had a wasted journey, because they did not find the Portuguese *fustas*, which had already left because of the Turkish galleys that guarded that coast, to tell them news of what was happening in Ethiopia. On seeing the Portuguese that he had wanted so much, Dom Christovam decided to go after Granh straight away, and so he left fourteen Portuguese who were very badly wounded on a very secure mountain in the care of the governor of the land, <[f. 124v/114v]> whom they call *Tigrê mohôn* (who had them very carefully tended and abundantly supplied with whatever they needed), and he marched on for ten days until he arrived at the mountain where Granh was hiding, which was very high and impregnable. Since winter was already beginning with heavy rains (it seems to have started earlier than usual that year), the empress and her people advised Dom Christovam to overwinter at the foot of another mountain called Oflâ, which lies just inside the kingdom of Tigrê, nearly in Angôt, and in sight of Granh's mountain, because from there they could stop provisions getting to him except from the direction of the sea, whence little would reach him, and in the meantime the Prester John would arrive, since that was his route. Dom Christovam thought it good and wrote to him straight away, telling him what had happened and that he should hurry to get there so that Granh should not escape them. He sent a mulatto called Aries Diaz with this letter, both because he knew the language of the land, as he had been in Ethiopia before with Dom Rodrigo de Lima, and because his colour would help him to get through more easily. The empress then commanded the local people to make houses for everyone, which they did very diligently and finished them quickly, because they were small and made of wood, of which there was no lack there, and thatched with straw. And they brought provisions and everything else that they needed in abundance, because they liked the Portuguese very much.

While Dom Christovam was here, he was visited at the end of winter by a Jew who had been the captain of a very secure mountain called {Oatî} <Oatê>, in the province of Cemên, which was close by, and he told him that there were a lot of horses on that mountain with very few Moors guarding them; therefore, if he wished, he could take the mountain with 100 Portuguese by going in secret by a route that he knew and he would come back very quickly with all those horses. He also told him that the Prester John had to come along that road as there was no other, and that he was bringing so few men that he would not be able to get past with those Moors there. Dom Christovam was very sad to hear that, because he had thought he was coming with a large force. He asked the empress whether what the Jew was saying was correct and she said that it was, but that made him more {[f. 130v]} fearful, although he did not show it. He decided to clear the way for the Prester John, with whom he very much wanted to join forces, and to {see whether he could} take those horses, which would be very useful to him for the war. Thus, leaving the camp in good order, he took Manoel da Cunha with 100 Portuguese and left at midnight in secret, so that Granh would not know that he was missing. Marching at full speed, he reached a large river that they call the Tacacê, which we talked about in Chapter 27, which in winter carries a lot of water and has a fierce current. Nevertheless, they crossed it on rafts and air-filled skins and then, without being detected, they scaled the mountain with the Jew guiding them. On top, however, they found many <[f. 125/115]> more Moors than he had said, because there were 3,000 foot soldiers and 400 horse and, on seeing the Portuguese, they very quickly took up arms. Dom Christovam then mounted his horse, as did eight Portuguese who also had them, and they attacked together with those on foot. At this, the Moorish captain, whom they called Cid Ahamêd, which means Lord Ahamêd, rode ahead of his men on a fine horse and charged at Dom Christovam. He too galloped to meet him with so much force that, even though the Moor was also coming with all his might, he very soon killed him and then charged into the Moors, cutting many of them dead on either side. The rest of the Portuguese did the same with such force that, even though there were a large number of Moors,

285

they made them fall back. They continued slaughtering them for a long time, and very few of those that they missed escaped alive, because the Jews who lived there killed them.

Once {all} that was finished, the Portuguese withdrew, thanking God for giving them such a great victory without any of them dying, at which all the Jews who lived on the mountain were greatly amazed. When the Jew who was guiding them saw what they had done, which to him seemed beyond human strength, he said that the only possible explanation was that the Portuguese had true faith, since God was helping them so much, and so he became a Christian together with twelve brothers, his captains of those lands. Because he had always been loyal to the Prester John even though he was a Jew, Dom Christovam let him remain captain of that mountain as he was before, charging him that he should send a message to the Prester John with great haste to say that the mountain had now been taken and that he should come soon without fearing the danger of the road. Here Dom Christovam took plenty of booty that the Moors had been keeping, since it was a very secure place, including many slaves, 300 mules and eighty select horses, which he valued above everything else, and then, overjoyed, he returned. He crossed the River Tacacê as he had done before, but afterwards, as the road was very rough and the horses were going slowly, he left {[f. 131]} thirty Portuguese with them and went on ahead with all the rest with the utmost haste, so that his delay should not cause trouble in case it became known that he and all those Portuguese were away from the camp.

While all that was happening, Granh was not wasting time. Rather, on seeing that so many of his men were dead and those remaining were so frightened that they would not dare face the Portuguese again, he made great efforts to bring in new men from other parts, especially Turks. For that purpose, he wrote to the pasha of Zebîd, a land on the other side of the straits, in Arabia, telling him of the difficulties he was in and how few Portuguese there were and asking him to assist him with as many Turks as he could, for he too was a vassal of the Grand Turk and should not want to let the lands he had won be lost, and he sent him a large amount of gold, with <[f. 125v/115v]> promises of more afterwards. On seeing that, the pasha, who had 3,000 Turks to guard the straits, sent him 700 or, as some claim, 900 men with arquebuses, including thirty horse with golden stirrups and ten pieces of field artillery. Many Arabian Moors came as well, sent to him by other Arabian lords who were friends of his. A large number of Ethiopians also joined him. The Turks reached Granh the same night that Dom Christovam arrived back in his camp, and straight away the following day he came down from the mountain to show off his force, which was so large that it covered the plain, and he pitched his camp so close to the Portuguese that the Turkish artillery, which they fired off at once, reached them.

Seeing the large reinforcements that had reached Granh, Dom Christovam took counsel on what best to do. They all said that they could certainly not withdraw, because the local people would rise up against them at once and not only would they not give them provisions, but they would not let them pass, either, and Granh would not let them go; they would be forced to fight, but they should not do so until the Portuguese arrived with the horses, which might take two days, and meanwhile they should defend themselves as well as they could in their camp, which they had fortified that winter with good palisades. Having reached that agreement, they sent a message at once to the Portuguese bringing the horses to come with the utmost speed, because Granh had come down with many men and was showing signs that he wanted to give battle straight away. They prepared themselves and strengthened their position all that day and night, which was not light work for those that had returned weary from their journey. However, not even that was enough to achieve their intention, which was to defend themselves until the horses arrived to give battle, because they could not avoid it before then, as we shall see in the next chapter.

# CHAPTER XXXIV

## How Granh gave battle to Dom Christováo and what the outcome was

{[f. 131v]} Seeing himself with so many magnificent and well-armed men, and knowing how few Portuguese there were, Granh felt very sure that victory would be his and so decided to give battle at once. Therefore, as dawn broke the following day, which was 28th August 1542, he set off for Dom Christovam's camp with all his men in battle order and 900 Turks with ten artillery pieces in the vanguard. Realizing his intention, Dom Christovam also drew up his men and sent them to their stations with the order that they should defend themselves there without going out into the field until the horses reached them, as they had agreed previously. As the Turks came within gunshot range, <[f. 126/116]> a very fierce and hard-fought battle started, with artillery and harquebuses firing back and forth, which lasted for several hours; many Turks and some Portuguese died and others were wounded. Eventually Granh's troops closed ranks and the Turks came so close to the palisades that they wounded and killed many men with their harquebuses. Dom Christovam could see the great damage they were causing and that they were liable to demolish his palisades, since these were not as strong as they needed to be to withstand such a great multitude and force of men, so he decided to make some sorties and then withdraw again. He was the first to sally, taking with him fifty Portuguese harquebusiers, and attacked some 100 Turks and other Moors who were on that side with so much force that he pushed them back a long way, killing and wounding many of them. But, so as not to go too far, and because many men were charging at him, he withdrew again. Then four of his Portuguese were killed and almost all the rest came back wounded, as he was himself, with a gunshot in one leg.

As Dom Christovam came in, Manoel da Cunha sallied with his men on another side and pushed the Turks back a good distance, as they were the ones giving most trouble, as they had come very close to the trenches. After he had fought for a long time with great valour and courage, killing and wounding many Turks, five of his Portuguese were killed and others wounded while they were withdrawing. The other station captains also made their sorties in order and, each time, they pushed the Moors and Turks a long way back across the field, causing them great damage, but on withdrawing they usually lost men and many came back wounded. And thus they laboured excessively until after midday, when the empress's house was so full of the wounded that there was no more room for them, and she and her maidens tied their wounds and shed many tears of great anguish and affliction, both at seeing such a lamentable sight and as it seemed to them that the time was coming when they would fall into the hands of those cruel {[f. 132]} enemies, because they had already come so close to the palisades that they were shooting cannon balls into the house, where they had wounded two women.

At that moment, although badly wounded, Dom Christovam was diligently running from one station to another encouraging the soldiers and showing such great valour and courage as might be expected from such an illustrious and courageous captain, worthy of being placed among those whose deeds had earned them the highest reputation and fame in the world. As he could see that the Turks had come so close that they were causing terrible damage inside the camp, he commanded Francisco d'Abreu to attack with his men on that side and his brother, Inofre d'Abreu, to sally with his in order to come swiftly to his aid when he wanted to withdraw, so that the Turks would not have room to cause too much damage. The valiant captain Francisco d'Abreu thus went out and fought so <[f. 126v/116v]> bravely that he made the Turks and Moors turn back, and he pushed them across the field, killing many of them. But as he had chased them further than he should, he was shot as he was pulling back and he fell dead. His brother then attacked and pushed back the Turks who were coming at him but, as he was raising his brother's body, he too was shot dead. Thus those two, who were not just brothers but loved each other dearly in life, were not separated in death, nor will they be separated in glory [for they will have great glory], since they suffered such labours and died fighting in defence of the holy faith.

Dom Christovam felt his heart pierced by this disastrous event and the loss of such excellent captains. Seeing that he had already lost four of them and many of his men, and that most of those who were left could not fight because they were badly wounded and that the Turks, who could see that, were very arrogantly closing in, he took those he could find who could accompany him, and there were very few of them. Leaving orders with Manoel da Cunha to advance with his men as he withdrew, he attacked with such force and fought so fiercely that soon there was no Moor or Turk left who dared face him; instead they all turned tail. And he slaughtered them like sheep, so much so, as some who were there stated, that if he had then had the horses that he had left back on the road, victory would no doubt have been his, but in all his camp he only had eight horses, and they had fought with them all day. Even so, he chased the Moors a long way and, when he felt his men were very tired, he withdrew again. At that, the Turks turned and came after them shooting, and they managed to kill some Portuguese and broke Dom Christovam's right arm. {[f. 132v]} Manoel da Cunha then arrived and, with his help, they withdrew, though many of them were wounded and all were so weary that they could barely move, and no one could take up arms any more. Even so, Dom Christovam, forgetting his wounds, was encouraging them and urging them to reach the palisade, which they did with great spirit. And twice they threw the Turks out, for they were getting in with great strength and speed, and all the Moors were charging at them and pounding them hard.

As things were going in that manner, and as it was already very late, the Portuguese said to Dom Christovam that they could do no more and that they should retreat up the mountain, but he did not want to do that at all. Instead, he picked up his sword in his left hand and very bravely went to the side where there were most Moors, telling his men that anyone who wanted to follow him should do so. The Portuguese could see what he intended and stopped him with brute force, giving him many reasons why he should retreat and try to save his life and that of his other companions who still had theirs, for if they stayed alive that loss could later be made good. And seizing him <[f. 127/117]> by the arms, they put him on his mule and took him up the mountain, with the patriarch and the empress going in front. Then the Turks entered the camp and found more than forty

Portuguese in the houses, so badly wounded that they could not move, and they began to slaughter them cruelly. But one of them was in the house where they had stored a lot of gunpowder that they had made during the winter and, to stop the Turks from using it against the Christians, he dragged himself along as well as he could and took a fuse that was alight on the ground and set light to the gunpowder, with the result that he and the Turks who had got in were burnt to death. Other Turks and Moors chased after those who were fleeing, and with arrows and stones killed some Portuguese who could not walk fast, since they were badly injured and weary, but as night soon fell and the mountain was covered with thick forest the rest escaped. The patriarch went with some Portuguese in one direction and the empress went with some others in another direction and they were saved, but Dom Christovam and fourteen Portuguese accompanying him set off along another track and walked all night with great difficulty, both because the track was rough and because they were all badly wounded and very weary.

When dawn broke, they left the path for fear that those who were following them would find them, and they crept into a thickly wooded valley. In the most secret part of it they found a small spring flowing out of a gorge, and there they helped Dom Christovam off his mule so he could rest and be treated, for they had not been able to do so until then. Since they had no medicine of any kind, they killed the mule that he had been riding and used its tallow to treat him and themselves, for they were all {[f. 133]} badly wounded. By then, twelve Turks and twenty Arabs on horseback had already gone past looking for Dom Christovam, as they had heard he had gone that way. Since they could not find him or any trace {on the path} <of him>, they turned back. But as they came opposite the place where Dom Christovam was, an old woman who seemed barely able to walk crossed the path in front of them. They went to catch her, as they wanted to hear any news, but she slipped through the forest from one thicket to another and they could not catch her. On reaching the valley, she ran to the trees where Dom Christovam was with the <other> Portuguese <very fast>, and as the Moors were following, determined not to lose her, they suddenly came upon them. They all rushed in together, shouting loudly, and captured them; only one escaped, as he was not so badly wounded. They did not see the old woman again, so the Moors said that Mohammed had sent her to lead them to the Portuguese.

Having captured them, the Moors recognized Dom Christovam at once by the arms that he bore, which they had often seen in battle. So they took him with great joy and happiness and presented him to Granh, who was in his tent amid great <[f. 127v/117v]> rejoicing and had 170 Portuguese heads in front of him, because he gave a large reward to anyone who brought him the head of a Portuguese, and so no Portuguese was left on the field whose head had not been taken. Showing them to Dom Christovam, {he said}, 'Here are those with whom you wanted to take my land from me. Do you now recognize how childish you have been? For such daring I want to do you a great honour.' And he then had him stripped naked, his hands tied behind his back, and cruelly whipped. After that they hit him in the face with their slaves' shoes and, taking him round the camp to the captains' tents, they did him many other insults and injuries. When they had all finished amusing themselves with him, they returned him to Granh's tent. Granh then commanded that they should make candlewicks of his beard with wax and set light to them, and they should pull out his eyelashes and eyebrows with the same tweezers that Dom Christovam had sent him before: he said he had kept them for that purpose. All that the brave and Catholic captain suffered with admirable patience, giving thanks to God, and with his eyes fastened on the heavens he begged Him to forgive his sins and offered Him his soul. Granh then commanded that he be untied and, mockingly, covered with a filthy rag, telling him amongst other things that he would pardon him from death and do him honours and favours and would let him embark for India with all his men who were still alive, on condition that he summoned them all to come to him from wherever they were. To that Dom Christovam replied, 'If you, Moor, realized who the {[f. 133v]} Portuguese really were, you would not say such vanities. You can do what you like with me, for I am in your power. But rest assured that even if you gave me half your lands I would not make a single Portuguese come to you, because the Portuguese do not live with Moors, who are dirty and enemies of the holy faith of Christ my Lord.' The Moor was so infuriated at this response that, rising from where he was seated, he pulled out his sabre and cut off his head.

When the Turks heard of the death of Dom Christovam, they were highly aggrieved, because they had wanted to take such a brave and valiant captain, the brother of the governor of India, alive to the Grand Turk. So they went to Granh's tent and asked how he could do such a serious thing without taking counsel. They came to such bitter words that they almost broke with him, and they decided to leave at once to embark for Zebîd and take Dom Christovam's head and thirteen Portuguese prisoners, but they left him 200 Turks, because that was what the Grand Turk had commanded, on account of the tribute that he paid him every year. At night, before they left, one of the Portuguese escaped and went to meet the empress and told her everything about Dom Christovam's capture and death that I have reported. People even say that he told her that as soon as the Moor had cut off his head, there rose a spring of water from the very spot where his body fell and his blood was spilt, and even now <[f. 128/118]> they talk a lot in Ethiopia about that spring and they say that, when the Christians ruled that land (for now there are some heathens there that they call Gâlas, who do not allow anyone in), many sick people used to go there out of the great devotion they had for Dom Christovam, and by washing in that water they were cured of various diseases.

They also say that, on the same day and at the very time when Dom Christovam died, a huge tree that was in the cloister of a monastery of monks was wrenched from the ground and turned upside down, its roots in the air, even though it was a very quiet, calm day; the monks were astonished and ascribed it to some great mystery, which is why they noted the day and time, and later they heard that Dom Christovam had been killed at that same moment. As the tree dried up, the monks cut off its branches to be used in the monastery, but six months later, on the day when the Portuguese fought Granh again and killed him, the tree turned itself over and, planting its roots in the earth, as they had been before, it at once put out green leaves. When the Portuguese heard that, they went to see the tree and found it had new leaves, and the monks told them that it had happened just like that. When I asked some monks about this recently, they told me that they had heard other older monks recount it as something that was quite true. They attribute all these {[f. 134]} things to God's wanting to honour His servant and to show how much he had pleased Him in life and death, and they all, great and small, still hold and proclaim him to be a great martyr. One can piously believe that, on account of the enormous patience with which he suffered everything and the great hatred of our holy faith with which that enemy of it took his life. Emperor Seltân Çaguêd, who is now alive, often gives him this same title. Since I wished to remove his bones to send them to India, I asked him to order a captain of his who was near that land to assist some Portuguese who were going there for that purpose, and he wrote him a very eulogistic letter. Among other things, he told him that it was not appropriate to leave the bones of that holy martyr in the field and that he should do everything possible to find them and deliver them to the fathers of the Society, so that they could put them in their church with the honour they deserved. But it was all in vain no matter how hard they searched, by trying many different means and even bribing the heathens, because these heathens are very false and were plotting to kill the Portuguese and the local people who came in with them, as some people who knew of the plot revealed to them. So they returned empty-handed, after wasting a large quantity of goods.

From what we have said, it is clear to see how far from the truth was the information that Friar Luis de Urreta was given about what happened to Dom Christovam and his soldiers in this last battle, for he describes it in these words, on page 360:

*While the Christians had surrounded the Moorish King Gradahametes, one must <[f. 128v/118v]> surmise that the mountain where he was backed onto the Sea of Arabia, over which he sent his ambassador to the Moorish kings, asking them for a favour and additional men and arms, informing them of the danger in which he was and the damage that the Portuguese had done to him. He was joined by many men well equipped with arms and harquebuses and eight field pieces, with which aid he reinforced his army, and adopting battle order he came down from the mountain in search of the Portuguese. He found them, as he was found by them, scattered across the fields: some in tents and others in huts, without any battle order or military discipline, and the Moor Gradahametes suddenly attacked the unwary Christians, some of whom were asleep, as it was at night, others were stunned by the artillery, others were careless, and all were unprepared. In the end, although they put up some defence, they eventually started to fall back and then to retreat until, unable to resist any longer, they fled, happy to be holding on to their {[f. 134v]} lives. Captain Christoval de Gama fled too, but he was captured in a wood by some soldiers who were pursuing him and taken to the Moorish King Gradahametes.[1]*

The author is right in what says here about the substantial aid that the Moor received from Arabia, as I said above, although he could have added that 900 Turks came among the Arabians. But as for the carelessness, negligence, disorder and lack of military discipline through which he says the Portuguese were taken unawares and asleep, as it was night, and the remissness and weakness with which he shows they fought and fled, it was not as he describes, but as we have already recounted. Anyone who pays careful attention to what we have said will find that, once Dom Christovam da Gama had landed on the Red Sea coast and begun to march through Ethiopia to the point where God permitted him to be defeated, nothing at all of what one might desire in a great and excellent captain was lacking in the way he fulfilled his duties, nor did his soldiers ever fail to show the valour and courage of those who are most famed by the histories for having it in abundance. Leaving aside the fearful battles that they won and the notable victories that they achieved, who will not be amazed at what they did in this last battle, for just 335 Portuguese, counting the two who came later with a message from the *fustas* that had

---

[1] Urreta, *Historia de la Etiopia*, excerpt (with some brief passages omitted) from bk I, ch. 32, pp. 260–61. Páez quotes this passage in Spanish.

arrived in Maçuâ to learn news and could not return – because, of the 400 who had originally set out, thirty-seven were already dead and thirty others had stayed behind on the road from Cemên with the eighty horses, and the Ethiopians who were with the empress did not help them at all that day – who, then, will not be astonished that just 335 Portuguese could do battle with 900 Turks as well armed <[f. 129/119]> as we have already mentioned and with countless Arabians and other Moors on foot and on horseback, from sunrise to sunset without ever having a single moment of rest or stepping back from the constant activity, with captains taking turns to sally from the palisades to fight the Moors on the battlefield, as we have described, killing many and routing them every time they sallied, and not securing victory only through lack of horses on which to pursue them? There is no doubt but that they did all that like excellent knights, who showed the greatest courage that there could be, so that it seemed that the Lord had given them superhuman strength. Therefore, we can very rightly proclaim them to be worthy of everlasting memory and fame, and we can strongly condemn everything that the author so unjustly attributes to Dom Christovam, since he was captured and killed, as we have said, after performing such extraordinary feats that they are an honour to the Portuguese name.

How the Portuguese who escaped from the battle joined the empress and later the Prester John and gave battle to Granh

After that sad and painful tragedy in which the wheel of such great happiness and good fortune dissolved like smoke after such propitious successes and marvellous victories, the Portuguese who had escaped from the battle were left scattered through the forests. As night soon came upon them and they did not know the paths, each one went where his fate took him. The best served were those who were able to follow the empress because, as she had with her local people who knew where they could take refuge, they easily found safety by taking to a very secure mountain. But of the ones who had been left in the forests, a group of ten or twelve were making their way along the next day, travelling slowly since they were badly wounded and weary. At about ten o'clock they were seen by a large party of Moors on foot and two on horseback who were searching the countryside, and they came after them furiously at once. Two of the Portuguese who were less badly wounded, who were called Fernam Cardoso and Pêro d'Almansa, told the others to run and hide in the forest, since they could not fight, while the two of them stayed fighting until they died or were captured; they offered themselves willingly so that the others could be saved. <[f. 129v/119v]> Thus determined, they turned towards the Moors with their shields and lances in their hands and made a pact together that, if they were captured, they would not give away the ones who had gone ahead no matter how much they were tormented.

The two Moors on horseback were drawing near. When they were close, they stopped to wait for the ones on foot so they could seize them, and they told them that they should give up their arms and they would not kill them. When the Portuguese saw so many men and that they were carrying so many bows and arrows, they said to each other that it would be better to give themselves up, because they would surely be killed by the arrows and stones before they could reach them with their lances, and if they gave themselves up perhaps the Moors would turn back and the others would be saved. So one of them, who already knew a little of the local language, told the Moors to keep their promise and take their arms away. And as they approached {[f. 135v]} to hand them over, they felt a new spirit within and both of them suddenly said, 'Holy Mary, are we to kill ourselves with our own arms?' As they said these words, each one struck his Moor such a blow that they both fell to the ground, one dead and the other very badly wounded, while their horses did not stir. When many of the foot soldiers saw that, they started to run away, even though there were many of them. So the Portuguese mounted the horses and went after them a little way to show that they meant to pursue them. But as the Moors ran further away and were hidden by the forests, they both turned back and went in search of their companions, whom they soon found. They were all amazed to see them, because they expected them to be dead or captive by then. When they heard what had happened, they called it a miracle and thanked God for such a great favour. Putting the most seriously wounded on the horses, they went on with great difficulty until, with the Lord's mercy, they managed to reach the mountain where the empress was with some other Portuguese.

The empress had already sent out many local people to search the roads and forests and to direct any Portuguese that they found to where she was, and to try to have news about Dom Christovam, for all they knew was that he had left the battle badly wounded. These people brought back some Portuguese and, the next day, the ones with the horses arrived as well. Until then, they did not know of the defeat, and so they were grief-stricken and shed many tears to see their companions so badly wounded and in such a terrible state. At that moment the Portuguese soldier who had escaped when they captured Dom Christovam arrived and, soon afterwards, the one who had fled from the Turks after his death. And they recounted what had happened <[f. 130/120]> in the manner that we described in the previous chapter. That grieved everyone so much that, forgetting all their other hurts and losses, they wept only for this one with the greatest, most heartfelt pain and anguish. No less great was the grief felt by the empress and the tears that she shed with her ladies and maidens for Dom Christovam's death, because she wept for him for many days as if he had been her own son, the emperor. She would accept no consolation, even though she tried to give as much to the Portuguese as she could.

[1]They stayed on this mountain for a few days to heal their wounds and rest and for those who were scattered around to be brought in; about 120 men gathered. They heard news that Manoel da Cunha with fifty Portuguese, without knowing which way they were going, had entered the lands of the *bahâr nagâx*, where {[f. 136]} they were very well received. The empress then decided, on the advice of the Portuguese, to go to {Oatî} <Oatê> mountain in Cemên, which Dom Christovam had captured in the winter, because they would be safer there and would have everything they needed in abundance, for not only is it very secure and almost impregnable, but on top it has broad fields of crops and enough grass for many cattle and water in great abundance from springs and streams that never dry up. So they went there and the captain that Dom Christovam had left on that mountain received them with much love and goodwill, liberally giving them all not only what was necessary but whatever else they requested for other particular reasons.

Ten days after the empress and the Portuguese had come to that mountain, or twenty days, as some say,[2] the Prester John arrived at its foot with such a small and dejected band of men that, if the mountain had not already been taken, not only would he not have been able to take it from the Moors, but he would not have dared near it. When the Portuguese learnt that he was so close, they came down in formation, carrying the banner of Our Lady of Mercy as their standard. When they reached him and he saw how they were and that there were so few of them, and when he heard of the defeat and death of Dom Christovam, his sadness and grief were as great as if his only son and heir to the empire had died, to the extent that afterwards he could not be consoled, because he had come with a great desire to see Dom Christovam on account of the great fame that he had heard of him. Nonetheless,

---

[1] New paragraph made by the editors.

[2] The latter figure is given by Guerreiro (see 'Adição à Relação das coisas de Etiópia', p. 376), in which he apparently followed the information given by Gaspar Correia, since his declared source mentions 10 days (see Castanhoso, *Dos feitos de D. Christovam da Gama*, ch. 20, pp. 54–5).

he received them with great honour and spoke very kindly, consoling them and saying that they should not consider themselves foreigners or abandoned in his empire, because he held it on account of the king of Portugal, his brother, since it had been bought with the blood of his Portuguese, who were true Christians. He then provided them with copious clothing, tents, mules and orderlies to serve them, and whatever else they needed.

<[f. 130v/120v]> He stayed on this mountain for a few months while men gathered to him. When he had some 500 horse and 8,000 foot, it seemed to the Portuguese that with those men he could give battle to the Moors, so they begged the emperor to help them avenge Dom Christovam's death. He doubted very much whether that could be done with so few men, but later, on hearing that the Turks had returned home leaving no more than 200 with Granh, and as the Portuguese were very insistent, he decided to follow {[f. 136v]} their counsel. He therefore sent word to the fifty Portuguese who had gone to the lands of the *bahâr nagâx* to come and join him as quickly as they could and, on the way, to bring the weaponry that Dom Christovam had left on Damô mountain, where the empress had taken refuge, on which he had left his spare weapons since it was a very good stronghold. But when the emperor's servants arrived, they did not find the Portuguese there, because they had thought that all the others were finished by then and that they could not reach the place where the emperor was, so they had set off towards Maçuâ to wait for any *fustas* on which they might embark for India. So the servants returned, but they did bring the weapons, which were very important because they had very few.

When the emperor realized that he should not wait for those Portuguese, who were now too far away, he left the mountain on 6th February 1543 with the ones he had with him, 120 or 130 of them, including some cripples whom the emperor told to remain behind, but they refused to do so as they wanted to die with their companions. He wanted to appoint one of them captain, but they would not accept that either, saying that as they had lost such a captain as Dom Christovam da Gama, they would not have any other save him and the banner of Our Lady of Mercy. With these Portuguese and his own 500 horse and 8,000 foot soldiers, he went in search of Granh the Moor, leaving his mother the empress on that mountain. On reaching the province of Oagrâ, he came across one of the Moor's captains with 300 horsemen and 2,000 on foot, and he commanded that they should attack them before dawn, with fifty Portuguese on horseback in the vanguard. They soon defeated them, killing the captain and most of his men and taking many prisoners. From them they learnt that Granh was a little further ahead, in the kingdom of Dambiâ near the lake through which the Nile flows, with his wife and children, for as he had left them there a long time previously and as the land there was fertile, he had come <[f. 131/121]> to be with them shortly after he had defeated Dom Christovam. He soon learnt that the emperor was on his way and that he was bringing some Portuguese with him, at which he was very surprised because he thought that they were all dead, and his men were not a little afraid, because they knew how brave the Portuguese were and understood very well that they were coming only to avenge the past. He made ready with great haste and, on parading his men, found that he had 13,000 men on foot and horse and 200 Turks.

When the emperor came within sight of the Moors, he pitched {[f. 137]} camp in a land that they call Oinadagâ and, before giving battle, they spent a few days in skirmishes, in which seventy Portuguese usually sallied on horseback and performed wonders. Once, when a famous Moorish captain came at them with 200 horsemen, they killed him in the first encounter together with twelve very brave horsemen and turned the others back; Granh was heavy-hearted at that, because he had been his best captain. The emperor's field general was also a great horseman and made very good sorties with his men, in which the Moors always came off worse. When Granh saw the serious damage that this captain was inflicting on him, he decided to lay a trap to kill him by treachery. So he commanded that four Turks, who were good harquebusiers, should go that night and hide by a stream that ran beside the emperor's camp, and at dawn two horsemen should go with a white flag and pretend that they wanted to tell the captain something in secret and try to come over to him, and, when he came out, the Turks would shoot him. They did so in such a way that it seemed that the two horsemen left their camp stealthily, and standing next to the stream they called out to the captain by name. The captain, who was already on his horse at that hour, sent to ask what they wanted. They answered that they had something that would be much to his advantage and that they could only tell it to him. When he heard that, he approached with many men and, on seeing that there were only two of them, he thought that they wanted to come over to him or give him some important news, so he told everyone to stay behind. Taking only two servants with him, he came to the edge of the stream and, while he was asking what they wanted, the Turks shot him with their harquebuses and killed him, and then they all ran off as fast as they could. When the captain's men heard the gunshots and saw the Moors running away, they realized it had been a trap and many of them raced after them on horseback, but they could not reach them because the Turks had horses ready for them nearby and many others came out of their camp to take them in. So they returned with their dead captain.

The emperor sorely felt the loss of this captain, because he had been very valiant and had shown and passed on his bravery to others; so, when they saw he was missing, many lost heart and considered victory impossible, and they tried to flee the camp in secret. {[f. 137v]} <[f. 131v/121v]> But there were those who told the emperor what was happening, so he decided to give battle the following day, fearing that if he delayed he would be left all alone. At dawn, he commanded that they should all draw up in battle order. The Portuguese joined them and raised the Mercy banner and, kneeling, they all commended themselves to God, begging him by the merits of the Virgin Our Lady of Piety, who was painted on it, to help them against their enemies and to receive the souls of those who He decided should end their lives in that battle. They stood up, formed ranks and took their place in the vanguard, as the emperor had granted, taking with them 250 *Habexims* on horseback and 3,500 on foot. The emperor took the rearguard with another 250 horse and 4,500 foot. In this manner they went forth to meet the Moors, who were already coming also divided into two battalions: Granh was in the first with 200 Turkish harquebusiers, 600 Moorish horsemen and 7,000 foot soldiers; in the rearguard was a great captain with 600 horse and 6,000 foot.

As the two sides met, they both attacked with great force and battle was joined fiercely. But the Turks, charging on one flank, were carrying the *Habexins* before them. When the Portuguese saw that, they very swiftly turned on them and killed many, and the rest drew back some distance until they joined the other Moors. But the Portuguese would not leave them alone, because they wanted to have them, so seventy of them that had horses went amongst them doing wonders, and many of the emperor's men went with them so as not to be shamed. The battle raged for a long time, but the Portuguese fought with such extraordinary bravery that they turned the Turks and Moors who were in that area. When

Granh saw that, he himself came to help with a son of his – a young man – and those who were accompanying him, and he made them all stop and fight. While rallying them he came so close that the Portuguese recognized him, and at once they all charged in his direction and fired so many shots at him from their guns that one hit him in the chest and he fell forwards onto his horse's saddlebow. His men saw this and came to his aid and, lowering their standards, they fled with him, but afterwards they left him on the ground, as they would rather ride unencumbered to save their own lives than pointlessly carry {[f. 138]} the body that would be the cause of their deaths, because his army at once began to fall into disarray and flee. Only the captain of the Turks resolved to die fighting and sell himself for a fair price, and so, rolling up his shirtsleeves, with bare arms and a broad scimitar <in his hands> and his round shield {in his hands}, he attacked five *Habexins* on horseback and gave them plenty of trouble. As one of them tried to spear him, <[f. 132/122]> he grabbed the lance out of his hands, and he cut the horse's legs from under another, so they no longer dared get close to him. At that point a Portuguese rode up and wounded him badly with his lance, but he grabbed hold of that too so strongly that he could not be made to let go, and he came so close that his scimitar struck the Portuguese on one knee and cut his sinews, crippling him; the Portuguese then took his sword and finally killed the Turk.

Meanwhile, the emperor's men were chasing after the Moors and slaughtering them. But the Portuguese were mainly occupied with the Turks, for they did not care so much about the others since they wanted the Turks so much, and so, of the full 200, no more than forty escaped. They went to Granh's wife, who, on hearing of the rout, took refuge with 340 horsemen who were in her guard. She took the treasure that her husband had taken from the emperor and escaped, since everyone was busy killing and taking booty from the field and camp, where they found a large number of Christian captives, especially children and women. That was a great joy and happiness for them, because some found their sisters, others their wives and others their children, whom they had no hope of ever seeing again. Everyone's pleasure was so great that it was like a dream. Recognizing that such a great mercy had come to them through the Portuguese, they threw themselves on the ground and kissed their feet, bestowing many blessings and thanks on them. The emperor too granted them many honours and showed that he owed them more than he could give, because he could see that they had given him back the empire, which had been so entirely lost that nobody had thought that it could ever be regained. And it was a wonderful thing that, even though this battle had been so fierce and the Portuguese had <always> been in the vanguard right from the start, facing the Turkish guns and the Moorish hordes, not one of them had died in it. That shows without doubt that the Virgin of Piety (to whom they had commended themselves before joining battle) had pity on them, and {[f. 138v]} obtained this great mercy for them from the Father of Mercies.

Everything that we have said in this chapter and in the others concerning Dom Christovam da Gama is from information given by reliable eye-witnesses, so more credence should be given to them than to whoever informed Friar Luis de Urreta about this story, which he recounts, on page 361, so differently from the way in which it in fact happened, as the reader will see in his words, which are as follows:

*While these things were happening in the kingdom of Adel, the Prester John came down* <[f. 132v/122v]> *with a vast army, which covered the fields, the mountains and the valleys and blocked out the light from the earth, in which there were more than 600,000 men. Three or four days' journey before arriving in the kingdom of Adel, he encountered many of his men who were fleeing, together with some Portuguese, who gave him the sad news about all that was happening and of the death of Don Christoval de Gama. Great was his anger and vexation at this misfortune but, rather ashamed at showing his grief at such trifles, he composed his appearance and, with a feigned laugh, said, 'Well, in truth, in truth, Gradahametes, one day you shall pay for so many wrongs, and punishment will not be long in coming. O illustrious Captain Gama, you were fortunate, for you suffered such a glorious death! Rejoice, for you have an emperor who will avenge your death. And I give my word that neither my brother the king of Portugal nor your brother the viceroy of India will ever be able to complain of me.' All that numerous multitude marched off at full speed, joyful and happy and leaping with pleasure, and they fell upon the Moors, whom they encountered so unawares that they were still dancing a thousand jigs for their past victory. But they soon turned to bitter tears, because while King Gradahametes was leaping and bounding, a fortunate bullet caught him in mid-air, went though his ribs and left him dead on those fields. With their king dead, all his men's hearts died, and on seeing the multitude of men charging at them, they fled, weakened, faint-hearted and debilitated, their hearts and minds shocked by that surprise. But the valiant Ethiopians fell on that battalion of Moors, wounding and killing them with all the fury and anger that avenging so many wrongs required. It was a judgment and terror to see and hear the fearful sound of the trumpets and drums, the booming of the harquebuses, the roaring of the bullets, the ferocity of the horses, the breaking of lances, the falling and shouting, the yells, the wails, the sighs, the bloody wounds, {[f. 139]} the merciless killing, the rivers of blood, the gunpowder, the smoke, the confusion, and this is war.[1] Emperor Claudio, {spirited}  and valiant, dressed in a strong cuirass extending half way down his legs, made of elephant hide, with his hardened round shield and iron-tipped spear, wearing his visor and helmet with a band of crimson hanging from his head (the ancient manner for Prester Johns to go into battle), fought his way through the tightest hordes of the enemy and dealt with them in such a way that he left not one that did not die at his hands or flee from his hands. Almost all the Moors died, uttering screams that rent the skies and calling to their Mohammed but, since he is in Hell, he did not hear them.[2]*

<[f. 133/123]> Up to here are the words of Friar Luis de Urreta, which, according to what we have said with certainty, lack a good deal in the truth of the story, because in the first place Dom Christovam's defeat did not take place in the kingdom of Adel, but (as we have said) in Oflâ, the borderland of the kingdom of Tigrê with Angôt, a long way from Adel. The Prester John did not come with 600,000 men, as he says, for even if the Moors had not taken control of almost all his empire by then, but it were flourishing and at peace, he would not have been able to gather even half the number of men that whoever informed him invented. He only ever had so few men that it would have been impossible for him to recover his empire if the Portuguese had not come. As their books tell, when his father David (who was also called Onâg Çaguêd) died in the kingdom of Tigrê, on Damô mountain, where Dom Christovam found Empress Zabelâ {Oenguêl} <Oenguîl>,

---

[1] In Urreta's text, this last clause is a question: 'And is this war?' (Urreta, *Historia de la Etiopia*, bk I, p. 363).
[2] Urreta, *Historia de la Etiopia*, excerpt (with several omissions) from bk I, ch. 32, pp. 361–3. Páez quotes this passage in Spanish.

who had taken refuge there for fear of the Moors, as it was a very secure place, he was there chosen to be emperor at the age of eighteen, and he had so little power that, when he was attacked four or five months later by one of Granh's captains, who was called Amîr Ozmân, he was defeated and only escaped with great difficulty. He went to the kingdom of Xâoa with just eighty men and stayed there, always on the run from one strongholds to another, with so few men that, although Dom Christovam had been in his lands for more than a year (for he had arrived in July 1541 and the battle in which he was defeated was on 28th August 1542) and had often sent word for him to come, since he too was coming down to meet him, he never dared to do so until he heard that Dom Christovam had taken the mountain of Oatî in Cemên province. He was not so far away that he could not have come to join Dom Christovam in less than a month, but he did not do so for fear of some Moors who were between them, and when he did come he brought very few men, as we said above. After joining the Portuguese on that mountain and staying there {[f. 139v]} for so long, he was only able to gather 8,000 foot soldiers and 500 horse, and such that they would not have dared fight Granh if the Portuguese had not encouraged and importuned them so much. And they were even ready to run away on the day before the battle, when they saw that the captain that Granh had killed by treachery was missing.

It was also mere imagination that the Prester John, on hearing of Dom Christovam's death, put on the display of bravura and threats against Granh that the author mentions. Nor did he consider the death of Dom Christovam and the other Portuguese to be such trifles that he should be ashamed to show the great sadness and mortal grief that this news had caused him. He was quite right to show his grief, because not only did he have very little hope left that he could recover his empire, but all good reason and gratitude required him to show sorrow and grief, for such a great lord as Dom Christovam da Gama had come with the Portuguese <[f. 133v/123v]> to aid him at a time of great need and, after performing so many wonders and fighting so valiantly, as we have seen, he poured out his blood and ended his life in his service. Nor did the emperor with his men suddenly fall upon the Moors, whom they found dancing jigs for their past victory, as he says, for he seems to think they had only just won their victory, whereas six months had already passed, and Granh was no longer in the place where the battle had taken place, but far away in Dambiâ. And he was not unawares, for he knew very well that the emperor was coming for him and they spent a few days before the battle in skirmishes. The emperor did not have armour made from elephant hide, because he did not wear any such thing, and there is nobody now who says that he joined in the battle, but he remained in the rear-guard. Even if he had joined in, it would be great exaggeration to say that he dealt with the Moors in such a way that he left not one that did not die at his hands or flee from his hands; instead of his hands, one should understand the hands of the Portuguese and the rest of his army. And not as many Moors died as he says, because many escaped and went away with Granh's wife.

# CHAPTER XXXVI

## Of some things that happened after the Prester John defeated Granh and of the exequies that he performed for Dom Christovão and the other Portuguese who died

When the emperor found that victory was his, he at once commanded that his tents be erected along the great Lake Dambiâ, which was nearby, while the soldiers chased the Moors and collected the booty, of which there was plenty, from the field. He entered his tents with loud music [{f. 140}] and rejoicing, very pleased with such a success, his only concern being that he did not know what had become of Granh. Although everyone assured him that he could not escape with his life, because he had been carried off mortally wounded, even so he could not remain calm since he was such a great enemy. But God wished to give him perfect joy, because a captain of his, who was called Calîd, soon came galloping in, celebrating loudly, because he was bringing Granh's head, which was easily recognized. Putting it in front of the emperor, he asked him to keep the promise that he had made, which was that he would give his sister in marriage to any Ethiopian who killed Granh and, if it were a Portuguese, he would do him very great favours. But somebody said that he had not killed him, but that he had found him already dead when he cut off his head, so the emperor ordered an investigation, and they found that the Portuguese had wounded him, for nobody else had harquebuses. Even though the captain assured them that he had killed him and that he was alive when he came and cut off his head, and he offered to prove it, they decided that, apart from the fact that there were many who claimed that they had found him dead, even if the captain could prove what he was claiming, that would not be sufficient for the emperor to be obliged to give him his sister, since the Portuguese <[f. 134/124]> had mortally wounded him and he had found him lying on the ground, for otherwise he would not have been able to get close to him. So the emperor did not give him his sister, but rewarded him for the present with other things. Nor did he do the Portuguese the favours he had promised, because he did not know which of them had wounded him, but if that could be proved he would be true to his word.

He then had the head placed on a long lance so that everyone in the camp could see it. Afterwards, he sent it to his mother the empress, who had remained on the mountain in Cemên, and from there it was to be taken to the other lands, so that nobody could doubt that he was dead. When the empress saw the head, she gave many thanks to God for releasing her empire from the hands of such a great and cruel tyrant and allowing her to see {with her own eyes} the punishment that he deserved for the inhumanity with which he had treated Dom Christovam da Gama, whom she loved as a son. And so, with great joy and happiness, she ordered many celebrations, and she was helped in these by the fifty Portuguese who had gone to Maçuâ, because, as they found no vessels to take them to India but learnt of the message that the emperor had sent them, they turned back and had already reached the place where the empress was. Having celebrated victory for a few days, she went to where her son was, taking the Portuguese with her. And they welcomed them all with great splendour and excitement, for until then they had only occupied themselves with music and festivities at seeing themselves free of that great tyranny and harsh captivity. The emperor also received the Portuguese very kindly with displays of love, considering himself highly obliged to them for what they had done for him, and he commanded that they should be abundantly supplied with everything they needed.

{[f. 140v]} At that time there came a message for the emperor from a great lord, who was called *Erâz* {Deganâ} <Deganô>, the father of *Bahâr Nagâx* Isaac, who had long ago sided with Granh since it seemed to him that it was no longer possible to restore the empire, and the Moor had held him in such esteem that he had made him his son's steward and captain of many men. Having escaped from the battle with Granh's son, when he heard that the father was dead, he sent word to the emperor that if he would pardon him he would deliver the Moor's son to him. Even though having that young man in his hands was such an important matter, the emperor would not grant a pardon because of the great displeasure and just indignation that he felt towards him for having sided with the Moors and fought for a long time against the Christians. Later, however, through the intercession of his son Isaac (to whom the emperor refused nothing, because he had brought him the Portuguese), he pardoned him and granted him safe passage. He then came at once, bringing the young man with him, who the emperor commanded should be treated well but kept under close guard.

When another great Moorish captain heard how the emperor had pardoned *Erâz* {Deganâ} <Deganô>, he also sent many people to intercede on his behalf to obtain a pardon and safe passage. <[f. 134v/124v]> The emperor granted this for certain reasons, even though he had become a Moor and had badly destroyed the land. But when he entered the camp, the emperor learnt that he had been one of those who had captured Dom Christovam and badly wanted to kill him, but he did not do so because he had granted him safe passage. The Portuguese wanted to do so even more, because they had recognized him straight away, and they were furious to see him before their eyes every day. So they went to the emperor and begged him dearly to have him killed, because he deserved it so much. But he answered that he could not do such a thing because he had given him {safe passage} <his word>, and he tried to satisfy them with kind words, by which they clearly understood that he would not mind if they killed him. So two of them went to the Moor's tent and stabbed him to death, and the emperor did not mind and nobody mentioned it to him. The emperor also had some of those who were with the Moor killed, but afterwards he granted a general pardon because, if he were to kill all those who deserved death, few – or at least few great men – would remain in all his empire.

The emperor stayed in that place for two months, during which time some great men who had been with the Moor came over to him, and then he went three leagues further to a town that lay close to the same lake, since it was a more comfortable place to spend the winter, which was already approaching. Distributing his warriors in the places around, he allocated a place to the Portuguese that was very close, where they were abundantly supplied with what they needed. And they went to the palace every day, because the emperor enjoyed that very much. At the end of August, on the same day on which Dom Christovam da Gama had died, he decided to perform some solemn exequies for him, as they do when a year has passed, and so a few days previously he had it announced {[f. 141]} throughout his lands that all the poor people should gather there for that day. More than 6,000 came, and they put up many tents in the fields where, at the emperor's command, they were given splendid food to eat and clothes to wear. He also had 600 or more monks come, and they performed their rites very solemnly in their customary manner, which we shall describe in the second book, and he ordered they be given plentiful alms. When winter was over (it usually finishes during September, as we have said), he gathered all his warriors, who now amounted to some 2,000 horse and 20,000 foot, and he went with them throughout all the lands that the Moors had conquered from him so as to finish reducing and pacifying them. It took him a long time and not a little trouble to do so, because there were still many Moors in those lands.

Friar Luis de Urreta recounts some of these things on page 363, but in a different manner, since the information that he had on this subject was very contrary to the truth in every way. It will therefore be necessary to report his own words, <[f. 135/125]> which are those that follow on from the ones that we included in the previous chapter, thus:

*The Prester John was not content with this punishment, nor was his desire for vengeance satisfied with the deaths of those Moors, but, like a thunderbolt and brimming over with fury as he recalled the death of his brother, he decided once and for all to rid himself of such a tiresome and vexatious enemy. So, entering the kingdom of Adel, he left no town or village that he did not burn and raze to the ground. So many Moors died at the hands of the Ethiopian Christians that they would say as an amusing exaggeration, 'What infernal bosom could be large enough to receive so many devils as entered there?' It is enough to say that, although it was a very densely populated kingdom with countless people and so large that it was 300 leagues around, scarcely 4,000 people were left alive. He destroyed fortresses and built new ones at the most important crossings. He brought people from Ethiopia to populate that kingdom, and gave the ports to the Portuguese, together with their fortresses, so that they could guard them against the Moors from Arabia and take in the fleets from Portugal on their way to and from India. That was the end of the king of Adel's wars.*[1]

That is what the author says. All of it, however, is mere fiction traced in the mind of the one who informed him, because not only did Emperor Claudio not do those things in the {[f. 141v]} kingdom of Adel, but he never went there in his life. Nor did the Moors lose so much with Granh's defeat and death that they could not have defended themselves very well, had he gone there. Rather, the Moor who succeeded Granh as *guazîr, scilicet* 'governor', came from there with an army against Emperor Claudio a few years later and, on giving battle, defeated and killed him not very far from where he had his court, as everyone says and his history recounts, as we shall report in Book 3. However, I think it highly likely that Friar Luis de Urreta was not informed in this way, but that he got confused with Joam Balthesar's papers, for he himself says that he took the story from them and that they were badly mixed up. Thus he attributed to Emperor Claudio the deeds that his father David performed in Adel (which we shall see in a story to be

---

[1] Urreta, *Historia de la Etiopia*, bk I, excerpt from ch. 32, p. 363. Páez quotes this passage in Spanish.

included at the beginning of the third book[1]) and he added a good deal more, as he did to other things that Joam Balthesar told him, as he himself testified later in a petition that he sent to His Majesty King Dom Phelippe, complaining that they had added four times more than he had said, the transcript of which was seen by Father Fernam Guerreiro of our Society, as he states on folio 268 of the addendum that he made to the Annual Report for 1607 and 1608.[2]

---

[1] See bk III, ch. 2, vol. II below.
[2] Guerreiro, 'Adição à Relação das coisas de Etiópia', p. 290.

# CHAPTER XXXVII

## How Emperor Claudio excluded the Patriarch Dom Joam Bermudez and made his seat in the kingdom of Ôye

<[f. 135v/125v]> Once Emperor Claudio, or by his other name Atanâf Çaguêd, had reduced the lands that the Moors had taken to his obedience and had pacified his empire, he saw himself free of the anguish and fears that had always made him flee from one place to another. When he should have been more grateful to Our Lord God for the great mercies that he had received from His merciful hand and submitted to the Holy Roman Church with all his heart, following the doctrine taught by the holy Patriarch Dom Joam Bermudez – whom he had received as such three years previously and to whom he had given the patriarchal lands, which are very extensive – he revealed instead how far he was from giving such obedience and from following that doctrine and from not accepting a patriarch from anywhere but Rome, as he himself wrote to King João III of Portugal that his father, Emperor David, had commanded him to do, {[f. 142]} because he had another patriarch brought from Alexandria, so as to exclude the one he had from Rome. At the same time, the monks of a large monastery plotted to defame Dom Joam Bermudez, whose holy life troubled them greatly. While he was at court they took some silver objects from their monastery church and, entering the patriarch's house, which was nearby, they managed to conceal them secretly among his clothes. Afterwards, they went to the emperor and said that those objects were missing from the church and that nobody could have taken them except the patriarch. The emperor then sent for him and told him, in front of the monks, that he should listen to what they said. Without any fear of God, they repeated their claim that those objects were missing and that nobody could have taken them except him. The patriarch was highly surprised and said that such a thing had never even crossed his mind, and he did not know how they dared think that of him. The monks asked the emperor to have his house searched and his servants questioned to find out the truth, and the patriarch did not mind since he was innocent. So some of the emperor's servants went with the monks and, while looking through the things in the house, they came across the objects among his clothes, and they took them to the emperor. The patriarch then said that that could only be the evil-doing of people who wished him ill, because he had never taken those things and he had no reason to do so. The emperor clearly understood that the patriarch would not do such a thing, but even so he found the case very strange, and it gave others cause to talk a great deal.

The patriarch saw all that and realized that he could not expect the emperor <[f. 136/126]> or even his own people to do anything about the charge, so he decided to return to India. Some say that he excommunicated the emperor in his presence and cursed the lands through which he passed, except the kingdom of Tigrê, which, they say, he spared at the request of some Portuguese who were accompanying him: since they held his saintliness in great esteem, they considered the lands that he cursed to be lost, and so they begged him to spare Tigrê so that if some Portuguese ever came they would find somewhere to enter, and so he left it. And he said he could see some black ants entering the emperor's lands and destroying them, and it seems they were some very black heathens that they call Galâs, who shortly afterwards started coming closer and making raids, causing great damage to the land, and they continued this so much that they came to destroy all the lands that the patriarch had cursed, which are three or four kingdoms and a few provinces, the best that the emperor had. Today, they are the absolute lords of those kingdoms, and no one can take them from their hands {[f. 142v]} and, what is more, they are always attacking the rest of the country, killing many people and taking property without count. If they were all to unite and attack together, not even the emperor {would be able to face them}, but since they do not have a king (as we said before in chapter 1) they never unite. Instead, those who are from one caste or family often fight with those of another, and Our Lord God allows this so that they do not completely destroy this ancient Christianity. Even though it is infected with {many} <some> errors, there have always been some good people who have condemned them and wept for them, begging the Lord for mercy, and today more than ever, and so I hope He will have mercy on them and come to their aid. They say that everything I have mentioned about the patriarch Dom Joam Bermudez is the truth, and some sons of the Portuguese who arrived with the patriarch have told me that they often heard it from their parents.

At the same time as these things were happening between the patriarch and the emperor, the latter made his seat in the kingdom of Ôye, as it was a very secure land and one that he liked most. Settling his camp on a beautiful plain near a mountain that they call Zêf Bâr, he soon had a large city built. It was not so well laid out or of such splendour and beauty as those of Europe, where there are such large stone houses and sumptuous palaces of marvellous design and architecture, but it had such different buildings that many of them could {more rightly} be called shepherds' huts than {houses} of the emperor's court, because they were round, very cramped and low, and instead of walls they had some rough poles placed upright and plastered inside and out with mud, and roofed with straw. Not even the great men's houses were different from these except in being <[f. 136v/126v]> larger and having walls of stone and mud, with better timber above, and others in not being round but long, though all with just one floor. The most that the polity and greatness of the emperor could achieve was to build a two-storey house, but a very miserable one hardly suited to an imperial person. They called it a *gamb*, which is the name they give to any two-storey house, while a round one that is not is a *bêit*, and a long, single-storey house is a *çacalâ*. Emperor Claudio stayed in this city most of the time for twelve or thirteen years, at the end of which there came a Moor from Adel, called Nur, with an army, and he killed him in battle, as we mentioned at the end of the last chapter and will describe in the third book.[1] Since he had no children, he was succeeded in the empire by a brother of his who was called Minâs, who moved the court from that city, and so it soon declined. And later the Gâlas took all that kingdom.[2] So the site of that city has been deserted for so many years that no vestige of it can be seen.

[1] See bk III, ch. 3, vol. II below.
[2] See Fig. 17.

# Book II

[BOOK II OF THE HISTORY OF ETHIOPIA, WHICH DEALS WITH THE FAITH THAT THE PRESTER JOHN AND HIS VASSALS PROFESS, THE ECCLESIASTICAL RITES AND CEREMONIES THAT THEY PERFORM AND OTHER MATTERS RELATING THERETO][1]

---

[1] Book II of ARSI, MS Goa 42 is written in a different hand from bks I, III and IV.

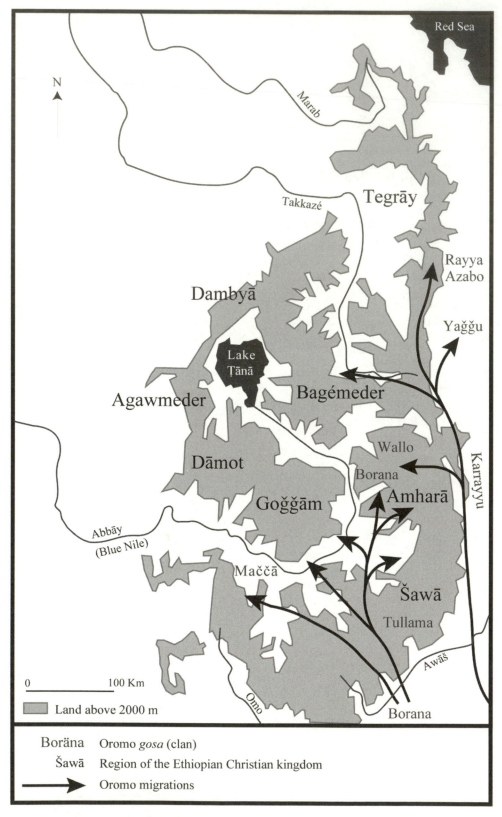

Figure 17. Map of the Oromo migrations in the sixteenth and seventeenth centuries.
Drawn by H. Pennec and M. J. Ramos. Base map: R. Oliver, Geography section, City of London
Polytechnic (Pankhurst, 1982).

# CHAPTER I

## On the origin of the Christian faith and religion in Ethiopia[1]

The Prester John's[2] vassals are very proud of the nobility and antiquity of their emperors, and they are so sure that they descend from Solomon that they do not think there can be any controversy about it, as we said in chapter 2 of the first book. Thus, in the nobility of their descent and antiquity they would put them first before all the kings in the world. But they feel no less honoured in also being sure that their empire was the first to publicly and universally receive the holy faith of Christ Our Lord, without the contradictions and difficulties that there were in {other} <certain> kingdoms before it could be finally introduced, which they recount in their books in the following words:

*Before Queen Sabaá[3] went to Jerusalem to hear the wisdom of Solomon, all the people of Ethiopia were heathens and worshipped different idols. But when she {[f. 143v]} returned from Jerusalem she brought them the story of Genesis, and they lived under the Law of the Jews until the coming of Christ, submitting to its rites and ceremonies and keeping God's commandments. Later, the cause of their being Christians was the fact that Queen Candace's eunuch went to Jerusalem to worship at the feast of the Passover, because the heathens who received the Law of the Jews went to Jerusalem for Passover, since it was not lawful for them to sacrifice in their land, but only in the place where God's name was invoked. For that reason, then, Queen Candace's eunuch went from Ethiopia to Jerusalem to celebrate the feast of the Passover and, as he was returning, the Angel of the Lord spoke to Philip, saying, 'Arise, go towards the south to the way that goes down from Jerusalem into Gaza the desert.' He went there and found an Ethiopian, a eunuch of Queen Candace of Ethiopia, who was the treasurer of all her wealth and had come to worship in Jerusalem, whence he was returning home in a carriage. When Philip approached the carriage, he heard that he was reading a prophecy of Isaias and he asked him whether he understood what he was reading. He replied that, if nobody taught him, how could he understand, and he begged <[f. 137v/127v]> Philip to get into the carriage, which he did. And taking the opportunity from what he had asked about that prophecy, he preached Jesus Christ to him and converted him and, informing him about the matters of the faith, he baptized him. Then the Spirit took Philip away and the eunuch never saw him again. Continuing on his way rejoicing and content at all that had happened to him, he reached Ethiopia and his lady's house and, when he told this story, they believed in the Gospel by the grace of Jesus Christ.[4]*

[1] See Glossary (Ethiopia).
[2] See Glossary (Prester John).
[3] See Glossary (Queen Saba/Queen of Sheba).
[4] See Acts of the Apostles 8:26–39. Francisco Álvares also recounted this episode from what 'their books say' 100 years before Pedro Páez. See Álvares, *Prester John of the Indies* ch. 38, pp. 149–51. See Glossary (*Kebra Nagast*).

Up to here are the words of a very old book kept in the church of Agçum in the kingdom of Tigré, where Queen Candace had her seat, and they say that she had that church built and that it was the first and most sumptuous that there has ever been in Ethiopia, as is very well shown by its {[f. 144]} ruins, as we described at length in chapter 22 of the first book. But it must be pointed out that this queen, whom we call Candace, is called Handeke by Ethiopians, but I have not found anyone who could tell me the proper name of her servant. Everyone, however, believes in the tradition that he was a eunuch, and the name given him in that old book that tells his story and in the text of the Acts of the Apostles itself, which is Heceu, has no other meaning than eunuch. So what Friar Luis de Urreta asserts on page 381,[1] that the Ethiopians consider and always have considered it a certainty that this holy man was not a eunuch, but perfect and entire in all his parts, was mistaken information and, as a consequence, he wrongly rejected the opinion of Saint Jerome, Saint Athanasius, Saint Augustine and other doctors that he mentions there, who all state that he was a eunuch, if in this part (as it seems) we are to give credence to the books and scholars of Ethiopia. The one who converted him was Saint Philip the Deacon, according to the holy doctors, apart from Albert the Great who believes it was Saint Philip the Apostle.

The doctors and saints raise another doubt, as to whether this eunuch was {a heathen, or} already converted to Judaism when he went to Jerusalem. Friar Luis de Urreta, on p. 383,[2] cites many serious authors on both opinions and follows those who say he was a heathen. But the people of Ethiopia hold it as quite certain that when this eunuch went to Jerusalem he was already converted to Judaism and the book of his history says so clearly since, as we mentioned above, it states that the reason he went to Jerusalem was because it was not lawful for heathens who received the law of Moses to sacrifice in their land, but only in the place where God's name was invoked.

When that book has finished recounting what we have mentioned about the eunuch, it continues in this manner:

*Many years after that, a merchant came {[f. 144v]} from Tyre with two servants, one called Fremenatós[3] and the other Sydrácos. And the merchant fell ill and died near the sea in the land of Ethiopia, and therefore they brought the young men <[f. 138/128]> to the king and {he} <the king> liked them very much and commanded that they should stay with his sons. They wondered greatly at {the ways of} the people of Ethiopia <and their ways> and asked how they believed in the faith of Christ, because they saw them praying and worshipping the Holy Trinity and their women had the sign of the Holy Cross on their heads. They gave many thanks to God that He had done that people such a great mercy that they believed without preaching and received the faith without an apostle. They stayed in the king's house for as long as he lived. And at the time of his death he freed them and gave them leave to go wherever they pleased, and so Sydrácos returned to his land of Tyre and Fremenatós went to the patriarch of Alexandria, desiring him to remedy the salvation of the people of Ethiopia, and he told him everything he had seen and how they believed without the teaching of the*

---

[1] Urreta, *Historia de la Etiopia*, bk II, ch. 1, entitled 'On the origin that the Christian faith and religion had in Ethiopia, and how it has been preserved until our times', pp. 379–94.

[2] Urreta, *Historia de la Etiopia*, bk II, ch. 1.

[3] See Glossary (*Abba* Çalamâ/*Abba* Salamá/*Abbā* Salāmā I/Fremonatôs/Frémenāṭos/Saint Frumentius).

*apostles. The patriarch was overjoyed and gave thanks to God for the great mercy that he had done them in showing them His holy Law and His holy faith. Then he said to Fremenatós, 'You will be their shepherd, because God has chosen you and raised you up.' And, ordaining him a priest, he made him bishop of Ethiopia. On returning to that country, he baptized its inhabitants and ordained many priests and deacons to assist him. He was esteemed and venerated by everyone and, because he brought them peace, they called him* Abbá Salamá *(which means 'Father of Peace', or 'Peace-loving'). His arrival in Ethiopia was during the reign of the brothers Abrá and Asbá, who received the teaching of justice as dry land receives rain from heaven.*

That is what I found in that book about the origin and progress of the Christian faith and religion in Ethiopia.[1] And in another book kept in the same church in {[f. 145]} Agçum, which deals with Queen Saba and the emperors who succeeded her, it is said in the catalogue of them[2] that in the reign of Amiamid (which was a long time after these two brothers Abrá and Asbá), many holy religious men entered Ethiopia coming from Rum. Some people understand this word 'Rum' to mean Rome; others affirm that it does not mean Rome but {a} <another> land called Rum ruled by the Turk, which is why the Turks are called Rum, although while I was captive among them they told me that the name Rum is not given to those who are Turks by nationality, but rather to those who are by caste Christians.[3] But even if those religious men were from that land, they would certainly have obeyed the Roman Church and taught its doctrine, since they were saints, and they could not have been saints otherwise, and that is enough for us, even if they did not come from Rome. Nine of them, whose names we gave in chapter 5 in the first book, settled in the kingdom of Tigré, where they built many churches that the people now call by their names, and some even think that only these came to Ethiopia. They performed many miracles, <[f. 138v/128v]> through which they finished converting the people of that kingdom. From the things that they tell now, I believe that the Christian religion flourished very much in Ethiopia at that time and that not only they, but many of their disciples were saints, and that many bodies of monks that have remained whole since time immemorial in the province of Bur in the kingdom of Tigré are theirs. Later, however, from the dealings and contact that they had with the Jews that there have always been in Ethiopia to this day, and because their prelates came to them from Alexandria infected with errors, they caught so many from them that they have some in almost all the sacraments and mysteries of our holy faith, as we shall see in the following chapters. Therefore, everything that Friar Luis de Urreta tries to prove throughout the second book of his *Historia Ethiopica*[4] – that the Prester John and his vassals have always been very good Catholics and obedient to the Roman Church and that, although for a long time they were unaware of certain of its ceremonies, even so, {[f. 145v]} as regards faith in the mystery of the Holy Trinity and in the fourteen articles and sacraments, they have always,

---

[1] The excerpt translated reflects an Ethiopian tradition distinct from that of the synaxarion.

[2] See bk I, ch. 5, above.

[3] 'Rum', ultimately derived from 'Roma', was the Arabic and Turkish name for the Eastern Roman Empire, then the name of the Seljuk Sultanate of Rum in Anatolia, and later was the name given to the Orthodox Christians in the Ottoman Empire.

[4] Urreta, *Historia de la Etiopia*, bk II, 'Which deals with the Christian Faith and Religion and holy ceremonies that are kept in Ethiopia'.

from the beginnings of the Church until today, kept themselves pure and sincere, in the same way as they believe in the Catholic Church – all that is based on false information which, as he says, was given to him by the Ethiopian Dom João Balthesar.

It must also be pointed out that what the author claims at the end of chapter 1 and in chapter 2 of the second book[1] – that the Prester John's Ethiopian vassals attended many councils that he mentions there, principally the Florentine Council during the time of Pope Eugene IV, where he says they made a protestation of faith in the name of the Prester John and all his empire – was of little avail, even if it were true (which I very much doubt), because not only have they for many years not kept what was decreed at those holy councils and what he reports they protested – and they do not keep it today – but rather they have held and still hold almost the very opposite to be the true faith.

He says something else in the same place of which I have been unable to find any recollection in Ethiopia, even though I have asked the emperor and many monks and elderly great men who have always lived in the emperors' palaces. It is that Emperor Alexandre III sent twelve knights of Saint Anthony, including Dom João Balthesar, together with twelve priests, to give obedience to the supreme pontiff, Gregory XIII. Many of those whom I asked consider this to be a fable, because they could not have been unaware of it or failed to hear something about it, because it was so short a time ago when the embassy was sent and so many people went with it. I think they are right and that, if such an embassy was taken there, that João Balthesar made it up on the way, like many other things that he told the author Friar Luis de Urreta, because I am not the one saying there were twenty-four ambassadors, but it would not have been possible to send even one without at least some of the great men knowing about it, since there is little secrecy in this land. Apart from that and the fact that there has never been such an Alexandre III in Ethiopia, it is mere fiction and fable that there are knights of Saint Anthony in Ethiopia, as we shall see later. So, when I once mentioned to the emperor what <[f. 139/129]> Friar Luis de Urreta says about them in the last chapter of book {[f. 146]} 3,[2] he laughed heartily and said, 'It seems that that João Balthesar saw some order of knights in your lands like the one he depicts here and was motivated by it to want to honour our land by saying that there was a similar one here. But the truth is that there has never been such a thing.' One may conclude from that that, just as he invented that the ambassadors were knights of Saint Anthony, so he also invented the embassy as he wished.

Having said that, I shall explain chapter by chapter what I have found in many general disputations and private conversations that I have had with the country's principal scholars, both ecclesiastical and lay, since 1603, when I arrived in Ethiopia. I shall report their errors simply and without any form of embellishment, for even in very light-hearted matters it is not appropriate for a religious person to resort to it, and certainly not in such a serious thing as it would be to slander a whole Christian nation and such a great emperor who is so famous throughout the world by resorting to embellishment or words that exaggerated matters in such a way that they might appear to be errors when they are not.

---

[1] Urreta, *Historia de la Etiopia*, bk II, ch. 1, pp. 390–94, and ch. 2, entitled 'Of the protestation of Faith made by the Ambassadors of the Prester John in his name and that of all his Empire in the Florentine Council, over which Pope Eugene IV presided', pp. 394–403.

[2] Urreta, *Historia de la Etiopia*, bk III, ch. 6, entitled 'Of the foundation and proceedings of the military and monastic order of the knights and monks of the glorious father Saint Anthony the Abbot', pp. 705–31.

# CHAPTER II

## Which describes how the Ethiopians deny that the Holy Spirit proceeds from the Son[1]

The Ethiopians display very great devotion to the Holy Trinity, which in their language they call *Quedézt Celacé*, 'Holy Trinity', and not 'Tinhiniah' as Friar Luis de Urreta says on page 405,[2] because they have many churches dedicated to it, and on the seventh day after the beginning of each month they hold a feast to it and once a year they celebrate it with great solemnity, and at the beginning of their books, which are all written by hand since they do not have printing, and in the letters that they send out of the empire, they commonly start with these words: '*Bazma Ab üa Üald üa Manfaz Quedúz ahâdu Amlác*', which means 'in the name of the Father and of the Son and of the Holy Spirit one God.' And almost every time that they begin some work or they are amazed at something, they repeat the same words, so that very commonly they have them in their mouths, thereby confessing that the three divine persons are really distinct and that there is supreme equality among them. But, like the Greeks, they deny {[f. 146v]} that the Holy Spirit proceeds from the Son, claiming that He only proceeds from the Father, with such pertinacity that, when in former times a monk tried to defend the idea that He also proceeded from the Son, they stoned him to death like Saint Stephen, since they thought that one should not even hear such a sacrilegious thing as uttering that the Holy Spirit also proceeded from the Son.

I heard about this as soon as I arrived in Ethiopia and, understanding the pertinacity with which they defended such a great error, I have tried to dissuade them of it by clearly showing them the truth through the holy scriptures, the holy councils, the authorities of saints <[f. 139v/129v]> and reasoning, always seeking opportunities to talk to them on this subject, and my companion fathers here have done the same, and through that the Lord has been served, for many scholars, both religious and lay, have been won over so that they have abandoned the error in which they lived and today they firmly believe that the Holy Spirit proceeds jointly from the Father and from the Son. The principal ones of these are the emperor and a brother of his called Celá Christós, and today he has the title of *erás*, which means 'head', because he is the head of all under the emperor. At first he was so contrary to our holy faith that, as he himself often tells me now, our beliefs seemed to him worse than those of the Moors, but since he has understood them he has received

---

[1] For the theological controversies between Jesuit missionaries and the Ethiopian Church, see Glossary (religious controversy).

[2] Urreta, *Historia de la Etiopia*, bk II, ch. 3, entitled 'In which the Ethiopians defend themselves as regards the articles of the faith that pertain to the divinity and holy sacred mystery of the Holy Trinity: in which they believe that which the Roman Church proposes, without ever having had any error at all', pp. 404–21.

them with such affection and believes them so firmly that he sometimes risks death to defend them and, now that he already confesses and takes communion with us, he says publicly that the faith of the Roman Church is the true one and that nobody can be saved outside it. When people contradict him in this matter, however great scholars they may be, he proves them wrong through his reasons as if they were children, because he is a man of great understanding and very well versed in the books of Ethiopia. With that and the great authority that he has over everyone, he achieves good results and reduces many people, and particularly those obliged to him are very steadfast in the faith and also speak out publicly, like their lord, confessing and defending the truth of our beliefs, and they face the dangers that arise against them with great confidence in the holy faith that they profess. Thus, when Celá Christós received news in late November 1617 that some very powerful heathen Gâlas[1] were coming to attack some lands that he has on the other side of the Nile, he summoned one of his captains called {[[f. 147]]} Ascader and told him that he should take his men over there at once while he gathered the rest together to follow behind him and, giving him his banner in front of many people, he strongly recommended to him that, if he had any encounter before he arrived, he should bear himself with the prudence, valour and courage that he expected of him. The captain took the banner and raised his sword, saying, 'With this I shall fight for my lord until I die, without turning my foot backwards. And if the enemy wounds me in the back and I escape from their hands, my lord must think no more of me and never see me again.'

On hearing this, Celá Christós said to him, 'It will avail you little if you fight for love of me: fight for the faith of Saint Peter that is taught by the Roman Church and then God will give you victory and all your affairs will prosper. And I too will do you many honours and favours. Do you not know how many He has done me, always bringing down all my enemies at my feet, since I began to follow and defend this holy faith? For He will do the same for you if with all your heart you follow it and fight for it.' The captain replied, 'My lord, you have reminded me of something very good: I say that I shall not fight save for the holy faith of Saint Peter and for it shall I die. And if I fight for any other reason, even if God gives me victory and destroys my enemies, may He take away <[f. 140/130]> my lord's desire to do me honours and favours because of it, and I shall not thank him for them, even if he does me any. I am very obliged to my lord for one thing, and I thank him for it more than for everything he has done for me, which is to have led me to know God and to understand what His holy faith is, so that I may be saved, for I did not know it before, nor did I know where I was going.' Then *Erás* Celá Christós said, 'If you fulfil with your deeds that which you promise with your words, to fight for the holy faith of Rome, everything will befall you very well. Go with the Lord's blessing.'

With that Captain Ascader took his leave. And the next day he received the blessing of a father, a companion of mine who is usually with *Erás* Celá Christós,[2] and he gave him a monk who was converted and reduced to our holy faith a long time ago to accompany him and direct him in the matters of his soul. He crossed the River Nile with great difficulty, since it was very swollen and raging, and after a few days he caught sight of the Gâlas, who were in large numbers and well armed, like men who had left their [land][3] solely for the

---

[1] Oromo peoples; see Glossary (Gâla/Galâ/Galla/Oromo).

[2] Father Francisco António de Angelis.

[3] The word for 'land' is missing in the manuscripts.

purpose {[f. 147v]} of fighting and destroying the Christians. He too put his men in order at once and gave battle, and he wrote to his lord of his success in the following words:

*Before we gave battle to the Gâlas, who came split into many squadrons, I commanded all my soldiers to worship the Holy Cross which was on the banner and to make every effort to fight, not out of greed to find spoils or for any other reason, but because these were cruel enemies of the Holy Cross and the law of Our Lord. Having encouraged them with this, we gave battle, bearing the banner of the Holy Cross before us. And I affirm before Our Lord God that it was neither through our spears nor through our bows and arrows but by the means and miracle of the Holy Cross that we achieved victory so easily that soon most of them were put to flight with such great fear that, leaving their women and children and all their cattle, they sought nothing else but to save their lives. Others, though at first they had come like ferocious lions, delivered themselves into our hands as if they were gentle lambs.*

At this time *Erás* Celá Christós was already on his way with a large army and, after crossing the River Nile, he joined up with this captain and went in search of the Gâlas that had escaped, who had already re-formed again, with many others joining them so resolute in fighting that they offered him a pitched battle, but with divine favour they were defeated and many were killed. The *erás* pursued them for {two} <eleven> days, causing great slaughter, capturing women and children and taking countless cattle, as he himself then wrote to me so that I might give thanks to God for all the many great mercies that He was doing him, and he attributed them all to his having received the doctrine and faith of the holy Roman Church and having defended it with such good heart, which he confesses and affirms publicly.[1]

<[f. 140v/130v]> The emperor also does a great deal, always seeking to accept our beliefs and to adjust his to them, without ever missing an opportunity to praise and declare them as we have taught them to him. Thus, one day in the palace when there were many great men and monks with him, including the most important one in Ethiopia, whom they call *ichegué*,[2] who is the head of the religion {[f. 148]} of *Abbá* Taquelá Haimanót, he said that he thought that those who claimed that the Holy Spirit proceeded only from the Father were not right, and that the doctrine of the Portuguese was the true one, stating that He proceeds from the Father and from the Son. {Everybody} <They> interrupted at once, saying that he should not {bring} <say> such a thing, because it was contrary to the true faith. He gave some reasons in proof of what he said, but they contested them all and presented others to counter them. Then the emperor said, 'Call Father Pedro Paez, and he will show you clearly that what I say is the truth.' One of them replied, 'Lord, he cannot show such a thing, nor give a reason that is not specious and that we do not demolish straight away.' The emperor said (as I was told later by a friend of mine who was present), 'Not only will you not demolish his reasons, but you will not even know how to respond to them.'

---

[1] See bk IV, end of ch. 19, vol. II below. The episode was recorded in the Chronicle of Susnëyos (Pereira, *Chronica de Susenyos*, II, pp. 191–200). The abbreviated histories place this episode in the sixth year of Susnëyos' reign (Foti, 'La Cronaca abbreviata dei Re d'Abissinia in un manoscritto di Dabra Berhan di Gondar', p. 112; Basset, *Études sur l'histoire d'Éthiopie*, pp. 128–9).

[2] See Glossary (ichegué/icheguê/*eččagé*).

I was at court at the time, as I usually {am} <was>, and so he had me called at once. When I {entered} <arrived>, he had me sit near him and asked whether the Holy Spirit proceeded only from the Father or whether He also proceeded from the Son.

I replied, 'Lord, He proceeds from the Father and from the Son, and this truth is declared by sixteen general councils and determined by an article of faith; it is clearly deduced from the {holy Gospel} <Gospels> and from Saint Paul, who says that the Holy Spirit is the Spirit of the Father and of the Son,[1] which is why all the holy doctors and even the books of Ethiopia teach it so.' A monk called *Abba* Marcá (who, as he was one of the oldest, and he thought he could answer best, spoke for everyone) said, 'The books of Ethiopia do not teach that the Holy Spirit proceeds from the Son, and one cannot say such a thing, which is contrary to our holy faith.' 'The principal book of Ethiopia', said I, 'is *Haimanót Abbó*' (which means 'Faith of the Fathers', because it is made of parts of homilies of Saints Athanasius, Basil, Chrysostom and other saints). 'This book says in many places that the Holy Spirit proceeds from the Father and from the Son.' The monk replied that there was not such a thing in all the *Haimanót Abbó*. When I asked them to bring the book, it came at once and I showed two places that I had already noted where it says 'proceeds from the Father and from the Son' and, in sixteen places, 'spirit of the Father and of the Son.' He replied, 'I have never seen such a thing before. This book is wrong. Bring another.' When it came and he found that it said 'proceeds from the Father' and the word 'and from the Son' had been scraped off, which is easy since the writing is <[f. 141/131]> on parchment, {[f. 148v]} he then said, 'This one is right.' I answered, 'At first it also used to say "and of the Son". This is where it has been scraped off.' The emperor said, 'That is true: *Azáx* Çadenguíl scraped it off. Bring another.' They brought five more and in all of them it said 'proceeds from the Father and from the Son.' Finally, a new book came which had 'proceeds from the Father' in all the places, and they all approved of it, saying that that one was right. I replied, 'They have recently copied this one from the one that has been scraped. The old ones are the true ones, which were copied from the books of the saints themselves.' The monk said, 'No, this one is right. Let all of them be corrected by it.' I answered, 'There can be no greater evil than to remove words from the books of the saints or to add to those that they say, in order that those who do this can show that they teach what they want, or so that their doctrine is not contrary to it. And since this is such a pernicious and serious matter, Saint John closed his Apocalypse by saying, "If any man shall add to these words, God shall add unto him the plagues written in this book. And if any man shall take away from the words of it, God shall take away his part out of the book of life, and out of the holy city, and from these things that are written in this book."[2] Then the emperor, showing annoyance, said, 'Nobody shall take words away from the books. Leave them as they were, for they are the books of the saints.' And so they all fell silent.

Seeing that they were not continuing {the conversation}, I said, 'Let us leave the *Haimanót Abbó* and move on to the Holy Gospel, for we shall find this truth clearly shown there too, because Christ himself, speaking of the Holy Spirit, says in Saint John, chapter 16, "he shall receive of mine, and shall shew it to you."[3] The Holy Spirit can take

---

[1] The writer was perhaps thinking of Matthew 10:20, John 16:14–15 (which he mentions several times) and Galatians 4:6.

[2] Apocalypse 22:18–19.

[3] John 16:14.

receive from the Son without receiving His essence. Therefore He received not only the essence of the Father, but also that of the Son.' The monk answered, 'When {Christ} <He> says "he shall receive of mine," He is speaking only of knowledge.' 'It is true', said I, 'that He is speaking of knowledge, but if the Spirit receives the Son's knowledge without receiving His essence, then He is not God but a creature.' He replied that they too had their explanations for this passage and with that he closed up, without giving any or wishing to respond. So I said, 'Then {[f. 149]} give me your response, Your Reverence, to what {Christ} Our Lord said, in the same chapter in Saint John and the next: "All things whatsoever the Father hath, are mine."[1] Thus, everything that the Father has the Son has, except the relationship of fatherhood. As the saints say, the Father has the attribute of being the origin of the Holy Spirit, so the Son also has that attribute, and therefore the Spirit proceeds not only from the Father but also from the Son.' He turned to the others and said, 'Do you not see, do you not see what a fallacy he takes from the Gospel?' I replied, 'Your Reverence, show me where the fallacy is. They are all words of the Gospel, from which one cannot take a fallacy.' <[f. 141v/131v]> 'That way', he said, 'the Holy Spirit had two fathers.' I replied, 'It does not follow, because the Holy Spirit does not proceed from the Father as being formally the Father, for then the Holy Spirit would be the Son, but from the Father as having a common essence with the Son, and so necessarily the Holy Spirit also proceeds from the Son.' He insisted that it was a fallacy and that there was no need to reply, but the others understood very well that he was saying so because he had no reply. I saw that, so I said, 'Since Your Reverence does not want to reply to my arguments, tell me how the Father begets the Son and how the Holy Spirit proceeds from the Father, for then I shall clearly show you that the Holy Spirit necessarily proceeds from the Son as well, or that there is no difference at all between Them and so They will not be three persons but two.'

Another monk said, 'Allow us to gather our monks together so that we can reply to that.' The emperor then intervened and said, 'That is a very good pretext. If the priest had said, "Allow me to gather my priests together so that we can reply," his excuse would have had some weight, because he is on his own. But there are so many of you and you still ask us to allow you to gather more? Reply, because that excuse is to no avail.' Another one, a close confidant of the emperor, said, 'We know these matters very well. Let the priest tell us, so that we can see how the Portuguese understand them.' To which I replied, 'Your Reverences have to reply because I asked first, and afterwards I shall reply to whatever you ask me.' But he insisted so much that I did not want them to think that I was making excuses so as not to show our beliefs or because I did not dare do so in front of them, {[f. 149v]} so I told them in the following words:

'Your Reverences know very well that, as Our Lord God is in every way perfect and blessed, He must necessarily understand and love, for we see that the most perfect thing that there is in us is understanding and love and in this we surpass the animals. And God can only have His glory and blessedness through understanding and loving Himself, because He did not gain one jot of glory from all the things that He created, nor would he lose any even if He annihilated them, just as a burning candle does not gain any light even if it lights many others, nor does it lose any when they are put out. Do you see, then, that as Our Lord God is in every way perfect He must necessarily understand? And because He

---

[1] John 16:15.

understands there must also be present in Him the thing that is understood and known, which is present in His mind as a most perfect portrait and drawing of this same thing. We see this clearly from experience because, when we sit and consider the trees and flowers, we have them so present that it hardly seems there is any difference between them and the image that we form inside ourselves. And if someone had the power to give being and life to the image that is inside his understanding, without doubt it would be a most perfect flower, or other thing contemplated. <[f. 142/132]> But even though our understanding is too weak to do that, at least it makes such a perfect and finished drawing of the thing it knows that there is no painter who can make such a perfect portrait with a brush as our understanding makes.

'Therefore God understands Himself, and in this understanding He makes a most perfect drawing of Himself. This drawing cannot be outside Him, because His portrait cannot be made perfectly in any created thing, for all things are finite and He is infinite. He gives being to this drawing and, as it is inside God, He gives it His own Godly being, and this act whereby God portrays Himself is called by the holy doctors begetting, and the drawing is called the Son, who is God like the Father, as infinite and eternal as {[f. 150]} He is, and this begetting is called eternal because one can never understand God to be not knowing and drawing Himself. In this act, God shows His riches and omnipotence, and in it He communicates to His Son all His greatness, His beauty, His wisdom, power and virtue, because He communicates into all His creatures only a drop of His infinite perfections. And not only does God understand Himself, but He must also necessarily love Himself, as I have said. The Father, then, on seeing the beauty, the goodness, the virtue and the riches in His Son whom He begot also as He is, as wise as He is and as mighty and omnipotent as He is, loves that Son whom He produced so much in His likeness. And the Son, also seeing all the greatnesses and treasures of the Father from whom He sees that all His infinite riches and goods come, necessarily loves His Father who begets Him. And this love, with which the Father loves the Son and the Son loves the Father, is love produced and is the person of the Holy Spirit. And just as God's understanding is infinite and begets the infinite Son, so God's {loving} <love> is infinite and mighty and produces an infinite and mighty love. These are the three persons that we say there are in God and there cannot be more than one single Son and one Holy Spirit, because in God there is no more than one understanding and one {loving} <love>. Your Reverences see here how, just as the Father produces the Holy Spirit, so the Son also produces Him, for it is the same love with which the Father loves the Son and the Son the Father. So on all points we must affirm and believe that the Holy Spirit proceeds from the Father and from the Son, because otherwise we would be unable to make any distinction between the Son and the Holy Spirit, and thus they would not be three persons but two.'

They listened very attentively to all this, and when I had finished they made no rejoinder to anything that I had said, but one of the great lords who was there came out with this ineptitude: 'So can Your Reverence tell us whether the darkness is a corporeal creature or not?' I answered, 'Lord, what does the darkness have to do with the Holy Spirit with whom we are dealing? {[f. 150v]} Your Lordship may say that it is a corporeal creature or that it is not, for little hangs on that.' He said, 'We wish to know what opinion Your Reverence has on this.' 'As for me', I replied, 'I do not think it is a corporeal creature, but just deprivation of light.' <[f. 142v/132v]> He said, 'Then that which the Jews affirm, that the darkness is a corporeal creature, is not true.' I replied that the authority of the

Jews was very weak and that not everything they affirmed was true, for they affirm that the Messiah has not yet come and that there is no Trinity of persons in God, and they hold as very certain many other things that are contrary to our holy faith. 'But, Your Lordship, listen to one of the reasons on which I base myself to say that the darkness is not a corporeal creature. If this room were closed up so that no light entered at all, this corporeal creature would be in it and, if it were opened up, it would suddenly be unmade. And every time burning candles were removed and placed here at night, that corporeal creature would be made and unmade, which does not seem possible in good philosophy.' Laughing, the emperor said, 'That is a fine corporeal creature that can be made and unmade so often and so easily!' Then the monk *Abbá* Marcá intervened saying, 'Why are we wasting time on something so unimportant as whether the darkness is a corporeal creature or not?' And with that the conversation ended and we all left.

A few days later, a cousin of the emperor called Belá Christós, who had well understood the truth of our beliefs, said, 'Your Reverence should not waste any opportunity to tell everybody how the Holy Spirit also proceeds from the Son, because, although many people used to hold it as certain that He only proceeded from the Father, they are now beginning to understand that He has to proceed from the Son as well.' And when I went to visit *Abbá* Marcá to see whether by speaking to him in private I might lead him out of that error, as I had led him out of others, as we shall see later, {[f. 151]} he showed me a place in the Nicene Council that they have, where it said, 'The Holy Spirit proceeds from the Father and not from the Son.' I said, 'There is no such thing in the Nicene Council, and they did not deal with this question of the Holy Spirit there, because that error did not yet exist, nor was it raised until a hundred years or more later, as can be seen in many authors; so this word 'and not from the Son' has been added.' He answered, 'That is true; they added it here in Ethiopia.' I showed him then what great evils resulted from adding words to the holy councils and other books that teach the true faith, and I explained to him at length how the Holy Spirit proceeds from the Father and from the Son, at which he was satisfied. And although he did not dare to publicly confess this truth for a long time, he now confesses and affirms it without anyone challenging him.

I might mention many other things from private conversations that I have had at times with some ecclesiastical and lay scholars who pertinaciously defend the idea that the Holy Spirit proceeds only from the Father, but what we have said will be enough to <[f. 143/133]> show how far Friar Luis de Urreta was mistaken in what he asserts, on page 416, in these words:

*This Catholic truth in which the Church believes, contrary to the Greeks, that the Holy Spirit proceeds from the Father and from the Son, is one that the Ethiopians believe, hold and profess with great fervour against the same Greeks, saying,* 'Spiritus Sanctus Paracletos Deus vivus, qui ex Patre et Filio procedit.'[1]

The author says this based on a protestation of faith that he claims some ambassadors from the Prester John made in the Florentine Council,[2] and he reports it on

---

[1] Urreta, *Historia de la Etiopia*, from bk II, ch. 3, p. 416 ('Holy Spirit Paraclete, the living God, who proceeds from the Father and from the Son'). Páez quotes this passage in Spanish.

[2] See Glossary (Council of Florence).

page 397.[1] But that protestation does not contradict what we have said, that the Prester John's Ethiopian vassals maintain that the Holy Spirit proceeds only from the Father, because, even if we concede that those who said they were the Prester John's ambassadors did not feign many of the things that are mentioned there in order to be well received by our people and to have their faith approved by them, as they readily do wherever they may be and as we have shown throughout Book 1 in those things that the Ethiopian João Balthesar put into the head {[f. 151v]} of that same author, and in the behaviour we have witnessed here in certain monks who have been to Rome, where they probably said that they professed the holy faith of the Roman Church but, after returning here, speak like the other monks of this land; even if we concede that that embassy was real and all that they professed was true, it does not follow that since then they have perfectly kept all the things that they protested there. The truth is that they have long held and still hold this heresy that the Holy Spirit proceeds only from the Father, and many others that we shall see later.

[1] Urreta, *Historia de la Etiopia*, bk II, ch. 2, entitled 'Of the protestation of the Faith that the Ambassadors of the Prester John made in his name and in that of all his empire in the Florentine Council, presided over by the Supreme Pontiff Eugene IV', pp. 394–403.

# CHAPTER III

## Which reports the errors that the Ethiopians maintain on the sacrosanct humanity of Jesus Christ Our Lord

The Prester John's Ethiopian vassals affirm that the human nature in Christ Our Lord is equal to the divine nature and that it is everywhere, and they say that, after the human nature is united with the divine person, it cannot be said that in Christ there are two natures, but rather one nature {one will and one begetting}. And they hold Dioscorus, who taught these great errors, to be a saint and, as such, they make a great feast for him every year, and as for Saint Leo the Pope, because he says that there are two natures in Christ, without being mixed, confused or separated, {two in all [...]}, they hold him in great abhorrence and call him names that are very alien to Christian people.[1] So when I was talking to an old monk about him, I said he had spoken of this matter through the mouth of Saint Paul and that he had been a most saintly man; to which he replied with extraordinary impatience at hearing this, 'He was nothing but a Satan.' I am not greatly surprised that they abhor him so much, since <[f. 143v/133v]> the doctrine of their books, which they hold to be the true faith, {incites} <excites> them to that, because, as we said in chapter 24 of the first book, they have added to the homilies of saints that they have in the book that they call *Haimanót Abbó* many things from heretical patriarchs {[f. 152]} of Alexandria, and one of them, who is called Theodoseós, says these words in chapter 2: 'We do not separate, like that accursed enemy Leo, who separated Him who was not separated and said two natures, two intents and two works in one Christ.' And a little further on, he again says, 'This accursed and treacherous Leo said two natures and two works; and in saying one person, in this the accursed wished to conceal his error, in saying one person.' And another, whom they call Cenutheós, says this: 'Those who speak and think, like the low, dirty, Jewish, bad council of those who gathered in Chalcedon, at which was Leo who has no law, a ferocious wolf, thief, destroyer of souls.' And another called Philatheós also says, 'They do not believe, like the Jewish council of those who gathered in Chalcedon and the book of treason of Leo the liar.'[2]

In addition to that, in a book that they call *Mazaguébt Haimanót*, which means 'Treasury of the Faith', they say the following of the Council of Chalcedon, because it declared as faith the doctrine of Saint Leo on the two natures, wills and operations in Christ Our Lord and condemned Dioscorus: 'There gathered together 630 foolish

---

[1] See Glossary (Dioscorus I; Leo I, Pope).
[2] See Glossary (*Haimanót Abbô/Hāymānota Abbaw*).

321

masters, with vanity and pride, wishing to be double the number of the 318 just men of the faith.'[1] And a little further on it says:

*They took out a word from Nestorius, who put two persons in Christ, one of the son of Mary and the other of the son of God, and they said that by their union they formed one person. They left this because of Father Cyril's excommunication[2] and composed it from the words of Father Cyril and the words of Nestorius, and so they said Christ one person, two wills, two natures, two intents, of the Godhead and of the manhood. They said that the Godhead performs work of Godhead, and the manhood work of manhood, by two paths: one works wonders and the other suffers infirmities, and therefore the manhood is less than the Godhead.*[3]

Up to here are words from that book.

I could mention many other similar things from their books, which I shall leave out for brevity's sake. It will be enough to recount, {[f. 152v]} in confirmation of my intention, what I went through with the principal scholars of Ethiopia, both ecclesiastical and lay, in some general disputations that I had with them over many days in June 1604 in the presence of Emperor Za Denguîl[4] and many lords, when he was in a land that they call Ondegué, beside the great lake that divides the kingdom of Gojam from that of Dambiá. In them we dealt with almost all the errors that there are in Ethiopia, and <[f. 144/134]> principally these of which we are speaking, which were among the first that they brought up. The emperor had me summoned to his palace for this purpose; he made me sit near him and said that he would like to hear something about the matters on which the Ethiopians had controversy with the Portuguese, to see whether it was true that there was such a great difference as they said. I replied that they could ask what they wanted, and I would tell them how we understood it. At once a monk said, 'We have a great difference in many things, particularly in that they say that there are two natures in Christ and that the human nature is not equal to the divine.' I replied that yes, we said that, and that was the Catholic faith, because leaving aside what Saint Paul says in many places, that God shed His blood for the Church, that He redeemed us with His precious blood, in which he clearly shows that there are two natures in Christ, because God, as God, has no blood; He is spirit. Therefore, He who is God and shed blood must necessarily have two natures. Also, in his Epistle to the Romans, chapter 8, he says that God spared not even His own Son, but delivered Him up for us all,[5] and later, in chapter 9, that Christ Our Lord is of Jewish parents according to the flesh, and that He is also God over all things.[6] How much more clearly could Saint Paul say that Christ Our Lord has divine and human nature? Saint John teaches the same in his first Epistle, in very clear words.[7] But leaving aside all

[1] See Glossary (Council of Chalcedon; and *Mazaguêbt Haimanôt/Mazgaba Hāymānot*).

[2] See Glossary (Nestor/Nestorius; and Cyril of Alexandria).

[3] See Cerulli, *Scritti teologici etiopici*, p. 77. This passage from the *Mazgaba Hāymānot* was repeated by Almeida ('Historia de Ethiopia a alta', Beccari, *RÆSOI*, 5, pp. 126–7). Páez translated the same excerpt, with slight variations, in bk I, ch. 11, p. 152, above.

[4] Guerreiro, *Relação annual*, III, f. 167/p. 124). See bk IV, ch. 6, vol. II below.

[5] Romans, 8:32.

[6] Romans, 9:4–5.

[7] 1 John 4:9–10 and 13–15.

that, let us go to the Holy Gospel, which is the source from which they took this truth to proclaim to the world. {[f. 153]} When Christ Our Lord was speaking with Nicodemus, as Saint John recounts in chapter 3, he said to him, 'And no man hath ascended into heaven, but he that descended from heaven, the Son of man who is in heaven,'[1] in which He clearly showed that He has two natures, for this one that was speaking and knew and said that He was the son of man was not then in heaven but on earth with Nicodemus, nor was He God, but man; because God cannot be seen or touched with the bodily senses, nor had He descended from heaven, but had been born on earth of the Virgin Our Lady, Luke 2. And despite all this, He Himself affirmed that He had descended from heaven and that then, when He was speaking on earth, He was in heaven. Therefore, Christ Our Lord had another nature, apart from the human one, according to which He could be in heaven when in the human nature He was on earth. And later, in chapter 9, Saint John says that when Christ Our Lord found that man who had been blind from birth to whom He had shortly before given sight, He asked him, 'Dost thou believe in the Son of God?' He answered, and said, 'Who is he, Lord, that I may believe in him?' And Jesus said to him, 'Thou hast both seen him; and it is he that talketh with thee.' The man who had been blind said, 'I believe, Lord.' And falling down, he adored him.[2] How much more clearly could Christ Our Lord show that He has two natures, since the one whom the blind man after receiving his sight saw, heard and adored says that He is at the same time the Son of God?

<[f. 144v/134v]> One of the laymen replied to this, 'After the Resurrection, only one nature was left.' 'Which of them?' I said. 'For if one was lost, it would have to be the human, but that is against the Holy Gospel. Otherwise, tell me, who was it that on the eighth day after the Resurrection was among the disciples and told Thomas to be not faithless? Whose were those wounds that He showed to him and offered him to touch? For the Godhead cannot be seen by bodily eyes or be touched by hands or have wounds; therefore, that which He offered him to touch and which he saw was not the Godhead but the flesh; and even so that very one whom he could see confessed to being God and his Lord, John 20.[3] How much more clearly can we be shown that Christ Our Lord after the Resurrection had two natures, divine and human? Apart from that, who was it that, according to Saint Luke in {[f. 153v]} his last chapter, appeared to the disciples after His Resurrection and, when they were troubled thinking that it was a spirit, said to them, "*Quid turbati estis, et cogitationes ascendunt in* {*corda vestra*} <*cordibus vestris*>?[4] See my hands and feet, that it is I myself; handle, and see: for a spirit hath not flesh and bones, as you see me to have."[5] Therefore, there can be no doubt that He truly had human nature, and you do not deny the divine either. You should know that the main reason why, after the Resurrection, Christ Our Lord stayed on earth for forty days, eating and drinking, conversing and interacting with his disciples, was to show that He truly had human nature for them to understand that that very person whom they had seen crucified and dead had become alive again.'

---

[1] John 3:13.
[2] John 9:35–8.
[3] John 20:25, 27, 28.
[4] 'Why are you troubled, and why do thoughts arise in your hearts?' The Latin Vulgate Bible has '*corda vestra*'.
[5] Luke, 24: 38–9.

At that he did not reply to me, but began to speak to the others about the interpretation of these passages. I said to him, 'These are all clear words from the Gospel.
What interpretation have they? But to cut our conversation short, answer me just this: is
Christ Our Lord today perfect God and perfect man or not?' He did not want to answer,
but tried to mix in other things, until the emperor said to him, 'Why do you not answer?
Can you deny that Christ is perfect God and perfect man?' He then answered that it
could not be denied. 'Therefore', said I, 'He has perfect divine nature and perfect human
nature.' {Another answered,} 'We do not deny that in Christ there is divine nature and
human nature, but after they were joined, it cannot be said that they are two, but one.' I
replied that that was to say that they are two and that they are not two. 'Since in Christ
there truly is divine nature and human nature, which are distinct, why can it not be said
that there are two? If you mean to say that of Christ Our Lord one cannot say two, but
one, that is very true, because {[f. 154]} there is only one single person, and this is what
Saint John mainly intends <[f. 145/135]> to show in his first Epistle, but in this one
Christ are two most perfect natures, divine and human.' He repeated that the natures
cannot be said to be two, but one, after they were united and became equal. I said that on
account of the union they did not stop being two perfect and distinct natures and that I
was very surprised that they claimed that these two natures were equal, for the Gospel
taught us the opposite, and Saint Athanasius (whose doctrine they told me they
followed) expressly declared it in his *Symbol*, saying that Our Lord Jesus Christ is equal to
the Father in Godhead and less than the Father in manhood. One of them responded,
'What false witness you bear to Saint Athanasius!' I told him to read his *Symbol* carefully
and he would find those very words in it, but that we did not need the authority of Saint
Athanasius, where that of Christ Our Lord was so explicit, for He says in a passage in
Saint John, chapter 10, that He is equal to his eternal Father and He and the Father are
one,[1] and in another, in chapter 14, that the Father is greater than He,[2] in which He
teaches us that He has divine nature, according to which he is equal to the Father, and
human nature, according to which He is less than He. He answered that, when He said
that He was less than the Father, he spoke out of humility, because, according to his
manhood, He was also equal to Him, as Saint Mark manifested in his last chapter, saying
that when He went up to heaven, He sat on His right hand,[3] which is the same as saying
that He is equal to Him, and He did not sit as God, but as man. 'Christ Our Lord would
not mislead us out of humility', I said. 'He declares in affirmative words that He is less
than the Father, and He as man cannot be equal to Him, because there are many things in
God that it would be contradictory to apply to the creature, {[f. 154v]} such as His being
not created, a pure act, infinite and other similar things. In addition, many things
contrary to the Holy Scripture would follow, such as having in the world two omnipotent, immense and infinite beings, the Godhead and the manhood of Christ Our Lord.
Apart from that, Saint John and Saint Paul clearly teach us that, as man, He is less than
the Father, because Saint John, in his first Epistle, chapter 2, says that He is our advocate
with the Father,[4] and Saint Paul, in Romans 8, affirms that He is at God's right hand and

---

[1] John 10:30.
[2] John 14:28.
[3] Mark 16:19.
[4] I John 2:1.

intercedes for us.[1] If He were equal, He could not be an advocate or intercede. And in 1 Corinthians, chapter 15, he says that, when the Father has subdued all things unto the Son (which will be on the Day of Judgment), even then the Son shall be subject to the Father.'[2]

They began to interpret these passages, but when the emperor saw that they were not making any headway he interrupted them and asked me how that passage in Saint Mark was understood, because sitting on God the Father's right hand seemed to denote being equal to Him. I replied that it only meant that He as <[f. 145v/135v]> God has the same glory, honour and power as the Father, and to Him as man the Father Himself gave more glory, more honour and more power than to all the saints and angels. 'But even if we said that sitting at His right hand meant reigning, judging and governing all things with equal power and honour, it does not follow that the human nature is equal to the divine, because this was not given to the human nature in itself, but within the divine person, and so one cannot say that the human nature in itself is sitting on the Father's right hand, but that it is the human nature of that divine person who is sitting on God the Father's right hand. As in the Incarnation, just because God was made flesh, manhood was not then God, but the manhood of God; but taking it all together, we can concretely say this man is God and is sitting on God the Father's right hand. {[f. 155]} I shall explain better by means of a comparison: when Your Majesty sits on your throne to judge and govern your empire, you wear your imperial robe, but even so one cannot say that the robe is sitting and is judging and governing, but that it is the robe of Your Majesty, who is sitting, judging and governing.'

'I have enjoyed listening to you very much', said the emperor. 'That is enough for today.' He rose, because it was already very late, and everybody left, leaving only a close confidant of his called Lac Mariam and a very scholarly monk called *Abbá* Zá Manoel and myself. And in front of them the emperor said to me, 'I must be simple, because I do not understand very well that the creature cannot be equal to the Creator. However, I should like you to show me that last passage that you quoted from Saint Paul.' I said where it was, and the monk at once showed it in his book, and it said, 'When all things are subject to him, then it will be seen that the Son is less than the Father', because in some of their books this is added. 'What need have we of more reasons', said the emperor, 'when Saint Paul speaks so clearly? Go away and rest.'

The following day, the emperor commanded that all the scholars should gather again and among the first things that they asked was whether there were two wills in Christ Our Lord. When I answered that there were, one of them laughed as if he had heard some very great absurdity. I told him that he had confessed that very thing the previous day, when they conceded to me that Christ is perfect God and perfect man, a very certain truth that could not be so if He did not have both divine will and human will together, for the will is such a great perfection that nobody can be perfect without it, and the Lord Himself saw fit to remove our doubts by teaching us in the Gospel in clear words that He has both divine and human will, because in chapter 6 of Saint John He says, 'I came down from heaven, not to do My own will, but the will of Him that sent Me'; and in Saint Matthew

---

[1] Romans 8:34.
[2] 1 Corinthians 15:28.
[3] John 6:38.

26,[1] Saint Mark 14,[2] {[f. 155v]} <[f. 146/136]> and Luke 22[3] He says, 'Father, if Thou wilt, remove this chalice from Me: but yet not My will, but Thine be done.' How much more clearly could He tell us that He has human will with which He complied and submitted to His eternal Father's will, which is the same will that He has as God? He replied that here 'will' was understood to mean natural affection. 'It cannot be understood', said I, 'to mean anything but "will" itself, because just as He speaks specifically of the will of the Father, saying that He came to do the will of Him that sent Him, and that the will of the Father be done, so He also speaks specifically of the human will, saying, "I came down from heaven, not to do My own will, but the will of Him that sent Me."' 'It would be a fine thing', he said, 'for us to put two wills in Christ, so that He might will two contrary things at once.' I replied that I did not think that the divine will and the human will in Christ were like his will and mine, by which he could will one thing and I something contrary, but that they were very united and concordant and the human will always subjected itself to the divine and obeyed it in everything, as Saint Paul explains very well in Philippians 2,[4] saying that He humbled himself, becoming obedient unto death, even to death on the cross.

During all this conversation, which was long because they mixed in many inapposite things, the emperor paid close attention and formed a good idea of the truth, as he had the previous day as regards there being two natures in Christ Our Lord, and so he said that we should pass on to something else, as it was not necessary to dispute any further on this. 'If Your Majesty will give leave, I should like them to tell me just this, whether Christ Our Lord has a perfect rational soul.' One of them replied that He had a most perfect one. 'Well, one of the most perfect things that the rational soul has', said I, 'is the will, to the extent that it is the will that chooses or rejects the good {or} <and> evil that the understanding represents to it; therefore the soul of Christ Our Lord has a will, for without one it would not be perfect. Moreover, when Our Lord God said, 'Let us make man to our image and likeness', Genesis 1,[5] He made man like Him in soul, placing in it (which is a single substance) three inseparable powers, which are understanding, will and memory, {[f. 156]} just as He being a single, most simple substance has three persons, those of the Father, the Son and the Holy Spirit. You also concede that in Christ Our Lord there is divine will, and therefore you must necessarily confess that in Him there are two wills, divine and human, but very united together, as I have already said.' He replied that if they were so united that the human always followed that which the divine willed, they were no more than a single will. 'You infer very badly', I said, 'because even if this union is so great and the human will follows that which the divine one wills, even so it does not lose its being, just as, because you may unite and subject your will to that of the emperor, even so it does not lose its being, which is as perfect after it was subjected as it was before.' The emperor said that we were to speak no more on the matter, and so we went on to deal with other errors that they have regarding rational souls, which I shall report later in their place.

<[f. 146v/136v]> All that we have said shows quite clearly how little information Friar Luis de Urreta had about these things, for he defends the Ethiopians on page 424, saying,

---

[1] Matthew 26:39.
[2] Mark 14:36.
[3] Luke 22:42.
[4] Philippians 2:6–8.
[5] Genesis 1:26.

'The Ethiopians, as Catholic Christians obedient to the sacred councils and in particular the Chalcedonian Council, confess and believe in two perfect, incommutable, distinct natures, divine and human.'[1] But so that one may see even better how far the Ethiopians are from this, I shall tell in the next chapter what happened in years past to Emperor Seltan Sagued, who is alive today, for wanting to make his people receive this Catholic truth, that in Christ Our Lord there are two most perfect natures, divine and human. I am sure that the reader will like to see this, even though it is long, because, apart from its being a delightful story, he will find no little opportunity to praise Our Lord for the great mercies that He has granted to this emperor and to *Eráz* Celá Christós, his brother, sometimes delivering them from death and, what is more, giving them knowledge of His holy faith, and he will beseech the Father to grant this greatest of the mercies that He did him also {[f. 156v]} to all the others of that empire, enlightening their understandings, so that they may put aside their errors and submit to His holy Church.

[1] Urreta, *Historia de la Etiopia*, bk II, ch. 4, entitled, 'En el qual se prosigue la defensa de los etiopes quanto a los articulos de la fe, que pertenecem a la humanidad santa de nuestro redemptor Jesu Christo, en los quales tienen la misma fe de la Iglesia romana, si los errores que muchos los han impuesto' ['Continuing the defence of the Ethiopians as regards the articles of the faith, which pertain to the holy manhood of our Redeemer Jesus Christ, in which they have the very faith of the Roman Church, without the errors that many have imputed to them'], pp. 422–34.

# CHAPTER IV

## Continuing the proof that the Ethiopians deny two natures in Christ Our Lord

Even though certain monks and great men learnt the truth of our holy faith in the disputations that I had with the scholars in the presence of Emperor Za Denguil, nevertheless, when others later realized that the emperor had received the faith, they stirred up the people and killed him, as we shall say later in book 4.[1] Therefore those monks and great men did not dare speak in public about it, although they communicated with me in secret. But after Emperor Seltan Sagued took possession of the empire, he greatly desired to know the basis of the controversies that we have with them, and so sometimes he asked me when he was alone, and other times he had other monks whom he trusted ask me in his presence, and it pleased Christ Our Lord that in this way he came to understand our beliefs well. When discussing them with Celá Christós, his brother, he told him that they appeared very good to him and that everything we said we proved with the Scripture. He replied, 'Lord, there is no need to listen to their things, which are so different from ours that we cannot accept them in any way whatsoever.' The emperor said, 'Do not fail to listen to them, because they are not as our monks say, and pay very careful attention if you hear anything contrary to the Scripture.' From that time on, he began to question me in detail, and he did the same with any of the other fathers that he found, more out of curiosity <[f. 147/137]> to see whether there was anything to seize on in order to mock our beliefs rather than to adopt them. But on finding them so consistent with reason and the Holy Scripture, and seeing that we all taught one and the same thing, he clearly understood {[f. 157]} that the doctrine of the Roman Church was the true one and so he determined to follow it and to die for it. Therefore he told the emperor that previously he had been very mistaken, but that there was no doubt that the faith we taught was the true one, at which the emperor was very pleased. He then met a cousin of his, who was called *Abeithum* Bela Christós, whom everyone held to be an oracle in matters of scholarship, even though he was a married man. And in truth, in curiosity and continual study he could compete with many of the scholars in our lands. This man, having also understood the truth of our holy faith, told the emperor the same as his brother had told him, and he began to speak of this with other scholars, and so the news spread that he and the emperor's brother approved of our doctrine.

When the monks who were on our side in secret heard in this way that they had such great lords in support, they too began to speak without fear and said to the emperor that

[1] See bk IV, ch. 9, vol. II below.

he should command the scholars that were at court to gather in his presence and that they would show them clearly through the Scripture that there are two natures in Christ, divine and human, without being mixed or confused. The emperor was very pleased to hear this and at once commanded that they should all gather in his palace on a certain day, which they did, at a time when a father and I chanced to be with the emperor. He made a speech to them in very good, well-chosen words, in which in brief he told them that he had heard that there were two very different faiths among them, only one of which could be the true faith, and that, among other things, some told him that there were two natures in Christ and others that there was only one. He wished to know the truth of this, so as to make everyone follow it uniformly, for it was not good that there should be such a great difference in matters of faith. They all replied that this was a very important and necessary thing.

As they then began to debate the question, those who were {[f. 157v]} on our side proved their opponents wrong through the Scripture and reasons based on it, so that they could not reply save with ridiculous things. One of them, seeing himself in a very tight spot, said, 'I shall explain myself through a simile: just as when they place iron in the fire it becomes so alight and fiery that one cannot say that there are two natures there, but just one, so too, after the divine nature united to itself the human one, they became such that one cannot say that they are two natures, but one.' The emperor's brother replied laughing, 'Your simile is very pertinent for proving our intent.' And a monk called <[f. 147v/137v]> Marcá said, 'By that you have declared what we say, that there are two natures in Christ because, when the divine nature united to itself the human one, the latter did not lose its being, just as the iron when it unites with the fire does not lose its nature. Otherwise, tell me, what is it that weighs there, the iron or the fire? What is it that the hammer strikes, the iron or the fire?' They spent most of the day on these things and rose without having finally settled on anything.

They met two or three more times afterwards, and the opponents were {so} proved wrong that they came to confess two natures in Christ, though believing more with the mouth than the heart, as was seen later. Only one of the monks there showed his obstinacy the whole time, affirming that in Christ there was no more than one nature, so the emperor delivered him to others so that they could show him the truth more slowly, and he commanded that it be proclaimed that thenceforth, on pain of death, nobody should say that there was only one nature in Christ, but rather two very perfect ones, divine and human. Another day, when I was with the emperor, they brought the obstinate monk. And *Abbá* Marcá said to him, 'Have you now understood the truth of what we say? Why do you dispute something that is so clear in the Scripture?' He said some things in reply, in which {[f. 158]} it seemed that he meant that he had now understood that there were two natures in Christ. But before he had finished explaining, he suddenly became so ashen that, black as he was, his face turned white, and he began to dishonour *Abbá* Marcá. The latter then said to the emperor, 'Lord, how can this man be allowed to dishonour me in front of Your Majesty? May the emperor command that justice be done for me.' He then appointed judges for him, and one ruled that he deserved death for being so intemperate in front of the emperor; two others said that he was an ignorant man and it was enough to flog him, and the emperor approved of this. And so they gave him many good lashes in the palace compound in front of many people. Even though the punishment was for the dishonour that he had uttered and his insolence before the emperor, most people thought that it was because he had affirmed that there was only one nature in Christ, and so they were frightened, fearing that if the emperor were angered he would also command that the proclamation he had made be carried out.

At this time, their patriarch was far away in other lands. When he later came to court, those monks who had earlier confessed to two natures in Christ, because they had been proved wrong, went to him straight away and told him that they had been forced to say that but, as he was their head, he should bring back their faith. Other great men also urged him to do so in secret, and offered him every favour and help. He therefore went to the emperor and showed that he was very offended that anything should be decided in matters of faith without his being present. The emperor replied that he had only wanted to find out the truth in order to avoid a schism but, if he thought that <[f. 148/138]> what had been settled was not right, he would have them all gather once more and debate the question anew. The patriarch said that that was necessary, and indicated the day on which, at the emperor's command, they all gathered before him in the palace. As {[f. 158v]} those who were on our side began to put forward their arguments and bring to bear passages from the Scripture, the patriarch saw that he could not respond, stood up and said that he was excommunicating all those who affirmed that there were two natures in Christ. The emperor's cousin, *Abeithum* Bela Christós, said, 'Matters of faith are not determined in this way, but by first looking very carefully at what the saints say and what the Holy Scriptures teach. Your Lordship should not be so hasty in matters of such {great} importance; hear our reasons and then, with mature counsel, you will decide what you think should be followed.' The emperor also told him to sit down and said that both sides should calmly put forward their doubts and the reasons on which they were based, the better to be able to declare the truth. He sat down then and, after many disputations, as he could not reply to the passages in the Scripture that they put to him, he came to concede that there {are} <were> two natures in Christ Our Lord. Thus the emperor again commanded that a proclamation be issued, saying that the books had been examined again and they had found as before, that there {are} <were> two most perfect natures in Christ, and so thenceforth nobody should teach the contrary, on pain of death.

The matter did not end with all these proclamations; instead they secretly sought ways to undo what they had settled and to say that there was no more than one nature in Christ; the patriarch, particularly, was furious, since he had not said that there are two natures in Christ from his heart, but only because he could not reply to the passages in the Scripture. Knowing full well that all these things were due to us, since we had taught them to the emperor and the others who defended them, he decided to close all doors to us, so that nobody could discuss them with us. With that in mind, he waited {[f. 159]} for a day when there was a large gathering of people in a large church that stands on the right in the palace compound. Coming out to the door, because there were many people outside, he called for their attention and had a kind of standard raised, and he said that by the power he had from Saint Peter and Saint Paul he excommunicated anyone who took the faith of the Portuguese or entered their churches or spoke to them about matters of faith. There happened to be a Portuguese there, and a monk who was on our side went up to him and made fun of his excommunication, saying, 'Portuguese, tell this *abuna* of ours[1] that he should excommunicate by the power he derives from Dioscorus, and he should leave the

---

[1] The expression '*abuna* of ours' is redundant, since the suffix '*-na*' already denotes the possessive 'our'.

power of Saint Peter and Saint Paul, which lies in Rome.' The Portuguese told me what was happening at once, <[f. 148v/138v]>, since I too was at court. The next day I went to the emperor and said to him, 'Your Majesty should see what the patriarch is doing to us. Yesterday he pronounced excommunication in front of the palace, like that.' The emperor replied, 'Do not worry about that, Your Reverence; I shall deal with it.' He at once commanded a great man who was there to go to the palace magistrates (who are responsible for having the emperor's orders proclaimed) and tell them to issue a proclamation that anyone who wished to join the faith of the Portuguese could do so publicly. He went, but they replied that they could not issue such a proclamation without first hearing it from the emperor's own mouth, because the patriarch had pronounced excommunication not only against those who took the faith of the Portuguese but against those who entered their churches. I was still with the emperor when this reply came back, and he was very angry and told them to issue the proclamation at once as they were commanded, for they did not need to hear it from his own mouth. They did so, but much against their will, because they too privately believed that there was only one nature in Christ.

The {[f. 159v]} patriarch and those on his side were incensed by this proclamation; they were so furious that they could not conceal it, but they waited for the right moment to vomit the poison that they were brewing in their hearts. It came when the emperor went with an army against some heathens that had rebelled and, even though many of them had submitted to him at once, he stayed to overwinter near them in a land called Achafér, so as to leave things more settled.[1] In the meantime, they tried to persuade the patriarch to lay excommunication on anyone who said that there were two natures in Christ and, taking no heed of the emperor, he did so, because he had many great men on his side, including one of the emperor's brothers called Iemana Christós, who at that time was very powerful, because he had been made *erás* and thus everyone depended on him so much that they did not dare to go against him in anything, least of all in his saying that there was one single nature in Christ, because they too held it to be the true faith. When the emperor heard this, he was very offended and wrote to the patriarch at once asking how he could do that, since he had previously declared in his presence, together with so many monks and scholars, that there were two natures in Christ, and he had even laid excommunication on anyone who said there was just one. If he had found something new, he should tell him, so that the monks and scholars could meet once again to examine it, before undoing that which they had declared after so much counsel. The patriarch replied that he should pay careful attention to the beliefs of the Portuguese priests, because they were like those who offer a drink of sugar mixed with deadly poison in a golden chalice. The emperor wrote back that he was not asking him about that, but how, without counsel, he had changed that which <[f. 149/139]> they had settled after so much counsel, and that he should reply to the point, for it was so important, because matters of faith should not be changed in that way. {[f. 160]} But he refused to answer and to give up what he was doing together with some monks and lay great men, which was to try to incite those present, by means of highly embellished words, and those absent, by means of letters, to revolt against the emperor and his brother Celá Christós, saying that they were abandoning their ancient faith and taking that of the Portuguese.

---

[1] See bk IV, ch. 19, vol. II below; see also Pereira, *Chronica de Susenyos*, ch. 33 (Ethiopic text).

One of those to whom they wrote, among others, was the viceroy of Tigre; even though he was the emperor's son-in-law, those things alarmed him so much that he joined their side at once and, very angrily, he resolved to persecute us, since he understood that everything derived from us. He therefore commanded that they should seize the property of everyone who had joined our faith, not only in our time but also in that of the former fathers, sparing not even the property of women who were married to Portuguese, threatening them that if they did not return to their faith, he would have their ears {and noses} cut off. And to trouble us further, he entrusted the enforcement of this to some men who were very much against us, who took such a good opportunity to show the great hatred that they had for us. They committed many cruelties in seizing the property, even leaving honourable women naked, in this way paying us back for the many good deeds we had always done them, by helping them in their needs and tribulations with much charity and not a little trouble. But our followers suffered all these robberies and tribulations and inhumanities with great patience and joy, determined to offer to the knife not only their ears and noses, with which the viceroy wished to frighten them, but even their necks, rather than fail by a jot in the faith of that Lord in whom they had placed their hopes.

A father who {[f. 160v]} was in Tigré[1] wrote to me at once about all these things, and it was at the same time that the emperor had sent word to me that, as soon as the winter permitted (for it was very bad at the time), I should go to meet him. Therefore, even though it was raining heavily, I set off without waiting any longer. When I arrived he welcomed me with great joy, because he was looking forward to my arrival even though he was not obliging me to go because of the winter, and he told me what he had written to the patriarch and what he had replied.

I too told him what was happening in Tigré and said how badly the viceroy was repaying the Portuguese for what their forefathers had done in Ethiopia, for he was ordering that even the property of their wives should be seized, even if they were local women. He showed such great sorrow to hear this that his eyes brimmed with tears, and he said, 'I know very well whence all these things are coming and who has written to the viceroy to encumber us, as is his custom. <[f. 149v/139v]> They stirred up the people against Emperor Za Denguil, my brother', (for he calls him thus, although he was just a cousin) 'by saying that he had abandoned his faith and taken that of the Portuguese, and so they killed him. Now they want to do the same to me. If God has given him leave, may His will be done, and if not, there is nothing they can do to me. As for the viceroy, I shall command him not to interfere again in matters of faith and to return at once all the property he has seized, because otherwise people will be very angry later, and he has certainly made me very angry by behaving in this fashion towards the Portuguese.' I kissed his hand for the favour and told him that his enemies would not prevail, because Our Lord had clearly shown that he had chosen him to do Him a great service, which was to reduce this empire, for with very little effort on his part He had given into his hands thirteen rebels {[f. 161]} who had so far risen up strongly in different places, each one seeking the empire, as well as victory over many other enemies, and he should be sure that God would help him in such an important matter and that, through it, He would make him prosper and would perpetuate the empire in his descendants. And I told him how it had come about

---

[1] Father Lourenço Romano. Páez refers to the same letter in another one that he wrote in July 1614 (Beccari, *RÆSOI*, 11, p. 321).

that the House of Austria had given rise to so many kings, but that matters in the service of God always had difficulties and contradictions in the beginning, and the devil would certainly bring many to bear on this matter that the emperor had begun, because he could see the great harm that it would do to him. But he should not be angry, because God would overcome them all and raise up the truth, at the same time honouring those who defended it. To that he replied that, once he had fully understood the truth, he had grown very calm in his heart and determined to defend it, and that, however adverse things might be, he would strive until his death to introduce the holy faith of Rome into his empire. He then wrote to the viceroy of Tigré that he was very surprised that, although he knew that the Portuguese fathers were his close friends, he should treat them in that manner, and that he should not interfere again in matters of faith, and that he should at once return all the property he had seized. And so that he should not try to delay matters, he sent the letter by a servant of his, but even so there was no lack of excuses for him not to be sent back.

Another day, when I was not present, some of our friends[1] said to the emperor that there were many murmurs in the camp because he was favouring the things of the Portuguese <and their> faith so much that many people were stirring against him. He answered, 'That is of little importance, because whatever they can do cannot go beyond death. That is something we cannot escape, for tomorrow or the next day it will {necessarily} come to all of us; hence, if necessary, let us die for the truth straight away.' And turning to a priest who understood our beliefs well and who already confessed <[f. 150/140]> with us, he said to him, {[f. 161v]} 'Why do you not speak freely of what you know? Are you afraid?' 'Yes, Lord', he answered, 'I am afraid of these people, because they are troublesome.' The emperor said, 'Do not be afraid. Speak out publicly; those who want to will make good use of it and, as for those who do not, it will be their fault. Do not keep it to yourself.'

When the emperor saw that the patriarch did not reply, he wrote to him again to come to him at the end of winter. And he commanded that all the superiors of monasteries and the scholars in the neighbouring kingdoms of Gojam, Begmederi and Dambeá should also go at the same time, so that they could finally determine the matters of faith. At that, the common people became even more agitated; they were saying that, since the emperor did not want to accept what the patriarch ordered, everyone should stand together and say as they had done before that there was only one nature in Christ, and die for it. They also said that some young monks were taking up sword and shield and were practising, saying that they would die for their ancient faith. When he heard this, Iemana Christós, the emperor's brother, who was in the kingdom of Begmederi, wrote to him to persuade him with many reasons that he should not go ahead with the matters of faith, but that he should command everyone to follow the patriarch's doctrine, or he would lose his empire. His mother too, who was in another part, wrote to him in the same vein, because the monks had put it into her head that he and his brother Celá Christós would die if they insisted on wanting to introduce the faith of the Portuguese.

The emperor was very sad that they should write to him in this way, and with his brother's letter in his hand he said in my presence, very angrily, that what had begun must be concluded at once, without waiting any longer, and he summoned {[f. 162]} Celá

---

[1] A note in the margin of BPB, MS 778, says 'enemies'.

Christós, who was nearby in the kingdom of Gojam. He hurried back, bringing with him the principal monks of that kingdom, who were all determined to die for our holy faith, at which the emperor was overjoyed. He took counsel with them as to what they should do, and they told him that he should appear indifferent to both sides, affirming that all he wanted was for the truth to be declared so that he could make everyone follow it, and that it was up to them, the scholars to declare it, and so they would clearly show through the Scriptures that there are two natures in Christ. On leaving the palace they all gathered in the house of the emperor's cousin, *Abeit Hum* Bela Christós, and they summoned me and proposed the authorities and reasons that they thought their opponents would use, which were ridiculous, and they wrote the response and the authorities in the Scripture and reasons that I indicated to them to confirm our beliefs.

A few days later, Celá Christós fell sick with very bad pleurisy, which hurt the emperor and all our friends to the very soul since he was such an important person and, if <[f. 150v/140v]> he died, the monks would say that God had killed him for defending our faith. He was therefore bled four times and he took some medicines, but despite all that on the night of the seventh day he was so weak and oppressed by the disease that he thought he was dying, so he ordered everyone else to go out, leaving just me with him (for I usually accompanied him). He said to me, 'I see that I am reaching the end. I certainly do not mind dying, but I am very sorry the matters of faith remain like this. If they had been concluded and I had died the next day, it would have been a great consolation; now those monks will say that, because I would not give these things up as they asked me, they killed me with their prayers, which some monasteries are saying publicly, and they take the altar stones on their heads begging Our Lord to remove this from my heart or to kill me. And they say {[f. 162v]} that they did the same in the time of Emperor Za Denguil and that God heard them and killed him. Confess me, Your Reverence, and may His {holy} will be done.' I replied that I had very great confidence in the divine mercy that would give him health, but that it was good for him to confess, and I instructed him in the way in which he should prepare himself, because to me he did not appear to be as close to the end as he thought. And so it was, because the next day he felt better, and so he told me that since Our Lord was doing him the mercy of relieving him, he would put off the confession until he could do it with more preparation and calm, as he did later. Then his mother heard that he had fallen ill and she was very upset, because she loved him very much as the youngest of her sons and because he deserved it for his excellent qualities, and she ended up believing what the monks were telling her, that God would punish him for defending the faith of the Portuguese. And so she wrote to him that she had already found that which she feared so much, and that he should ask for God's forgiveness for the past and propose to mend his ways, and when she had news that he was better, she wrote to him again, exhorting him with many words to stop defending the beliefs of the Portuguese and to follow the patriarch's doctrine, since God had given him health so that another, worse punishment should not befall him. He mentioned it to me, laughing at how easily the monks put whatever they wanted into her head.

When the time that the emperor had appointed for the scholars to gather arrived, the patriarch came with many monks. Many monastery superiors also gathered, and they brought so many companions with them that all that could be seen in the camp were bands of monks. Many nuns also came, for here they can go where they please, and so they, like many of the monks, were telling everyone that they had come to die for their {[f. 163]} old faith, since others were trying to change it, and the impact this had on the ignorant people was not so little that those who defended our side were not in considerable danger. I too was warned that I should look out for myself because they were going to kill me, <[f. 151/141]> and some people advised me to leave the camp, which I did not do for various reasons, and principally because it was necessary to encourage some of those on our side and to show them the authorities in the Scripture and in the saints that prove the truth and dismantle the opponents' arguments. Such was the temerity of certain monks that they plotted in secret to kill the emperor and his brother Celá Christós the first time many went out <together> on horseback and then to do as they wished with the matters of faith and everything else; the emperor heard of this and so, disguising his actions, he remedied the situation by scattering them.

Once all the monks and scholars had gathered, they asked the emperor to set the day on which the disputations would begin, and he ordered that it should be on 29th September 1613, the day of the glorious Archangel Saint Michael. On that day, the patriarch and all the others went before the emperor and, before anything was proposed, the emperor said that he was very displeased with the patriarch because, having previously declared together with the scholars that the true faith was that there were two natures in Christ, divine and human, united in the divine person, and having pronounced excommunication against anyone who said otherwise, because of which he had had it proclaimed that everyone should practise in that manner and that nobody should henceforth teach the contrary, he had then gone back to announcing that there was no more than one nature in Christ, without waiting for him to return from war or sending him any word or gathering together the scholars who had been present previously. The patriarch replied that he had never said that there were two natures in Christ rather than one. The emperor was surprised and asked how he could assert such a thing, for he had said it in front of him and many scholars and had settled it with excommunication, so he could not make the excuse {[f. 163v]} that it was a slip of the tongue, because almost all those who could bear witness to it were there. The patriarch replied that they could not bear witness against him, because they were all his opponents. The emperor said, 'That is no reason for the truth of what I say to remain thus; judge whether what he says is enough for them not to bear witness.' He appointed judges, and they decided that since he, the patriarch and father of them all, stated that they were his opponents, that was enough for them to be considered suspect. The emperor therefore remained silent, but even so the patriarch was considerably discredited. Celá Christós then rose and asked for justice against a lay scholar, because he had previously affirmed that there were two natures in Christ and, while speaking with other scholars, had said that anyone who said the contrary should be excommunicated twice over, but then he had gone back to affirming that there was only one. He replied that it was nothing of the sort, because he had always held that there is only one nature in Christ. But he was soon defeated and proved wrong, with many witnesses, and therefore the emperor had him arrested. That was sorely felt <[f. 151v/141v]> by our opponents, because he was of great assistance to them, not so much on account of his scholarship but for the abundance of his words, for he was very talkative. He was later released, however, because they were saying that the main speaker on their side had been removed deliberately so that they could not prove the truth, but the outcome of this was that everyone could clearly see how the patriarch had denied what he had previously affirmed.

They spent that day on this and other disputations, doing nothing but propose the question. The next day Celá Christós and the others on his side clearly proved that there are two natures in Christ Our Lord by using their own books, Saint Paul and the Gospel. When the opponents saw they had been proved wrong, they said that they would not reply or listen to those things, but only that which their master Dioscorus had taught them, that there is one single nature in Christ, and that all their forefathers had kept that in Ethiopia, and that the emperor should also have them keep it {[f. 164]} and should not come to them with a new faith. Celá Christós said, 'Therefore you do not want reason, but force. It must not be like that. You must listen and reply.' 'We cannot', they said, 'because we have Dioscorus's ban of excommunication not to listen to Leo's beliefs.' Celá Christós replied, 'What use is that excommunication against what the Gospel teaches us? You and we have Saint Paul's excommunication not to accept anything against his teachings, even if an angel were to come and say it. Judge which excommunication we should abide by: that of Saint Paul or that of Dioscorus?' The judges said that it should be that of Saint Paul, that they should look carefully at what he taught and keep that. The opponents protested, shouting that Dioscorus's doctrine was not contrary to Saint Paul's, for otherwise they would have to have a disputation about that, and he had ordered them not to do so; so the emperor should judge.

The emperor then commanded them all to be silent and said, 'Matters of faith are not decided by shouting, and doubts cannot be resolved except by question and answer. Those who have difficulties should put them forward and the others should reply so that the truth can be declared, for that is what we seek.' Then everybody left, because it was already late, and they were saying publicly that the others wanted to make them change their faith and give them two gods, and that the emperor was a perfect Portuguese, together with many other things in which they clearly showed their pride and pertinacity. Even the emperor's own servants were saying that he did not want justice, but to defend the beliefs of the Portuguese in every way. Thus the mutiny was growing from one hour to the next.

When the patriarch saw that the main strength of those who said that there {are} <were> two natures in Christ Our Lord was the emperor's brother, he decided to look for possible ways to separate him from them, and he set some great persons to persuade him to desist and, later, he himself went to his {[f. 164v]} house and threw himself <[f. 152/142]> at his feet, begging him to stop insisting on those things and to drop out. He made him rise and said that, if someone had killed his brother or insulted him very seriously, his intercession would at once have made him give up everything, but matters of faith cannot be given up because of entreaties, and he should not speak to him of that. The patriarch said that he should note how many emperors and great scholars there had been in Ethiopia who had taken this path, that he should not want to take a different one and leave behind him the reputation that he had made them change the ancient faith, that he should stop now, and that he would state publicly that he knew more than he did and that he had concluded that from his reasoning. Celá Christós replied that he was not seeking honours, nor was he changing the ancient faith, but rather he was defending it, as he had shown from the Gospel and Saint Paul and the very books that had come to them from Alexandria, and that he was not alleging it from the books of Rome. The patriarch said, 'Who knows whether these books that came from Alexandria were made by some heretic? All I want is for you to leave it to us, without helping one side or the other.' He kept insisting like this from the morning until midday, when Celá Christós told him not to tire him further, because he would defend there being two natures in Christ until his death, since that was the true faith. Furious at this, the patriarch left and, gathering his monks, they decided not to listen but to shout that it should be as it had been before, and they also incited the lay scholars to do the same.

The next morning, Celá Christós summoned me and told me what had happened with the patriarch; he said he was very sad because they did not want to listen to reason or look at their own books, but to carry things by mutiny. Even his servants were rising against him, so he was afraid that they might kill him during the night, and he was sure that the emperor and he were not a step away from death, so it was necessary to say many prayers and consider very carefully what counsel they {[f. 165]} would take. As I too saw that things were turning for the worse, I told him that I did not think they should try to carry the situation by force, because the emperor did not have the strength to do so at that time, but that they should do all they could, in the best way possible, to make the others listen to their reasoning and look at the books, for in that way they would give in more gently. If in the end, however, it appeared to them that they would not be able to achieve what they intended, the emperor should find a way to leave the question open, without deciding either one thing or the other, saying that it was a point of great importance and that it required long examination and thorough consideration before it could be resolved, and that as there were such varying opinions, they should all take another careful look at the books so that afterwards they might be better able to decide which of the two beliefs was true. Once all that fury had passed, people would soon cool down and they could gradually persuade the main ones of the truth, <[f. 152v/142v]> or they could put that off until the emperor was strong enough. He replied that they would do that, but they should not stop entreating Our Lord to help them. I continually did so and wrote to the other fathers to do the same, and the Portuguese and boys from the seminaries assembled in the churches every day and said litanies with this intent.

When the patriarch had instructed his monks in what they were to do, he went with them to the palace and asked the emperor to order the others to assemble so that they could finish resolving what had been started; he ordered it for the eve of the glorious Saint Francis, whom I strongly entreated on that day and the next on which they were debating to intercede with the Lord for our cause to be successful. After Celá Christós and those on his side had again proved that there are two natures in Christ Our Lord, based on Saints Chrysostom, Basil, Athanasius and many other ancient saints that they too have in their books, the others replied that they would not accept these saints. After many arguments, Celá Christós said, {[f. 165v]} 'Then give me a reply to what the Holy Gospel says, since you give no credence to the saints. When Christ Our Lord in the garden begged with such great anguish for that chalice to pass from Him, when He sweated blood, suffered and died, when He said on the cross, "My God, why hast Thou forsaken Me?" and then to His disciples, "I ascend to My Father and to your Father, to My God and your God," how did He say and suffer all these things? As man or as God?' They answered as man. 'Therefore He has human nature', he said, 'and the divine nature was never separated from it, after it united it to itself.' They conceded it all. 'Therefore in Christ there are two natures, divine and human', he inferred. They replied that it was not so because, after they were united, they cannot be said to be two, but one. 'You', said Celá Christós, 'are affirming two contrary things, that there are divine and human natures in Christ without being exchanged or mixed, and that there is no more than one nature. If you mean that there is only one Christ, I too say that, for He has only one person, but in Him there are two most perfect natures.'

They remained in these disputations for a long time, and when the patriarch and his followers finally saw themselves proven wrong and that they could not reply, they threw themselves at the emperor's feet, shouting that it should be as before, that he should not change their ancient faith that had been kept and defended by so many emperors. Seeing that they did not want to carry the matter by reason but by mutiny, he did not dare say clearly that they should settle on two natures, but that it should be proclaimed that they had seen the books and that everybody must obey what was in them. Celá Christós and his followers replied, 'That, my lord, is what we intend, that they should keep what is in the books, because the only thing that they teach (as <[f. 153/143]> we have shown) is that there are two most perfect natures in Christ Our Lord, divine and human.'

It was {[f. 166]} proclaimed as the emperor commanded, but a monk that was there shouted out that it meant that things were as they had been before, and therefore many people later affirmed that, just as previously they had held that there is only one nature in Christ, so that was what they were to believe. However, the patriarch and those who were on his side in the disputations understood very well what it meant and so they left feeling very angry, although they concealed it as much as they could, saying publicly that people should go on believing as before that there is just one nature in Christ. Nevertheless, there were some among them who understood the truth very well, that there are two natures in Christ, and although they did not dare confess to it out of shame for what they had already said, they later affirmed it in public.

The following Sunday, the emperor summoned a monk and a great man, who were leaders of those who defended that there was only one nature in Christ, and in private he had them speak with his brother Celá Christós, in his presence, for a long time, and he pressed them to the extent that they were forced to concede very absurd things, and therefore the emperor said to them, 'Such is the law that you have, that to defend it you have to {accept} <concede> such false ideas.' The monk tried to reason with the emperor, but at the end of his speech the emperor inferred from what he was saying that the divinity had died, and the monk replied that it was so. On hearing this, the emperor was so furious that, although he was a very serious and temperate man in speaking, he shouted, 'How can we put up with this? If the divinity in Christ died, then the Father and the Holy Spirit died as well. How can the divinity die?' He rose, clearly in a rage, and went to another room, and therefore they left without daring to say a word in reply.

A short time later, the emperor returned to his court in Dambia, leaving matters settled in those lands that had rebelled. When Holy Week arrived, he sent many candles and incense to the churches, {[f. 166v]} as has always been the custom at that time, and particularly to the large monastery that is on an island in the lake of Dambia, which they call Saná.[1] When the person taking them, who was a great man, arrived, five monks came out and said to him that in their church they would not burn candles from someone who said that there were two natures in Christ; they would not take them no matter how much he insisted, telling them that it was a matter of great scandal, and that the emperor would not let that pass without punishment. They did not let him confess and take communion in that church, because he too said that there are two natures in Christ.

---

[1] See Glossary (Canâ/Çaanâ/Çanâ/Ṭānā Qirqos).

When he saw that neither entreaties nor threats were to any avail, he returned and reported <[f. 153v/143v]> everything that had happened to the emperor, who was very annoyed and commanded that those monks should be brought to him at once. Given the circumstances, they thought that when they arrived he would have them killed or give them some {other} <very> serious punishment. They came and, while they were outside the palace, the emperor summoned many monks and great men of the court and said that they should judge what those monks deserved, for the affront and dishonour that they had done him; and if any Moor or heathen had sent them wax for the church, they would have taken it, but his they had rejected with arrogant and contemptuous words. They all, one by one, said, 'At the end of winter Your Majesty gathered the principal scholars of Ethiopia, and after all the disputations they had, you had it proclaimed that all should say as you had declared previously that there are two natures in Christ' (for although the proclamation was in the form that I mentioned above, they understood very well what it meant). 'Not only did they go against this command, but they committed a great disrespect and insult to the emperor, for which they would deserve death. But since they are ignorant men and of little {[f. 167]} understanding, it would seem appropriate for the emperor to use his customary clemency with them.' His mother also interceded for them, and she was aided by other great ladies who had quietly gathered there for that purpose, and so the emperor pardoned them.

We have shown very well the pertinacity with which most Ethiopians defend the idea that there is only one nature in Christ, but because after all this they were yet to reveal much more clearly how deep-rooted this heresy is in their hearts, through what they did against the emperor and his brother Celá Christós, I shall report it in the next chapter.

# CHAPTER V

## How the Ethiopians decided to kill Emperor Seltan Sagued and his brother Cela Christós for saying that there are two natures in Christ Our Lord

When the patriarch and the others on his side saw that the emperor and his brother Cela Christós would not give up what they had started, but would seek in every way that they could to stop people saying that there is one single nature in Christ Our Lord, rather than two, they decided to kill them and make another emperor, one that would no longer allow matters of faith to be called into question, but would let them continue as before. So that they could better carry out their intent, they chose as leaders of their conspiracy not men who might in some way have grievances against the emperor, but a <[f. 154/144]> brother of his called Iemaná Christós, to whom the emperor had granted supreme command over the empire, after himself, by making him *erás*, as we have already mentioned, and another of the most famous of the captains and other people that there were in Ethiopia, called Iuliós,[1] a very arrogant, proud man and much more ungrateful towards the emperor, because the emperor had brought him up as a boy and had raised him up so much that he gave him his {own} first daughter as his wife as well as vast lands and wealth, {[f. 167v]} and he loved him to the extent that he continually excused everything he did and considered suspect those who complained of him, and he hardly ever refused him whatever he asked for, and he was so besotted with him and did him so many honours that everybody said that all he lacked was the imperial crown; and in return for all this he held such great hatred for him in his heart that he was the principal one of those who sought and desired his death, displaying great zeal in his deceitful and false faith.

The emperor's brother was not helping in this because he wanted the empire, since he knew very well that it did not belong to him and that they would not give it to him, because he is not the son of the emperor's father, but of his mother; but he thought he was making a great {sacrifice} <service> to Our Lord by helping to kill his brothers, since they were deserting the faith that he held to be true. Because the conspirators understood very well what these two lords had in their hearts, they were not afraid to take them as leaders for what they intended, but in secret and in such a way that, even if the emperor knew that they privately believed that there is only one nature in Christ Our Lord, he would not imagine that their evil could reach such a point that they would seek his death, nor that they would join his opponents in that way.

---

[1] See Glossary (Iuliós/Yolyos).

With the same secrecy, they stirred up almost all the people at court against the emperor, and when the patriarch saw that he had so many on his side, he went to a church that stands inside the first palace compound and, without a care for the emperor, he pronounced excommunication against anyone who said that there are two natures in Christ and against any servants who served or obeyed such people in any way, but they should leave them immediately and wives should separate from their husbands. On hearing this, and realizing (as he himself told me later) that the patriarch intended that his people should not obey him, the emperor flew into a rage and sent word demanding to know how he could do such a serious thing {{f. 168}} and that he should at once remove that excommunication, which ignorant people thought was binding on them, or else he should watch out for his head. That frightened the patriarch, and he announced that he was removing the excommunication, but he sent word to the emperor that he needed to talk <[f. 154v/144v]> to him about matters of faith. He answered that he could do so whenever he wished. So the following morning the patriarch convened his followers and, entering the first palace compound, he sat on his chair under a tree. The compound then filled with people, even though it was large, and all of them were carrying concealed weapons. When they were all assembled, he sent word to the emperor that the word that they were using for 'nature' meant 'person', and so they could not say that there were two in Christ, but just one. That was merely a ruse to find a way to catch and kill the emperor or, at least to depose him and expel everyone from court straight away and appoint another, as some were already beginning to suggest, because the word that they use, which is '*bahari*',[1] does not mean person, but nature, and '*acál*'[2] is person.

The emperor's brother, Celá Christós, was with him at the time and on hearing the message he said, 'Lord, these men have gathered here very arrogantly, thinking that they have the strength to finish what they intend. Give me leave, Your Majesty, and I shall go and kill three or four of the leaders of this mutiny with my sword, and you will see how nobody dares say anything else.' The emperor said that it was not appropriate to do things like that and, with the counsel of those who were there, he answered that if that word that they used to say that there were two natures in Christ Our Lord meant 'person', then he would command that they should no longer use it. The patriarch sent word again that they should declare their faith and how they should speak. The emperor replied that the true faith was that Christ Our Lord was perfect God and perfect man, and everyone should say it thus. The patriarch was not content with this, but rather he twisted and turned with questions and answers. {{f. 168v}} Seeing that he could not find anything on which to catch him, he went away saying that that was what he wanted, that they should not say 'two'.

Although the patriarch tried to put this story about so that the common people would think that he had achieved his intention, he and the principal people on his side understood very well that the emperor was saying that there were two natures in Christ Our Lord and that he had it so set in his heart that there was no way that he would ever change. Therefore his son-in-law Iuliós finally resolved with many others to kill him. So that they would be even firmer in their accursed intention, he took oaths from the captains of the

---

[1] See Glossary (religious controversy).

[2] In ARSI, MS Goa 42 the last letter of this word might be read either as a somewhat open 'b' or as a more rounded 'l' than the others on that folio or on adjacent ones. The term '*akab*' has not been found in any glossary.

emperor's right hand and left hand, who had many men, and almost all the great lords of the court and, to the oath he added excommunication for a eunuch called Cafló, the first person in the empire after the *erás*, on whom everyone depended a great deal, because on account of <[f. 155/145]> his office the emperor would do nothing without his counsel; indeed he was so absolute that he <often> made decisions {on many things} against the emperor's will and they stood firm. Since he could enter the emperor's chamber at any time he wished, he promised to kill him very easily, on condition that Iuliós took it on himself to kill Celá Christós. They agreed all this in great secrecy. Iuliós asked the emperor for leave to go to the lands where he had his seat, which {was} <is> a province that they call Oagrá, two days' journey from the court, and he gave it. So he went in order to try and carry out what they had plotted from there, as soon as he found the opportunity.

At that time it happened that some 500 Moorish horsemen fell out with their king and fled into some secure lands belonging to the emperor. As that seemed to the eunuch a good place to kill the emperor, safer for him than inside {[f. 169]} the palace, because the captains would come over to him as soon as he killed him, he decided to make him go there by saying that those Moors should not be there and that, since they were fleeing from their king, who was a friend, and had entered those lands without permission, the emperor should take those horses and punish them, or send them to their king; he added that in order to do that more discreetly it would be good if the emperor went himself, letting it be known that he wanted to amuse himself hunting for a few days. He insisted so much that the emperor came round to it, and so he went off with all haste. He did not catch the Moors, however, even though the captain of the vanguard did fight with them, because they fled when they saw how many men there were and, as they had good horses, they easily reached safety. The emperor therefore turned back sooner than they had expected and so the eunuch did not dare do anything, because he was waiting for Iuliós to declare his uprising first.

When Iuliós saw that the emperor was leaving those rugged lands, he issued a proclamation in the province of Oagrá, where he was, that whoever wished to defend the idea that there were two natures in Christ should go off to the emperor or his brother Celá Christós, but that those who were zealous about their ancient faith and believed that there was only one nature in Christ should follow him. With that, a large number of men joined those he already had and he marched off to the nearby kingdom of Gojam, where Celá Christós was, very confident that he could kill him, both because of the large force that he had with him and because he had also come to an arrangement with many people in that kingdom. But just before he crossed the River Nile into Gojam, the patriarch went to him and told him that it was not good counsel to go <[f. 155v/145v]> and fight Celá Christós, who had many men; he should turn to go against the emperor, whose horses were tired and most {[f. 169v]} of whose soldiers had already gone to their homes; once the emperor was dead it would not be difficult to kill Celá Christós; and he was sure that if he killed the emperor God would forgive him his sins and would do him great mercies, because the emperor had deserted his faith; and if he died in battle, he would be a martyr. When he had finished telling him this, he made a speech to the whole encampment, exhorting them to fight valiantly against the emperor and to try to kill him because, if they did so, all their sins would be forgiven, however bad they might be. He then pronounced excommunication against anyone who left that camp or who did not follow Iuliós and obey him. He earnestly begged him to deliver to him the five of us fathers who were here, and he promised to do so. And he said he wanted to have our heads cut off in front of him, or he would put us inside our church with the Portuguese and burn us all there together, because we were the ones who had made the emperor and those on his side change their faith. And with this agreement he went with him and, on the following days, on the way, he renewed his ban of excommunication for nobody to leave the camp.

When the emperor heard what Iuliós had done and that he was going through Gojam determined to fight Celá Christós, he hurried to get there. When he reached a point a day's journey from where I was, I went to visit him. He ordered everybody out of his tent and said to me, 'Look at what they are doing to me, Your Reverence. Even my son-in-law, whom I have raised up so much, is trying to kill me. What counsel do you give me? What shall I do?' I answered, 'What counsel can I give you, Your Majesty, as you understand the matters of your people so well and know from experience how to proceed? But what comes to my mind right now is that if the hearts of this camp are with Your Majesty, you can safely go along this road, because Iuliós will not dare to fight, {[f. 170]} and send a message to Celá Christós not to fight him until Your Majesty arrives, but to block his way so that he cannot cross over to the Gâlas and then come back with them to destroy the land. But if you fear that some may be in concert with Iuliós, it would seem a good idea for Your Majesty to summon your captains and say to them, "Iuliós is going to fight Celá Christós, so let us take this other road, which is a short cut, to join up with Celá Christós, so that we can arrange things so that nobody dies." Once Your Majesty joins Cela Christós, neither will these men dare do anything, nor will Iuliós be able to escape.' Then he said, 'There is no need to fear <[f. 156/146]> the men in this camp, because they are all with me of one heart.' I answered, 'Lord, since the emperor has a pure heart, he thinks that everyone else has too. I have heard it said as something quite certain that Iuliós was claiming that all the officers in this camp were in concert with him, apart from seven of those who have less power, whom he had not dared contact in case he was found out.' 'That cannot be the case', said the emperor. 'He spreads these rumours on purpose to make me fall out with my people. I think it would be better to go along this road after him and command Celá Christós to come from the other side so that he cannot escape from us. As for the other roads to the Gâlas, I have already ordered them to be taken. Your Reverence should return home and write very quickly to Tigré, to the Portuguese captain, to tell me at once what is happening there.' That was because he did not have much confidence in the viceroy there, who, people said, was {courting} <corresponding with> the conspirators.

The following day, after I had taken my leave of the emperor, he commanded a captain with harquebusiers to go at full speed to help {[f. 170v]} Celá Christós, in case Iuliós wanted to give him battle. But when he encountered Iuliós on the road, he turned back and sent word quickly to the emperor that he was coming, and therefore the emperor marched more slowly and in order. On coming close to Iuliós, he commanded that they should find somewhere more suitable for them to fight, and the eunuch with the other captains in the conspiracy chose a valley from which the emperor could not flee on horseback, because in front, where the enemy would come, it was very flat, and behind there were some very high bluffs. But the emperor, who is a great warrior, said that it was not suitable and he went on to a high hill that had many large rocks at its foot, where the horses could not charge, for it was the horses that he most feared.

The next day, Iuliós arrived with many men on foot and on horseback, and he encamped on the plain rather more than a gunshot away from the emperor. The following morning, which was 11th May 1617,[1] he drew his men up in order. When his wife saw this, she begged him insistently and tearfully not to fight, for she would make friends for him with the emperor her father; but he replied that he did not want his friendship, but his death. Then, weeping to see if she could soften his heart, she said, 'Lord, do not go in haste; eat before you go.' He answered, 'First I will bring your father's head and, once I have put it here in front of us, I shall eat to my heart's content.' And he began to arm himself straight away. Meanwhile, the patriarch was standing with a cross in his hand, tossing many blessings at every squadron from a high spot. When Iuliós had finished arming himself, he put on spurs, {[f. 171]} <*bus exutus, et ipse capite obtruncatur,*>[2] something very unusual <[f. 156v/146v]> in Ethiopia, and mounted on a beautiful large horse he rode in front of the army with the horsemen whom he most trusted. Well before he reached the emperor's troops, which were also already drawn up in order, he charged furiously. When the captain of the emperor's right hand saw this, he withdrew with his men to one side, and the captain of the left and the eunuch, who both had many men, left them in their places. Thus the enemy came through the middle without any resistance, shouting, 'Where is the emperor? Where is the emperor?' until they came close to his bodyguard, which was very small and all on foot. But they attacked with very great spirit and, to show how little it takes to bring down the proud people of this world, Our Lord God allowed one of the least of those soldiers, who had never been in battle before, to throw a stone which hit him next to his left eye and knocked him off his horse and, as his mail rose up a little when he fell, he followed it up in there with his spear and, falling on him at once, he cut off his head, and the most presumptuous and arrogant captain that there was in Ethiopia came to his end like Goliath. They also killed some of the horsemen accompanying him and, when the emperor's other captains charged at the rest, they at once took flight as they had seen their general killed.

When the soldier cut off Iuliós's head, he took it straight to the emperor. On seeing it, he immediately ordered the retreat to be sounded, but the soldiers did not obey so quickly that they did not first kill many men and the patriarch himself, who remained at his post without fleeing, either because he was very disturbed to see the rout, as some say, or because he thought {[f. 171v]} that nobody would dare do him any harm. And in truth many passed him by without even touching his robe, and it might be that they left him because they were on his side in the matters of faith but, when a horseman came who had goodwill towards him on these same matters, he struck him in the neck with his lance, knocking him down, and those who came behind stripped him of his clothes and left him with nothing whatever. And he lay there for a long time, insistently begging anyone who passed for some water, because it seems all the blood he was losing from his wound was making him very thirsty. But he did not find even that small refreshment at such an anguished time: rather, instead of water, they shed whatever blood was left in him by cutting off his head, and so he had a wretched end and his naked body was left unburied for two days. They took his head at once to the emperor, and he had it put in front of him on the ground, on a mat, next to that of Iuliós. And so those who were such friends in life were not separated in death, <[f. 157/147]> and they found the same death that they wanted to give to us. Afterwards, the emperor commanded that seven of Iuliós's main

---

[1] A note in the margin of BPB, MS 778 reads 'death of Iulios ... 1617 ... II of May'.

[2] This extraneous fragment of Latin appears to mean '... put aside and he was decapitated'. It may be a jotting about the decapitation of Grāññ described later in this paragraph.

servants, who were brought captive to him, be beheaded, and he pardoned the rest. He proclaimed that all the horses, helmets, mail and valuable weapons, of which there were many, should be brought to him, and the rest the soldiers could keep. In that way many of them became rich, because all of those in Iuliós's army had brought their gold, silver and most valued fabrics with them, since they thought they would be safer there since they were so sure of victory, so much so that when they left to give battle they ordered that a meal be made ready for them because they would soon be back for dinner. {[f. 172]} That is what I was told later by the Portuguese who were with the emperor, because when they pursued the enemy they entered their tents and found the tables laid and the food ready.

The next day, Celá Christós arrived with a large army, and they all came in with their lances lowered as a sign of regret that they had not been in the battle, even though they had come as fast as they could to be there. But it seems that the Lord ordained it so that they should not attribute victory to their strength but count it as heaven sent. And, in fact, that is how all the dispassionate ones there saw it, especially the emperor, because when I went straight away to congratulate him on it, he said to me, 'Look at the great mercy that Our Lord has done me, Your Reverence. Although this man came with so many men on foot and horse and 120 harquebuses, He delivered them all to me, without their killing a single one of my men. Is that not a very great miracle?' I replied that I too regarded it as such and that the Lord had performed it to show His pleasure that His Majesty was defending the beliefs of his holy faith. He then continued his speech, giving many thanks to God for the mercies that he was doing him, but he was not joyful at the victory, nor did he celebrate it much, but rather he dressed in black velvet, showing his sorrow at the loss of those who had died. And in truth, if they had repented and been faithful, it might have been considered a very great victory, because they were valiant horsemen.

When he had finished this, the emperor began to make enquiries about those who had joined the conspiracy, and he found so many that he had to dissemble with many of them. He only publicly denounced and banished some, among them Iemaná Christós, whose life he pardoned since he was his brother, even though he very rightly deserved death. However, although some people knew of that eunuch's doings, they did not dare denounce him since they were very afraid of him. {[f. 172v]} He too had those he most feared discreetly killed, including a monk who had known of his conspiracy with Iuliós and had pronounced excommunication on them both to make them carry it out, and a servant of his who had carried the messages. Even so, he did not consider <[f. 157v/147v]> himself safe and so, fearing that in the end his treason would become known and he would not be able to escape, he resolved to do anything to kill the emperor and Celá Christós, who at the time was at court with only a few men. To achieve his purpose, he told the emperor that he wanted to parade the soldiers that he had under him and asked for permission to bring them in front of the palace and he would see them from the veranda. He was counting on then entering and killing him, which he could do easily since the emperor was unsuspecting and had very few guards at the doors, and then he would go straight away with his large force of men and kill Celá Christós, who would not be able to resist at all. But although the emperor was far from imagining such treason, he said that it was not necessary and he was not in favour of it.

Seeing that this attempt had been unsuccessful, the eunuch ordered a large quantity of wine – which is made of honey here, and it arrived in five or six days – so that he could invite Celá Christós to dinner and, when he was merry with the wine, kill him and then go straight to the palace to kill the emperor. To do that, he had arranged with a young page to open the door to him at whatever time he arrived, because he had to come and deal with some very secret business with the emperor. But, shortly before the day on which he had resolved to do this, it pleased Our Lord for the emperor to hear some rumours, and so he had him seized and had it proclaimed that everybody who knew anything about him should come and tell it, on pain of death. At once many people testified that he wanted to kill the emperor {[f. 173]} and all his sons and Celá Christós, and then raise another emperor as he wished. So he had him beheaded in the palace compound, and the whole court applauded and celebrated, since everyone felt as though a very heavy yoke had been lifted from their necks, because of the way he oppressed them in everything, treating them with excessive violence and making everyone bow their heads so that they could not oppose him, and if he heard that anyone, however great, opposed him in anything, he would look for a way to destroy him and swallow him up like a wolf. Since he was like that in life, Our Lord God permitted that in death his body should be thrown out to the wolves in the field and that it should find no resting place but a wolves' den, where his kinsfolk put him and closed it up with rock, and they took him there in secret at night, since the emperor had forbidden anyone to bury him.

I have reported all these things both because they are worthy of memory and so that the reader may see more clearly how very mistaken Friar Luis de Urreta was when, on page 424 of his *Historia*,[1] he said that the Ethiopians, as Catholic Christians, confess and believe that there are two perfect natures in Christ, incommutable <[f. 158/148]> and distinct; because even today many of them are so very far from this that, even though they see the great providence that Our Lord God has for those who defend His holy faith and the manifest punishments that He meted out to the main leaders of those who persecute it, they do not change their purpose, nor do they recognize them as such; rather, some affirm that the patriarch and Iuliós, together with the others that died in that war, were martyrs. And if the emperor were now to die, which God forbid, I am certain that they would kill *Erás* Celá Christós at once and that they would not even spare us, as he {[f. 173v]} himself has sometimes told me.

---

[1] Urreta, *Historia de la Etiopia*, bk II, ch. 4.

# CHAPTER VI

## Which deals with the errors that the Ethiopians have regarding rational souls

Now that we have seen what the Ethiopians say about the sacrosanct manhood of Christ Our Lord, it will be appropriate to mention briefly what they affirm regarding His most holy soul and other rational souls, which are three extremely serious errors. The first is that Our Lord God does not create rational souls, but that they come from the parents and that even Christ Our Lord's soul was taken by the Holy Spirit from the most holy soul of the Virgin Our Lady, because God only created Adam's soul; and others say that He made it from the four elements. The second error is that, when the most holy soul of Christ Our Lord descended into hell, it brought out not only those of the holy fathers who were in Abraham's bosom, but also {all} those of the damned in hell. The third is that all the souls of the holy fathers, however great they may be, are in the earthly paradise, without enjoying glory, and they must wait there until Judgement Day, when they will be united with their bodies and will enter heaven together; and the souls of the damned are not in hell, but in another place, and they will not be tormented until they are joined with their bodies.

These three errors are condemned by the doctors and saints as heresies, and, leaving aside many others, the glorious Saint Thomas, speaking of the first in part 1, question 118, article 2, says that it is heretical to affirm that God does not create intellectual souls, but that they come from the parents.[1] And Saint Augustine, in *Liber de hæresibus* chapter 79, dealing with the second error, affirms that it is a heresy.[2] As for the third, it is condemned in the Florentine Council, last session, and in the Tridentine Council, session 25.

I have often dealt with all these errors in {[f. 174]} disputations and private conversations with the principal scholars of Ethiopia and sometimes in the presence of Emperor Seltan Sagued. I asked them on what they based themselves for the first one, and they answered that it was the Scripture, for Genesis 2 says that when Our Lord God had finished <[f. 158v/148v]> creating everything, He rested on the seventh day, which means that from then on He did not create anything at all, and to affirm that God creates all rational souls would be not to give Him rest, but to keep Him forever busy creating all the thousands of souls that would be needed to infuse into bodies every day throughout

---

[1] Thomas Aquinas, *Summa theologica*, I, question 118, article 2, 'Utrum anima intellectiva causetur ex semine' ['Whether the intellectual soul is produced from the semen'].

[2] Augustine of Hippo, *De hæresibus ad quodvultdeum*, liber unus, caput 79, 'Alia, descendente ad inferos Christo credidisse incredulos, et omnes exinde existimat liberatos' ['Another heresy believes that upon Christ's descent into Hell the unbelievers believed and all were liberated from Hell'] (Müller, *The De Haeresibus of Saint Augustine*, p. 115).

the world. I responded that the divine Scripture there meant nothing more than that on the seventh day Our Lord God stopped creating any more new things or in a new way than that in which He had created the others, but He still governs and multiplies the works that He made in those first days. Thus Christ Our Lord says in Saint John, chapter 5, that His Father and He work until now.[1] Therefore it is not inconvenient that He now creates souls, because they are not new things, nor does He create them in a new way than that in which He created the first soul, and God is not kept busy in creating so many every day because, as David says in Psalm 148, He only spoke, and they were made: He commanded, and they were created.[2] In this same way He could create a thousand other worlds if He wished. Later I brought him some authorities from the saints that they know about, such as Saint Chrysostom, who in *Homilia 23 in varia loca Matthei* says that the soul neither begets nor is begotten, nor does it know any other father than Him by whose will it is created;[3] and Saint Hilary, who, in book 10 *On the Holy Trinity*, says that the soul of man is the work of God and flesh is always born of flesh.[4] But these authorities had little effect on him, because as they do not have these books, they think that {[f. 174v]} we are making false allegations. Therefore, moving on, I brought them some passages from the Scripture that prove this truth, such as Job chapter 33: 'The spirit of God made me, and the breath of the Almighty gave me life';[5] and David, in Psalms 32 and 99: 'He made us, and not we ourselves.'[6] Likewise Solomon, in Ecclesiastes, last chapter, where he says, 'Remember thy Creator in the days of thy youth, before the time of affliction come, ... And the dust return into its earth, from whence it was, and the spirit return to God, who gave it';[7] and Machabees, chapter 7, book 2, where it is told that when Saint Felicitas was exhorting her seven sons to go and suffer with good spirit the torments that they were given and die for the law of God, she told them among other things that she had not given them their soul, but the Creator of the world.[8] A monk responded that they would be excommunicated if they {accepted} <received> the doctrine that God creates souls and so it was not necessary to waste time disputing on this matter, and these passages did not mean that which I inferred. Others, however, understood the truth very well, and not even the others who defended the opposite were able to deny it, <[f. 159/149]> but rather came to concede it, because I brought them authorities from their books and from the very one from which they pray in one of their Masses, and I proved to them that if the souls of the children came from the parents, they would not be immortal, and so now many of them believe and confess publicly that God creates them.

Their second error has its basis in their own heads, when they say that, by virtue of the blood of Christ Our Lord, not only were the souls of the holy fathers that were in Abraham's bosom brought out, but so were those of the damned, and to say they were not is to dishonour the blood of Christ.

---

[1] John 5:17.

[2] Psalms 1:8.5.

[3] John Chrysostom, 'Homiliæ in Matthæum 23–24', *Opera omnia*, 7.

[4] Hilary of Poitiers, *De Trinitate libri duodecim*, bk 10:20, '... cum anima omnis opus Dei sit, carnis vero generatio semper ex carne sit.'

[5] Job 33:4.

[6] Psalms 32[33]:9 and 99[100]:3.

[7] Ecclesiastes 12:1 and 7.

[8] 2 Machabees [Apocrypha, Maccabees]: 7:22–3.

I sometimes showed how false this is to many people by means of passages from Scripture, authorities of saints and reasoning, and some received it, convinced of the truth, in particular the emperor and his brother Celá Christós. When {[f. 175]} certain monks heard that, they made great efforts to dissuade them, and they brought the emperor a book which, without stating whether it was also speaking of the hell of the damned, said that Christ Our Lord had brought out all the souls. The emperor replied that that only meant that He had brought all the souls out of Abraham's bosom. They said that it also meant the souls of the damned. Then I said, 'If that is so, then the evil ones were more fortunate than the holy, for the latter had always borne the yoke of God's law on their necks, although it is so heavy that Saint Peter, in Acts 15, says that neither their fathers nor they could bear it,[1] and apart from that they suffered countless troubles, wandering in deserts, as Saint Paul says, distressed, afflicted, some put to the sword, others cut asunder, others flayed;[2] so if the others – despite having no duty with God's law, but killing, robbing, indulging their appetites as much as they liked and reaching the end of their lives with great prosperity and abundance of all things, many of them worshipping idols and sacrificing their sons and daughters to devils, as David says in Psalm 105[3] – should have their souls brought out together with those of the holy men who were in Abraham's bosom to receive the reward of glory, then the former were more fortunate than the latter. That cannot be said, for Our Lord God does not make those who are evil equal to those who are good but, as the divine Scripture tells us at every step, He gives to each one according to his works; and because the works of the evil deserved eternal fire, He had condemned them to that, and as they were already there, the blood of Christ Our Lord did not redeem them, because in hell there is no redemption at all. A monk then said, 'Leave us alone, Your Reverence; do not interfere now in our causes.' I therefore fell silent, but the emperor replied in such a manner that in the end they had nothing to say.

<[f. 159v/149v]> Another time some monks jointly accused {[f. 175v]} one of the emperor's cousins, who was called Edá Christós, of having said that Christ Our Lord only brought out the souls of the holy fathers that were in Abraham's bosom. And he came to me quite distressed saying that they wanted the emperor to appoint a judge against him and that they were determined to have him killed. He asked me to advise him on what he should do and how he should respond. I answered that since he was defending the true faith and he was such a great lord, then he should have spirit and heart and they would not be able to do anything against him or even know how to reply to him, so he should freely say that that is the truth and he would prove it with authorities from the saints, reasoning and the Holy Scripture. And I pointed out to him certain saints and passages, such as that of Solomon in Ecclesiastes 9: 'the dead know nothing more, neither have they a reward any more';[4] which means that in that which Our Lord God determines, when men die, there is no change afterwards, nor do they receive a further reward: if they deserve glory and have nothing to purge, He gives it to them at once; if they deserve hell, He casts them into it forever. And further on, in chapter 11, he says, 'If the tree fall to the south, or to the north, in what place soever it shall fall, there shall it be,'[5] because by 'south'

[1] Acts of the Apostles 15:10.
[2] Hebrews 11:8–38.
[3] Psalm 105 [106]:19–39.
[4] Ecclesiastes 9:5.
[5] Ecclesiastes 11:3.

he means heavenly glory and by 'north' the punishments of hell, and so he means that those who have once fallen into those punishments will never come out of them. Again, in Ecclesiasticus 24, speaking about divine wisdom, he says that she promised to behold all that slept and to enlighten all that hoped in the Lord.[1] Those that hoped in the Lord were only those who were in Abraham's bosom, because those who were in hell did not hope in the Lord, rather, many of them had never heard of the Lord, because they were idolatrous heathens and spent all their lives in the gravest sins, and so Christ Our Lord did not enlighten them; they remained there in their darkness and torments. Saint Jude declared the same thing to us at the beginning {[f. 176]} of his Epistle, saying that the bad angels are in everlasting chains, just as the people of Sodom and Gomorrah are in the punishments of hell for their sins.[2] This is also clearly deduced from chapter 11 of Saint Matthew, where Christ Our Lord says that it shall be more tolerable for Tyre, Sidon and Sodom than for Corozain, Bethsaida, etc., meaning that the latter will have greater punishment on the Day of Judgment than the former, because, having heard the doctrine that He preached and seen the marvels and miracles that He wrought, they did not repent their sins and do penance, for if the people of Tyre, Sidon, etc. had seen those marvels, they would have repented and done penance, but since they did not see them, their guilt is less than that of the other cities, and so will their punishment be on the Day of Judgment.[3] <[f. 160/150]> Hence, since they will have torments then, it follows that Christ Our Lord did not bring them out of those that they already had, when He descended into hell, because, if he had brought them out then, he would not put them back in on the Day of Judgment. The same may be deduced from what was shown to Saint John, in Apocalypse 14, when, speaking of the idolaters that died before Christ Our Lord (as he declared later in chapter 17), he says that the smoke of their torments shall ascend up for ever and ever, neither have they rest day nor night.[4]

After I had finished instructing him in what he had to do and say, he asked me to go to the emperor, so that I would be present, because the monks would come soon to ask him for a judge. I went in with him right behind me and soon one of the more important monks came in and began to say in a loud voice, 'May the emperor give me justice against Edá Christós, who dishonours the blood of Christ by affirming that when He descended into hell He only brought out the souls of the holy fathers.' Edá Christós replied, 'Lord, I do not dishonour the blood of Christ, but rather I hold it in great veneration and I defend the truth. This monk dishonours the justice of Our Lord God, which had condemned to everlasting torments {[f. 176v]} the idolatrous heathens and those who broke His holy law and spent all their lives in sins, by saying that later they were saved. Tell him to respond, Your Majesty, and let the priest be the judge, for I shall clearly show from the Holy Scripture that what he affirms is false.'

The monk was very angry and said, 'Why should the priest be our judge? Is there perhaps nobody among us who can be as good as he?' And since he began to dispute with more liberty than was appropriate in that place, the emperor angrily said to him that they should both go away, for it was not up to them to determine those things. So the monk

[1] Ecclesiasticus 24:45.
[2] Jude 1:6–7.
[3] Matthew 11:21–4.
[4] Apocalypse [Revelations] 14:11 and 17:8.

left without getting a judge, and he did not ask for one again since he could see that the emperor was on our side, but all the time many of them dispute against us and against those who hold this truth.

Regarding the third error, when I arrived in Ethiopia, people commonly held it as certain that the souls of saints, however great they may be, are in the earthly paradise without enjoying glory, and that they must wait there until the Day of Judgment, when they will be united with their bodies and enter heaven together; and that the souls of evil people are not in hell, but in another place close to the earthly paradise, and that they will not be tormented until they are joined with their bodies. They were so certain of this that nobody ever doubted it. But once the fathers and I started explaining this topic in public disputations and private conversations, <[f. 160v/150v]> we clearly showed them in passages in Scripture and by reasoning that the souls of saints that have nothing to purge enter heaven as soon as they die and enjoy the glory that their works deserve, and that the souls of those who die in mortal sin go straight to hell, where they are tormented. Many have received this truth and believe it, but there are many more {[f. 177]} who still remain in their error. Thus, when I was with the emperor a short time ago, some monks came in and began to talk about this topic, and although I gave them reasons and places in Scripture to which they were unable to reply, they did not appear to be convinced, until I brought them authorities from their own books, which they could not deny. And so the emperor said to them, 'Why do you insist on something that the father has proved so well with the Scriptures and your own books?' And so the principal one of them answered that it could not be denied.

From what we have said, it can clearly be seen how false the information was that Friar Luis de Urreta had on this topic, for on page 420 of his *Historia Ethiopica* he says that the Ethiopians do not have this error, saying, 'The Ethiopians, with Catholic feeling, believe and maintain and have always believed that the souls of the good, unless they have something to purge at the point when they leave this life, see the divine essence and enjoy God as the blessed.'[1]

---

[1] Urreta, *Historia de la Etiopia*, excerpt from bk II, ch. 3, pp. 404–21. Páez quotes this passage in Spanish.

# CHAPTER VII

## Which shows how the Prester John's Ethiopian vassals have for a long time been schismatics disobedient to the holy Roman Church

When I have asked many of the principal scholars and elders of Ethiopia how long they have been disunited from the Roman Church, they have replied that since the time of Dioscorus. This is what they all say, and it seems to be true, because they have always followed his writings and accursed doctrine and venerate him as a saint, and they hold Pope Saint Leo, who condemned him, to be a heretic, as was said in chapter 3 of this second book. Although Emperor David, who later called himself {[f. 177v]} Onág Çagued, wrote letters to the supreme pontiff and the kings of Portugal in 1524 showing that he wished to unite his empire to the holy Roman Church, this did not take effect because he died before the arrival here of the Portuguese with whose help he wished to do it. Although his son Claudio (whom they called Athanás Çagued when they made him emperor) received as patriarch Dom João Bermudez, <[f. 161/151]> who came with Dom Christovão da Gama[1] and other Portuguese in 1541, it seems he only did so to buy time with the Portuguese, of whom he had such great need at that time, because after they had delivered his empire from the tyranny of the Moors and subjugated all his enemies, when he should have shown himself to be more grateful to Our Lord who had done him such great mercies and to the Portuguese who had undertaken so many labours for him, he then showed how far he was from receiving the holy faith of the Roman Church or obeying his patriarch, because he brought another from Alexandria and Dom João Bermudez returned to India, leaving him excommunicated, as we said in chapter 10 of the first book. To show more clearly that, even though he apparently accepted Dom João Bermudez as patriarch, he was not minded to obey the Roman Church, I shall report some of the things that happened from that time onwards, when he clearly showed his mind.

First of all, when Father Master Gonçalo Rodrigues of our Society entered Ethiopia with Ambassador Diogo Dias in 1555, by order of Dom Pedro Mascarenhas, who was viceroy of India at the time, to arrange and prepare this Emperor Claudio for the arrival of the patriarch, {[f. 178]} Father Dom João Nunes Barreto[2] of our Society, and his companions, who were already making ready in Portugal,[3] he sought to do so very diligently, showing him through reasoning and obligation that he had to receive the patriarch and his companions and give obedience to the holy Roman Church, and reminding him of

[1] See Glossary (Christoval da Gama).
[2] See Glossary (João Nunes Barreto).
[3] Páez returns to this subject at greater length in bk III, ch. 4, vol. II below. See Glossary (first Jesuit mission).

the letters that he himself had written to Portugal and Rome, in which he promised to unite with the holy Church of Rome. And to move him more to do so, he made a treatise[1] in which, with passages from Scripture and clear reasoning, he showed how great were the errors of Ethiopia and the truth of our holy faith and how all Christians were obliged to obey the supreme Roman pontiff, and he presented it to him. But it was to no avail, as the father himself affirms in a long letter that he wrote from Goa to the fathers of the Society in Portugal on 13th September 1556 and which Father Fernão Guerreiro of our Society reports in the *Annual Report on the things that our fathers did in East India in the years 1607 and 1608*, page[2] 281, where, after recounting many things that happened to the emperor, he says the following:

*Finally, when many arguments had been made on both sides, with the Portuguese present, I told him through the captain that what I sought in that written paper that I had given him was to know his <[f. 161v/151v]> intent as regards giving obedience to the Roman pontiff and receiving the scholars and religious men that the king of Portugal, his brother, wished to send to him, because if he did not want them and did not wish to obey, there was no reason for them to come to his kingdom; that His Highness should see whether he wanted to give obedience, as he had given it and sent it to His Holiness, when he was in such-and-such a place. To that he replied that he had religious men and scholars in his kingdom and therefore he had no need of those of the king {[f. 178v]} of Portugal, and he certainly had never given obedience to the Roman pontiff, for the obedience that Gaspar de Magalhaes had taken had not been given by him, but an Arab monk, who translated his letters for the king of Portugal, had made a mistake and had not understood them. Finally, he concluded that he only wished to obey the patriarch of Alexandria, whom he had always obeyed. Therefore, seeing his deliberation and obstinacy, I took my leave of him.[3]*

Up to here are the words of Father Master Gonçalo, in which it can be seen that, although Emperor Claudio received Dom João Bermudez as patriarch, it was not from the heart, since he says that he never gave obedience to the pope, and had only ever obeyed the patriarch of Alexandria. Even though the father returned to talk to him on other occasions, he was only able to obtain permission for the fathers to come and a promise that he would hear them. After he had left the court for India, where he arrived in September 1556, an honourable Portuguese called Afonso de França[4] – who had been the father's interpreter both in the treatise that he wrote[5] and when he was speaking to the emperor, since he knew the language well and was always at court – wrote him a letter, in which he tells him about a long disputation that he had with the emperor on matters of faith and clearly describes his obstinacy and perfidy, then ending the letter with these words:

*From which I understand that the king would rather be a vassal of the Moors, like the Dioscorian peoples, which are those of Alexandria and Egypt, than give said obedience to the*

---

[1] See Glossary (*Tratado sobre todos os erros de Etiópia* [*Treatise on all the errors of Ethiopia*]).

[2] 'Folio' would be more appropriate.

[3] Guerreiro, 'Adição à Relação das coisas de Etiópia', f. 282v/p. 307. Páez transcribes Gonçalo Rodrigues's letter in full in bk III, ch. 4, vol. II below.

[4] See Glossary (Afonso de França).

[5] See Glossary (João Bermudes).

*holy pontiff, and he never wished to reveal this truth before to Your Reverence so as not to make you so disconsolate that you might desist from performing the duties required of your office.*[1]

Emperor Claudio always showed this same stubbornness and obstinacy {[f. 179]} until his death, as the fathers of the Society who arrived in Ethiopia later, in March 1557, with Father Bishop Dom Andre de Oviedo, bore witness in a joint letter that they wrote to Rome in the year 1562 to Father Diogo Lainez, the General of the Society at the time, and Father Fernão Guerreiro reports it <[f. 162/152]> in the *Annual Report* mentioned above, on page[2] 294. Having recounted in detail the course of their journey and arrival at the emperor's court, they say:

*After some speeches, the bishop gave him the letters from the governor of India and from our patriarch and others, and the king, taking them, began at once to show his displeasure at the matters of his reduction, from which he was so far as Rome is from Ethiopia. But since he was noble and discreet and friendly towards the Portuguese, he concealed his displeasure, although not to the extent that he did not give clear indications of his real feelings and perfidy. However, he always behaved very temperately towards the bishop.*[3]

Further on, having dealt with the disputations that the father bishop had with the emperor's scholars in his presence, and how all of them appeared ignorant compared with the bishop, although they shouted out trying to show that they had won, they continue in this manner:

*As the father bishop could see how little progress he was making in this matter, he took all the main subjects and points of their errors and set out to write upon them, and he presented these documents to him, to which the king replied by writing other documents on these, resolving at the same time that he would not obey Rome. And, after he had stated this abundantly and shown his displeasure with the bishop and said publicly that he would not accept the First Council of Ephesus, which the bishop was urging him to embrace, but instead only the customs and faith of his forefathers, the bishop took his leave {[f. 179v]} of him determined* (saltem ad tempus)[4] *to make room for his displeasure. The king gave these very clear indications of his real feelings at the end of December '58, and directly in the following January of '59 the bishop took his leave of him, and shortly afterwards, in the month of February, there arrived in this land the Moors that here they call 'Malacais*[5] *(who are perhaps the Amalecites), and in the month of March that year and on the Thursday of Holy Week, the king encountered them and his men fled from him and left him on the field, where the wretched man died and, with him, our captain with eighteen Portuguese, and the victory of the Moors was so unexpected that*

---

[1] Guerreiro, 'Adição à Relação das coisas de Etiópia', f. 286/p. 312.

[2] Folio.

[3] Guerreiro, 'Adição à Relação das coisas de Etiópia', f. 295v/p. 323. This letter was Páez's main source on the early years of the first mission to Ethiopia, and he quotes from it at length in bk III, chs 4, 5 and 7, vol. II below.

[4] Latin: 'at least for the time being'.

[5] The Islamized population of 'Adāl. *Malaçai* (the writer has omitted the cedilla) was the Portuguese form of the local word *malassaye*, from *'slamawi*, 'Islamized'. The name is associated on phonetic grounds with the Amalecites of the Bible (enemies of the Hebrews, who lived in Sinai, e.g. Exodus 17:8–16, 1 Kings [1 Samuel] 15:1–9).

*their captain, attributing it to God alone, dismounted from his horse and celebrated the triumph of his victory riding an ass.*[1]

All these are the words of the fathers of the Society, which clearly show how far Emperor Claudio always was from obeying the holy Roman Church. But because Father Bishop Dom Andre de Oviedo, in speaking of him and his vassals, declared that very thing in a sentence that I have in my <[f. 162v/152v]> hand, signed by his own hand, I shall report it here in his own words, which are as follows:

*Andreas de Ouiedo Dei et Apostolica Sedis gratia Episcopus Hieropolensis, ac coadiutor Reuerendissimi in Christo patris et domini Joannis Barreto Patriarchæ Aethiopiæ.*[2] *Because just as it helps to publish and to praise good acts so that they may be imitated, so it also helps to tell and to reject public evils so that people may flee from them; therefore, we have publicly preached in Ethiopia the matters of the faith and written them down, and they have come to the notice of many or most of those who have wished to know them, and until now they have not {[f. 180]} wanted to receive our doctrine or the faith of Rome, rather in Oye last year, by the Cross, it was proclaimed that nobody should enter our church on pain of death, and to keep to the customs of their forefathers. And it appears to us that they do not err out of ignorance and they have many things that are not good, nor pleasing to Our Lord, we therefore define and by sentence declare that the people of Ethiopia in common, great and small and scholars and others of the Abyssinian people, do not wish to obey the holy Church of Rome, being obliged to do so like all Christians, as the Church of Rome is the head of all the Churches (and the pope of Rome father and pastor and superior of all Christians) and they are rebaptized many times and for many causes, which is contrary to the truth of the faith. Likewise, they publicly keep the Sabbaths and formerly they did not keep them in Ethiopia, and they circumcise themselves and they also circumcise many slaves and others that they make Christian, and many refuse or hold it a sin to eat the meat of swine and hare and other things, which was from the law of Moses, which in {these} <our> things already ceased by the death of Christ, and they divorce by justice against reason and against that which Christ commands in the Gospels, and many hold it a sin for men who have union with their wives to enter churches the following day, whereas this is not a commandment of Christ or of the Church. And many scholars stubbornly defend that in Christ there is one single nature and one operation and that the manhood of Christ is equal to the Godhead, which is contrary to the faith and the Gospel and the Synods, which say that Christ has a single person, two natures and two operations and two wills and that Christ according to the Godhead is equal to the Father and according to the manhood is less than the Father; {[f. 180v]} and in common they hold a feast on the 14th day of, it seems, our September for Dioscorus the defender of Eutyches the heretic, both of them condemned by the Church and for that reason they should not have a place in <[f. 163/153]> Ethiopia for Dioscorus. And they maintain other things against the faith of Rome, which they should not do, because there is only one faith and the faith of the Church of Rome by the promise of Christ cannot err.*

---

[1] Guerreiro, 'Adição à Relação das coisas de Etiópia', f. 296/p. 324. This passage was repeated in full by Almeida ('Historia de Ethiopia a alta', in Beccari, *RÆSOI*, 5, pp. 381–2).

[2] 'André de Oviedo, by the grace of God and the Apostolic See the Bishop of Hieropolis, and coadjutor of the Most Reverend in Christ Father Dom João Barreto, the Patriarch of Ethiopia'.

*Wherefore we admonish our spiritual sons to distance themselves from these and other errors that those of Ethiopia maintain and not to fall into them, and we refer the Ethiopians to the judgment of the Church and of its superiors with regard to punishing them in their persons and goods in public or in secret, or to have mercy on them, as they see fit and with whom they see fit, in full or in part, chiefly if there be repentance, which God may grant them through His mercy.*

*Done in the Docomo in Ethiopia, on the second day of February 1559*
*Gonçalo Cardoso – Apostolic Notary*
*Andreas Episcopus Hieropolensis.*
*Published in our Church in the Docomo on 2nd February 1559.*[1]

Up to here are words of the sentence of Father Bishop Dom Andre de Oviedo, who later became patriarch, and they and the rest of what we have said very clearly show that in Emperor Claudio's lifetime neither he nor his vassals obeyed the {holy} Roman Church, and his brother Minás, who succeeded him in the empire and was called Adamás Sagued, never gave obedience. Rather, for the four years that he lived as emperor, he persecuted the Catholics very {severely} <cruelly>, and he made many recant through his threats and cruelties, as the fathers of the Society affirmed in the same letter that we began to report before the sentence {[f. 181]} and shall continue in book 3, where we shall deal on purpose with this Emperor Adamás Sagued.

After Adamás Sagued died, he was succeeded by his son Emperor Zerça Denguîl, who was called Malác Sagued and reigned for thirty-three years, but, even though he did not persecute the Catholics like his father did, he never gave obedience to the Roman Church, because, despite having sent a man to India in 1576 and later, in 1593, a monk called Taclá Mariam to Rome, via Cairo – he was taking a letter from the captain of the Portuguese, Antonio de Gois by name, to His Majesty, and from the fathers to His Holiness and to the general of the Society[2] – the emperor did not write, nor did he intend to unite with the Roman Church, but to obtain assistance from the Portuguese against the Turks and some heathens called Gâlas who were seriously troubling his empire, as the old Portuguese who knew his nature and understood his intentions very well now testify.

This emperor was succeeded by a bastard son of his called Iacob, a seven-year-old boy, and therefore the empire was governed by the Empress Mariam Siná and Athanateus, her son-in-law, for almost seven years. And during this time they did not try to unite <[f. 163v/153v]> with the Roman Church. Rather, on receiving a letter that came to them from the Coast of Melinde by land from the fathers of Saint Augustine, in which they exhorted them to unite with the king of Portugal, they replied that they needed no more than a few craftsmen of various crafts, and all the great men were of the opinion that they should not admit any Portuguese at all.

In May 1603 I arrived in Ethiopia shortly after Iacob had begun to govern, and soon afterwards, in September, they deposed him {[f. 181v]} and sent him prisoner to the ends of the empire, to a kingdom that they call Nareá, and they elected a cousin of his, who was

---

[1] This letter was also transcribed by Almeida ('Historia de Ethiopia a alta', Beccari, *RÆSOI*, 5, pp. 383–4). Páez quotes this letter in Spanish.

[2] A letter dated 1596 and signed by a group of Portuguese states that Takla Māryām was sent by them to Rome in 1591 (see Beccari, *RÆSOI*, 10, pp. 391–3).

called Za Denguil. The Portuguese were very upset at this because, as they told me, he was very much against the matters of our holy faith, but after he understood them by means of the disputations that I held with his scholars in his presence over many days, of which I have often spoken, he then decided to give obedience to the holy Roman Church and to subject all his empire to it. But this did not take effect because, when his vassals realized this, the principal ones rose up against him and gave him a pitched battle on 13th October 1604 and killed him, as we shall say in book 4. After that they brought back Iacob; I often met him and gave him to understand our beliefs. He too wished to unite with the Roman Church, but before he could do so he was killed in battle on 10th March 1607 and the empire passed to a cousin of his who was called Susniós, and is now called Seltan Çagued. I continued with this one as well for a long time, clearly showing him the truth of our holy faith. He determined to follow and defend it until he might die doing so, and thenceforth, until today, he has with great fervour and diligence sought every means possible to make his vassals accept this holy faith and obey the holy Roman Church. He has never been able to do so entirely; rather they have tried to kill him many times because of this, especially in May 1617, as we said in chapter 5 of this second book.

There is therefore no doubt at all that for a very long time the Prester John's Ethiopian vassals have <always> been and still are {schismatics} disobedient to the holy Roman Church.

{[f. 182]} From what we have said, it can very clearly be seen how little information Friar Luis de Urreta had of the matters of Ethiopia, since in chapter 5 of the second book of his *Historia* and in chapter 1 of the third book he tries to prove that the Ethiopians have never been schismatics or refused to obey the Roman pontiff, and in confirmation of that, speaking of the time when Francisco Álvares[1] and Ambassador Dom Rodrigo de Lima entered Ethiopia, which was in 1520, he says this, on page 449:

*After that they went to Rome, and Pope Clement VII commanded <[f. 164/154]> in a private brief that the most senior archbishop should be* abuna *and apostolic nuncio, and in all things should substitute for the Pope, and on his death he should be succeeded by the oldest, most senior one. Paul III, Pius V, Gregory XIII and Sixtus V all confirmed this post, and these supreme pontiffs commanded that if there should arise any business of importance on which the nuncio was unable to decide, then they should go to Rome for the declaration, or else to the apostolic nuncio in Lisbon or, if that was not possible either, they should go to Goa, whose prelate would resolve the case with the theologians of that city and give the reply, giving him all his powers for that purpose. And they are governed in that way in Ethiopia today.*[2]

Up to here are words of the author. But in Ethiopia there are no archbishops or bishops, and the *abuna* is always an Egyptian and is sent by the patriarch of Alexandria, who resides in Cairo, and since I been here I have known two sent by him, and so, even if Pope Clement VII did issue that Brief (if he did) and the other supreme pontiffs that he mentions did confirm it (which they will know in Rome if it is true), the command

---

[1] See Glossary (Francisco Álvares).

[2] Urreta, *Historia de la Etiopia*, excerpt from bk II, ch. 5, entitled 'In which it is proved that the Ethiopians have never been schismatic or refused to obey the Roman Pontiff but rather have always recognized him as head since the primitive Church', p. 449. Páez quotes this passage in Spanish.

contained in it did not take effect, nor could it have done, because there were no such archbishops.

Similar to this is what he says on page 616,[1] that Emperor Mena (who was in fact called {[f. 182v]} Minás] wrote to Pope Pius V and made all the members of the Grand Council write to him as well with much submission and tears, with great Christianity and religion, all confessing to be Catholic Christians and sons of the Roman Church, and at the same time renewing their obedience to him and asking him to send the Tridentine Council. Emperor Minás could hardly have written these things to Pius V because not only was he such a cruel persecutor of the Catholic Church and enemy of its holy faith, as we have seen and shall see at length in the third book, but he died in February 1563, and Pope Pius V was elected in January 1566, and therefore even less could Pius V write him the letter that the author puts on page 578,[2] which he says was written in November 1570. There is no truth in what he puts on page 459[3] about the Prester John's ambassador, whom he names Zagazabo – who was actually called Zaga Sa Ab, which means 'Grace from the Father' – that he told King João III of Portugal that the Ethiopians had, ever since the beginnings of the primitive Church, acknowledged and confessed that the Roman pontiff was the first bishop and that until that day they had obeyed him as the vicar of Christ. There is no truth in this, for not only has much of what he said in Portugal since been found to be very different, but the Ethiopians readily show that they follow the same things as the people in whose land they happen to be.

---

[1] Urreta, *Historia de la Etiopia*, bk III, ch. 1, entitled 'In which is put a defence and Apology of the Catholic faith and Christian religion that the Ethiopians have always kept: and which deals with the Christianity of the Christians of Asia and of all the provinces of the world', pp. 571–623.

[2] Urreta, *Historia de la Etiopia*, bk III, ch. 1.

[3] Urreta, *Historia de la Etiopia*, bk III, ch. 5.

In which it is declared how the Ethiopians circumcise themselves, keep the Sabbath and other Jewish ceremonies[1]

One of the things to which the Ethiopians cling most strongly even today is circumcision, to the extent that, as they say themselves, if there were any among them who were uncircumcised, they would be considered heathens, {[f. 183]} and so they use the word *colafá*, which means 'uncircumcised', as a great insult. When they buy heathen slaves, until they are circumcised, under no circumstances will they eat from the plates that the slaves eat from or drink from the cups that they drink from without a priest blessing them first, or at least washing them very well, because they think they become contaminated.

They circumcise {boys} at eight days old, and sometimes girls too, ordinarily in the parents' house, and women commonly do this. And when we ask them why they do it, since circumcision is now finished, some answer that they found it thus from their parents, others that it is for beauty, others because the Law commands it. Christ profits them nothing, for this means that He has not yet come, since circumcision was a sign that He would come, Genesis 17,[2] and so those who are circumcised are obliged to fulfil all the Law, as Saint Paul says in Galatians 5.[3] They reply that Saint Paul also says there that neither circumcision avails anything, nor the prepuce, but faith that works by charity, and so being circumcised is nothing. To this I retorted that, if such were the meaning of that passage, the apostle would contradict himself in a few words by saying, 'if you be circumcised, Christ shall profit you nothing', and then, 'being circumcised is nothing'; it is the same as saying you may not circumcise yourselves and you may circumcise yourselves. What Saint Paul intends there is to undeceive the Galatians, who, being heathen by caste, after being converted and after the Law of Christ Our Lord was published, put their hope in keeping circumcision and ceremonies of the Law, since they thought that without it grace would not be sufficient for their salvation. He also intends to explain to them that neither being circumcised nor keeping the prepuce avails them anything for this hope, unlike faith that works by charity, because hope of salvation does not come from circumcision or from the prepuce, but from faith with works, for without works even faith is dead, as Saint James says in chapter 2.[4]

{[f. 183v]} When they hear these things and realize that they have nothing to say in reply, they resort to saying that they do it for beauty's sake, to which we reply that this

---

[1] The content of this ch. was repeated by Almeida ('Historia de Ethiopia a alta', Beccari, *RÆSOI*, 5, pp. 133–6).
[2] Genesis 17:9–14.
[3] Galatians 5:2–6.
[4] James 2:17.

excuse is not enough for <[f. 165/155]> them to be able to do something that scandalizes most Christians and which Saint Paul seriously prohibits in so many places and the apostles prohibited in that famous council that they held in Jerusalem, which is reported in the Acts of the Apostles, chapter 15. With these and other things that we brought them in general disputations and private conversations, many came to confess that it was right not to be able to practise circumcision and some are now not circumcising their sons and the heathen slaves that they buy, including the emperor, who had one son and three or four grandchildren born after he heard our doctrine, and he commanded that they should not be circumcised and so they were left, but the others are so hard-headed that there is no way that we can persuade them to give up circumcision.

The Ethiopians also commonly keep the Sabbaths and many monks do so with such observance and rigour that it seems they would rather allow themselves to be put to death than break it. They start to keep it on Friday evening like the Jews, and throughout that day some of them do not come out of some tiny huts that they have inside the veranda that they ordinarily build round the church, nor do they talk to anybody until evening, when they go to eat. In particular, in a monastery with many monks that is called Bisam, which is about one and a half days' journey from the port of Maçuá, they eat meat on Friday evening, because they say that the feast of the Sabbath has already begun, and (they say) the inhabitants of the province of Amacem and the other lands near the Red Sea do so as well, in imitation of them. When I arrived in Ethiopia, in the first disputations that I had with the scholars in the presence of Emperor Za Denguil, the first thing that they asked me was why we did not keep the Sabbath. I answered that it was because the Sabbath was the principal Jewish ceremony and the principal figure of the Old Testament, as Saint Paul explained to the Colossians, {[f. 184]} chapter 2,[1] and, since the ceremonies and figures of the Old Testament ended with the coming and death of Christ Our Lord, people could no longer keep the Sabbath and Saint Paul therefore severely reprimanded the Colossians and Galatians in the epistles that he writes to them, because they kept the Sabbath.[2] When I mentioned to them these passages and others in the Holy Gospel showing that all this is finished, and explained to them the reasons why the holy Church keeps Sunday instead of the Sabbath, some of them came to confess that it was right not to be able to keep it. Emperor Za Denguil, who was a man of great understanding, had it proclaimed that nobody should keep the Sabbath from that time onwards and they were already beginning to break it, particularly at court, but as they killed him shortly afterwards they soon went back to their old custom, until the emperor who is now alive came to the throne, <[f. 165v/155v]> and as he understood our things he too proclaimed that nobody should keep it, and many people are now making an effort. Were it not for the bad example and doctrine of the monks, keeping the Sabbath would have been abandoned altogether by now, but they put it into the common people's heads that they have an obligation to keep it, to the extent that because of this there was a major uprising against the emperor a short time ago, as we shall say at the end of book 4.

Not only do the Ethiopians circumcise themselves and keep the Sabbath, as we have said, but they do not eat certain things that used to be prohibited by the Law, such as hare and rabbit, and they show great aversion to the Portuguese because they have heard that

[1] Colossians 2:16–17.
[2] Galatians 3:1–5.

they eat them. And although some people eat wild boar and fish without scales, there are not many who do; the rest, especially monks, will not eat them at all. They consider women who have given birth to be unclean for forty days, if they have had a son, and eighty if a daughter, and during this time they may not enter the church, nor can {[f. 184v]} menstruating women, and not even married couples who have lain together at night may enter church the following day and, if it happens that one of them dies soon after and is found by the other, they do not bury that person in the church, but in the churchyard, and they complain a lot about the Portuguese because they do not keep these things.

From that it can be seen how false Friar Luis de Urreta's information was since, wishing to defend the Ethiopians against what we have mentioned about them, after many arguments that he could well have done without, he says on page 473:

*As soon as the supreme pontiffs commanded them not to perform such ceremonies, they immediately bowed their heads and obeyed the apostolic mandates, so that they no longer circumcise themselves or keep the Sabbath.*

And a little further on, speaking about pork, he says:

*They have complied with the Roman Church in everything and now they eat it, and they have profited so much from it that they hold it to be the most delicious and most coveted food, so that they also give it to the sick, and they do not purge anyone who is not when they give him pork to eat. The reason is that, since it is a moist meat, it is more suited to the dry climate of that land, and also because they raise their swine on dates, because there are no acorns there.*[1]

This is what the author says, but it is all very different from the truth of what happens here, because there are no dates, nor do they give pork to the sick, nor can the healthy even stand the sight of it, apart from some that only eat it when it is wild. <[f. 166/156]> With regard to abandoning circumcision and no longer keeping the Sabbath, they have never obeyed the apostolic mandates, because they have always circumcised themselves and they keep the Sabbath until today, as we have said.

{[f. 185]} I point out that it is also impossible to accept the doctrine that he mentions on page 467,[2] where, to excuse the Ethiopians' circumcision, he says that they may circumcise themselves for devotion's sake and so as to resemble Christ, so that there is neither respect for the Law of Moses nor any scandal. This cannot be accepted because, apart from the fact that they know very well that the Portuguese are scandalized and even so they do not stop circumcising themselves, nobody can do for devotion's sake something that is prohibited by some divine law, because then they are not works of devotion but sins and offences against God; otherwise it would often be lawful to break the law, saying that we did so out of some devotion to God, which cannot be. So when Saul excused himself for offering a sacrifice, not just out of devotion but by force of necessity, the prophet Samuel reprimanded him severely, 1 Kings 13, and said that because he had not kept

---

[1] Urreta, *Historia de la Etiopia*, excerpts from bk II, ch. 6, entitled 'Of the books called Manda & Abethilis, dealing with circumcision and observance of the Sabbath and other rites that the Ethiopians used to keep and the end that they had, with other ecclesiastical customs', pp. 460–81. Páez quotes this passage in Spanish.

[2] Urreta, *Historia de la Etiopia*, bk II, ch. 6.

God's commandments his kingdom would pass to someone else. And another time when, out of devotion, he kept the Amalecites' best animals to sacrifice to God, Samuel said to him, in chapter 15, 'Doth the Lord desire holocausts and victims, and not rather that the voice of the Lord should be obeyed? For obedience is better than sacrifices.'[1] So God's precepts must not be broken, not for any devotion. And therefore one cannot say that it is lawful for the Ethiopians to circumcise themselves for devotion's sake.

Since we are talking about this subject, I thought I would also give some news here of a new sect that has arisen in Ethiopia, the followers of which circumcise themselves and keep the Sabbath in honour of the Father and Sunday in honour of the Son and Monday in honour of the Holy Spirit, all three days with great solemnity, and they have many other Jewish ceremonies that they were taught by a monk called {[f. 185v]} Za Christós, which means 'Of Christ'; but later his disciples said that he was in fact called Ze Christós, which means 'The Same Christ', and in 1602 he came out saying that he was Christ the true Messiah promised in the Law, and he gathered twelve companions whom he called apostles and gave them the same names as those of Christ Our Lord, and said that he would die crucified and rise again on the third day, together with many other things. When he heard this, Emperor Za Denguil commanded he be seized and, as he did not abandon this perverse deception, he had him beheaded early in 1604, so that they should see that he did not die crucified, and he ordered them to keep the body for seven days <[f. 166v/156v]> without burial, so that they could not say that he had risen again on the third day, as he had promised. He also wanted to have his disciples killed as well, but the great men begged him to spare them, because that man had deceived them and they now knew their error and were repentant, and so he pardoned them. But although they pretended for a while, they later went to a kingdom that they call Amhará, to the province of Olacá, and perverted many people, saying that that man was Christ and had risen again and that he had appeared to them many times and commanded them to keep Saturday, Sunday and Monday, as we have said; the property of the ones who joined them was held in common as in the times of the primitive Church. Emperor Seltan Sagued told me that, and I said to him that it was necessary to remedy that straight away, and that it would be good to have them all brought and split up among the monasteries, so that they could show them how wrong they were and teach them. But he was not able to do so since he was very busy with those who had risen up against him because he was defending our holy faith, as we said above in chapters 4 and 5. {[f. 186]} And these revolts were very convenient for those people because, since they found nobody to oppose them, they taught their errors in public. In the province of Olacá they dedicated the church of a large monastery to their master, where many monks and nuns gathered from many parts (for nuns can wander wherever they like here); many married men also went with their wives and children and said that they were going to be saints and, when they arrived, the men were put in one part and the women in another.

On learning what was happening, *Erás* Celá Christós, the emperor's brother, who also governed the province of Olacá, wrote to the emperor that it was growing fast, and he replied that he should at once send someone who could convince them of their error by means of the Scriptures and, if in the end they did not want to be reduced, he should punish them rigorously. He therefore sent a very noble man of great understanding and

---

[1] 1 Kings [1 Samuel] 13:10–14 and 15:22.

well versed in the Scriptures, whose name was Fecura Egzi and who had been reduced to our holy faith a long time before. He seized many of them and sent two of those monks to *Erás* Celá Christós so that he could have more news of their beliefs. When they arrived, he summoned me to his house, since I happened to be there on some business, and, in the presence of many monks and great lords (who had gathered to hear such a great novelty), he told me to explain to them how blind and wrong they were. I therefore started to prove to them through the Scriptures that Christ Our Lord was the true Messiah and how all the things that were prophesied about the Messiah were fulfilled in Him. They replied that they did not deny <[f. 167/157]> that Christ Our Lord was the true Messiah, but that He Himself had become flesh once again, joining with the first flesh, and had died for us. I asked them in which place in Scripture they found that Christ would become flesh twice and die twice and how the two fleshes were joined. {[f. 186v]} They replied that he himself had said so to his twelve disciples (for these two were not of the twelve, but of those who had joined him later), and that nothing was impossible for God, for even we can put on two vestments when we wish to. I asked them how in a matter of such importance they could in that way believe the words of a man of whom no Scripture spoke and who did not do <such wonderful> works by which one might believe him, for even Christ Our Lord, despite doing such wonderful works, said that they should consider the Scriptures, for they gave testimony of Him; and I asked them whether the doctrine that He had taught us was true. They replied that it could not be lacking in anything, because He was the Son of God. 'Because He knew that things like these would happen', said I, 'He Himself forewarned us in the Holy Scripture, in Matthew 24, saying that we should take heed that no man seduce us, for many would come in His name saying, "I am Christ," and they would seduce many, and that if anyone were to say to us, "Here is Christ, or there," we should not believe him.'[1]

With these and other things that I said to them but leave aside now so as not to be too long, they came to confess their mistake and affirmed that even beforehand they had had some doubts about those things and that, now that Our Lord God had enlightened them, they were ready for any penitence that they might wish to give them. I replied that if they were saying that with true repentance, they would certainly be pardoned, because God does not want the sinner to die, but to be converted and live, and whenever he is sorry for his sins, he shall no longer remember them. When they went away, I warned *Erás* Celá Christós that they should not be left together but in different monasteries, and that they should not allow them to speak to people from outside until they had instructed them well and could see that they were sound in what they said.

{[f. 187]} A few days later, Fecurá Egzi came and told me that those twelve disciples of the one who made himself Christ had put it into many people's heads that he really was, and that, this second time, he had taken flesh of the gentile people to unite it with the Jewish people, and that he had risen again and spoken to them many times; but some were saying that the first flesh that he had taken from the Jewish people had not died again now; others that it had also died with the second flesh. Fecurá Egzi said that he had laboured for many days with them to reduce them, showing them the Scriptures and giving them <[f. 167v/157v]> many reasons, and as they had nothing to reply, they retreated into the idea that what that man had taught them was the truth and they would

---

[1] Matthew 24:4 and 23.

not accept anything else at all. In the end, therefore, he told them that if they did not abandon such a simple, gross error, he would have them thrown off a rock that is near that monastery, and they took no heed of that. To see whether they would be afraid when they arrived there, he had them all taken there and many of them stood on the highest point of it and said, 'If you will leave us be in our faith, we shall keep it, and if not, we shall throw ourselves off from here.' He replied that they should decide to accept the truth of what he had shown them, or else he would have them thrown off without fail. On hearing this, they picked up some children of theirs who were nearby and, before anyone could come to their aid, they threw them down the rock and flung themselves straight after them, so that they were all dashed to pieces.

When he saw such folly, he hurried to the others, threw himself at their feet with great sadness and begged them not to persist in that, for they would waste their lives and souls, since it was a great trick of the devil, but they were not in the least moved, and later they ignored his pleas and those of many monks whom he had asked to come for that purpose {[f. 187v]} from {other} <many> places. He therefore commanded that they should throw them off the rock, and in all 488 men and women died. One of those who had thrown themselves off of their own free will happened to fall down a part that was not so high and so she did not die, although she nearly did; they carried her back up and asked her how she was not afraid to throw herself off such a high rock to dash her body to pieces and lose her soul, to which she answered that she did not see rocks but very fine beds on which to lie down; and so they left her to see whether, from what she had experienced so much to her own cost – that those were not beds but hard rocks – she might finally realize that it was all a trick of the devil and so be reduced.[1] And they say that there are still many others in hiding and that it will be very difficult to finally put out this fire.

---

[1] I.e. repent and be converted.

# CHAPTER IX

## Which deals with the errors that the Ethiopians have in the holy sacrament of baptism

Since we have already seen the errors that the Ethiopians have in the articles of the holy faith, it is now appropriate to report those that they have in the holy sacraments, beginning with holy baptism, as it is the first of them all and, principally, it was instituted so that we might be pardoned the first guilt of original sin and, consequently, it is bestowed on us in order to enter the Church of Christ and to participate in the remaining sacraments. In this sacrament, [certain] Ethiopians {... excessively...} keep the true form when they baptize, {... there are some} but [most], including monks, baptize <[f. 168/158]> without knowing it. When by chance I recently asked some monks who live about half a league from the court (and they should therefore have been better aware of even more difficult matters) what words they said when they baptized, they replied the following: 'I baptize thee in the Holy Spirit.' {[f. 188]} And when I asked them how they could do such a serious thing as that, because they did not say the words that Christ Our Lord commanded in the Gospel, they replied that it was because nobody had taught them. When I asked more specifically about these things, they affirmed to me that they [ordinarily used these and other unauthentic forms][1] and that there were many who baptized without saying all the words, particularly in the lands governed by the *bahar nagax*. That does not surprise me very much because even in the emperor's court a short time ago, in one of its main churches, a monk who was baptizing a heathen lad said, 'I baptize thee in the name of the Father and the Holy Ghost.' When the godfather asked why he did not also mention the Son, he laughed and said that that would be the Portuguese way, and that he would not mention Him.

They baptize boys after forty days and girls after eighty and priests always perform it. Apart from some learned monks and other lay people who, on account of the communication they have had with the old Portuguese and what they have heard from us, baptize children at any time if they are in danger of dying, the rest will not baptize them before that time at all, even if they are dying. They usually do not put on holy oils but a liquor that they get from oleaster wood, which they chop up very fine and put in a pan with holes in the bottom, then they set light to it on top and collect the fluid that drips through the holes below, and this they call *zeite*[2] and with it they anoint the children that they baptize {without blessing them...}. Moreover, if somebody becomes a Moor or idolatrizes with heathens, they will not accept him into the Church again without first baptizing him, and even Christians who are captured by heathens are baptized when they return, because they have eaten and drunk with them.

---

[1] Noted in the margin in a different hand in ARSI, MS Goa 42.
[2] *zayt*, oil.

{[f. 188v]} Every year they rebaptize themselves on Epiphany Day in memory of the fact that Christ Our Lord was baptized in the Jordan on that day, and, as they tell me, they say the form of the sacrament and consider it true baptism, and so {sometimes} <at the same time> they baptize there the children who have never been baptized when on that day they reach the age on which they customarily baptize them. I did not content myself with asking many of them how they celebrated this festival and the ceremonies they performed in it, but I wrote it down as I was told it by the abbot of a monastery, a friend of mine, who performs this office every year, as follows. Those who do not live near a lake have the streams dammed so that enough water is held back to reach the chests of the people who are to be baptized. The day before the festival, {some} two or three hours before sunset, the abbot goes there with his monks and clergy, taking a cross <[f. 168v/158v]> and altar stone[1] and the books that they normally use for their offices inside the church and, when they arrive, they place the altar stone on a wooden altar that they have fashioned inside a tent or a shelter that they make near the water. Some monks adorn themselves with the richest ornaments that they have in the church, a deacon takes up the cross on a long staff and, singing and censing, they plant the staff bearing the cross in the water, in the part where it enters the pool. And then they sing the Psalms and other things and they read the whole of the Acts of the Apostles and the Gospel of Saint Matthew or Saint Mark, and they even told me that in some places they read all four, beginning the first facing east, the second west, the third north and the fourth south. They spend the evening doing this until night-time, when they take out the cross and place it on the altar and withdraw to a tent or shelter, where they have a splendid supper in their manner.

After midnight, they get up and, lighting candles, they chant their offices, as they do in the church on great feast days, and they say a dry Mass[2] with music in their manner. And meanwhile they confess if the previous evening {[f. 189]} they were unable to confess, or the most devout of them do, since the rest do not care about that. As the sun rises, all the monks and clergy go to the edge of the water, and the abbot or the monk officiating in his place puts oil on the cross and then, touching the water with it, makes the sign of the cross, saying, 'In the name of the Father and of the Son and of the Holy Spirit one God.' Making the sign of the cross again, he says, 'One Holy Father, one Holy Son and one Holy Spirit.' Having done that, he hands the cross to someone else and removes all his clothes behind a cloth serving as a screen, while he enters the water; two priests follow him until the water comes up to their chests and, placing him in the middle, each one puts a hand over his head, without touching it, and says, 'I baptize thee in the name of the Father, the Son and the Holy Spirit', and he dips his head into the water three times. Then he baptizes the other two, saying those words. Meanwhile, all the other priests are in the water singing and clapping as a sign of festivity and then they baptize each other, repeating the form. Others say that they do not say the form for the priests, but they just plunge themselves in the water, but with deacons and lay men and women the priest puts his hand on their heads and plunges them in three times while saying the form of baptism.

When they were baptized in these general baptisms, the emperors (who had never failed to take part until the current one stopped in 1609, after I showed him that people

---

[1] See Glossary (altar stone/*tābot*).
[2] A mass without consecration or communion.

should not be rebaptized) put up a tent next {at the water's edge} <in the water> and the patriarch would baptize them in the pool, {going in} with a small cloth girded at the waist and everyone else naked. Francisco Álvares says on folio 121[1] <[f. 169/159]> that he saw this and that the baptism begins at midnight, but it seems that they did so to show him more splendour, or so that there would be time to be able to baptize all the people, as there must have been many of them; but now they only start at sunrise. And if there are so many people that they cannot baptize them all because it is too late, they say to the ones that are left, 'We give you leave to baptize yourselves. Come in: may baptism come to you.' And then they all get into the water together {[f. 189v]} and they consider themselves baptized. And if for any reason some are left without being baptized on that day, they are baptized ten days later, when they also hold a {large} festival in the church, because they say that Our Lady died on that day and that she went up to heaven on 19th August. They call all those ten days following the baptism 'astareo', which means 'appearance', because the Holy Spirit appeared in the form of a dove on Christ Our Lord when he was baptized, and therefore they also call the glorious Transit of the Virgin 'Astareo Mariam'. And they do not content themselves with being baptized on this day or on Epiphany Day, but many who want to show themselves to be most devout are also baptized in church on the day of the Resurrection of Christ Our Lord, and the water in which they are to be baptized is kept inside the church all Holy Week.

I have spoken to the scholars of Ethiopia on this subject on many occasions, some of them in the presence of Emperor Seltan Sagued, and I have proved to them at length, through Saint Paul, the Councils and reasoning based on Scripture, that they must not be baptized more than once. The main source is the passage in Hebrews 6: 'non {rursus} <rursum> iacientes fundamentum',[2] etc., where the apostle clearly says that it is impossible for those that have sinned after baptism to be again baptized or for those that have sinned after confirmation to be again confirmed, because these are foundations that cannot be laid more than once. I also asked them whether this general baptism that they perform every year was true baptism, like that which a person who has never been baptized receives, and they replied that it was. 'Hence', said I, 'one might infer the falsehood of that which Our Lord affirmed through Saint Matthew, chapter 18, and Saint John, chapter 20: "Amen dico vobis, quaecumque alligaveritis super terram," etc.,[3] because if a sinner goes and confesses just before that baptism, however much the confessor denies him absolution it will be to no avail, because he will then go and be baptized and will be forgiven everything and will be in a better situation than if he had been absolved, because he becomes new again, which cannot be achieved through penitence, as Saint Paul says in Hebrews 6, saying, {[f. 190]} "Impossibile enim est," etc. "renovari ad poenitentiam."[4] "Id est novum fieri,"[5] as Saint Chrysostom explains.'

---

[1] Álvares, *Prester John of the Indies*, ch. 96, 'How the Prester John sent to tell those of the embassy and the Franks to go and see his baptism, and of the performance which the Franks played for him, and how he ordered that I should be present at the baptism, and of the nature of the tank, and how he desired the Portuguese to swim, and gave them a banquet', pp. 345–6.

[2] Hebrews 6:1, 'not laying again the foundation.'

[3] Matthew 18:18, 'Amen I say to you, whatsoever you shall bind upon earth ...'. The reference to John 20 appears to be a mistake by Páez.

[4] Hebrews 6:4–6, 'For it is impossible ... to be renewed again to penance.'

[5] 'that is, to become new.'

On hearing these things, some replied that they did so as a reminder that they were <[f. 169v/159v]> baptized. 'In that way', said I, 'priests can also be ordained every year so as not to forget that they are ordained. The Jews do not forget that they are Jews, nor the Moors that they are Moors, so should Christians forget that they are baptized? If people had such poor memories, it should be enough to see so many children being baptized and to confess and take communion so many times, professing that they are Christians, for them to remember it. That is not a good excuse to defend such a serious thing as being rebaptized, for Saint Paul spoke against some that wanted to do so, saying that it would be like recrucifying Christ, because insofar as it is, on their part they crucify him again: "{*rursus*} <*rursum*> *crucifigentes*,"[1] Hebrews 6.' With these conversations and those that my companion fathers had with them many times on this same subject, many have now stopped being rebaptized, but others still do, as we have said. From that it may be seen how wrongly Friar Luis de Urreta says, on page 486,[2] that people falsely ascribed to the Ethiopians that they were rebaptized every year on Epiphany Day, and that Francisco Álvares – who affirms that he saw the baptism and that they said the form of this sacrament – was mistaken since he did not understand the language, and that they merely said certain blessings and prayers with which they blessed the water of the pool. But the truth is that, in addition to these blessings, they say the form of the sacrament of baptism when they baptize there.

---

[1] Hebrews 6:6, 'crucifying again.'

[2] Urreta, *Historia de la Etiopia*, bk II, ch. 7, entitled 'Of the holy sacrament of baptism, in which the Ethiopians keep the faith of the Roman Church, without having the errors that people ascribe to them', pp. 481–7.

# CHAPTER X

## On the holy sacrament of confirmation and extreme unction and on that of penance

I have brought all these holy sacraments together in this chapter because I have little to say about the first two: the Ethiopians do not perform them at all, and I have been unable to find anyone who could tell me whether at any time they knew about confirmation, because they say that their books do not deal with {[f. 190v]} it and they do not know what it is. I am not very surprised at this ignorance, even though Christ Our Lord instituted this holy sacrament, as shown in Saint John, chapters 16 and 20,[1] where He promised and gave the Holy Spirit to the apostles, and even though the apostles performed it. In the early Church, by special commission or dispensation, they did so just by placing their hands on the baptized, and they received the Holy Spirit in this way, as stated in Acts 18 and 19.[2] It had to be done in that manner at that time in order to perfect the faith and confirm it, but once the Church was sufficiently well established, and that extraordinary way of receiving the Holy Spirit ceased, they would anoint people with holy oil, as the usual method instituted by Christ for confirming the faithful. Despite all that, the Ethiopians' ignorance of confirmation is hardly surprising, because they penetrate the Scriptures so little that they do not even understand other much clearer things that are in them, and most of them are so unscholarly that, although they have very few books, they do not know what is in them; thus they often argue against certain things <[f. 170/160]> of ours that their own books teach as well. It is more surprising that they do not perform the sacrament of extreme unction, which Saint James in his Epistle, chapter 5, says should be given in these words, which many of them know by heart: 'Infirmatur quis in vobis', etc.[3] Here the apostle clearly shows that this sacrament, like the others, was instituted by Christ, as he resolutely affirms that the sick person's sins shall be forgiven him. A monk also assured me that one of their {Sinodos}[4] <books> ordered that the sick should be anointed, although it was not done and he did not know if it ever had been done.

As we come to the sacrament of penance, the Ethiopians believe that someone who has sinned mortally after baptism is obliged to perform it and to be reconciled with God by

---

[1] John 16:13–14 and 20:22. In the Ethiopian Orthodox Church, the sacrament of confirmation is administered immediately after baptism.

[2] Acts of the Apostles 18:25 and 19:2–6.

[3] James 5:14, 'Is any man sick among you?'

[4] The *Sénodos* is a compilation of canon law that forms part of the Ethiopian Orthodox New Testament. (See Bausi, ed., 'Il sēnodos etiopico', *CSCO–SAE*, 101–2, Louvain, 1995.) Páez considers it apocryphal and not authoritative.

means of confession, and therefore some of them confess often, whereas {others} <some> do so very late, and some never. And if they go for many years without confessing, their vicar does not ask them why they do not do so. When they come to confess, they do not begin with the confession 'I, a sinner', etc., nor do they say anything except, 'Father, I have sinned; release me', which is the same as 'absolve me.' Some confessors ask the penitent {[f. 191]} what they are to absolve him for, and he mentions {two or three} <three or four> sins, such as 'I have lied' or 'I have broken the feast day' and they absolve him, even though he may still have many others. He does not usually declare how many times he has committed the sin that he is confessing, nor do they ask him that, and some confessors absolve people who just say 'I have sinned, I have sinned.' They also say that sometimes many people come together and ask the priest for absolution, and when they all say 'I have sinned, I have sinned', he tells them to say some prayer and then utters the form of absolution [which is not the true form][1] for all of them together. Most of them do not confess simple fornication, since they do not hold it to be a sin, to the extent that unmarried people often agree to live together for a while, and they go to a priest and the young man says, 'I have agreed to live with this woman this summer. Bind her with excommunication not to leave me, and I too will be bound by excommunication not to leave her.' He binds them with excommunication not to leave one another for all that time.

The confessor often knows that the penitent is currently cohabiting and that he will not leave his woman, and even so he absolves him. And it is not just idiot monks that do this, but some of the *abunas* are so ignorant that they not only absolve them when they are cohabiting but tell them not to throw out their women, as I was told by a Greek who had been in Ethiopia for years. When he was reduced to our holy faith in 1604 he told me, before confessing, that he had three women and was not married to any of them, and when he had confessed with *Abuna* Pétros, who was the *abuna* at the time, he had told him that he had them and the *abuna* had answered that he should not throw them out, for they would be lost; instead, he should keep them, but <[f. 170v/160v]> make them equal, {and} <but> he would absolve him. Later, he said to Emperor Zadenguil as a joke, when I was present, 'Lord, this father is very strict. I went to confess with him and, because I told him that I had three women, he would not confess me; he tells me to marry one and throw the others out. Our *abuna* is more liberal because, when I told him in confession that {[f. 191v]} I had them, he gave me leave to keep them, on condition that I made them equal, and he absolved me.' The emperor, who at that time had already decided to give obedience to the {holy} Roman Church, said to him, 'What kind of Christianity is yours? If you have three women, do what the father orders you to do.' And while *Abuna* Simão[2] – whom they killed on 11th May 1617, as we said in chapter 5 – was confessing a great lord who had secretly had two houses of another lord burnt down, he obliged the lord to tell him that he had burnt them down and he would pardon him, and that is what he did. The owner of the houses told me this afterwards, and said that the lord had had them burnt down in order to kill him inside and that it was God's will that he had not been there that night, and he revealed a very great aversion to him.

Although the ignorance that we have mentioned is commonly found among confessors and penitents, there are some people (as I have been told) who, when they confess,

---

[1] Marginal note written in a different hand in ARSI, MS Goa 42.
[2] See Glossary (Simam/Simão).

declare the number of their sins, not just those that they have committed in deed, but also in word and in thought, and sometimes the confessor also asks them this. But they seldom or never oblige the penitents to pay for the damage they have done or to restore the property of others that they have taken; they merely say, 'Do not do that again.'

They do not worry about usury, since it is common among them, and when I asked whether the confessors had any summa of cases to guide them, they told me that they had no book dealing with this; they went by doctrine and by their *Sinodos*. The penances that they give are sometimes very lenient for serious sins and other times unbearable for very minor things. A reputable man once told me that because he had laughed in church a monk had given him a penance of bowing 1,000 times so that his head touched the ground each time, between two o'clock in the afternoon and nightfall; when he refused to do this penance because the time was too short, he commanded him to do it on pain of excommunication; {he did it} for fear of the excommunication. And {[f. 192]} he told me that he had been so tired that he could not move, even the next day. These obeisances are what they most usually give as a penance. They also tell them to recite fifty psalms, and sometimes all 150, every day for a whole year, and sometimes to fast every day for three or four years, and ordinarily they do not take communion until they have fulfilled it.

When they confess, the confessor and the penitent both stand unless the things they have to say are so lengthy that they sit down together; when the confession is over, they get up and he absolves him standing. Some of the most scholarly monks that they have wrote down for me the form of absolution that they use, and it is this: 'So-and-so, servant of God, may Jesus Christ give you leave and pardon you your sin through the mouths of Peter and Paul <[f. 171/161]> and may He release you from the prison of sin.' Another monk said it to me like this: 'Servant of God, so-and-so, may the Paraclete pardoner of guilt and sin pardon you all your sins.' And another said: 'May you be released by the mouth of Our Lord Jesus Christ, by the mouths of Peter and Paul, by the mouths of the 318 true men of the faith.'

When people fail to confess their sins in full, it is because they think that they are still fulfilling their duty by doing that, because the monks do not teach them, and most of them do not know enough to be able to do so. If they did teach them, they would confess not only all their sins but the circumstances as well, however minor they may be, as can be seen in many people who show themselves to be very scrupulous about very small things and so desirous of salvation that they even confess very serious sins out loud to their *abuna* in front of anyone who wishes to gather there. There are ordinarily many people present, because he sometimes comes out in public for this purpose, and he sits on his chair with many people on either side of him. Those who want to confess come through the crowd one at a time. As one gets close, he says in a loud voice, 'Lord, I have done such-and-such a thing', which are usually the worst sins that he has committed in his life, and then he bows his head, waiting for the penance, and the *abuna* raises his {[f. 192v]} staff with both hands and gives him three or four hard blows on his back, saying, 'You have done that and you do not fear God? Give him thirty lashes over there.' He then moves away and goes to receive them from the hands of two men who always walk in front of the *abuna* with some long strips of leather tied to sticks. When they have given him six or eight lashes, those present plead for him and the *abuna* then says that it is enough and absolves him. Then another one comes up, and he dispatches him and all the rest who want to confess as he did the first one.

371

What I have said was related to me both by some Portuguese who witnessed it and by some local people who were present on some occasions. They told me that when one man came to confess he asked the *abuna* to hear him in secret, because he could not {reveal} <say> what he had to say in public, and he answered, 'Will you not say it afterwards in front of the angels? Why do you not say it now in front of men?' So he told him that he had stolen a number of cows. Their owner, who had been unable to find out who had taken them, was there and heard this, and he accused him of theft before a judge, and the man not only returned the cows he had taken, but paid a lot of property as a fine. Therefore, since they confess such serious sins in public and at such risk, there is no doubt that <[f. 171v/161v]> they would be more likely to confess all the smaller ones in secret, with all the circumstances, if they had someone to explain to them that it was necessary to do so for their confession to be valid.

Friar Luis de Urreta, in chapter 8 of his second book,[1] seeks to defend the Ethiopians by saying that, although for a long time they had no knowledge of the sacraments of confirmation and extreme unction, once the Roman Church taught them the doctrine of these sacraments they accepted it with great joy, and they have performed them ever since with the diligence that the Florentine and Tridentine Councils demanded. He says that they have always used the sacrament of confession {[f. 193]} with all the thoroughness that the holy Church proposes and they confess all their sins without leaving out any of them, and they include all their circumstances and conditions. If somebody happens to fall into sin, he goes to confess at once, for otherwise those who see him are scandalized; and there is no one, no matter how distracted, who does not confess at least twice a week, and the most devoted and withdrawn usually confess every day. Their confessors are governed today by the *Summa* of Sylvestre[2] as well as others, which were sent to them from Rome by Father Friar Serafino of the Order of Preachers, who was the general of his holy religion. He also says that the confession that the penitents say to the priest is the same as one used by the Roman Church, but they begin with Psalm 78: '*Salvum me fac Deus*', etc.,[3] and then they say, 'I, a sinner, confess to God', etc., while kneeling, with the confessor seated as a judge. We have already shown above how contrary all this is to what actually happens.

---

[1] Urreta, *Historia de la Etiopia*, bk II, ch. 8, entitled 'How the Ethiopians had no knowledge of the sacraments of confirmation and extreme unction and in that of penance they kept the faith of the Roman Church', pp. 487–93.

[2] Urreta is referring to the two-volume *Summa Silvestrina* by Silvestro da Prieria Mazzolini (c. 1456–1523). Several re-editions of this work were issued during the 16th century.

[3] Psalm 68 [69]:2, 'Save me, O God.' The writer has mistakenly attributed this passage to Psalm 78 [79].

# CHAPTER XI

## Which deals with the most holy sacrament of the Eucharist and the ceremonies that the Ethiopian priests perform in their mass

The Ethiopians have very great devotion and reverence for the ineffable sacrament of the Eucharist, because they believe that once the priest has said the words of consecration (which, as some monks have told me, are almost the same as those the Catholic Church says) the bread stops being bread and the wine stops being wine, and beneath their accidents is really and truly the body and blood of Christ Our Lord, hypostatically united with the person of the divine Word. As well as believing this and confessing that, although the human nature was united with the divine, it was not changed or mixed, many here affirm that there is only one single nature in Christ, <[f. 172/162]> as we said in chapters 3 and 4.

They consecrate in leavened bread, and to make it they have a little building outside the church to the east, close to the back of the choir, {{f. 193v}} and if sometimes there is no room there they move it slightly to the north. There is nothing in this building other than what is needed to make the bread and wine that they use; in it, a monk grinds the flour, which is hard work when there is a large amount, because they do not have a mill. Sometimes they also give it to an honourable widowed or married woman who lives near the church to grind. When it is time to make the bread (which is always a little before Mass, and they find it very strange that we do not make the hosts every day), then a priest goes and kneads it with leaven and, if there are usually only a few people to take communion, he makes a bread the size of a paten[1] and little more than a fingerbreadth in thickness, and if there are many he makes it two fingerbreadths thick and as large as necessary, because they only make a single bread for consecration, except on certain major feast days when they make three. They mark this bread with five small crosses made with a cross-shaped wooden signet. Then he makes some other small breads that they give to everyone as holy bread. Afterwards, they bake them on a large earthenware dish and, when they are done, they put the one to be consecrated in a small copper bowl and the others in a little basket that they have for this purpose.

They make the wine from raisins in the same building a little before the Mass, in the following manner: they take the dried raisins that they keep all year and, after washing them, place as many as they think will be enough in a bowl, squeeze them by hand in more water, and then strain it through a clean cloth. In some churches where they have not very many raisins, they add so much water (as the monks have told me) that it barely turns red,

---

[1] Concave metal disc used to cover the chalice and on which the host is placed during mass.

even though the raisins are always black, and they themselves have even told me that they often add so much water to four or six raisins that there is enough to say Mass and to give communion to many people, for here they do so *in utraque specie*.[1] Hence once can clearly see that they do not consecrate it, for it is not wine but water; even so, they worship it when they say the words of consecration.

{[f. 194]} When the time comes to say Mass (which is in the morning on days that are not fast days, and in the afternoon about two hours before sunset on Wednesdays and Fridays, when they fast, and at sunset during Lent), the priest says certain prayers over the vestments. These consist of a long robe with sleeves and no collar, in the Turkish fashion, often the very same caftans that the lords buy from the Turks and give as offerings <[f. 172v/162v]> to the churches. They put this on first and on top of it another, which they call *motaát*, which also comes down to the feet in front and drags about a cubit behind; it is cut like a cope but with less skirt. They only wear these two vestments, since they have no amice, stole, maniple or girdle. I am aware that Francisco Álvares says in his *Historia Ethiopica*[2] that the vestment is just the width of the piece of fabric from which it is made, with a hole in the middle through which they put their head, without any other artistry; nowadays, however, it is as I have said.

After those prayers that the priest says over the vestments every time he says Mass, he vests himself, and the deacon likewise, and another priest who assists puts on only the first one, which serves as an alb, and the subdeacon puts on another (I say subdeacon, because they give this name to the one who assists, even though many affirm that they do not have this order, as we shall say later). Sometimes the priest, deacon and subdeacon say the Mass without another priest, but without these three they do not say it at all and they find it very strange that among us the priest says Mass just with acolytes, without a deacon or subdeacon.

While they are robing, a deacon and subdeacon go to the little building where the bread and wine are. In his right hand the deacon takes the cup of wine covered with a cloth and in his left a jug of water for washing hands, and the subdeacon takes in his right hand a basket containing the bread to be consecrated, wrapped in a cotton cloth, and the other breads to be given to the people as holy bread, and in his left a bell. When those who remained in the chapel have finished robing, the priest starts by saying 'Alleluia' in a loud voice and says a long prayer and, when those who are ready to bring the bread and wine hear this, they come in ringing the bell. All the people inside the church bow their heads when they hear this, {[f. 194v]} saying, 'Holy, Holy, Holy, God of Gods, who is now and ever shall be in heaven and on earth.' When they reach the altar, the priest who is to say the Mass takes the bread and covers it with a cotton cloth, which serves as the corporal and is always black or red so that any relic that may fall on it may be more easily seen. Then the deacon assisting at the Mass takes the wine, and the subdeacon holding a candle in his left hand and a thurible in his right begins to walk round the altar, which is always in the middle of the chapel, followed by the others, while the priest says this prayer in a loud voice: 'Our Lord God, who didst receive the sacrifice of Abel in the desert and of Abraham on the mountaintop and that of Elias on Carmel and the widow's coin in the

---

[1] 'In both species', i.e. unlike the Catholic practice at that time by which only the priest received the wine.

[2] Álvares, *Prester John of the Indies*, ch. 12, 'Where and how the bread of the sacrament is made, and of a procession they made and of the pomp with which mass is said and of the entering into the church', p. 84.

temple, likewise receive the sacrifice of this Thy servant.' And the deacon bearing the chalice with the wine says <[f. 173/163]> Psalm 22, '*Dominus regit me*', etc.[1] When they have finished going round, the priest places the bread on the paten, which is inside a large copper bowl that they put on the altar stone, which they call *Tabot*,[2] and the deacon pours the wine into the chalice, which is made of silver in the principal churches and copper in the others.

After that, the priest says, 'Christ our God, who, when Thou wast called, didst go to the marriage in Cana of Galilee and Thou didst bless them and make their water wine, likewise make this wine that is before Thee, bless it that it may be joy, contentment and life to our soul and body and forever dwell with us. Father, Son, Holy Spirit, there is no other God but Thee.' And he continues, over the chalice, 'God our God, Jesus Christ, truly God and man who did not separate His Godhead from His manhood, who spilt His blood through His will by His doing, place, O Lord, Thy holy hand over this chalice, make it clean and sanctified; may it be made Thine honoured blood; may this be for the life and salvation and redemption from sin of Thy people. Amen. Blessed be God the Almighty Father and blessed be the only Son, who was born of Saint Mary for our salvation, and blessed be the Holy Spirit the Paraclete, our hope. Glory be to the Father, to the Son, to the Holy Spirit, now and forever. Amen. One Holy Father, one Holy Son, one is the Holy Spirit. Praise the Lord all peoples, praise Him all peoples, because His mercy has been confirmed on us and His {[f. 195]} truth remains forever. Glory be to the Father and to the Son and to the Holy Spirit, for ever and ever. Amen.'

After that, the deacon says in a loud voice, 'Rise up and pray.' And then the priest says, 'Peace to you all. Let us praise the Maker of all that is good, God the merciful, Father of Our Lord God and Saviour Jesus Christ, because He came to our aid, received us and made us strong and made us reach this hour. Let us beseech Him to watch over us on this holy day and henceforth for all the time of our lives in peace. Almighty God, our God.' The deacon says, 'Entreat and beseech, all of you, that God may forgive us and receive the prayer and petition of His saints for love of us. Make us worthy, Lord, to partake in the blessed mystery and forgive us our sins.' And then, all those who are in the choir (where only those who have orders can enter) say once, 'Kyrie eleison.' And the priest says, 'O Lord God Almighty, we bless Thee on all works, for love of all works and in all works, because Thou hast delivered, helped and watched over us and hast made us come to Thee, and Thou hast received us and made us strong and hast made us reach this hour, wherefore we beseech and beg Thee <[f. 173v/163v]> for Thy gifts. O lover of peoples, give us that we may fulfil this holy day and all the time of our lives in peace; through Thy fear deliver us from all envy and from all temptation and from all the works of the Devil and counsel of evil people and from the rising-up of the secret and public enemy. Remove it all, Lord, from me and from Thy people and from this Thy holy place. Grant us all Thy gifts, Thou who gavest us the power to tread upon asps and basilisks and upon all the power of the enemy; do not lead us into temptation, but deliver us from evil, with grace and peace and the love of the people and of Thine only Son, Our Lord Jesus Christ, in whom Thou hast honour and power, and with the life-giving Holy Spirit, who is equal {with Thee} <with Thy Son>, for ever and ever. Amen.'

---

[1] Psalm 22 [23], 'The Lord ruleth me.' ['The Lord is my shepherd', in the Authorized King James Version.]
[2] See Glossary (altar stone/*tābot*).

He then continues over the bread and the chalice, 'O Jesus Christ, the head, participant from the beginning, Thou art pure Word of {the Father}<faith>, bread of life who camest down from the {heavens} <heaven> and camest forward to be the spotless lamb for the life of the world, we beseech and beg Thee for Thy gifts. O lover of the children {[f. 195v]} of men, show Thy face upon this bread and upon this chalice which are placed upon this table for this priestly invitation. Bless them, <clean them> and sanctify them and convert this bread into Thy pure and holy flesh which has joined with this chalice and may Thine honoured blood be equal participation for all of us, medicine and salvation for our souls and bodies, because Thou art the king of us all, Christ our God. To Thee we give the highest praises, to Thee belong glory, adoration and power, and to Thy gentle, good Father and to the life-giving Holy Spirit, now and for ever and for all centuries. Amen.'

When these prayers are finished, the deacon says, 'Rise up for the prayer' (not for them to sit and rise, because they remain standing), and the priest says, 'Peace be unto you all.' Then he puts incense in the thurible and goes round the altar, censing and saying, 'Glory and honour to the Holy Trinity, Father and Son and Holy Spirit, at all times, now and for ever and ever. Amen. O everlasting God, who hast neither beginning nor end, who art great in Thy knowledge, mighty in Thy works and wise in Thy counsel, who art in all parts, we ask, <Lord,> and beseech Thee to be with us in this hour; show Thy face upon us and purify our hearts and sanctify our souls; forgive the sins that we have done willingly and unwillingly and make us offer pure sacrifice, living sacrifice, and may the spiritual incense enter the house of Thy holy glory.' <[f. 174/164]> The deacon says, 'Rise up for the prayer'; and the priest says, 'Peace be unto you all.' And he moves on with the thurible, taking the subdeacon in front of him with a candle, and the deacon behind him with Saint Paul in his hand. The deacon goes outside the chapel door and reads one of Saint Paul's epistles, while the priest goes right round the outside of the chapel, on a cloister-like external veranda[1] which the lay people can enter, since they cannot go into the chapel, censing all round and saying, 'Holy, Holy, Holy, perfect God of Sabaoth, the earth is full of sanctifications of Thy glory.' Then he repeats the same as above: 'O everlasting God, who hast neither beginning nor end', etc. When he re-enters the chapel, the deacon stops reading and goes in {[f. 196]} after him and, when he reaches the altar, the subdeacon goes outside and reads a piece of the canonical epistles from the same place, and meanwhile the priest at the altar repeats again, 'O everlasting God, who hast neither beginning nor end', etc., and he adds, 'Thou art Our Lord and our God; to Thy holy apostles Thou didst declare the glory of the Gospel of Thy Messiah and gavest Him countless gifts of Thy grace, and Thou didst send them to preach throughout the universe; the richness of Thy grace and mercy is unknown. Give us grace, Lord, to tread their paths and to follow in their footsteps and to be worthy to partake of their inheritance and to be like them for all time and to be strong in their love. And watch over Thy holy Church that Thou hast built through them, and cast Thy blessing over the sheep of Thy flock; increase the fence of Thy vineyard that Thou didst plant with Thy holy right hand, in Jesus Christ Our Lord, with the Holy Spirit, for ever and ever. Amen.'

---

[1] After the Aksumite period, church layout became predominantly circular, comprising three distinct areas, with the holy of holies in the centre and an ambulatory veranda around the outside.

When the subdeacon goes out to read his lesson, he is followed by the priest who assists at the Mass with just the alb and he stays on the inside. When the subdeacon has finished reading, he hands the book to him and goes to the altar, and he stays reading the Acts of the Apostles. Meanwhile, the priest at the altar says, 'O Lord Jesus Christ, our God, who didst say to Thy holy disciples and pure apostles, "Many prophets and just men have desired to see the things that you see, and have not seen them, and to hear the things that you hear, and have not heard them. And blessed are the eyes that see the things that you see."[1] And so, like them, make us worthy to hear and to fulfil the word of Thy Holy Gospel, through the prayers of the saints.'

Then the deacon says, 'Let us pray.' And the priest says, 'Remember once more, Lord, those who asked us to remember them at the time of our prayers and petitions that we make to Thee. O God Our Lord, give rest to those who have died <[f. 174v/164v]> before us and give health to the sick, because Thou art life and our hope and our deliverer and the resurrection of us all, and to Thee we give the highest praise. Glory be to the highest, for ever and ever.'

Then he puts out his right hand to the east and, turning it to the west, to the north and to the south, he makes a cross, {[f. 196v]} saying, 'May God in the highest cast His blessing on us all and sanctify us with spiritual blessing and make us enter the holy Church with the diligent angels that serve and praise Him for ever and ever.' At this point, the priest who was outside reading from the Acts of the Apostles comes back and, putting the book in its place, takes the Gospel from a shelf near the altar (on the altar there are no books at all, because everything they say {at the altar} <there> is learnt by heart) and, opening it at the part to be read, he gives it to the priest who says the Mass and he takes it with both hands and places it on his left shoulder and goes out to the place where the others read, saying, 'Holy Gospel in which so-and-so' (naming the evangelist from whom he will read) 'gave tidings, word of the Son of God.' And going out through the door, he reads the Gospel for that day. They do not mix the evangelists; instead they read from one evangelist for a whole year and then from another the following year, and so they finish reading them in four years.

After reading the lesson for that day, he returns to the altar saying, 'We also ask Almighty God the Father, Our Lord and Redeemer Jesus Christ, we ask and beseech Thee for Thy gifts, O lover of the peoples. Remember, O Lord, the peace of the Church, holy congregation of the apostles, which will remain until the end of the world; bless all the people and all the cattle with the peace that is in the heavens, and put it in our hearts and in it give us the peace of our lives. Give Thy peace to our king N. and to his army and to his princes and lords. O King of peace, give us peace, because Thou hast given us all things and we know no other but Thee; we name and call on Thy holy name so that it may live in our souls in the Holy Spirit, and may deathly sin not attack us, Thy servants and all Thy people.'

After that, the deacon says, 'Rise up for the prayer', and the priest says, 'Peace be to you all.' And those who are in the chapel and outside it say the Creed, and meanwhile the priest says, 'Rise up, O my Lord God, and may Thine enemies scatter and those who abhor Thy holy and blessed name flee from Thy face; and may Thy peoples be blessed with the blessing of the thousands of thousands that do Thy will with grace and peace of {[f. 197]}

---

[1] Matthew 13:16–17; Luke 10:23–4.

love for the people, of Thine only Son, Our Lord and our God Saviour, Jesus Christ, with whom Thou deservest glory and honour and power, <[f. 175/165]> and with the life-giving Holy Spirit, who is equal with Thee now and for ever and ever', etc. 'Great and ever-lasting God, who didst make people without corruption, and didst diminish death, which first came into the world through the envy of the Devil, in the coming of Thy Son, our God and Lord and Saviour Jesus Christ, and didst fill all the earth with peace from the heavens, with which the choirs of angels praise Thee, saying "Glory to God in the highest and on earth peace to men of good will."[1] O Lord, if Thou wilt, fill our hearts with Thy peace and cleanse us of all stain and all envy and all evil work and the memory of evil that causes death, and make us worthy to kiss one another with holy kisses and to receive without punishment Thy holy celestial bread, which is without death, in Jesus Christ Our Lord, with the Holy Spirit, for ever and ever. Amen.'

On finishing this prayer, he begins one of twelve different Masses that they have for feast days and holidays. The one that I shall put here, which is one of the shorter ones, was, they say, made by the apostles, but they have added some words pleading for their patriarchs and others.

## Mass of the Apostles

The priest who says the Mass turns to face those who are in the chapel and blesses them with his right hand, saying, 'God be with you.' Turning to the altar and giving blessing, he says, 'Bless our God.' And then he continues, 'We bless Thee, Lord, in Thy beloved Son, Our Lord Jesus, whom Thou didst send to us in the last time, Thy Son the Saviour and Redeemer, angel of Thy counsel, this Thy {holy} Word in whom Thou didst all things through Thy will.' The deacon says, 'For love of the blessed and holy Pope Marcos' (here he names the patriarch of Alexandria alive at the time) 'and the blessed Pope N' (here he names his *abuna*). The priest says, 'To them and to the {works} <souls> of all give rest and have mercy on them. Thou didst send Thy Son from heaven into the Virgin's womb and He was made flesh and was in her belly; {[f. 197v]} Thy Son was made known by the Holy Spirit to Thee and to those who are standing before Thee, thousands and thousands of saints, angels and archangels and Thine honoured animals that have six wings: seraphim and cherubim; with two of their wings they cover Thy face and with two Thy feet and with two they fly, from the beginning to the end of the world; all of them to sanctify and praise Thee for ever, with those who sanctify and praise Thee. Receive also our Mass from us who say to Thee: Holy, Holy, Holy, perfect God of Sabaoth, heaven and earth are full of the sanctification of Thy glory. Thy holy Son came and was born of the Virgin to do Thy will and for the people to sanctify Thee; He stretched out His hands <[f. 175v/165v]> to suffer pain and to unbind the sick and those who trusted in Thee, and He delivered Himself, by His will, to suffer in order to take away the power of death and to break the chains of the Devil and to tread in hell, in order to guide the saints and to plant order and to declare His resurrection. And on that night when they delivered Him, He took bread with His holy, blessed and immaculate hands and raised His eyes to heaven and to Thee, His Father, and blessed it and broke it and gave it to His disciples, saying, "Take and eat this bread of My body, which for you is broken for forgiveness of sins." Likewise He gave the blessed and sanctified chalice to his disciples, saying, "Take and drink of this chalice; it

---

[1] Luke 2:14.

is My blood which for you shall be spilt in remission of sins." Now also, O Lord, remembering Thy death and Thy resurrection, we trust in Thee and give to Thee this bread and this chalice, blessing Thee, for Thou didst that for our delight, so that we might stand before Thee and serve Thee; and we ask Thee, O Lord, and beseech Thee to send the Holy Spirit of virtue over this bread and this chalice and to make it His house and the blood of Our Lord Jesus Christ, for ever and ever. And also grant to all those who partake of it that for them it may be for sanctification and the redemption of sin, for ever and ever.' While saying these words, he wets the tip of his thumb and makes a cross with it on the bread from one side to the other, and says, 'Grant us that we may unite in Thy Holy Spirit and heal us in this bread so that we may live in Thee for ever. Blessed be the name of God and blessed be he who comes {[f. 198]} in the name of God.' And they all repeat the same words, beginning with 'Grant us that we may unite', etc.

The deacon says, 'Rise up for the prayer.' And then the priest says, 'Peace be unto you all', and, giving thanks, he blesses it and breaks it (here he breaks the bread, taking a little from the top, where the first cross is, and then from the bottom, and after that from the right-hand side and then from the left; then with his finger he removes the crust of the bread where it is marked with the middle cross and puts it whole into the chalice), and says this prayer: 'We also beseech Almighty God the Father, Our Lord and Saviour Jesus Christ, to grant that we partake of the holy mystery with His blessing, and that it fortify us and that none of us soil himself, but to make it a delight for all those who receive the holy mystery of the body and blood of Christ, Almighty God, our God.' The deacon says, 'Let us pray.' And then the priest says, 'God, who art almighty, give us strength in receiving of Thy holy mystery and do not allow any of us to soil himself, but bless us all for ever and ever.'

<[f. 176/166]> The deacon says, 'While standing up, raise up your heads.' And then the priest says, 'Everlasting God, knower of the secret and of the manifest, may Thy people bow their heads before Thee. We revere Thee and we open the depth of Thy heart and flesh; look down from the dwelling that becomes Thee and bless them; incline Thy ear and hear their prayers; make them firm with the virtue of Thy right hand; help and cover the evil sickness; be their guard for body and soul; increase in them and in us Thy faith and the fear of Thy name, in Thine only Son for ever.'

The deacon says, 'Worship God with fear.' And then the priest says, 'O almighty Lord, Thou art who shall heal our soul and body, because Thou sayest so through the mouth of Thine only Son, Our Lord, our God and our Saviour Jesus Christ, who said to our Father Peter, "Thou art Peter; and upon this rock I will build my church, and the gates of hell shall not prevail against it. And I will give to thee the keys of the kingdom of heaven. And whatsoever thou shalt bind upon earth, it shall be bound also in heaven: and whatsoever thou shalt loose upon earth, it shall be loosed also in heaven."[1] May {[f. 198v]} Thy servants, my parents and my brothers, be loosed and free, in the mouth of the Holy Spirit and also in my mouth, Thy sinful and guilty servant. God Our Lord, who takest away the sins of the world, receive the penance of these Thy serving men and serving women, and light in them the light of everlasting life, and forgive them their sins, because Thou art merciful and a lover of men. Thou art God, our God, and merciful and of peace, far from wrath, and very merciful and truly just. If we sin against Thee, O Lord, in our words or in

---

[1] Matthew 16:18–19.

our hearts or in our deeds, forgive and edify, because Thou art good and a lover of peoples. Because Thou art God, our God, loose us and all Thy people. Remember, O Lord, our honoured and holy Pope *Abbá* N.' (here they name the patriarch of {Alexandria who is currently alive) 'and our blessed and holy Pope N.' (here they name the patriarch of} Ethiopia). 'Our God, watch over them for us for many years and long times, with justification and peace. Remember, Lord, our King N. and loose him from the prison of the sins that he has committed both knowingly and in ignorance; subject his enemies and throw them at once under his feet. Remember, Lord, all the popes, bishops and clerics, deacons, subdeacons, exorcists and cantors, men and women, children, old men and young and all the Christian people; fortify them with the faith of Christ. Remember, O Lord, and loose those that have slept and rested in the true faith; gather their souls in the bosom of Abraham, Isaac and Jacob; and deliver us from all blame and malediction, and from all negation, and from all excommunication, and from all false oaths, <[f. 176v/166v]> and from all union with rebels and heathens. Give us grace, O Lord, heart, judgment and understanding, so that henceforth for ever we may shrink and flee from any evil work that tempts. Grant us that we may do Thy will at all times, and write our names in the book of life in the kingdom of heaven with all the saints and martyrs, in Jesus Christ Our Lord, with whom and with the Holy Spirit Thou hast glory and power, now and for ever and ever. Amen.'

{[f. 199]} The deacon says, '*Necer*' ('look'), and the priest says, 'Lord, forgive us, Christ', and then all the men and women say the same, chanting, and the priest repeats it twice more, and each time the others do as well. {Then} the priest says, 'Truly, holy flesh of Our Lord God and Saviour Jesus Christ, who gives Himself for life, salvation and redemption of sin to those who partake of it with believing. Truly, honoured blood of Our Lord God and Redeemer Jesus Christ, who gives Himself for life, redemption and salvation from sin to those who partake of it with believing. Because this is His flesh and {His} blood, of Emmanuel, our true God, I believe and confess until my last breath that this is the flesh and blood of Thine only Son, Our Lord and our God and our Saviour Jesus Christ, which He took from the Lady of us all, holy and blessed Mary, and made it one with His Godhead, without mixing, without separating, without changing, and He bore witness, with good testimony, in the time of Pontius Pilate, and He gave it up of His own will upon the holy cross, for the life of us all. I believe that His Godhead was not separated from His manhood at any time, not even for the blink of an eye, and He gave it up for us, for life, salvation and the redemption of sin for ever. I believe and confess that this is the flesh and blood of Our Lord and Saviour Jesus Christ, to whom belong glory and honour and worship, with His good, merciful Father and the {life-giving} <justifying> Holy Spirit, at all times, now and for ever and ever. Amen.'

When he reaches this point, he takes a small piece of the bread, saying, 'Holy flesh of Emmanuel, our true God, which He took from the Lady of us all', and he eats it. And then the deacon gives him a little of the blood in a silver or copper spoon, saying, 'This is Christ's blood.' And then he gives communion to the priest who assists at the Mass and the latter takes the spoon in his hand and drinks of the blood, and then he gives communion to the deacon and the priest who assists at the Mass gives him the blood, and then to the subdeacon and the ones who are in the chapel, who are those who have orders, and then he hands the chalice to the deacon, who stands on the right of the one who says {[f. 199v]} the Mass, with the priest who assists <[f. 177/167]> on the left, and he takes one side of the bowl in which goes the paten with the sacrament covered with black or red cotton cloth, and one of the priests that are there unvested takes the other side, and the one who says Mass puts out his hands and places them over the cloth with which the sacrament is covered, and the subdeacon goes in front with a cup, which he puts in front of the chalice when the deacon gives the blood, so that no drop may fall on the ground. And, on coming to the chapel, or rather, church door, the priest gives the sacrament of the body to the lay men and women, saying, 'Holy flesh of Emmanuel, our true God, which He took from the Lady of us all.' And the one communing says, 'Amen, amen.' And then the deacon gives the blood in the spoon, saying, 'This is the blood of Jesus Christ, for life of the flesh and soul and for everlasting life', and the subdeacon puts a little water into the palm of the hand of the person who has communed, who rinses his mouth with it and swallows it, and sometimes he pours water into his mouth from the jug, which has a spout. And everybody stands when they take communion.

When they have finished giving communion to everyone (because ordinarily everyone who is there takes it even if they have not confessed), they return to the altar. If {part of the} <any> sacrament is left, the one who says the Mass consumes it and then washes his fingers with water in the chalice and drinks it. He washes the paten and chalice and gives that water to the priest who assists at the Mass to drink; then he washes the chalice again and gives it to the deacon, and then he washes his hands over the paten and gives it to the subdeacon to drink. Having done that, he rubs the palms of his hands with incense and, holding them to form a cross, he gives them to all the priests who are there to kiss, saying, 'The power of Peter's hand', and the one who kisses them responds, 'As with the first sacrifice of Abel, receive.' And he places his palms on the foreheads of the deacons and subdeacons and then gives them to them to kiss, saying, 'Paul's blessing.' When I asked why they said it in one way for Saint Peter and another way for Saint Paul, they answered that it was because Saint Peter was a priest and Saint Paul a deacon.

I took all of this from a book that they gave me[1] {[f. 200]} in a large monastery, and the monks told me that all the prayers and ceremonies reported here, from where they bring the bread and wine from that little building in which they are made up to where I have put the title 'Mass of the Apostles', are said and done in all the other Masses, and that some of them have more ceremonies than this one, and that they commemorate Dioscorus in them. They do not say more than a single Mass in any church, even though there may be many priests in it, and they find it very strange that many Masses are said in one day in our churches, and in public, in view of the people, without a curtain. They say a Mass for the dead (as the monks told me) and, as we have seen in this one, they plead for them, and even so they deny purgatory, <[f. 177v/167v]> as we shall see later. They call Mass *cadacê* and the most holy sacrament *corbân*, which means holocaust.

Friar Luis de Urreta puts a Mass in chapter 9 of the second book of his *Historia Ethiopica*,[2] and mentions the ceremonies that the Ethiopians perform in it. But he was mistaken in many of the things that he says there, such as that since the beginning of their Christianity they have consecrated in azyme, *scilicet* unleavened bread; and that they now use hosts like us, large ones for the priests and small ones for the people to commune; and

---

[1] Probably a missal of the Orthodox Church (*Maṣḥāfa qeddāsē*).

[2] Urreta, *Historia de la Etiopia*, bk II, ch. 9, entitled 'Of the holy sacrament of the Eucharist, in which they kept the purity of the Catholic faith', pp. 494–516.

that formerly they made wine to say Mass from raisins, leaving them to soak for ten days, and then they would dry them and squeeze them in a screw-press, but that they no longer do so, because they have a great abundance of grape wine. He also says that, although the ornaments with which the priests said Mass used to be just a very close-fitting alb, and the chasuble used to be like a tight scapular with an opening for the head, they now use all the ornaments with which the Roman Church celebrates Mass. He says that at a certain point in the Mass the people say out loud the Creed that the Roman Church chants, without a word different; the priest pleads for Saint Peter's living successor in Rome; and he gives the bowl with the sacrament to the deacon covered with a pall, and the chalice with the blood to the subdeacon, and they give communion to the priests who are near the altar, and then to those with greater and lesser orders, and then, at the church door, to lay men and women; and, although lay people used formerly to commune *sub utraque specie*, this is no longer done, ever since the Supreme Pontiff Paul III {[f. 200v]} commanded them in his Briefs that they should commune only with the species of bread, as the Roman Church does, and they obeyed fully at once. He also states that in the past they used not to keep the most holy sacrament in the churches or to take it to the sick, because, as they took communion most days, if they fell sick, their last communion served as viaticum, as they said, but now they keep the most holy sacrament in the churches and take it to the sick, following the style of the Roman Church in everything.

The author says these and other things (which I leave out since they are of lesser import) in that chapter, but they are all very different from what in fact happens here, because, as we have seen above, they have always consecrated in leavened bread until today, and if they are to say Mass in the morning, they make the dough at night, adding leaven, and when they fast and say Mass in the afternoon, they make the dough in the morning with leaven. They do not use hosts like us, and have never had iron moulds, which is why Emperor Seltan Cegued wished to see ours and commanded us to make hosts in front of him, and he praised them highly; <[f. 178/168]> some lords who were present did the same and one said, 'This is a very good thing, for it can be consumed without chewing; relics of our sacrament are always left between our teeth.' And a lady said, 'This is a thing of heaven; it seems that our monks use their feet to knead the bread that they make for the sacrament.'

They do not soak the raisins or squeeze them in a screw-press, but shortly before Mass they wash them and throw away that water, then squeeze them in some more water with their hands and strain it {through a cloth} <by hand>, as we have said. They have never (they say) used grape wine to say Mass, and do not use it now. And the ornaments are not like those of the Roman Church, but like those that we described above; and in the Mass they do not chant the Creed as the Roman Church has it, but rather they commonly deny pertinaciously that the Holy Spirit proceeds from the Son, as we said in chapter 2 of this book. The priest does not plead in the Mass for Saint Peter's living successor in Rome, but for the patriarch of Alexandria. And the deacon does not give the communion of the body {[f. 201]} to the clergy or to the lay people, but of the blood, and the priest who says the Mass gives it of the body, for they all still commune *sub utraque specie* today. Therefore, if the Supreme Pontiff Paul III commanded that they should commune only with the species of bread (as the author says), they have not obeyed. Nor do they follow the style of the Roman Church in keeping the most holy sacrament in the churches and taking it to the sick, because they do neither one thing nor the other. And it is a very weak excuse to say that they used not to take it because, as they took communion most days, if they fell sick, their last communion served as viaticum, because they might be sick for a year or two so that they could not go to church. The worst thing is that not only do they not commune while they are sick, no matter how lengthy their sickness, but very few confess, because their monks tell them – as I myself have heard – that, since they cannot do penance because of their sickness, confession avails them nothing, and so they die without it.

Those whom justice had condemned to death never used to confess at all. But a short time ago I alerted Emperor Seltan Sagued to how bad this was, and persuaded him to order his judges to make those they condemned to death confess before suffering. The vicars and monks also are so negligent when they teach the people the procedure required in order to receive the holy sacrament that, as they told me, there are married men who often commune without ever having confessed in their lives. Among those who were reduced to our holy faith, I found some more than twenty years old who told me they took communion every week and they had never confessed in their whole lives, since they did not know it was necessary to confess one's sins before communing.

Which reports what the Ethiopian priests pray in place of our
canonical hours

Since we have seen the ceremonies that the Ethiopian priests perform in their Masses, it is
now appropriate to relate what they pray {[f. 201v]} in place of our canonical hours, so that
anyone who wishes to know about these things in detail can see them here taken from their
own books. As far as possible I shall keep to the way they say things, although in the
passages they have mixed in from Scripture some words do not entirely agree with our version. Starting with the matters that they ordinarily sing two hours or an hour and a half
before dawn, they do not first say as we do the *Pater Noster*, *Ave Maria*, *Credo*, *Domine
labia mea aperies*, etc., but, singing in their manner, they repeat *Alleluia* three times and
then: 'I bless and rise up, in the name of the Father and of the Son and Holy Spirit, taking
as my staff three names; even if I fall, may He raise me; even if I walk in darkness, God will
{enlighten} <raise> me; in Him I trust. We bless Thee, Lord, and glorify Thee. We bless
Thee, Lord, and trust in Thee. We submit to Thee, Lord, and serve Thy holy name. We
worship Thee, to whom every knee makes obeisance and every tongue submits. Thou art
God of gods and Lord of lords, God of every flesh and of every soul. To Thee we call, as Thy
Son taught us, saying, "When you pray, say this: *Pater noster qui es in coelis*,"[1] etc. And they
say it in full and then, 'Blessed be God, God of Israel, who alone did great wonders, and
blessed be the name of His holy glory and may His glory fill all the earth. So be it. So be it.'

'Holy, Holy, Holy, perfect God of Sabaoth, the heavens and earth are full of the sanctification of Thy glory, God who was before time and will be for ever. Holy God, who is
glorified by the diligent and sanctified by the saints. Holy God, who is feared by the
cherubim and at whose majesty the seraphim tremble. Holy God, who turns the lightning
and makes the thunder loud. Holy God, who casts down darkness in the evening and light
in the morning. Holy God, who made the sun rule over the day to give us light from the
sky. Holy God, who made the moon and stars fulfil at night that which He had ordered.
Holy God, who makes His angels spirits and His ministers burning fire. Holy God, who
stretched out the heavens like a tent and established the earth over the waters. Holy God,
who made Adam to His image and likeness. Holy God, who ordered Abraham and swore
to Isaac and kept the promise {[f. 202]} to Jacob. Holy God, who was sold like Joseph to
measure out the food to the people. Holy God, who gave Law to Moses. Holy God, who
sanctified the priesthood of Aaron. Holy God, who anointed David with the unction of
the kingdom and priesthood. Holy God, who breathed on the prophets, to make them
<[f. 179/169]> hear His holy word. Holy God, whom the angels glorify and the powers

---

[1] Matthew 6:9, 'Our father who art in heaven.'

praise.' Then they say some verses from Psalms 104 and 117, in the manner of respon-sories, thus: '*Confitemini Domino et invocate nomen eius. Alleluia*',[1] etc. And then they say, 'Glory be to the Father and to the Son and to the Holy Spirit. Alleluia, in all time and at every hour. Glory be to the Father and to the Son and to the Holy Spirit. Alleluia in all times and moments. Glory be to the Father and to the Son and to the Holy Spirit. Alleluia in all times and years. Glory be to the Father and to the Son and to the Holy Spirit. Alleluia to the holy Church, for ever and ever. Alleluia. To Him belongs glory, from generation to generation.'

'I praise thee, O Virgin, full of praise, as much as my mouth can praise thy greatness. The tongue of the cherub cannot fully praise thee and the mouth of the seraph will not fully declare thy greatness. The narrowness of thy womb became broader than the heavens and thy splendour was brighter than the sun's. Thou art pure gold, treasure of nature. Blessed art thou, Mother of God. Thou art praised by the mouths of the prophets and glorified by the apostles; the crown of James's blessing and the praise of the House of Israel, thou proceedest from the kingdom of the root of Jesse; pure flower from the trunk of David, through thee all the saints smell sweet. We bow to thee, O Queen, and raise our eyes to thy Son, mighty of all time. Stretch forth thy hands and bless each of thy servants. <Lord> forgive us {Christ}.' This they repeat twelve times. 'Bless us, Our Lord God, from the highest heaven. Receive our {prayers} <hearts>. Forgive us, Lord, and have mercy on us all.' This they repeat three times. 'We plead with God the Father, Almighty Lord, and our Saviour Jesus Christ for our sick brothers; may He remove from them all sicknesses and spirit of disease and, life prevailing, give them health, O Almighty God, our God.'

The deacon says, 'Let us pray', and then a priest says, 'Our God, Almighty God, {[f. 202v]} Father and Lord and our Saviour Jesus Christ, we ask and beseech Thee to give life to our sick brothers and to remove from them the spirit of disease; make all pains and sicknesses leave them and may they find health at once. Visitor and healer of the soul and body, remove from them all the things of the foul spirits that trouble and oppress the soul, give peace and rest, remove all the diseases from this house and from us, give perfect health to all those who pronounce Thy holy name and salvation to our souls, in Thine only Son, with whom and with the Holy Spirit Thou hast glory for ever and ever.'

'Remember, Lord, the promise of Thy holy servants, the promise of Abraham, Isaac and Jacob, Thy faithful servants, to whom Thou gavest hope of justification and life and didst swear on Thyself. Remember, Lord, the zeal of Moses, Thy servant, who with Thy <[f. 179v/169v]> wonders became great among the Egyptians and found favour in Thy sight and received the Law from Thy hands. Remember, Lord, the justification of David, whom Thou Thyself didst praise, saying, "I have found David, My servant, a faithful man according to My heart." Remember, Lord, the work of Thy holy prophets, to whom thou gavest Thy spirit, and they called like a trumpet proclaiming Thy birth. Remember these, for-give Thy people and bless Thy inheritance, raise up Thy strength and come to deliver us.'

'Hear us, our God and Lord, God of our fathers: we do not see or hear, nor did our fathers tell us that there was any other God than Thou. May those who worship idols and those who glory in their gods be confounded. Our soul hopes in God, because He is our helper and refuge. Come to me, O Virgin, with thy beloved Son Jesus Christ, to bless us. Come to me, O Virgin, with Adam, Abel, Seth and Enoch, holy fathers of the appointed

---

[1] Psalm 104 [105]:1, 'Give glory to the Lord, and call upon his name. Alleluia.'

ancient fathers. Come to me with Noe and Sem, who found favour before the Highest. Come to me, O Virgin, with Abraham, Isaac and Jacob, thy fathers who generated the glory of the whole world. Come to me, O Virgin, with Moses {[f. 203]} and Aaron the priests, who were like thee in the time of the old Law. Come to me, O Virgin, with Josue the prophet and prince, who made the sun stand still before Gabaon and divided the inheritance unto the Hebrews. Come to me, O Virgin, with Samuel who brought David from among the sheep and anointed him with the oil of his horn. Come to me, O Virgin, with David, our father the singer. Come to me, O Virgin, with Isaias and Jeremias, the highest in their words and preachers with virtue. Come to me, O Virgin, with Elias and Eliseus, prophets of Israel. Come to me, O Virgin, with Ezekiel and Daniel of good visions, who proclaimed the mysteries of heaven. Come to me, O Virgin, with Ananias, Azarias and Misael, who would not obey the king's command but only God in heaven, and prayed within the fire. Come to me, O Virgin, with all the prophets of Juda and Samaria and Babylon, who called like trumpets for thy Son. We praise thee, O Virgin, just as the Angel Gabriel, saying, Blessed art thou and blessed is the Fruit of thy womb. Rejoice, full of grace, God is with thee, blessed art thou and blessed is the Fruit of thy womb. Rejoice, source of joy, blessed art thou and blessed is the Fruit of thy womb. O Lord, forgive us, Christ.' This they repeat twelve times.

'We praise God who is glorified with the glory of the saints. He is praised by the company of joyful angels; He is served by the souls of the just; He is worshipped by the holy Church, saying, "Glory to God in the highest and on earth peace to men of good will." <[f. 180/170]> Holy, Holy, Holy, God who dwells in the highest and sees the heart of the abyss, the cherubim cannot see His majesty. Holy God, who is of three faces and one nature, almighty of one counsel. Holy God, who is {three in} <one> union, is glorified by the diligent, fire of life that cannot be touched or seen with the eye, subtle spirit. We worship His Trinity with one {[f. 203v]} adoration and we give Him glory. Holy God, for the walls of his house are flames and the floor snow, to Him belongs adoration. Holy God, for the priests in heaven are standing around Him, giving Him glory, worshipping Him and trembling before His throne. Holy God, whose house is lightning of His glory, before Him runs the river of fire. Holy God, who does not sleep, diligent, glorified among the saints, the seraphim surround Him like a rainbow; to Him alone belongs glory. We submit to thee, O daughter of David, honour of all the world, second in the heights, Virgin mother. We submit to thee, O daughter of David, second in heaven, of whom the sun[1] was born, thou gavest birth to God. We submit to thee, O daughter of David, house of the holiness of the Son, throne of gold. We submit to thee, O daughter of David, dressed in a robe of gold and light. We submit to thee, O daughter of David, pure crystal, scent box with which the priests anoint themselves. We submit to thee, O daughter of David, enclosed garden, sealed fountain, daughter of the prophets. We submit to thee, O daughter of David, new heaven, mysterious ark, vessel of gold and silver. We submit to thee, O Mary our mother and mother of Our Lord. Thou art our honour and glory.'

'Plead, plead for us, prophets full of spirit, trumpet of the Trinity. Plead for us, apostles, pipes of gold, keys of justice and of the vineyard fence. Plead for us, martyrs strong in battle, stars, bright torches of the Church. Plead for us, just sons of Sion. Plead for us, company

---

[1] The sun was used as a metaphor for God in the early Christian Church, and features in both western and eastern Christian painting, including in Ethiopia.

of the virgins and nuns. Plead for us, company of joyful angels, who do not sleep and glorify Him without ceasing. Plead for us, popes and priests and deacons, who are of good faith. Plead for us, men and women, children and elders. Plead for us, Abraham, Isaac and Jacob, fathers of the people, lords of the faithful. Plead for us, John the virgin, {[f. 204]} preacher of the Gospel. Plead for us, blessed Stephen, pillar of faith, who didst clearly see the mystery of the Trinity of the heavens. Plead for us, virtuous George, fighter, miracle-worker, star of honour between heaven and earth. Plead for us, Taquelá Haimanot, our father, tree of Lebanon, worker in the spirit, follower in Anthony's footsteps. Plead for us, Phelipe, our father, pious of heart, pure as a dove, who grew with the spirit of wisdom. Plead for us, our Father Estateus, follower <[f. 180v/170v]> of the sun. Plead for us with the prayer of Michael, our virgin father and martyr, master of the order and rule, sweet tongue, follower of the apostles. Plead for us, Iared the priest, singer of verses and viol of the Church.[1] Plead for us, holy spiritual Church, treasury of wheat without tares.'

'Jesus Christ, sweet of name, who didst call Saint Paul, call to Thy mouth; Jesus Christ, sweet of name, salt of Paul's priesthood, remove our stains with Thy divinity; Jesus Christ, sweet of name, brightness of Paul's teaching, enlighten with Thy beauty the darkness of our hearts; to Thee belong honour and glory and adoration of men and of angels. O Peter, to whom it was granted to be the rock of faith, open to us, Peter, so that we may enter the house of Christ's marriage. O Peter, chief of the doctors to whom was given power in the heavens and on earth, bless our company. O chief of shepherds, bless our inheritance, chief of all the apostles, because to thee He said, "Feed my sheep." Thou, O Lord, art glorified and the name of Thy glory is wonderful; Thou didst make the foundations of the prison shake; Thou didst loose the bands of Saint Paul; loose us, O Lord, from the enemy's prisons. At night raise up our hands in the temple before the Gospel.'

If it is a Sabbath day, at this point one of the priests present reads a lesson from the Gospel of Saint Matthew, chapter 25, beginning *'Tunc simile est regnum coelorum decem virginibus'*, etc., to where it says *'Quia* {[f. 204v]} *nescitis diem neque horam'.*[2] And if it is not a Sabbath day, they leave out this Gospel and continue with the following:

'Because He gave Law to Moses and He made His Sundays for honour and sanctification of the divine Trinity. To him belongs praise, because He breathed into the prophets and sanctified His Sundays so that they might be close to us, and He renewed that which was old. Higher than the high, Holy among the saints, the fragrance of the incense of the diligent apostles is offered to Thee; those who have been sanctified glorify Thee with Thine ordination.' Here a deacon says, 'Rise up for the prayer.' And then a priest says, 'Peace be unto {us} <you> all.' And he reads a lesson from the Gospel of Saint Mark, chapter 13, beginning with the words *'De die illo* {et} <vel> *hora* {nemo} <meno> *scit'*, etc., as far as *'Omnibus dico vigilate'.*[3]

'Make us worthy to enter the Sunday of Thy Sundays and may we be called to Thy feast, with all Thy saints; may we praise Thy Gospel, bearing Thy cross. We also plead with Almighty God the Father and Lord and our Saviour Jesus Christ for the fruits of the earth: may He make them <[f. 181/171]> grow with blessing and give riches in abundance, God, our God.' A deacon says, 'Let us pray.' And then a priest says, 'God, our God,

[1] See bk II, chs 19 and 22, below.

[2] Matthew 25:1–13, 'Then shall the kingdom of heaven be like to ten virgins ... because you know not the day nor the hour.'

[3] Mark 13:3–27, 'But of that day or hour no man knoweth ... I say to all: Watch.'

who art our Almighty God, we ask and beseech Thee to make the fruits of the land grow with Thy blessing. Hasten to make them be harvested for Thy poor people and for all those who utter Thy holy blessed name, in Thine only Son, with whom and with the Holy Spirit Thou hast glory, for ever and ever.'

'Those of you who fear God, do not disdain, because His name alone has risen up. At midnight, pray, because the stars in the sky, the brightness of the sun and of the moon, the lightning and clouds, the angels and archangels and all the choirs, the depths, the sea, rivers, springs, fire and water, rain and wind and all the arms of the just glorify God, and those who always pray {are counted} <sit> in God's heart. Therefore, in doing this, you faithful, join with one another and pray and beg Our Lord, because he commanded this {[f. 205]} with the promise of His Word.'

'Sweet of tongue, fragrant like incense, Paul guided the blind. True master, who with the hem of Thy robe healed the sick, stretch forth Thy right hand and bless us who are gathered, just as the tree that grows beside the stream of water was made green again by John and rose up; may the proceeding of his word be like a bunch of grapes. Give us part of the Gospel of grace, the sources of the Law of the Gospel river, the olive branches and the vine branches proceed from a trunk; may the Son's apostles bless us on the Sunday, by stretching forth their hands.'

A deacon says, 'Rise up for the prayer.' And then a priest says, 'Peace be unto you all.' And he reads a lesson from the Gospel of Saint John, chapter 3: '*Erat autem homo ex phariseis Nicodemus*', etc., to where it says '*quia in Deo sunt facta*.'[1] This Gospel is read only on Sundays and on the other days they leave it out. And they continue as follows: 'Alleluia, alleluia, alleluia. We call thee star for the Sun of Justice made thee grow, for He made thee sleep on His breast. We call thee star for He kissed thee with His mouth and girded thee with His girdle. We call thee star for He showed thee His secrets and gave thee the Gospel of His grace. We call thee star, John, who like thee;[2] we ask thee to plead for us.'

'Because His name alone rose up, and at this time all the creatures fall silent a little so that they may praise Him; the stars and waters stand still for an hour and all the choirs of angels serve God at this time; with the souls of the just they glorify God. Alleluia. All the choirs of spiritual angels, who are like the burning of the fire and are {surrounded} <crowned> with a flame of virtue, the cherubim glorify, the seraphim sanctify and the archangels sing and the company of angels serves His glory, and they all say with one voice, "Holy, Holy, Holy, perfect God of Sabaoth." <[f. 181v/171v]> The heavens and earth are full of the sanctification of Thy glory. This Church has the order of angels, like the heavens. The Church is like the house of the Highest and the holy Virgin, with the wheel of fire that the cherubim bear, in place of the four sides of the throne, four elements from which {[f. 205v]} Adam was created: earth, water, air and fire. In place of the cherubim we have four evangelists who speak of the divinity and, through the pipe of glory, partake of the fountain from the mouth of the living Son of God. In place of the man, Matthew, because he {recounted} <contains> the birth of our Redeemer of the seed of David, king of Bethlehem in Juda; of the lion, Mark, because he roars like a lion in the lands of Egypt, preaching the Gospel until he makes them leave their idols; of the calf, Luke, because he spoke of sacrificing the clean calf; of the eagle, John, {who flies high and preaches}

---

[1] John 3:1–21, 'And there was a man of the Pharisees, named Nicodemus ... because they are done in God.'
[2] This clause is apparently incomplete.

<because he preaches high and of> high things and enters the doors of heaven and speaks the secrets of the divinity, sings with the angels and sees the mystery of the diligent. In place of the seraphim we have priests, ministers of the mystery, who give living communion and sweet-smelling acceptable incense; in place of the archangels, we have virgins who have been happy with purity and have rejected the pleasure of this world.'

'Now let us also beseech the lover of men, saying, "Forgive us, Lord, for love of all Thy saints, for love of the cherubim, Thy horses, and seraphim, ministers of Thy house, for love of Thy faithful Michael and Gabriel, proclaimer of Thy manhood, for love of the Angel Raphael, keeper of all Thy commandment, and for love of all the company of angels who serve Thy divinity, for love of the blessed prophets and for love of the preaching apostles, for love of the victorious martyrs, for love of the pure virgins and for love of the perfect religious, for love of the sweet-tongued priests, and for love of all the perfection of the company of a single saintly woman who is above all the Churches, and principally for love of Mary, Thy Mother, who is the glory of our fathers, for love of her belly that Thou didst have, and for love of her virginity which she did not lose in giving birth to Thee, for love of her knees on which Thou didst lie, for love of her breasts which made Thee grow, and for love {[f. 206]} of her hands which touched Thee, and for love of her feet which walked with Thee, for love of her bright eyes and ears which heard the good news of the angel Gabriel, for love of the soul and flesh that Thou didst take from her and didst unite to Thy divinity without changing or separating or mixing, as our fathers have taught. Glory be to Thee, adoration be to Thy Father, greatness be to Thy spirit, and mercy be to Thy people, for ever and ever. Amen."'

'Our honour and glory and the strength of our salvation is Jesus Christ, {the teaching} <fine steel> of our peace, in whom we trust, the strength of our salvation, in which <[f. 182/172]> we rest. The cornerstone of life is Jesus Christ. A good yoke and a light weight is Jesus Christ. The path to His Father, the door to His begetter is Jesus Christ. Our ship that waves cannot reach, our treasure where no thief can approach nor moth corrupt, is Jesus Christ. Good seed that bears fruit in the flesh of the good is Jesus Christ. The pontiff that stands over the saints is Jesus Christ. Morning star, sun of justice is Jesus Christ. May He find the peace of His Father for us who believe in Him and confess. Lord, forgive us, Christ.' They repeat this twelve times.

## Prayer for the king

'We also plead with Almighty God the Father and Lord and our Saviour Jesus Christ for the lover of God our King N., to keep him and his kingdom, without sickness, with peace and justification, Almighty God, our God.' The deacon says, 'Let us pray.' And then the priest says, 'God, our God, who art almighty, we ask and beseech Thee to be good to the king of this land, lover of God; give him grace and subject his heathen enemies who oppose his rest, and breathe into his heart the good of Thy holy Church, and may he at once find Thy health for us. O Lord, give him heart, that he may have only Thee for God, without error of the faith in Thine only Son, with whom and with the Holy Spirit Thou hast glory, for ever and ever.'

{[f. 206v]} 'Michael, plead and pray for us. Saint Gabriel, make our prayer rise up. Ye four spiritual creatures, glorifiers and doctors, plead for us. Celestial angels, plead for us. Prophets, apostles, just men, martyrs, plead for us. <Prophets, apostles, just men, martyrs, plead for us.> Ye twenty-four priests and also heaven, plead for us. Society of saints and martyrs, plead for us, that He may give us part and inheritance to us all. Mary Our Lady, who gave birth to God, because thou didst find grace before Him, thou didst find grace and virtue of the Holy Spirit, plead for us. May thy Son share with us His peace; may He cause us to be with the saints in open paradise and ornate rest.'

'Raise your hands at night in the temple and bless God, and in Sion glorify Jesus, the saint of Israel. Holy, Holy, Holy, God of Sabaoth, our God is glorified by the cherubim and sanctified by the seraphim and praised by the archangels. His kingdom is cleaned of foulness. Holy God of Sabaoth, our God, who mounts fiery horses and walks on the tops of clouds, His tents are flames and His wheels are tremor. Holy God of Sabaoth, our God, who in sparks is marvellous, and in flashes is praised, and speaks in fire, the sound of His thundering wheels. Holy God of Sabaoth, our God, His glory is of Himself and His praise is of Himself, almighty Himself and the sword of vengeance in His hand; may the justice of those who suffer force come from His house. Holy God of Sabaoth, our God, who ordered the brightness to go round and knows <[f. 182v/172v]> whence it rises. Holy God of Sabaoth, our God, who disdains the proud and raises up the poor. Holy God of Sabaoth, our God, who scattered the clouds, who wets the earth and makes the sea dry up, who does what He wants and fulfils it as he wishes, without there being anyone who can withstand Him. There is no one who can say to Him, "Thou didst this badly and this well." Let us praise glorified God, who glorified Himself. Alleluia, alleluia, alleluia. The water was as a wall to them on either side. Alleluia to the Father, alleluia to the Son, alleluia to the Holy Spirit. Blessed be {[f. 207]} God; He is wonderful: He threw the horse and the rider into the sea. Plead for us, Mary, candle of the world, glorified in the heights. Plead for us, Mary, crown of the pure, brightness of the saints. Plead for us, Mary, scent box of the priesthood and kingdom. Plead for us, Mary, well of honour, vessel of mystery. Plead for us, Mary, channel of joy, vessel of prophecy; I shall praise thee seven times each day, because thy love has pierced my heart. The peace of the Angel Gabriel, my Mary.' (Here they say the *Ave Maria*.) 'Alleluia, alleluia, alleluia, because He saw the humility of His handmaiden and made power with His arm; because God chose Sion and made it flow to be His dwelling place. This is my resting place for ever.'

'The angels praise Mary within the curtains and say to her, "Peace be with thee, Mary." As she lived in a poor house, as a poor man He came down from the heavens to her, pleased with her beauty, and He was born of her. In the sixth month the Angel Gabriel was sent from God.' (Here a priest says the Gospel *'Missus est angelus'*, etc. as far as *'fiat mihi'*, etc.[1] And then they all continue.) 'The angel said to her, "Peace be with thee." Gabriel said to her, "Peace be with thee, Virgin Mary." Peace be with thee, for thou gavest birth to God. Peace be with thee, holy Mary. Peace be with thee, blessed Mary. Peace be with thee, pure Mary. Peace be with thee, divine dwelling-place. Peace be with thee, perfect tabernacle, sister of the angels. Peace be with thee, mother of all the people. Peace be with thee, Our Lady Mary. Peace be with thee, peacemaker. Peace be with thee, dressed in the golden robe of different colours. Peace be with thee, silvered feathers of {doves} <bustards>. Peace be with thee, door of the east and mother of brightness. Peace be with thee, brighter than the sun and higher than the mountains. Peace be with thee, Mary the chosen and honoured one. Peace be with thee. Plead for us to thy Son and our Redeemer, Jesus Christ, that He may release us when He comes with the glory of His Father, with His

---

[1] Luke 1:26–38, 'The angel [Gabriel] was sent ... be it done to me [according to thy word].'

holy angels, and when He has the sheep stand on the right hand and the goats on the left, that He may have us stand at His right hand with Stephen the martyr and John the Baptist and with all the saints and martyrs for ever and ever.' Here a priest reads {[f. 207v]} the Gospel of Saint John, chapter 19, '*Stabat autem iuxta Crucem*',[1] etc. And then they say the following:

'Peace be with thee, ark of Noe. Peace be with thee, rod of Aaron. Peace be with thee, <[f. 183/173]> viol of the Psalms of David. Peace be with thee, honour of Solomon. Having hope in thy blessing, with an offering we make reverence to thee. May God save thee, Mary, our mother and Our Lady. Thou art the glory of our fathers. Fight the enemies of our souls with the sword of perdition. Come, pass among us dressed in brightness with the Child in thy arms. The peace of thy Son be with us today, with reverence. Peace to all thy beauty, for the memory of thy name, sweeter than the honeycomb. Thou art Maria, daughter of Adam, who filled the breadth of the world, with reverence. Peace be to thy beauty, which causes wonder, with reverence. Peace', etc. In this manner they praise each member of the Virgin and her birth and presentation, with the rest of the feasts, on which they spend a long time,[2] and then they say:

'May the prayer and pleading of Mary free us from the wrath of her Son. Lord, forgive us, Christ.' They say this twelve times, and then the *Credo* and at the end, 'Alleluia, we praise Thee, Lord, and glorify Thee, we bless and glorify Thee. Thy name manifests Thy Word. Thy kingdom has no end, O Lord, king for ever. We praise Thee, {Lord,} and glorify Thee, king for ever. We bless Thee, glorified be Thy name, king for ever; Thy Word does not fail, and Thy kingdom has no end, O Lord, king for ever, who judgest rightly, without exception of persons, mercy in Thy hand. We beseech Thee, Lord, to hear us, alleluia. Forgive us, Lord, and have mercy on us. O Lord, for Thy holy name that was uttered over us, for Thy holy name, forgive us, Lord and have mercy on us, alleluia. We defend the Lord with Thy shield, that we may be diligent and fight with Thine enemy; cover us with the shadow of Thy wings, defend us with the wood of Thy cross and do not shame us, O Lord, before Thee. May all His works bless God. Thou art glorified <for ever> and the highest {for ever}. Let us bless the Father and the Son and the {[f. 208]} Holy Spirit. Alleluia to the Father, alleluia to the Son, alleluia to the Holy Spirit, who delivered Ananias, Azarias and Misael from the fire, likewise deliver us from all our opponents.'

'O principle of grace, Jesus Christ, virtue and wisdom of the Father, Thou art the lamb of God who bears the sins of the world; have mercy on us, because Thou camest down from heaven with the measure of the wisdom of Thy Father to deliver our vessel of clay and didst make Thyself mortal and corruptible. And He goes with wings of wind, who makes His angels spirits and His ministers burning fire, who looks at the earth and makes it tremble, who touches the mountains and they smoke with the spirit of Thy grace; content Thy {people} <Father>. Thou, Almighty <[f. 183v/173v]> God, our God, yes, Our Lord God, with the spirit of Thy grace, gladden Thy people, because Thou art the helper of the troubled, and make the most difficult things, ornament of the apostles, wealth of the poor, hope of the hopeless, raiser of the dead, virtue and wisdom of Thy Father, we bless Thee now and for ever and ever.'

---

[1] John 19:25, 'Now there stood by the cross ...'
[2] This type of praise follows the traditional model of *malke'e* poetry.

'For the prayer and petition of Our Lady Mary, have mercy on us, O Lord. For the virginity and purity of the body of Our Lady Mary, have mercy on us. For the pleading of Our Lady Mary, have mercy on us. For the pleading of the Church, in which the blood and flesh of our Saviour are shared, have mercy on us. For the pleading and power of Peter and Paul, torches of the world, and the blood that they spilt, have mercy on us. For the virginity and purity of John, Thy beloved, have mercy on us. For the virginity and torments of Thomas, apostle and martyr, have mercy on us. For the lashes and imprisonment of Matthew, Thy disciple, have mercy on us. For the prayers and pleadings and martyrdom of Bartholomew, Thine apostle, have mercy on us. For the prayers, pleadings and death on the cross of Andrew and Philip, their heirs, have mercy on us. For the prayers and death of Matthew the evangelist and James the son of Zebedee, have mercy on us. For the death of James, {[f. 208v]} thy brother, have mercy on us. For the death of Nathanael and the {pleadings} <death> of Thaddeus, preacher of the Gospel, have mercy on us. For the death and martyrdom of Mark and {Luke} <Matthew> the evangelists, whose fragrance was like incense, have mercy on us. For the blood of the victorious martyrs and miracles of the blessed just men, have mercy on us. For the pleadings of the diligent angels that do not sleep and glory of the cherubim and seraphim, have mercy on us. Forgive us, Lord, have mercy on us.'

'Give peace to Thy people, Thy holy Church. Lord, forgive us, Christ. *Nunc dimittis servum tuum*.[1] Alleluia, alleluia, alleluia. Release us with Thy right hand, in peace, Lord. Alleluia, alleluia, alleluia. Release us with Thy right hand, *quia viderunt oculi mei salutare tuum*.[2] Alleluia, alleluia, alleluia.' And they say thus all the verses, adding three alleluias, and at the end they add, 'Defend us in the wood of Thy Cross.'

On every day of the week, except the Sabbath and Sunday, they also say the following:

'O fountain of wisdom, fragrant tongue, Paul, plead for us, alleluia, alleluia, alleluia, <[f. 184/174]> that we may follow the trail of thy doctrine and have a share in thy inheritance. O Peter, head of all the saints, torch of the world, lord of the Christians, alleluia, alleluia, bless thy company with the power of thy hand. Alleluia, alleluia. Master apostles, resplendent stars, plead for the remission of sinners, cause your mercy to be {seen} <heard> in the morning.' A deacon says, 'Rise up for the prayer.' And a priest says, 'Peace be unto you all.' And then he reads a passage from the Gospel.

And on the Sabbath alone the following is added:

'After God finished speaking with Moses, He gave him the tablets of the promise, whose writing and making were of the Lord and the keeping of Sundays was carved.[3] Seek out Sion and embrace her and speak within her, alleluia, alleluia, alleluia. The prophets are her strength and the apostles her lamp and the saints and martyrs accompany her, alleluia, alleluia, alleluia. These are branches of vines and the river of the Gospel of the kingdom, alleluia, alleluia, alleluia. Work, then, my brothers, because you know not the hour when the new Lord of the house will come. {[f. 209]} Work, then, my brothers, that

---

[1] Luke 2:19, 'Now thou dost dismiss thy servant.'
[2] Luke 2:30, 'Because my eyes have seen thy salvation.'
[3] The text has probably been manipulated here by Páez.

He may not find you asleep at night or at daybreak. Work, then, my brothers, have your loins girded and your lamps lit. Work, then, my brothers, may grace and peace be multiplied unto you in Jesus Christ. Work, then, my brothers, raising up the virtue of the Gospel and glorying you with the grace of the cross. Work, then, my brothers, trust in God and lean on Him as the prophet, from morning until night, entrusted Israel to God. Lord, forgive us, Christ.' This they say twelve times.

### On Sundays only, the following is added:

'"{*Abiiciamu*} <*Anunciamus*> *opera tenebrarum et induamur arma lucis*,"[1] as Saint Paul said. "If we hope in His death, may we be like unto His life, let us hasten to enter into His rest."[2] John the virgin, outstanding among the diligent, John the virgin, glory of the saints, John adorned with brightness, trumpet that sounds in Ephesus, plead for us and for the remission of sinners, alleluia, alleluia. The apostles of peace, torches of the world, participants of torments, cast down from above pipes filled with mercy.' Here a deacon says, 'Rise up for the prayer.' And then a priest says, 'Peace be unto you all.' And he reads the Gospel of Saint John, '*In principio erat Verbum*',[3] etc., and then, 'Peace be with Thee, Sunday of brightness and splendour, Sunday of mystery, head of the times, alleluia, alleluia, alleluia, just as John bore witness that Thou wast called, memory of the resurrection of Emmanuel. Lord, forgive us, Christ.' This they repeat twelve times.

### <[f. 184v/174v]> They say the following every day:

'Bless us, O Lord our God, we praise Thee.' (Here they say the *Credo*.) And then, 'Peace be with thee, our glory and honour. Peace be with thee, Mary, crown of our glory. Peace be with thee, fortress of our salvation. Peace be with thee, garden of roses.' In this manner they salute the Virgin Our Lady many times and {then} some angels, and finally, they say some verses that deal with the humility of Christ Our Lord and the arrest in the garden and what He suffered in the house of Caiphas. And with that they finish what they sing in place of our matins.

### {[f. 209v]} When dawn breaks, they sing the following:

'Holy God, holy powerful, holy living, immortal God, who was born of Saint Mary the Virgin, have mercy on us. Lord, holy God, holy powerful, holy living, immortal God, who was baptized in the Jordan and was crucified on the tree of the cross, have mercy on us. O Lord, holy God, holy powerful, holy living, immortal God, who rose up from the dead on the third day and went up to heaven with glory and is on the right hand of His Father and will come again with glory to judge the living and the dead, have mercy on us. Glory to the Father, glory to the Son, glory to the Holy Spirit, now and evermore and for ever and ever. Amen, amen. So be it, so be it. Holy Trinity, living God, have mercy on us. To the true God belongs glory, to Thee, Lord, maker of all invisible things. God, open up our souls. We give Thee glory of the morning, Lord. To the wisdom of the almighty and merciful God, edifier of the soul, we give the glory of Him who was born before time.

---

[1] Romans 13:12, 'Let us [therefore] cast off the works of darkness, and put on the armour of light.' The copyist of BPB, MS 778 incongruously replaced the word '*abiiciamus*' ('let us cast off') with '*anunciamus*' ('we announce').

[2] Hebrews 4:11.

[3] John 1:1, 'In the beginning was the Word.'

Word of the Father, who rests in His saints, and Thou art glorified with the glory that the choirs of angels give to Thee without ceasing, to Thee who wast not made by hand, creator of the hidden, invisible, pure and holy, who didst say to us the hidden and holy wisdom and didst give us hope of the brightness that is never lost; glory and praise we give Thee, and pure sanctity we say, Thy servants, and the people glorify Thee.'

'God of brightness, giver of life, head of understanding, head of perfect grace, maker of the soul, profitable giver of the Holy Spirit, treasury of wisdom, master helper of the saints and foundations of the world, who receivest the prayer of the pure, to Thee we give glory. Firstborn and only son, Word of the Father, the graces that Thou didst give to us who call Thee are Thine. Pure Father without stain, to the souls that trust in Thee Thou givest pleasure, with the visit of the angels. Brightness that was before the world, our guardian, treasure that is never corrupted, Thou didst lighten the darkness that we had through the determination of Thy Father; Thou didst bring us out of the deep {[[f. 210]} <[f. 185/175]> into the brightness and from death Thou didst give us life and deliver us from servitude. With Thy cross Thou didst make us come to Thy Father above the heavens. With {Thy} <the> Gospel Thou didst guide us and with the prophets Thou didst console us. To Thee, our God, Thou didst make us come, but give us brightness, Lord. To Thee, our God, we give praise without ceasing, saying: We are Thy servants and the people praise Thee. Three times we give Thee this praise from our mouths with Thy kingdom for ever. Jesus Son of God, who is above all things with the Father, every creature praises Thee with terror and trembling; all the souls of the just are leaning on Thee, who didst calm the waves of the furious rivers, who from perdition didst make us a port of life, rest at the end of the race, and hope of eternal life. Thou didst deliver those troubled at sea, and those of the desert Thou didst heal with grace; Thou accompaniest those who are in harsh prison, Thou didst loose us from the chains of death; Thou consolest the poor and sad, and those who labour Thou releasest with Thy cross, and Thou removest Thy wrath from us who trust in Thee. We praise and glorify Thee, Lord, whom the prophets and apostles praised in hiding. Grant us that we may fulfil Thy commandments by doing Thy will, that we may rest in Thee in the dwelling place of life. Lord, visit thy mercy upon all, great and small, princes and people, the shepherd with his flock, because Thine is the kingdom, blessed Lord, our God. Glory be to the Father, to the Son and to the Holy Spirit, since before time, now and for evermore, and for ever and ever, and from generation to generation without end, and for all time. Amen.'

This is what they sing in the morning, but I have been unable to find what they say at the other hours and in the evening in place of vespers, although I have tried hard, because, as they say it all by heart, it is not easy to find the book in which it is written, and they did not want to tell it to me by word of mouth. I even took what I have reported above from a book that a monk, a friend of mine, gave me covertly in great secrecy. But in a synod that they call the synod of the Apostles, in commandment 5, they are ordered to say the office above, as well as the prayer of the terce in honour of Christ's lashes; the sext since He was crucified at that hour; the prayer of the none, because He expired then on the cross and the earth quaked; the evening prayer, for the Lord gave them the night to rest from the day's work; and the night prayer, so that God may deliver them from the sons of darkness. Hence it can be seen that they appear to have all the hours as we do.

## On the sacrament of ordination and the ceremonies that the *abuna* performs when he ordains

In all the lands that the Prester John rules there is no one who may give orders apart from a single bishop, whom the Ethiopians call *abuna*, which is an Arabian word that means 'Our Father'. He always comes to them from Egypt, sent by the patriarch of Alexandria, who usually resides in the city of Cairo because of all the business that he has with the pasha of the Turks, on whom he depends in almost all his affairs. And when Ethiopia asks him for an *abuna*, he commands the Egyptian monks of the order of Saint Anthony, who are in Cairo, to assemble and they present to him one or two monks of their order that seem to them to be most suitable and he chooses and confirms the one that he thinks is the most qualified of the two.

I know that Friar Luis de Urreta says, on page 439,[1] that the Ethiopian monks of Saint Anthony that live in Jerusalem put forward the one who is to come to Ethiopia as *abuna*, but he was mistaken, if we are to give credence to the Egyptians who come from there with the *abuna* himself. They assured me that no Ethiopian monks were involved in his election in any way, but just Egyptian ones. *Abuna* Simão, whom they killed here in May 1617, as we have already said, also assured me that neither he nor any of his predecessors was a patriarch, but just a bishop. The *abuna* tries to leave Turkish lands in complete secrecy, because if they are aware they do not let him come without paying a great deal of money. And if it comes to their notice once he has left, they oblige the patriarch there (so they say) to pay. Because of these difficulties, the emperor sometimes sends gold from here for him to give to the Turks to obtain permission for him to come. But even if they give it to him, he hardly ever comes by sea, both because it is a long voyage and so that the pasha of Suaquém cannot block his way to take some goods from him, for the Turks are never short of an excuse to do that. Therefore, he comes overland with great difficulty and danger of falling ill, because of the deserts and the heat {[f. 211]} on the journey, which they say ordinarily takes forty days.

When the *abuna* arrives in Ethiopia, they receive him with much festivity and honour. And the emperor always does him great honour, because whenever he enters his presence, <[f. 186/176]> the emperor rises to his feet and, coming close, the *abuna* touches him on the forehead with a little silver cross, which they always carry in their hands, and gives it to him to kiss. And then they ordinarily sit on the floor on carpets, although the emperor always rests on brocade or velvet cushions. The lands that they give him are very large and beautiful and always the same ones, because they have been marked out for that since

---

[1] Urreta, *Historia de la Etiopia*, bk II, ch. 5.

ancient times, and he has plenty of income from the churches. He also takes from every-one that he ordains a block and a half of salt, and sometimes two, which are two and a half fingerbreadths wide by eight long and are used as currency. Here in Dambiá they ordinar-ily give thirty for a certain weight of gold, which must be worth one *cruzado*. And this mounts up considerably because there is always a huge multitude of people being ordained, especially in the lower orders, because he sometimes – in fact, often – gives orders even to children at the breast. Once the advertised time arrives to give orders and many people have assembled from various parts, he puts it off for several days and makes them work gathering firewood and other things that he needs, and the ones who come from afar suffer with that, because the provisions they have brought run out. Once, when I was with the emperor, they made a complaint to him about *Abuna* Simão, because he had been detaining those who had come to be ordained for many days and was making them work, bringing him firewood and helping in a house that he was building, and since they were now tired and short of supplies, they all gathered in the evening and sang the litanies where he could hear them, beseeching God to move his heart so that he would dispatch them. The emperor was angry and said, 'I do not know how these things do not move him.' One of the great men jokingly replied, 'Lord, is he not Egyptian? It is hardly surprising that he is not moved by pleadings and prayers, since his forebears were not moved with all the plagues that God gave them in the time of Moses.' {[f. 211v]} The emperor then sent word to him that he should not keep those people waiting any longer but should give them orders, because they were complaining bitterly, and therefore he ordained them sooner than he would have done.

When he is going to give orders, he has a large tent erected in a field, because there is no room in the churches to organize all the people that are commonly ordained. Sometimes, however, when there are not so many, he does it in a church that has a good-sized yard in front of it. They are told to sit in three rows, usually, and are counted to see how many blocks of salt will be collected from them, and an inked seal is stamped <[f. 186v/176v]> on their right arms, near the hand. Then the *abuna* sits on his chair at the door to the church – or tent, when he gives orders in one – and reads a little from a book in the Arabian language. And then those who are to be ordained come up one by one and he cuts off a few hairs from their heads, which seems to be the first tonsure, and if one of them comes with a shaven head (as many do), he touches him on the head with the scissors, and they leave through the other side of the tent, which is also open. When they have all gone past, he reads from the book again and they go past again in order, as before. And he performs certain ceremonies and says some words, which I have never been able to discover, because the one who keeps the book would not show it to me at all or tell me what they were.

In this manner he gives all the orders together, except priesthood, which he gives on another occasion. For these first ones there is no prior examination at all, because they are given their orders even if they cannot read. A monk gave me the names of the orders writ-ten down, and they are as follows: doorkeeper, *aceitâ haueheû*; exorcist, *mecémerân*; reader, *anagunz têz*; acolyte, *caoarê mahetôt*; subdeacon, *nefquê diacon*, which means 'half-deacon'; a deacon they call *diacôn*; a priest, *cassês*, but it is an Arabian word; and priest-hood, *quesnâ*. I have reported this, because Friar Luis de Urreta, on page 520,[1] gives all

---

[1] Urreta, *Historia de la Etiopia*, bk II, ch. 11, entitled 'Of the sacrament of ordination and of the ceremonies with which the *abuna* ordained. Of the virgin and married priests that there are in Ethiopia', pp. 519–31.

these orders names that are so unheard-of in these lands that, when I mentioned them to some people to see whether they knew them, they {[f. 212]} found them very funny, as if they had been invented on purpose.

In the case of those to be ordained to say Mass, the *abuna* first has them examined by some Egyptian ministers that he has, and on those that they pass they stamp a mark in black ink on their right arms with a seal; but the examination is so easy that they fail very few or none at all, even if they barely know how to read, because they try to learn to read the texts on which they will be examined, which are particular passages: the beginning of the Gospel of Saint John, the beginning of chapter 2 of the Acts of the Apostles, and the beginning of chapter 23 of the Acts. They have to read out a little from these three passages, because there are certain letters in them which are difficult to pronounce for those who do not know how to read well. Those who come to be ordained also resort to another trick, which is for all those from the same land to gather together with the ones who know how to read in front; as the examiner sees the ones who can read well, he passes everyone from that land to make it less tiring. Hence many of those who say Mass can barely read, as I saw when I went to a large monastery to see the ceremonies of their Mass. The one who was saying it sang some things by heart and, when he came to read the Gospel from the book, he made such poor progress <[f. 187/177]> that another monk had to come and read it to him, but the second one stumbled only a little less than the first, and so another came to his aid and corrected him where he went wrong until he finished. I asked one monk, who is one of the greatest scholars that they have, whether they made those who were being examined explain any passages of Scripture, or whether they asked them about any issue of theology; he laughed and said, 'Neither the examiners nor the *abuna* himself know how to do that, so how could they ask them? They just examine them on reading.'

After the examination, the ones to be ordained sit on the ground in a row and the *abuna* sits on his chair and reads a little from the Arabian book. Then they go up one by one in order and put their faces on his hands and leave by the other door of the tent; then they come back in and he blows on their faces and, in this way, he performs {[f. 212v]} other ceremonies on them, such as blessing them with a cross that he holds in his hand, making them touch the altar stone and anointing them with oil, and lastly he makes a speech to them, telling them not to serve laymen, not to bear arms, not to indulge in other women, etc. Then the *abuna* says Mass and they all commune. He ordains the lame, the crippled and the blind, and I know some of these. When I asked why they ordained blind men for the Mass, since they could not celebrate it, a monk answered that it was so that they could excommunicate {and assist} and confess and sing in church.

All clerics are married, but they get married before being ordained for Mass, and to a virgin woman. If this wife later dies, they cannot marry again, and if they do (which often happens), the *abuna* suspends their orders, but they keep the wife at home. They also assured me as something that is quite certain and well known by everyone that if they offered a bribe the *abuna* would give them permission to say Mass again and keep that wife. They told me about one cleric who, as his first wife had died and he had married another, went to the *abuna* and said to him, 'Lord, I could not help marrying a second time; take away the priesthood that you have given me.' He replied, 'You are a good man; be calm. Say Mass and stay with this woman, for I give you permission.' The cleric said, 'I do not want to say Mass or to stay with this woman.' The *abuna* then commanded him on pain of excommunication to say Mass and not to leave the woman. I am not very surprised that the *abunas* behave in this way with the clergy, in view of the very little that they know <[f. 187v/177v]> and the bad example they ordinarily set in this matter.

Many are very finical about the orders that the *abuna* gives and assert that he does not give subdeacon's orders, even though in Ethiopia they have a name, which is *nêfqué diacôn*. I insisted to some monks that were talking about this and to *Eráz* Cela Christós, the emperor's brother, that that could not be so and that they must be mistaken, because since he gives all the orders together {[f. 213]} up to deacon, and since he speaks in another language, they would not understand his words, nor would they really notice whether he was giving subdeacon's orders or not; but they contradicted me all the same, insisting on what they had said. Moreover, when I was once alone with Emperor Seltan Sagued, he told me that he had serious doubts about the priesthood in his land, but he did not explain to me on what they were based. Father Patriarch Dom Andre de Oviedo also had very serious doubts and even said that there was a substantial alteration in the sacramental forms used by the *abunas* in administering orders. Father João Álvares of our Society wrote to me about this from Rome on 29th December 1605, when he was assistant for Portugal; his words were as follows, regarding a monk, Taquelâ Mariam by name, who went from here to Rome via Cairo:[1]

> Because the father patriarch had given a warning both here and there that there was a substantial alteration in the forms of the sacraments in this Ethiopia, in that they had either been maliciously corrupted or become altered with time, in this case it seemed best, on the good advice of the fathers, to ordain him sub conditione. When I took up the case with Cardinal Saint Severino, of good memory, protector of these nations, he told me that it would be very difficult, but as he was very zealous of the universal good of the Church, he gave in and ordered me to test said Taquelâ Mariam, because he felt that he would not pass. I did so and I too found it very difficult; however, when I explained to him the secrecy with which it would be done and the likelihood that he was not ordained, he gave in. Permission was sought from His Holiness, who gave it willingly to the cardinal, and a bishop whom he had in his house, who was very zealous of these things, ordained him sub conditione in his chapel in great secrecy. With that this good man changed completely and became the most joyful, happy and relieved man that Your Reverence could imagine, a sign (in my view) that he had not been properly ordained the first time. The reason for requesting such secrecy was so that it should not become known there that he considered the sacraments from there to be invalid and therefore he was being ordained {[f. 213v]} validly here, which would be a reason for them to treat him badly. He was prudent and very modest; it was a loss that he died.

Up to here are words from Father João Álvares; and a little before these he says, 'This monk was returning to Ethiopia via Portugal and died on the journey.'

<[f. 188/178]> I have never been able to get hold of the book by which the orders are given[2] (as I said above), despite having even *Eráz* Cela Christós intercede for this purpose. But Father Patriarch Dom Andre de Oviedo would not have written to Rome that there

---

[1] Guerreiro mentions the episode, but does not transcribe the letter; see 'Adição à Relação das coisas de Etiópia', f. 273v, p. 296.

[2] See Grébaut, *Rituel éthiopien de prise d'habit* (14th-century Ge'ez liturgical text).

was a substantial alteration in the forms of the sacraments if he had not been very sure of it, nor does it seem likely that many monks and laymen in Ethiopia would have the doubts that they have without good grounds. One thing is quite certain and well known by everybody, which is that once, when *Abuna* Petrôs, who died in 1607, was giving orders and was already tired because he had done many and he still had a large number to ordain, he had it proclaimed that all those who had gathered there to take orders at whatever level were ordained, because he was conferring orders on them, and the blocks of salt that they customarily pay were collected and they went away, feeling sure that they were now ordained. Somebody was extremely scandalized by this and went to tell the emperor, who was Malâc Sagued at the time. He summoned the *abuna* and said he found the case very strange and told him to gather together all those who had been there before to whom he had not given orders and to ordain them. But it is possible that some were from very distant lands and did not hear that they were being commanded to return, and they continued saying Masses and hearing confessions without being ordained. Before this *Abuna* Petrós, they say that another called Marcos did the same. Therefore, since the *abuna* is as idiotic as this, it would not greatly surprise me if he left out essential things in the forms of the sacraments without noticing.

It may be seen from what we have said in this chapter how little information Friar Luis de Urreta had on these matters, since on some of them he affirms the opposite. In chapter 11 of the second book of his *Historia*, after mentioning {[f. 214]} the ceremonies with which he says the *abuna* gives orders, he puts these words:

*The reader will rightly have noticed, in this manner of giving orders, how correct they are in ceremonies, as well as some things contrary to any good arrangement, such as ordaining altar boys and other minor orders. They also used to ordain the lame, crippled, blind and people with other bodily defects in the four minor orders. But for these and other abuses we shall not condemn them outright as heretics, as some {strict} qualificators do, because they did so out of ignorance. Since the Church ordered them not to do so, they have obeyed like good children and they now ordain in the manner of the Church of Rome, with the same rites and ceremonies, the bishops and archbishops giving orders to their parishioners in their dioceses, because it is their particular office to consecrate not just men but temples, vessels and vestments, although the four <[f. 188v/178v]> minor orders are {these days} given by spiritual abbots, vicars or priests by special commission of the supreme pontiffs. As for ordaining boys to all orders up to the deaconate, they were wrong to do so and they have therefore stopped, but they were truly ordained. As regards ordaining the lame, blind and crippled, they have stopped and no longer do so.*[1]

The author says this, but he is very much mistaken, because they still ordain boys to the four minor orders and as altar boys, and the lame, crippled and blind to the priesthood. Therefore, if the Roman Church did command them at any time not to do so, they have not obeyed her command. And there is no one in Ethiopia who gives any orders other than the *abuna*, because he is the only bishop and the abbots and vicars are not permitted to give the four minor orders, as we shall say later.

---

[1] Urreta, *Historia de la Etiopia*, excerpt (with omissions) from bk II, ch. 11, pp. 522–3. Páez quotes this passage in Spanish.

A little further on, he says that in Ethiopia there are virgin clerics and others who are married, and he deals with them at length and says that in each of the four parishes that they make in each city there are thirteen virgin priests, *scilicet* who are not married {[f. 214v]} and never have been and are like regular clerics. Twelve are subordinate and the other is the superior, ordinarily the vicar. To be admitted to this dignity, they all have to be noble and fifty years old, and have to show that they are mortified, composed and religious men, and so, before they are accepted, they are made to spend three years within the cloister (because the parish churches are like a monastery with its cloister), and they practise humble works and mortification. At the end of this time he is put in a chapterhouse, and if he is accepted he is sent to the bishop with testimonials from the priests and parishioners, for these also give their vote. He goes on an elephant, seated in a very rich kind of litter, in the manner in which the Prester John and the prelates of Ethiopia customarily travel; he is accompanied by his kinsfolk and friends and in this manner presents himself to the bishop, who receives him with great honour. After seeing if his letters dimissory are sufficient, he ordains him on Wednesday for the Epistle, on Friday for the Gospel and on Saturday for the Mass. Then he returns to his church with the same retinue and all the priests come out to welcome him, dressed in the ornaments in which they say Mass, and their superior, opening a book of the Gospels, makes him swear everlasting obedience to the Roman Church and observance of the primitive Antiochian Church. Having done that, he says a new Mass with great solemnity and then they perform many ceremonies with him, <[f. 189/179]> in the end covering his face with a black veil that comes down to his chest (a custom of virgin priests always to keep their face covered with a veil) and, as if dead to the world, they say to him, '*Requiescat in pace*.'[1] In each city, the Prester John gives these priests more than half a league of land, where they build houses and villages, plant and sow, and have vegetable plots and gardens, where they live {[f. 215]} with serving folk, except for women, who cannot enter.

Of the married priests, he says that there can be thirty-two in each city of the empire and that they were allowed this at one of the Antiochian Councils, at the request of an emperor whom the Ethiopians call João the Holy, where at the same time they were given permission to be married, on condition that they made a vow of conjugal chastity when they were ordained *in sacris*, that they had not had more than one wife, that she had not been a widow, and that if she died they could not remarry. At the end of the chapter, he says that Supreme Pontiff Gregory XIII, in some apostolic briefs that he dispatched to Ethiopia, which were brought by João Baltesar, commanded virgin priests to dress in the Roman manner and to have a priest's tonsure, because previously they had shaved their whole heads and had long beards, unlike lay members, who shave their beards and leave their moustaches and hair long. He ordered them to wear four-cornered birettas, because previously they had worn round ones, and to wear a cassock and mantle in the Roman manner, because previously they had worn long robes little different from those of the secular priests, and to wear rochets.[2] And he declared that it was not his intention that married priests should enjoy these privileges.

The author says these and many other things, but they are all mere fiction invented by whoever informed him, because there are no such virgin clerics in Ethiopia and there

---

[1] 'Rest in peace.'
[2] Rochet – a vestment similar to a surplice.

never have been (as everyone says), and they have never seen a tame elephant here or a litter. Even if there were such clerics, they would not make them swear everlasting obedience to the Roman Church, since they are separated from it and hold its doctrine to be false, as we saw in the first chapters of this second book. Therefore, if the Supreme Pontiff Gregory XIII dispatched some briefs to Ethiopia, as the author says, it would be through false information from João Balthesar, {[f. 215v]} for they have not heard of any such briefs here or of four-cornered birettas, <[f. 189v/179v]> and nobody dresses in the Roman manner; instead, many of them dress almost in the Turkish manner, especially the *abuna*. All the clerics are married, and if they contented themselves with their wives it would be a very good thing, but they do get married before they are ordained, and to a virgin woman, as we said above. They shave their whole heads and let their beards grow, as many secular priests do, and generally none of them shaves off his beard. They do not differ from them in dress: those who can wear a white cotton caftan with a tall, tight-fitting collar, and over it another made of cloth from our lands or silk that they get through the Turks, and on their heads a round or long biretta of any colour that they find, and sometimes on top of it a turban like that of the Moors; they wear long, narrow trousers down to their shoes. Those who are poor only wear a white cotton cloth, with which they cover themselves, and calf-length breeches; they go bare-headed and barefoot. But they all carry in their hand a slender iron or black wooden cross about a span in length, which is specific to the clergy, although nuns also carry one. I wanted to find out when these married priests had their origin, but I could not find anyone who could tell me, for what Friar Luis de Urreta says on page 526,[1] that the Prester John whom the Ethiopians call João the Holy obtained permission for clerics to be married, is false, because there never was such a Prester John in Ethiopia, as we shall say at the end of this book.

To what we have reported from the author here – that the bishops and archbishops give orders to their own parishioners – I thought I should add what he says a little further on in chapter 12. There he says that the archbishops of this empire are twelve in number and the bishops seventy-two, and that there have never been either more or less since the beginning of Christianity in this land, despite the land being so broad that there could be many more, because in this way they preserve the memory {[f. 216]} of the twelve apostles and seventy-two disciples. He also says that the oldest archbishop acts as supreme pontiff and is the apostolic nuncio for the whole of Ethiopia, under specific briefs from Clement VII and Paul III and other Roman pontiffs, and that in addition to these prelates, who govern the spiritual side of Christianity in Ethiopia, there are titular patriarchs, archbishops <[f. 190/180]> and bishops who are consecrated but do not hold churches or sheep, and these attend the Grand Council and are elected by the Prester John under briefs that he has for this purpose from the above-named pontiffs.

Up to here are words of the author,[2] but in them and in almost everything else that he says in that chapter there is not one word corresponding to the truth of what happens here, because there are no such archbishops or bishops apart from the *abuna*, and there never have been, nor an apostolic nuncio, nor those patriarchs that attend the Grand Council, nor even priests, for they are all secular. Thus, if the Roman pontiffs did issue

[1] Urreta, *Historia de la Etiopia*, bk II, ch. 11.
[2] Summarized by Páez.

those briefs, they would have done so based on false information that the petitioners had given them with the intention of making a name there for themselves and their land, by showing that they had such a form of government here and that they were obedient to the Roman Church. And there are no abbots that ever give minor orders, nor can they. There was only some doubt about the general of the monks of *Abba* Taquelá Haimanot, whom they call *icheguê*, which is the title of the office; but when in 1615 he started saying that he had the power to ordain, the *abuna* of the time stood up to him and, when he made a complaint about it, they judged that only the *abuna* had the power to give orders, and thus the *icheguê* was excluded.

# CHAPTER XIV

## Which deals with the errors that the Ethiopians hold regarding the holy sacrament of marriage and the ceremonies that they perform in it

{[f. 216v]} Although Christ Our Lord taught so clearly in the Holy Gospel how insoluble consummated marriage is after baptism, saying that husband and wife are not two but one flesh, and what God has joined together let no man put asunder, Matthew 19,[1] and that he who puts away his wife and marries another commits adultery, and if the woman leaves her husband and marries another she commits adultery, Mark 10, Luke 16,[2] despite all that it is very common among Ethiopians for the husband to leave his wife and marry another and for the wife to marry someone else. To do this it is only necessary for them to go before the emperor's judges and for the husband to say, 'I cannot stay with this wife: she is very wilful; she speaks to me as she likes and she is breaking up my household', or other, similar things. Or the wife may say, 'I cannot put up with this husband, because he is giving me a very bad life; in particular he dishonours me and even <[f. 190v/180v]> beats me.' And if these causes are confirmed, they then judge that they should separate and marry whomever they like. If they both ask for permission to separate, they split the property that they own and they each take their half, but if only one says he or she wants to separate, this one takes no property at all: it all goes to the other. In addition, if the husband is away for two or three years and the wife goes to the judges and says that her husband has been absent for so long and she has nothing to eat and cannot wait any longer and wants to marry someone else, they give her permission to do so.

The *abuna* hands down the same decisions when they go to him with these complaints, and the Egyptians say that the patriarch of Alexandria does the same, because when a wife has quarrelled with her husband in such a way that she does not want to stay with him, if she is not given permission to marry someone else she will leave the faith and become a Moor. But they also leave their wives and marry others without making these complaints, and wives often leave against their husbands' will and marry others, without there being anyone to oblige {[f. 217]} them to return to them, as I myself have sometimes seen.

If a man finds that his wife has committed adultery, he may leave her and marry another without any kind of complaint or note, because it is common doctrine among their doctors that Christ Our Lord gave permission for this when he said, in Matthew 5, 'whosoever shall put away his wife, excepting for the cause of fornication,'[3] etc. Many now understand the opposite, however, ever since we showed them through disputations and

---

[1] Matthew 19:6.
[2] Mark 10:1–12; Luke 16:18.
[3] Matthew 5:32.

public speeches how great an error this is, because these words do not mean that the bond of marriage is loosed because of fornication, but that a man who separates from his wife because of fornication does not sin, for otherwise an adulteress would be more fortunate than an innocent wife, because the adulteress would be loosed from the law of marriage and could lawfully marry someone else, while a chaste, innocent wife who was falsely shown to be adulterous could not marry someone else, since she would not be truly loosed from the law, nor could she stay with her husband, since he would be married to someone else. Husbands would often commit adultery on purpose in order to be free of their wives and be able to marry others, and wives who had become bored with their husbands would do the same. But the most holy and pure law of Christ Our Lord does not provide paths for sin, and so it certainly cannot be said that the bond of marriage is loosed because of fornication.

<[f. 191/181]> But what need have we to give reasons for this, when the doctrine of Saint Paul is so clear, in Romans 7 and 1 Corinthians 7?[1] He says that the wife is bound to all the law while her husband lives, so that if she goes with another she will be an adulteress; and that to those that are married, it is not he but the Lord who commands that the wife must not depart from her husband, but, if she does depart, she must remain unmarried or be reconciled to her husband; and the husband must not put away his wife. Here {[f. 217v]} Saint Paul is speaking of the woman who leaves her husband for some just cause of divorce, such as fornication or heresy, and he says that she cannot marry anyone else, but that she must stay as she is or be reconciled to her husband. Therefore the bond of marriage is never loosed until death, neither because of fornication or for any other reason; and here Saint Paul is speaking of the wife who leaves her husband with just cause and, clearly, not of one who leaves without such cause, because he would not have said of the latter that she should stay as she was or be reconciled to her husband, but that she should stay as she was until she was reconciled to her husband and she must in any case return to her husband, because Saint Paul could not give permission for an unjust divorce against the express precept of Christ Our Lord. And if in the same chapter he does not permit those who are married to abstain from the commerce that they owe to each other, except for a time by mutual consent so that they may give themselves to prayer and then return together as before, how could he permit the woman to stay away from her husband against his will without any just cause? There is no doubt, therefore, that he is speaking of the woman that has left her husband with just cause, and that he is saying that this woman cannot marry anyone else, but must stay as she is or make friends again with her husband. With these and other issues that we have brought to these Ethiopians, many have come to understand this truth and firmly believe it; however, an incomparably greater number say the opposite and hold it to be something quite certain.

Regarding the ceremonies that they perform at their marriages, I asked many monks and secular men and they said that when a young man wants to marry a maiden, he sends honourable men to talk to her parents and presents them with goods according to his ability. When {[f. 218]} he obtains <[f. 191v/181v]> their and her consent, he gives a surety that he will not break her arm, eye or feet or do her any other notable harm and that she will not lack the necessary things to wear and eat, and if he should fail in any of these, they can claim from the surety. But when the parents deliver their daughter, they always give

[1] Romans 7:2–3; 1 Corinthians 7:10–11.

her much more property than they received from the young man, and after their deaths she inherits her parents' estate if only she is left, and if she has brothers and sisters she gets the part due to her in accordance with the rules of the kingdom, because the eldest always takes twice as much as each of the other brothers and sisters.

A few days before they marry, they hold a feast in the young man's house and in that of the maiden's parents, playing music and singing night and day. If the young man is a deacon, the woman has to be a virgin. And they both go to church accompanied by their kinsfolk and friends and, while she stays in the place of the women (which is in the cloister or veranda, if the church has one, or if not then before reaching the first curtain, beyond which lay people cannot pass, as we shall say later), he goes inside and there they give him the vestments that the deacon wears to assist at Mass, and he takes them in his arms to the priest, who is robed to say Mass, who blesses him, saying, 'Blessed be Almighty God the Father and blessed be the only Son Jesus Christ, who was born of the Holy Virgin Mary, and blessed be the Holy Spirit the Paraclete. Glory and honour be to the most holy Trinity, Father, Son, Holy Spirit, for ever and ever.' Then the deacon makes obeisance to the altar and vests himself and assists at the Mass, and after he has communed, they take the communion to her at the church door and he gives her the blood. When Mass is over, two priests lift him off the ground and another two her, and they hold them thus while they sing some canticles and then they carry them like this a until they are a little way from the church. When the priests put them down, {[f. 218v]} two young laymen put him on their shoulders and the one acting as godfather puts her on his back and they carry them to their house if it is nearby, or they go on mules if it is a long way away, accompanied by all those whom they brought before.

If the bridegroom is a layman, neither he nor his bride go to church, but if he wants a blessing, which they often do not seek, he goes to the vicar's house and he blesses him there briefly, and he returns. Sometimes the vicar also goes <[f. 192/182]> to the couple's house to bless them, but not often. And if the bride is in another land, the bridegroom goes to fetch her on a mule, accompanied by people on mules or horses, according to their status, and many on foot with arms and musical instruments. They ordinarily sleep there no more than one night, and in the morning they bring her back with them on a well-adorned mule; if she is a great lady, the bridle is decorated with gilded silver set on crimson velvet, and the whole mule is covered with brocade or other silk so that one can only see the part of its head that the bridle does not cover and the lower half of its legs. The bride always comes dressed according to her rank, and even if she is not of very high rank, she wears good clothes, because they lend her some if she does not have any, and she puts on a turban so that only her eyes show, with a tall, silk hat on her head and a veil, ordinarily red, with ends so long that they hang down her back to her waist – the usual fashion for ladies when they travel. But sometimes she wears a burnous with a cowl on her head, and then she does without a hat. A man goes on either side of her to hold on to her and control her mule if necessary, because she does not hold the reins in her hand.

{[f. 219]} When she arrives at the bridegroom's house, they hold a great feast and the bride and groom do not leave the house for at least ten days, sometimes thirty, and all this time they are accompanied by two men, whom they call *miçôs*, who are like godfathers. And when the bride and groom come out, after either ten or thirty days, a monk goes there and sprinkles them with holy water. When I asked a monk why they performed that ceremony, he answered that it was because of the sin that they committed when they consummated their marriage, since she was a maiden. I explained to him then that in the venerable sacrament of marriage there is no sin, for it is instituted by Christ Our Lord, and it gives grace with which the natural love of the married couple is perfected, and it sanctifies them and confirms the indissoluble union that they are obliged to have until death.

If the bride or groom is the emperor's kin and they are at court, on the day when he is to take her home they both go to the palace, he accompanied by noblemen and she by ladies, and the emperor gives them both many <[f. 192v/182v]> rich robes, and then they go to the bridegroom's house with a large retinue, with the emperor's drums and shawms going in front, and for a few days they hold a great feast and give food and drink to everyone who comes.

When the husband dies, if he has an unmarried brother, he often marries the wife – this often happens among less noble people – and if the brother is married, he also sometimes takes her home and keeps her as a wife, because he says that he is the one who will inherit his brother's wife. When I went to a province in the kingdom of Tigrê called Hamacêm, the governor of the province put me up for two days. When I learnt that together with his own wife he also had as such the wife of a deceased brother of his, I took him aside and told him how serious a matter that was, to which he replied that he had done so because that was the custom in the land {[f. 219v]} and he had not thought it was bad, but that he would send her home and not have any more relations with her. He did so straight away, and she was very angry at that. Likewise, there are others who have them without ever being punished for it. I only found one monk, in the kingdom of Gojam, who denied a couple the sacraments because the man was also keeping the wife of a deceased brother of his.

I am aware that Francisco Álvares says in his *Historia Ethiopica*, folio 25,[1] that, even though the emperor's justice does not forbid anyone to have many wives, and in fact some men have, such people are not given sacraments and they are not allowed to enter the church. But it seems to me that in those days they were stricter about this matter than now, because when *Erás* Cela Christós issued a command in the kingdom of Gojam, where he is viceroy, that those who had left their lawful wives and married others should abandon the latter and take back the former, and that sacraments should not be given to those who had more than one wife, they took it very hard, and he was unable in the end to implement it; indeed, as a monk told me later, they still have not stopped confessing and giving communion to those who openly have many wives at the same time.

Francisco Álvares also says in the same place[2] that he saw two marriages, and that they put a bed with curtains in a meadow and, when the bride and groom sat on it, three clerics came and walked round them three times, singing <[f. 193/183]> some kind of verses with alleluias, and then they cut some hair from the bridegroom's head and some from the bride's and, after wetting it with honey wine, put the bridegroom's hair in the place where they cut off the bride's and hers in the place where they cut off his, and they sprinkled them with holy water, and then the wedding festivities began. He says that on another

---

[1] Álvares, *Prester John of the Indies*, ch. 20, 'Of the town of Barua, and of the women and its traffic, and of the marriages which are made outside the churches', p. 105.

[2] Álvares, *Prester John of the Indies*, chs 20–21. Álvares also includes some notes on divorce and on the widow marrying her brother-in-law in ch. 21: 'Of their marriages and benedictions, and of their contracts, and how they separate from their wives, and the wives from them, and it is not thought strange', pp. 107–8.

occasion he saw *Abuna* Marcos perform it, but it was at the church door, and he had a cross in his hand and censed all round the bed, and then 'he put his hands on their heads, saying that they should keep {[f. 220]} what God commands in the Gospel and that they should remember that from that time onwards they were not two separate people but two in one flesh, and that their hearts and wills had to be like that as well'. Up to here are words from Francisco Álvares, but it seems that since he was a foreigner from such distant lands they wanted to show him this ceremony in their marriages, just as they deliberately showed him a good deal that was extraordinary in other matters that he recounts in the same book. {Or it may be that they used to do that at that time, but now there is no such thing, and I have not been able to find anyone to confirm such a custom, although I have asked many people.}

Someone who totally contradicts what we have said is Friar Luis de Urreta, who, in chapter 10 of his second book,[1] says that the Ethiopians neither have many wives, nor have ever had more than one, nor do they leave the lawful ones, and that there is no nation that punishes adultery more rigorously when a case is found among them. But his information was wrong, as it was on almost every other subject, because there have always been men in Ethiopia who have openly had many women, and there are today, and others who leave their lawful wives and marry others, as we have said above. And the only punishment that an adulteress has is to shave her head and give up her property, and with that she is free to marry someone else or do whatever she likes, and they do not give any other punishment to the adulterer than to pay a fine, as we said in chapter 16 in the first book.

---

[1] Urreta, *Historia de la Etiopia*, bk II, ch. 10, entitled, 'Of the Sacrament of marriage, and of the ceremonies that the people of Ethiopia keep in it'], pp. 516–19.

# CHAPTER XV

## Which deals with the making of the temples that there were in the past and there are today in Ethiopia and the reverence that they have for them[1]

We saw in the previous chapter how the Ethiopians go about the venerable sacrament <[f. 193v/183v]> of marriage, which signifies the indissoluble union and conjunction of Christ with the Church. It will now be appropriate to see how they go about making their temples, {[f. 220v]} the reverence and veneration that they have for them, and the extent to which the ancient churches were more sumptuous than those of today, as is well shown by the ruins of some and by others that are still standing. Starting with those that I have seen, the church of Saint Mary of Sion, which was built in ancient times (as they say) by Queen Candace in a place that they call Agçûm in the kingdom of Tigrê, was of great majesty and beautiful architecture, as shown by its ruins and testified by the ancient books that are kept in that monastery, which report in detail all its making, although I have only noted down its measurements. They say that it was 184 spans wide, 250 long and sixty-four high; the thickness of the walls was fourteen and the main door was fourteen high. They started to build it forty-nine years after the birth of Christ Our Lord and finished it in the year 92.

Francisco Álvares says on folio 44 of his *Historia*[2] that he saw it and that it had five naves covered with a cupola and painted, and seven chapels with their altars to the east, well arranged, and that it had a choir like ours, but so low that one's head almost reached its cupola and choir loft, although they did not use it. But all this has now collapsed and only the outer walls are left to a height of two cubits, and in the middle they have made another, much smaller church, although with three naves with square, very thick columns, and it is very dark since the windows are poor and it is roofed with thatch. One reaches it up the same steps as to the old church, which are ten in number and made of very beautiful, long stones. The other things that might be noted here that beautified the old church were included in chapter 22 of the first book, when we were dealing with the cities. There

---

[1] This chapter and the next contain brief descriptions by Francisco Álvares of the monolithic churches of Lālibalā, carved out of the rock from the 12th century onwards. The site, which was given World Heritage status in 1978, takes its name from the king of the Zāgwé dynasty who is attributed with the miraculous construction of the temple complex. It was originally called Roḥā after the holy city in Syria (Edessa or Roha) conquered by the Mongols in 1144. Páez has partly transcribed Álvares's descriptions, rendering in Portuguese passages that he has taken from his copy of a Spanish translation of the *Verdadeira informação*, but he has omitted some passages and adapted others. We have therefore decided not to italicize the long apparent quotation from Álvares's book that is given here.

[2] Álvares, *Prester John of the Indies*, ch. 38, pp. 151, 153.

is one thing worth mentioning with regard to this church, which is that it is said {[f. 221]} that the church was begun to be built in honour of the Virgin while Our Lady was still alive, like the chapel of Our Lady of the Pillar in Zaragoza in Spain.

<[f. 194/184]> Some six or eight leagues from this church, to the west, in the province of {Aorât} <Torât>, there is a monastery that they call Alleluia, on a high mountain, the church of which was also dedicated to Our Lady. It has now fallen down, but the outer walls remain standing to a height of some three cubits. When I measured the space between them, I found it was 132 spans long and 105 wide. It appears to have had many naves, and they say that it was very beautiful. The church they have now is round, small and dark. But leaving the ones that are now in ruins, we shall speak of some that still stand in the province that they call Oror, and the people of Ethiopia celebrate them as a thing of great wonder, and Francisco Álvares, on folio 66,[1] went much further, saying that there are so many church buildings carved out of the living rock that it is not possible that others like them, or so many, might be found anywhere in the world. If he had seen the temples, or rather, the Devil's houses that the heathens in East India have dedicated to various idols, some hacked out of the living rock, others built in stone, he would have refrained from including such an exaggeration. In one dedicated to a monkey, which I think is in Coromandel, those who have seen it claim that just the cloister that serves to gather the cattle to be sacrificed has 700 columns of worked marble, larger and much thicker than any that can be seen today in Spain, because, they say, in circumference and length they are as big as those that Agrippa put in his Pantheon, which they now call the Rotunda, in Rome. I have questioned {[f. 221v]} local people who have seen these buildings in Oror, and they do not depict them as being as large as Francisco Álvares says. Nevertheless, I shall report here the things that he wrote, to which more credence should be given, since for the sake of curiosity he noted down measurements and everything else and so he was not speaking in the dark, unlike the people I questioned, not one of whom was able to tell me those things.

Francisco Álvares says, then, that the churches are Saint Emmanuel, Saint Saviour, Saint Mary, the Holy Cross, Saint George, Golgotha, Bethlehem, Mercoriôs, the Martyrs and Lalibelâ. This last one was named after an emperor who had them made and is buried in the church of Golgotha, which is the one that has the least work. This church of Golgotha is hewn out of the rock and must be 120 spans long and seventy-two wide. The vault or roof of the church is supported on five columns, {two on each side} and one in the middle; the ceiling of the church is as flat as its floor; the walls have many windows and as much carving work as <[f. 194v/184v]> a goldsmith can do in silver. On the left as you enter through the main door, before you reach the main chapel, there is a tomb made in the rock itself which, they say, is in the likeness of the sepulchre of Christ Our Lord, and so they hold it in great veneration. On the other side are two relief images, carved in such a way that they are almost separate from the wall: one is of Saint Peter and the other of Saint John. This church also has a chapel, which itself is almost like a church, with naves and six columns, three on each side, and is very well worked; the middle nave is very high and has good arches, windows and doors, one main and one side door, apart from the one that serves the large church. This chapel is square and must be fifty-two spans each side. It

---

[1] Álvares, *Prester John of the Indies*, ch. 54, 'Of the great church buildings that there are in the country of Abuxima which King Lalibela built and of his tomb in the church of Golgotha', pp. 205–21; and ch. 55, 'Of the fashion of the church of St Saviour, and other churches which are in the same town, and of the birth of King Lalibela, and the dues of this country', pp. 222–6.

has another square chapel twelve spans each side with many windows and finished above like a papal mitre. The altars of this church {[f. 222]} all have their columns, with corridors above them. It also has a square cloister round it, as high as the church, and you enter through a tall passageway carved in the same rock, thirteen spans wide. All this is carved out of a single number rock,[1] without anything else being added: the columns, the altars and the verandas above them are worked in it, together with everything else.

The church of Saint Saviour is separate and also hacked out of the rock, and it must be 200 spans long and 120 wide. It has five naves, each one with seven square columns, four spans wide on each side, and the walls are well carved, the vaults are high and the middle one is higher than the others. On the ceiling there were many curiosities, like skylights, roses and flowers and other things all very well carved. In the walls there were many openings well cut inside and out with abundant tracery showing very fine workmanship. The main chapel is very high, and so is the altar ceiling, which is on four columns with its corridors all round. The main door starts with thick arches which gradually become narrower; the door is no more than nine spans high and four and a half wide. The side doors are worked in the same way, but are not so wide. Outside the main door is a vaulted portico on seven columns standing twelve spans from the wall of the church, with some moons on them, and there are arches from one to another; they must be two lances tall from the ground to the top.[2] <[f. 195/185]> There is no difference at all in the whole of this rock out of which this church was carved: it all seems to be a single piece of marble. Its cloister is also very well worked in the rock and each side must be sixty spans long, apart from the wall that stands opposite the main door, which must be a hundred. The {[f. 222v]} entrance to this church is through the same rock, in which a passageway has been made that is eighty spans long and wide enough for ten men to walk in a row, shoulder to shoulder, and it must be rather more than a lance in height; in the ceiling there are four skylights which let in plenty of light; and from this entrance to the church there is a plot of land where they have a house and sow barley.

The church of Our Lady, while not so big as that of the Saviour, since it is no more than eighty spans long and sixty-four wide, is beautiful and has three naves, the middle one being higher than the others. In each nave there are five columns with their arches on which the vaults are supported. In the middle of the crossing there is another very high column supporting the corridors,[3] which are so well worked that they seem to be pressed in wax, and at the front of each nave is a chapel with its altar. Outside the church are six pillars, two against the wall and four separate, with their arches, on which are supported some square platforms, fifteen spans on each side. There is a fine cloister as tall as the church. Opposite the main door is a large house, also made out of the same rock, and in it they give food to the poor. To the right of this church is another the same size, with three naves on columns and made of the same rock, and it is called the church of the Martyrs. To the left of the church of Our Lady there is another, smaller one, sixty-eight spans long, with only one nave with three columns supporting the ceiling and just one altar. It is called Holy Cross, and it has neither cloister nor portico nor anything other than a dark passageway carved out of the same rock, which comes out a very long way away.

---

[1] The original Portuguese has '*pedra número*', which may be a copyist's mistake for '*pedra mármore*', marble.

[2] The half-moons carved in the stone decorate the platband above the colonnade.

[3] The meaning of 'corridors' in these descriptions is unclear; the tall central column in the church of Saint Mary (Béta Māryām) supports only the centre of the barrel vault above the main nave.

The church of Saint Emmanuel is small, but {[f. 223]} curiously carved; it has three naves and the middle one is higher. The ceiling, which is flat like the floor, is supported on five columns, and it is forty-two spans long and twenty wide, and all made from a single rock. The church of Saint George is some distance away from the others, but also carved out of the rock like them, and near it, in the same rock, is a pool of water and they say there is a spring there. Francisco Álvares does not describe the other churches, but he says that he was told that they were all made in twenty-four years and that the master craftsmen were white men. Up to here are his words.

<[f. 195v/185v]> Those people of this land that have seen these churches told me that they were all carved out of the rock on a not very high hill that they call Lalibelâ, named after the emperor who had them made, and he died in June and was buried there. The common people hold him to be a saint. In October they make a large feast there to a Gabrâ Christôs, whom they hold to be a very great saint, and it means Alexius, and they say that he was the son of Theodosius, king of Constantinople, and his mother was the daughter of a king of Rome. It seems they are {confusing} <understanding> the story of the Roman Saint Alexius. A great multitude of people gathers at that time from many places, because the monks there put it into their heads that anyone who goes there once will be saved, and if he goes seven times not only will he be saved, but also his children and grandchildren, and some extend it even further.

There are other churches <that were built> not in rock {that were built} a long time ago, which I shall leave out because their architecture is not such that it merits description.

The churches that they build in these times are all made of stone and mud, for no lime goes into them. Some are longer than broad, but not many, because commonly they are round and small and, although some of them {[f. 223v]} start square at the bottom, as they go up a little they put <wooden> timbers across the corners inside so that they can then raise the wall in the round for four or five cubits. Surrounding it, some six or eight cubits from the church wall, they make a kind of low cloister, with many doors, and so it is shaped like the church. It is roofed with straw laid on the timber, which comes from the very top of the church passing down over the cloister walls, so that all churches, despite having three doors, are so dark that not even at midday can one read inside without a candle, and so there are many bats that roost in them. Although the timber is rough, few churches have an internal ceiling. In some of the long ones, they hang a curtain right across from wall to wall a short distance from the altar, which is always placed in such a manner that one can walk around it. Nobody is allowed inside this curtain while Mass is being said, apart from priests and the deacons assisting at it. Another curtain is hung separate from this one, and the deacons who are not assisting at Mass and those who have <[f. 196/186]> minor orders stay between the two; laymen stay outside this second curtain. In round churches there is ordinarily only a single curtain, because laymen and women stay in the cloister round the outside.

Women do not go to certain monks' churches because they are inside the monastery compound, which they cannot enter, but in those places where the monks' church is like this they have another to which the women go, which they call the women's church, not because men do not enter it, but because women can enter it as well, but only in the part that we have said is theirs. Some say that in the past there were churches that only women could enter, but now there is no such custom, and men can also enter them all.

Churches are commonly looked after by {[f. 224]} monks and canons together. The canons, whom they call *debterôch*, or *debterâ*[1] if there is just one, may or may not be priests, but they are all married and in their dress do not differ from laymen. However, they ordinarily carry a small iron or black wooden cross in their hand, and when they enter into the service of some church, when they are young, they make a letter with a razor on their right shoulder and another on the left by which it can be seen that they are from that church; so if it is the church of Saint Mary, on the right shoulder they put a 'D' and on the left 'M', meaning 'of Mary'.[2] If one of these canons has to move to another church, the superior of the one in which he used to be has to bear witness that he was his, and the superior of the one that he enters puts new letters on him to signify the name of his church. But there are some monasteries where canons do not enter the churches, and only monks look after them. And on the altar stone of each church they write the name of the saint to whom it is dedicated.

Whenever they put a new altar stone in a church, and when they put one in a newly built or rebuilt church, if they want to change its patron saint (which they often do), they take the stone there with great festivity. And if it is in a large monastery where they want to do it with more pomp, they take the stone to where the emperor is (either at court or in his camp) – after the *abuna* has consecrated it, for nobody else in Ethiopia can do that – and they put it in some church or decent place, and from there the emperor commands that it be taken to the monastery <[f. 196v/186v]> with music and festivities and accompanied by all the nobility, provided the monastery is nearby; if it is a long way away, they go some distance from the city or camp and then turn back, and the monks carry on with the people who want to accompany them out of devotion. The emperor always gives at least a valuable piece of fabric to cover the stone, and a priest carries it on his head, and if a deacon helps him, the priest places it on his head and takes it off so that the deacon does not touch it with his hands, even though the stone may be wrapped in silk cloths: he can only hold the parts {[f. 224v]} of the cloth covering it that hang down on either side. A short time ago, when I was with the emperor, a number of monks came in from a large monastery that is on an island that they call Çanâ, in Lake Dambiâ,[3] and said that they had just rebuilt their church, which had fallen down, and that they wanted to change its patron. Previously it had been dedicated to a martyr named Charcôs, and they now wanted to dedicate it to Jesus, and when the first altar stone had been placed in that church, the emperor at the time had commanded that it be taken there from the court with festivities. Now that they were changing the patron, they were asking if he would command that this stone too be taken from the court with festivities, and they had brought it with them for that purpose. Thus he issued the command at once and donated a piece of brocade with which they covered it, and all the cavalry and many footsoldiers with their arms marched out, with the emperor's shawms and drums in front, and accompanied them for a good distance.

Churches in the past used to have many valuable ornaments, as Francisco Álvares states on folio 18,[4] speaking of the monastery church of Bisan, where he says that at one feast he saw the cloisters decorated with brocades and velvets and the monks in procession

---

[1] See Glossary (*debtera*/*debterâ*/*dabtara*).

[2] 'D' for *dabr* (mountain, monastery) and 'M' for *Māryām* (Mary), i.e. Dabra Māryām.

[3] See Glossary (Canâ/Çaanâ/Çana/Ṭānāa Qirqos; and Lake Dambiâ/Lake Ṭānā).

[4] See Álvares, *Prester John of the Indies*, ch. 14, 'How the monastery of Bisam is the head of six monateries, of the number of the monks, and ornaments of the *tascar* which [is a feast] they make for [one Abbot] Felipos, whom they call a saint', p. 89.

wearing many capes of the same material and carrying fifty silver crosses, and they had a large gold chalice; and he also saw much of this in other churches. But almost all of them are now poor, because the Moors were lords of most of Ethiopia for twelve to fifteen years at the time of the Moor Granh, who killed the Portuguese as we described at the end of the first book, and afterwards the Turks and the heathens called Gallas made many incursions and there were also major wars among them. As a result, the churches were robbed, their revenues diminished and the emperors and princes were so impoverished that they could not return them to their former state. <[f. 197/187]> Instead of bells, they have some hanging stones a span or less {[f. 225]} in width, four fingerbreadths thick, and long; when struck with other small stones they can be heard over a very long distance and they ring in such a way that, to someone who did not know that they were stones, they might sound like bells. In some monasteries, instead of these stones, they have three boards tied together, which make a loud noise when struck against one another.

As for the respect and reverence that they have for the temples, it is considerable, and so, when they reach the door, they take off their shoes and enter barefoot, even the emperor himself. While Mass is being said, they keep very quiet: they do not laugh or talk to one another, and they certainly never spit inside; nor do they allow dogs to come inside the fence. If people travelling on horseback have to go past a church, they usually dismount before reaching it and walk for some distance past it. Thus, when Emperor Seltan Sagued with all his court came to our church[1] in October 1618, he dismounted some distance before reaching it and, at the door, he had a page take off his shoes and he kissed the door and, entering barefoot, he stood and prayed, showing great devotion. And he and the noblemen who entered the church heard Mass and the sermon in silence, and they praised it all very much. When he left, the emperor also saw our house and ate in it, and afterwards he gave us a very good plot near the lands that he had given us when he was made emperor, so that we could build another church in our style, for the one that we had was small and in the local style, and he added the lands surrounding the plot. And because here in Dambia there is no timber that is any good except at their churches, he commanded that they should cut down some very fine cedars for us from them, and he gave them good alms in return, and he said that we should not put any other kind of timber in our church. And his brother, *Eras* Cela Christôs offered to cover all the expenses for it, begging us dearly not to put in anything at all from our house, and he said he would also make the brocade, velvet and damask ornaments and would give extensive lands.

When we saw how much the emperor wished to see the style and design of our churches, we tried to make {[f. 225v]} the best one that we possibly could, all built out of cut stone, although it is small, because the body of it is only twenty-eight spans wide by seventy-two long, and the chapel twenty-four wide by thirty-two <[f. 197v/187v]> long. Even so, because it and the sacristy are made of very good red stone, the arch and body of very white, well cut stone, the façade and side doors decorated with eight fluted columns, and the pedestals, capitals and friezes and everything else all polished and very well worked, it pleases everyone who sees it so much that they say it is not a work of the earth but of heaven. It has its choir with railings and woodwork, a font for baptisms and two for holy water all beautifully carved; it is very light, with windows on both sides, well decorated on the outside with roses and mouldings in the same stone. It has a terrace roof

---

[1] The first church at Old Gorgorã (see Beccari, *RÆSOI*, 11, pp. 414–15.

and a number of columns above the parapet to finish it off, some topped with a pyramid above the capital, interspersed with others topped with balls; in the middle of the columns and finishing touches on the façade, it has a very beautiful cross with a pedestal worked in the same stone, with plenty of tracery. It also has its tower on the right-hand side of the façade, with a fair-sized copper bell that came to us from India. It was finished this March, 1620.[1] The emperor came at once to see it with all his court from two days' journey away, where he now resides, and he heard Mass and a sermon on those words of Saint Luke, '*Hodie huic domui salus facta est*',[2] and then he examined it very slowly, twice going up to the terrace and praising it very much and wishing to gather all the Portuguese here so that the church would be fuller. Then he donated the best carpet he had for it and 100 *cruzados* for an ornament. And he has decided to build a large church in the same style as this one on another, better site. Doing us a favour and honour, he placed his tent within our compound and stayed to sleep here that night.[3]

On many of their church altars they do not usually put images, because they always build them almost in the middle {[f. 226]} of the chapel, but they paint many images on the walls in various colours, particularly red, white, green and yellow, for they do not use black much as they do not like this colour, and so they never paint a black face, except for the Devil and some heathens that they call Gallas. They paint their saints' faces on a red ground. This shows just how ridiculous a fiction Friar Luis de Urreta paints on page 557, when talking about the images in Ethiopia in these words:

*All the images are brush painted and all of them are black, so that they paint God and Christ and the Virgin, the angels and all the saints black. They paint the <[f. 198/188]> Passion of Christ and the Supper, and in it Christ and the apostles are black and the Jews, executioners and Judas are white. They paint Saint Michael black and the demon under his feet white. What is amusing is to see a painting of the Last Judgment in which God and the angels and all the blessed are black and the demons and the damned in hell are very white, because since they are black, they want the saints to look like them, because they hold it to be the best colour.*[4]

This is what the author says, but it seems that the one who informed him was inclined to tell lies, like this one, which is so enormous. The people of this land, particularly the nobles, are not so black, with squashed noses and thick lips, as he makes them out to be there, but they are generally very well presented, brown in colour, with thin lips, proportionate noses and large, beautiful eyes, as we said in chapter 1 of the first book, although in some lands that the emperor rules there are ugly kafirs that the *Abexins* have as slaves.

---

[1] This is the Church of Old Gorgorã (Beccari, *RÆSOI*, 11, p. 406; Pereira, *Chronica de Susenyos*, I, p. 259 (Ge'ez text); II, p. 199 (Portuguese translation). See Pennec, *Des jésuites au royaume du prêtre Jean*, pp. 171–5.

[2] Luke 19:9, 'This day is salvation come to this house.'

[3] See the letters by L. Azevedo (3 July 1619) and D. Mattos (2 June 1621) in Beccari, *RÆSOI*, 11, pp. 413, 416 and 485.

[4] Urreta, *Historia de la Etiopia*, excerpt from bk II, ch. 14, entitled 'Of the greatness and majesty of the temples of Ethiopia and of the great reverence in which they hold them and of the adoration of holy images', pp. 546–58. Páez quotes this passage in Spanish.

## On the style and ceremonies that the Ethiopians keep at burials and on the error that they have regarding purgatory

Now that we have seen the respect and reverence in which the Ethiopians hold their temples, it will be appropriate briefly to describe the manner and the ceremonies with which they bury their dead. Leaving aside their extremes of behaviour at deaths, the men throwing themselves on the ground and the women tearing out their hair and scratching their faces – because we spoke about this and the way in which they weep in chapter 21 of the first book, when dealing with some customs that they have – leaving that aside, then, when somebody dies, if it is an ordinary man, they take two long poles and put shorter ones across between them, like a ladder, and they lay him on top wrapped in a shroud and cover him with any cotton cloth that they find. With four men carrying him on their shoulders, his kinsfolk and friends, men and women, accompany him, weeping aloud and saying, 'Woe is us that he has fled, woe is us that he has fled', and other things of that kind. Thus, when I was once with Emperor Seltan Çegued in the highest part of his palaces, the steward said to me, 'Does Your Reverence not hear what those people are saying? They are carrying the deceased bound up and they say he has fled.' When they reach the church or monastery where he is to be buried, the clergy or monks come out to the door (for they never go to his house) and bring a cross and thurible, but not <[f. 198v/188v]> holy water, which they do not use at burials, and one comes robed as when he is going to say Mass, and they say many prayers for him and then bury him in the cloister or veranda of the church.

If the deceased was a nobleman or lord, {[f. 227]} they take him on his own bed or another narrow one, tying two long poles underneath it and, on top, {some} <two> slender arches which, when covered with a cloth, resemble our kind of tomb. These men are ordinarily buried in monasteries and they sometimes carry the body for one or two days' journey. The monks come some way outside the monastery to receive him, one of them in front, robed and carrying cross and thurible, and they say some prayers for him and in that way take him to the church, where they sing more prayers and bury him inside, as I have seen, and some are buried near the altar, as the monks have told me.

For monks they have a much longer office than for laymen, and they bury them in their own habits, covering their faces with the cowl and then wrapping them in a thin leather shroud that they make from goatskins, once sewn together and stained red. Some whom they hold to be more saintly, whom they call *bataois*,[1] ask before they die to be buried with a knife in their girdle, and the monks put one there because they have great respect for

---

[1] Latinized form of Ge'ez (singular *bāḥtāwi*, plural *bāḥtāwiyān* ), hermit monks.

415

them and they ask for it very insistently. The reason is that they have always mixed closely with Jews until the time of this emperor, and one of the many fables that the rabbis have put into their heads is the one that they have concocted around those words from Psalm 103, '*Draco iste, quem formasti ad illudendum ei*'.[1] They say that at the beginning of the world Our Lord God created two fishes of immense size, male and female, but He saw that, if by generation they multiplied, they would hinder navigation, so he killed the female and stored it so that with it he could invite the just to a splendid feast after the resurrection; meanwhile he plays with the male {[f. 227v]} for three hours every day. And they say that this is what those words from the Psalm mean, and some of these ignorant monks believe it so firmly that they plead to be buried with a knife, so that they will have one to cut that fish with when God invites them after the resurrection.

When the emperor dies, they carry him as well on his bed arranged like a tomb, accompanied by a large retinue, because not only do the princes and great men do, but also all the noble lords that are nearby, <[f. 199/189]> all covered with mourning and with their heads shaven, as is their custom at the death of their parents, to show their great sadness. I saw the burial procession for the son of this Emperor Seltan Çagued, a prince called *Abeitahun* Canafra Christós, who was just twenty years old. From where he died they went a day's journey to put him on an island that they call Çanâ in Lake Dambia, where there is a large monastery. He was accompanied by all the court cavalry and many ladies, all covered with mourning, with the emperor's banners and drums in front playing mournful music.

On the day of burial, not only of the emperor but of any great man, many alms are given and, at least in the church where he is buried, they recite the Psalms of David in their entirety every day for thirty days, as well as other prayers (for they do not say Masses for the dead, as several monks have told me), and they are given alms for that. On the last of the thirty days, they slaughter cattle and feed the monks and many poor people who always gather there. On the fortieth day they take a large quantity of candles and incense to the church and slaughter many more cattle and give substantial alms. They also give more on the eightieth day and when a year has passed, but not so many, and they call this *tascâr*,[2] which means 'remembrance', and *fetât*, which means 'release'. Emperor Atanaf {[f. 228]} Çagued, who was first called Glaudios, *scilicet* Claudeo, made a very solemn remembrance for Dom Christovão da Gama on the first anniversary of his death, which was on 28th August 1542. To make it more splendid, as required by the gratitude that he wished to show and owed to Dom Christovão {for all} he had done for him, he had it proclaimed throughout the lands a few days in advance that all the poor people should gather there on that day, and more than 6,000 came (according to a Portuguese who was present), and they put up many tents for them in the field where, at the emperor's command, they regaled them very splendidly with food and clothing. He also had 600 or more monks come, and they very solemnly sang the Psalms and prayers that they have for this office, and he commanded that they be given abundant alms.

In the past, the emperors were buried in the kingdom of Amharâ, not on the mountain where they kept their sons, which is called {Guigên} <Guigêm> Ambâ, but in a church

---

[1] Psalm 103 [104]:26, 'This sea dragon which thou hast formed to play therein.'
[2] See Glossary (*tascâr/tazkâr*).

that they call Mecâna Celace or in Atronê Ça Mariâm,[1] <[f. 199v/189v]> which were both burial places of the emperors, as it says in the history of Emperor Onâg Çagued;[2] but after the Moor Granh burnt these two churches, which would have been in the 1530s, more or less, they were never again buried there, but in others: Emperor Onâg Çagued on a mountain in the kingdom of Tigre, which they call Ambâ Damô,[3] which is so secure that one cannot climb up except by means of ropes, where there is a very large monastery of monks. His son, Emperor Atanaf Çagued, was buried in a church called Tedebâba Mariam[4] that he had had built in the kingdom of Amharâ; his brother, Emperor Adamâs Çagued, in the same church; the latter's son, Emperor Malac Çagued, in a monastery on the island that they call Çanâ, in Lake Dambiâ; his nephew, Emperor Zadenguil, was buried in a little church in Dambia, and ten or twelve years later Emperor Seltan Çagued, his cousin, transferred his body, which was found to be entire, to {[f. 228v]} the monastery on that island of Çanâ.[5] Emperor Iacob was buried in the kingdom of Gojam in a church that they call Nazareth. For the emperor, they not only recite the Psalms and everything else that is customary in the church where he is buried, but they also perform this office in all the churches in the empire, with as much solemnity as they can.

Although the Ethiopians give so many alms and have so many prayers said for their dead – and they call this office *fetât*, *scilicet* release, by which they mean that after this life they may be released from their sins by means of alms and prayers – even so there are many who deny purgatory, so much so that in some disputations that I had with the principal scholars in the presence of Emperor Zadenguil in June 1604, when I said for some reason that there was a purgatory, one of them, who was called *Azax* Zadenguil, burst out laughing in such a way as if I had said an unheard-of absurdity. I asked him why he was so surprised at what they themselves affirmed through their deeds and admitted in their words, since they gave so many alms and said so many prayers for their dead and called it *fetât*, release, for if they could not be released and their alms and prayers were to no avail, why did they do it and why did they call it 'release'? He replied that they did that so that the dead person's property <[f. 200/190]> might be well used. I said that it would be well used on his wife and children, who were often poor, and since it did not benefit the dead, it would be better to offer it for the living so that while they were here they might obtain some mercies from the Lord. He replied that as long as the property was well spent in death and in life it could be done, but that I should explain to him what purgatory was. When I saw that he did not want to respond to the point, I told him that purgatory is a certain place where {[f. 229]} souls remain after this life, as if in prison, purging what they have left behind here, so that pure and clean they may enter the bliss of heaven, where nobody may enter with stains. 'Show me', he said, 'the passage in Scripture from which you take this.' I asked him whether they considered the books of Machabees to be holy like the other books of the Holy Scripture. He answered that they did. 'Well, in the second book of Machabees, chapter 12', I said, 'it tells that Judas Machabeus sent 12,000 drachms

---

[1] See Glossary (Mecâna Celace/Makānā Śellāsē; and Atronê Ça Mariâm/Atronsa Māryām).

[2] The Chronicle of Lebna Dengel.

[3] The monastery of Dabra Dāmo (founded in the 6th century), east of Aksum.

[4] See Glossary (Tedebâba Mariam/Tadbāba Māryām).

[5] Monastery of Ṭānā Qirqos, on Lake Ṭānā. Páez's statement that Za Dengel's body was moved to Ṭānā Qirqos contradicts his claim in bk IV, ch. 9, vol. II below that it was taken to Dāgā Esṭifānos monastery, also on Lake Ṭānā. See Glossary (Çanâ/Çaanâ/Saná/Ṭānā Qirqos).

of silver to Jerusalem for sacrifices to be offered for those who had died in a war, and Scripture says then, "*Sancta est salubris {ergo} <est> cogitatio pro defunctis exorare, ut a peccatis solvantur.*"[1] Therefore, after this life there is a place where the souls that were not fully purged and satisfied for their sins here are in a kind of prison, until either through the punishments that they suffer there or through the sacrifices and prayers that the living offer for them they can be fully satisfied; for otherwise sacrifices {and prayers} will have been offered in vain and Scripture must have been wrong in praising such prayers. And we call this place purgatory.'

When he saw that this passage was convincing, he said, 'Give me this word "purgatory" in the Gospel or in Saint Paul; as for this, I will not listen to it.' I answered that, since he had admitted that these books were holy, why would he not listen to them and believe what they taught? When he insisted that I should give him this word in the Gospel or in Saint Paul, I told him that he knew very well that not everything that Christ Our Lord taught and not all the marvels that he did are written in the Gospel, for Saint John says at the end of his Gospel that, if everything were to be written, the world would not be able to contain all the books. 'Therefore, perhaps Christ Our Lord said the name <[f. 200v/190v]> of this place that we call purgatory and it was not written down but, however it may be, it is enough to take it from the Holy Scripture {[f. 229v]} that there is such a place. And to satisfy you with the Gospel and Saint Paul, Christ Our Lord says through Saint Matthew, chapter 12, that there is sin that shall not be forgiven, neither in this world, nor in the world to come. Therefore it follows (speaking with good prudence, as the Lord spoke on all things) that there are sins that are forgiven in the world to come by means of the prayers and suffrages of the Church and, consequently, some place where souls remain where they can be helped by these suffrages. This is taught by many doctors and saints in this passage and they also deduce it from what the Lord said in Matthew 5 and Luke 12: "*Amen dico tibi: non exies inde donec reddas novissimum quadrantem.*"[2] Saint Paul, too, in I Corinthians 3, says that the fire shall try the work of each one, whatever it may be: "*Uniuscuiusque opus quale sit ignis probabit: si cuiusque opus manserit, quod superaedificavit mercedem accipiet; si cuius opus arserit, detrimentum patietur ipse autem salvus erit, sic tamen quasi per ignem.*"[3] And in chapter 15, he says, "*Quid facient qui baptizantur pio mortuis si mortui nom resurgunt? Ut quid baptizantur pro illis?*"[4] Here the apostle is speaking of the baptism of tears and penance, and he means "What will they do, those who pray, fast, give alms and afflict themselves for the dead, if they do not rise again?" In this, Saint Paul clearly shows that, after this life, there is a place where these things avail souls.'

To all this he replied, laughing, that it did not satisfy him. 'Then if Scripture, which is so clear', I said, 'does not satisfy you, what will satisfy you? Tell me why it does not satisfy

---

[1] 2 Machabees [Apocrypha, Maccabees].2:46, 'It is therefore a holy and wholesome thought to pray for the dead, that they may be loosed from sins.'

[2] Matthew 5:26, 'Amen I say to thee, thou shalt not go out from thence till thou repay the last farthing...'. Also Luke 12:59.

[3] 1 Corinthians 3:13–15, 'The fire shall try every man's work, of what sort it is. If any man's work abide, which he hath built thereupon, he shall receive a reward. If any man's work burn, he shall suffer loss; but he himself shall be saved, yet so as by fire.'

[4] 1 Corinthians 15:29, '[Otherwise] what shall they do that are baptized for the dead, if the dead rise not again at all? Why are they then baptized for them?'

you, or answer me this: can a man die with venial sins or without giving full satisfaction for the mortal sins that he has confessed?' He would not reply to this until the emperor said to him, 'Why do you not reply? Is it not true that a man can die when he has just confessed many mortal sins?' He then replied that it was true. Then I said, 'So this man does not go to hell for the venial sins, <[f. 201/191]> for God does not condemn a man to eternal punishment for such little cause, nor {[f. 230]} for the penance that he should have done to give satisfaction for the mortal sins that he has confessed, because they do not deserve hell since the confessor has absolved him of them, and Christ Our Lord says, "Whatsoever you shall loose upon earth, shall be loosed also in heaven",[1] etc. And this man cannot enter heaven either, whether he died just with venial sins or just without having given satisfaction for the mortal ones that he confessed, because with these debts and stains, even though they may be from very minor sins, one cannot enter heaven, as Saint John says in the Apocalypse, chapter 21: "*Non intrabit in eam aliquid coinquinatum, aut abominationem faciens, et mendacium*",[2] just as nobody with dirty feet, even if it is just with the dust of venial sins, may enter that celestial holy city of Jerusalem, where the squares are made of very fine, pure gold and the rest of precious stones. Therefore it is certain that there is some place where, after this life, souls may be purged and cleansed in order to enter heaven, and we call this place purgatory.' Since the emperor understood the truth very well, he said before the other could reply, 'Why should we waste any more time on this, etc. What I wish to know is whether the souls of the saints are already in heaven enjoying glory, or are they waiting in the earthly paradise or somewhere else until Judgment Day, so that together with their bodies they may go and enjoy it?' And so we left the matter of purgatory and went on to this other subject, which we debated for a long time, and I showed them, through passages from Scripture and reasoning, that the souls of the saints are in heaven enjoying glory, and the souls of the wicked are in hell. And the chance arose to speak on this matter on several other occasions in the presence of Emperor Seltan Çagued, as we said in chapter 6.

I am well aware that Friar Luis de Urreta, in his second book, chapter 15,[3] affirms many things contrary to those that we have said here. For example, when someone dies, four married priests that serve in the parish go to fetch him with cross, holy water and thurible and after saying some prayers for him {[f. 230v]} <[f. 201v/191v]> they take him to be buried. When they arrive at the church, they place him by the door and all the virgin priests come out and sing for him and throw holy water and cense him, and then they take him to the cemetery where they bury him (because they have never buried the dead inside their churches, except those who died with the reputation of being saints and martyrs). The next day they say Mass for him in the cemetery itself, in the chapel that is always there, because they never say Mass for the dead in the churches, but every Monday in the year (if it is not occupied by one of the saints that they celebrate) the whole divine office is for the dead in the cemetery, because of all nations in Christendom the Ethiopians are the most devoted to the souls in purgatory. Lay people do not give alms for the Masses or pay for burials, and there is no obligation to give anything for any ministry. The clergy

[1] Matthew 18:18.

[2] Apocalypse 21:27, 'There shall not enter into it any thing defiled, or that worketh abomination or maketh a lie.'

[3] Urreta, *Historia de la Etiopia*, bk II, ch. 15, entitled, 'Of the style and ceremonies that they keep at burials. On holy water, instituted by Saint Matthew the Apostle and Evangelist in Ethiopia', pp. 558–70.

support themselves from the lands that the Prester John gives to them, which are many and very large; they just have some collecting boxes and alms chests at the church door, into which people can put alms if they wish, and these are shared among the priests. The emperors too are buried in a cemetery on Mount Amharâ, where the emperors' sons are, and there they say Masses and perform their offices for them; and when they are taken to be buried they go in a litter carried by an elephant covered with mourning and accompanied by all the priests of the city of Sabbá, with 1,000 guardsmen, until they reach the mountain.

Up to here are words by the author,[1] in which he clearly shows how little information he had about things here, because neither do the priests go to the house of the deceased to fetch his body, nor is there such a distinction between married and virgin priests, as they are all married. They do not use holy water at burials, as they themselves have told me, and they only bury a few poor people in the cemetery, but everyone else inside the church. For every one that they bury, they are given two cloths made locally, which are sometimes worth two *cruzados*, sometimes a little less, and if they are not given them they will not bury the person; and they will not recite psalms or do the other things that they customarily do unless they are paid very well. And they do not have the alms chests at the church doors that he mentions at the end of the chapter. The emperors are never buried {[f. 231]} on the mountain he refers to, <[f. 202/192]> but in the churches that we named above, and they are not taken to be buried in a litter on an elephant, as they have never seen a tame one, as we have said, nor do they know what a litter is. The things with which he ends that chapter are similar: he says that in each bishopric the bishop and the chapter appoint four of the canons to meet three times a week with four vicars from the parishes of the city where the bishop resides, in order to deal with whatever arises and seems necessary for the spiritual governance of the bishopric, and they hold the office of provisors and judge all complaints. The same happens in the archbishops' metropolis. And every six years the archbishop meets with his suffragan bishops and they hold provincial synods, and sometimes all twelve archbishops and seventy-two bishops of Ethiopia meet with many spiritual abbots of Saint Anthony in the city of Sabbá for the universal reformation of the churches of Ethiopia, over which the most senior archbishop presides as legate. This is what Friar Luis says. But we have already shown several times that it is all mere fiction, for there is no such form of governance, nor are there archbishops or bishops other than the one who comes to them from Cairo, whom they call *abuna*, and this one is sent by the patriarch of Alexandria.

---

[1] Translated into Portuguese and summarized by Páez.

# CHAPTER XVII

## Which deals with the religions[1] that some authors place in the part of Ethiopia over which the Prester John rules

We have often made passing mention of the monks of Ethiopia in this *History* without describing what their religions are, so as not to interrupt the thread of what we have been saying. Now that we have dealt {[f. 231v]} with ecclesiastical matters, it will be good to see which religions are claimed by some authors to exist in Ethiopia, although no trace or memory can be found of them (and afterwards we shall say how many there really are, and which ones). The first one that occurs to me is that of the glorious patriarch Saint Augustine. Friar Luis de Urreta, in the first book of his *Historia* on page 213, and in book 3 on page 708,[2] says that its friars are in Ethiopia today, but that when they arrived they were not of this sacred religion, but some hermits and anchorites <[f. 202v/192v]> from the Thebaid, who came with the name of Saint Augustine but were in fact heretics. And so they began at once to teach that the Holy Spirit does not proceed from the Son, that there is no purgatory and that the saints do not see God until the Day of Judgment. When Emperor Claudio learnt that, he delivered them to the priors of Alleluia and Plurimanos monasteries, who convinced them of their heresies and worked hard to reduce them, but some remained obstinate and the emperor had some of these thrown to the lions and others buried alive, while the ones who had been reduced were to be kept in those monasteries to be indoctrinated. Meanwhile, the emperor wrote to the most reverend general of the religion of Augustinian friars, who was Father Master Friar Thadeo Perugino, asking him to send him the constitutions of his sacred religion so that those anchorites might profess it, and he would cast those who refused out of his lands. The most reverend general replied, sending him the constitutions, which were translated into the Ethiopic language. The hermits professed in the hands of the priors of those monasteries according to the style of the Augustinian fathers' constitutions. Some monasteries of them exist, although they are few and poor, and they live in the deserts and lead a hermit life. Friar Luis confirms this in another tome, which he published in 1611: on page 5[3] he says that the chronicles of this sacred religion mention that {[f. 232]} there are many monasteries of their Order in Ethiopia.

[1] I.e. religious orders.

[2] Urreta, *Historia de la Etiopia*, bk I, ch. 21, entitled, 'On the Latin Council which deals with matters relating to Europe. It includes a mission made by thirteen Fathers of the Society of Jesus, with a letter written by the Holy Father Ignacio to the Prester John, emperor of Ethiopia', pp. 192–219; ibid., bk III, ch. 6.

[3] Urreta, *Historia de la sagrada orden*, 1611, ch. 1, 'How the religious of the sacred Order of Preachers went to preach in the kingdoms of Ethiopia, monarchy of the emperor called Prester John of the Indies', pp. 1–21. The text has been summarized by Páez.

This is what Friar Luis de Urreta says, but in Ethiopia there are no such friars or any recollection that there ever have been, as I was told by a number of old men whom I questioned thoroughly when the most reverend Father Friar Aleixo de Meneses,[1] who was archbishop of Goa in 1605, wrote to me to find out whether Alleluia monastery belonged to Friars of Saint Augustine. To satisfy myself further, I also asked a very old monk who was like the general of the monks that here they call the monks of Taquelâ Haimanôt, and he answered, in the presence of many monks, that he had been the superior of that religion for many years (for that post is for life, and the one who holds it is called *icheguê*), and he had never seen such friars, nor had he heard that they were in Ethiopia. I was told the same thing by another monk <[f. 203/193]> who for a long time had been the prior of the monastery that Friar Luis calls Plurimanôs, which is in fact called Debra Libanôs, which means Monastery of Lebanon. Hence there is no doubt that there are no friars of Saint Augustine in the Prester John's lands today and there never have been, because it would not be possible for these very old monks never to have heard of them at all, especially if, as Friar Luis says, they arrived at the time of Emperor Claudio, who died sixty-one years ago, as of this year 1620, and he had reigned for eighteen years, and the very same priors in whose hands the author says those friars professed affirm that they have never heard of them. As for when he says that the chronicles of this sacred religion mention that there are many monasteries of their order in Ethiopia, they must be in other lands of Ethiopia, for they are very broad, but not in those over which the Prester John rules, because the people of this country would necessarily have heard of them if there were any.

In the same chapter in which he speaks of this religion, which is the last one in his third book, he deals at length with a {[f. 232v]} military and monastic order of knights and monks of the glorious Father Saint Anthony, which, he says, was founded in Ethiopia by the Prester John called João the Holy in about 370, so that they could fight the Arians in honour of the holy Trinity, and he gave them as a device the figure of the cross that the glorious Saint Anthony gave to his disciples, in the form of a tau 'T'.[2] He says that Emperor Phelipe VII, who succeeded João the Holy, gave this order many privileges and revenues and added to the knights' insignia some little flowers trimmed all round with gold thread like a galloon, to differentiate them from the monks. He also imposed a law that all his vassals of any rank and position, except doctors, were from that time onwards obliged to give one out of every three sons to serve the religion of Saint Anthony; this was and still is kept so strictly that not even the kings are exempt from this law, but when their sons receive the habit, they go to serve the imperial princes who live on Mount Amharâ, while other men's sons serve in the war. The order has a monastery in every city, such that in all the monasteries there are 2,500 of them; in each abbey there are no more than twenty-five. However, there is no fixed number of military knights, and so there are <[f. 203v/193v]> abbeys with 500, 1,000 and 2,000 or more knights commander, who will necessarily be of lordly and noble rank. These knights join the abbeys at the age of sixteen to eighteen, and the abbeys have to take them, since everyone is obliged to give one out of every three sons to the Order. As soon as they take them in they send them to war, where they spend nine years' novitiate: three in the Red Sea garrisons, guarding the

---

[1] See Glossary (Aleixo de Meneses, Friar).

[2] From the Greek *tau*, the letter *T*; the canons of Saint Anthony wore a white, T-shaped cross on their habits.

coasts of Ethiopia from the corsairs that come from Arabia; three on the island of Meroe, which looks towards Egypt, where they maintain a garrison so that if the Turk tries something he will not find them unprepared; and the other three on the frontier with the kingdom of Bornó, which is a very powerful enemy of the Prester John and borders his lands. At the end of the {[f. 233]} nine-month[1] novitiate, the captain gives him a letter for the procurator of the abbey where he was given his habit, who attends the court of the grand abbot or master of the Order of Meroe Island, in which he tells him that that novice has nobly completed his probation and attendance at war. And the procurator then extracts enough information about his life, habits and service and reports on everything to the grand master, who, on his advice, approves the novitiate and writes to the *abba* of the abbey where they gave him his habit to give him his profession. And he, obeying this mandate, robes himself in his pontificals and comes to the church door, where the knight arrives with a large retinue. After many ceremonies the military abbot rises and, with four of the most senior knights commander, he strips him of the arms he is wearing and they dress him in a black robe down to his feet, with a cross, and over it they put on him a black cowl, which is a habit with many folds at the neck and long sleeves, like that of the monks of Saint Benedict, and on it there is also another blue cross.

After this, the spiritual abbot takes him by the hand and all the knights in procession enter the church with him and, kneeling before the holy sacrament in the presence of everyone, he makes a solemn vow of eternal obedience and fidelity to the Roman apostolic see and, at the same time, to the Prester John and the abbots of his Order to go to war whenever he is commanded to do so and to keep the constitutions of his religion and the canons and decrees of the Florentine Council of Eugene IV. <[f. 204/194]> Having finished this vow, he then makes an oath on the hands of the spiritual abbot not to go to or fight in wars between Christians, not to take holy orders and not to marry without express permission from the Roman pontiff, although the Prester John and the apostolic nuncio may, under briefs they have from the Roman See, relax this oath on good grounds. Thenceforth, he does not leave the monastery for the city without permission from the military abbot, and he must go in his habit, accompanied by four servants. And the spiritual abbot is responsible for giving all the knights the {[f. 233v]} necessaries for their support, but as there are many of them they do not eat all together like the monks, but divided into squadrons.

The grand abbot holds the office until he dies and always resides on the beautiful island of Meroe, which Prester John Claudio and afterwards Alexandre III, in our days, gave in fee simple to the Order of Saint Anthony. He wears a large blue cross right across his chest, which nobody else can wear; he is served with great majesty, because just for his own personal service he has 100 knights commander and 200 others who serve him. He is the absolute lord of this large island that the River Nile forms and thus he owns all its revenues and the mines there, of which there are many, and so every year he receives nearly two million from the minerals and tributes from the peoples, because on this island there are three kingdoms, also counting the duties paid by the Moors and Jews from all over Africa who pass through on their way to Mecca and by those who want to go from Arabia to other kingdoms in Africa, because they necessarily have to go via this island. The grand master lives on this revenue and the rest is kept in the Order's treasury for war expenses,

---

[1] *Sic*, for 'nine-year' (Urreta, *Historia de la Etiopia*, bk III, ch. 6, p. 716).

because the Prester John spends nothing on them in the wars that come about. The other abbeys have their own separate revenues.

This is, in brief, what Friar Luis de Urreta says in that long chapter, and with it he ends his *Historia Ethiopica*. That is very apposite, because a History of so many and such enormous lies as we have seen up to here and will see later could not be closed more appropriately or sealed with any other seal than such a fabulous fable as to say that there is such a military order in Ethiopia, for there is not and never has been, and so everything he says about it is mere fiction. I have only mentioned this so that the reader may see how little credence should be <[f. 204v/194v]> given to information from Joam Balthesar, whom Friar Luis says he follows. I can testify that there is no such military order in Ethiopia now {[f. 234]} because in the nineteen years that I have been here – and I have always been in the palace of the emperors that there have been during this time – I have never seen a monk or knight of this order, which would not have been possible if they existed, because they would necessarily have had to come to the emperor often, especially if they had a monastery in the imperial city, as he says. I also asked many old men and they said that they had never seen such knights or heard that said order ever existed in Ethiopia, or that the emperor had any garrisons at all on the Red Sea coast; nor did they know of that island of Meroe, or that the River Nile had an inhabited island. Even so, for even stronger proof, one day when I was with Emperor Seltân Çaguêd, {who is alive today,}[1] I mentioned some of these things, which he applauded and said, 'It seems that that João Balthesar saw some military order like that in Spain and, to give greater authority to our land, he said that it existed here too, but the truth is that there has never been such a thing, nor in all the River Nile that we govern is there such an island of Meroe or any other inhabited island, because the ones it forms are so small and unhealthy that nobody can live on them.'

In addition to these two religions that Friar Luis places in Ethiopia, he says in many parts of his *Historia* that his own order, that of the glorious Father Saint Dominic, is here as well, and that is what he especially tries to prove in another history, which he published in 1611 and titled *History of the Sacred Order of Preachers in the Remote Kingdoms of Ethiopia*.[2] The first argument is, as he states on page 3, that the bulls that certain supreme pontiffs issued to his sacred religion mentioned Ethiopia among the kingdoms in which Dominican friars were preaching; and so he says that in this there can be no doubt at all, and that the only difficulty is whether the friars of Saint Dominic who entered Ethiopia founded monasteries and whether they persist today, because he found some people who cast doubt on it, to whom he replies {[f. 234v]} with these words, on page 5: 'I shall prove by means of many doctors and experience and eye-witnesses that those holy friars who entered Ethiopia founded monasteries, which persist today with much religion and greatness, and to deny that is to deny the midday sun and to belong to the sect of those academic philosophers who cast doubt on everything.'[3] He then refutes Francisco Álvares, who spent six years in Ethiopia, for saying in his *Historia* that in the lands of the Prester John there were no friars other than those of Saint Anthony, <[f. 205/195]> and he cites some historians who (he claims) say that the Orders of Saint Anthony and Saint Dominic are found in the lands of the Prester John, and others who say that they that they have seen in Rome friars of the Order of Preachers who had come

---

[1] The fact that this phrase was omitted from the BPB, MS 778 copy of the text may indicate that it was produced after the death of Susneyos, i.e. after 1632.

[2] *Historia de la Sagrada Orden*. The 'Order of Preachers' is the First Order of Dominicans.

[3] Páez quotes this passage in Spanish.

from the lands of the Prester John. He also says that in the Royal Archive in the city of Valencia there is a manuscript book that says that on 10th April 1515 there arrived in the monastery of Preachers of that city eight Dominican friars who were all black and said that they were from Ethiopia and were vassals of the emperor called Prester John.

He confirms this on page 7, saying that 'Dominicans from the monasteries of Ethiopia'[1] arrived in the Monastery of Preachers in Valencia on many other occasions and said they were from the Alleluia and Plurimanos monasteries. And there were friars from Ethiopia in the General Chapter held in Barcelona in the Monastery of Saint Catherine, a martyr of the Order of Saint Dominic, in 1574; and Dominican friars from Florence and Venice go on missions to Ethiopia, just as in Spain they have the custom of sending friars to the Indies; and, when he was writing the book that he published in 1611, {[f. 235]} the master of novices in Alleluia Monastery was Friar Marcos de Florença, who was from Florence and a 'son of the habit' of Saint Mark's Monastery, and he had signed the originals that the author was translating, together with Friar Miguel de Monrojo and Friar Matheus Caravajal, who were born in Ethiopia, the sons of certain Spaniards who {lived in} <had come to> the country. Further on, on page 11, he says that there were Dominican friars from Ethiopia at the Chapter that the general, Friar Pablo Constable, held in Rome in 1580.

The first religious of Saint Dominic who came to Ethiopia, he says on page 13, were eight in number and left Rome on 1st May 1316, with powers to be inquisitors of the faith <[*Idem dicit Ludou a Paramo De Orig. Off. Ste Inquis. Lib. 2. Cap. 19. Sed non de femina*]>,[2] taking in their company an elderly woman who wished to suffer martyrdom by preaching the Gospel. Her virtue and the opinion that people had of her saintliness and {life} <virtue> were so great that the prelates of the Order of Saint Dominic gave her permission to do so, as she was a religious of the Third Order of Penance, who are commonly called *beatas*. Thus they went together to Jerusalem and, after visiting the holy sites, turned their course towards Ethiopia, travelling on foot, eating what they were given as alms, and walking among infidels <[f. 205v/195v]> with such discomfort, hunger and poverty and being treated so badly as anyone might imagine. But the Lord, who would guide them for the great good of the souls of Ethiopia, brought them there safe and happy, and they soon learnt the language of the land and began to preach, confirming their doctrine with many miracles. And, {[f. 235v]} when news of them reached the Prester John, as a good Christian he gave many thanks to God for having brought those holy men to them for the good of his vassals, and he sent his welcome to them and at the same time gave them permission to build monasteries throughout his land, promising to grant them all the privileges that they enjoyed in the Latin Church and accepting the powers that they brought as inquisitors. When they heard this excellent message, they returned their thanks to the emperor, and with his good grace and applause came more than 600 leagues into Ethiopia, as far as Lake Cafates, which is where the River Nile rises, and they built many monasteries in the kingdoms of Gojam, Cafates and Saba. And they gave the habit of the sacred religion to many men, who became such good disciples that they were able to be masters of virtue and saintliness to the rest, of whom many were enlightened in miracles, in particular the glorious saint Taquelá Haimanót, to whom they gave the habit in

---

[1] Phrase quoted in Spanish.

[2] 'Ludovico a Paramo says the same in *De Origine et Progressu Officii Sanctae Inquisitionis* [Madrid, 1598]. Bk 2, Ch. 19. But not about the woman.'

the monastery dedicated to Saint Stephen, which these holy religious men had built on an island in Lake Cafates called Haic, which means fresh water.

The holy *beata* was not idle either, for she built a convent of nuns of the Order of Saint Dominic that they called Bedenagli, in which more than 5,000 nuns live today, and it is now called Saint Clare's Convent. At the same time she gave the habit of the Third Order of Penance to many virtuous and exemplary women desirous of journeying to perfection, and today there are many of them throughout Ethiopia.

The author says on page 29[1] that no mention is made of these holy friars' names in the chronicles of the Order of Saint Dominic, because it was impossible {[f. 236]} to record such a large number of preachers as left every day for unknown lands with the blessing of their prelates, and in Ethiopia they only know the name of one of them, who was called Friar Pantaleão. They gave the other seven names in their language, which <[f. 206/196]> are: Arghai, Grima, Licanos, Sama, Aleph, Assen and Aguloa, and they called the *beata* Imata. One can easily see that these names are not of the Latin Church, nor are they proper names in Ethiopia, but the names of offices and dignities, because they gave each one the name of the office that they saw he had in the monastery that they built, and it stuck, and they are invoked by these names as glorious saints.

Friar Luis de Urreta says all this in the places mentioned in order to prove his intention that the friars of Saint Dominic arrived in the Prester John's lands in the past and that they are here now and have many monasteries here. But, despite all his evidence, the truth is that in all the lands of Ethiopia ruled over by the emperor that they commonly call the Prester John there are today no monasteries or friars of Saint Dominic, or even a recollection that they ever entered these lands. I have made extraordinary enquiries about this, but have been unable to find anyone who knew of them or had heard that they had ever come to these lands. Leaving aside many others from whom I sought information, one old monk who for many years was the prior of Dêbra Libanôs, which the author calls Plurimanos, and a short time ago succeeded to the position of *icheguê* on the death of the one we mentioned above, and he is the general of the monks of Taquela Haimanôt, assured me that he had neither found in his Histories {[f. 236v]} nor had he heard tell that friars of Saint Dominic had ever come here, and many of his old monks who were present said the same. Afterwards I went on purpose to Alleluia Monastery, which is in the kingdom of Tigrê, and talked to the prior. He told me that he was called Taoâld Madehên (which means 'The Saviour is born') and that he was 131 years old and had been the prior of that monastery for forty years, and that he did not know that friars of Saint Dominic or of Saint Augustine had ever entered these lands; he said that his predecessor had been called Gâbra Maraoî (which means 'Servant of the Bridegroom') and had been the prior there for fifty-eight years, and he had never heard him talk of such friars. Hence it shows very clearly that these monasteries of Dêbra Libanôs and Alleluia are not of Saint Dominic or Saint Augustine, and there is no other place that is theirs, for if there were, someone would certainly know of it, because the land is not so vast that they do not know one another very well. Where the author says that those friars came more than 600 leagues into Ethiopia after receiving the message from the Prester John, even <[f. 206v/196v]> if it were true that they did come, he was greatly mistaken about the

---

[1] Urreta, *Historia de la sagrada orden*, ch. 2, 'How the religious left for the holy city of Jerusalem and visited the sacred sites and with revelation from God went to preach in Ethiopia', pp. 21–30.

distance, because from whichever side they may have come it is not even 200 leagues to where the Nile rises.

As for his argument that the bulls that certain supreme pontiffs issued to his sacred Order mentioned Ethiopia among the kingdoms in which the friars of Saint Dominic were preaching, it carries no weight at all because, as this name of Ethiopia is so broad that, as we mentioned at the beginning of this *History*, it includes many other {[f. 237]} lands much larger than those over which the Prester John rules, it does not follow that just because they used the name Ethiopia they meant precisely the lands of the Prester John. And if one wished to insist that they really were talking about them and that they had reliable information that those religious did arrive here – and I do not know how it could be proved – I would reply that any memory of them had disappeared so completely that there is nobody today who knows anything about them or has heard of them. Hence those friars who he says were at the general chapters and who were there in the monasteries that he names, and who claimed to be Dominicans, if they really were from this land, must have said whatever they liked in order to find a good welcome and some interest, just as João Balthesar did in other things that he invented in his reports, as we have seen. And here again this seems to be the case in what he says on page 8: when João Balthesar left here, which Friar Luis says elsewhere was in 1606, the master of novices in Alleluia Monastery was Friar Marcos de Florença, who was from Florence and had signed the originals that the author was translating, together with Friar Miguel de Monrojo and Friar Matheo Caravajal, who were born in Ethiopia, the sons of some Spaniards; the fact is that neither were those friars in Alleluia Monastery at that time, nor is there any recollection of them, according to the monks of the same monastery, who were raised there and are now very old. Therefore it seems that he deliberately had the papers that he gave to Friar Luis de Urreta signed somewhere else, in order to make them look genuine and obtain some profit from them. Something else that is false is Friar Luis's claim that friars of Saint Dominic from Florence and Venice go on missions to Ethiopia, just as in Spain they have the custom of sending friars to the Indies; leaving <[f. 207/197]> aside the difficulties and dangers of the journey, if that were the case they would have undertaken some mission or other in the nineteen years that I have been here, or at least some of those who had come previously would have been found here, but {[f. 237v]} I have not seen any, and there is no recollection that any have ever arrived here. As for the authors that he quotes, who say that there are monasteries of Saint Dominic in the lands of the Prester John, I reply that the information on which they based themselves was just as false as that which he has had from João Balthesar.

It follows from what we have said that the author unjustifiably refuted Francisco Álvares when, on page 7, he said that he had gone beyond the limits and jurisdiction of the truth by saying that there were no friars in the lands of the Prester John save those of the Order of Saint Anthony, and that, when Prester John David saw in the governor's letters that the king of Portugal had founded monasteries of Saint Dominic and Saint Francis in the lands he had conquered, he specifically asked him who these saints were and requested that he translate their lives into his language. I also have no doubt that in order to affirm that there were no friars of Saint Dominic in these lands he would have made very careful enquiries, because in the prologue to his *Historia Ethiopica* he swears that the things he wrote down on information received were from people who knew them very well. In addition, the Prester John would not have asked so specifically who Saint

Dominic was if there had been monasteries in his lands and the friars from them were his confessors and inquisitors, as the author often claims that they always were; rather, he would have said, 'We too have monasteries of that sacred religion here and we are guided by its doctrine'; but since he had no knowledge of such a religion and the Inquisition has never existed in these lands and they do not know what it is, that is why he asked.

Another thing the author says, that only one of the eight religious of Saint Dominic who entered these lands in former times kept his own {[f. 238]} name, which was Pantaleão, and the others were called in the local language Arghai, Grima (which should really be said Arogaôi, *scilicet* 'Old', Guerima), and that they gave the habit to *Abba* Taquelâ Haimanôt, is in all respects false, because these monks, of whom there were nine, entered the kingdom of Tigrê many years before the glorious patriarch Saint Dominic was born, as is shown in the ancient histories of Ethiopia that are kept in the monastery in Agçûm in the kingdom of Tigrê, <[f. 207v/197v]> from which I took the catalogues of the emperors that were included in chapter 5 of the first book, and which state the time when they came. And I found the same thing in another book of ancient histories that Emperor Seltân Çaguêd, who is now alive, showed me. Both these books, when setting out the catalogues of the emperors, say that in the time of Emperor Amiamîd nine saints entered Tigrê: *Abbâ* Pantaleão, *Abbâ* Arogaôi, *Abbâ* Guerimâ, *Abbâ* Alef, *Abbâ* Cehemâ, *Abbâ* Afcê, *Abbâ* Ademaatâ, *Abbâ* Oz (who was later called *Abbâ* Gubâ, *scilicet* 'Father Puffed-Up', because he made a church on a hill and stayed there alone) and *Abbâ* Licanôs. Some say that many others came at the same time and spread out around the empire, but the books that I have seen mention these nine and no more. After Emperor Amiamîd the catalogues show twenty-two emperors for whom they do not put the time that they reigned, plus a woman who reigned in Tigrê for forty years, and in the time of the last of these emperors, who in the first catalogue is named Delnaôd and in the second Armâ, the line of Solomon's descendants was cut and the empire was seized by a great man named Zagoê, who was married to a kinswoman of the emperor, who was just a boy. The descendants of this Zagoê held the empire {[f. 238v]} for 340 years; despite the fact that the catalogue does not show so many, everybody says – and Emperor Seltân Çaguêd has assured me – that many years are missing in it, and that it is certain that they held the empire for 340 years. Later, the first of Solomon's descendants to succeed to the empire again was called Icûnu Amlac, and from him until the present year of 1622 we can count 355 years and three months; adding to that the forty that that woman reigned in Tigrê and the 340 that the family of Zagoê held the empire, it makes 735 years and three months, leaving out the twenty-two emperors for whom it is not known how long they held the empire, whereas the glorious Saint Dominic passed away little more than 400 years ago.

Regarding these nine holy religious, those books do not state which Order they belonged to; they only say that they came from Rum, which people commonly say is Rome, and so, when the *icheguê* came to the emperor with many monks in {1620} <1610> to persuade him to command that we should not teach anyone except the Portuguese, he said to them, 'Why do you persecute the fathers, when you are their disciples? Your History says that nine came from Rome, <[f. 208/198]> and that your founder Taquela Haimanôt was the disciple of one of them.' And he would not grant what they wanted, but said instead that we should teach everyone, because our doctrine was the true one. Nevertheless, there are people who think that Rum is a land of the Turks, and hence they were called Rum. At the end of the history of *Abba* Taquela Haimanôt, which we shall mention later when we deal with it in the appropriate place, it says, 'Abba Anthony gave the habit to Abba Macarius; Abba Macarius gave it to Abba Pachomius; Abba Pachomius gave it to Abba Arogaoî, Abba Arogaoî came to Ethiopia and gave it to Abba Christôs Bezâna; he gave it to Abba Mazcâl Moâ; he gave it to Abba {[f. 239]} Joannî; and he gave it to Abba Iesus and to Abba Taquela Haimanôt.' And everyone says that this Abba Arogaoî is the same one that we mentioned above among the nine saints of Tigrê, and therefore these monks greatly pride themselves on coming from them, even though they call themselves monks of Taquela Haimanôt, since he is held by them to be a great saint. In view of that, it is doubtful that those nine religious came from Rome, and it also follows that those eight friars of Saint Dominic that Friar Luis de Urreta says came from Rome – even if were true that they entered this land – did not give the habit to Taquela Haimanôt, and it was a long time before the glorious Father Saint Dominic was born, because the third abbot after Abba Arogaoî gave the habit to Taquela Haimanôt, and Abba Arogaoî arrived in Ethiopia 735 years ago plus the time that twenty-two emperors reigned, which is not stated in the catalogue.

{On top of} <With> everything that we have said, for me the real proof that the monks who are in these lands of the Prester John are not of the sacred religion of Saint Dominic was seeing that, apart from a few who have been reduced through our public disputations and private talks, all the rest are schismatic and hold on to many heresies, as we have seen in this book. They are so obstinate in them that, when Emperor Zadenguil wanted to give obedience to the holy Roman Church after the public disputations that I had in his presence with his monks and scholars on the matters of our holy faith, they stirred <[f. 208v/198v]> up the people against him and killed him, when the principal captains fought him in a pitched battle. Likewise, when Emperor Seltan Çaguêd, who is alive today, wanted to make them give up their heresies and receive our holy faith, they attempted {[f. 239v]} to kill him four times and in one of these attempts they fought a pitched battle with him and he miraculously achieved victory, as we said in chapter 5 of this second book. To that can be added the great licentiousness that they commonly display, in that they openly cohabit, and they cast out some women and take others, to the extent that the emperor's principal secretary once said to me in the presence of a very serious monk, 'Father, in this land of ours, the monks have better luck in matters of the flesh than married men, because if we have to do what the Gospel orders we cannot leave our wives until death, but they leave one woman and take another whenever they like.' I asked him why he spoke in that manner, because he had been confessing with us for a long time and publicly defended our holy faith. He replied, 'So what? It is common knowledge. This monk has already had twelve.' The monk tried to laugh it off, saying that I should not believe him because he was talking nonsense. But the secretary retorted that it was true. On another occasion, when I was asking Emperor Seltan Çaguêd how many monks there were in the monastery that they call Dêbra Libanôs, he answered that previously there had been many, but now there were only a few. A monk of the religion of Taquela Haimanôt who was there joined in, saying, 'There must be a good 3,000 even now, if they all get together.' The emperor, although he is a very serious and modest man, then said, 'Yes, if you count their children too; but with just the monks, there cannot be so many.'

The licentiousness of the monks reaches such an extreme {[f. 240]} that, because women cannot go inside the monastery compound, they put them up in a number of houses nearby, and they call those houses alênguê, which means 'worldly place'. And they

429

go there whenever they like, without the superiors or the *abuna* putting a stop to it, because he is even worse – at least, the ones I have known have had children, and when they killed the last one, they found he had seven wives, as we said at the beginning of this book. Emperor Seltan Çegued and *Eráz* Cela Christôs, his brother, have worked hard and are still working to remedy <[f. 209/199]> this in some way. They commanded that those who were found in that situation should be fined, and when they saw that this was not enough, they even commanded that those in that situation should not say Mass on pain of excommunication; there is now a lot of murmuring and defiance over this. May Our Lord help them in their holy purpose, for it does not seem that they will be able to achieve what they intend. Not that this is anything new among the monks now, because Father Master Gonçalo Rodrigues of our Society of Jesus, who was the first of our Society to arrive in Ethiopia in 1555, wrote in a letter to Portugal[1] the following year that, when he went with some Portuguese to visit the superior of Dêbra Libanôs, he found that the monastery was very large and there were many nuns near the monks, and it was said that there were many children among them. That clearly reveals how little this has to do with the sacred Order of Saint Dominic. And the same father, straight away saving the honour of this holy religion, added these words: 'The order of these monks is not that of Saint {[f. 240v]} Francis nor even less of Saint Dominic, but is called the Order of Taquela Haimanôt, who was a man of that name, whom the *Abexins* here hold to have been a great saint canonized by them.'

---

[1] See Guerreiro, 'Adição à Relação das coisas de Etiópia', f. 285, p. 310. Páez quotes other passages from the same letter in bk II, ch. 7, above, and bk III, ch. 4, vol. II below.

# CHAPTER XVIII

## Which describes how many religions there are in Ethiopia and whom they consider to have been their founders, their manner of government and life and how they deal with novices

In all the lands of Ethiopia over which the Prester John rules, there are no more than two religions: one that they say is of *Abba* Taquela Haimanôt, which means 'Plant of the Faith', and the other of *Abba* Stateûs. And the monks of both religions greatly pride themselves on having their origin in *Abba* Arogaoî, one of those nine holy religious that we said in the previous chapter entered the kingdom of Tigrê in ancient times, which they affirm as being beyond doubt, because the histories of both testify to it. But they have taken them as founders because they gave the habit to many monks and are held by them to be illustrious saints enlightened in miracles.

The way of life of all these monks is almost the same, but they have major differences in many things, such as over some lands that are in the possession of <[f. 209v/199v]> those of *Abba* Stateûs but which those of *Abba* Taquela Haimanôt say belong to them. Most of all they dispute over precedence, because although the monks of *Abba* Stateûs admit that they lived at another time and that *Abba* Taquela Haimanôt died first, because they find it in their history that, when *Abba* Stateûs went to Armenia, {[f. 241]} Our Lord God revealed to him that *Abba* Taquela Haimanôt had died, even so they claim that *Abba* Stateûs began first. Those of *Abba* Taquela Haimanôt deny that and put forward arguments to prove that their founder began first, and so they spend their time in disputes without ever finally resolving the matter.

I have tried very hard to obtain the histories of these two founders, but I have only succeeded in finding that of *Abba* Taquela Haimanôt, which I shall put in the following chapter. I could not get hold of the history of *Abba* Stateûs because, not only are there few books of it, but they will not lend them, since they think that we want them to see if we can find something in them to criticize or to refute their errors, because they have seen that we refute them with other books of theirs. But what the monks from the kingdoms of Gojam and Tigrê, where they have their main monasteries, have assured me without any discrepancy at all is that *Abba* Stateûs was born in a land of the kingdom of Tigrê called Cerâ, and, after building many monasteries and giving the habit to a large number of monks, he wanted to teach and spread the holy faith, so he embarked for Armenia, where he stayed preaching until he died. Since he did not leave anyone in his place here to be superior over everyone – or if there was one, he did not last long – the priors of the monasteries are not dependent on any other, but when it sometimes happens that the prior of Biçân Monastery, which is near the port of Maçuâ, comes with others to visit the emperor or on some business, the custom is that he enters first and takes the principal place inside.

The prior or abbot of the monastery, whom they call *mêmeher*, which means 'master', holds the position {[f. 241v]} until his death, although sometimes they remove him for serious reasons and elect another, or when he is so old that he cannot attend to the duties of his office. He is elected by the votes of the monks of that monastery alone, and they then take him to the emperor, tell him how they have chosen that one to be their master and ask him to command that the customary ceremonies be performed, which are to robe him, over his habit, in a blue collarless robe reaching down to his feet and to place a gold crown two fingerbreadths tall on his head. And then, accompanied by the monks, they take him like that outside the first palace enclosure, and there they proclaim to everyone present, ordinarily a large crowd, that he has been given responsibility for their monastery. Then he returns with the same retinue and kisses the emperor's hand <[f. 210/200]> and afterwards takes off the crown and the blue robe. If his monastery is a large one, the emperor gives him a good bolt of cloth and a mule. When he returns to his monastery, they take him to the church and, at the entrance to the chapel, he sits on his predecessor's chair with a cross in his hand, while all the monks stand, and then a vested deacon sings aloud that verse by David: '*Etenim benedictionem dabit legislator, ibunt de virtute in virtutem, videbitur Deus eorum in Sion.*'[1] And everyone repeats it, singing, and they say it three times, the deacon and the others *alternatim*. And then the deacon reads the Gospel of Saint Matthew, starting from '*Vos estis sal terrae*' until he reaches '*et glorificent Patrem vestrum qui in coelis est*'.[2] Then he rises and blesses everyone and they take him with much festivity to the house of the previous abbot, because the monks do not live in cells {[f. 242]} like those of Europe, but each in his separate house, as we shall say below. But sometimes they perform this ceremony as soon as they elect him, before taking him to the emperor. And if it sometimes happens that they vote for two and the vote is tied, they take the case to the emperor and the one who returns with the position is commonly the one who has more people at court to speak to the emperor for him, that is, either through friendship or by means of bribes (for bribes work better than anything else here with people at court), because these people inform the emperor as they see fit, and they ordinarily make him choose the one they want, and once he commands that he be given the crown that we mentioned, it is all over.

The monks of *Abba* Taquela Haimanôt have not only monastery abbots but also a superior who is like a general, whom they call *icheguê*, and they elect him by voting, as we have already said. He visits the monasteries of his whole order and, when he cannot, he has them visited by a monk; if he finds something that deserves punishment he hands it down, which commonly means a fine, because the monks have some private property, as we shall see later, although he also gives {other penances} <some penance> when he sees fit. But despite all their visits there has been little reformation, because monks cohabit openly today just as they used to before.

When differences and complaints arise among them, they ask their *icheguê* and sometimes the *abuna* for a judge but, whichever of them appoints him, the judge cannot enter

---

[1] Psalm 83[84]:8, 'For the lawgiver shall give a blessing, they shall go from virtue to virtue: the God of gods shall be seen in Sion.' (The word '*legislator*' is an error for '*legis dator*'.)

[2] Matthew 5:13–16: 'You are the salt of the earth ... and glorify your Father who is in heaven.'

to perform his duties without first speaking with the lord of the land on which the monastery stands, {[f. 242v]} or with whomever he has put in his place, and he gives a man <[f. 210v/200v]> who attends the taking of witnesses and the other investigations performed by the judge; in the end he passes judgment as he sees fit and then the judge hands down his decision, and so this man plays some part in the way the judge sentences the guilty party. And if either party objects to the decision, they take it to whoever appointed the judge, and it ends there.

Furthermore, sometimes in these complaints and generally in those they have with lay people, they ask the emperor's tribunals or the viceroy of the region where the monastery is to appoint a judge. This judge also has to ask the lord of the land to provide a representative and, when they take the decision back to those tribunals, if they find that the monk deserves flogging or death they pass sentence, but it is not carried out without confirmation from the emperor or the viceroy who appointed the judge. I once saw two monks whom Emperor Seltan Cegued had ordered to be flogged, and they were given a very good lashing, one in front of the palace and the other in the field in front of the emperor's tents, because it had been proved that he was plotting to kill him. And a viceroy of Tigrê once sentenced a monk to be speared to death, because when a captain of his was near the monastery fighting a rebel who, despite having many men, could not harm the captain because he was in a secure position, the monk guided the rebel's men along a path that they did not know and they came upon the captain unexpectedly from behind and defeated him, killing many men and stealing many valuables that were kept in the monastery. Soon after the sentence had been carried out I happened to be arriving {[f. 243]} from another land to visit the viceroy and saw the dead monk. It is very common for the emperor's judges to pass sentence on monks and clerics when they deserve it and to carry out their sentences like this.

It may be seen from this what little value there is in the interpretation that Friar Luis de Urreta, in the third book of his *Historia*, page 708, gives of what – as he claims there – Illescas wrote in the life of Clement VII,[1] that in Ethiopia there is no ecclesiastical immunity and that secular justice punishes the lay, the religious and the clerics, and of what Francisco Álvares says in his *Historia Ethiopica*, that he saw certain monks flogged in front of the Prester <[f. 211/201]> John's tents. Friar Luis responded that they had mixed them up with a certain kind of hermits that there are in the deserts in Ethiopia today, who, although they wear a habit and carry out great penances, are purely secular and so they can give up the habit whenever they like, and they do not have a specific habit indicated for them, because some wear tanned skins and others yellow cotton cloths, but they have some monasteries where this habit is given to those who ask for it, and some elders who are priests and minister the sacraments; these hermits, who are secular, despite their penances and way of life, are seized and punished by secular justice just like other secular people, and unlike the priests and religious, for there is no nation that has greater respect for them.

These imaginings of the author are not enough to convince me that the ones that Francisco Álvares saw flogged were not real monks but those hermits that he depicts because, although I have not found the words to which he refers – since he {[f. 243v]} does not quote the exact place, and the copy of Francisco Álvares's *Historia* that I have is

---

[1] Gonzalo de Illescas, *Historia pontifical y catholica*, 2 vols, Salamanca, 1569; Burgos, 1578.

not divided into chapters and has no index since it is very old – this writer does say on page 78 that he saw a monk flogged at court for bringing some letters from the princes on mount Amhará, and he shows clearly that the monk was a priest, because he says that they asked him where he had been ordained to say Mass. Whatever Francisco Álvares may have said, however, what really happens is that the Prester John's justices arrest clerics and monks and punish them according to their guilt. And in Ethiopia there is neither the kind of hermits that Friar Luis says there are today, nor the countless solitaries and anchorites that he claims are in the deserts, some followers of Saint Moses the Ethiopian, others of Saint Paul the first hermit, of Saint Hilarion, Saint {Panuphio} <Pancephio>,[1] Saint Macarius and Saint Onuphrius. There are no solitary followers of any of these in the lands of the Prester John; all those who live in the deserts are monks of the religions that we have been talking about, of *Abba* Stateûs and Taquela Haimanôt, and these wear habits as he describes, some made of yellow cotton cloth, others of skins like the chamois of Spain, but coarser, and others of black or white cotton cloth. In this there is nothing particular to distinguish between those of the desert and those of the towns: each one wears a habit of the colour and cloth that he wants or can afford, and so some wear very expensive silk cloths over their habit. However, those monks of the desert [who want to appear to be more penitent always wear yellow skins, like thick <[f. 211v/201v]> chamois.][2] They have their monasteries there and, in order to be freer from communication and dealings with other people, they have obtained decrees from the {[f. 244]} emperors that nobody may farm or settle within certain limits a long distance from their monasteries. Ordinarily they perform great penances in those monasteries, and increase them particularly in Lent, because then they go out in pairs or larger groups to fast under trees or in caves, and they eat nothing but a few herbs or vegetables at night and drink water, and some go two days or longer without eating or drinking. They wear iron cilices and do other very extraordinary things, but what can all this profit them, since they are schismatics and heretics, and without faith it is impossible to please God? As Saint Paul says, '*Sine fide autem impossibile est placere Deo*', Hebrews, 11.[3]

The monks from monasteries in towns go off to the desert monasteries when they like, without their superior being able to prohibit them from doing so, and later they return to the town when they please. The common people regard them as saints and therefore give great credence to everything they say, and they themselves want to be seen as such, since they put it into the heads of the ignorant and even many who appear to be discriminating that they have great revelations and that Our Lord shows them things that are yet to come. So some people go to them as if to oracles and, although they find out every day how false and mendacious their dreams are, they never disabuse themselves, even when they often see that those they held to be saints give up the habit after their penances {[f. 244v]} and openly marry. I know one who spent six years in the desert, wearing skins and performing great penances, to the extent that in addition to the ordinary ones that the others usually do he spent certain hours of the day praying with his head on the ground and his feet in the air, and now he is married with several children. When I once explained to him that it was a great sacrilege to give up the habit and live in that way, he

---

[1] Possibly a copyist's error for 'Paphnucio', Saint Paphnutius.
[2] Written in the margin in ARSI, MS Goa 42.
[3] Hebrews 11:6, 'But without faith it is impossible to please God.'

replied that he had given up the habit because originally they had made him take it against his will and because subsequently he had married since he felt he could not live in chastity. The same excuse is given by all those in town monasteries who marry and give up the habit (and they are not few in number), and there is no one who will put a stop to it. It is true that <[f. 212/202]> monastery superiors force some people to take the habit, because they consider it a great honour to give the habit to large numbers and so, if the boys that they teach do not want to be monks by entreaty, they take some of them prisoner and ill treat them in other ways until they say yes, and others they persuade to take the habit, for in that way they will achieve honour among the lords. Therefore they often give someone the habit without a novitiate or any kind of examination other than his saying that he wants it, as some monks told me. One of them was an old abbot who for nearly forty years has been the abbot of one of the oldest and largest monasteries in Dambiâ, {[f. 245]} and he told me that all this perdition of the monks had come about because they used to give the habit in this way, without the probation that they had had previously, which they tell me was as follows.

When in former times they took in a novice, they gave him seven years' probation, having him serve in the monastery and perform laborious duties while still wearing secular clothing. During this time he was at liberty to leave if he could not face that way of life, and the monks too would dismiss him if they thought he was not suited to their religion. But if he decided to persevere and the monks were satisfied with him, they would accept him and give him the habit in the following manner: first he confesses with the abbot of the monastery, who then blesses the water and baptizes him, saying, 'So-and-so, I baptize you in the name of the Father, the Son and the Holy Spirit', and they anoint him with oils, with only the monks being present in the church, because they do not allow any secular person to enter; and taking him before an altar, where a vested priest and ministers are waiting, they begin to sing that verse by David: '*Illumina oculos meos ne unquam abdormiam in morte, ne quando dicat inimicus meus prevalui adversus eum*', Psalm 12.[1] Then from Psalm 33: '*Accedite ad eum et illuminamini, et facies vestrae non confundentur.*'[2] And so they go on taking a few verses from many other Psalms. When that is over, the priest blesses incense, saying two prayers, and then the deacon says a prayer for the patriarch {[f. 245v]} of Alexandria and the *abuna*, and then the priest continues, praying for those present and the people. After this, the priest takes some scissors and cuts some hair from five parts of his head, in the form of a cross, saying the *Pater noster* and Psalm 50. Then the abbot says this prayer over him: <[f. 212v/202v]>

'Almighty God, who art in heaven and seest all things and knowest what is hidden in man's heart, look down from Thy holy glory upon Thy servant So-and-so who has come to seek Thee and to submit to Thee. In his life as a monk, straighten his path, give him complete patience and keep from him all thought of this world, and when he prays keep from him evil deeds, and receive his prayer through Thy mercy. Give him, Lord, the light of Thy grace, because he has sought Thee with love and with his heart. Make him flee the appetites of this world, be fit for Thy spiritual vineyard and not turn back, nor think of the love of this world. Give him patience in his labours and to submit with purity to Thy

---

[1] Psalm 12 [13]:4–5, 'Enlighten my eyes that I never sleep in death: Lest at any time my enemy say: I have prevailed against him.'

[2] Psalm 33 [34]:6, 'Come ye to him and be enlightened: and your faces shall not be confounded.'

command and Thy will, for the love of Thy name which has been invoked over him and to do what is best and to seek the holy mysteries, to possess joy without end and to find a share of the kingdom of heaven, with Thine only Son Our Lord Jesus Christ, for ever {and ever}. Amen.

'Almighty God, Father of Our Lord Jesus Christ, we beseech Thee, O lover of men, {[f. 246]} look down upon Thy servant So-and-so, who is humbled before Thy glory, bless him and sanctify him and bind him to Thy holy cross and {add him to} <raise him up with> the celestial armies. And when he puts on the *azquemâ* [1] may he show himself naked of the things of this world, and make vain love abandon him. Give him spiritual humility and a pure heart and good thought, love and patience. Keep from him all representations of the demons and cast them under his feet. Give him power to be able to tread on serpents, placing Thy living fear in his heart so that thoughts of the flesh may leave him, and cleanse his body and soul so that he may be pure without any evil. Light and keep the candle of his works so that he may not be lost. Ensure that in the last hour he is ready to put on a clean robe, with Thine only Son, Our Lord and Saviour Jesus Christ. Glory be to Thee, to Him and to the Holy Spirit for ever. Amen.'

Then they bless the girdle, a leather strap, with very lengthy prayers and read lessons from the end of the Epistle to the Ephesians, starting at '*Induite vos armaturam fidei* {*Dei*}', etc., as far as '*ut in ipso* {*audeam*} <*audirem*> pro- <[f. 213/203]> *ut oportet me loqui*',[2] and from Saint Peter and from the Acts of the Apostles, and then from the Gospel of Saint Matthew: '*Ecce nos reliquimus omnia*', etc., {and from Saint Mark: '*Ecce nos dimisumus omnia*', etc.,} and from Saint John: '*Pater, venit hora, clarifica filium tuum*', etc.[3] And then they say '*Kyrie eleison*' four times and a prayer. After that, while giving him the habit and girdle, they say two prayers, and while he is girding himself they say another in which it mentions that he should be girded with a girdle that cannot be loosed, and then another very long one, asking that, just as the Lord sent {[f. 246v]} the Holy Spirit unto His apostles, so may He send Him also unto that servant of His, and may He place His right hand on him and keep him as a son. In addition to these prayers, they have others suited to those who are virgins and others for widowers to whom they give the habit. When that is done, they bless the cowl, saying the *Credo* and some Psalms and 'Alleluia' three times, and they cense, saying a prayer and then another very long one. Then the abbot takes the cowl in his hand and says a prayer, and when he has finished they read a large part of the Epistle to the Hebrews, starting at '*Est autem fides sperandorum substantia rerum*', and from the first Epistle of Saint Peter: '*Charissimi, obsecro vos tamquam advenas et peregrinos*' to '*Beatius est magis dare quam accipere*', and then the priest reads the Gospel of Saint Luke, 19: '*Homem quidam nobilis abiite in regionem longiquam*', etc.[4] The abbot then puts the cowl on him and, with his hand on his head, says, 'Behold, here I have put on your head

---

[1] Páez provides a description of this ornament in the penultimate paragraph of this chapter.

[2] Ephesians 6:11–20, 'Put you on the armour of God ... so that therein I may be bold to speak according as I ought' ('*audirem*' is a copyist's error in BPB, MS 778).

[3] Matthew 19:27, 'Behold we have left all things.' Mark 10:28, 'Behold, we have left all things.' John 17:1, 'Father, the hour is come, glorify thy Son.'

[4] Hebrews 11:1, 'Now faith is the substance of things to be hoped for.' 1 Peter 2:11, 'Dearly beloved, I beseech you as strangers and pilgrims.' The second quotation that Páez attributes to 1 Peter is in fact from Acts 20:35, 'It is a more blessed thing to give, rather than to receive.' Luke 19:12–28, 'A certain nobleman went into a far country.'

this cowl of humility, which is appropriate for penance, so that you may give forth honourable fruit with the help of Our Lord Jesus Christ; glory be to Him and to the Father and to the Holy Spirit, now and for ever. Amen.' And then he continues, 'We beseech Thee, Almighty Lord, that through Thy mercy Thou deliver Thy servant from the death of this world and set him on the path of justification, that Thou deliver him and release him from the temptation of the Devil. Keep his soul in purity, Lord, so that he may espouse the Holy Spirit, and make him always remember Thy command and fulfil it. Give him patience, courage, humility, goodness, faith, hope and charity, in Thine only Son, Our Lord and Saviour Jesus Christ, for ever. Amen.'

{[f. 247]} <[f. 213v/203v]> When he has finished this prayer, he reads I know not what things that the book says are appropriate for monks, but they would not show them to me, and he asks him three times if he can take that burden upon himself and fulfil all those things, and each time he says he can, and then he commands him to lie on the floor and he lies in the way that the corpse lies in the grave, to show that he has died to the appetites of the flesh and to all the things of the world and lives for all that is good, and he says a prayer over him. Then the vested priest says many more and, when he has finished, he starts the Mass and gives communion to the one who has received the habit. After Mass, they take him with rejoicing to eat with the abbot.

I found all this in a book that an abbot lent me, and he told me that some monks did not want to take the cowl together with the habit, giving some excuses of humility, but ordinarily it was so as to go and take it in another monastery, because afterwards he could stay in whichever of the two he liked. And they necessarily have to share the lands of that monastery with him, as we shall say later.

In addition to the habit and cowl, they have another thing that they call *azquemâ*, which is like a very slender plait that they make from three strips of parchment; they wear it round the neck so that both ends come in front to be tied to a little copper ring that they have on the girdle, and some of them put tiny wooden crosses on it. This *azquemâ* cannot be given to the monk until he is thirty years old, and before receiving it he must serve for one year doing whatever the monks want him to do; when they give it to him, it is with many ceremonies and various prayers, and they hold it in great esteem and consider it to be something of great honour.

{[f. 247v]} Also in that book is the way in which the habit must be given to a nun, and it sets out many prayers and says that they should cut hair from five places on her head, as they do when they give the habit to a monk, and another one should shave her whole head and then they should give her the veil, which is almost like a monk's cowl. Although nuns never used to live in a monastery here, as they do in Europe, <[f. 214/204]> but each one in her own separate hut, so that their residence was like a town or village, depending on how many there were, even so they say that they used to be attached to some monastery of monks and that they had a superior whom they obeyed. Now, too, there are some who live in their huts near monasteries and the abbots have some superintendence. But usually they live where they like, separate from one another, so that they are more like *beatas* than nuns; the worst thing is (so they say) that both those who live together near monasteries and those who live separately are commonly more worldly than before they became nuns.

# CHAPTER XIX

## Which reports the history of *Abba* Taquela Haimanôt, as told by the books of Ethiopia

Friar Luis de Urreta writes this history in chapter 9 of a volume that he published in 1611 on the saints of Ethiopia,[1] and on page 131 he says that *Abba* Taquela Haimanôt was born in the famous city of Saba, the capital of all Ethiopia, illustrious since {[f. 248]} it was the largest in the whole land, populous since it had served for a long time as the court of the emperors, and most noble since it had been built by Queen Saba when she returned from visiting the holy temple of Solomon. His father, who was called Sacasab, was the king in this metropolitan city of the kingdom of Saba and he married the daughter of a king of Ethiopia, who was called Sarra, a maiden of extreme beauty and great honesty and virtue. And in the holy state of matrimony they lived for many years in a state of virginity, imitating the matrimonial state of the Virgin Mary and Saint Joseph, but later, while she was at prayer, an angel appeared to her and said that it was God's will that they should consummate their marriage, because He wanted to give her as a son a faithful plant that would bear fruit throughout Ethiopia. Appearing also to King Sacasab, he commanded him the same on God's behalf. The saints obeyed God's command and Sarra conceived and in due time gave birth to a son, to whom at baptism they gave the name Tacleaimanot, which <[f. 214v/204v]> means 'Fruitful Plant'. After that they again continued their good desires of chastity for the rest of their lives, occupying themselves in prayer.

When the holy young man reached the age of twenty, God took his parents in order to give him the reward of his virtues. Despite being so young, rich and powerful and the king of a great kingdom, since {[f. 248v]} good desires had {always} flourished in him, he feared lest they be in vain, and with this fear he renounced the kingdom into the hands of the Prester John and, so that his vassals would not oblige him to become king again, he went to the *abuna* of Ethiopia, who was called Athanasius, so that he might ordain him with all the holy orders up to the holy priesthood, and the *abuna* did so, since he had had a revelation and commandment from heaven to do that. He took his leave of the *abuna* and, taking his blessing, went off preaching around the kingdoms of Ethiopia. And he entered the kingdom of Damôt, which at that time belonged to Moors, and converted the king and all his vassals, and the Prester John sent many priests and bishops there, and this kingdom remains in the faith of Jesus Christ to this day. Leaving that kingdom in their good hands, his intention was to move on to others held by infidels, but an angel of the Lord appeared to him and told him that it was God's will that he should become a religious of

---

[1] Urreta, *Historia de la sagrada orden*, ch. 9, 'Of the prodigious life, portentous miracles and glorious death of Saint Thacleaymanoth, inquisitor and friar of the Order of Preachers', pp. 129–64.

the order of Saint Dominic. He bowed his head to the divine commandment and said that the divine will would be done in all things, and then there appeared a beautiful cloud and, raising him up high, it took him to an island called Haic, which is in the great Lake Cafates, and set him down at the door of Saint Stephen's church, which was a monastery of the friars of Saint Dominic, and the prior was the holy Father Friar Argay, one of the eight religious who had entered Ethiopia preaching. The saint went in and, prostrating himself at the prior's feet, asked him with many tears for the holy habit, and recounted to him what the angel had told him and the miracle of the cloud.

{[f. 249]} The religious received him with extraordinary joy as if he were an angel coming from heaven, and they gave him the holy habit. Seeing himself a religious, he began to make a new life, even though the old one had been a very good one. He exercised himself in humility, in fasting and in constant prayer. When the year of novitiate was over he professed in the hands of the prior, the holy Friar Argai, and as a professed religious he shone in all the virtues. In the forty years that he spent in the religion, he never ate meat, even if he was ill. His fasting was continuous all his life, and he ate nothing <[f. 215/205]> but raw herbs once a day and drank just water. During Lent, Advent and the fifteen days before the Assumption of Our Lady he would only eat on Sundays, and what is more, he did not sleep for seven consecutive years. Divine Majesty honoured him with prodigious miracles and gave him the gift of prophecy; when he was about to say Mass, an angel would come down from heaven and bring him the wine and host and would assist him. Often during Mass they saw him raised up high in the air. When he was going to some city to preach, wild lions, tigers, bears and many other animals would come out to him on the road and lie at his feet like gentle lambs and would follow him and accompany him on the way, without doing him or those he met any harm; many kinds of birds, too, would follow him and fly round his head waiting for his blessing. When he arrived at the place where he was going, he would bless the animals accompanying him and, bowing their heads, they would return to their forests without doing any harm. His miracles are beyond count: he gave light to the blind, healed cripples, cleansed lepers, delivered those oppressed by the Devil and raised many people from the dead.

{[f. 249v]} Saint Taquela Haimanôt founded the famous monastery of Plurimanos and was its prior, setting a great example in virtues. He vested many nobles in the habit of Saint Dominic there, including some kings' children, such as Saint Phelipe, Saint Elça and Saint Clara. From there he once went to visit the Christians in the kingdom of Damôt and, on his way back to his monastery, he was brought a girl whom the Devil was cruelly torment-ing and, making the sign of the cross over her, he commanded the Devil to come out and leave her alone, and he did. Her parents took her back home with great joy and lay her on a bed to rest, but when they left her alone the Devil took possession of her again even more strongly and, pulling her from the bed, threw her on the fire, where she was burnt to death. When her parents came in they were overcome with grief, as might be expected. Leaving her there, they hurried after the saint, who was already far away and when they reached him they threw themselves at his feet in floods of tears. They told him what had happened and begged him <[f. 215v/205v]> to have pity on them and help them. The saint was moved by their tears and turned back, and when he saw that sad sight, he raised his eyes to heaven begging God for His favour; then he took the girl by the hand and raised her alive and well, unmarked and with no trace of burning, and delivered her to her parents. At once he commanded the Devil to appear visibly in front of everyone in order to receive punishment for his temerity. The Devil obeyed at once and appeared in the figure of a man, and the saint said to him, 'What diabolical daring of yours was this to burn this child, who had been redeemed by the blood of Jesus Christ? Well, so that henceforth you will obey the commands of priests, I command you in the name {[f. 250]} of the holy Trinity to serve the Monastery of Plurimanos in the figure of a visible man for a period of seven consecutive years, doing all the menial work that the prior and his religious command you to do, and in particular you will ring the bells at all the canonical hours, you will sweep the church, and you will arrange the lamps.' The Devil could not withstand the divine virtue operating through the saint and so he went in a great fury to the monastery and served in it meticulously for all the seven years in the body of a visible, ugly man, so that everybody could see him and speak to him and he would answer. This is something that every child in Ethiopia knows and is a most certain and true tradition.

While this glorious Saint Taquela Haimanôt was ill with the sickness of which he died, and was speaking to his son Saint Phelipe and many other religious of the rewards that God keeps in heaven for His servants, he said to them, 'I know something from experience, because for twenty years without interruption, seven times a day, according to the number of canonical hours, I have been taken in the hands of angels to heaven, where I have heard the angelic music and enjoyed that gentleness and delight, and so I say as someone who has experienced it that all the penances and labours are as nothing compared to the reward that you will have.' As his last hour came, with the religious standing all round his bed, he said, 'Make room, my children; I can clearly see my Lord Jesus Christ entering this room with his most holy Mother and our glorious Father Saint Dominic, with many saints.' Then, with all the religious prostrate on the floor, that room was filled with the sweetest fragrance, and our {[f. 250v]} Master Christ came to Saint Phelipe and Saint Elça, who were <[f. 216/206]> on their knees, and made a cross with His divine hands on each of their foreheads. Sweet celestial music could be heard, and as that happy soul left its body it was received in the arms of its Master Christ and taken to heaven with eternal glory, after forty years of the habit, at over seventy years of age, in the year of the birth of Christ 1366. In the place where they put his body there rose a spring of clear water, and the sick who drink from it are healed of all their diseases.

Forty days after his death, while Saint Phelipe and Saint Elça were in the church praying after matins, Saint Taquela Haimanôt appeared and said to them, 'You, my son Phelipe, will succeed me in the priorship and in the end, through martyrdom, you will come and enjoy God in my company. And you, my son Elça, will be prior and will suffer great labours in performing the holy office of inquisitor and, although you will not die like your brother Phelipe, you will follow him on the path of glory.' And, taking his leave of them, he disappeared.

Friar Luis de Urreta writes these and many other things in chapter 9 with a great abundance of words, and I thought it best to summarize them here so that if the reader could not find his book he could see how differently he depicts the history of Taquela Haimanôt from the way we shall report it soon, taken from the books of Ethiopia, and at the same time to show briefly how far many of these things are from the truth of what happens here. First, {[f. 251]} *Abba* Taquela Haimanôt was born in Zorêr, a land of the kingdom of Xaoa, and not in the famous city of Sabâ, for there is no such city in Ethiopia, nor any recollection that there ever has been. He was not the son of a king, but of a priest who was called Zagâ {Za Ab} <Zaab>, which means 'Grace of the Father', and not Sacasab, as he says. This man was a descendant of the priests who had come from Jerusalem to Ethiopia with Menilehêc, the son of Solomon and Queen Saba, of whom we spoke at the beginning of the first book, and therefore in the history of Taquela Haimanôt it says that he traces his origin to Sadoc the priest, the son of Abiatar. His mother was not the daughter of a king, either, but of an honourable man, and she was called Sara, but her father-in-law Heôtbenâ gave her the name Egziareâ, which means 'God has chosen her'. They did not live in the state of matrimony in virginity, but instead the history says that Egziareâ was very sad because she was barren <[f. 216v/206v]> and in church she was always begging God to give her children, and when she gave birth there was great rejoicing in her house because she had borne a son, having been barren, and when they baptized him, they gave him the name Feçâ Sion, which means 'Joy of Sion', and not Taquela Haimanôt, as Friar Luis says, because his history says he was given this name much later by an angel.

As for his claim that when his father died he renounced the kingdom and, so that his vassals would not oblige him to become king again, he went to *Abuna* Athanasius and he ordained him to say Mass, he could hardly have renounced something that he did not have, and the one who gave him orders {[f. 251v]} was *Abuna* Guerlôs, and he went to him before his parents died. When he went to the kingdom of Damôt to preach, they were not Moors there but heathens, and their king was called Motolomê, and the Prester John did not send priests and bishops there, for there were no bishops in Ethiopia and the priests that he left in Damôt after they had been converted were some that King Motolomê himself, when a heathen, had taken captive from the land of {Zorêr} <Zorey>, where he had been born. As for his claim that an angel appeared to the saint and told him to become a religious of the Order of Saint Dominic, and that he was then taken to a monastery of friars of Saint Dominic on the island of Haic and Prior Argay gave him the habit, and what he mentions later, that at the time of his death he saw Saint Dominic who had come with Christ Our Lord to his cell, it is mere fiction because, as we saw above at the end of chapter 17, *Abba* Taquela Haimanôt was not of the Order of the glorious Father Saint Dominic, ...[1] nor does it say in his history that he appeared to him, for that is something that it would not have left out, had it been true. And the prior who gave him the habit on the island of Haic was called *Abba* Iesus. No less fictional is his claim that an angel brought him the wine and host from heaven when he was about to say Mass, and that when he was going somewhere to preach he was accompanied on the road by wild animals and birds, because neither is it in his history, nor have I found anyone who has heard of it.

The monastery that he names Plurimanos, which as we have said before is actually called {[f. 252]} Dêbra Libanôs, was built fifty-seven years after the death of *Abba* Taquelâ Haimanôt, as the monks there affirm and as is stated at the end of his history, where it says that when he asked Christ Our Lord where He commanded that his body be buried, He replied that it should lie there for fifty-seven years and, after that time, that house would fall and its sons would build <[f. 217/207]> a great monastery nearby in his name and would move his body to it, and so he could hardly have been its prior, nor could the Devil have served there in his time. I also asked the general of that religion about it, as he had been the abbot in this monastery for many years, and he replied in the presence of many monks that he had never heard it said that the Devil had served there, and that it

---

[1] Three lines are struck through in the manuscript.

was a lie. Moreover, his history does not mention that he was raised up to heaven seven times a day to hear angelic music, nor does it mention the spring which Friar Luis says rose on the spot where he was buried, nor that afterwards he appeared to Phelipe and Elçâ. It just recounts that, when he was about to die, he ordered his disciples to gather and told them that Christ Our Lord had appeared to him and told him that his hour had come and that some of those who were present were to go with him. He ordered Elçâ to remain in his place and, three days after he had departed this life, a deacon died and, when they were about to bury him and the office of the dead had already finished, he returned to life and affirmed that he had been taken into the presence of his Father Taquelâ Haimanôt, who was in great glory, and that he was sending word that Elçâ should go to him and Phelipe should remain in his place, and having said that he died. Three months later Elçâ died and his disciples put *Abba* Filipôs in his place. And so that {[f. 252v]} the reader may, if he wishes, see these and the other things that are told about *Abba* Taquelâ Haimanôt, I shall now report his history as the books of Ethiopia tell it.

## History of *Abba* Taquelâ Haimanôt as the books of Ethiopia tell it

*In the name of God three in one, to whom glory and adoration are due. We write down the labours of our blessed and holy Father Taquelâ Haimanôt, Plant of the Father, Plant of the Son, Plant of the Holy Spirit, who is Thy Father Taquelâ Haimanôt who bore the name of the Trinity which comes on 10th August.[1] May the virtue of his prayer deliver us from evil and remove perdition from our lands, for ever and ever. Amen.*

*This Saint Taquelâ Haimanôt (which means 'Plant of the Faith')[2] was a descendant of Sadoc the priest, the son of Abiatar of Jerusalem, because Solomon sent his son Eben Ahaquîn to reign in <[f. 217v/207v]> Ethiopia and sent with him Azarias, Sadoc's son, to be a priest like his father, and he left Jerusalem with great rejoicing and honour, taking with him the Ark of Sion, God of Israel. And soon after arriving in the land of Tigrê, Azarias married the daughter of the honourable local family called Dêcamadabâi and begat a son whom he called Sadoc, like his father. Sadoc begat Levi, and Levi begat Hezberaâi; Hezberaâi begat Hezbeçahî. These priests taught the Old Law to the people of Ethiopia until the time when Tiberius was the emperor of Rome, and Herod the king of Galilee, and Baçên the king of Ethiopia, and Aquîn the priest. Then Our Lord Jesus Christ was born in Bethlehem in Juda. Achîn the priest begat Simon and {[f. 253]} Simão begat {Emberâm} <Euberam>. And 256 years after the Ascension of Christ Our Lord there came a merchant from Jerusalem and with him two boys, who were called Fremenatôs and Sydracôs, and they sheltered in the house of Embarîm the priest and that night the merchant fell ill and died soon after. And the boys served in the house of Embarîm and, one day, Fremenatôs said to Embarîm, 'Lord, I marvel at the customs of the people of Ethiopia, because they have circumcision and believe in Christ, and I do not see baptism or the sacrament of communion.' Embarîm replied, 'Our forefathers brought circumcision to us and the belief in Christ was taught to us by Queen Endaque (scilicet Candace);[3] no apostle has come to us to baptize us and give communion, but you go to the pope of Jerusalem, so that he may empower you to be our apostle.' And he gave him gold and silver for his journey.*

---

[1] In converting the date of this feast (24 Naḥāsé, 27 August) to the western calendar, Páez forgot to take the ten days of the Gregorian reform (1582 in Spain and Portugal) into account.

[2] Interpolation by Páez.

[3] Interpolation by Páez.

*With this, Fremenatôs departed from Ethiopia and, on arriving in Jerusalem, reported the customs of this land to Pope Athanasius, at which he greatly rejoiced. And he ordained him and made him bishop of Ethiopia and gave him the name* Abba Çalamâ, *which means 'Father of Peace', because he would bring peace between God and men. And so* Abba Çalamâ *returned to the Land of Agazî[1] and reached Embarîm 315 years after the birth of Christ Our Lord and baptized him and gave him orders of deacon and then priest and, changing his name, he called him Hezbê Cadêz. He commanded him to baptize all the people and said that he was giving him the powers of a bishop. And so he went baptizing* {[f. 253v]} *all the people of Tigrê and Amharâ and Angôt and teaching them the faith of Christ Our Lord, and they were very good Christians. Hezbê Cadêz begat Hezbê Bariê; the latter came from the land* <[f. 218/208]> *of Tigrê and made his seat in the land of Daont, which is called Baheranquedâ, where he married and begat Tecla Caat; the latter married a woman called Maquedelâ in Amharâ and begat seven sons, and his descendants are there to this day. One of these seven, who was called Azquelevî, baptized the people of Olacâ and Amharâ and the people of Manâbetê and Mauz. This Azquelevî married in Harbeguixê and begat Abailâ, who, after he had grown up, was sent by King Dignacîn to the land of Seuâ with 150 priests in order to baptize all those people, and when he arrived there they baptized 20,000 in one day and they built many churches; and Abailâ chose the land of Zorêr, where he married and begat Hârbaguixê, who begat Bacorâ Ceôn, who begat Hezbecadês, who begat Berhâna Mazcâl. In his time, the kingdom passed from those of Israel to Zagoê. Berhâna Mascâl begat Heôt Benâ, who begat Zara Ioannes, who is Zaga Ça Ab, who is the father of our holy father. Zaga Ça Ab married a daughter of the honourable people of that land, who was called Sara, and they were both God-fearing and said many prayers, fasted and gave considerable alms, and they loved each other, like Abraham and Sara and like Zachary and Elizabeth.*

*Sara was very beautiful and prudent,* {[f. 254]} *and so her father-in-law called her Egziareâ (scilicet 'God has chosen her') and from that day on she was called by that name. When Heôt Benâ died, Zaga Ça Ab and his wife were left with an abundance of the goods of this world, but Egziareâ was barren and they therefore began to celebrate the feast of Saint Michael the Archangel every month, and always gave food and clothing to the poor on those days. Egziareâ was very sad in her heart at being barren, and in church she always begged God to give her children, saying, 'O Lord Jesus Christ, O Lord of Saint Michael, Thou art creator of the angels, joy of the sad, hope of all the world; Thou art King of kings and Lord of lords, God of gods. Hear me, Lord, give me a son to serve Thee and do Thy will in all things.' Zagâ Ça Ab too was always busy praying in church and offering sacrifices and he gave many offerings. And one day Egziareâ said to him, 'Lord, I have something to tell you, and I should be very pleased if you would agree to it.' He said yes, he would agree to it if it was good. 'You see', she said, 'how our parents have died and we have no children to whom we can leave our wealth.* <[f. 218v/208v]> *Please let us give it to the Church and to the poor and set free our slave men and women so that God may release us from our sins.' Zagâ Ça Ab replied, 'O my sister, your cause is very good, but do not hasten to give everything in case you later regret it.' Egziareâ said, 'Brother, it is better that we hasten* {[f. 254v]} *to do good, so that we may praise the Lord in the sepulchre. Let us take of what pleases our flesh and give our soul and we shall*

---

[1] Partial translation of *Beḥéra Agāzi*, literally 'Land of the Free (Men)', the name for Ethiopia in Ethiopian written sources.

*serve our God.' When Zagâ Ça Ab heard these words, he said, 'O wife, great is your faith. You have spoken the truth; I shall do what you say at once.'*

*Taking this holy counsel, {Zagâ Ça Ab} <Zaga Çab> shared his wealth with the Church and the poor and, calling his slaves, he told them that they could go where they pleased, for henceforth they were freed men. On hearing this they wept loudly and said, 'Lord, what have we done? In what have we displeased you? If we have offended you in any matter, punish us and we shall mend our ways.' Zagâ Ça Ab said, 'You have not angered me in any way. May God bless you with the blessing of my fathers the priests, who went before Him in truth. If you wish to remain in my house, it shall not be as slaves, but as my kinsfolk; and the women slaves shall be called Egziareâ's kinsfolk.' On hearing this the slaves were overjoyed and kissed his feet and hands and they remained with him for a long time, with the men slaves as lords of the house and the women slaves as ladies.*

*At this time there rose a tyrant who was called Matolomê and his mother Aseldonê, and he reigned in the lands of Damôt, Ceoâ and Amharâ, as far as a large river called Gemâ. He destroyed many churches and worshipped idols and commanded that the maiden daughters of the lords be brought to him, and their {[f. 255]} fathers did not dare contradict him on account of the great fear they had of him. He was very strong in {war} <the land> and once, when overrunning the land of Zalâlgi, he surrounded the land of Zorêr. When Zagâ Ça Ab saw this and realized that he was coming to kill him, he fled by a different road, but one of Matolomê's horsemen followed him and, when he was close, threw his lance at him but missed. When he threw again, the lance turned back at him and wounded him in the arm. Despite that, he continued pursuing him, and when Zagâ Ça Ab reached a large lake he jumped in the water and the soldier came on his horse to the water's edge and waited for him to swim out, but on seeing that he did not appear, <[f. 219/209]> he thought he had drowned and went off to seek other prey. But Zagâ Ça Ab, a pure priest, received no harm under the water, but rather it was like a tent to him in which he sheltered, because Saint Michael was watching over him, although he could not see him, and so he shouted, 'O Michael, my hope, O Michael, my aid, where is thy strength? Behold, death has come to me here, and on the day of labour in thy feast, on which thou always gavest me so much joy, such great anguish has come to me.' And while saying this he wept very bitterly. Then Saint Michael showed himself to him clearly and said to him, 'Why dost thou weep, Zagâ Ça Ab? Behold, I, Michael, am watching over thee; be not afraid. The miracle was not very clear when I delivered thee from that soldier that was following thee, but it will appear now when I bring thee out of this water in peace, not for thy sake, but for the sake of a son that thou shalt have, who shall be the light of all the world, he shall be like unto me and I shall watch over him.'*

*Zagâ Ça Ab remained under the water {[f. 255v]} for three days and three nights, and at the end of them Saint Michael said to him, 'The destruction is over and perdition is past; come out.' And taking him by the hand he brought him out. And as he entered a church in Zorêr, Saint Michael disappeared. Then Zagâ Ça Ab saw the churches destroyed, the land lost, and heard that his wife and many other people had been taken captive, so he wept much more than before and his sadness was doubled. After that, those who had remained hidden in the caves joined him and together they wept again. Egziareâ, who had been taken captive by soldiers, was doing the same, and when they saw her great beauty they said that she deserved to be the king's wife. So when they came to Matolomê, they told him that they were bringing him one of the women that they had captured who was so beautiful that, if he married her, all the earth* *would submit to him. He rejoiced at this news and commanded that she be given very fine robes and gold jewellery and that they should bring her to him the next day. When the soldiers took her all this and plenty of food, she neither ate nor drank; instead, weeping bitterly, she would not raise her eyes from the ground. On seeing this, the soldiers said to her, 'O woman, why are you so <[f. 219v/209v]> sad? For you have been chosen to be our queen and lady.' She answered nothing, but from the bottom of her heart she was speaking to Christ, saying, 'O my Lord Jesus Christ, why dost Thou look at my sins and not remember the innocence of Thy servant Zagâ Ça Ab, who has served Thee with much purity, and why hast Thou delivered me into the hands of Thine enemies, who are so distant from Thee? O Lord, strength of the strong, {[f. 256]} show Thy strength over them today. O Almighty Lord, show Thy might over them today.' She remained like this until those soldiers fell asleep, and at once she tore off the robes that she had been forced to put on and, putting on her own, she started praying again with great anguish, saying, 'O Lord, God of all creatures and almighty, everything fills Thy divinity. Thou didst deliver Sara from the hand of the Pharaoh, Daniel from the lions' den, Susanna from the false elders, and the three young men from the fiery furnace of Babylon; now, Lord, show Thy strength also for me. Give glory to Thy name, Lord, and do not leave Thy servant in the mouths of these wolves. And thou, Saint Michael, how canst thou remain silent when seeing thy servant in such great anguish and peril? And this trouble came to me on the day when we were celebrating thy feast. Help me, helper of the poor.' At that, Saint Michael appeared to her and said to her, 'This has not come for thy perdition, but so that it may be seen how much I love thee. Of {this temptation}< these temptations> thou shalt be free, for the sake of a son that shall be born of thee.' She said, 'When will this be, Lord?' He replied, 'When God's will is done.' And with that he disappeared.*

*Egziareâ spent the whole night in prayer and, before dawn, she put on again the robes that she had cast off. When the soldiers arose, they took her to the king, who rejoiced when he saw her and decided in his heart to make her queen. And he said to the soldiers, 'Truly, you have brought a beautiful woman. I, the son of Aseldanê, shall give you riches enough for you and your children. Guard this woman well and give her whatever she wants, until I make her queen over all my wives.' The soldiers then took her away and {[f. 256v]} did as their lord had commanded them. Afterwards, Matolomê sent servants to his land, saying, 'Behold, return here in peace and rejoicing. Gather together and prepare <[f. 220/210]> 1,000 cows and 1,000 oxen with gilded horns and 1,000 with silver horns and another 1,000 that are hand-some. Also make ready 70,000 jars of grape wine and as many of honey wine, and let there be beer in as much abundance as water, and delicacies beyond count. And tell the people of Damôt to bring the tribute of my kingdom at once to Malbaredê (which was the house of their idols). 'And if you do not do entirely what I command, I shall cut off your heads.' They went with great haste and made ready everything that he commanded. Matolomê also hastened his journey and within eight days arrived in his land, where everyone welcomed him with great festivities and rejoicing. He told them all to gather the following day 'to sacrifice and worship our gods, who give us strength in time of war and sustain us in peace'. They all replied that they would do so, and that they would spend the whole night making ready what was necessary. But Egziareâ spent it in prayer, beseeching God to help and deliver her. When dawn broke, Matolomê commanded that they bring her to the house of their idols and he went there accompanied by the great men and followed by all his army. When they arrived, they stopped in front of the idols to worship them and then to raise Egziareâ there as queen. But just then Saint Michael came down from heaven like a fearsome thunderclap and, taking*

445

*hold of Egziareâ, carried her away from Damôt to the land of Zorâre, on 22nd August, three hours after sunrise; then he put her down near the church and disappeared.*

*{[f. 257]} When the soldiers heard the crash with which Saint Michael came down, their fear and dread were so great that 1,000 of them fell dead, together with 300 of the sorcerers who had gathered to sacrifice. And Matolomê was left totally insane, not knowing what he was doing or saying for a period of twenty-five years: thus he would command that men be killed and then that they be brought alive, and that a house should be built for him in the air, and other similar absurdities.*

*While Egziareâ was where Saint Michael had left her, Zagâ Ça Ab came out of the church, which he had entered to pray and offer incense for her. Seeing her alone and so richly dressed, he was very surprised and said to her, 'How are you, my lady? Where have you come from? I can see <[f. 220v/210v]> you are highly honoured: you must be a king's daughter. Why are you alone, without any servants?' She answered, without uncovering her face, 'While I was on the road, Matolomê found me and took my people and everything {we} <I> had, but God delivered me from his hands and, since I heard that he had captured the wife of a man called Zagâ Ça Ab, I have come to be his wife.' He replied, 'Why do you think that which cannot be? It is not lawful for a priest to do that. Besides, he is a low-born man and you are honoured; it does not become you to speak of that. What is more, he has sworn by God's holy name that if He does not deliver his wife, he will not marry another.' She said, 'How can she escape from captivity? I heard that the king wanted to marry her and make her queen.' He replied, 'Not only can He take her out of captivity, but He can also raise her from the dead.' As she could see his faith and constancy, she rose and uncovered her face, saying, 'Behold your wife Egziareâ.' When he heard this he was greatly astonished and, rising, {[f. 257v]} he kissed her feet and hands saying, 'O my sister, how did you come here? Who delivered you?' 'God's mercy', she replied. 'After I was separated from you, no harm came to me at all, because the Lord sent His angel, who watched over me and delivered me.' Then Zagâ Ça Ab raised his eyes to heaven, giving thanks to God and saying, 'Blessed be the Lord God of Israel and blessed be His name, for He has done such {a great wonder} <great wonders>.'*

*When the people of the land who had escaped from Matolomê heard this and saw Egziareâ dressed in such fine robes, they said to her, 'What is this, Lady? Who brought you here {like this} with such grandeur?' She told them everything that had happened to her and they praised God, who works wonders through His saints, and they spent much of the day giving thanks to Him, and afterwards they went home with joy. And Egziareâ told Zagâ Ça Ab that since she had been separated from him she had not eaten or drunk anything, at which he was very astonished, and he told her all that had happened to him as well, and they spent all that night talking about God and the angel. The next day, 23rd August, Zagâ Ça Ab finished his week[1] and went home and, that night, while he was in bed <[f. 221/211]> with his wife, she saw in her dreams a resplendent pillar that reached up to heaven and all the kings of the earth and bishops were around it, some bowing down to it, others accompanying it, and many birds of various colours were perched on it. At that moment Zagâ Ça Ab cried out and, waking up, she asked, 'Why did you cry out?' He answered, 'Out of wonder at the vision that appeared to me in my dreams. It seemed that I could see the sun come out from between us and with it countless stars, {[f. 258]} and they illuminated the whole world.' Egziareâ said, 'A marvellous thing is this; who can hear it? I too have seen wonderful things.' And she told him what*

---

[1] His week of priestly functions.

she had seen, and both of them, in astonishment, said, 'What is to come upon us at this time?' After that they went back to sleep, and Saint Michael appeared to Egziareâ and said to her, 'Thou hast conceived in thy womb that chosen son that I told thee would be born of thee, beloved of God and of the Virgin Mary His mother and of the angels, and much honoured.' Having said that, he disappeared from her and manifested himself to Zagâ Ça Ab, and told him the same thing. When morning came, he asked his wife if she had seen something the second time she had gone to sleep. She replied that she had, and recounted to him what Saint Michael had told her. He said, 'He announced the same thing to me as well.' They were greatly astonished at that. Then Egziareâ said, 'Lord, when Saint Michael brought me back, he commanded me to give to the poor the clothes in which I came and the gold and silver, keeping nothing, for God would provide for us.' Zagâ Ça Ab replied, 'So we had better do it at once.' And they did not neglect a single one of the things that the angel had commanded them to do.

Nine months later, on 30th December,[1] our father was born and a great feast was held that day in the house of Zagâ Ça Ab because his wife, who had been barren before, had given birth, and they gave many alms to the poor. Three days after their son was born, the child raised his hand to heaven and blessed God in a loud voice, saying, 'One Holy Father, one Holy Son, one Holy Spirit.' On hearing this, his mother was greatly astonished and said, 'O chosen son, this word was not suited to you {[f. 258v]} but to your father. You should only be suckling.' When the time of purification, which is forty days, was over, they took the boy to the temple {and baptized him}, giving him the name Feça Seon (which means 'Joy of Sion'),[2] because he made the Church rejoice with his doctrine and strong faith. When they returned home, Saint Michael said to Zagâ Ça Ab in a dream, 'This is the chosen son of whom I spoke to thee before, but his name is not Feça Seon, but another that is hidden from thee.' Zagâ Ça Ab replied, 'Tell me, Lord, what name is this?' Saint Michael said, 'I am not sent for this, but to explain to thee <[f. 221v/211v]> the vision that thou and thy wife had before. The sun that thou didst see coming out of thy house was this son of thine, and the stars that were with him are the sons that will be born to him in the Holy Spirit, and the resplendent pillar that thy wife saw reaching up to heaven is this same son, and where she saw that kings were bowing down to him, in truth they will bow down to him and will serve the peoples, and he will be the father of all the earth and, just as heaven rises from the earth, so his name shall be raised.' And having said that, he disappeared.

When Zagâ Ça Ab awoke from his sleep, he told his wife what Saint Michael had said to him, at which she was astonished and they said to each other, 'What will become of this boy? Why is the hand of God with him?' A year and three months later there was a great famine in the land of Seoa and in Zorêre, and when the feast of Saint Michael arrived Egziareâ said to Zagâ Ça Ab, 'What shall we do, for we have nothing at all with which to celebrate this feast as we are accustomed to?' As she said that, she showed that she was very sad, and Zagâ Ça Ab was just as sad to see her like that. So they both went to the church and prayed. Afterwards the boy began to cry, not wanting to suckle, {[f. 259]} so he went home and, on entering the house, the boy put out his hand towards a basket in which there was a very small measure of wheat, as if to say that they should give it to him. When they brought it to him, he put his hand over the wheat and at once it began to increase, so that twelve baskets were filled, and that day

---

[1] Páez has made a mistake in converting the calendar, which accounts for the period of four months (August to December) instead of nine (March to December).

[2] Interpolation by Páez.

447

*God's blessing came down upon the house of Zagâ Ça Ab. When his mother saw that, she brought him a jug in which there was a little butter and the boy made the sign of the cross and it became full, and from it they filled several others. The same happened with the salt, which from a small amount increased greatly. When Zagâ Ça Ab came in, his wife told him what was happening, at which he was very astonished and he began to praise God, saying, 'May the God of Israel be blessed, for He has visited and saved His people. What shall I give Thee, Lord, for this that Thou hast done for me, although I am a sinner?' And he kissed the boy and said to him, 'O my son, live many years so that you can always give me joy and consolation.'*

*After this, they prepared the blessing that God had given them to celebrate the feast of Saint Michael on 13th March, and they invited their kinsfolk, the people of the land and many poor people, and they fed them all with great abundance, at which everyone was amazed, since they did not know whence they had obtained it all at a time of such famine. And they said that after their son had been born to them, they had found this. But not only was it abundantly enough for the feast, but <[f. 222/212]> there was plenty left over to support the poor for as long as the famine lasted. This boy performed many other miracles by giving a blessing with his hand. And when he was older he learned the Psalms and the Church books so easily that it seemed as if he already knew them, because he had Christ in his heart and the Holy Spirit gave him wisdom, and so he always feared God and obeyed his commands, and not only did those who saw him love him, but also those who heard about him. He fasted continuously, and with that, together with the patience that he had in everything, he armed himself against demons. When he reached the age of fifteen, his father took him to the patriarch Abba Guerlôs, who was {[f. 259v]} in Amhârâ, at the time when the pope (that is, of Alexandria)[1] was Abba Beniamin; but before they arrived Saint Michael appeared to Abba Guerlôs in a dream and said to him, 'Tomorrow a white man will come bringing with him a son chosen for the kingdom of heaven. Give him deacon's orders and despatch him straight away.' With that he disappeared and when Abba Guerlôs awoke he was astonished at his dream. When morning came he went out and saw Zagâ Ça Ab, who was just arriving, and from afar he bowed down to him and commanded that they should call him in. He asked where his son was, for he was anointed by the Holy Spirit and through him victory would be given to kings, justice to princes, peace to priests and strength in the faith to the faithful. Zagâ Ça Ab was amazed to hear this from Abba Guerlôs. The patriarch said to him, 'Why are you amazed? Bring your son for me to bless him, as my God commanded me.' Zagâ Ça Ab returned at once to where his son had remained and brought him with great haste.*

*When Patriarch Guerlôs saw Feça Seon, he rose from his chair and embraced him and kissed him, at which everyone was greatly astonished and said, 'What have you seen in this boy, Lord, for you to rise from your chair?' He replied, 'This boy is honoured by Jesus Christ and by His mother the Virgin Mary, and Saint Michael watches over him with a fiery sword.' And he commanded them to lodge Zagâ Ça Ab and his son very well, and the next day as morning broke he said Mass and ordained Feça Seon as a deacon and then took him to his house, where he kept him for seven days without leaving his side, and in the end he gave him his blessing and sent him back to his land. On the journey, they arrived at a house where some people had gathered and Feça Seon said, 'Peace be upon this house; if there is a son of peace in it, may it rest upon him, and if not, may it return to us.' When the people heard this they were very angry, {[f. 260]} and one got up and struck him a few blows. <[f. 222v/212v]> The*

---

[1] Interpolation by Páez.

saint said, 'Why do you do this? Instead of peace do you give me blows?' And he said to Saint Michael, 'Dost thou not see what this man is doing?' And he had not finished saying these words when that man was lifted into the air, where he was whipped very hard without being able to see who was doing it. And he shouted out, 'Forgive me, boy, for although you are small in body, your work rises up to heaven. I did not know and I wronged you; forgive me and I shall serve you from now on.' Feça Seon said, 'Do you know the justice of God, which He metes out at once to those who do evil?' He answered, 'Yes, sir.' The saint said, 'He who raised you up for this torment shall put you down.' The lashes then stopped and he was put down on the ground and he showed the marks of them, like burns from a fire. And he begged them to stay in his house, but he thought in his heart that they were sorcerers. Feça Seon recognized his evil and said to him, 'We are not what you think, but God's servants.' He begged them to forgive him and, taking them to his house, he gave them everything they needed in great abundance, and very joyfully he said to them, 'God has brought you for my good.'

The next day, all those people came to see them and humbly asked them, for the love of God, to forgive them the wrong that they had done them. They replied, 'God forgive you. Henceforth, do not act like that; have love for one another and for pilgrims, because love covers the multitude of sins. If you do not do so, what will you answer on the Day of Judgment, when Christ Our Lord says to you, "I was hungry, and you gave me not to eat: I was thirsty, and you gave me not to drink. I was a stranger, and you took me not in"?'{[f. 260v]} They replied, 'May your God be in our hearts so that we may fulfil everything that you have said to us.' And they took their leave of them, and twenty-four persons accompanied them. When night over-took them on the journey before they could reach the town, they took shelter in a cave but they found no water, though they were all very thirsty. Feça Seon moved away a little and, praying, said, 'Lord God who didst hear me yesterday with that man, hear me also today in the need for water that we have. Thou art He who drew water from the stone when the people of Israel were thirsty; help us also now.' As he said this, he shed so many tears that they fell on the ground, where at once a spring of delicious water rose up, for which he gave thanks to God, and he called his people, saying that he had found water, and they all drank without knowing that it was miraculous. The next morning they left there and, continuing their journey, <[f. 223/213]> they arrived in peace in their land, Zorâre, where Egziareâ received them with great joy at seeing that her son was now a deacon. And Zagâ Ça Ab told her what the patriarch had said to him and everything that had happened to him on the journey, and he gave thanks to God for so many wonders.

As he grew older, Feça Seon occupied himself in hunting, riding and archery, at which he was so skilled that he never shot an arrow in vain. Seeing him thus, his parents tried to marry him to a daughter of the principal family in the land, but he told them that they should not speak of such a thing, because he had offered his purity to Christ. However, his parents did not give up, but instead brought that maiden to their house for him to marry her. But soon after-wards she died, and he rejoiced at being free to be able {[f. 261]} to keep his purity, because he had not set his thoughts on worldly things. Shortly after that, he went to where Patriarch Guerlôs was and told him that they had made another faith and another custom of the Church and that they were baptizing boys before circumcising them. On hearing this, Guerlôs gave him his blessing and said to him, 'Because you are zealous of God's things, like Elias the prophet of Israel, you will be a new apostle and will destroy idols and all evil spirits will be cast out by your command. And you will make many people put aside the worship of demons and worship Christ Our Lord, by the grace of the Holy Spirit, which is upon you.' And then he *ordained him to say Mass and made him the prior of all the lands of {Seoâ} <Sion>, giving him his powers for that purpose, and he sent him in peace, with honour, to his land.*

*While Feça Seon was in Amharâ with* Abba *Guerlôs, Saint Michael appeared to Egzihareâ. 'Behold, what thou didst see before has come about. This son of thine is that pillar of light that thou couldst see, and the birds that were perched on it are the sons that will be born to him in the Holy Spirit; and according to the steps that it had, so will be his holiness, and none of those that thou didst see will be lost. And that tyrant who captured thee will become a very good Christian through his doctrine, and will be cured of his insanity through his intercession; and those who died then will live again through his prayer. And he will be the father of many saints. I have told thee this because thou lovest me.' And he disappeared. She recounted everything to her husband and they gave many thanks to God for having given them such a son. Shortly afterwards, Feça Seon arrived, now a priest. When his mother asked him on what day he had been ordained, she realized that Saint Michael had appeared to her on that very day, {[f. 261v]} and they then held a great feast and gave many alms to the poor. But then, on 12th August, <[f. 223v/213v]> his mother Egzihareâ went to her resting place, and on the 16th so did his father, Zagâ Ça Ab. May the blessing of these two elders, pure as doves, and the blessing of their wise son be with us for ever and ever. Amen.*

*Finding himself an orphan, Feça Seon wept bitterly. And he occupied himself in praying night and day and he read the holy books of the apostles and fulfilled his duties as a priest. And he remained in his father's house for seven years with great riches. One day he went hunting in the countryside with many people and, as he moved away from his companions, Saint Michael appeared to him at noon, wearing a very fine robe; on seeing him, the saint fell on his face as if dead, but Saint Michael raised him up and made the sign of the cross over him, and then he lost his fear and could see the angel clearly, and he said, 'Who art thou, Lord, whom I see with such grandeur?' He replied, 'I am the angel of God's strength who watches over thee at all times, without ever leaving thy side. I am he who pulled Zagâ Ça Ab from the depths of the water, for love of thee. I am he who delivered Egzihareâ from captivity, for love of thee. But now, why art thou a hunter, for this exercise is not becoming for priests, but rather for lay people? The office of the priest is to teach the faith and to correct the common people. Henceforth, be not a hunter of animals, but of souls for God. He gives you the power to raise the dead, heal the sick and cast out demons. And thy name shall not be Feça Seon, but Taquela Haimanot, which means 'Plant of the Father and of the Son and of the Holy Spirit.' And while Saint Michael was saying this, {[f. 262]} Our Lord Jesus Christ showed Himself to him seated on the angel's wings in the form of a very beautiful young man. Seeing this, Taquelâ Haimanôt was astonished, and Our Lord said to him, 'How art thou, my friend?' The saint replied, 'Who art thou, Lord?' And He said, 'I am Jesus, Saviour of the world, who created thee. I am He who blessed thee in thy mother's womb. I am He who blessed thy hand to fill thy parents' house with wheat flour, butter and other things at the time of famine. I am He who crucified the man in the air and scourged him in My wrath, when he wronged thee. I am He who made the spring of water rise from the dry earth when thou wast thirsty and besought me. I am He who has given thee virtue and strength until today and will give thee much more hereafter.' Saying this, He blessed him and breathed three times on his face, and said, 'Receive the Holy Spirit. <[f. 224/214]> Whatsoever thou shalt bind upon earth, shall be bound also in heaven; and whatsoever thou shalt loose upon earth, shall be loosed also in heaven. He that heareth thee, heareth me. I gave this power first to the apostles and from them it came to the bishop and he gave thee power to bind and to loose, to plant and to root up. That*

450

which I have done for thee is not so that thou mayst leave aside the word of the bishop, but to show thee the love I have for thee. Behold, I have given thee command and a new name through the mouth of Saint Michael, in order to send thee to a new people, whom My holy apostles did not reach. And thou art not less than them in any work, because I have made thee a new apostle, for thee to call all men to me. And may Michael, My angel, be thy help in all things and never leave thy side. And I shall be with thee all thy life.' And saying this He gave him the salutation of peace and rose up to heaven, and the holy Taquelâ Haimanôt watched Him until He {[f. 262v]} disappeared from sight. And the saint lay on the ground and blessed God, saying, 'Blessed be the name of the Lord in heaven and on earth, for He has given me more grace than was due to me, a sinner.' And from that day he was filled with Holy Spirit and virtue.

When this was finished, he joined his companions and said to them that it was best to return home, because it was late. Seeing the light on his face, they were afraid and said, 'Why must we return home without catching anything?' The saint said, 'Let us go, because henceforth it is not becoming for us to hunt animals of the wilderness, but of the house instead, which are lost sheep.' But they did not understand that he was talking about the souls of men, and he did not reveal his vision to them. While they were going home, they said to one another, 'Did you see this man's face? He left us at the third hour and we did not see him until the ninth,[1] and he was shining so brightly that we could not look at him. We do not know what it was.' And our Father Taquelâ Haimanôt spent the night rejoicing in the Holy Spirit who was upon him and, as morning broke, he began to gather together the possessions of his house, and in eight days distributed it among the poor, widows and orphans. When the people of the land and his kinsfolk saw this, they came to him and asked him why he was throwing his property away all at once. He answered that he was not throwing it away but adding to it, so that it would be his legacy. And he asked them, 'Do you know my name?' They replied that they knew very well that it was Feça Seon. He said that he no longer had that name, because the angel of heaven had commanded that henceforth he should be called Taquelâ Haimanôt. When they heard that, they said that it was a very good name, and they called him by it ever after.

<[f. 224v/214v]> Our Father Taquelâ Haimanôt began at once {[f. 263]} to follow the path of the apostles and, having nothing to do with property, friends or kin, he went to preach the Gospel and left his house open, saying, 'Lord Jesus Christ, behold, I have left my house open, so that Thou mayst open the kingdom of heaven to me. Henceforth I shall have no help but Thine for my weakness.' And with that he departed like a brave soldier, saying in his heart, 'For what shall it profit a man, if he gain the whole world, and suffer the loss of his soul?' And he remembered the Lord's words, 'He that loveth his life shall lose it', etc.[2] And everywhere he went he preached, saying, 'The kingdom of heaven has come: believe in the Gospel of the Son of God.' And his news was heard in all the lands and many men came to him and received his blessing. And they brought the sick and cast them at his feet and he healed them with God's virtue. And when the people saw that he was performing miracles in the name of Jesus Christ, they followed him with all their heart and left behind their errors and were entire in the true faith. Hearing that in a land called Catatâ they worshipped the trees and rocks, birds and

---

[1] Liturgical hours, calculated from dawn (6 a.m.); i.e. 'he left us at 9 a.m. and we did not see him until 3 p.m.' Such time-keeping is still in everyday use in Ethiopia.

[2] John 12:25.

*wild animals and fire, he went there with great zeal. As he began to teach, the peoples of that land heard Christ's name and became very angry, but the saint suffered patiently, seeing that they did not know what they were doing. He asked them whom they worshipped, and they answered a tree, because a voice from it spoke to them saying, 'I created you', and it said, 'I am your god.' Our father said to them that when they went to worship they should take him with them. Since they thought that he wanted to worship their god, they took him there the next morning at daybreak. As they arrived near the tree, the demon that was inside it shouted out, 'Why have you brought me this evil man, who is called Taquelâ Haimanôt?' They then asked the saint if he was Taquelâ Haimanôt, 'for in our {[f. 263v]} land there is no such name. Stay, do not come with us, so as not to anger our god.' And they made him stay on the path while they went to perform their worship. On seeing this, Taquelâ Haimanôt turned his face to the east and began to pray, saying, 'Behold, Lord, the demon's pride. See what he is doing to Thy people. I beg Thee, Lord, to bind this proud demon with the hand of Thy servant, sending Saint Michael to help me, as Thou didst promise, and do not permit the demon to move from that tree without being shamed in front of these people that he has so deceived. And may that tree come to me, roots and all. O Lord Jesus Christ, Thou art my faith and my work, show the virtue of my faith today, so that the strength of my work may be manifested before all these people gathered here.'*

*<[f. 225/215]> Having finished his prayer, he went to the tree and said, 'In the name of my Lord Jesus Christ, whom I worship, I command you to come out with your roots and to follow me, bringing the demon that speaks in you, so that men may see the strength of my God.' At once the tree uprooted itself with as mighty a noise as thunder in midwinter and went to the saint, striking those it could reach with its roots so hard that it killed twenty-four and the rest fled in great fear. When the tree reached the saint, the demon shouted out, 'Where shall I flee from you, O evil man? Is not all the land of Celâlgi enough for you, that you also come here to rob me of my servants?' Then Saint Michael came down from heaven with his sword and bound the demon, who shouted, saying, 'I beg you, Michael, for God's sake, do not give me labour, but rather death. Let me go, and I shall never again come to where this evil man is.' Saint Michael replied, 'I shall not let you go {[f. 264]} until Taquelâ Haimanôt stops.' Then the demon shouted out for the saint to wait, because he had to speak to him. He stopped and commanded the tree that was following him to stop, and he said to the demon, 'Why do you make people go astray and persuade them that you created them?' He replied, 'Do you not know that I am a liar and the father of lies, and that I tell lies to all those that believe me, as is my custom? Let me go and I promise you I will not return again to where you are.' The saint said, 'Since you deceived the people of this land, tell them now, "In the past I led you astray with lies; from now on worship Our Lord Jesus Christ with His Father and Holy Spirit."' The demon replied, 'I cannot utter those names.' The saint said, 'If you cannot utter the names of the Trinity, tell them, "Worship and serve the Creator of the heavens and of the earth, who created you and me."' Then the demon told the people of the land, 'In the past I led you astray with lies; from now on serve the Creator of the heavens and of the earth, who created me and you. Whoever follows me goes down to hell together with me.' When he had said that, Saint Michael released him and he fled straight away like a gust of wind.*

*<[f. 225v/215v]> When those who were gathered saw such a great miracle they marvelled greatly, but they did not see the angel, just Taquelâ Haimanôt, to whom Saint Michael said, 'Be strong, for thou wilt overcome everything with the virtue of thy God.' Having said this, he gave him the salutation of peace and rose up to heaven, and all the people of the land came to*

*our father and, throwing themselves at his feet, said, 'O light of life, teach us the path of salvation.' Taquelâ Haimanôt replied, 'Come, my children, follow me; believe in God who created you.' And they said, 'Yes, we believe {[f. 264v]} as you tell us.' And he baptized them in the name of the Father and of the Son and of the Holy Spirit. And afterwards he went to where the bodies lay of those whom the tree had killed and he prayed, saying, 'O Lord Jesus Christ, who raised Lazarus from the dead after four days and the son of the widow of Naim, Thou art God of the strong and resurrection of the dead; Thou canst do everything. Send Thy mercy from {heaven} <the heavens> so that these dead may arise.' And as dew came down from heaven onto the dead, they all arose, as sound as before, and with them {fifteen} <the> men who had died a long time before arose from their graves and made obeisance to the saint, throwing themselves at his feet. When he asked them when they had died, they replied that it had been in the time when Abrahâ and Azbahâ reigned. And Taquelâ Haimanôt asked them, 'Were you baptized in the name of Christ?' They replied that they did not know what baptism was and that they did not know Christ at that time. 'Well, whom did you worship?' asked the saint. They replied, 'A tree that was there and it spoke to us, saying, "I created you," and while we worshipped it we died and they took us to hell and we were left in the fire that never goes out.' Taquelâ Haimanôt asked them, 'Why did the god that you worshipped not deliver you?' They answered that he could not even deliver his own head. He asked them, 'How have you come here now?' They replied that, through his prayer, God's mercy had been sent over those dead people and that it had also embraced them, who had been beneath. 'We beseech you now, O saint of God, do not make us return again to those great torments in which we dwelt.' Taquelâ Haimanôt marvelled greatly when he heard this, and said to the people, 'Behold this miracle. If I had spoken to you, you would not have believed me. Here it has been recognized that your god can save neither himself nor others.' {[f. 265]} He also asked the others <[twenty-four]> who had arisen from the dead, 'And you, where have you been?' They replied <[f. 226/216]> that, when their souls had left their bodies, the evil angels were taking them to the fire and he had come on a fiery horse and fought them, and then Saint Michael had come down from {heaven} <the heavens>. 'And he said, "Give these souls to that man." And they released us at once. And you brought us back and now we are before you, as you see us. Tell us how we can save and deliver ourselves from these torments.' The saint said to them, 'Believe in God and be baptized in His name, so that you may attain eternal life.' They all replied, 'We believe in God; baptize us.' The saint rose up and baptized them in the name of the Father, the Son and the Holy Spirit. And 12,345[1] people were baptized that day, and Taquelâ Haimanôt stayed baptizing that day until the sun was about to set. And then he said Mass and gave them communion.*

*After that, Taquelâ Haimanôt called the fifteen men who had died previously and said to them, 'You were raised from the dead so that these people might see the virtue of my God. Go now and sleep until the day of common resurrection.' They then threw themselves at his feet, weeping and saying, 'Lord, do not send us back to that land of torments.' Taquelâ Haimanôt replied, 'Do not weep, for henceforth you will not go to the land of torments, but to {that} <the land> of peace, because whosoever believes in Christ and is baptized is saved, and whosoever*

---

[1] In this number and in five others in this narrative of the life of Takla Hāymānot, Páez uses the Portuguese word 'conto' (literally, 'million') apparently to represent the value of the Ethiopic symbol for '10,000' used in the text from which he was translating. The latter value, which is adopted here, corresponds to the numerals given in the Ethiopic text and English translation published by Budge (*Life of Takla Hâymânot*, I, p. 85 *et seq.* and II, f. 58.b.1 *et seq.*).

*does not believe is damned; and whosoever eats his flesh and drinks his blood shall have ever-lasting life.'* {[f. 265v]} *As he said that, they died, and the saint buried them and they went to everlasting life, as he had told them.*

*When day broke, many people, men and women, {old} men and boys, came to Taquelâ Haimanôt to {hear} <see> the marvels that God was working through His servant. And they said, 'Behold, we all believe in the God that you worship.' On hearing this, the saint gave many thanks to God and went down with them to the river that they call Meeçât and blessed the water and baptized them in the name of the Father, Son and Holy Spirit. That day 603,049 people were baptized. And the Holy Spirit came down in the shape of a white dove upon them, but on no one more than Taquelâ Haimanôt, and the faces of those who had been baptized shone brightly.*

*When he had finished baptizing them, he at once began to teach them clearly how God made {heaven} <the heavens> and the earth and all that is on it, <[f. 226v/216v]> and how He created Adam in His image and likeness, and how he was cast out of Paradise for eating of the forbidden fruit, and how God later punished his children with the flood because they had committed many sins, and no more than seven souls were saved, and to their descendants he gave the Law and prophets, and they did not keep the Law well. And later God Himself came down from heaven and was born of the Holy Virgin Mary, and at the age of thirty He was baptized by Saint John in the Jordan and, going out into the desert, He fasted for forty days and forty nights. And thus he told them all the mysteries. As they listened to these words, they entered their hearts like oil into bones and, throwing themselves at the saint's feet, they said, 'Thanks be to God, for He has given us the light of life.' And he gave them the body and blood of the Son of God.*

*When the prince of the land, who was called {[f. 266]} Derasguêd, heard what Taquelâ Haimanôt had done, he was very angry, because those who worshipped that tree used to give him 300 pounds of silver. When they told the saint that the prince was very angry, he said to his faithful, 'Bring axes and come with me.' And coming to the tree, which he had left stand-ing, he commanded it to fall, and it fell at once, and he told them to cut it up to make a church from it. Just then the prince arrived very haughtily and said to our father, 'Are you the one who is putting our land to waste?' The saint replied, 'I am not the one putting it to waste; instead it is being saved by means of a poor servant.' The prince said, 'If you are not putting my land to waste, who gave you permission to cut down this tree and lose the king his tribute?' And he looked so indignant that it seemed he would devour the saint. Even so, those men did not stop cutting it up, but a splinter flew up and caught him in the right eye. He fell down like a madman in great pain and shouted to his god, saying, 'Lord, I did not command it, nor did I come to cut down the tree, but this evil man who is unknown to us has put the land to waste and tried to take over thy command. Forgive me, Lord.' The demon then shouted from far away, saying, 'Derazguêd, Derazguêd, henceforth leave the land to this man, for I can do nothing with him, because he is very strong. What shall I tell you of the torments that I have found for his sake? I cannot save you from his hand, nor even myself. Today I tell you in truth that you and your peoples must serve him, for you will not see me again.' And saying that he disappeared.*

*<[f. 227/217]> When those who were present saw this, they were afraid and the prince told them, 'I believe in this man's God; you must beg him to forgive me for the arrogance that I showed him and heal me of this sickness.' They begged the saint insistently to {[f. 266v]} forgive him. He replied, 'If he does not believe in God with all his heart, he will not be healed*

*of his sickness.' They said that he had already declared that he believed. He then commanded them to bring him, and when he arrived he raised his voice, saying, 'I believe in your God; servant of God, heal me of this sickness.' Our father then touched his eye with his hand and it was healed at once. When the prince saw that he was healed, he threw himself at the saint's feet and said, 'Truly, your God is all powerful. Tell me how I can be saved.' The saint said to him, 'Believe in God with all your heart, and you and your household will find everlasting life.' The prince replied, 'I believe with all my heart.' The saint said to him, 'If you fully believe, rise up and cut this tree.' And he did so with great fervour. And they built a church in the land of Endeguên, in the place called Zateibêr, using that tree to make all the doors, windows, columns and everything else needed for the church. Then Taquelâ Haimanôt baptized the prince, his wife and all his household, and he gave him the name Bamina Christôs and his wife Acrôcia. And those who were baptized in the land of Catatâ numbered {645,387} <645,347>, because many came from many other lands on account of the fame of the miracles that the saint performed, and they were baptized.*

*As such a great multitude of people had gathered round our father, he sent word to the priests of his land of Zorêre saying, 'Come to me, because I have taken a large prize from the Devil and have brought many into the house of God, and I want you to watch over them.' They did so at once and when they arrived he put that church in their hands. And he travelled round that land of Catatâ for a long time teaching the faith of Christ, casting demons out of bodies and healing the sick. And when it was time to fast, he fasted for forty days and kept many other fasts without eating except on Sundays, and then only herbs {[f. 267]} from the field, making no difference between the sweet and the bitter; and when he had finished fasting he would return to the people to teach them the faith. He did this for three years, with Saint Michael always accompanying him. Once, when he was in <[f. 227v/217v]> the wilderness, he heard a voice from heaven that said, 'Taquelâ Haimanôt, Taquelâ Haimanôt.' He replied, 'Behold Thy servant', because he knew it was the word of God. He said to him, 'Go to the land of Damôt to do thine office. And in this wilderness a large church shall be built later by a son that will be born to thee from the Holy Spirit, who will be called Tadeus.'*

*When the fast was over, our father came out of the wilderness and gathered all the people of Catatâ together and said to them, 'Be firm in the faith of Christ that I have taught you. I am going to where my God has sent me. If His will be done, I shall return to you.' On hearing this, they began to weep, saying, 'To whom will you leave these new plants of yours? Who will give us the water of the doctrine of faith to drink? What father shall we find like you, guardian of the soul and body?' He replied, 'I cannot fail to do what my God commands me to do. Be not sad; dwell in the fear of God and hope in Him and He will do what you wish, because he who firmly believes in Him finds everything. Seek God and you will find Him; love Him with all your heart and with all your soul and love one another as yourselves and in that way you will know yourselves, as you are servants of God.' They said, 'Our father, if you leave us in flesh, do not leave us in spirit, because you are our support before God.' And as they all wept bitterly, he took his leave and went on his way, without wanting to accept anything from them. And where he came to sleep {[f. 267v]} that night, Christ Our Lord appeared to him and said, 'O my friend Taquelâ Haimanôt, be not afraid, because wherever thou goest I shall always be with thee.' And with that He disappeared. Continuing his journey, he arrived in the lands of Seoâ, where he preached the holy Gospel, and then he went down to Endestê and reached a large mountain called Oifât. Climbing to the top, he found many demons shouting loudly* and, as he made the sign of the cross, they all disappeared like smoke in the wind. And the saint spent the whole night in prayer.

When morning came, the people of the land came up the mountain with cattle and many kinds of food and they began to make offerings, as was their custom. When Taquelâ Haimanôt saw that he burned with zeal for God's honour and shouted out the names of the Father, the Son and the Holy Spirit, at which they were all very astonished. And he said to them, 'Why do you worship demons and ignore Him who created the heavens and the earth and everything in them?' They replied, <[f. 228/218]> very afraid, 'Lord, we have never heard these words in all our lives.' Our father said to them, 'Until now you have done this because you did not know; from now on worship God, lest you be damned.' They replied, 'If we stop worshipping our god, he kills our sons and daughters and destroys our lands; and that is why we worship him.' Taquelâ Haimanôt asked them, 'Where is your god, so I may look at him?' They replied, 'He does not show himself by day, only by night.' The saint said to them, 'He truly shows himself in the darkness because he abhors the light, so that his works cannot be seen; and in this you can recognize that he is all darkness.' And he asked them how they recognized him when he came to them. They replied that he came with a loud crash like {[f. 268]} thunder, dressed in fire, sitting on a wolf, and many others followed him on wolves, spitting fire from their mouths. The saint said, 'He is worse than his horse.[1] Let us wait for him to come. If he beats me, I shall worship him, and if not you shall worship my God.' They replied that they would worship Him, if he won. When it was already very late, he came on a wolf with the customary noise, and as he arrived Taquelâ Haimanôt made the sign of the cross, and straight away he and all those accompanying him fled and vanished like smoke, saying, 'Who is this man who persecutes us?'

All those who were there marvelled, and throwing themselves at the holy father's feet said, 'Truly your God is stronger than the strong; it is He who defeats them all.' The saint commanded them to rise and said to them, 'Be not afraid. Henceforth worship God the Father and His Son Jesus Christ and the Holy Spirit, because He does not like it when someone is lost, and so He waits for everyone to do penance. He does not want cows or goats slaughtered for him, because He does not eat their flesh or drink the blood of animals. Worship Him with all your heart, because He is God of every creature and there is no other God <in heaven> but He {in the heavens}, on earth or in the sea. He kills and gives life; He raises up and casts down. Believe in this King so that you may find everlasting life.' And he preached to them until dawn came. They said, 'If this god of ours that you defeated comes to kill our children and destroy our lands, what shall we do?' The saint replied, 'If you fully believe in God, he cannot reach you, because he is very weak. Go and call the people of the land, and let them bring all their sick {[f. 268v]} so that they can see the strength of my God, who will heal them.' They went with great joy and told the other inhabitants of the land what was happening. <[f. 228v/218v]> And then they gathered their sick, who were twelve cripples, thirteen hunchbacks, seven possessed by demons and ten blind people, and brought them to our Father Taquelâ Haimanôt. When they came in sight, the demons in them started shouting, 'What do you want of us? Why do you persecute us? Is it not enough that we have left you the land of Calâlgi and Catatâ? Where are we to flee from you? Leave us alone now; do not give us trouble and we shall leave of our

---

[1] 'Horse' (*faras*) is the term used for a person possessed by spirits in the possession rituals of the Ethiopian *Zār* cult.

own will.' The saint said to those bringing the sick, 'Come quickly.' And as they came, the
demons fled and he healed the rest of the sick.

When they all saw that they were healed, they threw themselves at the saint's feet, saying,
'Bless us, our father.' He replied, 'I shall not bless you without first baptizing you in the name
of my God.' They all said, 'Father, we shall do whatever you command; baptize us.' And the
saint baptized them in the name of the Father and of the Son and of the Holy Spirit and
commanded that they build a church, and afterwards he gave them the body and blood of
Christ in it, and Saint Michael assisted him like a deacon. He remained with them for nine
months, teaching them the faith, and then Saint Michael said to him, 'Rise up and go and do
what thy God has commanded thee.' He then gathered together the people of the land and
said, 'Be firm in the faith that I have taught you and love one another and be in peace, because
I am going to where my God commands me.' On hearing this, the people of the land wept
bitterly, saying, 'To whom will you leave us, our father and master?' And the saint departed
from them with many tears and went to the lands of Ennarêt and destroyed the idols, and he
went on {[f. 269]} to Oiraguê and Catâl and arrived in the land of Bilât, where he found a
notable sorcerer whom the people of the land had raised up as king and held in great veneration, because when he told them that there was to be some difficulty or some good, they would
find it. When our father went up to where he was seated on a gilded chair, richly attired and
with a large retinue, he approached him and struck him a blow that knocked him from his
chair, saying, 'O deceitful man, son of the Devil, why do you lead astray the people that Christ
redeemed with His blood?' He was unable to reply at all, but instead lay there trembling,
thinking a bolt of lightning had struck him.

When the king's servants saw what Taquelâ Haimanôt had done, they threw themselves
on him and struck him many blows until he bled from his nose and ears; then they beat him
with very thick sticks until they killed him, and they threw his body under a tree for the wolves
to eat. At this, Saint Michael came and said, 'Taquelâ Haimanôt, Taquelâ Haimanôt, rise
up.' And the saint rose up as if from sleep and as the angel touched his wounds he was healed,
and he said to him, 'Go and fight that <[f. 229/219]> sorcerer, for thou shalt win.' So the
saint went very confidently and found him again sitting on his chair and struck him another
blow that knocked him off his chair. He broke his hand in the fall and shouted for his servants,
who came and seized the saint and flogged him with chains until his bones showed, and they
asked, 'Where are you from? What office have you? Did we not kill you yesterday? Who raised
you up? Is your sorcerer perhaps stronger than ours?' {[f. 269v]} The saint said, 'In truth my
God is stronger than yours. I neither know nor came to do sorcery, but to remove yours. Nor do
I have to say to dogs where I come from; indeed, dogs are better than you, for they know their
lords.' They then flogged him again until they broke his body to pieces, and they threw him
dead into a cave; but Saint Michael raised him again as before. And he worked on them for
forty days without eating or drinking, but he was not able to lead them onto the path of truth.

After forty days, when Taquelâ Haimanôt saw the hardness of their hearts, he prayed to
God, saying, 'Lord Jesus Christ, Thou art He who sent me from my land to teach new peoples,
and wherever I go it is at Thy command. I have now come to these that know Thee not and
they have done me the evils that Thou knowest. Judge them, Lord, and command the earth to
swallow them up with Dathan and Abiron; show Thy strength over them.' Having finished
his prayer, he went up a mountain, where he found many sorcerers offering sacrifices to their
king. Going amidst them, he said in a loud voice, 'I command the earth, in the name of my
God, to open and swallow up these evil people.' And it opened at once and they and their king

*went down to hell alive. And Taquelâ Haimanôt praised the Lord, saying, 'Today thou hast given joy to my heart. Thou art truly God of gods and King of kings.' And then he went to where the sorcerers had been worshipping and found many gold and silver idols, and he smashed them with a stone. The next morning he heard a voice from heaven saying, 'There will be born to thee a spiritual son by the name of Anorêos; he will convert those that remain here and will build a church in this place.'*

*{[f. 270]} Our Father Taquelâ Haimanôt then left that land and went to Damôt, where he destroyed many idols, cast out demons and healed the sick, through which many were converted, including a prince who was called {Cafaraudîm} <Cafamandim>. But when the king of the land heard what was happening, he commanded that the saint and the prince be seized and brought to him. As they were being taken, the prince said <[f. 229v/219v]> to the saint, 'This king has been as if insane for twenty-five years because of a woman that he captured from the land of Seoâ, whom he wanted to marry, and so he had her taken with great honour to the door of his idol and, while I was there watching with a large crowd of people, there came a great thunderbolt and took her up to heaven. Many died of fright and the king has been left as if insane from that day to this. If you heal him, I think he will forgive us, otherwise he will have us killed.' The saint laughed and said, 'Fear not, for God will deliver us from this king's hand. As for that woman, I shall tell you later, when you behold the glory of God.' And when they arrived before King Matolomê, after much talking, he commanded that they be thrown {twice} off a high rock, and Saint Michael delivered them both, and for this and many other miracles that the Lord did for love of his servant, the king was converted. And the saint healed him of all his sickness, and so the king had it proclaimed that everyone should stop their worship of idols and should worship the God of Taquelâ Haimanôt, and that henceforth if anyone had an idol in his house he would be thrown off the rocks. When King Matolomê was baptized, 102,099 others were baptized as well, and the king was given the name Feça Seon.*

*After this, the king had many {[f. 270v]} churches built throughout his kingdom, but he had doubts about the resurrection of the dead. Taquelâ Haimanôt brought him many arguments and passages from Scripture to persuade him of it, but he was not satisfied, saying, 'How can it be that the body can be raised up again after it has been made dust? It is now fifteen years[1] since 1,000 men of my army and 300 sorcerers died. If you can make them rise again, then I shall believe.' And the saint asked, 'For what reason did so many men die?' 'Do not ask me that', answered the king; 'but make them rise up if you want me to believe.' 'Since you do not want to tell me', said the saint, 'I shall say it. You captured a woman from the land of Seoâ and, as you wanted to marry her, you gathered your men together before your idol in order to make her queen and to make her worship the idol, and while she was standing there among them all, there came what seemed like a thunderbolt from heaven and carried her away under your eyes. And those men died of that fright and you were left as if insane from that day until I healed you.' The king said, 'O saint of God, who told you that?' He replied, 'My God, who knows everything.' The king asked if he knew that woman's land. He replied, 'Not only the land, but her as well, because after she was taken from your presence, she gave birth to me.' The king marvelled and threw himself at his feet, <[f. 230/220]> making great obeisance to him and saying, 'I thought they had taken her to heaven.' Then the saint went to*

---

[1] It was 25 years, according to the previous paragraph and the account of how the soldiers died and the king was left insane (bk II, ch. 19, p. 446 above).

where those men had died and, having prayed, he said in a loud voice, 'Rise up, through the virtue of my Lord Jesus Christ.' And 1,000 men then emerged and threw themselves at the saint's feet, saying, 'Bless us, Lord, for we died because of your mother and now we rise again through the virtue of your arm.' The saint asked them, 'Where have you been?' They replied that they had been in the torments of hell and that even if 10,000 suns entered there they could not enlighten one man in that darkness. On hearing this, everyone was very afraid, and {[f. 271]} the king said to our father, 'Woe is us; does all this await us?' The saint said to him, 'Do you now believe in the resurrection of the dead?' He replied that he did. 'Tell me what I must do so as not to go to those torments.' The saint replied, 'Fear not, for henceforth you will not be damned, because he who believes in the Son of God will have everlasting life.' And he baptized those who had risen and commanded them to go throughout that land preaching the resurrection of the dead.

Taquelâ Haimanôt stayed in the lands of Damôt for twelve <months> and spread the faith of Christ as far as the River Gehon, and all the lands neighbouring Damôt believed in Christ through his doctrine. Then he went up a mountain and fasted for forty days without eating anything, other than some herbs of the field on Sundays, making no difference between the sweet and the bitter. And on Easter Saturday, at night, when it was midnight, Christ Our Lord, came down with Saints Michael and Gabriel, and His mother Mary and the twelve apostles and many saints from heaven, and said to him, 'How art thou, my friend Taquelâ Haimanôt? May the peace of My Father and the Holy Spirit be with you. Rejoice, for thy name is written in the Book of Life. I have come to give thee joy today, because thou hast given Me joy with so many souls that thou hast brought to Me. Whosoever gives bread or offers incense or even a cup of water in thy name passes with thee to the kingdom of heaven, and whomsoever thou callest in thy work, I shall deliver him. And He gave him a herb and water of life, saying, 'Eat and drink.' With that his soul rejoiced greatly, so that it seemed to him that he had not fasted a single day. He also said to him, 'Go to the land of Amharâ and wait there until I speak to thee and Saint Michael will be with thee.' And He kissed him on the mouth and, placing His hand over him, He blessed him and then went up to {[f. 271v]} heaven. Taquelâ Haimanôt said, 'Lord, blessed be Thy name, for Thou hast given so much grace to this Thy servant.'

After this, the saint went to King Feça Ceon (for he had called him that at his baptism)[1] and said to him, 'Be firm in the faith of Christ and be diligent <[f. 230v/220v]> in watching over the churches. I am going to where my God has commanded me.' On hearing this, the king wept bitterly and said, 'O our father, to whom do you leave your land that you delivered from the Devil and taught the holy faith?' The saint replied, 'I cannot fail to do my Lord's command.' And he then summoned all the priests, whom the king had previously brought captive from his land, and said to them, 'Keep your faith well and be diligent in watching over these sheep and teach them the truth and fear of God.' They replied, 'We shall go with you, because after God we have our hope in you.' The saint said, 'You cannot go. Watch over my sheep, for this is the will of God.' And with this he departed, and the king and all his army followed him, weeping. The saint said to them, 'Go back, my children, and do not weep, for although I leave you in flesh, I shall not leave you in spirit; I shall always remember in my prayers.' With this they took their leave and returned to their lands. And the saint, going on his way, came to the land of Zorerê, where previously he had converted many people, and they

---

[1] Interpolation by Páez.

*came out to receive him with great joy. And he had them bring out their sick and he healed them all by making the sign of the cross over them.*

*As Taquelâ Haimanôt continued his journey, he met a monk and asked him where he was from and where he was going. He replied that he was from Amharâ, but that he did not know where he was going. The saint said, 'God has sent you to me, so that you may guide me to your land. Turn back {[f. 272]} with me.' The monk replied, 'Why should God have sent me to you? I cannot turn back.' No matter how much the saint begged him, {he would not,} and he said to him, 'If God did not send you to me, go away, but if He did send you, He will stop you from going any further.' With that the saint went off and the monk remained there, unable to go one way or the other, and so he shouted to him to wait. At this, the saint heard a voice from heaven saying, 'Forgive him, because he did that without knowing.' So the saint went back and said to the monk, 'The Lord has forgiven you your sins.' The monk then threw himself at his feet and begged his forgiveness. The saint made him rise and they went on, talking about God's matters. They came to a house where they took shelter, and the lord of the house had a son possessed by a demon and begged them to pray for him, and the monk asked the saint very much to heal him, and so he made the sign of the cross, saying, 'Come out, accursed spirit, through the virtue of my Lord Jesus Christ, whom I worship.' And the demon came out, yelping like a dog, and the boy was healed. When his father saw this, he threw himself at the saint's feet and gave him many thanks <[f. 231/221]> and put them up that night with great joy. In the morning he announced the miracle, and so everyone brought their sick, who numbered thirty-nine, and they put them at the saint's feet and he healed them, at which everyone rejoiced, praising God who had given his servant such great virtue.*

*As Taquelâ Haimanôt moved on, that monk asked him on the journey if he was a man or an angel, because he marvelled at what he had seen him do. The saint replied, 'Do not say that, my brother. How can a little ash be an angel?' And he made the monk swear not to tell anyone what he saw on the journey. {[f. 272v]} Soon afterwards, they reached the monk's land and monastery, and the monks asked him, 'Where does this guest who is with you come from? He looks like an angel of God. When did you meet him?' He replied, 'I met him yesterday in the land of Ceoâ.' They said, 'How did you get here in two days?' He replied that he did not know, but they did not believe him, because it was a two-week journey. They entered the church and prayed, and slept together that night, and in the morning the monk took the saint to the abbot of the monastery, who was called Abba Michael. And when he saw the saint, he marvelled at the brightness of his face and, rising from his chair, he gave him the salutation of peace and made him sit near him and said, 'You are Taquelâ Haimanôt, in whom the Holy of Holies was praised.' The saint replied, 'My father, who told you the name of this sinner?' Abba Michael said, 'Last night the Holy Spirit told me your name and virtues. Stay here with me until the Lord calls you to do His bidding.'*

*Taquelâ Haimanôt then began to imitate the works of those saints and served everyone, occupying himself in arduous, humble things, fetching water and firewood on his back and grinding flour with his hands, through which he gave all his brothers rest, and they all blessed him. Despite all this work, he recited many Psalms and worshipped God every day, bowing his head to the ground 1,750 times, and sometimes many more. And he fasted all week, so that he became as dry as a stick. He continued thus for seven years, and at the end of that time they brought a man possessed by the Devil for Abba Michael to heal, but he was not able to cast out the Devil. The monks said to Abbot Michael, 'Taquelâ Haimanôt will heal him, if you command him to, {[f. 273]} because he is like an angel of God and has healed many people of their diseases by touching them.' And the monk who had come with him on his journey* <[f. 231v/221v]> *also recounted what he had seen. Then Abba Michael summoned him and, when he arrived, the Devil threw the man to the ground, and he lay there trembling. The abbot said to the saint, 'My son, heal this man, because God has given you leave.' The saint replied, 'How can I, a sinner, heal him? May God, whom you serve, heal him through your prayer.' And as he said this the Devil came out shouting, 'Is it not enough that I have left you the land of Ceoâ, that you come to Amharâ to persecute me? Where am I to flee from you? I cannot find rest anywhere.' And revealing himself to everyone in the shape of a monkey, he disappeared, vanishing like smoke, and never again returned to that man. And the saint said to the abbot, 'This man was healed through your prayer.' He replied, 'It was not through my prayer, but through your humility and the grace that you have been given.' And throwing himself at his feet, he asked him to tell the story of his life. And he told the brothers to go away, and when they were alone he recounted it all without concealing anything. On hearing this, Abba Michael gave thanks to God because he had brought him such a man, and he said to him, 'From now on, you will not occupy yourself in the offices that you have had until now, but with your brothers in the church.' He replied, 'I will not give up my office until I know God's will.' And so he continued as before.*

*This miracle soon became known throughout the lands of Amharâ, and they brought all their sick and cast them all at his feet and, when he put his hand over them, they were healed, at which all the monks marvelled. In addition, {[f. 273v]} when a nephew of* Abba *Michael died, he went with the monks and they made a great lament over the dead body. When they told Taquelâ Haimanôt that the abbot's nephew had died, he went there and wept with them and the abbot said to him, 'Man of God, if you will, you can raise this man from the dead, as I understand from the virtue that God has given you.' The saint replied, 'How can I, a sinner, raise the dead?' The abbot said to him, 'Do not say that, son, but pray to God, for He will hear you.' Then he prayed and recited the Gospel and then he shouted in a loud voice, saying, 'Rise up, by virtue of my Lord Jesus Christ, so that men may see His strength.' The dead man then rose up and threw himself at the saint's feet, saying, 'Forgive me, father, for I abhorred you previously with envy of your miracles, and I thought that when* <[f. 232/222]> *our father died you would take his place, and now you have taken me from hell and given me life.' The saint said to him, 'God is merciful and forgives us all, but you did not do well.' Those who were present marvelled greatly and praised God, and all the people of the land honoured the saint and held him in great veneration.*

*When Taquelâ Haimanôt saw the honours that they were doing him, he was very sad and wept bitterly, and he spoke to Christ Our Lord, saying, 'Lord, why did I show these things? Why do they honour me in vain? Lord, send me now somewhere else, where I may save my soul with quietude.' As he said that, Saint Michael appeared to him and said, 'How art thou, my {[f. 274]} friend Taquelâ Haimanôt? Behold, God commands thee to go to the church of Saint Stephen, the first martyr, which is in Haic,[1] and there thou shalt find a holy man who is called* Abba *Iesus. He will make thee the yoke of the religion. Come, for I shall guide thee.' Saying this, the angel passed on. {And the} saint went to Abbot Michael and said to him, 'Behold, my things have become known here. Give me permission, father, to go where God commands me to go, and remember me in your prayers.' When he heard this, Abba Michael wept bitterly, saying, 'In what have I displeased you, my son, or in what have your brothers*

---

[1] See Glossary (Saint Stephen's/Dabra Esṭifânos).

*upset you?' He replied, 'O my holy father, they have not upset me in anything; all that is taking me is God's command.' And all the brothers gathered together, weeping and begging him not to leave them. The saint replied, 'Forgive me, brothers, I cannot fail to fulfil God's commandment. Bless me.' And they said, 'God bless you and straighten your path. Do not forget us in your prayers.' He answered, 'How can a sinner profit my holy fathers? I just say to you to have patience, humility and fear of God in everything, because these three things lead to everlasting life, and guard yourselves against the envy, pride and scorn of others.'*

*With this Taquelâ Haimanôt took his leave, having spent ten years with them. As he went away, Saint Michael guided him by carrying a pillar of light in front, and he went thus until he came to the place to which he had been sent. On arriving at the shore of the lake on which the monastery stands, he found no boat to carry him across, and he prayed to God. Then Saint Michael appeared to him clearly, walking on the water, and said to him, 'Come, follow me.' So he stepped forward and they both crossed over the <[f. 232v/222v]> water as if{[f. 274v]} it were dry. The angel entered the church and went to the abbot, who was called* Abba Iesus, *and said to him, 'Behold, a man of God is at the church door. Have him come in and welcome him and give him a monk's habit.' And with that he disappeared. At that moment the door-keeper entered and said that there was a man at the church door and he did not know how he had come across. 'Call him in', said the abbot, 'for his coming is God's work.' He came in, and when the abbot saw him he marvelled at the light of his face and the grace that was in him and, rising from his chair, he gave him the salutation of peace, saying, 'Welcome, man of God.' And then he asked him how he had come and for what. He replied that he had come at God's command so that he might give him the habit, and soon afterwards the abbot gave it to him. After that he occupied himself in prayer and reading the Psalms, and he worshipped God night and day 30,950 times until he even sweated blood like water, and he fasted all week, eating nothing but a few herbs of the field on Sundays.*

*Taquelâ Haimanôt remained there in this manner for many years and worked night and day, remembering what Christ had said: 'If any man minister to me, let him follow me; and where I am, there also shall my minister be.'[1] While he was exercising himself in these things, the angel of God came and took him to a house that shone more brightly than the sun, so broad and long that even if the people of the whole world had gathered there they would not have filled it. And it had many columns of various colours and so resplendent that they took the sight from one's eyes, and in each one of those columns there appeared all the others as if in a mirror, and the floor was like glass and the ceiling shone like the sun. On coming to the middle of the house, he was afraid, because he saw three chairs and the one in the middle was larger and more{[f. 275]} beautiful than the others, and over them was a kind of rainbow, and on the middle chair was a garment of light with a tongue of fire, and on it was written 'Alleluia to the Father, alleluia to the Son, alleluia to the Holy Spirit'. And on the right-hand chair there were seven crowns, each one different from the others. As he was very afraid at seeing that house, the angel said to him, 'Be not afraid, for I am commanded to explain the things of this house to thee.' And at once all his fear was removed, and he asked the angel how large that house was and who dwelt in it. And he replied, 'First see what thou hast not yet seen and then I shall tell thee who its lord is.' When he saw many names written on the columns, <[f. 233/223]> he asked who they were whose names were written there, and how many columns there were and 'What are those chairs for?' The angel answered him, 'This house is*

---

[1] John 12:26.

*thine and the middle chair and the garment on it and the crowns are thine, and thy sons who will come after thee will sit on the chairs on the right hand and on the left hand. The columns on the right hand number 450,000 and the ones on the left the same, and the names written on them are of the children that thou shalt have in spirit, until the end of the world.'* He replied, *'Who am I, a sinner, to achieve such grace?'* The angel said to him, *'God gives grace to whomsoever He wishes.'*

After that, the angel took him up to heaven and made him enter within the curtain. And he stood in front of the throne of the <Holy> Trinity and he worshipped and heard a voice from the throne, which said, *'Taquelâ Haimanôt, Taquelâ Haimanôt, may thy lot be with My twenty-four priests.'* And they gave him a gold thurible like theirs and his glory was like theirs and his vestment was like theirs; and he clearly saw {[f. 275v]} God in the Trinity, and He said to him, *'As thou hast loved Me, so I shall love thee, and as thou hast honoured Me, so I shall honour thee, and I shall make thy name exalted and honoured. In truth I tell thee that whosoever believes in thy prayer shall be saved through love of thee, and whosoever offers what he can in thy memory, I shall make him great in heaven and on earth, and whosoever finds himself in some temptation and calls out thy name, I shall deliver him from it, and whosoever serves thy church, I shall {pay} <serve> him with My seven archangels, and wherever the book of thy miracles is read and thy name is called, there shall be peace and mercy for ever.'* On hearing this, the saint worshipped and glorified Him, and said, *'Thanks be to Thee, Lord, who hast given me all this by Thy will and not for my works.'* And then the angel brought him back to where he had been before.

With these things his heart lit up so much in the love of God that he did not sleep, and he occupied himself night and day in reciting the Psalms and reading the books of the prophets and apostles. While he was like this, there came to him the desire to seek other holy lands and to discover the custom and perfection of a monk. And at this the angel who always watched over him shone before him and said to him, *'Go and do as thou hast thought.'* Taquelâ Haimanôt asked him where he should go. And he said to him, *'Go to the land of Tigrê and climb a mountain called Damô and there thou shalt find a holy man by the name of Ioannî, and from his hand thou shalt take the cowl and* azquemâ' (this is always worn <[f. 233v/223v]> instead of the scapular),[1] *for until then he had taken no more than the habit. When he heard this, he went to his spiritual father and told him of his desires and what the angel had said to him, and for that reason* Abba Iesus wept bitterly, saying, *'Why are you leaving me? I did not look on you as a son, but as an honoured father; but, since it is so, go in peace and take the cowl {[f. 276]} and* azquemâ *in that monastery. And later you will give them to me and you will be my father. Wait today, because there is no man to take you to the other side of the lake.'* He replied, *'There is no man greater than God. If He is with me, there is no one who can block my way, nor water or anything else.'* And with this he got ready to go, and the abbot accompanied him to the edge of the water; Saint Michael was there already and said to him, *'Come, follow me.'* And they went across the water as if on dry land. When Abba Iesus saw that he marvelled greatly and said, *'Lord, great are Thy miracles in Thy saints.'* And he returned to his house praising God.

Taquelâ Haimanôt went on his way, having stayed there for ten years, and he reached the monastery of Mount Damô, which is of one of those nine saints who came from Rum and Egypt during the reign of Alamidâ, the son of Seladobâ, before Jazêm. Those nine are stars of

---

[1] Interpolation by Páez.

*light that illuminated all the lands; some of them sowed in the morning and reaped in the afternoon, others brought water in sieves without spilling it, and they performed many other miracles. When Taquelâ Haimanôt arrived at the monastery, Abbot Ioannî asked him where he had come from and he replied that it was from a distant land. He asked him what he was called and who had given him that monk's habit. He answered that his name was Taquelâ Haimanôt and the habit had been given to him by* Abba Iesus, *who dwelt on an island in a lake.* Abba Ioannî *said, 'In truth, you are the son of my son, because I engendered him in spirit.' And he blessed a cowl and an* azquemâ *and gave them to him. As our father took it, he began to perform the miracles of those nine saints, as if he had begun to be a novice without knowing how to perform miracles, and he prophesied things that were going to happen well in advance, and thus* {[f. 276v]} *he was like the angels in their glory, the prophets in their spirit and the martyrs in being cast down from rocks, and he adapted to all those with whom he dealt and brought them to the path of salvation.*

*Taquelâ Haimanôt spent twelve years in that monastery. And at the end of that time, the angel of God appeared to him and said, 'Leave here and visit all the monasteries in the land of Tigrê and the saints in the desert, because in them* <[f. 234/224]> *thou shalt find profit.' He went at once to* Abba Ioannî *and told him what the angel had said to him. He replied, 'You came here first at the angel's command, now go likewise. God be with you.' And he accompanied him as far as the descent from the rock, which is so high that thirty cubits of rope are needed to reach the ground. And while the abbot and monks remained at the top, our father began to descend the rope, and as it broke, he was given six wings and he flew six leagues away. Seeing this, the monks returned to their monastery, praising God. And our father went into the desert of Oalî, where he found many holy monks. Gathering all together they asked him, 'Why have you come here, since you are much more honoured than we are?' The saint replied, 'Do not say that, my fathers, for you are much more than I am.' They said, 'In truth, we have never seen a man who has been given as much grace on earth as you. Many saints will be born of you and you will be the father of many peoples.' The saint replied, 'May {my} God's will be done.' And he stayed with them for forty-five days, fasting. And then he took his leave and went to the monastery of Haoazên and asked the elders there for their blessing. They replied, 'It is not becoming for us to bless the man who has been blessed by the hand of God; but bless us with your holy hand, for {the Lord} God has sent you for this.' And they begged him so much that he gave them his blessing and, receiving their blessing as well, he took his leave.*

{[f. 277]} *From there, he visited other monasteries and healed many sick people until he reached the Erterâ Sea (*scilicet*, Red Sea)[1] and, finding no ship on which to cross it, he prayed and the angel Saint Michael appeared to him, as was his custom, walking on the water. And as he followed him, they both crossed it in one hour and, arriving on the other side, the saint found a dead man and blessed him, saying, 'O {dead} man, if you are a Christian, rise up in the name of my Lord Jesus Christ, whose cross I bear.' And the dead man rose up at once, as if from a dream, and said, 'I am a Christian of the people of Sion and I worship God. My death was from lack of water, as I was going to Jerusalem.' The saint said, 'If you are going to Jerusalem, follow me.' And he went with him as far as the sepulchre in Jerusalem, the patriarch of Alexandria being* Abba Michael. *And he went to him and made obeisance to him and, and he said to him, 'Welcome, man of God, Taquelâ Haimanôt.' The saint replied, 'Bless me, father, for I have come to receive your blessing. Who told you my name?' He said, 'The*

---

[1] Interpolation by Páez.

*angel told me it today.' And he gave him his blessing, saying, 'May you be blessed in the bless-*
*ing of my fathers the apostles and in the blessing of my fathers the patriarchs who sat on the*
*chair <[f. 234v/224v]> of Mark.' And the saint kissed his hands and feet and the patriarch*
*kissed him on the head and told him to go back to his land, for he was to be the father of many*
*monks and many churches would be built in his name. The saint replied, 'I have not come to*
*go back, but to die in your hands.' The patriarch told him, 'Go back, because God has kept that*
*lot for you.' He replied, 'So be it, I shall do what you command me, for you are my father under*
*God.' And, taking his leave of him, he visited all the holy places {[f. 277v]} and then went to*
*the desert of Cihôt and Azquêtez and received the blessing of the monks who dwelt there.*

*While Taquelâ Haimanôt was with those saints, the angel of God appeared to him and*
*said, 'What sayest thou, Taquelâ Haimanôt?' He replied, 'I want to stay here.' The angel said*
*to him, 'It is not thy lot: go to the land of Ethiopia and give the monk's habit to those who ask*
*thee for it, because only those chosen for heaven will come to thee.' And so he returned to*
*Ethiopia, bringing with him that man that he had raised up. Arriving in Tigrê, land of*
*Ethiopia, that man said to the holy father, 'Give me the monk's habit, for I am determined to*
*serve God.' Our father replied to him, 'Can you do the work of the saints?' He said, 'Our God,*
*who can do everything, will give me strength.' And so he gave him the habit and gave him the*
*name Araiacagahú, and he persevered always with great saintliness. Afterwards, he gave the*
*habit to many men and built many monasteries in the land of Tigrê which are called by his*
*name to this day. And from there he went twice more to visit the holy places in Jerusalem and,*
*on the last time, the patriarch Abba Michael said to him that he should not return again, but*
*he should settle in some place in the desert. And so, on coming to Tigrê, he climbed up to the*
*monastery of Mount Damô and received the blessing from Abbot Ioannî. And from there he*
*went to a mountain called Cantorâr, where he fasted for forty days, and he decided to remain*
*there, because the land was deserted, but the angel of God appeared to him, 'What art thou*
*thinking, Taquelâ Haimanôt? This is not thy lot; later many sons of thine will dwell here.*
*Go to Abba Iesus and do what he tells you.'*

*Very early the next day he went as the angel had commanded and, arriving at the edge of the*
*lake, he found no boat and went across above the water. He came to Abba Iesus, who was very*
*joyful to see him, and he {[f. 278]} asked him who had given him the cowl and azquemâ. He*
*replied, 'Lord, Abba Ioannî of Mount Damô.' He said, 'Then give me the cowl and azquemâ,*
*because I wish to receive it from your holy hands.' And Taquelâ Haimanôt <[f. 235/225]>*
*gave it to him, because the angel had commanded that he should do what he told him. And so*
*the series of our {saints} <fathers> is this: Abba Anthony was given the monk's habit by the*
*angel Saint Michael; Abba Anthony gave the monk's habit to Abba Macarius; Abba*
*Macarius gave it to Abba Pachomius; Abba Pachomius gave it to Abba Aragoaî; he came to*
*Ethiopia and gave the habit to Abba Christôs Bezâna; he gave it to Abba Mascal Môa; he*
*gave it to Abba Ioannî; and he gave it to Abba Iesus and to Abba Taquelâ Haimanôt. And*
*then Taquelâ Haimanôt gave cowl and azquemâ to Abba Iesus, as we have said.*

*Taquelâ Haimanôt took his leave of Abba Iesus and went to the land of Amharâ. And,*
*arriving in Arabihâ, he found there a high mountain which is called Dadâ, which he climbed*
*with his disciple Araicagahû, and he found a very large serpent, which opened its mouth and*
*was about to swallow the saint, but he made the sign of the cross and it fell into three pieces. He*
*told his disciple to measure its length, and he found it was 175 cubits. Then the people of the*
*land who worshipped that serpent came and, finding our father at prayer, they asked him how*
*he had come up there and whether he had cast out the serpent that they worshipped. He*

*replied that he had climbed up by God's will and that he had not cast out the serpent, but that he had killed it by God's virtue, and his disciple would show it to them. They all went with him and marvelled, and they asked the disciple how he had killed it. He replied that his master had made the sign of the cross and it had died at once, at which they were very afraid. And they went to the king of the land and told him that a very handsome monk was on the mountain* {[f. 278v]} *and that he had killed the serpent that they worshipped. The king went with them and, when he arrived, he said to our father, from afar, 'Man of God, give me leave to approach.' The saint replied, 'Come.' As he came close, he made obeisance and asked him to give him his blessing. The saint* {said} <replied>, *'I shall not bless you without knowing what* {faith} <law> *you hold.' He replied, 'I am a Christian by name, but I worshipped this serpent. When I heard how you killed it with the sign of the cross, I realized that God is with you and therefore I have come to do what you command me to do.' The saint said, 'When you stop worshipping the Devil and are baptized in the name of my God, then shall I bless you.' He replied, 'Baptize me, father, and give me your blessing.' Then the saint went down to the River Zohâ and, blessing the water, he baptized him and 3,000 men, apart from women and children,* <[f. 235v/225v]> *and gave them communion and commanded that they should make a church on the mountain where he killed the serpent, in honour of the four evangelists, which stands there to this day.*

*While he was here, Taquelâ Haimanôt heard a voice from heaven telling him, 'Taquelâ Haimanôt, go to the land of Ceoâ, because few of the faithful that thou didst gather there are left. Visit them and teach the faith, as before, and thy grave shall be there. And thy sons will multiply like the sands of the sea and the stars of heaven, and a monastery like Jerusalem will be built in thy name, and thy name will be heard throughout the land.' Then the saint called all the people of the land and said to them, 'I am going where my God commands me. Keep his commandments well so that you may be well in soul and body. And may my son Araicagahû be your father in my name.' When they heard this, they wept bitterly and his disciple begged him with many tears to take him with him, but the saint said to him, 'I am leaving you by God's command. This is your lot, for ever.' And he left him his* {[f. 279]} *cross and staff, saying that he would be the father of many religious. And with that he took leave of everyone and set off for Ceoâ. And everywhere that he passed, he taught the faith and said, 'Do penance, because the kingdom of heaven is coming; blessed are those who believe in the Son of God; blessed are those who weep for their sins, because they shall be saved from the torments.' And when they heard his words, many were baptized. When the saint came to Ceoâ, he gave the monk's habit to sixteen, including a cousin of his, the son of one of his father's brothers. Later, as he was walking with a disciple of his beside a lake, an evil spirit came out of it and began to torment his disciple. Our father then made the sign of the cross, saying, 'Come out of my son, evil spirit.' And he fled from him at once and, as he was about to jump back into the water, the saint made the sign of the cross and he remained on the bank, unable to jump in. Our father came up and took hold of him, saying, 'Why do you dare to enter my son? What is your name?' He answered, 'Because I thought you were like other men. My name is Baharâ Aliâm.' Our father asked him if he wanted to go with him or stay where he had been before. He replied, 'When you made the sign of the cross, I lost my power; I can no longer go back to where I was.' So Taquelâ Haimanôt took him with him and circumcised him and, taking him to a church, gave him the name of Christôs Hareiô (scilicet* 'Christ Has Chosen Him').[1] *After he*

---

[1] Interpolation by Páez.

*had served there for some* <[f. 236/226]> *time, he gave him the monk's habit and he was loved by God all his life until he died and entered the kingdom of heaven.*

{[f. 279v]} *Soon afterwards,* Abuna *João came to Ethiopia and summoned Taquelâ Haimanôt and wanted to make him bishop and give him half of Ethiopia, but he would not accept, saying that such dignity was not becoming for a sinful man such as he. And after staying there for three weeks, he received the* abuna's *blessing and returned home. When he converted a sorcerer's son, the father was very angry and gathered many sorcerers, and they came to kill the saint, some growling like bears, others roaring like lions and barking like dogs. But the saint came out and went among them and said in a loud voice, 'In the name of God whom I worship, I command the earth to open and swallow up these workers of evil.' At once it opened and swallowed them up, and it became known throughout the land of Ceoâ, and they received his doctrine with great love as far as the land of Guerareâ. Many demons also came to his door screaming, at which his disciples were very afraid, and the saint came out and made the sign of the cross and they fled, saying, 'You have shamed us.' Later, while he was at prayer, a two-horned serpent came to him and was about to swallow him, but when he made the sign of the cross it split down the middle and fell dead. He then called his disciples and told them to measure it, and it was seventy cubits long, and he affirmed to his disciples that Christ had commanded him to tell them that anyone who killed a serpent on a Thursday or a Sunday would have forty years of sins forgiven.*

*A prince whom our father had converted was sick and, when the hour* {[f. 280]} *of his death was upon him, he said, 'I see my Father Taquelâ Haimanôt and you others do not see him; thanks be to God who has shown him to me.' And then he died, while our father was a long way from there. Many saints also bear witness that he visits his children at the hour of their death, and all the souls who call for him, be they righteous or sinners, go to him, because the soul of a righteous man does not enter its inheritance until it comes to him and, on seeing him, the soul cries out, saying, 'My father, my father', and he replies, 'Behold your father', and then it comes to him* <[f. 236v/226v]> *and after that enters its inheritance. And the soul of the sinner is not taken to hell without first coming to our father, and when it comes to him it cries out, saying, 'My father, my father', and when he sees it, if he finds some good work such as calling for the ancient fathers or for him, he pleads with his God in accordance with the opinion he has formed and makes it go to everlasting life.*

*When Taquelâ Haimanôt was old and unable to walk from one place to another teaching the faith as had been his custom, he made a hut in the desert, so low and narrow that it was only big enough for him to stand up inside. And in the walls he put more iron nails with very sharp points to the inside, so that two points pricked him in the back, two in one side and two in the other and two in the chest. And so he stood inside without leaning one way or the other for many years, without eating or drinking except some herbs and water on Sundays, so that eventually one foot rotted and fell off, and his disciples took it and wrapped it in a cloth and buried it in the church near the altar. Then he stood on the other foot for seven years, and for four he did not drink water, so that he was nothing more than skin stuck to his bones. At this point Our Lord Jesus Christ came to him and, with Him, Our Lady* {[f. 280v]} *and fifteen prophets, twelve apostles and many saints from heaven clothed in light, and He said to him, 'How art thou, My friend Taquelâ Haimanôt? I have come today to take thee to the rest and joy that will have no end. I say to thee, in truth, that whosoever gives alms in thy memory and calls on thy name, I shall forgive him, and not only him but his descendents to the tenth generation. And whosoever builds a church in thy name, I shall build it for him in the kingdom of* heaven. And whosoever writes the book of thy miracles, or has it written, believing in it, I shall write his name in the Book of Life. And whosoever takes in some guest in thy name, I shall take in when he comes to Me. And whosoever gives food and drink in thy name, I shall give him the bread of life to eat and the spring of blood that issued from My side to drink. And whosoever celebrates thy feast day with joy, I shall seat him with Me at the feast of 1,000 years. And whosoever offers incense, wine and oil to the church, I shall accept his prayer and forgive his sins. And whosoever visits thy tomb, I shall reward him as if he had visited my tomb in Jerusalem.' Our father replied, 'I give thanks to Thee, my Lord, who hast done me so many mercies. They are not for my merits, but for the love that Thou hast for men. Where, Lord, dost Thou command that my body be buried?' The Saviour said to him, 'It shall be buried here for {fifty-seven} <fifty-four> years and then this house shall fall and here, to one side, thy sons shall build a great monastery in thy name, and they shall translate thy body to it. And I shall watch over those who will be there and hear their prayers, and those of thy sons that die in these deserts I shall count among the martyrs.' <[f. 237/227]> And so saying, He gave him the salutation of peace, kissing him three times, and rose up to heaven in great glory.

Taquelâ Haimanôt ordered all {[f. 281]} his sons to gather. 'Behold, the wedding feast has arrived: make yourselves ready to go in your wedding garments and be not like the one who did not wear a wedding garment. He who does not wear the garment of good works shall not go in to the celestial wedding, because my Lord Jesus said to me today that the time of my death has arrived and that some of you will go with me.' When his disciples heard this, some of them rejoiced and others wept because he had to leave them. Our father exhorted them to scorn the world and its things and charged them to love one another, because the love of the spirit cleanses the flesh and soul, and if they kept that they would truly be his sons. He ordered Elçâ to take his place and be father to them. And as he said this, his sickness became much worse. And that night, 27th August, there came a light and a fragrance so great and sweet that it took the heart, and Christ Our Lord appeared to him with His Mother and Saint Michael and Saint Gabriel and twenty-four priests with thuribles in their hands and many angels with candles. And when our father saw the Saviour, he worshipped Him, kneeling as if both his legs were sound. And the Saviour said to him, 'O My friend, all thy works are written in Jerusalem.' And as He said that, the soul left Taquelâ Haimanôt's body and Christ Our Lord received it and said, 'Pure soul, come to Me.' As He rose up, the angels sang, 'May he who worked in the world live for ever. This is the day that the Lord made: let us enjoy it and rejoice in Him.' And so they took him. And he came into his inheritance for ever, and the Saviour gave him the garment that the angel had shown him, with the tongue of fire that spoke of divinity and the seven crowns on account of his faith and other virtues. He lived in this world for 103 years and four days.

All his sons were left weeping, and they wrapped his body in a shroud and buried him, with two priests singing, as is the custom. And three days later {[f. 281v]} a deacon died, who was a cousin of our father by the name of Amd Mascâl, and they wrapped him in a shroud and took him to be buried. And when they had finished the office of the deceased, he moved, and so they opened the shroud and asked what it had been. He replied, 'I died, as you saw, and I was taken before the Lord of truth, and from there they took me to our Father Taquelâ Haimanôt and I saw him with so much glory that human tongue cannot describe it, <[f. 237v/227v]> and his crown shone seven times more brightly than the sun. And he commanded me to tell you, "Let Elçâ come to me and Phelipe take his place, because in his time my things will become manifest in all the earth."' As he said this, his soul left his body *again and they buried him. And three months later Elçâ died and his disciples put our Father Phelipe in his place, as they had been commanded, and the grace of Taquelâ Haimanôt was shown in him, because from him there came fourteen shepherds who manifested the faith and ensured that it was kept.*

*May the prayer of our Father Taquelâ Haimanôt, honoured master, deliver us from the strength of the enemy and from evil things for ever and at all times. Amen.*[1]

Up to here are words from the history of Taquelâ Haimanôt, in which there is no lack of apocryphal things, as there is in many of their histories. And if he was a saint, as all Ethiopians hold for certain, it is clear to see that some worse things have been added to justify their errors. For instance, when he went to be ordained to say Mass, he said to Patriarch Guerlôs that they had made another faith and {another custom} <other customs> of the Church by baptizing boys before circumcising them, and the patriarch gave him his blessing and said, 'Because you are zealous of God's things, like Elias the prophet of Israel, you will be a new apostle.' And after he had ordained him to say Mass, he made him prior of all the lands of Ceoâ and gave him his powers for that purpose. It seems that they added this in order to justify circumcision, to which most of them cling very strongly, and to ensure that {[f. 282]} the common people would not give up being circumcised, since that man that they all hold to be a great saint says that it is making another faith to baptize boys without circumcising them. There is also that fabulous tale that, as he was walking beside a lake, a demon came out of it, entered his disciple and began to torment him; when Taquelâ Haimanôt saw that, he made the sign of the cross and the demon fled at once. As he was about to jump back into the water, he made the sign of the cross again and the demon remained on the bank, unable to jump in. Taquelâ Haimanôt came up and asked him if he wanted to go with him or stay where he had been before, and he replied, 'When you made the sign of the cross, I lost my power; I can no longer go back to where I was.' So Taquelâ Haimanôt took him with him and circumcised him and, after he had served for some time, he gave him the monk's habit, and when he died he went to heaven. A monk of Taquelâ Haimanôt's Order gave me an answer to this, that the one that was in the lake was not a demon but a human sorcerer and he lived in the water by means of the devil's art, but the name <[f. 238/228]> that the history gives him, which is *ganên*, just means 'evil spirit', and if he had not been one he could hardly have entered Taquelâ Haimanôt's disciple, nor would he have said 'Come out of my son, evil spirit', as is recounted there.

It is not surprising that they added this, because they often do so in their books so that they can later justify their errors, even in the holy councils. When they find words against them in the {book} <books> of the saints, they remove them, as they did in the monastery of Agçum in the kingdom of Tigrê, where, because Father Patriarch Andre de Oviedo took some authorities from those books with which to refute their errors, many monks gathered together and scratched out everything that they thought was against them. And soon after I arrived, I went to see those books for the same purpose as the father patriarch, and a monk, who was a friend of mine, told me this and showed me many passages where

[1] According to Cerulli, Páez must have used the so-called long version of Takla Hāymānot's hagiography. A summary of his hagiography was published by Budge, who added some variants of the text (Budge, *Life of Takla Hâymânôt*). See Cerulli, 'Introduction', p. vii. For other editions of the story, see Conti Rossini, 'Il gadla Takla Haymanot secondo la redazione Waldebbana'.

words had been scratched out, and as the books are made of parchment they can do this easily. Moreover, since I have been here, {[f. 282v]} a book that they call *Haimanôt Abbô*,[1] which means 'Faith of the Fathers' and is considered a great authority among them, used to say that the Holy Spirit proceeds from the Father and from the Son, and they have scratched out this word ('and from the Son'); and in the Nicene Council they have added 'proceeds from the Father and not from the Son', and many of them stubbornly defend this.

---

[1] See Glossary (*Haimanôt Abbô*/*Hāymānota Abbāw*).

# CHAPTER XX

## Which deals with the monastery that they call Dêbra Libanôs

Formerly in Ethiopia there were many renowned monasteries with <very> large revenues and large numbers of monks but, because of the damage that the Moors did to them at the time of a captain who came from the kingdom of Adêl, whom they called Grânha, who was killed by the Portuguese who came here with Dom Christovão da Gama in 1541, as we said at the end of the first book, and because of the destruction that was caused later by some heathens that they call Gâlas, who have taken a large part of the empire, many monasteries have closed down entirely and others are in such decline that, compared with what they used to be, there is hardly anything left of them apart from their names. Those that still have some substance are that of Bisân, of the family of *Abba* Stateûs, which is in the kingdom of Tigrê, a day's journey from the port of Maçuâ; and, five or six days' journey inland from there, the one that they name after *Abba* Guerimâ; and, some two <[f. 238v/228v]> and a half leagues from there, another in Agçum belonging to monks of *Abba* Taquelâ Haimanôt. And these monasteries still have not even a third of the monks that they used to have. In the lake of Dambiâ, among other islands, there are three called Dagâ, Çanâ and Dêbra Mariam, and each of them has its monastery of *Abba* Taquelâ Haimanôt. In the kingdom of Gojâm, there is one called Dimâ and, nearby, another of the family of *Abba* Stateûs {[f. 283]} which they call Dêbra Ore, and another called Calalô. I shall leave out the rest, of which there are many, because they are not so well known and because I only mean to deal with Dêbra Libanôs monastery and Alleluia monastery, of which we shall speak later, since they are the most famous that there have ever been in Ethiopia.

Dêbra Libanôs (which has always been the foremost of all the monasteries in this empire) means 'monastery of Lebanon', because *dêber* means 'monastery', although it also means 'mountain'. <but because they ordinarily build monasteries on mountains in Ethiopia, for that reason they also came to call the monastery> Thus they call Mount Tabor *Dêbra* Tabor and the Mount of Olives *Dêbra* Ceît. Some think instead that *dêber* properly means 'mountain', but because they ordinarily build monasteries on mountains in Ethiopia, for that reason they also came to call the monastery *dêber*. And when they want to say 'the monastery of such-and-such a place', they add this letter 'a' and say *dêbra*. However it may be, Dêbra Libanôs is the same as monastery of Lebanon. It is situated on the flat top of a large, secure mountain in the kingdom of Xâoa and, as its monks now affirm, it was built by a monk by the name of Ezechias, fifty-seven years after the death of *Abba* Taquelâ Haimanôt. His history also bears witness to this, because at the end it says that, when he was about to die, Christ Our Lord appeared to him; he asked Him where He commanded that his body should be buried, and the Saviour said to him, 'It shall be buried here for fifty-seven years and, after this time, this house shall fall and here, to one side, thy sons shall build a great monastery in thy name, and they shall translate thy body to it, and I shall watch over those who will be there.' And the monks say that it happened like that, and later an emperor {[f. 283v]} made the church much larger as it was the burial place of Taquelâ Haimanôt. But this monastery building is not like the monasteries of our Europe, because each monk lives in a house by himself, and ordinarily the houses <[f. 239/229]> are very small, round and roofed with straw, so that the monastery looks like a village. And all the other monasteries in Ethiopia are like this, but some have a circular fence and formerly women could not go inside the fence, but now few monasteries keep to this.

The histories do not say how many monks there used to be in that monastery, and they themselves do not know either; some old monks and the one who is now like their general told me that formerly there were many monasteries in that district subordinate to this one, and that the number of monks in them all would have been 10,000 or more, but they did not know the exact number of those who used to live inside the monastery compound. It therefore seems that when they say that Dêbra Libanôs had 9,000–10,000 monks it does not mean that they all lived within the monastery compound, but that they were also counting the ones in the monasteries that were subordinate to it in the surroundings. Nor do they now know how much income it had; they just say that the emperors gave them many good, extensive lands and the abbot {of the monastery} took a certain part of them and the rest he shared among the monks, so that each one knew which lands were his and he had them worked and collected the produce in his house, and from it he fed and clothed himself and spent it as he saw fit. As for the <~~abbot~~> young men, until the abbot allocated them lands he would feed them in his own {[f. 284]} house, all of them together at one table and he at another, but with a curtain between them so that they could not see the abbot eating. They all keep this same custom now. When a <~~property~~> monk dies, if he has left some monk property that he earned by writing or teaching boys or by some means other than what was provided by the lands that feed the monastery, it is inherited by his kinsfolk, while the land and all the rest reverts to the monastery; if, however, the monk left children (as often happens) and one of them wants to be a monk, he takes the lands and other property that belonged to the monastery.

They do not want to say how many monks live in Dêbra Libanôs now; all they say is only a few. Just one of them said that there must be forty, and if there are that many it sounds rather a lot, because those lands are now almost deserted because of the continual incursions by the Gâlas, who come in whenever they like meeting no resistance at all, and they kill everyone they find. The monks have therefore come to the kingdom of Gojam and elsewhere, leaving no more than forty, or maybe fewer, in that monastery, and those stay there because that is the burial place of their founder and a secure place, for otherwise not one would be left there.

<[f. 239v/229v]> Friar Luis de Urreta deals at length with this monastery of Dêbra Libanôs in chapter 3 of the book that he entitled *History of the sacred Order of the Preachers in the remote Kingdoms of Ethiopia*,[1] and on page 35 he calls it Plurimanos and

---

[1] Urreta, *Historia de la sagrada orden*, ch. 3, entitled 'On the foundation of the great Monastery of Plurimanos, where nine thousand friars reside; on its mode of government, and origin, and on its topography and building', pp. 30–40.

says that Taquelâ Haimanôt founded it for the Ethiopians who had professed the religion of Saint Dominic, above the great {[f. 284v]} Lake Cafates, where the Nile rises, between the lake and the Mountains of the Moon, in the kingdom of Malemba. It was such a fertile land that near the monastery the Prester John had built an imperial city for his seat, thirty years before the time when he was writing, which was in 1611, and had called it Zambra. He says the monastery is so large and its architecture such that it has more than eighty dormitories, each with 120, 150 and in some cases 200 cells; at one end of them is the main church and at the other end the refectory, but each one has its own church and house of novices. From one dormitory to the next there is a cloister, because the whole building consists of rooms on one floor. Each wall is more than 500 paces long and it is two miles round. The dormitories have their own enclosures in which they close themselves in at night, and they cannot go from one to another without permission. There is a main entrance common to the whole monastery and it has a fence that separates it from the vegetable plots and gardens. In the refectory there are tables like ours and they are over two miles long; there are ten pulpits where ten lectors read without hindering one another, and everyone can hear them very well. For every three tables there is a serving table and a window through to the kitchen, in which there are cooks allocated to every three tables, and their servers allocated to them. And so they all start and finish their meal together. On weekdays, one dormitory goes to the choir of the main church of the monastery on one day and another dormitory goes the next day, in turn; the other dormitories each go to the church in their own dormitory. But on Sundays and feast days, they all go together {[f. 285]} to the main choir and there is enough room. The church is more than 600 paces long and the width and height are consistent with the length. There are all the crafts necessary for the service of the house within the monastery enclosures, such as tailors, shoemakers, weavers, carpenters, blacksmiths, stonemasons and farmers.

Up to here are the author's words, but it is all mere fiction drawn in his imagination or in that of the one who informed him, because there is no such style of building or division of dormitories as he depicts either in Dêbra Libanôs monastery or in any other in Ethiopia, but instead little round houses separate from each other, as we said above. They do not eat together in a refectory, but each one eats in his own house, and even though the young men that the abbot supports until they are given lands eat together, they are not read to at table, nor do they know what a pulpit is, for they do not have them even in churches, because they never preach, and if some monk says something by way of <[f. 240/230]> a speech, he sits on a stool, and they very rarely do that. And the monastery was not founded by *Abba* Taquelâ Haimanôt but by another monk by the name of Ezechias, fifty-seven years after his death; nor was it for friars of the Order of the glorious Father Saint Dominic because, as we proved above in chapter 17, neither there are friars of {[f. 285v]} Saint Dominic in the lands of the Prester John today, nor is there any recollection that there ever have been. The monastery is not founded near the lake through which the River Nile passes (for it does not rise in a lake, as we said in chapter 26 in the first book), but some eight days' journey from this lake. And in all the lands ruled by the Prester John there is no kingdom called Malemba, nor such a city of Zambra, as we also showed at the end of chapter 20 in the first book. To say it all in a word, virtually none of the many words that he writes about this monastery of Dêbra Libanôs corresponds to the truth of what there used to be in the past or what there is today.

# CHAPTER XXI[1]

## On the foundation of Alleluia Monastery

After the monastery of Dêbra Libanôs, which, as we have said, belongs to monks of *Abba* Taquelâ Haimanôt, the most famous one that there used to be in Ethiopia in the number of its monks was Dêbra Hallelô, which means monastery of the Alleluia, belonging to monks of *Abba* Stateûs, of whom we spoke earlier at the beginning of chapter 18.

This monastery is in the kingdom of Tigrê, on a very high mountain near the River Marâb. All around are high, rugged mountains and the valleys are so hot and unhealthy that people do not dare live in them, but just on the mountaintops, and from there they go down to till them; they also till in the mountains in certain areas where there is enough space. The monastery is on the very top of that mountain, and its former buildings were like those we described above at Dêbra Libanôs: little round houses separate {[f. 286]} from one another. I went to see them, because it is not more than a day's journey from our church at Fremonâ,[2] and they have almost all fallen down; I think there must have been about 600 of them. The old church, which was dedicated to Our Lady, also fell down a long time ago. I measured its overall size, because the foundations can still be seen, and it was 132 spans long and 105 wide. Within this outline, they have made another much smaller one, but large enough for the monks now, because no more than ten live there and, as they told me, there are twenty in the monasteries and churches subordinate to this monastery. I asked them how many monks there had been there in the past. They answered that their books did not say and they themselves did not <[f. 240v/230v]> know, but they had always heard that there were many of them. They showed me an old book that dealt with things of that monastery, and where it talked about its founder it said this:[3]

Abba *Samuel, who was born in Marabâ in Tambên* (this is a province in the kingdom of Tigrê),[4] *was a disciple of* Abba *Antônz, who was in Maedarô* (this is in the middle of Tigrê)[5] *in the monastery of Ambâ Tambûc, and there he did great penances: by day he worked and at night he lay in a little water with a rock on his back, was scourged a great deal and always wore a cilice. After he had been there for a long time, he asked his master for leave and went off alone into the deserts, where he found a completely white lion which, with a joyful expression, guided him through the wilderness* {[f. 286v]} *to another high mountain, where it disappeared. When he wanted to go further on to see if he could find somewhere better, God told*

---

[1] Incorrectly numbered '22' in the manuscripts.
[2] See Glossary (Fremona/Fremoná/Fremonâ/Māy Gwāgwā).
[3] The *gadl* has been published: Colin, 'Vie de Sāmu'ēl de Dabra Hāllēluyā'.
[4] Interpolation by Páez.
[5] Interpolation by Páez.

*him to go back and settle there and build a church, because He would make him the father of many saints. Soon many men started coming to him from various places, and he gave them a rule and way of life. And the first thing with which he charged them strongly was silence, followed by union among them as if they were limbs of a single body, that they should help one another, and the foot should not complain that it had not been made the head. Then he distributed the offices and made a church in which they all worked with great fervour and devotion.*

*On the Monday after Easter he went into a room where he remained standing up against a wall, praying, without eating or drinking for fifty days, until Whitsunday. And when a disciple of his came in on that day, he told him he should go to church, but he replied that he could not, and he should take him by the hand. As he did so, he found that the clothes on his back had been eaten away by worms, as had his flesh down to the bone. On seeing this the disciple began to weep loudly, but he told him to be quiet, and soon he saw him whole again, and he commanded him not to reveal that until after his death.*

The book recounts many other marvels about him. And later it says:

*Realizing that the time of his death was approaching, he asked Our Lord what he should do with his disciples. And He answered that he should give them his blessing, for it was now time to come to Him. And so he gave many blessings to those present and then* {[f. 287]} *he fell ill and commanded that those absent should come. Then an angel appeared to him and told him to appoint another in his place, and he made them a speech in which he charged them with the things that he wished them to keep, and he appointed Za Iesus as their master, and on* <[f. 241/231]> *saying this, he expired. And many angels came down in the company of Our Lady to receive his soul, and David came in front of her, singing* 'Pretiosa in conspectu Domini mors sanctorum eius.'[1]

Further on, the book says that *Abba* Antônz, the master of this *Abba* Samuel, showed this mountain to his disciples from afar, for it appeared with majesty, and he told them that its name was Hallelô, and he prophesied everything that later occurred.

This is what I found in that monastery, but some time later I asked a local man that I trusted to go and ask them again. And they told him that they did not know the number of monks that there had been in the past, but that they had heard that around the old church there were 1,230 monks' houses, while others said 4,000, and that the churches subordinate to this monastery numbered ninety-one and that there were twelve monks who heard complaints and visited in place of the abbot, and when one of them visited lands he was accompanied by 1,000 monks, and when the abbot went to the emperor on business he was accompanied by 150 monks wearing burnouses and riding mules; but the income he had is not known, because he gave some lands to each monk, from which he fed himself and spent on his needs.

{[f. 287v]} Friar Luis de Urreta says in chapter 4 of the *Historia Ethiopica* that he wrote on his sacred religion[2] that

---

[1] Psalm 115 [116]:15, 'Precious in the sight of the Lord is the death of his saints.'

[2] Urreta, *Historia de la sagrada orden*, ch. 4, entitled 'Of the foundation of Alleluia Monastery, where seven thousand friars live; of the manner of its governance and the design of the building', pp. 41–9.

*this Alleluia Monastery was founded by Friar Bertolameu de Tivoli, who was born in Italy and was a friar of the Order of Saint Dominic. The reason was that, when he was consecrated bishop in Rome, they gave him the title of a city called Dangala in Nubia, a province bordering Ethiopia on the northern side. And, since these Nubians had formerly been Christians and at that time there was some trace of the Christian faith and religion there, he determined like a good shepherd to go to the aid of his sheep, and so he departed from Rome in the year 1330 or so, at the time when Saint Taquelâ Haimanot was building the monastery of Plurimanos. He took in his company two regular clerics and two lay brothers of his same order. On arriving in Jerusalem they visited the holy sites and then went on to Nubia, where he and his companions converted many Moorish infidels and heathens and reduced innumerable Christians. When the holy bishop saw such copious fruits, he determined to build a monastery of the order that would serve as a seminary for apostolic preachers to teach the doctrine to those peoples. But since he could not find a suitable place in Nubia, because of its barrenness and lack of water, particularly where <[f. 241v/231v]> he was living, he went to see a sumptuous temple that was nearby, within Ethiopia, in the kingdom of Tigrê Mohon. It was public knowledge and received tradition that Queen {[f. 288]} Saba had built it when she returned from Jerusalem. And it is designed in the shape of a cross, signifying the mystery of the Holy Cross that God revealed to her.*

*The land where this temple stood was fruitful and lush, covered with the most beautiful groves and with ornamental, artful loops of rivers and springs, and so the good prelate found it most agreeable. He therefore sent one of the priests, who was called Florencia, with one of the brothers to the Prester John, who was Phelipe VIII, and asked him for that temple as a favour, together with the land needed to found the monastery. With great love and goodwill, the Prester John gave him the temple and as much land as was necessary not only for the house but for the gardens, vegetable plots and fields to support them, and commanded that he should be paid all the building expenses, because he held it to be a great mercy from God that they should wish to build a monastery in his realm, seeing that they were Dominican friars, for whom they had long had great devotion in Ethiopia. The religious of Plurimanos also came to help them as brothers and sons of the great Father Saint Dominic, and in particular Saint Taquelâ Haimanôt was their only patron.*

*The bishop was delighted with such a good decree and, as he began with his own hands to dig the foundations for the monastery, angelical voices were heard in the air singing 'Alleluia, alleluia' with sweet harmony, and because of this auspicious miracle it acquired the name of Alleluia.*

*It must be more than 700 leagues from the monastery of Plurimanos, {[f. 288v]} because almost the whole of Ethiopia lies between them. And this monastery has 7,000 religious and its enclosure is nine miles round and, apart from the main monastery, there are also six others inside it, each with 1,000 or more religious and all the necessary workshops and buildings, churches, cloisters, dormitories, refectories, kitchens and everything else that is required; and in each monastery there is a prior and superior and the other officers. On the feast days of Saint Dominic they all go in procession <from the monasteries> to the Alleluia church, where they sing the divine offices, and then each community returns to its monastery. On non-feast days, each monastery takes turns to sing the canonical hours in Alleluia {church} <monastery> on one day, while the other monasteries stay in their own churches. Some days they all eat together in a very large refectory that they have for this purpose, arranged in the same manner as that of Plurimanos monastery. Within the Alleluia monastery enclosure*

*<[f. 242/232]> there are many woods and many wildernesses, where there must be more than a hundred hermitages with hermit monks, like those in Plurimanos monastery.*

The author also says, on page 68,[1] that *every year the friars from Alleluia and Plurimanos monasteries undertake missions to kingdoms of Moors and heathens and in Ethiopia as well and, on the day following the feast of All Saints, the priors name those who will go and tell them to which kingdom and city, and the company that each one will take. They customarily name 1,500 to 2,000. {[f. 289]} Those from Alleluia monastery go to Nubia, the kingdom of Bornô and other kingdoms, as far as Cairo and the Arabian ones. Those from Plurimanos monastery go preaching through all the kingdoms of Congo, Angola, Anzicana, Barames and the many provinces that there are in the Cape of Good Hope, as far as the Mountains of the Moon, which is in the kingdom of Monomotapa, Maitagazo, Sofala, Arneta, Tibut, Sibit and many other provinces, and also through the kingdoms that lie along the coast of the eastern ocean up to the Red Sea, which makes almost 1,000 leagues. These missions last seven months, and many monks, burning with the zeal of the honour of God and the good of others, spend years on their mission, going as far as the East Indies and reaching the kingdom of Siam, Pegu and the great kingdom of China, which makes a journey of more than 3,000 leagues.*

He confirms this on page 73,[2] saying that in the papers he was translating it was written that in Plurimanos monastery there were ancient writings that mentioned that in about 1390 there were Dominican friars who went preaching as far as China, and they were martyred there by the heathens.

He also says, on page 88,[3] that he found it written in a report given to His Holiness Gregory XIII that

*in November 1580 there was {[f. 289v]} a great multitude of Moors in the main square in the city of Mecca listening to one of their number who was preaching to them, and, at that moment, there arrived there two Dominican friars from Alleluia monastery who were preaching and fulfilling the obedience of their mission. When they saw those people listening to so many absurdities and all those souls being lost, and inspired with the courage that divine love gave them, they broke into the crowd with their crosses in their hands and, contradicting the infernal alfaqui,[4] they disabused all the people of the error in which they lived and that they would go to hell. Many more alfaquis came up <[f. 242v/232v]> and stirred up the people against the friars, and so they seized them and with a lot of shouting took them to the prison. But there were more than 2,000 merchants from the kingdoms of Africa there, who were in the habit of taking shelter at Alleluia monastery and who were obliged to the fathers of that holy house for their good works when they passed that way. When they recognized that the friars were from Alleluia monastery, they charged through the people with weapons in their hands and pulled out the friars and took them to their district, which is enclosed, and defended them there,*

---

[1] Urreta, *Historia de la sagrada orden*, ch. 6, entitled 'On the studies and Theology and manner of teaching of the Friars Preachers of Ethiopia, on the missions that they undertake to preach in the land of heathens and Moors, which is something worth reading', pp. 64–92.

[2] Urreta, *Historia de la sagrada orden*, ch. 6.

[3] Urreta, *Historia de la sagrada orden*, ch. 6.

[4] Expert in Islamic religious law.

*saying that those religious were from Alleluia, where they gave hospitality to the merchants that were there, and without that hospitality and religious alms it was impossible for goods to reach the city of Mecca. Having heard this and other arguments, {[f. 290]} the sheikh, or governor, ruled that for the sake of general peace they should be banished from the city at once. And so it was done, and the merchants gave them men to protect them until they were out of danger.*

Up to here are words of the author, in which there is nothing that is not mere fable, because, first of all, Alleluia monastery was not founded by Friar Bertolameu de Tivoli, from Italy, but by *Abba* Samuel, from the kingdom of Tigrê, as we saw above. Nor is the monastery of monks of *Abba* Taquelâ Haimanôt, but of *Abba* Stateûs. And at the time when Friar Bertolameu left Rome, which he says was in the year 1330 or so, Taquelâ Haimanôt was not building the monastery of Dêbra Libanôs, which he calls Plurimanos, because as we saw at the end of the previous chapter, it was in fact built by another monk who was called Ezechias, fifty-seven years after Taquelâ Haimanôt died. And the temple was not built in a cross, as we saw above; nor could the Prester John Phelipe VIII have given lands for the monastery because, as Emperor Seltân Çaguêd told me, there has never been an emperor of this name; nor is it called Alleluia for any reason other than what *Abba* Antônz said to his disciples, according to its history. And for many years no {[f. 290v]} more than ten monks have lived in this monastery, and not 7,000 as he says, and today there is no recollection of the actual number that there used to be, because neither do their histories state it, nor can the monks themselves say any more than we have mentioned above. He also depicted the monastery buildings as he wished, because there were never any such divisions, but little round houses separate from one another, as we said.

<[f. 243/233]> Equally false is what he says about the missions that the monks of these monasteries undertake every year to the provinces that he names, because not only have they never been there but they do not even know their names and, according to Emperor Seltân Çaguêd, they have never been beyond the kingdom of Nareâ, of which we spoke above, and from there to the Cape of Good Hope, which he would have them reach, there are unending forests and deserts inhabited by wild beasts through which it is impossible to pass. As for now, they would not go a league from their houses to confess, unless there was a reward. I have only seen one monk who was travelling among some heathens that live in the kingdom of Gojam, teaching and, as he was such a rarity, Emperor Zadenguil did him many honours and favours; but afterwards he gave up the habit and went around on a fine horse, very well dressed as a layman, and he told some great men in my presence that one could not eat {[f. 291]} and drink without a woman. Here the author also puts the Mountains of the Moon in the kingdom of Monomotapa and yet, because João Botero[1] put them in that same kingdom, he says on page 298 of the first volume that he must have been delirious with some fever; and on page 246[2] he puts them in Gojam and affirms that the River Nile rises in them. To his claim that the papers he was translating said that there were ancient writings in Plurimanos monastery that mentioned that Dominican friars went preaching as far as China, I must reply that the monks of that monastery know

---

[1] See Botero, *Relaciones universales del mundo*, 1st part, bk 3, p. 121.
[2] Urreta, *Historia de la Etiopia*, bk I, ch. 28. See Páez's refutation in bk I, ch. 26, above.

nothing about such writings, nor that there have ever been friars of Saint Dominic in Ethiopia, as we have said already. It is not very surprising that he found this lie in <~~these~~> those papers since, as he states on page 8, they were also signed by the master of novices at Alleluia, Friar Marcos, born in Florence, and Friar Miguel de Monrojo and Friar Matheo Caravajal of the same monastery, sons of Spaniards, and yet such friars never existed there, as we saw in chapter 17. As for what he says he found in the report given to His Holiness Gregory XIII, that two friars of Saint Dominic from Alleluia monastery entered Mecca and contradicted the alfaqui, etc., they must know of that report there in Rome; what I heard from many Moors while I was a captive eight days' journey inside the gates of the Strait of Mecca is that they do not allow Christians to enter that city under any circumstances, on {[f. 291v]} pain of death, and if anyone enters covertly and they find him, they kill him without any clemency. Therefore, they would hardly have allowed friars to enter wearing habits and with crosses in their hands. If even then they wish to affirm that those friars did enter and that the information is correct, I reply that we can find at least two patently false things here: one, that they were friars of Saint Dominic from Alleluia monastery, because there have never been friars of Saint Dominic in it; <[f. 243v/233v]> and the other, that Moorish merchants travelling from the kingdoms of Africa to Mecca go via Alleluia monastery and take shelter there, and there can be nothing more absurd than that, as we shall see. It is true that monks from these monasteries go on pilgrimage to Jerusalem and some go on from there to Rome, but there is no such thing as the preaching missions that he claims.

The author deals at length with the way in which they shelter merchants in Alleluia monastery on page 61,[1] where he says that

*this monastery is the key to almost all of Africa, because all those that live in the west of it, if they want to do business in Cairo and the Arabias, and all the Moors who go to the house of Mecca, and the merchants from Manicongo, Borno, Biafra and many other kingdoms that he names there, including those from Fez, Morocco and the great lower Libya, cannot travel to Egypt or great Cairo or visit the house of Mecca without going via Alleluia monastery, because the rest {[f. 292]} is uninhabitable. Counting merchants, travellers and serving folk, some 10,000 men must go there, and they must take 4,000–5,000 camels, 6,000 mules and 3,000 asses, all laden. Before reaching Alleluia monastery, they travel for over twenty days without finding a drop of water, and after the monastery they go almost as far again without any, and so they are forced to stop there. The religious receive them with great charity and stable all their pack-animals and feed them on dates, barley and other grain; and they put the people up in large guest houses that they have for this purpose, and give them beds and meals of bread, meat, rice and fruit, with everything else that is needed, and those who arrive sick are taken to the hospital, and all of this at no charge at all. All these merchants and travellers are Moors or Jews or heathens, and they spend four to six days there, where they stock up with water and the things needed to sustain them, and they are given everything free of charge, but they always give the religious some of the goods they are carrying and they are very devoted to them and call them saints, and they respect Saint Dominic highly, because they see that the religious revere him, calling him 'father', and while they are there, they preach to them and teach them, so that many of them convert to the faith of Christ.*

[1] Urreta, *Historia de la sagrada orden*, ch. 6.

This, in brief, is what Friar Luis de Urreta says there, but it could not be a {[f. 292v]} more fabulous fable, because such a caravan of merchants does not go via Alleluia monastery and never has done, as the monks themselves affirm, and I can testify that over the last nineteen years <[f. 244/234]> I have neither seen nor heard of such a thing, despite having spent part of this time in the residence that we have a day's journey from this monastery; and there is no sign there of such stables and guest houses. In all those lands, there is not a single palm tree, let alone such an abundance of dates that they give them to the pack-animals; instead, the Moors bring them as a great present for the emperor from Arabia and some other parts. Even less is rice found there, because there is none at all in all the lands ruled by the Prester John. As for a hospital where they could put the sick Moors and Jews from that caravan, they could hardly have had one, because there is not even one for Christians in all of this Ethiopia. The lands around the monastery are not so short of water as he says, because from whichever side one approaches it, over many leagues, one will not find a day's journey without water, except when coming from the kingdom that they call Dequîn. But leaving aside all that, what greater absurdity can there be than to claim that, in order to go to Cairo and Mecca, merchants from the Arabias, Manicongo, Borno, Fez, Morocco and Libya are absolutely forced to go via Alleluia monastery? Why should they make a detour of many hundreds {[f. 293]} of leagues and cross great deserts and vast forests? And in order for the reader to see this better, I shall describe where the monastery is in the kingdom of Tigrê. Demarcating it by some port on the Red Sea – because to speak exactly in degrees we have no instruments here with which to measure elevation or anything with which to see it – the most suitable port they have is Maçuâ, which they commonly call Dalec, because the customs house of Maçuâ used to be on another island called Dalêc. Coming then from the port of Maçuâ to Alleluia monastery, one travels almost west-south-west, to use the language of sailors, which is much more towards the west than towards the south; one can reach it in four days if one travels fast, or five if slowly. As for the kingdom that he calls Borno, according to what he says in all the places where he speaks of it, it can only be the one that here they call Dequîn and its inhabitants Balôus, and this kingdom lies much closer to Cairo than Alleluia monastery does, so that those who come from Borno to this monastery are not going towards Cairo, but rather coming away from it and they have to turn back. Therefore, the author was very much mistaken in everything he says here.

# CHAPTER XXII

Which declares how groundlessly Friar Luis de Urreta counted among the saints of his sacred religion the monks of Ethiopia whose lives he reports in the second volume

{[f. 293v]} <[f. 244v/234v]> Friar Luis de Urreta's principal aim in the second volume of his *Historia Ethiopica* is to show that the religion of the glorious Saint Dominic has many prodigious saints in the lands ruled by the Prester John. And so, as he begins to deal with their lives, on page 129, he says:

*The flow and course of the history has brought us to that which I so greatly desired, which is to write the heroic lives and prodigious marvels of those illustrious and glorious saints, divine phoenixes of Ethiopia, suns that beautify and enlighten the starry sky of the religion of the glorious Father Saint Dominic. This protracted narrative has been flowing towards this end alone and aiming at this target alone.*[1]

On page 105,[2] he affirms that in this land of Ethiopia alone there are more martyrs than in all the rest of the {Religion} <Order> of Saint Dominic, although it has had many thousands, and even more than all the other religions put together, because the martyrs from the two monasteries of Dêbra Libanôs and Alleluia add up to 300,000. But so that it may be clearly seen how groundlessly he places the fathers of these monasteries among the saints of his sacred religion – for he canonizes them as such – I shall here briefly mention some of the many things that he tells about them, leaving out the life of *Abba* Taquelâ Haimanôt with which he begins, because we dealt with it above in chapter 19.

Beginning, then, with Friar Phelipe, whose life he puts in chapter 10,[3] he says on page 169 that

*he is a martyr saint and the son of a king called Glariacas in Ethiopia. When he reached* {[f. 294]} *the age of discretion his parents, the king and queen, took him with a large retinue to the monastery of Dêbra Libanôs, which he calls Plurimanos, in order to receive the habit of Saint Dominic, which the holy father Taquelâ Haimanôt gave to him with great pleasure, since {through} <with> prophetic spirit he knew the great treasures that divine mercy had*

---

[1] Urreta, *Historia de la sagrada orden*, excerpt from ch. 9, p. 129. Páez quotes this passage in Spanish.

[2] Urreta, *Historia de la sagrada orden*, ch. 7, entitled 'On the innumerable martyrs that the Religion of Preachers has in the kingdoms of Ethiopia; some notes are provided on this subject', pp. 93–110.

[3] Urreta, *Historia de la sagrada orden*, ch. 10, entitled 'On the miraculous life and heroic martyrdom of the glorious Saint Philip, friar of the Order of Preachers and apostolic inquisitor', pp. 165–207.

*kept in that boy. At the age of sixteen, after a few years as a novice, he professed in the hands of the prelate, Saint Taquelâ Haimanôt, with great shows of devotion, and in due time he received holy orders from the hands of the patriarch of Ethiopia, who was called Iacob. And he said his first Mass in the monastery of Dêbra Libanós and, when he raised the holy sacrament, everyone saw him lifted more than two cubits into the air and his body remained suspended up high, but he neither noticed nor knew of it until the prior told him, when he asked him about it. Afterwards, when he was about to say Mass (as with his master Taquelâ Haimanôt), an angel came down to administer to him and assist in it, bringing him the bread and wine from heaven to consecrate, and he attended for the whole time that that holy sacrifice lasted.*

Further on, on page 179, <[f. 245/235]> he says:

*This glorious saint was marked with the holy sign of the cross by two fingers of Christ at the death of Saint Taquelâ Haimanôt, and he succeeded him in the priorship and also in the office and dignity of apostolic inquisitor, as Taquelâ Haimanôt was and all the priors of Dêbra Libanós[1] and Alleluia monasteries are.*

*{[f. 294v]} When he was inquisitor, it happened that a Christian king, whose kingdom was near Dêbra Libanós monastery and who was subject to the Prester John, openly married two women and lived with them, causing public scandal throughout Ethiopia. The {holy inquisitor} <saint> took note of this and, at a meeting with the patriarch and some religious in a church, he summoned him, reprimanded him and threatened to excommunicate him and have the Prester John deprive him of his kingdom if he did not leave the concubine and stay with his lawful wife. Since this was to no avail, he then excommunicated him in the church, putting out candles and ringing bells and commanding that news of this be given to the people. The king was so angry at this that he at once gathered the men of his palace and, in a great rage, went to the church where the Inquisition Council was being held and, as swords started slashing, the patriarch and inquisitor fled with their religious, some of them wounded, and went to another kingdom. But the inquisitor was able to find ways to confirm the king's excommunication in the churches and public places of his court. Not even that was enough to stop him persevering in his sin for three years, although God punished him by not giving rain in that kingdom throughout that time, and so Saint Phelipe gathered a large army from the places subject to Dêbra Libanôs with the intention of waging war as against a schismatic. When the king saw that he was coming with such a large army, and seeing that his vassals were not going {[f. 295]} to help him, he sent an ambassador to the holy inquisitor, saying that they should avoid the deaths that there would inevitably be in the war and that the Prester John should judge the case, and he would abide by his ruling. The inquisitor came on hearing this and went to the Prester John, and the king sent his proxy, who was an apostate monk. When the Prester John had heard both of them, he handed down his ruling, commanding the king at once to give up the second woman with whom he was cohabiting. Shortly afterwards, God punished the monk who was the king's proxy by covering him with leprosy, and he died eaten up by worms. When the people saw that and realized that it was God's punishment, they began to rise up against the king and deny him obedience, and so the king deceitfully sent word to the inquisitor to come and <[f. 245v/235v]> absolve him and pacify his kingdom and he would do what he commanded him. The holy inquisitor thought that he was speaking*

---

[1] 'Plurimanos' in Urreta's text.

*from his heart, and so he went with his companions, but when he arrived before the king he commanded that the saint be stripped, tied to a column and flogged, which his servants did so well that he was left as if dead, and as such they delivered him to his friars for them to bury him. But as they took him to Dêbra Libanôs, by God's will he came back to life and was healed. On hearing that, the schismatic king went to the monastery with soldiers and, catching everyone unawares, went in after the saint. He found him in the church, prostrate before the holy sacrament, entrusting his soul to the Lord, and he commanded them to beat him to death where he was. {[f. 295v]} As his soul left his body, sweet music and gentle chanting was heard in the air. His martyrdom was on 4th November, and on this day his feast is celebrated throughout Ethiopia.*[1]

The author says these things in that chapter, as well as others that are not relevant, which I shall leave out so as not to tire the reader. And for the same reason I shall only briefly report what he says at length about the other friars of Dêbra Libanôs.

In chapter 11,[2] the author deals with Elça. He says he was an inquisitor and was born in the famous city of Saba, the son of kings subject to the Prester John, and that when he was ten he asked Saint Taquelâ Haimanôt for the habit, and they gave it to him with great pleasure, because they were informed that they were divine callings. When he reached the age when he was to receive priestly orders, he felt unworthy of such high dignity, and Saint Taquelâ Haimanôt had to command him to be ordained out of obedience; then, before saying his first Mass, he asked for leave to go and prepare himself in the wilderness, where he spent forty days and nights without eating or drinking, always in fervent prayer, during which he was taken in spirit to heaven, where he saw and heard mysterious things. While he was in his rapture up in heaven, he celebrated his first Mass, with angels singing and the twenty-four elders who are so celebrated in the Apocalypse serving as ministers and patrons, dressed in white and with gold crowns on their heads and harps in their hands, with sweet fragrances. {[f. 296]} The holy Prior Taquelâ Haimanôt was also carried up to heaven at the same time and was present at the new Mass and enjoyed that music and sweetness. Later the prior summoned him and asked him where he had been, but he dared not reveal the mercies that Our Lord had done him until the holy prior told him that he had been present in <[f. 246/236]> heaven at his new Mass, but even so he wanted him to sing in the monastery the next day and give communion to all the religious, as is the custom in Ethiopia. When the time came, he vested himself and, when the sacristan was about to prepare the hosts {and wine}, he said, 'That job is not necessary, for they will be more worthily provided by others.' And then the archangel Saint Gabriel appeared visibly before everyone, bringing hosts made of very white bread for all those who were going to commune, as well as wine. And the angel did not only do it {that time} but whenever Saint Elça was the celebrant. When he raised up the holy sacrament, he rose five cubits into the air, to the astonishment of Saint Clara and the others who were present, and it was not just at this Mass, but the same thing happened to him at many others.

After the glorious martyrdom of Saint Phelipe, he was made prior of Dêbra Libanôs. And this saint was one of those whom Christ Our Lord marked with the sign of the holy

---

[1] Urreta, *Historia de la sagrada orden*, ch. 10, pp. 170–95, abridged by Páez in Portuguese.

[2] Urreta, *Historia de la sagrada orden*, ch. 11, entitled 'On the life and great miracles of the glorious inquisitor Saint Elsa, religious of the second Order of Preachers', pp. 207–34.

cross on the forehead with His fingers, to indicate that he was to be a prior, and he governed in that position for forty years. His saintliness was so great {[f. 296v]} that the Prester John chose him as his confessor, and he performed this office so well and so much to the satisfaction of all Ethiopia and to the emperor's pleasure that ever since then it has been the custom for the Prester Johns to confess with friars from Dêbra Libanôs. He performed many miracles during his life and, when he was already old and tired, one night of the Assumption of the most sacred Virgin, while he was at prayer, he begged God with many tears to take him to Himself and, while he was engaged in this fervent petition, Our Lady appeared to him and told him to rejoice, for one year from that day he would leave this miserable life and go up to enjoy glory in heaven. At this news he was overjoyed and spent all that year in prayer and contemplation. When the last hour of his pilgrimage arrived, with all the religious gathered together, he spoke to them, encouraging them in the service of God and in keeping their religion. Once he had received the sacraments of the Church with great devotion, on the day of the Assumption of Our Lady, his most holy life came to an end. And they placed his holy body in a golden coffin embellished with precious stones next to the glorious Saint Phelipe and Saint Taquelâ Haimanôt. He died in the year of our redemption 1416 at over seventy years of age, having spent forty as the prior of Dêbra Libanôs.

<[f. 246v/236v]> And in chapter 12,[1] Friar Luis de Urreta {[f. 297]} reports the life of *Abba* Samuel and makes him too an apostolic inquisitor and friar of the sacred religion of Saint Dominic, and says that he was born in a city called Esumin, subject to the Prester John, in Ethiopia. His father was called Estevão and his mother Isabel, and they were the most illustrious persons in that city. At the age of eighteen he received the habit of the Order of Preachers in the monastery of Dêbra Libanôs, and when his novitiate year was finished he professed and shone with many great virtues, and God wrought many miracles through him. Once while he was sitting beside a surging river – one of the many that rise in the great Lake Cafates and flood like the Nile – reading Saint John's Gospel, he fell asleep with the sound of the waters and, while he was asleep, the river rose, as all those that flow out of that lake do. The waters overflowed their banks and spread out over the land, flooding all the fields on all sides, and the saint was left surrounded by very deep water as if in a room, with the waters acting like crystal walls, harder than diamond. And he remained there until the flood subsided without wetting his clothes or the book.

After he had spent some years in the company of the other religious in Dêbra Libanôs, he asked his prelate for leave and, with one companion who wished to follow him, he went to a very distant wilderness, where they lived in caves for forty years, eating raw herbs once a day and drinking water. {[f. 297v]} For three hours every day he was carried up in spirit to heaven in the company of the angels, and one of the twenty-four elders that Saint John mentions in the Apocalypse gave him the holy communion of the Eucharist. Once it happened that the great Lake Cafates swelled up, as it regularly does, and burst out over its usual shores with such force that, although the saint was some leagues away from it, it reached him and destroyed a chapel that he had made there, and he withdrew to a safe place, thus being delivered from the wild flood of water that was carrying all before it. Once the waters had retreated, the saint found the chapel destroyed and the lamp lost, and

---

[1] Urreta, *Historia de la sagrada orden*, ch. 12, entitled 'On the admirable life of the glorious father Saint Samuel, apostolic inquisitor and friar of the sacred Religion of Preachers', pp. 235–57.

he set off for a city named Belasa to fetch another. To get there he had to cross a lake ten miles wide and, making the sign of the cross, he stepped onto the lake and walked over the waters as if they were solid land. <[f. 247/237]> In addition, when he was walking through those deserts and felt tired, he would call the tiger and lion, elephant and rhinoceros, and they would {come at} <obey> his command and he would mount them as if they were gentle asses and continue his journey; and if he came to some river of the many that there are in the Mountains of the Moon, he would call an elephant or rhinoceros and cross the river on them.

After forty years of his hermit life, an angel appeared to him and commanded him on God's behalf to leave the desert and go {[f. 298]} and preach in his own land, because it needed his teaching. The holy father obeyed at once and, on arriving there, his preaching bore much fruit, and fame of his holiness spread so that many people gathered to him, wishing to imitate his way of life, and therefore he had to found a monastery in the city of Essumin, where he gave the habit of the glorious father Saint Dominic to more than 400 novices. Later, when the prior of Dêbra Libanôs died, they elected him, and so he was forced to go there, and he was received like a true portrait of his glorious father Saint Dominic, and he governed that monastery in a most holy manner until, at the ripe old age of almost eighty, on 12th December 1430, he exchanged this mortal life for the immortal and blessed one.

In chapter {17} <18>,[1] he puts the life and martyrdom of a saint that he calls Taclâ Varet, which should be Taquelâ Haureât, which means 'Plant of the Apostles'. He says he was born in the city of Saba; his mother was called Elena, the Prester John's sister, and his father was a great prince. When he was eight years old he went to Dêbra Libanôs and asked for the habit of the sacred religion of Saint Dominic and, since the religious had had news of him, they gave it to him, considering that it was a special favour from God and mercy from heaven to have been given that boy. He at once began to lead an angelic life and, on reaching the age to receive the holy priesthood, he had to be commanded to accept it out of obedience, {[f. 298v]} because he did not consider himself worthy of such an ineffable dignity. Having lived in the monastery for some years with great saintliness and having performed many miracles, he decided to ask his prelates for leave to go and live in the desert; and it was granted. There he made great penance and received great favours from Christ Our Lord, one of which was that an angel came to him every day while he was in that desert and put him on a white, transparent cloud, and he was taken to Jerusalem where, with great devotion, he visited those <[f. 247v/237v]> holy places where our redemption was made, and he returned to his hermitage on that same cloud, making a journey of more than 900 leagues.

When the happy end to his holy life was approaching, Christ Our Lord appeared to him and told him to leave that desert and go and preach in a nearby kingdom, giving him the news that he would be martyred there and that, through martyrdom, he would enjoy glory. He went at once to fulfil the divine command and, entering that kingdom, he preached the evangelical doctrine with great fervour and converted many people to the holy faith. When he was saying Mass one Christmas Day and had just finished

---

[1] The reference here is wrong in both manuscripts. It should be to Urreta, *Historia de la sagrada orden*, ch. 13, entitled 'The life and glorious martyrdom of Saint Thaclavaret, religious of the sacred Order of Preachers, who was born in Ethiopia', pp. 258–77.

consecrating, the queen of that kingdom arrived and, taking the chalice, washed her hair and forehead with the precious blood of Christ Our Lord. On seeing such sacrilegious temerity, and burning with divine zeal for the honour and reverence of Christ's blood, the saint cut off {[f. 299]} her hair with some scissors and scraped her forehead until she bled. The queen rushed out weeping and making much ado and, covered with blood as she was, she presented herself to the king her husband, who was a very hot-tempered, violent man. When he saw her like that, he went in a great rage straight to the church where the priest was. After dishonouring him with insulting, intemperate words, he ordered his guardsmen to kill him. And so, with swords and halberds and partisans they cut him to pieces at once, while the saint was kneeling in prayer saying, '*In manus tuas Domine*', etc.[1] As he expired, sweet chants of angels were heard in the air and angels also appeared visibly, and in precious cups they collected the blood that flowed from his wounds. Once he had expired, everyone saw his body rise up and be carried through the air in the hands of angels for many leagues to the monastery of Dêbra Libanôs, where the angels themselves put him in an honoured grave, at which many miracles were performed. And every year on Christmas Day, the day of his martyrdom, an angel comes down visibly in human form and places in the refectory ten most beautiful citrons in front of the religious, which they divide up into many parts and share among the people, and the Prester John is present at this miracle almost every year. Serafino Rosi reports that a friar from Ethiopia swore to him that he had often been present at this miracle and that he had seen the citrons come down and had eaten a share of them.

{[f. 299v]} God did not wish that king's evil to remain unpunished for a long time; instead, soon afterwards, as he was returning <[f. 248/238]> home with all his guard and close friends, and the air was clear and the sky serene, suddenly it was covered with very dark clouds and it began to rain heavily, with frightful thunder and lightning, and so many thunderbolts fell that they killed the sacrilegious king and all his cruel retinue, their miserable bodies being burnt to cinders and their souls sent to eternal torment.

In chapter 14[2] he puts the life of Saint Andre, martyr and apostolic inquisitor, and friar of the Order of Preachers, and says that his mother was the Prester John's sister and his father was one of the most illustrious princes in Ethiopia. When he reached the age of twenty he went to Dêbra Libanôs monastery, the prior there being Saint Phelipe the martyr, and received the habit of the glorious Father Saint Dominic from his hands. And then he started many {fervent} <fine> penances, and at the age of thirty he was promoted to the holy priesthood, which office he performed with such purity and fervour of spirit that often, while he was the celebrant, they saw him miraculously raised off the ground, and many other times he was surrounded by angels while he said Mass and one of them would serve him, assisting him at the altar and preparing the host and wine for him to consecrate. He was present at the death of the glorious father Friar Elça and, in the presence of many others, he made the sign of the cross on his forehead, saying that he was to be the prior of that monastery. And so he was, because he succeeded Saint Samuel in the priorship and performed many miracles. {[f. 300]} Once, while he was saying Mass in the monastery, he rose into the air in view of everyone and stayed there so long that many

---

[1] Psalm 30 [31]:6, 'Into thy hands [I commend my spirit: thou hast redeemed me], O Lord.'

[2] Urreta, *Historia de la sagrada orden*, ch. 14, entitled 'The life and miracles of the most glorious father Saint Andres, martyr and apostolic inquisitor, friar of the Order of Preachers', pp. 277–92.

people came to see the novelty of the miracle, and then he came down and finished the Mass. The heat was so great that everyone was afflicted by the great thirst that they were suffering, so the saint sent for the water that they had prepared for the religious to drink and, when he cast a blessing over the jars, it was multiplied so that not only was there sufficient for those that were there, but there was enough left over for all the religious and, what is more, the water was miraculously turned into precious wine, at which everyone gave thanks to God, for thus he comes to the aid of his servants.

In one of Ethiopia's kingdoms, a king was governing who was a Christian in name only, because he openly lived with and was married to two women. And since the glorious father Saint Andre was prior, he succeeded to the holy office of apostolic inquisitor, so he went to where that king was and <[f. 248v/238v]> lovingly reprehended him to give up that infernal life through which he was scandalizing all his kingdom, but the king took no notice of those loving admonitions. When the holy inquisitor saw his obstinacy, he began to reprimand him severely, threatening him with divine justice and the obligation of his office; however, since this libidinous vice becomes more cruel the more it is indulged, the king furiously commanded one of his guard to kill the holy father there and then. But just as the temerous soldier raised his arm with his sword drawn to wound the saint, his arm was cut off and fell to the ground, and {[f. 300v]} at this punishment the sad man threw himself at the saint's feet and with many tears begged his forgiveness for his guilt, beseeching him to put his arm back. The holy father was moved by his tears and picked up the arm from the ground and, making the sign of the cross, put it in its place and it remained as if it had not been cut off. But not even with this great miracle did the accursed king come to his senses, but instead he commanded another soldier to take his life at once, which he did, striking the saint's head with a sword and splitting it in two; as the saint said the sweet name of Jesus, he gave up his soul to the Lord and, although the wound was so cruel, not a drop of blood fell to the ground, because the angels collected it and embalmed the holy body with precious unguents.

The Lord did not let His martyr's blood call out in vain without the tyrant king getting the punishment that he deserved for his guilt, because, as he was sitting on his royal chair, he suddenly fell to the ground as if struck down from heaven, and he remained with his head stuck to the ground and his feet in the air for a long time without being able to change his position, no matter how hard he tried, so it seems that the demons were holding him like that. Finally he ended his miserable life with loud screams and infernal anguish.

In chapter 15[1] he deals with a woman whom he calls Imata, the founder of a nunnery called Bedenagli. And he says she was a *beata* of the Third Order of Saint Dominic, and that she left Rome in the company of those eight holy religious men who journeyed to Ethiopia, as was said above. The Ethiopians call her {[f. 301]} Imata, which means 'Servant of God', and so high was the opinion that everyone had of her saintliness that they gave all nuns the generic name 'imatas', just as in Spain and Italy they are called 'sisters'. The nunnery <[f. 249/239]> called Bedenagli that she founded lies between the great Lake Cafates and the Mountains of the Moon, a little more than a quarter of a league

---

[1] Urreta, *Historia de la sagrada orden*, ch. 15, entitled 'Of the glorious Imata, founder of the magnificent Monastery of Bedenagli, where 5,000 nuns live; of the design of the building and customs of the nuns', pp. 293–306.

from the monastery of Dêbra Libanôs. She withdrew there with fifty maidens, daughters of high-ranking people, who received the holy habit of Dominican nuns, and this number persisted in the nunnery until her blissful death. And then the glorious Zemedemarea, whose name means Clara,[1] was elected prioress of the nunnery, and in her time, with the help of her spiritual father, Saint Taquelâ Haimanôt, the nunnery grew to the number of 300 nuns. And after the death of Taquelâ Haimanôt, when Saint Phelipe the martyr succeeded him in the priorship, with his help the number of nuns rose to 5,000, and the same number still remains today. The dormitories, refectories and choir are in the style of Dêbra Libanôs monastery and it is governed in the same way, and so it is easy to understand how a prioress can govern such a large number of nuns. Those that have professed and are veiled wear black-and-white habits and a white coif made of cotton, and a black veil on top that covers the face down to the bust and shoulders. Formerly they were not enclosed but could leave the house, {[f. 301v]} but now they comply with it very strictly by commandment of the general of the Order of Preachers, Master Friar Vicente Justiniano.

Novices can go out to sell what the nuns make in the nunnery, because some of them weave veils and coifs, and others taffeta, grogram and serge, and they do good business with it; and the coifs and veils are highly regarded by the Turks and Moors and the Turks even value them for their turbans, and so they take them as merchandise to Cairo and Alexandria. These nuns set such a holy example that nothing like an offence to God has ever been heard of in Ethiopia and no scandal has ever happened, which is all the more reason to esteem those good religious women. When they take the veil, they do not speak to anybody, even kinsfolk, and secular people cannot see their faces; and so they do not have locutories and only women are allowed in their churches.

Up to here are words of Friar Luis de Urreta, in which, as we have seen, he assumes it to be quite certain and verified that these monks are of the sacred religion of Saint Dominic. But he is very much mistaken, because both this and the rest of what he says about them is totally false. As we have <[f. 249v/239v]> said several times and proved above in chapter 17, *Abba* Taquelâ Haimanôt, who (as he himself affirms here) gave them the habit, was not a friar of Saint Dominic; and his statement that Friar Phelipe succeeded Taquelâ Haimanôt in the priorship is not so, because it was Elça who succeeded him; {[f. 302]} and the latter was not prior for forty years, as the author says, but for three months, as mentioned at the end of the history of Taquelâ Haimanôt, and after him Brother Phelipe was prior. Nor were these or any other prior apostolic inquisitors, because there has never been an inquisition in Ethiopia, and they do not know what it is; thus each one speaks as he wishes about matters of faith and every day they come with new heresies, without there being a prelate to deal with this, and the emperor cannot do anything with them, even though at our insistence he works hard to remove their errors and introduce our holy faith. That shows how much of a fable it is to say that, since Friar Phelipe held the office of inquisitor and a king who was currently married to two women did not want to obey him, he gathered a large army from the places subject to Dêbra Libanôs, where he was prior, and went to fight him; and here it would not have been considered right of him if he had gathered such an army, because it was not his place but the emperor's to do so.

---

[1] Urreta, *Historia de la sagrada orden*, ch. 16, entitled 'On the prodigious life and grandiose miracles of the glorious virgin Saint Zemedemarea, which in our way of speaking means Clara, a nun of the sacred Order of Preachers', pp. 307–44.

As for the miracles that he tells of these friars, I could not find one of them in the *Flos Sanctorum* of Ethiopia, which they call the *Senqueçâr*.[1] But they told me that there was a particular book dealing with Taquelâ Haimanôt's disciples, and I could not get hold of it, so I shall not mention anything about them here. I only say that, if all the miracles that {[f. 302v]} the author recounts are to be given the credit that some of them deserve, then they have none, but rather they are patently fabulous. One example is the one he tells of *Abba* Samuel, who was sitting beside one of the many rivers that rise in the great Lake Cafates, which flood like the Nile, and while reading Saint John's Gospel he fell asleep and the river rose, as all those that flow out of that lake do, and the waters overflowed their banks and flooded the fields, and the saint was left in the middle as if in a room, with the waters acting like walls, and he remained there until the flood subsided without wetting his clothes or the book. This is a fabulous lie, because no river rises in the lake that he calls Cafates (which they actually call *bahar*, which means 'sea'); the Nile just passes though one side of it, as we said in Chapter 26 of the first book; and the Nile does not rise so suddenly while it goes through the Prester John's lands (as he imagines it does), but rather it takes a long time to become swollen, and once it is in full spate it does not spread out, because it always makes its course between mountains or in very deep ravines.

<[f. 250/240]> Also patently false is his claim that Lake Cafates once swelled up so much, as it regularly does, and burst out over its usual shores with such force that, although the saint was some leagues away from it, it reached him and destroyed a chapel that he had made there, and he {[f. 303]} withdrew to a safe place where he was delivered from the waters. The author could not have depicted a greater lie, because when this lake floods it is not like the ocean tide, which in some places rises with great force and floods large tracts of land, but it rises very slowly, a little every day, and this is also well after the beginning of winter; after it has finished rising, it does not spread out anywhere to the extent that a man can barely throw a stone across by hand; and when it goes down, it is so slow that very little can be seen each day, so that it is not like the ocean sea, which in our lands rises and falls in twelve hours, but from early July it starts to rise until October, and after that it falls again very slowly. Therefore the lake flood could hardly destroy *Abba* Samuel's chapel, which was some leagues away from it. I shall leave aside the claim that when he was walking through those deserts and felt tired, he would call the tiger and lion, elephant and rhinoceros, and he would mount them, because the reader may believe what he pleases about this, because they easily invent these stories here. A short time ago, a monk who had been wandering in the desert for years said in the kingdom of Tigrê that the empire belonged to him and that the emperor could not stand up to him, because even the lions obeyed him {[f. 303v]} and there in the desert he would mount them to go from one place to another.[2] Because of that a large number of people gathered around him, and he was about to enter Tigrê as if he were its lord; but a man who was not even a captain yet went out and seized him and took him to the emperor, who commanded that his ears and nose be cut off, and now he is wandering around without anyone taking any notice of him.

Similar to these tales is what he says about *Abba* Taquelâ Haureât, that every year on Christmas Day, which was the day of his martyrdom, an angel comes down visibly in human form in his honour and, in front of the monks in the refectory of Dêbra Libanôs,

[1] Synaxarion.

[2] Humble obedience by wild animals is a biblical topos that is widely used in Ethiopian hagiographies.

he places ten most beautiful citrons, which are shared among the people. I could not find anyone who knew anything about any such citrons, although I asked some monks of the same religion, including one called *Abba* Marcâ, who is highly renowned among them, and he told me he was eighty years old and had been brought up as a boy in Dêbra Libanôs and had never seen such citrons. And the captain who until just recently was captain <[f. 250v/240v]> of the Portuguese, who is called João Gabriel,[1] a man of very good character, told me that when he was young he had spent three years in that monastery without interruption, learning the books of Ethiopia, and he had never seen such a thing, and until now – he is seventy year old – he had never heard anyone mention it, even though he has usually been in the emperors' palace; and the emperors have not been to that monastery for many {[f. 304]} years, let alone every year. And since I arrived in Ethiopia, which was in 1603, not one of the three that there have been in this time has been there. Therefore, what the monk from Ethiopia swore to Friar Serafino Rosi, that he had often been present at this miracle, was just as correct as what Friar Luis de Urreta, on page 56 of the first volume,[2] affirms that João Balthesar from Ethiopia swore to him affirmatively and with much exaggeration on all that is sacred, that on Mount Amharâ they keep a gold chest containing a piece of the tablets written with God's finger which were broken by Moses because of the people's idolatry, and which he had often held in his hands. That (as we explained at length at the end of chapter 3 in the first book) is a fable and lie, because there has never been such a thing in Ethiopia; instead, her scholars also affirm that no recollection remains of the tablets that Moses broke, which clearly shows how little credit should be given to his oath.[3]

As regards what the author says about that woman Imata, the founder of nuns in Ethiopia, we need not dwell on that because it is very clearly a fable that that woman came from Rome, since we proved above in chapter 17 that the religion of Saint Dominic is not and never has been in the lands ruled by the Prester John and that the monks with whom he says that woman came from Rome {[f. 304v]} were more than 300 years before the glorious father Saint Dominic was born. The name Imata, which ought be Amâta, and means 'Maidservant', is not common to nuns, because they ordinarily keep their name from baptism, when they call many women Amâta Christós, 'Maidservant of Christ', Amâta Michael, 'Maidservant of Michael'. And then they are not nuns, but married women. Nor is there that kind of refectory and choir that Friar Luis depicts; nor do they wear a veil that reaches down to the bust; nor are they enclosed today, nor have they ever been enclosed, but each one goes where she likes, because their manner is much more like *beatas* than nuns. And if they kept the honesty of *beatas* it would be a great boon, but it is not so; instead, many of them live in such a way that lay people say that once they become nuns <[f. 251/241]> they are more worldly than if they were not. They commonly become nuns after being widowed, and they stay in their house as before, and even if they are maidens and want to retreat, there is no other way than to be near some monastery of monks, in their little houses separate from one another, and they can go at will wherever they wish.

---

[1] See Glossary (João Gabriel).

[2] Urreta, *Historia de la Etiopia*, bk I, ch. 5, pp. 46–65.

[3] Ethiopian Christian tradition still considers the chapel of Saint Mary of Sion in Aksum to be the place where the tablets of the ten commandments are kept.

As for the taffeta, etc., which he says they weave, it is a fable, because in Ethiopia there is no silk and they do not know how to weave taffeta. Wool is very scarce and coarse and they do not know how to work it, and so they only use it to make some blankets, far worse than those they use in our land to cover horses. There is abundant cotton here, but they do not know how to use it to make the coifs and veils that the author says {[f. 305]} they take to the Turks; instead, the coifs, veils and fine clothes that are worn in Ethiopia come here through their ports from India.

In chapter 18[1] he also deals with Empress Helena,[2] and he says that she married Emperor Alexandre II and was the mother of Emperor Naum and the grandmother of Prester John David, and that afterwards she was a religious of the Third Order of Penance of Father Saint Dominic, and that just as Saint Helena is the honour and glory of the whole Catholic Church, the Blessed Helena is the honour of the Ethiopian Church and the glory of the Order of Preachers and the singular beauty of the holy state of the religious women that they call *beatas*. Here too, Friar Luis had faulty information, because Empress Helena was not the wife of Emperor Alexandre II, for in Ethiopia there have not been two Alexandres, but in fact she married Emperor Naôd and never gave birth, because although David was Emperor Naôd's son, he was not Empress Helena's, but a bastard. And because she raised him, since she had no children, it may be that people did not know and said that he was her son, or perhaps she called him that as an honour. And she could not have been a religious of the Third Order of Saint Dominic because, as we have said, they do not know of it here and have never heard anything about their sacred religion. Thus, everything he says in chapter 20,[3] about how {[f. 305v]} the Brotherhood of the Holy Rosary was founded in Ethiopia, and that today there are many of them, and they persist with considerable grandeur, it is all fable, because there is not and never has been a Brotherhood of the Rosary in these parts, nor do they know what it is.

---

[1] Urreta, *Historia de la sagrada orden*, ch. 18, entitled 'On the blessed Helena, empress of Ethiopia, religious of the Third Order of Penance of the glorious Father Saint Dominic, which we call *Beatas*', pp. 379–91.

[2] See Glossary (Helena/Elena).

[3] Urreta, *Historia de la sagrada orden*, ch. 20, entitled 'On the Brotherhood of the Holy Rosary of the most Sacred Virgin and on its foundation in the Kingdoms of Ethiopia', pp. 399–416.

# CHAPTER XXIII

## Which explains whether there have been any emperor saints in Ethiopia

It would have been far from me to waste time on this subject and to tire the reader with such unnecessary things had Friar Luis de Urreta not forced me to do so by canonizing <[f. 251v/241v]> seven emperors of Ethiopia, with whom he deals in chapter 3 of book 3 of his first volume,[1] as saints. He says that they are Saint Phelipe, the first Christian Prester John, Saint Emperor João, another João the Holy, Saint Phelipe VII, Emperor Saint Elesbaão, Saint Prester John Abraham, and the glorious Emperor Lalibela. But, because if I passed over what he says about these emperors in silence someone might think that it was all true, it seemed best to report briefly what he says about them and then to explain what the people of Ethiopia recount.

Thus, when the author speaks about Prester John Phelipe, he says:

*When Queen Candace baptized the princes of the house and blood of David on Mount Amharâ, the eldest was called Zacharias and at his baptism he decided to be called Phelipe, in memory of the glorious Saint Phelipe who baptized the eunuch. The histories of Ethiopia say that this holy emperor (to whom Queen Candace renounced {[f. 306]} the empire and then withdrew to a monastery) was a great defender and preacher of the Christian faith, because he was equally emperor and apostle. He built countless churches and endowed them with very large incomes. They say that God honoured him with miracles in life and in death, for since he so carefully sought to serve God, naturally God Himself would seek to honour him. He kept his virginity entire throughout his life, and he is buried on Mount Amharâ, in the temple of the Holy Spirit, where they bury the emperors of Ethiopia, and there he is honoured and revered as a saint.*

### Saint Emperor João

*After the holy death of Emperor Phelipe, since he left no sons as he had always kept virginal chastity, he was succeeded by his brother John, who is held to be a saint in Ethiopia and was one of the princes whom Queen Candace and the holy eunuch baptized on Mount Amharâ. He had been called Daniel, and at his baptism he wanted to take the name João. He was a most holy man and in everything sought to imitate the example left to him by his saintly brother and predecessor. He tried with all his might to spread the Catholic faith and to consolidate it in all {[f. 306v]} his kingdoms by banishing any trace or relics of idolatry; he*

---

[1] Urreta, *Historia de la Etiopia*, bk III, ch. 3, entitled 'On the Prester Johns and emperors of Ethiopia who are regarded and revered as saints', pp. 672–85; Urreta's book contains pagination errors.

492

built very sumptuous churches and in everything sought to follow the path of virtues of his saintly brother. Like him, he had wanted to keep his chastity, but the council and all the empire forced him to marry, because there were very few of the house of David. And so they found him a suitable wife with whom he had seven sons and two daughters, and in holy matrimony he led an angelic life, so <[f. 252/242]> that in Ethiopia they hold him to be a saint and always have done, even though the Ethiopian histories give no more information about him, as they are such ancient matters.

One of Emperor João's princess daughters was called Eufrasia and she kept her virginity all her life. For many years she lived in a cave in the desert, performing great penances and having contact only with God and the angels, without being seen by human eyes. In the cave where she performed her penance, today there is church built in her name and they have great devotion for her. The Martyrologium Romanum[1] mentions this Saint Eufrasia on 13th March, and although it says she was from the Thebaid, it is because it is close to Ethiopia, but in fact she was the daughter of the emperor of Ethiopia.

## The emperor saints of Ethiopia João the Holy and Phelipe VII

These two emperors lived at the time of Saint Basil, which was from 330 to 380 after the birth of Christ. They were very saintly princes and among the most famous that Ethiopia has had. João the Holy (for the Ethiopians give him this name because of his heroic saintliness {[f. 307]} and to differentiate him from other emperors who were called João) was so zealous of the Catholic faith that, on seeing in his time the rise of that heretical blasphemy of Arius, which denied the equality of the divine persons, making the Son less than the Father, he set up a military order of knights commander under the name of Saint Anthony the Abbot. And he wrote to his great friend Saint Basil asking him to send him the institutes and constitutions, which the glorious saint did very willingly, and the knights have kept them to this day. The purpose of this military religion in those times was to fight the Arians and to guard Ethiopia against such a blasphemous heresy, and it was such an important instrument that, although this heresy reached almost the whole world, it was unable to contaminate Ethiopia, despite its proximity to Egypt where it had been invented. This emperor saint built many churches dedicated to the Holy Trinity and made many laws for the good governance of Ethiopia, which are kept to this day. He died in the most saintly manner, uttering the name of the Holy Trinity, as an extremely staunch defender of its faith and purity. And God made him illustrious through many miracles.

This Emperor João the Holy was succeeded by Phelipe, the seventh in number of those who have <[f. 252v/242v]> had this name. He is held in Ethiopia to be holy and blessed and, just as he succeeded João in his position, {[f. 307v]} so he inherited his heroic virtues and holy zeal both in matters relating to the faith and as regards the good government of his kingdoms. He greatly expanded the military order of the Knights of Saint Anthony and gave them privileges and revenues just so that they might occupy themselves in fighting the Arians. He made many laws for the governance of the cities that are so good and holy that, to this day, when emperors are crowned they swear to uphold them; and in all the cities of the empire they have these laws written on a tablet and put up in the middle of the squares so that everyone may know them and the judges and governors may pass judgment according to them.

---

[1] Martyrologio Romano reformado conforme a la nueva razón del Kalendario y verdad de la Historia Ecclesiastica, f. 39v.

*He was a most exemplary prince, father and support for all and full of virtues. Content, he left this life for glory. These two emperors were buried in the temple of the Holy Spirit on Mount Amharâ, where they are venerated as saints.*

### Saint Elesbaam, emperor of Ethiopia

*Symeon Metaphrastes recounts in the History of Saint Arethas the martyr[1] and Nicephorus that, at the time of Emperor Justin, a king of the Homerites in Arabia called Dunaam, a Jew by law and belief, with all his followers, gathered a great army of Jews and heathens and besieged a city of Christians called Negra, in Arabia Felix.[2] Although he kept it surrounded for a long time, the Christians defended themselves vigorously and, when he saw that {[f. 308]} he could not succeed in the undertaking by force, he raised the siege and made peace, but then treacherously entered the city and his followers penetrated it secretly. And afterwards he began to persuade the Christians to become Jews and, when they did not want to accept his accursed counsel, he commanded his men to destroy the city and thus he made martyrs of all those who were in it.*

*This cruelty and treachery of the perfidious Jew came to the notice of Prester John Elesbaam, who was also king and lord of that city and much of Arabia. To avenge such a great evil, he gathered a copious army of Ethiopians and Arabians, all Christians, and went in search of the Jew Dunaam; giving him battle, he defeated him easily and killed all his men and cut him to pieces in payment for his cruelties. Emperor Saint Elesbaam, acknowledging that that victory had been God's, did not show himself to be ungrateful and, proclaiming God's mercies, sent his imperial crown to Jerusalem to the Holy Sepulchre of Jesus Christ and, renouncing the empire, became an ecclesiastic. Once ordained to say <[f. 253/243]> Mass, he put on a very coarse cilice and lived in a dark, frightful cave, where he spent the rest of his life without any living man seeing him. He performed incredible penance, eating nothing but raw herbs, and therefore God revealed him with many miraculous works. They hold him to be a very great saint in Ethiopia, and in the place and cave where he did his penance, though {[f. 308v]} extremely harsh and almost uninhabitable, a sumptuous church was built dedicated to this saint, to whom they have great devotion, as shown by the people who throng there and the frequency with which they receive holy communion in it. The Martyrologium Romanum mentions this saint on 22nd October,[3] and Metaphrastes on the 24th.*

### The miraculous life of Saint Abraham, Prester John of Ethiopia

*In the province of Ancona, which is a certain lordship in Ethiopia, there is a mountain that must be a climb of two leagues, and it is so rough and steep that to climb it one has to hold on to ropes that are tied there, and the path is so difficult that it takes more than half a day to reach the top. On top there is a cave and inside a very large church, like a cathedral with three*

---

[1] A version of this document by Symeon, bishop of the Persian Christians (Symeon Metaphrastes) was published by Esteves Pereira in *História dos martyres de Nagran*, pp. 1–31. In the same volume he also published the text of the *Martírio de Santo Arethas*, pp. 35–76.

[2] Urreta is referring to Yūsuf Dhū Nuwās, king of Himyar in southern Arabia and vassal to the Aksumite Negus Kâleb (known to the Greeks as Elesbaan); Dhū Nuwās massacred the Christians in the Arabian town of Nağrān in 518 or 523.

[3] Saint Elesbaan's feast is on 27 October (*Martyrologio Romano*, f. 176r–v). *Metaphrastes* is also the metonymic name for the collected lives of saints compiled by Symeon Logotheta in the tenth century.

*very well made naves with their chapels and altars. There are more than 200 clerics in it, and it is very wealthy. It is called Imbra Christos, which means 'Path of Christ'. In this church {there are two little dwellings carved out of the rock itself, in which Saint Abraham did penance, and he had that church made.} The histories of Ethiopia mention that this Prester John was a priest and he retreated to the cave that is inside this church, where he spent forty years hidden, and he said Mass every day and the angels brought him bread and wine with which to say it. Today, this emperor is painted at the high altar, dressed in priest's vestments {[f. 309]} as if to say Mass, with a hand coming through a window with bread and another through another side with a cruet, signifying the miracle that we have mentioned. They also said that while he was Prester John in Ethiopia he took no tributes <or labour> or duties from his vassals and, if he was given a gift, he would share it among the poor, while he supported himself on some lands that he worked. He performed great and rigorous penance in that cave and for forty years he only ate once a week, <[f. 253v/243v]> on Sundays, and always wore a cilice. The great fame of this emperor saint's heroic virtues spread around the world, to the extent that a patriarch of Alexandria came to Ethiopia just to see him and died in the church itself. Eventually the holy Abraham went to receive the reward for his labours from the liberal hand of God and, in death, God honoured him with many miracles. He was buried in the church itself, in a tomb that lies in the middle of it, four steps high, and in another tomb to the right, three steps high, the patriarch who came from Alexandria is buried, and in another tomb to the left is a daughter of Emperor Saint Abraham, who followed the penance of her father and is held to be a saint throughout Ethiopia.*

### The glorious Lalibelâ, emperor of Ethiopia

*Since the holy life, birth and {[f. 309v]} death of this blessed Prester John were so miraculous, they called him Lalibela, which means 'Miracle of the World', because all his life, his works and his virtues were miraculous and his miracles were many and marvellous. The histories of Ethiopia tell of him that, at the moment when he was born, countless bees came and covered him from head to foot, so that no part of the child could be seen uncovered, and the people who attended the birth, marvelling at such a miraculous thing, did not dare touch but could only look to see what would happen. The bees did him no harm at all but cleaned him of the filth and blood with which he had come from his mother's womb and, leaving him clean, they flew up to heaven and were not seen again. This was a sacred sign of great mysteries, because heaven made use of such announcements to reveal what was to be found in Saint Lalibela. This emperor saint kept his chastity all his life, which lasted for eighty years, remaining always a virgin, and so at the hour of his death he departed this life with the halo of virginity to receive his reward from the supreme remunerator. This purity and cleanness was foretold by the bees that covered him at birth, because the bee, as Saint Epiphanius notes, is a symbol of cleanness and chastity. Bees were also a symbol <[f. 254/244]> for some ingenious men, fond of works and of making buildings, because of the mysterious design by which they make their combs. Thus was Emperor Saint Lalibela, very attentive to the divine cult and most fond of building churches and prayer houses. It was he who with incredible effort made those {[f. 310]} miraculous temples all made out of a single rock which we mentioned in the second book, which are one of the greatest marvels that the world has ever had. And he is buried there in the church that they call Golgotha. In the end, rich in virtues, he departed this life and gave his soul into the hands of that Lord who had lent it to him until then. The Ethiopian histories say that God honoured him with many miracles and his holy body is held* *in great veneration and many people go to it on pilgrimage, since he is held by everyone to be a great saint.*[1]

This is what Friar Luis de Urreta recounts about these emperors of Ethiopia, whom he baptizes as Prester Johns. But, as may be seen from the catalogues that we put in chapter 5 of the first book, only Lalibelâ was emperor of Ethiopia and there is no recollection at all of the rest. Thus, when I asked many old men who were knowledgeable in the histories of Ethiopia, they told me that they did not know that there had been such emperors, apart from Lalibelâ. To satisfy myself further, I even asked Emperor Seltân Çaguêd, who is alive today, and he told me in the presence of many lords that none of his predecessors had had such names and that Lalibelâ was not of the royal house to whom the empire belongs, but a descendant of a tyrant by the name of Zagoê, who is also mentioned in the catalogues of emperors. I also asked if there had been any emperor saint in Ethiopia, and one of the great men replied with a laugh that there had not. The emperor said, 'How could {[f. 310v]} they be saints, when they died with three or four concubines beside them?' And upon this he talked for a good while about the licentiousness that there had been in the past. And afterwards *Erâs* Celá Christôs, the emperor's {brother} <servant>, told me, 'For the sake of modesty, my lord said <[f. 254v/244v]> that the past emperors died with three or four concubines beside them, but he could well have said twenty, because they had no lack of them.' In the past this was so usual and public that, apart from the empress, they always had two proper wives (apart from other concubines) in their houses, one to the right of the palace and the other to the left, and they called the latter *balteguerâ*, which means 'lady of the left hand'. They say that only Emperor David, who later was called Onag Çaguêd, did not have these concubines. And it may well be that the man who informed Friar Luis de Urreta, to whom he gives the name João Balthesar, was a kinsman of one of these that they call *balteguerâ* and, for honour's sake, he wished to be called João Balteguerâ, and Friar Luis de Urreta understood João Baltesar, because as the emperor told me the first time I mentioned him in his presence, 'This name is not from Ethiopia.'

What we have said should be enough for the reader to understand quite well how fabulous the things are that Friar Luis de Urreta says here, for in the lands that the Prester John governs there have never been any such emperors, except for Lalibelâ. Nonetheless, to see it even more clearly, the reader should know that what he states about the first of these emperors, Phelipe, whom Queen Candace {[f. 311]} baptized on Mount Amharâ and to whom she renounced the empire, is patently false because, as we said at the end of chapter 7 of the first book,[2] the first ones to be put on that mountain, {which is called Guixên,} were put there in about 1295, and Queen Candace lived at the time of the apostles. In what he says later about Saint Eufrasia, it would have been better if he had followed the *Martyrologium Romanum*, which says that she was from the Thebaid, because in Ethiopia there was no such Emperor João, whose daughter he says she was. It is also false when he says that the emperor he calls João the Holy set up a military order of knights commander

---

[1] Urreta, *Historia de la Etiopia*, excerpts, with many omissions, from bk III, ch. 3, pp. 674–85, translated by Páez into Portuguese.

[2] In BPB, MS 778, the long excerpt from 'hold on to ...', in the paragraph beginning 'In the province of Ancona' (f. 253/243), to here seems to have been written in a different hand.

to fight the Arians, because, as we showed in chapter 17 of this second book, there is not and never has been such an order of knights in Ethiopia. Nor are the laws that he says were made by Emperor Phelipe VII written on tablets in the squares, and he could hardly have made them because there never was such an emperor. In addition, if what he says about Prester John <[f. 255/245]> Abraham were true – that he had a cathedral church built where there are more than 200 clergy, and with the fame of his heroic virtues a patriarch of Alexandria came and they are both buried in that church – many people would {know} <have heard> about this, and yet everyone says that they have never heard of such things, or that there was ever such an emperor in Ethiopia.

Of everything that Friar Luis says about these emperors, the part that might seem most plausible is {[f. 311v]} what he says about Emperor Lalibelâ, but almost all of it is fable as well, because neither do the histories of Ethiopia say that he was covered by bees when he was born,[1] nor did he keep his virginity all his life, because everyone says he was married and had two sons: his wife was called Mascal Quebrâ and the sons were Emera Christôs and Naacuto La Âb. Nor is there much certainty about his saintliness; indeed, Emperor Seltan Çaguêd told me that he was not a saint, and only ignorant people spoke of that. The evidence is very weak, because in Ethiopia they venerate many people as saints who were very bad and died as they lived. In the kingdom of Tigrê, in the land they call Adecorrô, there is the grave of one that they call Isac, a place of great pilgrimage thronged by the common people because they hold him to be a saint; nevertheless, he spent more than twenty years in that kingdom rebelling against the emperors and eating up its revenue. When Emperor Adamas Çaguêd went there with an army, he called in the Turks from Maçuâ and, with them, fought him in a pitched battle and defeated him; thus the Turks took large amounts of booty and many Christian captives. A few years later, Emperor Malâc Çaguêd went against him with a large army and he again brought in Turks, but on giving battle he was defeated and ended up badly wounded. Seeing that he could not escape from those that were searching the battlefield, he told some men that were with him to cut off his head {[f. 312]} and bury it and to put it about that he had fled, and in that way they could eat off that kingdom for some time longer, which they {refused} <agreed> to do. So when the emperor's men arrived soon afterwards, they killed him and took his head. Although he lived and died in that way, the people of that land hold him to be a great saint, because they say he gave many alms. Many people also consider *Abuna* Simão and Iuliôs, who died <[f. 255v/245v]> in the way we described in chapter 5 above, to be saints. It is therefore not surprising that they also hold Emperor Lalibela, who made the churches that we described in chapter 15 of this second book, to be a saint. And to show how differently the books of Ethiopia recount his life from the way Friar Luis de Urreta reports it in his, I shall put it here in the manner that I found it in them.

## Life of Emperor Lalibelâ as told by the books of Ethiopia

*On 17th June, the blessed, pure watcher of the mysteries of heaven, Lalibela, emperor of Ethiopia, went to his rest. When this saint was born, his parents raised him in the fear of God and, when he became a young man, his brother the emperor saw that he was growing and*

---

[1] Ethiopian popular tradition does in fact associate King Lālibalā with swarms of bees, which are supposed to have miraculously carved out the famous monolithic churches during his reign.

*would possess his empire and sit on his chair, and envy crept into him and he summoned him. And when he came he made him stand before him and, seeking {[f. 312v]} excuses, commanded that he be given many lashes from six o'clock in the morning until eight or nine. Then he had him brought and, on seeing him, he and all his people marvelled greatly, because nothing had touched him, for the angel of God had delivered him. The emperor therefore said to him, 'Forgive me, my brother, for what I have done to you.' And they made peace and friendship. And God saw his torment that day and gave him the empire, and when he was in it, he thought how he could please God and he gave many alms to the poor. And since God could see the strength of his love, the angel of God appeared to him in a dream and showed him how he would make the ten churches in a different manner. And he did as God had shown him and, when he had finished building those churches, he passed the empire to his brother; and thus rested in peace.*[1]

Up to here are words from the book that tells the life of this emperor, and it does not say anything else, and if what Friar Luis de Urreta mentions were true, it would not have omitted it. One cannot even give credit to what this book says, because of the many lies it contains, one of which is that, when talking about the circumcision of Christ Our Lord, it says that Our Lady the Virgin begged Saint Joseph to bring a wise man to circumcise the boy and, when he brought him, Christ Our Lord held a long conversation with him and, in the end, raising His eyes to heaven and speaking to His eternal Father, He said, 'O Father, give me the circumcision that Thou didst give before to Abraham, Isaac and Jacob, without the hand of man.' And then He appeared circumcised {[f. 313]} without <[f. 256/246]> the hand of man. And His circumcision happened without it being known, and He showed His wisdom in that none of His flesh at all was cut off in the circumcision.

Of everything that Friar Luis de Urreta says about these emperors, only one thing made me take careful note. It was what he said about Emperor Elesbaam, because of the authors that he cites and because Cardinal Cesar Baronio, in his volume 7,[2] says that in 522 a King Elesbaan reigned in Ethiopia in the royal city of Auxume (which would seem to be the same as the one they now call Agçúm here). He recounts how he defeated the Jew and, in recognition of the mercy that God had done him in giving him such a great victory, he sent his crown to Jerusalem and, leaving his city at night, he went to a monastery of religious that was on a mountain, crept into a little house and stayed there for many years, performing great penances, until he departed this life. Because of this, and because the *Martyrologium Romanum* of Gregory XIII mentions this king of Ethiopia, Elesbaan, on 27th October, I diligently asked the old monks who might best be able to inform me of this, and they all agree that there has never been a king in these lands that had such a name, but that in a town in the kingdom of Tigrê, which they call Agçúm, which was once a very large city, there had once reigned a king called Caleb, of whom their books told the same story that the above-mentioned authors {[f. 313v]} attribute to Elesbaan. I therefore tried to obtain this book and found it in a very old monastery that is in Agçum itself, and speaking of King Caleb it says the following:

---

[1] Páez almost certainly translated this brief note on Lālibalā from the *Senkessār* (Synaxarion).

[2] Baronio, *Annales ecclesiastici*, Cologne, 1609, VII, items 23–4, pp. 99–100. The annals also contain a report of the martyrdom of the people in Najrān and the help sent by Elesbaan/Kāleb, items 22–66, pp. 99–110.

On the death of Tacenâ, king of Agçum, his son Caleb reigned, a wise, strong man of true faith. Timotheos, pope of Egypt and Alexandria, sent him a message about the people of Nagran, who had been killed by that tyrannical Jew named Finaâs, asking him to go to the aid of those Christians at once. And he first sent 10,500 well-armed soldiers from Ethiopia, but they died of thirst on the journey, and when the king heard this sad news he went in disguise to a holy man called Abba Pantaleão. On arriving, he kissed the wall out of devotion and tearfully begged him to plead to God for him and to tell him what he thought would happen to him, and he explained about those soldiers of his that had died. The saint then told him that he should go in peace, that he would defeat the enemies of the Christians, and that his soldiers' deaths had been the work of the Devil; he should go in the confidence that he would establish <[f. 256v/246v]> a church there and teach the faith of Christ, and then return home to salvation. The king rejoiced greatly at this, taking those words as being from God, and after receiving the holy man's blessing he gave one of his disciples a present of incense with ten ounces of gold hidden inside. When the disciple came with this, the holy man said to him, 'Why did you take it? Do you {[f. 314]} not know that there is gold inside? Leave it, leave it.' And turning to the king he asked him why he had committed that mistake. 'The Gospel says, "Give us this day our daily bread." Why did you give so much gold? We do not want to be rich. Give this to the poor and it will be kept for you in heaven. Go, for the prayers of Timotheos, pope of Alexandria, and the tears of Justin will accompany you. The sacrifice of the martyrs of Nagran, which has already reached heaven, will also go in your company, and God will give you victory.'

The king departed with great confidence in God and none in his own strength or in that of his soldiers. When the Jew learnt of that, he made some very large iron chains to prevent the passage of his ships, which numbered 171, including 103 large ones. When the king arrived at the place and his ships could not pass, there appeared to him a man like a hermit, with a beautiful, shining white face, and he made a gesture with his hand that they should pass to the right (the enemy did not see this vision), and when the king arrived there with eleven ships that hermit guided them. Seeing this, the Jew sent many men to prevent the ships from passing through, but the king fell on them and killed them and burnt their houses and razed everything he found in his path until he reached the place where the Jew was and captured him. The other part of the king's fleet knew nothing of this, and suffered many adversities and hunger; the men in it therefore prayed to God, who saw fit to hear them and showed them that monk, who took hold of the tail of an enemy horse in one hand and wounded it with the other. Then the enemies of Christ fled and the men from Ethiopia fell on them and killed many, until they reached the place where the king was and, as the Jew's men were trapped in the middle, the king killed many more than the others had killed.

When this was finished, they all gathered together and related what had happened to them both at sea and on land {[f. 314v]} and how the king had taken Finaâs. And the king said how a monk had made a gesture to him and his ships and had broken those chains by striking them with his foot, and first one ship and then the other ten had passed through, and the monk had walked on the waters as if they were dry land. And the king added that he thought that the monk had been the one who had been in the little house <[f. 257/247]> in his land, and that he had guided him to where the Jew was and that the monk himself had caught him and delivered him to him, so that he should keep him until the church was established and then behead him there. One of the king's princes said that, when a contrary wind came, that monk had stopped it with his rod. And another said that one ship had broken and that when

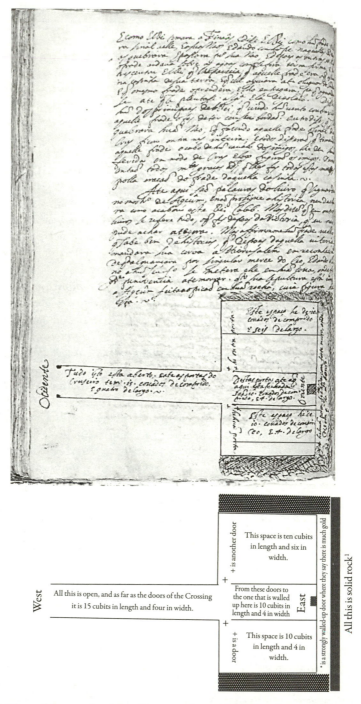

Figure 18. Plan of the tomb of the Aksumite king Kaleb (sixth century), in Aksum, included at the end of book II of the *História da Etiópia*.
ARSI, MS Goa 42, f. 314v.

[1] This phrase appears in BPB, MS 778, but cannot be seen in ARSI, MS Goa 42, which is tightly sewn close to the shaded area.

*that monk made the sign of the cross it became whole again. And they all said that when that monk had taken hold of the tail of an enemy horse, he had given it a wound in the shape of a cross and the enemy had fled at once. Then they all gave many thanks to God for having done them all these mercies on account of the prayer said by the monk in that little house.*[1]

Up to here are words from the book kept in the monastery in Agçûm. And it does not continue the history or explain how this King Caleb died, but they say that other books relate everything that he did after the victory, although I have not yet been able to find them. But an old monk, who knows the histories well, told me that after that victory he sent his crown to Jerusalem, in recognition of the fact that he had achieved victory by singular mercy from heaven; then, giving the kingdom to a son of his, he withdrew into a cave, where he performed great penance until he died. As for his grave, it is near Agçûm, hacked out of the rock, and it looks like this.[2]

---

[1] The version that Páez has translated displays a few differences compared with the version translated by F. M. Esteves Pereira. In the latter, for instance, there is no supernatural intervention in the figure of the monk. Páez has also used only the last part of the narrative, relating the part played by Kāleb or Elesbaan (see Pereira, *História dos Mártires de Nagran*). The source for this excerpt seems to be the *Gadla Ṗāṇṭāléwon* (Hagiography of Pantaleon), which gives a similar account of the saint's miraculous intervention in the events. Páez has abridged the text, omitting a substantial part of the dialogue between the king and the monk (see Conti Rossini, 'Vitae sanctorum antiquiorum'; Ethiopic text is found in vol. 9, pp. 48–52, and its translation in vol. 10, pp. 52–3 and 55–6).

[2] See Fig. 18.